T0224414

Lecture Notes in Computer Science   **8974**

Commenced Publication in 1973
Founding and Former Series Editors:
Gerhard Goos, Juris Hartmanis, and Jan van Leeuwen

More information about this series at http://www.springer.com/series/7407

Andrei Voronkov · Irina Virbitskaite (Eds.)

Perspectives of System Informatics

9th International Ershov Informatics Conference,
PSI 2014
St. Petersburg, Russia, June 24–27, 2014
Revised Selected Papers

 Springer

Editors
Andrei Voronkov
School of Computer Science
University of Manchester
Manchester
UK

Irina Virbitskaite
A.P. Ershov Institute of Informatics Systems
Novosibirsk
Russia

ISSN 0302-9743   ISSN 1611-3349   (electronic)
Lecture Notes in Computer Science
ISBN 978-3-662-46822-7   ISBN 978-3-662-46823-4   (eBook)
DOI 10.1007/978-3-662-46823-4

Library of Congress Control Number: 2015935417

LNCS Sublibrary: SL1 – Theoretical Computer Science and General Issues

Springer Heidelberg New York Dordrecht London

Printed on acid-free paper

Springer-Verlag GmbH Berlin Heidelberg is part of Springer Science+Business Media
(www.springer.com)

Preface

This volume contains the papers presented at PSI 2014: 9th Ershov Informatics Conference held during June 24–27, 2014 in St. Petersburg, Russia.

PSI is the premier international forum in Russia for academic and industrial researchers, developers, and users working on topics relating to computer, software, and information sciences. The conference serves to bridge the gaps between different communities whose research areas are covered by but not limited to foundations of program and system development and analysis, programming methodology, and software engineering and information technologies.

The previous eight PSI conferences were held in 1991, 1996, 1999, 2001, 2003, 2006, 2009, and 2011, respectively, and proved to be significant international events. Traditionally, PSI offers a program of keynote lectures, presentations of contributed papers, and workshops complemented by a social program reecting the amazing diversity of the Russian culture and history.

The PSI conference series is dedicated to the memory of the pioneer in theoretical and system programming research: academician Andrei Petrovich Ershov (1931–1988). Andrei Ershov graduated from the Moscow State University in 1954. He began his scientific career under the supervision of Alexandr Lyapunov. After that Andrei Ershov worked at the Institute of Precise Mechanics and Computing Machinery, and then became director of the Theoretical Programming Department at the Computing Center of the USSR Academy of Sciences in Moscow. In 1958 the Department was reorganized into the Institute of Mathematics of the Siberian Branch of the USSR Academy of Sciences, and by the initiative of the academician Sergei Sobolev Ershov was appointed the head of this department, which later became part of the Computing Center in Novosibirsk Akademgorodok. The first significant project of the Department was aimed at the development of the ALPHA system, an optimizing compiler for an extension of Algol 60 implemented on a Soviet computer M-20. Later the researchers of the Department created the Algibr, Epsilon, Sigma, and Alpha-6 programming systems for the BESM-6 computers. The list of achievements also include the first Soviet time-sharing system AIST-0, the multi-language system BETA, research projects in artificial intelligence and parallel programming, integrated tools for text processing and publishing, and many more. A.P. Ershov was a leader and a participant of these projects. In 1974 he was nominated Distinguished Fellow of the British Computer Society. In 1981 he received the Silver Core Award for services rendered to IFIP. Andrei Ershov's brilliant speeches were always in the focus of public attention. Especially notable was his lecture on "Aesthetic and Human Factor in Programming" presented at the AFIPS Spring Joint Computer Conference in 1972.

This edition of the conference attracted 80 submissions from 29 countries. We wish to thank all their authors for their interest in PSI 2014. Each submission was reviewed by three experts, at least two of them from the same or closely related discipline as the authors. The reviewers generally provided high-quality assessment of the papers and often gave extensive comments to the authors for possible improvement of their contributions. As a result, the Program Committee has selected for presentation at the conference 17 high-quality papers as regular talks, 11 papers as short talks, and 2 papers as system and experimental talks. A range of hot topics in computer science and informatics is covered by five keynote talks given by prominent computer scientists from various countries.

We wish to express our gratitude to all the persons and organizations who contributed to the conference: the authors of all the papers for their effort in producing the materials included here; the sponsors for their moral, financial, and organizational support; the Steering Committee members for their coordination of the conference, the Program Committee members and the reviewers who did their best to review and select the papers, and the members of the Organizing Committee for their contribution to the success of this event and its great cultural program.

The Program Committee work was done using the EasyChair conference management system.

December 2015   Andrei Voronkov
                                                                          Irina Virbitskaite

Organization

Program Committee

Marek Bednarczyk	Gdansk Branch of the Institute of Computer Science PAS, Poland
Frederic Benhamou	University of Nantes, France
Leopoldo Bertossi	Carleton University, Canada
Eike Best	University of Oldenburg, Germany
Nikolaj Bjorner	Microsoft Research, USA
Swarat Chaudhuri	Rice University, USA
Marsha Chechik	University of Toronto, Canada
Gabriel Ciobanu	Institute of Computer Science, Romanian Academy, Romania
Volker Diekert	Universität Stuttgart, Germany
Schahram Dustdar	Vienna University of Technology, Austria
Dieter Fensel	STI Innsbruck, Austria
Sergei Gorlatch	Universität Münster, Germany
Jan Friso Groote	Eindhoven University of Technology, The Netherlands
Arie Gurfinkel	Carnegie Mellon University, USA
Joost-Pieter Katoen	RWTH Aachen University, Germany
Konstantin Korovin	University of Manchester, UK
Maciej Koutny	Newcastle University, UK
Laura Kovacs	Chalmers University of Technology, Sweden
Gregory Kucherov	University Paris-Est Marne-la-Vallée, France
Kim Guldstrand Larsen	Aalborg University, Denmark
Leonid Libkin	University of Edinburgh, UK
Johan Lilius	Åbo Akademi University, Finland
Pericles Loucopoulos	Loughborough University, UK
Andrea Maggiolo-Schettini	Università di Pisa, Italy
Rupak Majumdar	Max Planck Institute for Software Systems, Germany
Klaus Meer	Brandenburg University of Technology, Cottbus, Germany
Torben Ægidius Mogensen	University of Copenhagen, Denmark
Peter Mosses	Swansea University, UK
José Ramón Paramá	University of A Coruña, Spain
Wojciech Penczek	Institute of Computer Science of PAS, Poland
Peter Pepper	Technische Universität Berlin, Germany
Alexander Petrenko	Institute for System Programming RAS, Russia

Paul Pettersson   Mälardalen University, Sweden
Wolfgang Reisig   Humboldt-Universität zu Berlin, Germany
Andrey Rybalchenko   Technische Universität München, Germany
Andrei Sabelfeld   Chalmers University of Technology, Sweden
Don Sannella   University of Edinburgh, Uk
Klaus-Dieter Schewe   Software Competence Centre Hagenberg, Austria
Konstantin Serebryany   Google, Russia
Natasha Sharygina   University of Lugano, Switzerland
Zhendong Su   University of California, Davis, USA
Mark Trakhtenbrot   Holon Institute of Technology, Israel
Irina Virbitskaite   A.P. Ershov Institute of Informatics Systems,
                                Russia
Andrei Voronkov   The University of Manchester, UK

Additional Reviewers

Alberti, Francesco	Grunske, Lars	Polrola, Agata
Alt, Leonardo	Haidl, Michael	Poulsen, Danny Bøgsted
Aman, Bogdan	Hatvani, Leo	Prüfer, Robert
Bacci, Giorgio	Horne, Ross	Rasch, Ari
Bello, Luciano	Höger, Christoph	Reutter, Juan
Bertrand, Nathalie	Johnstone, Adrian	Rohloff, Judith
Bollig, Benedikt	Keiren, Jeroen	Rollini, Simone Fulvio
Calvert, Wesley	Keshishzadeh, Sarmen	Schmaltz, Julien
Canciani, Andrea	Kim, Jin Hyun	Semini, Laura
Causevic, Adnan	Kincaid, Zachary	Steuwer, Michel
Chen, Xin	Knapik, Michał	Strathmann, Thomas
Chistikov, Dmitry	Kopecki, Steffen	Szreter, Maciej
de Vink, Erik	Korovina, Margarita	Tate, Ross
Del Tedesco, Filippo	Kuchen, Herbert	Torrini, Paolo
Dimitrakopoulos, George	Kullmann, Oliver	Tsarkov, Dmitry
Diéguez, Martín	Lasota, Sławomir	van Delft, Bart
Doganay, Kivanc	Li, Yi	Van Den Brand, Mark
Doh, Kyung-Goo	Lin, Anthony	van der Pol, Kevin
Dragan, Ioan	Lopes, Nuno P.	Van Der Werf,
Enoiu, Eduard Paul	Lorenzen, Florian	Jan Martijn
Fan, Guisheng	Meiländer, Dominik	von Styp, Sabrina
Fedyukovich, Grigory	Milazzo, Paolo	Vrgoc, Domagoj
Fleischhack, Hans	Moelle, Andre	Völlinger, Kim
Fu, Zhoulai	Mutilin, Vadim	Wilkeit, Elke
Gabbay, Murdoch	Nordlander, Johan	Winkowski, Jozef
Galletta, Letterio	Pardini, Giovanni	Xue, Bingtian
Gast, Holger	Patney, Anjul	Zantema, Hans
Gierds, Christian	Pedreira, Oscar	Zhong, Hao

The Laws of Concurrent Programming

(Abstract)

Tony Hoare

Microsoft Research Cambridge,
Cambridge, Great Britain

At the beginning of my academic career (1968), I wanted to express the axioms of sequential computer programming in the form of algebraic equations. But I did not know how. Instead I formalised the axioms as deduction rules for what became known as Hoare logic.

I now know how I should have done it as an algebra. Furthermore, I can add a few neat axioms that extend the algebra to concurrent programming. From the axioms one can prove the validity of the structural proof rules for Hoare logic, as extended to concurrency by separation logic. Furthermore, one can prove the deductive rules for an operational semantics of process algebra, expressed in the style of Milner. In fact, there is an algebraic time-reversal duality between the two forms of semantic rule. For me, this was a long-sought unification.

Big Data, Big Systems, Big Challenges:
A Personal Experience

(Extended abstract)

Vadim E. Kotov

Correspondent member of the Russian Academy of Sciences
Sunnyvale, CA, USA
vkotov@sv.cmu.edu

I have been fortunate to work in two remarkable research communities, Akademgor-odok in Siberia and Silicon Valley in California, and that my professional career stretched over two very different, yet both exciting epochs of the computer systems and science evolution: steady accumulation of knowledge and technology in 1960s–1980s and, then, "Internet Big Bang" and Information Revolution in 1990s–2010s.

In this talk, I track the trends in the development of large computer systems which I witnessed working first at Hewlett-Packard Laboratories and then at Carnegie-Mellon University, Silicon Valley Campus. This is not a general survey, I exemplify those trends by the systems in the analysis or/and design of which I and my colleagues participated.

The driving force behind the computer system progress is unprecedented accumulation of complex data and huge global data traffic. "Big Data" is a popular metaphor labeling the situation. It becomes difficult to process Big Data using traditional computer systems and applications. "Big Systems" that become the main trend in the current system architecture are required. They include: powerful data centers using tens of thousands servers; enterprise IT "systems of systems" consisting of globally distribute data centers; Grid and Utility Computing; Cloud Computing; Warehouse Scale Computers, Internet of Things (IoT), and coming exascale supersystems.

Contents

Descriptive Types for Linked Data Resources

Gabriel Ciobanu[1], Ross Horne[1,2(✉)], and Vladimiro Sassone[3]

[1] Institute of Computer Science, Romanian Academy, Blvd.
Carol I, No. 8, Iaşi, Romania
gabriel@info.uaic.ro
[2] Faculty of Information Technology, Kazakh-British
Technical University, Almaty, Kazakhstan
ross.horne@gmail.com
[3] Electronics and Computer Science, University of Southampton, Southampton, UK
vs@ecs.soton.ac.uk

Abstract. This work introduces the notion of descriptive typing. Type systems are typically prescriptive in the sense that they prescribe a space of permitted programs. In contrast, descriptive types assigned to resources in Linked Data provide useful annotations that describe how a resource may be used. Resources are represented by URIs that have no internal structure, hence there is no a priori type for a resource. Instead of raising compile time errors, a descriptive type system raises runtime warnings with a menu of options that make suggestions to the programmer. We introduce a subtype system, algorithmic type system and operational semantics that work together to characterise how descriptive types are used. The type system enables RDF Schema inference and several other modes of inference that are new to Linked Data.

1 Introduction

Linked Data is data published on the Web according to certain principles and standards. The main principle laid down by Berners-Lee in a note [2] is to use HTTP URIs to identify resources in data, e.g. *res:Andrey_Ershov*. By using HTTP URIs, anyone can use the HTTP protocol to look up (dereference) resources that appear in data in order to obtain more data. All URIs that appear in this paper are real dereferenceable URIs.

To facilitate interoperability, Web standards are employed. Data is represented in a simple graph-based format called the Resource Description Framework (RDF) [7]. In RDF, there is a notion of a *type*, for example *res:Andrey_Ershov* may be assigned the type *dbp:SovietComputerScientist*. RDF Schema [5] provides some simple mechanisms for organising these types into *hierarchies*. RDF Schema also enables the types of resources to be *inferred* in certain contexts.

If you ask the Linked Data scientist whether there is any link between types in RDF and type systems, they will explain that there is almost no connection. Traditionally, type systems are used for static analysis to prescribe a space of constraints on a system. In contrast, types in RDF change to describe the system instead of prescribing constraints on the system.

A. Voronkov and I. Virbitskaite (Eds.): PSI 2014, LNCS 8974, pp. 1–25, 2015.
DOI: 10.1007/978-3-662-46823-4_1

In this work, we provide a better answer to the question of the type-theoretic nature of types in Linked Data. We distinguish between a *prescriptive type system* and *descriptive type system*. In a traditional prescriptive type system, if a program is not well typed, then the program is rejected. In a descriptive type system[1], if a script is not well typed then the script can be executed but warnings are produced at runtime. The warnings present the user of the script with several options including expanding the type system itself to accommodate the script. Options can be selected interactively at any point during the execution of a script. Note that the user of a script is usually the programmer in this setting.

In Sect. 2, we present a motivating example of a scenario where descriptive typing can be applied to Linked Data to present meaningful warnings to a programmer that would like to interact with Linked Data.

In Sect. 3, we develop technical prerequisites for our descriptive type system. In particular, we require a notion of type and a consistent notion of subtyping. We develop these notions and present supporting results.

In Sect. 4, we continue the technical development of the type system. We introduce a simple scripting language for dereferencing resources over the Web and querying Linked Data in a local store. We devise an algorithmic type system that we use as part of our typing and inference mechanism.

In Sect. 5, we specify the behaviour of scripts using a novel operational semantics. The operational semantics allows us to refine the type system during execution in response to warnings. The operational semantics also enables us to formalise the examples in the motivating section. We describe an algorithm for deriving warnings based on constraints generated by the operational semantics and algorithmic type system. We conclude with a type reduction result that proves that, if the type system is sufficiently refined, then the script will run without unnecessary warnings.

2   Motivation for Descriptive Typing for Linked Data

We illustrate a scenario involving descriptive typing for scripts that interact with Linked Data. Descriptive typing generates meaningful warnings during the execution of a script, that can assist programmers without imposing obligations.

Suppose that at some point we would like to obtain data about Andrei Ershov. Our script firstly dereferences the URI *dbp:Andrei_Yershov* (in Russian Ershov and Yershov are transliterations of the same Cyrilic characters). From this we obtain some data including the following triples.

> *res:Andrei_Yershov   dbp:birthPlace   res:Soviet_Union.*
> *res:Andrei_Yershov   dbp:league   res:Kazakhstan_Major_League.*
> *res:Andrei_Yershov   rdf:type   dbp:IceHockeyPlayer.*

---

[1] The idea of descriptive types arose in joint work with Giuseppe Castagna and Giorgio Ghelli. Here we instantiate it for our Linked Data scripting language [6]. The development of descriptive types for the full SPARQL 1.1 specification will be given in a forthcoming paper by the above authors.

In the electronic version of this paper the above URIs are dereferenceable, allowing the reader to follow the links. The reader familiar with Ershov the academician will find the above data strange, but the script that performs the dereferencing has no experience to judge the correctness of the data.

The script then tries to query the data that has just been obtained, as follows:

> select $place
> where *res:Andrei_Yershov dbp:birthPlace* $place.

The above query uses a property *dbp:birthPlace* that can relate any person to any location. The database is aware, due to the DBPedia ontology [3], that *dbp:IceHockeyPlayer* is a subtype of *dbp:Person*. Hence the query is considered to be well typed. The query produces the result $place ↦ *res:Soviet_Union*, which appears to be correct.

Next the script tries a different query.

> select $book
> where *res:Andrei_Yershov free:book.author.works_written* $book.

Before the query is executed, it is type checked. The type system knows that the property *free:book.author.works_written* relates authors to books. The type system also knows, from the data obtained earlier, that *res:Andrei_Yershov* is an ice hockey player, which is not a subtype of author. The subject of the triple and the property appear not to match.

In a prescriptive type system the query would be automatically rejected as being wrong. In contrast, a *descriptive type system* provides warnings at runtime with several options to choose from other than outright rejection.

1. Change the type of *res:Andrei_Yershov* so that the resource is both an ice hockey player and an author.
2. Change the type of the property *free:book.author.works_written* so that ice hockey players can author books.
3. Change the subtype relations so that ice hockey player is a subtype of author, hence all ice hockey players are automatically inferred to be authors.
4. Change the data so that a different resource or property is used.

The default option for RDF Schema [14] is to infer that, because the subject of *free:book.author.works_written* is an author and *res:Andrei_Yershov* appears as the subject, then *res:Andrei_Yershov* must also be an author. The type of *res:Andrei_Yershov* would be refined to the following intersection of types.

> IntersectionOf(*dbp:IceHockeyPlayer*, *free:book.author*)

Academics can have colourful lives, so the above type may appear plausible to an observer unfamiliar with Ershov's life. However, this is a case of mistaken identity. Ershov the academician was never a professional ice hockey player.

The correct way to resolve the above conflict is instead to change the data. A query to freebase [4] and DBpedia [3] asking resources with name Ershov in Cyrillic that are book authors reveals that the intended Ershov was identified by *res:Andrey_Ershov* in DBpedia and *free:m.012s3l* in freebase.

We return to this example in Sect. 5, after developing the necessary technical apparatus.

3   Types and Subtyping for the Descriptive Type System

In this section, we introduce the types that are used in our type system. We explain the intuition behind each construct and how they are useful for describing resources. We also define how types are arranged into a hierarchy by using a subtype system.

3.1   Types for Classifying Resources

Many type systems are intimately connected to the form of data. For example, in XML Schema, the lexeme 3 has the type *xsd:integer*, whereas the lexeme ''Ershov'' has the type *xsd:string*. RDF does allow XML Schema datatypes to appear as objects in triples. Such literals should be typed prescriptively, since it should be forbidden to add a string to an integer or evaluate an integer using a regular expression.

Now consider the types of resources. Resources in RDF are represented by a URI that identifies the resource. The simplest answer is to say that the type of a resource is *xsd:anyURI*, in which case a prescriptive type system is sufficient, as defined in [6].

In this work, we draw inspiration from RDF Schema [5], which concerns types that classify resources. In RDF Schema, one resource can be classified using the type *dbp:IceHockeyPlayer*, and another using the type *yago:SovietComputerScientists*. Both resources are represented as URIs, so there is nothing about the syntax of the resources that distinguishes their type.

Notice that basic types themselves are also URIs. We use these basic types as the *atomic types* of our type system. The full syntax for types is presented in Fig. 1.

Type ::=	*atom*	*atomic type*
	owl:Thing	*top type*
	`IntersectionOf`(*Type*, *Type*)	*intersection type*
	`UnionOf`(*Type*, *Type*)	*union type*
	`Property`(*Type*, *Type*)	*property type*

Fig. 1. The syntax of descriptive types.

In Fig. 1, there are three type constructors, namely intersection, union, and property types. There is also a top type *owl:Thing* that represents the type of all resources.

Intersection Types. The intersection type constructor is used to combine several types. For example, acording to DBpedia, *res:Andrey_Ershov* has several types, including *yago:SovietComputerScientists* and *yago:FellowsOfTheBritish ComputerSociety*. In this case, the following intersection type can be assigned to *res:Andrey_Ershov*.

```
IntersectionOf ( yago:SovietComputerScientists ,
                 yago:FellowsOfTheBritishComputerSociety )
```

Intuitively, the resource *res:Andrey_Ershov* is a member of the intersection of the set of all resources that have the type *yago:SovietComputerScientists* and the set of all resources of type *yago:FellowsOfTheBritishComputerSociety*.

Property Types. The property type is inspired by RDF Schema [5], which enables the domain and range of a property to be declared. In RDF [7], the basic unit of data is a triple, such as:

$$res:Andrei\_Yershov \quad dbp:birthPlace \quad res:Voskresensk.$$

The elements of a triple are the subject, property and object respectively. Here the subject is expected to be of type *dbp:Person*, the object is expected to be of type *dbp:Settlement*, while the property is assigned the following type.

$$\texttt{Property}(dbp:Person, \ dbp:Settlement)$$

In RDF Schema, this type represent two statements: one that declares that the domain of the property is *dbp:Person*, and another that declares that the range of the property is *dbp:Settlement*.

Union Types. If we inspect the data in DBpedia, we discover that the following triple also appears.

$$res:Andrei\_Yershov \quad dbp:birthPlace \quad res:SovietUnion.$$

Observe that *res:SovietUnion* is not a settlement. We can use the union type to refine the above type so that the range of the property is either a settlement or a country. The refined type for *dbp:birthPlace*, involving union, is as follows.

$$\texttt{Property}(dbp:Person, \ \texttt{UnionOf}(dbp:Settlement, \ dbp:Country))$$

Notice that intersection would not be appropriate above. If we replace `UnionOf` with `IntersectionOf` in the above example, the range of the property is restricted to resources that are both a settlement and a country (e.g. Singapore), which is not the intended semantics of *dbp:birthPlace*.

Top Type. Intuitively the top type ranges over the set of all resources. If a resource has no descriptive type information, then it can be assigned the top type. The resource *yago:Random_access_machine* in the Yago dataset [16] has no type other than *owl:Thing*.

In Yago the following triple relates Ershov to the random access machine.

$$yago:Andrei\_Ershov \quad yago:linksTo \quad yago:Random\_access\_machine$$

The property *yago:linksTo* is very general, relating any resource to any resource, as indicated by the property type `Property`(*owl:Thing*, *owl:Thing*).

Notice that the syntax of types is liberally expressive. We can express type that are both atomic types and property types, allowing multiple uses of one URI. This design decision accommodates the subjective nature of human knowledge and data representation, without the system becoming higher order. A descriptive type system is expected to evolve, hence we do not want to restrict unforeseeable developments in its evolution.

3.2 A Subtype Relation Over Descriptive Types

Types form a lattice defined by a subtype relation. The subtype relation, defined in Fig. 2, determines when a resource of one type can be used as a resource of another type. This relation is important for both typing systems and for refining the type system itself, in response to warnings.

$$\frac{\vdash C \leq D}{\vdash C \leq \mathtt{UnionOf}(D, E)} \textit{ left injection} \qquad \frac{\vdash C \leq E}{\vdash C \leq \mathtt{UnionOf}(C, E)} \textit{ right injection}$$

$$\frac{\vdash C \leq E \qquad \vdash D \leq E}{\vdash \mathtt{UnionOf}(C, D) \leq E} \textit{ least upper bound}$$

$$\frac{\vdash C \leq E}{\vdash \mathtt{IntersectionOf}(C, D) \leq E} \textit{ left projection} \qquad \frac{\vdash D \leq E}{\vdash \mathtt{IntersectionOf}(C, D) \leq E} \textit{ right projection}$$

$$\frac{\vdash C \leq D \qquad \vdash C \leq E}{\vdash C \leq \mathtt{IntersectionOf}(D, E)} \textit{ greatest lower bound}$$

$$\frac{\vdash C_0 \leq C_1 \qquad \vdash D_0 \leq D_1}{\vdash \mathtt{Property}(C_1, D_1) \leq \mathtt{Property}(C_0, D_0)} \textit{ property}$$

$$\frac{}{\vdash C \leq \textit{owl:Thing}} \textit{ top} \qquad \frac{a \leq b \in \mathrm{SC}^*}{\vdash a \leq b} \textit{ atoms} \qquad \frac{\vdash C \leq D \quad \vdash D \leq E}{\vdash C \leq E} \textit{ cut}$$

Fig. 2. Axioms and rules of the subtype system.

Axioms. We assume that there are a number of subtype inequalities that relate atomic types to each other. For example, we may assume that the following subtype inequalities hold.

$$dbp{:}Settlement \leq dbp{:}PopulatedPlace \qquad dbp{:}Country \leq dbp{:}PopulatedPlace$$

$$yago{:}CitiesAndTownsInMoscowOblast \leq dbp{:}Settlement$$

These inequalities are inspired by the *rdfs:subClassOf* property from RDF Schema, which defines a reflexive transitive relation [14]. We call a subclass relation SC the set of *subtype assumptions*. We denote the reflexive transitive closure of SC as SC*. Notice that SC is a relation over a finite number of atomic types, hence SC* is efficient to calculate using techniques such as the Dedekind-MacNeille completion [13].

The relation SC* is used in the axiom *atoms* in Fig. 2. The *top* axiom states that every resource is of type *owl:Thing*.

Rules for Union, Intersection and Properties. Suppose that another hint from the type system leads to the type of the property *dbp:birthPlace* to be refined further. The hint suggest that the range of the property should include *dbp:Populated-Place.* From the subtype rules, we can derive the following inequality.

$$\vdash \begin{array}{l} \texttt{Property}(\ dbp{:}Person\ , \\ \qquad dbp{:}PopulatedPlace\ ) \end{array} \le \begin{array}{l} \texttt{Property}(\ dbp{:}Person\ , \\ \qquad \texttt{UnionOf}(dbp{:}Settlement,\ dbp{:}Country)) \end{array}$$

The proof follows from applying first the *property* rule, that swaps the direction of subtyping in each component, generating the following subtype constraint, and an axiom.

$$\vdash \texttt{UnionOf}(dbp{:}Settlement,\ dbp{:}Country) \le dbp{:}PopulatedPlace$$

The above constraint is solved by applying the *least upper bound* rule and *atoms* rule. The least upper bound rule generates two inequalities between atomic types that were declared to be in SC* above. The above subtype inequality between properties suggests that a property with range *dbp:PopulatedPlace* can also range over resources that are settlements or countries.

Now suppose that the following inequality is added to the relation SC.

$$yago{:}SovietComputerScientists \le dbp{:}Person$$

By the *left projection* rule and the above subtype inequality, we can derive the following subtype inequality.

$$\vdash \texttt{IntersectionOf}\ (\ yago{:}SovietComputerScientists\ , \\ \qquad\qquad yago{:}FellowsOfTheBritishComputerSociety\ ) \le dbp{:}Person$$

The above inequality suggests that Ershov can be treated as a person, although his type does not explicitly mention the atomic type *dbp:Person*.

The Cut Rule. A subtype relation is expected to be a transitive relation. To prove that subtyping is transitive, we include the *cut* rule in our subtype system and then show that any subtype inequality that is derived using cut can also be derived without using cut. In proof theory, this consistency result is known as *cut elimination.*

Theorem 1 (Cut elimination). *The cut rule can be eliminated from the given subtype system using an algorithmic procedure.*

Proof. The proof works by transforming the derivation tree for a subtype judgement into another derivation tree with the same conclusion. The transformation is indicated by $[\![\cdot]\!]$. The symbol π_i above a subtype inequality represents a proof tree with the subtype inequality as its conclusion.

Without loss of generality, assume that the rule applied at the base of the proof tree is the cut rule. The proof proceeds by induction over the structure of the proof tree.

Consider the case of cut applied across two axioms for atoms. Since SC* is transitively closed, if $a \leq b \in SC^*$ and $b \leq c \in SC^*$, then we know that $a \leq c \in SC^*$. Hence the following transformation simplifies atom axioms.

$$\left[\begin{array}{c} \dfrac{\dfrac{a \leq b \in SC^*}{\vdash a \leq b} \quad \dfrac{b \leq c \in SC^*}{\vdash b \leq c}}{\vdash a \leq c} \end{array}\right] \longrightarrow \dfrac{a \leq c \in SC^*}{\vdash a \leq c}$$

The above case is a base case for the induction. The other base case is when the top rule is applied on the right branch of the cut rule. In this case, the cut can be absorbed by the top type axiom, as follows.

$$\left[\begin{array}{c} \dfrac{\overset{\pi}{\vdash C \leq D} \quad \overline{\vdash D \leq owl{:}Thing}}{\vdash C \leq owl{:}Thing} \end{array}\right] \longrightarrow \overline{\vdash C \leq owl{:}Thing}$$

The result of the above transformation step is clearly cut free.

Consider the case where the left branch of a cut is another *cut* rule. The nested cut rule can be normalised first, as demonstrated by the transformation bellow.

$$\left[\begin{array}{c} \dfrac{\dfrac{\overset{\pi_0}{\vdash C \leq D} \quad \overset{\pi_1}{\vdash D \leq E}}{\vdash C \leq E} \quad \overset{\pi_2}{\vdash E \leq F}}{\vdash C \leq F} \end{array}\right] \longrightarrow \left[\begin{array}{c} \left[\dfrac{\overset{\pi_0}{\vdash C \leq D} \quad \overset{\pi_1}{\vdash D \leq E}}{\vdash C \leq E}\right] \quad \overset{\pi_2}{\vdash E \leq F} \\ \hline \vdash C \leq F \end{array}\right]$$

By induction, the resulting nested tree is transformed into a cut free derivation tree; hence another case applies. This induction step is symmetric when a nested cut appears on the right branch of a cut.

Consider the case where the *least upper bound* rule appears on the left branch of a cut. In this case, the transformation can be applied separately to each of the premises of the union introduction rule, as demonstrated below.

$$\left[\begin{array}{c} \dfrac{\dfrac{\overset{\pi_0}{\vdash C_0 \leq D} \quad \overset{\pi_1}{\vdash C_1 \leq D}}{\vdash \mathtt{UnionOf}(C_0, C_1) \leq D} \quad \overset{\pi_2}{\vdash D \leq E}}{\vdash \mathtt{UnionOf}(C_0, C_1) \leq E} \end{array}\right]$$

$$\longrightarrow \dfrac{\left[\dfrac{\overset{\pi_0}{\vdash C_0 \leq D} \quad \overset{\pi_2}{\vdash D \leq E}}{\vdash C_0 \leq E}\right] \quad \left[\dfrac{\overset{\pi_1}{\vdash C_1 \leq D} \quad \overset{\pi_2}{\vdash D \leq E}}{\vdash C_1 \leq E}\right]}{\vdash \mathtt{UnionOf}(C_0, C_1) \leq E}$$

By induction, the result of the transformation is a cut free proof. The case for the *greatest lower bound* is symmetric, with the order of subtyping exchanged and union exchanged for intersection.

Consider the case of the injection rules. Without loss of generality, consider the *left injection* rule. In this case, the cut is pushed up the proof tree, as demonstrated below.

$$\left[\begin{array}{c} \dfrac{\overset{\pi_0}{\vdash C \leq D} \quad \dfrac{\overset{\pi_1}{\vdash D \leq E_0}}{\vdash D \leq \mathtt{UnionOf}(E_0, E_1)}}{\vdash C \leq \mathtt{UnionOf}(E_0, E_1)} \end{array}\right] \longrightarrow \left[\begin{array}{c} \dfrac{\dfrac{\overset{\pi_0}{\vdash C \leq D} \quad \overset{\pi_1}{\vdash D \leq E_0}}{\vdash C \leq E_0}}{\vdash C \leq \mathtt{UnionOf}(E_0, E_1)} \end{array}\right]$$

By induction, the result is a cut free proof. The cases for *right injection, left projection* and *right projection* are similar.

Consider an *injection* rule applied on the left of a cut, and *least upper bound* rule applied on the right of a cut. This is a *principal case* of the cut elimination procedure. Without loss of generality, consider the left projection. The result of the transformation is that only the left premise of the union introduction rule is required; the irrelevant branch is removed by the elimination step, as demonstrated below.

$$\left[\!\!\left[\dfrac{\dfrac{\pi_0}{\vdash C \le D_0} \quad \dfrac{\dfrac{\pi_1}{\vdash D_0 \le E} \quad \dfrac{\pi_2}{\vdash D_1 \le E}}{\vdash \texttt{UnionOf}(D_0, D_1) \le E}}{\vdash C \le E} \right]\!\!\right] \longrightarrow \left[\!\!\left[\dfrac{\dfrac{\pi_0}{\vdash C \le D_0} \quad \dfrac{\pi_1}{\vdash D_0 \le E}}{\vdash C \le E} \right]\!\!\right]$$

By induction, the result of the transformation is a cut-free proof. The principal case for intersection is similar to union.

Consider the case of cut applied to two predicate subtype rules. In this case, the contravariant premises of each subtype rule are cut individually, as follows.

$$\left[\!\!\left[\dfrac{\dfrac{\dfrac{\pi_0}{\vdash D_0 \le C_0} \quad \dfrac{\pi_0'}{\vdash D_1 \le C_1}}{\vdash \texttt{Property}(C_0, C_1) \le \texttt{Property}(D_0, D_1)} \quad \dfrac{\dfrac{\pi_1}{\vdash E_0 \le D_0} \quad \dfrac{\pi_1'}{\vdash D_1 \le E_1}}{\vdash \texttt{Property}(D_0, D_1) \le \texttt{Property}(E_0, E_1)}}{\vdash \texttt{Property}(C_0, C_1) \le \texttt{Property}(E_0, E_1)} \right]\!\!\right]$$

$$\longrightarrow \dfrac{\left[\!\!\left[\dfrac{\dfrac{\pi_1}{\vdash E_0 \le D_0} \quad \dfrac{\pi_0}{\vdash D_0 \le C_0}}{\vdash E_0 \le C_0} \right]\!\!\right] \quad \left[\!\!\left[\dfrac{\dfrac{\pi_0'}{\vdash E_1 \le D_1} \quad \dfrac{\pi_1'}{\vdash D_1 \le C_1}}{\vdash E_1 \le C_1} \right]\!\!\right]}{\vdash \texttt{Property}(C_0, C_1) \le \texttt{Property}(E_0, E_1)}$$

By induction, each of the new transformations on the right above have a cut-free proof, so the result of original transformation on the left above has a cut-free proof.

For every cut one of the above cases applies. Furthermore, in each transformation a finite number of proof trees are considered after a transformation step, each of which has a smaller depth than the original proof tree; hence by a standard multiset ordering argument [8] it is easy to see that the procedure terminates. Therefore, by structural induction on the derivation tree, a cut free derivation tree with the same conclusion can be constructed for any derivation. □

Cut elimination proves that the subtype system is transitive. It is straightforward to prove that the subtype system is reflexive, by structural induction. Also, the direction of subtyping is preserved (monotonicity) by conjunction and disjunction, while the direction of subtyping is reversed (antitonicity) for property types. Monotonicity and antitonicity can be established by a direct proof.

Proposition 1. *For any type* $\vdash C \le C$ *is derivable. Also, if* $\vdash C_0 \le D_0$ *and* $\vdash C_1 \le D_1$ *then the following hold:*

- $\vdash \textit{IntersectionOf}(C_0, C_1) \le \textit{IntersectionOf}(D_0, D_1)$ *is derivable.*
- $\vdash \textit{UnionOf}(C_0, C_1) \le \textit{UnionOf}(D_0, D_1)$ *is derivable.*
- $\vdash \textit{Property}(D_0, D_1) \le \textit{Property}(C_0, C_1)$ *is derivable.*

$$
\begin{array}{ll}
term ::= variable \mid uri & script ::= \mathbf{ok} \\
& \mid \mathbf{where}\ term\ term\ term\ script \\
data ::= term\ term\ term & \mid \mathbf{from}\ term\ script \\
\quad\mid data\ data & \mid \mathbf{select}\ variable\colon type\ script
\end{array}
$$

Fig. 3. The syntax of scripts and data.

Theorem 1 and Proposition 1 are sufficient to establish the consistency of the subtype system.

Our subtype system is closely related to the functional programming language with intersection and union types presented by Barbanera et al. [1]. Our subtype system without properties coincides with the subtype system of Barbanera et al. without implication. Furthermore, properties can be encoded using implication, so our system is a restriction of the system presented in [1].

4 An Algorithmic Type System for Scripts and Data

We introduce a simple scripting language for interacting with Linked Data. The language enables resources to be dereferenced and for data to be queried. This language is a restriction of the scripting language presented in [6]; which is based on process calculi presented in [9,12]. We keep the language here simple to maintain the focus on descriptive types.

4.1 The Syntax of a Simple Scripting Language for Linked Data

The syntax of scripts is presented in Fig. 3. Terms in the language are *URIs* which are identifiers for resources, or *variables* of the form $x. RDF triples [7] and triple patterns are represented as three terms separated by spaces. The **where** keyword prefixes a triple pattern. The keyword **ok**, representing a successfully terminated script, is dropped in examples. Data is simply one or more triples, representing an RDF graph.

The keyword **from** *res:Andrei_Yershov* represents dereferencing the given resource. The HTTP protocol is used to obtain some data from the URI, and the data obtained is loaded into a graph local to the script (see [6] for an extensive discussion of the related **from named** construct).

The keyword **where** represents executing a query over the local graph that was populated by dereferencing resources. The query can execute only if the data in the local graph matches the pattern. Variables representing resources to be discovered by the query are bound using the **select** keyword (see [12] for the analysis of more expressive query languages based on SPARQL [10,15]).

4.2 An Algorithmic Type System for Scripts and Data

We type scripts for two purposes. Firstly, if the script is correctly typed, then we can check that it is well typed and execute the script without throwing any warnings. However, if the script is not well typed, we can use the type system as the basis of an algorithm for generating warnings. Scripts and data are typed using the system presented in Fig. 4. There are typing rules for each form of term, script and data.

$$\frac{\vdash C \leq D}{\text{Env}, \$x\colon C \vdash \$x\colon D} \; variable \qquad \frac{\vdash \text{Ty}(uri) \leq C}{\text{Env} \vdash uri\colon C} \; resource \qquad \frac{}{\text{Env} \vdash \texttt{ok}} \; success$$

$$\frac{\text{Env}, \$x\colon type \vdash script}{\text{Env} \vdash \texttt{select } \$x\colon type \; script} \; select \qquad \frac{\text{Env} \vdash script}{\text{Env} \vdash \texttt{from } uri \; script} \; from$$

$$\frac{\text{Env} \vdash term_0\colon C \quad \text{Env} \vdash term_1\colon \texttt{Property}(C, D) \quad \text{Env} \vdash term_2\colon D \quad \text{Env} \vdash script}{\text{Env} \vdash \texttt{where } term_0 \; term_1 \; term_2 \; script} \; where$$

$$\frac{\text{Env} \vdash term_0\colon C \quad \text{Env} \vdash term_1\colon \texttt{Property}(C, D) \quad \text{Env} \vdash term_2\colon D}{\text{Env} \vdash term_0 \; term_1 \; term_2} \; triple$$

$$\frac{\text{Env} \vdash data_0 \quad \text{Env} \vdash data_1}{\text{Env} \vdash data_0 \; data_1} \; compose \qquad \frac{\text{Env} \vdash term\colon atom}{\text{Env} \vdash term \; rdf\!:\!type \; atom} \; RDF \; type$$

$$\frac{\text{Env} \vdash term\colon C \quad \vdash C \leq D}{\text{Env} \vdash term\colon D} \; subsumption$$

Fig. 4. The type system for scripts and data.

Typing Data. To type resources we require a partial function Ty from resources to types. This represents the current type of resources assumed by the system. We write Ty(uri) for the current type of the resource, and call Ty the *type assumptions*. The type rule for resources states that a resource can assume any supertype of its current type. For example Ershov can be a person even though his type is the intersection of several professions, as illustrated in the previous section.

The type rule for triples assumes that a triple is well typed as long as the subject and object of a triple can match the type of the property type assumed by the predicate. Well typed triples are then composed together.

Triples with the reserved URI *rdf:type* in the property position are treated differently from other triples. In the *RDF type* rule, the object is an atomic type and the subject is a term of the given atomic type. This rule is used to extract type information from data during inference, and can be viewed as a *type ascription*. Further special type ascription rules could be added to extract more refined types based on OWL [11]; however the rule for atomic types is sufficient for the examples in this paper.

Typing Scripts. Variables may appear in scripts. The type rule for variables is similar to the type rule for resources, except that the type of a variable is drawn from the *type environment*, which appears on the left of the turnstile in a judgement. A type environment consists of a set of type assignments of the form

$x: C$. As standard, a variable is assigned a unique type in a type environment. Type assumptions are introduced in the type environment using the type rule for `select`.

The rule for `where` is similar to the type rule for triples, except that there is a continuation script. A script prefixed with `from` is always well typed as long as the continuation script is well typed, since we work only with dereferenceable resources. A prescriptive type system involving data, such as numbers which cannot be dereferenced as in [6], takes more care at this point. The terminated script is always well typed.

The Subsumption Rule. Derivation trees in an algorithmic type system are linear in the size of the syntax. The *subsumption* rule relaxes the type of a term at any point in a typing derivation. Since we can apply subsumption repeatedly it could give rise to type derivations of an unbounded size. By showing that subsumption can be eliminated, we establish that the type system without subsumption is an *algorithmic type system*.

Proposition 2 (Algorithmic Typing). *For any type assumption that can be derived using the type system, we can construct a type derivation with the same conclusion where the subsumption rule has been eliminated from the derivation tree.*

Proof. There are three similar cases to consider, namely when a subsumption immediately follows: another subsumption rule; or a type rule for resources, or a type rule for variables. In each case notice that, by Theorem 1, if $\vdash C \leq D$ and $\vdash D \leq E$, then we can construct a cut-free derivation for $\vdash C \leq E$. Hence, in each of the following, the type derivation of the left can be transformed into the type derivation on the right.

1. $$\frac{\dfrac{Env \vdash term\colon C \quad \vdash C \leq D}{Env \vdash term\colon D} \quad \vdash D \leq E}{Env \vdash term\colon E} \quad \text{yields} \quad \frac{Env \vdash term\colon C \quad \vdash C \leq E}{Env \vdash term\colon E}$$

2. $$\frac{\dfrac{\vdash Ty(uri) \leq D}{Env \vdash uri\colon D} \quad \vdash D \leq E}{Env \vdash uri\colon E} \ \text{where } Ty(uri) = C \quad \text{yields} \quad \frac{\vdash Ty(uri) \leq E}{Env \vdash term\colon E}$$

3. $$\frac{\dfrac{\vdash C \leq D}{Env, \$x\colon C \vdash \$x\colon D} \quad \vdash D \leq E}{Env, \$x\colon C \vdash \$x\colon E} \quad \text{yields} \quad \frac{\vdash C \leq E}{Env, \$x\colon C \vdash \$x\colon E}$$

For other type rules subsumption cannot be applied, so the induction step follows immediately. Hence, by induction on the structure of a type derivation, all occurrences of the subsumption rule can be eliminated. □

Since the type system is algorithmic, we can use it efficiently as the basis for inference algorithms that we will employ in Sect. 5.

Monotonicity. We define an ordering over type assumptions and subtype assumptions. This ordering allows us to *refine* our type system by enlarging the subtype assumptions; by enlarging the domain of the type assumptions; and by tightening the types of resources with respect to the subtype relation. Refinement can be formalised as follows.

Definition 1. *When we would like to be explicit about the subtype assumptions SC and type assumptions Ty used in a type judgement $Env \vdash script$ and subtype judgement $\vdash C \leq D$, we use the following notation:*

$$Env \vdash_{SC}^{Ty} script \qquad\qquad \vdash_{SC} C \leq D$$

We define a refinement relation $(Ty', SC') \leq (Ty, SC)$, such that:

1. *$SC \subseteq SC'$.*
2. *For all uri such that $Ty(uri) = D$, there is some C such that $Ty'(uri) = C$ and $\vdash_{SC'} C \leq D$.*

We say that (Ty', SC') is a refinement of (Ty, SC).

In a descriptive type system, we give the option to refine the type system in response to warnings that appear. The following two lemmas are steps towards establishing soundness of the type system in the presence of refinements of subtype and type assumptions. The lemmas establish that anything that is well typed remains well typed in a refined type system.

Lemma 1. *If $\vdash_{SC} C \leq D$ and $SC \subseteq SC'$, then $\vdash_{SC'} C \leq D$.*

Proof. Observe that only the atom rule uses SC. Also notice that if $a \leq b \in SC^*$, and $SC \subseteq SC'$, then $a \leq b \in SC'^*$. Hence if the subtype axiom on the left below holds, then the subtype axiom on the right below holds.

$$\frac{a \leq b \in SC^*}{\vdash_{SC} a \leq b} \qquad \text{yields} \qquad \frac{a \leq b \in SC'^*}{\vdash_{SC'} a \leq b}$$

All other cases do not involve SC, hence the induction steps are immediate. Hence, by structural induction, the set of subtype assumptions can be enlarged while preserving the subtype judgements. □

Lemma 2. *The following monotonicity properties hold for scripts and data respectively.*

1. *If $\vdash_{SC}^{Ty} script$ and $(Ty', SC') \leq (Ty, SC)$, then $\vdash_{SC'}^{Ty'} script$.*
2. *If $\vdash_{SC}^{Ty} data$ and $(Ty', SC') \leq (Ty, SC)$, then $\vdash_{SC'}^{Ty'} data$.*

Proof. For type assumptions, observe that the only rule involving Ty is the rule for typing resources. Assume that $(Ty', SC') \leq (Ty, SC)$. By definition, if $Ty(uri) = D$ then $Ty'(uri) = C$ and $\vdash_{SC'} C \leq D$ where $SC \subseteq SC'$. Hence if $\vdash_{SC} D \leq E$, by Lemma 1, $\vdash_{SC'} D \leq E$. Hence, by Theorem 1, we can construct a cut free proof of $\vdash_{SC'} C \leq E$. Therefore if the type axiom on the left below holds, then the type axiom on the right also holds.

$$\frac{\vdash_{SC} Ty(uri) \leq E}{Env \vdash_{SC}^{Ty} uri : E} \qquad \text{yields} \qquad \frac{\vdash_{SC'} Ty'(uri) \leq E}{Env \vdash_{SC'}^{Ty'} uri : E}$$

Consider the type rule for variables. By Lemma 1, if $\vdash_{SC} C \leq D$ then $\vdash_{SC'} C \leq D$. Therefore if the type axiom on the left below holds, then the type axiom on the right also holds.

$$\frac{\vdash_{SC} C \leq D}{\text{Env}, \$x \colon C \vdash \$x \colon D} \qquad \text{yields} \qquad \frac{\vdash_{SC'} C \leq D}{\text{Env}, \$x \colon C \vdash \$x \colon D}$$

All other rules do not involve Ty or SC, hence follow immediately. Therefore, by structural induction, refining the type system preserves well typed scripts and data. $\qquad\qquad\qquad\qquad\qquad\qquad\qquad\qquad\qquad\qquad\qquad\qquad\qquad\qquad\quad$ □

5   An Operational Semantics Aware of Descriptive Types

This section is the high point of this paper. We illustrate how descriptive typing is fundamentally different from prescriptive typing.

In a prescriptive type system, we only permit the execution of programs that are well typed. In contrast, in this descriptive type system, if a program is not well typed, then the program can still be executed. During the execution of an ill typed program, warnings are generated. At runtime, the program provides the *option* to, at any point during the execution of the program, *address the warnings* and *refine the type system* to resolve the warnings.

5.1   The Operational Semantics

The rules of the operational semantics are presented in Fig. 5. The first three are the operational rules for `select`, `where` and `from` respectively. The fourth rule is the *optional* rule that refines the type system in response to warnings. We quotient data such that the composition of data is associative and commutative.

Configurations. A configuration (*script, data*, Ty, SC) represents the state that can change during the execution of a program. It consists of four components:

– The script *script* that is currently being executed.
– The data *data* representing triples that are currently stored locally.
– A partial function Ty from resources to types, representing the current type assumptions about resources.
– A relation over atomic types SC, representing the current subtype assumptions.

Type assumptions and subtype assumptions can be changed by the rules of the operational semantics, since they are part of the runtime state.

Example of a Good Script. We explain the interplay between the operational rules using a concrete example. Suppose that initially we have a configuration consisting of:

$$\frac{\vdash^{Ty}_{SC} uri \colon C}{(\texttt{select } uri \colon C \; script, data, Ty, SC) \longrightarrow (script\{^{uri}/_{sx}\}, data, Ty, SC)} \; select$$

$$\frac{}{\begin{array}{l}(\,\texttt{where } term_0 \; term_1 \; term_2 \; script, \\ \quad term_0 \; term_1 \; term_2 \; data, Ty, SC)\end{array} \longrightarrow (script, term_0 \; term_1 \; term_2 \; data, Ty, SC)} \; where$$

$$\frac{(Ty', SC') \le (Ty, SC) \quad \vdash^{Ty'}_{SC'} data_1}{(\texttt{from } uri \; script, data_0, Ty, SC) \longrightarrow (script, data_0 \; data_1, Ty', SC')} \; from$$

$$\frac{(Ty', SC') \le (Ty, SC) \quad \vdash^{Ty'}_{SC'} script}{(script, data, Ty, SC) \longrightarrow (script, data, Ty', SC')} \; optional$$

Fig. 5. The operational semantics for scripts. Note that, in the *from* rule, $data_1$ is the data obtained at runtime by dereferencing the resource *uri*.

– a script:

> from *res:Andrey_Ershov*
> select \$place: *dbp:PopulatedPlace*
> where *res:Andrey_Ershov dbp:birthPlace* \$place

– some data $data_0$ including triples such as the following:

> *dbp:birthPlace   rdfs:domain   dbp:Person*
> *dbp:birthPlace   rdfs:range   dbp:PopulatedPlace*
> *res:SovietUnion   rdf:type   dbp:PopulatedPlace*

– some type assumptions Ty such that:

> $Ty(dbp{:}birthPlace) = \texttt{Property}(\; dbp{:}Person,$
> $\qquad\qquad\qquad\qquad\qquad dbp{:}PopulatedPlace\;)$
> $Ty(res{:}Andrey\_Ershov) = owl{:}Thing$
> $Ty(res{:}SovietUnion) = dbp{:}PopulatedPlace$

– an empty set of subtype assumptions.

The above script is not well typed with respect to the type assumptions, since the strongest type for *res:Andrey_Ershov* is the top type, which is insufficient to establish that the resource represents a person.

There are several options other than rejecting the ill typed script. We can inspect the warning, which provides a menu of options to refine the type system so that the script is well typed. At this stage of execution, there are two reasonable solutions: either we can refine the type of *res:Andrey_Ershov*, so that he is of type *dbp:Person*; or we can refine the type of *dbp:birthPlace* so that it can relate any resource to a populated place.

A further option is available. Since these are warnings, we can ignore them and continue executing the script. Assuming we choose to ignore the warnings at this stage, we apply the operational rule for from.

The rule involves some new data $data_1$ that is obtained by dereferencing the resource with URI *dbp:Andrey_Ershov*. This includes triples such as:

res:Andrei_Ershov rdf:type yago:FellowsOfTheBritishComputerSociety
res:Andrei_Ershov dbp:birthPlace res:SovietUnion

The rule must calculate (Ty', SC') such that $(Ty', SC') \leq (Ty, SC)$ and $\vdash_{SC'}^{Ty'}$ $data_1$. Again there are several options for resolving the above constraints, presented below.

1. Refine the type assumptions such that the resource *res:Andrey_Ershov* is assigned the intersection of *yago:FellowsOfTheBritishComputerSociety* and *dbp:Person* as its type.
2. Refine the type of Ershov to the type *yago:FellowsOfTheBritishComputer Society* and refine the type of property *dbp:birthPlace* such that it is of the following type:

    IntersectionOf(Property(*dbp:Person*,
    dbp:PopulatedPlace),
    Property(*yago:FellowsOfTheBritishComputerSociety*,
    dbp:PopulatedPlace))

3. Refine the subtype assumptions to SC' such that it contains the following subtype inequality:

    yago:FellowsOfTheBritishComputerSociety $\leq$ *dbp:Person*

The first option above is the default option taken by RDF Schema [5]. It assumes that, since the domain of the property was *dbp:Person*, Ershov must be a person. The second option above makes the property more accommodating, so that it can also be used to relate fellows of the British Computer Society to populated places. The third option is the most general solution, since it allows any fellow of the British Computer Society to be used as a person in all circumstances.

The choice of option is subjective, so is delegated to a human. Suppose that the programmer selects the third option. This results in the following configuration:

– a script where the leading from keyword has been removed:

    select $place: *dbp:PopulatedPlace*
    where *res:Andrey_Ershov dbp:birthPlace* $place

– some data $data_0$ $data_1$ including the new data obtained by dereferencing the resource *dbp:Andrey_Ershov*;
– a refined type assumption Ty', such that:

    Ty'(*res:Andrey_Ershov*) = *yago:FellowsOfTheBritishComputerSociety*

– the refined subtype assumptions SC' suggested in the third option above.

Having resolved the warning we are now in the fortunate situation that the remainder of the script is also well typed with respect to the new type and subtype assumptions. Thus we can continue executing without further warnings.

We apply the operational rule for `select`. This rule dynamically checks that the following holds.

$$\vdash_{SC'}^{Ty'} res{:}SovietUnion : dbp{:}PopulatedPlace$$

Since the above subtype judgement holds, the substitution is applied to obtain a configuration with the following script.

$$\textsf{where } res{:}Andrey\_Ershov \; dbp{:}birthPlace \; res{:}SovietUnion$$

Finally, since the triple in the `where` clause matches a triple in the data, we can apply the operational rule for `where`. This successfully completes the execution of the script.

Example of a Bad Script. Now consider the example in the motivating section. We begin with the following configuration, where the wrong URI has been used for Ershov:

– the following script:

       `from` *res:Andrei_Yershov*
       `select` $book: *free:book*
       `where` *res:Andrei_Yershov free:book.author.works_written* $book.

– some initial data $data_0$ including triples such as:

       free:book.author.works_written rdfs:domain free:book.author
       free:book.author.works_written rdfs:range free:book

– initial type assumptions Ty such that:

$$\text{Ty}(\textit{free{:}book.author.works\_written}) = \texttt{Property}(\textit{ free{:}book.author,} \\ \textit{free{:}book })$$

– an empty set of subtype assumptions.

The programmer has not yet realised that *res:Andrei_Yershov* represents an ice hockey player who is not the intended scientist. At runtime, the programmer initially ignores a menu of warnings that would enable the *optional* rule to be applied. One option suggests that the type of *res:Andrei_Yershov* should be *free:book.author*; another option suggest refining the type of *free:book.author. works_written* to the following type.

$$\texttt{Property}(\textit{owl{:}Thing}, \textit{free{:}book})$$

The programmer decides to ignore the warnings and continue executing the script. As in the previous example, we apply the `from` rule. This dereferences the resource *res:Andrei_Yershov* obtaining some new data $data_1$ including the following triple.

$$res{:}Andrei\_Yershov \quad rdf{:}type \quad dbp{:}IceHockeyPlayer$$

There is only one good option in this case, which that script automatically selects. It sets a refined type assumption Ty such that the following holds.

$$\text{Ty}'(res{:}Andrei\_Yershov) = dbp{:}IceHockeyPlayer$$

In the new configuration, there are still warnings that are induced by attempting to apply the *optional* rule. The following menu of options is presented to the programmer.

1. Refine the type assumptions such that the resource *res:Andrei_Yershov* is assigned the intersection of *yago:IceHockeyPlayer* and *dbp:Person* as its type.
2. Refine the type of the property *free:book.author.works_written* such that it is of the following type.

$$\texttt{IntersectionOf}(\ \texttt{Property}(\ free{:}book.author,$$
$$free{:}book\ ),$$
$$\texttt{Property}(\ dbp{:}IceHockeyPlayer,$$
$$free{:}book\ ))$$

3. Refine the subtype assumption to SC' such that it contains the following subtype inequality.

$$dbp{:}IceHockeyPlayer \leq free{:}book.author$$

The three options are similar to the options in the previous examples. The difference is that the programmer should be suspicious. The first option above may be plausible, but the programmer will be asking whether Ershov was really both an author and a professional ice hockey player. The second option above, which allows all ice hockey players to author books, is highly questionable. It certainly does not make sense to take the third option above and make every ice hockey player a book author.

A further reason to be alarmed is that, if the programmer attempts to ignore the strange warnings, then the script cannot be executed further. There is no resource that can be selected that enables the **where** clause to be matched.

Given the evidence, the programmer can conclude that there was a mismatch between the query and the resource dereferenced. The solution is therefore to change the scripts. By inspecting the data it is clear that the resource represents the wrong Ershov, hence the programmer decides to change all appearances of the troublesome resource.

5.2   Calculating the Options in Warnings Algorithmically

The *optional* operational rule and the operational rule for **from** are specified declaratively in the operational semantics. These rules permit any refined type system that satisfies the constraints to be chosen. We can algorithmically generate a menu of good solutions that fix some types while maximising others.

Firstly, we explain how the algorithm can be applied to generate the options in the examples above. Secondly, we present the generalised algorithm.

Example Constraints. Consider a system of constraints from the running examples. Assume that SC is empty and we have that Ty is such that:

$$\mathrm{Ty}(\textit{res:Andrei\_Yershov}) = \textit{dbp:IceHockeyPlayer}$$
$$\mathrm{Ty}(\textit{free:book.author.works\_written}) = \mathtt{Property}(\,\textit{free:book.author},$$
$$\textit{free:book}\,)$$

The aim is to calculate Ty$'$ and SC$'$ such that $(\mathrm{Ty}', \mathrm{SC}') \leq (\mathrm{Ty}, \mathrm{SC})$ and the following type assumption holds.

$$\vdash^{\mathrm{Ty}'}_{\mathrm{SC}'} \mathtt{select\$book:} \textit{ free:book}$$
$$\mathtt{where} \textit{ res:Andrei\_Yershov } \textit{free:book.author.works\_written } \mathtt{\$book}.$$

We then unfold the algorithmic type system, using type variables X and Y for types that could take several values, as follows.

$$\cfrac{\cfrac{\vdash \mathrm{Ty}'(\textit{res:Andrei\_Yershov}) \leq X}{\vdash \textit{res:Andrei\_Yershov}: X} \quad \cfrac{\vdash \mathrm{Ty}'(\textit{free:book.author.works\_written}) \leq \mathtt{Property}(X,Y)}{\vdash \textit{free:book.author.works\_written}: \mathtt{Property}(X,Y)} \quad \cfrac{\vdash \textit{free:book} \leq Y}{\mathtt{\$book}: \textit{free:book} \vdash \mathtt{\$book}: Y}}{\cfrac{\mathtt{\$book}: \textit{free:book} \vdash \mathtt{where } \textit{res:Andrei\_Yershov } \textit{free:book.author.works\_written } \mathtt{\$book}}{\vdash \mathtt{select\$book}: \textit{free:book } \mathtt{where } \textit{res:Andrei\_Yershov } \textit{free:book.author.works\_written } \mathtt{\$book}}}$$

From the above we generate the following constraints on Ty$'$, where X and Y are variables for types that must be solved.

$$\mathrm{Ty}'(\textit{res:Andrei\_Yershov}) \leq X \qquad \textit{free:book} \leq Y$$
$$\mathrm{Ty}'(\textit{free:book.author.works\_written}) \leq \mathtt{Property}(X,Y)$$

Also, since $(\mathrm{Ty}', \mathrm{SC}') \leq (\mathrm{Ty}, \mathrm{SC})$, we have the following constraints and SC $\subseteq$ SC$'$.

$$\mathrm{Ty}'(\textit{res:Andrei\_Yershov}) \leq \textit{dbp:IceHockeyPlayer}$$
$$\mathrm{Ty}'(\textit{free:book.author.works\_written}) \leq \mathtt{Property}(\textit{free:book.author}, \textit{free:book})$$

From the above, we can generate the following scheme for upper bounds on Ty$'$.

$$\mathrm{Ty}'(\textit{res:Andrei\_Yershov}) \leq \mathtt{IntersectionOf}(\textit{dbp:IceHockeyPlayer}, X)$$
$$\mathrm{Ty}'(\textit{free:book.author.works\_written}) \leq \mathtt{IntersectionOf}($$
$$\mathtt{Property}(\textit{free:book.author}, \textit{free:book})\,,$$
$$\mathtt{Property}(X, \textit{free:book})\,)$$

We use these upper bounds to generate the options that appear in warnings.

Maximise Type of Property. To generate the first option Ty_1, we maximise the type of properties by ensuring that $\mathrm{Ty}(\textit{free:book.author.works\_written})$ is equal to the upper bound on the property. This yields the following type inequality.

$$\mathtt{Property}(\textit{free:book.author}, \textit{free:book}) \leq \mathtt{IntersectionOf}($$
$$\mathtt{Property}(\textit{free:book.author}, \textit{free:book})\,,$$
$$\mathtt{Property}(X, \textit{free:book})\,)$$

We use the cut-free subtype system to analyse the above constraints. We apply the *greatest lower bound* rule, then the *property* rule to obtain the constraint $X \leq free{:}book{.}author$. From this constraint we derive the most general solution $X \mapsto free{:}book{.}author$. Thereby we obtain a refined type system such that.

$$\mathrm{Ty}_1(res{:}Andrei\_Yershov) = \texttt{IntersectionOf}(dbp{:}IceHockeyPlayer, free{:}book{.}author)$$

The above is exactly what RDF Schema would infer [14].

Maximise Type of Subject/Object. To generate the second option Ty_2, we maximise the type of the subject be setting $\mathrm{Ty}(res{:}Andrei\_Yershov)$ to be equal to the upper bound on the resource. This yields the following type inequality.

$$dbp{:}IceHockeyPlayer \leq \texttt{IntersectionOf}(dbp{:}IceHockeyPlayer, X)$$

As in the previous example, we unfold the rules of the algorithmic type system to derive the constraint $dbp{:}IceHockeyPlayer \leq X$. We then maximise the type of the property with respect to this constraint, yielding the most general solution $X \mapsto dbp{:}IceHockeyPlayer$. Thereby we obtain a refined type system such that.

$$\mathrm{Ty}_2(free{:}book{.}author{.}works\_written) = \texttt{IntersectionOf}($$
$$\texttt{Property}(free{:}book{.}author, free{:}book),$$
$$\texttt{Property}(dbp{:}IceHockeyPlayer, free{:}book) \ )$$

Extend the Subtype Relation. The final option is to add subtype assumptions to the type system. We can calculate these subtype assumptions algorithmically, by calculating the conditions under which the above two options are equal.

Let $\mathrm{Ty}_1 = \mathrm{Ty}_2$ if and only if $(\mathrm{Ty}_1, \mathrm{SC}) \leq (\mathrm{Ty}_2, \mathrm{SC})$ and $(\mathrm{Ty}_2, \mathrm{SC}) \leq (\mathrm{Ty}_1, \mathrm{SC})$. Now $\mathrm{Ty}_1 = \mathrm{Ty}_2$ if and only if the following equalities hold.

$$dbp{:}IceHockeyPlayer = \texttt{IntersectionOf}(dbp{:}IceHockeyPlayer, \ free{:}book{.}author)$$

$$\texttt{Property}(\begin{matrix} free{:}book{.}author \ , \\ free{:}book \ \end{matrix}) \ = \ \begin{matrix} \texttt{IntersectionOf}(\\ \texttt{Property}(free{:}book{.}author, \ free{:}book) \ , \\ \texttt{Property}(dbp{:}IceHockeyPlayer, \ free{:}book) \ ) \end{matrix}$$

By using the cut-free subtype system, we can calculate that the above equalities hold only if the following subtype inequality holds.

$$dbp{:}IceHockeyPlayer \leq free{:}author$$

Thus, if we include the above constraint in SC', then the original Ty satisfies the necessary constraints to enable the *optional* rule.

Note that the above algorithm does not always find a suitable set of constraints. For example, if we attempt to apply the *optional* rule before executing `from` in the above example of a bad script, we are led to the constraint.

$$owl{:}Thing \leq free{:}book{.}author$$

The above inequality cannot be induced by extending the set of subtype assumption, so there is no solution to modifying SC. This is a positive feature since, in an open world of knowledge like the Web, it makes no sense to state that every resource is an author.

Summary. The general algorithm works as follows.

1. We use the algorithmic type system and the constraint $(Ty', SC') \leq (Ty, SC)$ to generate a scheme for upper bounds on Ty'.
2. We generate the first option by, for every property, setting the type in Ty to be equal to the upper bound on constraints. We then solve the system of equalities using unification to obtain a suitable unifier. This is used to obtain solution Ty_1.
3. We generate the second option by, for every subject and object, setting the type in Ty to be equal to the upper bound on constraints. Again we solve the system of constraints using unification to obtain Ty_2.
4. We set $Ty_1 = Ty_2$ and solve the system of equalities to obtain a set of subtype inequalities over atomic types. If there is a solution, we extend SC with these constraints and fix Ty.

The second point above generates classes for resources as expected by RDF Schema [5]; hence RDF Schema is sound with respect to our descriptive type system. The third and fourth points above provide alternative, more general modes of inference. Thus the above algorithm extends RDF Schema inference.

If there is a solution to the fourth point above with an empty set of subtype inequalities, then the script can be typed without refining the type system. In this case, the constraints could be solved efficiently, using techniques in [17]. Further analysis of the above algorithm is future work.

5.3   Subject Reduction

There are two reasons why a system is well-typed. Either *a priori* the script was well typed before changing the type system, or at some point during the execution the programmer acted to resolve the warnings. In either case, once the script is well typed it can be executed to completion without generating any warnings other than unavoidable warnings that occur from reading data from the Web.

The following proposition characterises the guarantees after choosing to resolve a warning. In particular, as long as the data is kept well typed, then after choosing to resolving warnings the script is also well typed, with respect to the refined type system.

Proposition 3. *If* $\vdash^{Ty}_{SC}$ *data and the optional rule is applied, such that*

$$(script, data, Ty, SC) \longrightarrow (script, data, Ty', SC'),$$

then $\vdash^{Ty'}_{SC'}$ *script and* $\vdash^{Ty'}_{SC'}$ *data.*

Proof. Assume that $\vdash^{Ty}_{SC}$ data and $(script, data, Ty, SC) \longrightarrow (script, data, Ty', SC')$ due to the *optional* rule. Hence it must be the case that $(Ty', SC') \leq (Ty, SC)$ and $\vdash^{Ty'}_{SC'}$ script. Hence, by Lemma 2, $\vdash^{Ty'}_{SC'}$ data holds, as required.

We require the following substitution lemma. It states that if we assume that a variable is of a certain type, then we can substitute the variable for a resource of that type and preserve typing.

Lemma 3. *Assume that* $\vdash uri\colon C$. *Then the following statements hold:*

1. *If* $Env, \$x\colon C \vdash script$, *then* $Env \vdash script\{^{uri}\!/_{\$x}\}$.
2. *If* $Env, \$x\colon C \vdash term\colon D$, *then* $Env \vdash term\{^{uri}\!/_{\$x}\}\colon D$.

Proof. Assume that $\vdash uri\colon C$. The proof proceeds by structural induction on the type derivation tree.

Consider the case of the type rule for variables, where the variable equals $\$x$. In this case, the type tree on the left can be transformed into the type tree on the right.

$$\frac{\vdash C \leq D}{Env, \$x\colon C \vdash \$x\colon D} \quad \text{yields} \quad \frac{\vdash uri\colon C \quad \vdash C \leq D}{Env \vdash uri\colon D}$$

Hence, by Proposition 2, $Env \vdash uri\colon D$ holds in the algorithmic type system and clearly $\$x\{^{uri}\!/_{\$x}\} = uri$ as required. All other cases for terms are trivial.

Consider the case of the select rule. Assume that $Env, \$x\colon C \vdash \texttt{select } \$y\colon D$ *script* holds. If $\$x = \$y$, then $\$x$ does not appear free in $\texttt{select } \$x\colon D$, hence $Env \vdash \texttt{select } \$x\colon D$ *script* as required. If $\$x \neq \$y$, then, by the induction hypothesis, if $Env, \$x\colon C, \$y\colon D \vdash script$ holds then $Env, \$y\colon D \vdash script\{^{uri}\!/_{\$x}\}$ holds. Hence the proof tree on the left below can be transformed into the proof tree on the right below.

$$\frac{Env, \$x\colon C, \$y\colon D \vdash script}{Env, \$x\colon C \vdash \texttt{select } \$y\colon D\ script} \quad \text{yields} \quad \frac{Env, \$y\colon D \vdash script\{^{uri}\!/_x\}}{Env \vdash \texttt{select } \$y\colon D\ script\{^{uri}\!/_x\}}$$

Furthermore, since $\$x \neq \$y$, by the standard definition of substitution the following holds as required.

$$\texttt{select } \$y\colon D\ script\{^{uri}\!/_x\} = (\texttt{select } \$y\colon D\ script)\{^{uri}\!/_x\}$$

The cases for other rules follow immediately by induction. □

We also require the following result, the proof of which is straightforward.

Lemma 4. *Assume that* $data_0 \equiv data_1$. *If* $\vdash data_0$ *then* $\vdash data_1$.

The property that a well typed script will not raise unnecessary warnings, is formulated as the following subject reduction result.

Theorem 2 (Subject reduction). *If* $\vdash^{Ty}_{SC} script$ *and* $\vdash^{Ty}_{SC} data$, *then if*

$$(script, data, Ty, SC) \longrightarrow (script', data', Ty', SC'),$$

then $\vdash^{Ty'}_{SC'} script'$ *and* $\vdash^{Ty'}_{SC'} data'$.

Proof. The proof is by case analysis, over each operational rule.

Consider the operational rule for `select`. Assume that the following hold.

$$\vdash \texttt{select } \$x\colon C \; script \qquad \vdash data \qquad \vdash uri\colon C$$

The above holds only if $\$x\colon C \vdash script$, by the type rule for `select`. By Lemma 3, since $\$x\colon C \vdash script$ and $\vdash uri\colon C$, it holds that $\vdash script\{^{uri}/_x\}$. Therefore the `select` rule preserves types.

Consider the operational rule for `where`. Assume that the following type assumption holds.

$$\vdash \texttt{where } term_0 \; term_1 \; term_2 \; script \qquad \vdash term_0 \; term_1 \; term_2 \; data$$

The above holds only if $\vdash script$ holds, hence the operational rule for `where` preserves well typed scripts.

Consider the operational rule for `from`. Assume that the following assumptions hold.

$$\vdash^{\text{Ty}}_{\text{SC}} \texttt{from } uri \; script \qquad \vdash^{\text{Ty}}_{\text{SC}} data_0 \qquad \vdash^{\text{Ty}'}_{\text{SC}'} data_1 \qquad (\text{Ty}', \text{SC}') \leq (\text{Ty}, \text{SC})$$

The first assumption above holds only if $\vdash^{\text{Ty}}_{\text{SC}} script$ holds, by the type rule for `from`. Since $(\text{Ty}', \text{SC}') \leq (\text{Ty}, \text{SC})$, by Lemma 2, $\vdash^{\text{Ty}'}_{\text{SC}'} script$ holds. By Lemma 2 again, $\vdash^{\text{Ty}'}_{\text{SC}'} data_0$ holds. Hence $\vdash^{\text{Ty}'}_{\text{SC}'} data_0 \; data_1$ holds. Therefore the `from` rule preserves types.

Consider the case of the *optional* operational rule. For some initial configuration $(script, data, \text{Ty}, \text{SC})$, we assume that $\vdash^{Ty}_{\text{SC}} data$. The result then follows from Proposition 3. □

6 Conclusion

The descriptive type system introduced in this work formalises the interplay between runtime schema inference and scripting languages that interact with Linked Data. The system formalises how to build RDF Schema inference into scripts at runtime. The system also permits new inference mechanisms that refine the types assigned to properties and extend the subtype relation.

We bring a number of type theoretic results to the table. We establish the consistency of subtyping through a cut elimination result (Theorem 1). We are able to tightly integrate RDF schema with executable scripts that dereference and query Linked Data. This is formalised by a type system that we prove is algorithmic (Proposition 2), hence suitable for inference. We specify the runtime behaviour of scripts using an operational semantics, and prove a subject reduction result (Theorem 2) that proves that well typed scripts do not raise unnecessary warnings.

We also provide an algorithm for solving systems of constraints to generate warnings at runtime. This suggests a line of future work to investigate the optimality of the algorithm presented. The descriptive type system can be employed in expressive scripting languages [12], and extract more type information based on RDF Schema and OWL from data. This descriptive type system can coexist with a prescriptive type system for simple data types as presented in [6].

A subjective question is the following. At what point does the programmer stop ignoring the warnings and become suspicious? Many programmers are likely to ignore warnings until the script stops working. At this point, they will inspect the warnings and, based on their subjective human judgement, decide whether suggestions are consistent or conflicting. Most programmers will be happy to let fellows of the British Computer Society be people, but will have second thoughts about letting all ice hockey players be authors. The Web is an open world of subjective knowledge. Our descriptive type system assists subjective decisions that keep data and schema information consistent.

Acknowledgements. We are grateful to the organisers of the Ershov memorial conference, PSI 2014, for inviting this work to be presented as a keynote speech. The work of the first and second authors was supported by a grant of the Romanian National Authority for Scientific Research, project number PN-II-ID-PCE-2011-3-0919.

References

1. Barbanera, F., Dezani-Ciancaglini, M., de'Liguoro, U.: Intersection and union types: syntax and semantics. Inf. Comput. **119**(2), 202–230 (1995)
2. Berners-Lee, T.: Linked data. Int. J. Semant. Web Inf. Syst. **4**(2), 1 (2006)
3. Bizer, C., et al.: DBpedia: a crystallization point for the web of data. Web Semant. Sci. Serv. Agents World Wide Web **7**(3), 154–165 (2009)
4. Bollacker, K., Evans, C., Paritosh, P., Sturge, T., Taylor, J.: Freebase: a collaboratively created graph database for structuring human knowledge. In: Proceedings of the 2008 ACM SIGMOD International Conference on Management of Data, pp. 1247–1250. ACM (2008)
5. Brickley, D., Guha, R.V.: RDF vocabulary description language 1.0: RDF schema. Edited Recommendation PER-rdf-schema-20140109, W3C (2014)
6. Ciobanu, G., Horne, R., Sassone, V.: Local type checking for linked data consumers. In: Ravara, A., Silva, J. (eds.) WWV. EPTCS, vol. 123, pp. 19–33 (2013)
7. Cyganiak, R., Wood, D., Lanthaler, M.: RDF 1.1 concepts and abstract syntax. Recommendation REC-rdf11-concepts-20140225, W3C (2014)
8. Dershowitz, N., Manna, Z.: Proving termination with multiset orderings. Commun. ACM **22**(8), 465–476 (1979)
9. Dezani-Ciancaglini, M., Horne, R., Sassone, V.: Tracing where and who provenance in linked data: a calculus. Theor. Comput. Sci. **464**, 113–129 (2012)
10. Harris, S., Seaborne, A.: SPARQL 1.1 query language. Recommendation REC-sparql11-query-20130321, W3C. MIT, MA (2013)
11. Hitzler, P., Krötzsch, M., Parsia, B., Patel-Schneider, P.F., Rudolph, S.: OWL 2 Web Ontology Language primer (second edition). Recommendation REC-owl2-primer-20121211, W3C (2012)
12. Horne, R., Sassone, V.: A verified algebra for read-write linked data. Sci. Comput. Program. **89**(A), 2–22 (2014)
13. MacNeille, H.M.: Extensions of partially ordered sets. Proc. Natl. Acad. Sci. U.S.A. **22**(1), 45–50 (1936)

14. Muñoz, S., Pérez, J., Gutierrez, C.: Simple and efficient minimal RDFS. Web Semant. Sci. Serv. Agents World Wide Web **7**(3), 220–234 (2009)
15. Pérez, J., Arenas, M., Gutierrez, C.: Semantics and complexity of SPARQL. ACM Trans. Database Syst. (TODS) **34**(3), 16 (2009)
16. Suchanek, F.M., Kasneci, G., Weikum, G.: Yago: a core of semantic knowledge. In: Proceedings of 16th WWW Conference, pp. 697–706. ACM (2007)
17. Tiuryn, J.: Subtype inequalities. In: Proceedings of the Seventh Annual IEEE Symposium on Logic in Computer Science, LICS 1992, pp. 308–315. IEEE (1992)

2^5 Years of Model Checking

Edmund M. Clarke$^{(\boxtimes)}$ and Qinsi Wang

Computer Science Department, Carnegie Mellon University, Pittsburgh, USA
emc@cs.cmu.edu

Abstract. Model Checking is an automatic verification technique for large state transition systems. It was originally developed for reasoning about finite-state concurrent systems. The technique has been used successfully to debug complex computer hardware, communication protocols, and software. It is beginning to be used for analyzing cyber-physical, biological, and financial systems as well. The major challenge for the technique is a phenomenon called the *State Explosion Problem*. This issue is impossible to avoid in the worst case; but, by using sophisticated data structures and clever search algorithms, it is now possible to verify state transition systems with an astronomical number of states. In this paper, we will briefly review the development of Model Checking over the past 32 years, with an emphasis on model checking stochastic hybrid systems.

1 Model Checking and State Explosion Problem

Model Checking, as a framework consisting of powerful techniques for verifying finite-state systems, was independently developed by Clarke and Emerson [22] and by Queille and Sifakis [52] in the early 1980s. Over the last few decades, it has been successfully applied to numerous theoretical and practical problems [17,20,36,37,45,63], such as verification of sequential circuit designs, communication protocols, software device drivers, security algorithms, cyber-physical systems, and biological systems. There are several major factors contributing to its success. Primarily, Model Checking is fully automated. Unlike deductive reasoning using theorem provers, this 'push-button' method neither requires proofs nor experts to check whether a finite-state model satisfies given system specifications. Besides verification of correctness, it permits bug detection as well. If a property does not hold, a model checker can return a diagnostic counterexample denoting an actual execution of the given system model leading to an error state. Such counterexamples can then help detect subtle bugs. Finally, from a practical aspect, Model Checking also works with partial specifications, which allows the separation of system design and development from verification and debugging.

Typically, a model checker has three basic components: a *modeling formalism* adopted to encode a state machine representing the system to be verified, a *specification language* based on Temporal Logics [51], and a *verification algorithm*

This paper has been partly supported by the Office of Naval Research (ONR) under grant 29749-1-1141240.

© Springer-Verlag Berlin Heidelberg 2015
A. Voronkov and I. Virbitskaite (Eds.): PSI 2014, LNCS 8974, pp. 26–40, 2015.
DOI: 10.1007/978-3-662-46823-4_2

which employs an exhaustive searching of the entire state space to determine whether the specification holds or not. Because of the exhaustive search, when being applied to complex systems, all model checkers face an unavoidable problem in the worst case. The number of global states of a complex system can be enormous. Given n processes, each having m states, their asynchronous composition may have m^n states which is exponential in both the number of processes and the number of states per process. In Model Checking, we refer to this as the *State Explosion Problem*. Great strides have been made on this problem over the past 32 years for various types of real-world systems. In the following sections, we discuss major breakthroughs that have been made during the development of Model Checking, and then briefly review the work adopting these techniques for the analysis of stochastic hybrid systems, especially for probabilistic hybrid automata.

2   Major Breakthroughs

2.1   Symbolic Model Checking with OBDDs

In the original implementation of the first model checking algorithm [22], the transition system has an explicit representation using the adjacency lists. Such an enumerative representation is feasible for concurrent systems with small numbers of processes and states per process, but not adequate for very large transition systems. In the fall of 1987, McMillan made a fundamental breakthrough. He realized that by reformulating the original model checking procedure in a symbolic way where sets of states and sets of transitions are represented rather than individual states and transitions, Model Checking could be used to verify larger systems with more than 10^{20} states [18]. The new symbolic representation was based on Bryant's ordered binary decision diagrams (OBDDs) [14]. In this symbolic approach, the state graphs, which need to be constructed in the explicit model checking procedure, are described by Boolean formulas represented by OBDDs. Model Checking algorithms can then work directly on these OBDDs. Since OBDD-based algorithms are set-based, they cannot directly implement the depth-first search, and thus the property automaton should also be represented symbolically.

Since then, various refinements of the OBDD-based algorithms [10,16,35,54] have pushed the size of state space count up to more than 10^{120} [16]. The most widely used symbolic model checkers SMV [46], NuSMV [19], and VIS [13] are based on these ideas.

2.2   Partial Order Reduction

As mentioned in Sect. 1, the size of the parallel composition of n processes in a concurrent system may be exponential in n. Verifying a property of such a system requires inspecting all states of the underlying transition system. That is, $n!$ distinct orderings of the interleaved executions of n states need to be considered in the setting where there are no synchronizations between the individual processes. This is even more serious for software verification than for hardware verification, as software tends to be less structured than hardware. One of the most successful techniques for dealing with asynchronous systems is partial order reduction. Since the effect of concurrent actions is often independent of their ordering, this method aims at decreasing the number of possible orderings, and thus reducing the state space of the transition system that needs to be analyzed for checking properties. Intuitively, if executing two events in either order results in the same result, they are independent of each other. In this case, it is possible to avoid exploring certain paths in the state transition system.

Partial order reduction crucially relies on two assumptions. One is that all processes are fully asynchronous. The other is that the property to be checked does not involve the intermediate states. When coping with realistic systems where the processes may communicate and thus depend on one another, this approach attempts to identify path fragments of the full transition system, which only differ in the order of the concurrently executed activities. In this way, the analysis of state space can be restricted to one (or a few) representatives of every possible interleaving.

Godefroid, Peled, and Valmari have developed the concepts of incorporating partial order reduction with Model Checking independently in the early 1990's. Valmari's stubborn sets [60], Godefroid's persistent sets [33], and Peled's ample sets [49] differ on the actual details but contain many similar ideas. The SPIN model checker, developed by Holzmann [39], uses the ample-set reduction to great advantage.

2.3 Bounded Model Checking

Although Symbolic Model Checking (SMC) with OBDDs has successfully improved the scalability and is still widely used, OBDDs have multiple problems which restrict the size of models that can be checked with this method. Since the ordering of variables has to be identical for each path from the root of an OBDD to a leaf node, finding a space-efficient ordering is critical for this technique. Unfortunately, it is quite difficult, sometimes impossible, to find an order resulting in a small OBDD. Consider the formula for the middle output bit of a combinational multiplier for two n-bit numbers. It can be proved that, for all variable orderings, the size of the OBDD for this formula is exponential in n.

To further conquer the state explosion problem, Biere et al. proposed the Bounded Model Checking (BMC) using Boolean satisfiability (SAT) solvers [9]. The basic idea for BMC is quite straightforward. Given a finite-state transition system, a temporal logic property and a bound k (we assume $k \geq 1$), BMC generates a propositional logical formula whose satisfiability implies the existence of a counterexample of length k, and then passes this formula to a SAT solver. This formula encodes the constraints on initial states, the transition relations for k steps, and the negation of the given property. When the formula is unsatisfiable (no counterexample found), we can either increase the bound k until either a counterexample is found, or k reaches the upper bound on how much the transition relation would need to be unwound for the completeness, or stop if resource constraints are exceeded. As an industrial-strength model checking technique, BMC has been observed to surpass SMC with OBDDs in fast detection of counterexamples of minimal length, in saving memory, and by avoiding performing costly dynamic reordering. With a fast SAT solver, BMC can handle designs that are order-of-magnitude larger than those handled by OBDD-based model checkers.

As an efficient way of detecting subtle counterexamples, BMC is quite useful in debugging. In order to prove correctness when no counterexamples are found using BMC, an upper bound on steps to reach all reachable states needs to be determined. It has been shown that the diameter (i.e., the longest shortest path between any two states) of the state-transition system could be used as an upper bound [9]. But, it appears to be computationally difficult to compute the diameter when the state-transition system is given implicitly. Other ways for making BMC complete are based on induction [55], cube enlargement [47], Craig interpolants [48], and circuit co-factoring [32]. This problem remains a topic of active research.

An interesting variation of the original BMC is to adopt a Satisfiability Modulo Theories (SMT) solver instead of a SAT solver [24,59]. SMT encodings in model checking have several advantages. The SMT encodings offers more powerful specification language. They use (unquantified) first-order formulas instead of Boolean formulas, and use more natural and compact encodings, as there is no need to convert high level constraints into Boolean logic formulas. These SMT encodings also make the BMC work the same for finite and infinite state systems. Above all, high level of automation has not been sacrificed for the above advantages. CBMC is a widely used Bounded model checker for ANSI-C and C++ programs [42], having supports for SMT solvers such as Z3 [27], and Yices [28].

2.4   Counterexample-Guided Abstraction Refinement

When the model state space is enormous, or even infinite, it is infeasible to conduct an exhaustive search of the entire space. Another method of coping with the state explosion problem is to abstract away irrelevant details, according to the property under consideration, from the concrete state transition system when constructing the model. We call this approach *abstraction*. This simplification incurs information loss. Depending on the method used to control the information loss, abstraction techniques can be distinguished into either over-approximation or under-approximation techniques. The over-approximation methods enrich the behavior of the system by releasing constraints. They establish a relationship between the abstract model and the original system so that the correctness of the former implies the correctness of the latter. The downside is that they admit false negatives, where there are properties which hold in the original system but fail in the abstract model. Therefore, a counterexample found in the abstract system may not be a feasible execution in the original system. These counterexamples are called *spurious*. Conversely, the under-approximation techniques, which admit false positives, obtain the abstraction by removing irrelevant behavior from the system so that a specification violation at the abstract level implies a violation of the original system.

The *counterexample-guided abstraction refinement* (CEGAR) technique [21] integrates an over-approximation technique - existential abstraction [23] - and SMC into a unified, and automatic framework. It starts verification against universal properties with an imprecise abstraction, and iteratively refines it according to the returned spurious counterexamples. When a counterexample is found, its feasibility with regard to the original system needs to be checked first. If the violation is feasible, this counterexample is reported as a witness for a bug. Otherwise, a proof of infeasibility is used to refine the abstraction. The procedure then repeats these steps until either a real counterexample is reported, or there is no new counterexamples returned. When the property holds on the abstract model, by the Property Preservation Theorem [23], it is guaranteed for the property to be correct in the concrete systems. CEGAR is used in many software model checkers including the SLAM project [6] at Microsoft.

3   Model Checking and Stochastic Hybrid Systems

Stochastic hybrid systems (SHSs) are a class of dynamical systems that involve the interaction of discrete, continuous, and stochastic dynamics. Due to the generality, SHSs have been widely used in distinct areas, including biological systems, cyber-physical systems, and finance [12]. To describe uncertainties, randomness has been added to hybrid systems in a number of ways. A wealth of models has been promoted over the last decade. One class of models combines deterministic flows with probabilistic transitions. When state changes forced by continuous dynamics involve discrete random events, we refer to them as probabilistic hybrid automata (PHAs) [56]. PHAs are akin to Markov decision processes (MDPs) [8], which determine both the discrete and continuous successor states. When state changes involve continuous random events as well, we call them stochastic hybrid automata (SHAs) [29]. Some models allow that state changes may happen spontaneously, such as piecewise deterministic Markov processes (PDMPs) [26], which are similar to continuous-time Markov chains (CTMCs) [58]. Other models replace deterministic flows with stochastic ones, such as stochastic differential equations (SDEs) [5] and stochastic hybrid programs (SHPs) [50], where the random perturbation affects the dynamics continuously. When all such ingredients have been covered, there are models such as the general stochastic hybrid systems (GSHSs) [15, 40].

The popularity of SHSs in real-world applications plays an important role as the motivation for putting a significant research effort into the foundations, analysis and control methods for this class of systems. Among various problems, one of the elementary questions for the quantitative analysis of SHSs is the probabilistic reachability problem. There are two main reasons why it catches researchers' attention. Primarily, it is motivated by the fact that most temporal properties can be reduced to reachability problems due to the very expressive hybrid modeling framework. Moreover, probabilistic state reachability is a hard and challenging problem which is undecidable in general. Intuitively, this class of problems is to compute the probability of reaching a certain set of states. The set may represent a set of certain unsafe states which should be avoided or visited only with some small probability, or dually, a set of good states which should be visited frequently.

Over the last decade, research efforts concerning SHSs are rapidly increasing. At the same time, Model Checking methods and tools for probabilistic systems, such as PRISM [44], MRMC [41], and Ymer [65], have been proposed and designed. Results related to the analysis and verification of SHSs are still limited. For instance, analysis approaches for GSHSs are often based on Monte-Carlo simulation [11,53]. Considering the hardness of dealing with the general class, efforts have been mainly placed on different subclasses [1–3,29,30,34,50,56,62,66,67].

For a decidable subclass which is called probabilistic initialized rectangular automata (PIRAs), Sproston offered a model checking procedure against the probabilistic branching time logic (PBTL) [56]. The procedure first translates PIRA to a probabilistic timed automaton (PTA), then constructs a finite-state probabilistic region graph for the PTA, and employs existing PBTL Model Checking techniques. For probabilistic rectangular automata (PRAs) which are less restricted than PIRAs, Sproston proposed a semi-decidable model checking procedure via using a forward search through the reachable state space [57].

For a more expressive class of models - probabilistic hybrid automata (PHAs), Zhang et al. abstracted the original PHA to a probabilistic automaton (PA), and then used the established Model Checking methods for the abstracting model [66]. Hahn et al. also discussed an abstraction-based method where the given PHA was translated into a n-player stochastic game using two different abstraction techniques [34]. All abstractions obtained by these methods are over-approximations, which means that the estimated maximum probability for a safety property on the abstracted model is no less than the one on the original model. Another method proposed is a SMT-based bounded Model Checking procedure [30]. We will discuss these methods in detail in the following subsections.

A similar class of models, which is widely used in the control theory, is called discrete-time stochastic hybrid systems (DTSHSs) [4]. Akin to PHAs, DTSHSs comprise nondeterministic as well as discrete probabilistic choices of state transitions. Unlike PHAs, DTSHSs are sampled at discrete time points, use control inputs to model nondeterminism, do not have an explicit notion of symbolic transition guards, and support a more general concept of randomness which can describe discretized stochastic differential equations. With regard to the system analysis, the control problem concerned can be understood as to find an optimal control policy that minimizes the probability of reaching unsafe states. A backward recursive procedure, which uses dynamic programming, was then proposed to solve the problem [1,4]. Another approach to a very similar problem as above, where a DTSHS model doesn't have nondeterministic control inputs, was presented in [2]. Compared to former method, the latter approach exploits the grid to construct a discrete-time Markov chain (DTMC), and then employs standard model checking procedures for it. This approach then had been used in [3] as an analysis procedure for the probabilistic reachability problems in the product of a DTSHS and a Büchi automaton representing a linear temporal property. Zuliani et al. also mentioned a simulation-based method for model checking DTSHSs against bounded temporal properties [67]. We refer to this method as Statistical Model Checking (StatMC). The main idea of StatMC is to generate enough simulations of the system, record the checking result returned from a trace checker from each simulation, and then use statistical testing and estimation methods to determine, with a predefined degree of confidence, whether the system satisfies the property. Although this statistical model checking procedure does not belong to the class of exhaustive state-space exploration methods, it usually returns results faster than the exhaustive search with a predefined arbitrarily small error bound on the estimated probability.

In [29], as an extension of PHAs, stochastic hybrid automata (SHAs) allow continuous probability distributions in the discrete state transitions. With respect to the verification procedure, a given SHA is firstly over-approximated by a PHA via discretizing continuous distributions into discrete ones with the help of additional uncountable nondeterminism. As mentioned, this over-approximation preserves safety properties. For the second step, the verification procedure introduced in [66] is exploited to model check the over-approximating PHA.

Another interesting work is about stochastic hybrid programs (SHPs) introduced in [50]. This formalism is quite expressive with regard to randomness: it takes stochastic differential equations, discrete probabilistic branching, and random assignments to real-valued variables into account. To specify system properties, Platzer proposed a logic called stochastic differential dynamic logic, and then suggested a proof calculus to verify logical properties of SHPs.

Among these different models and methods mentioned above, of particular interest for this paper are PHAs. In the remainder of this section, we will review two kinds of interesting techniques - abstraction-based, and BMC-based methods - proposed for probabilistic reachability and safety analysis for PHAs.

3.1 Probabilistic Hybrid Automata

Before going into the details of model checking algorithms, we recall the definitions of PHAs as given in [56].

Definition 1. (Probabilistic Hybrid Automata) *A probabilistic hybrid automaton H is a tuple $(M, \bar{m}, k, \langle Post_m \rangle_{m \in M}, Cmds)$ where*

- $M := \{m_1, m_2, \cdots, m_n\}$ *is a finite set of control modes.*
- $\bar{m} \subseteq M$ *is the set of initial modes.*
- k *is the dimension of the automaton, i.e. the number of system variables.*
- $\langle Post_m \rangle_{m \in M}$ *indicates continuous-time behaviors on each mode.*
- *Cmds is a finite set of probabilistic guarded commands of the following form:*
  $g \quad \rightarrow \quad p_1 : u_1 + \cdots + p_n : u_n,$
  where g is a predicate representing a transition guard, and p_i and u_i are the

corresponding transition probability and updating function for the ith proba-
bilistic choice respectively (1 ≤ i ≤ n).

The semantics of a probabilistic hybrid automaton is a probabilistic automaton [56] which is formally defined as follows.

Definition 2. (Semantics of Probabilistic Hybrid Automata) *The semantics of a probabilistic hybrid automaton H is a probabilistic automaton* $PA[\![H]\!] = (S, \bar{s}, Act, T)$, *where*

- $S = M \times \mathbb{R}^k$ *denotes the (possibly uncountable) set of states.*
- $\bar{s} = (\bar{m}, 0, \cdots, 0)$ *is the set of initial states.*
- $Act = \mathbb{R}_{\geq 0} \uplus Cmds$ *describes the transition relation. Note that,* $\uplus$ *denotes the disjoint union.*
- T: *for each* $s \in S$, *it may have two types of transitions. The first one is from command* $g \rightarrow p_1 : u_1 + \cdots + p_n : u_n$ *by* $u(s)$ *when* g *is fulfilled. The second one is from time* t *by* $Post_m(s, t)$.

3.2 Abstraction-Based Methods

Zhang et al. presented an abstraction-based method for verifying safety properties in probabilistic hybrid automata (PHAs) [66]. The main underlying idea is to compute finite probabilistic automata (PAs) via abstractions for PHAs, and then estimate the reachability probabilities of the over-approximating PAs with the help of existing methods. In detail, the verification procedure works as follows. To construct a safe over-approximation for a given PHA, the method first considers a non-probabilistic hybrid automaton (HA) obtained by replacing probabilistic choices with nondeterministic ones. Then, this classical HA is abstracted into a finite-state abstraction, where PHAVer [31] can be employed. As the final step of the abstraction, the finite-state abstraction is decorated with probabilities via techniques known for Markov decision processes [25,38], resulting in a probabilistic finite-state automaton. Figure 1 illustrates the entire abstraction process for an example PHA. After building a safe over-approximation, the probability of reaching unsafe states in the probabilistic abstraction is estimated using value iteration [8]. Since it is computing over-approximations, the abstraction preserves the safety property: if the probability of reaching unsafe state regions in the abstracting probabilistic automaton is bounded by p, this is also the case in the original probabilistic hybrid automaton. In other words, p is a safe upper bound for the reachability probability of the original model, and if a safety property holds in the abstraction, it holds also in the concrete system. Otherwise, refinement of the abstraction is required to obtain a potentially more precise upper bound. The realization of this refinement depends on the exploited abstraction technique. For example, PHAVer computes polyhedra to cover the continuous state-space for each discrete location. Refinement can be done by reducing the maximal widths of these polyhedra.

To estimate the maximum/minimum probability of reaching a certain state region, Hahn et al. proposed another abstraction-based approach [34]. This approach considers two different abstraction methods - a game-based approach [43] and an environment abstraction [61]. Both methods abstract a given PHA by an n-player stochastic game, and allow us to obtain both lower and upper bounds for quantitative properties. In a bit more detail, the semantics of a PHA is firstly expressed as a (stochastic) 2-player game, where one player represents the controller and the other the environment. Both abstraction methods represent the obtained abstraction as a separate player in the game resulting in a 3-player stochastic game. Then, with the first method, this 3-player game is reduced to a 2-player stochastic game. The second method makes this new player collaborate with the player representing the environment in the PHA. By adjusting the strategy of the player denoting the abstraction to maximize (or minimize) the probability of reaching the target states, the upper (or lower) bound on the optimal reachability probability for the original automaton can be obtained from the abstraction. This approach establishes a verification as well as falsification procedure for probabilistic safety properties.

3.3   BMC-Based Methods

Fränzle et al. presented an fully symbolic analyzing method of probabilistic bounded reachability problems of PHAs without resorting to over-approximation by intermediate finite-state abstractions [30]. When reasoning about PHAs, the authors use the SMT solving as a basis, and extends it by defining a novel randomized quantification over discrete variables. This method saves virtues of the SMT-based Bounded Model Checking, and harvests its recent advances in analyzing general hybrid systems. This new framework is referred to as Stochastic Satisfiability Modulo Theories (SSMT). In detail, an SSMT formula Φ can be defined in this format: $\Phi = Q_1 x_1 \in \mathrm{dom}(x_1) \cdots Q_n x_n \in \mathrm{dom}(x_n): \phi$, where ϕ is a quantifier-free SMT formula. $Q_1 x_1 \in \mathrm{dom}(x_1) \cdots Q_n x_n \in \mathrm{dom}(x_n)$ is the *prefix* of Φ, binding variables x_i to the quantifier Q_i. Note that not every variable occurring in ϕ has to be bound by a quantifier. In the framework of SSMT, a quantifier Q_i is either a classical *existential* quantifier, denoted as $\exists$, or a newly introduced *randomized* quantifier, denoted as $\mathrm{\mathtt{H}}_{d_i}$, where d_i is a finite discrete probability distribution over $\mathrm{dom}(x_i)$. The notation d_i is usually a list $\langle (v_1, p_1), \cdots, (v_m, p_m) \rangle$, where p_j is the probability of assigning x_i to v_j. The semantics of an SSMT problem is defined by the maximum probability of satisfaction, which is designed for computing the maximal reachability probability. Formally, the maximum probability of satisfaction $Pr(\Phi)$ of an SSMT formula Φ is defined recursively as follows.

- $Pr(\phi) = 1$ if ϕ is satisfiable, and 0 otherwise;
- $Pr(\exists x_i \in dom(x_i) \cdots Q_n x_n \in dom(x_n) : \phi) = max_{v \in dom(x_i)} Pr(Q_{i+1} x_{i+1} \in dom(x_{i+1}) \cdots Q_n x_n \in dom(x_n) : \phi[v/x_i])$; and
- $Pr(\mathrm{\mathtt{H}}_{d_i} x_i \in dom(x_i) \cdots Q_n x_n \in dom(x_n) : \phi) = \sum_{(v,p) \in dom(x_i)} p \cdot Pr(Q_{i+1} x_{i+1} \in dom(x_{i+1}) \cdots Q_n x_n \in dom(x_n) : \phi[v/x_i])$.

To analyze PHAs, the probabilistic bounded reachability problems need to be encoded in SSMT formulas. The construction procedure contains two steps.

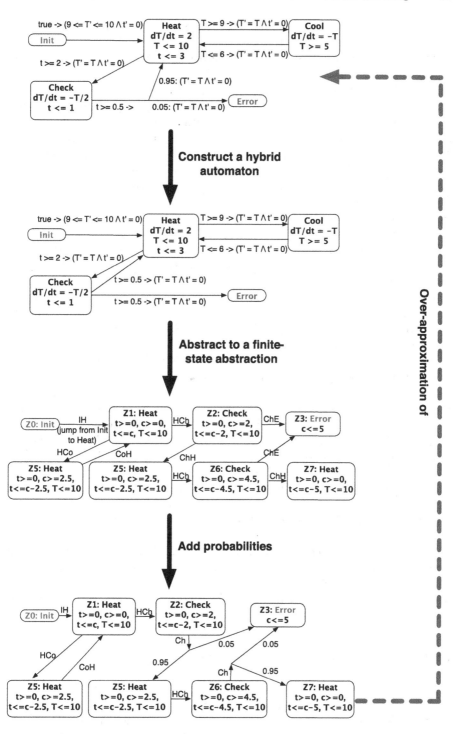

Fig. 1. Abstraction steps for a probabilistic hybrid automaton for the thermostat

First of all, akin to the SMT-based BMC, an SMT formula is used to express all runs of the given PHA of the given length k, ignoring both nondeterministic and probabilistic transitions. Quantification is then added to encode the missing nondeterministic and probabilistic choices. Existential quantifiers reflect nondeterministic choices and randomized quantifiers describe probabilistic transitions. With this encoding, the step-bounded reachability analysis of probabilistic hybrid automata is reduced to calculating the maximum probability of satisfaction of an SSMT formula. To compute the maximum satisfaction probability, an algorithm, which was discussed in [30], consists of three layers - a theory solver, an SMT solver, and an SSMT solver. The first two solvers are the same as the corresponding parts in widely used SMT solvers, such as Z3 [27], and CVC4 [7]. The last SSMT layer is an extension of the SMT layer to cope with existential and randomized quantification.

Another BMC-based approach to the falsification of safety properties was promoted by Wimmer et al. [64]. Although the stochastic models that they consider are discrete-time Markov chains (DTMCs), DTMCs are quite similar to PHAs except that the former do not support nondeterminism. Also, its analysis technique is closely related to the one in [30]. It works as follows. First of all, the given safety property is reduced to a state reachability one through removing edges from the given DTMC. Then, it encodes the behavior of the given DTMC with length k and the reachability property as an SAT formula as the case for SAT-based BMC. During this step, probabilistic transitions are treated as nondeterministic ones, and the transition probability matrix of the given DTMC is stored in order to be able to track the transition probabilities between states in the near future. Thereafter, the Boolean formula with the depth-bound k is solved by a SAT solver. If the formula is satisfiable, the returned satisfying assignment is used to extract a system execution of length k. The probability of this execution is computed according to the preserved probability matrix. After adding a clause representing the negation of the last returned assignment, the SAT solver is called again to find another execution reaching the target states. These steps are repeated until the SAT solver returns "unsat" for a modified formula for length k. Then, it generates a new Boolean formula for depth step $k+1$, and calls the SAT again. The overall procedure terminates if the accumulated probability of all collected system runs reaching the given unsafe states exceeds a given threshold, which is used to falsify the safety property. To reduce the number of calls to the SAT solver, the authors propose some optimizations. The most important one tries to detect loops in executions reaching the target states in order to achieve infinitely many runs from one solver invocation.

4   Conclusion and Future Work

Model Checking has proved to be a highly successful technology. Over the last 32 years, we have witnessed enormous progress on improving performance, on enhancing scalability, and on expanding applications in the area of Model Checking. The progress has increased our knowledge, but also opened many questions and research directions. Efforts are still needed to further conquer the state explosion problem in Software Model Checking. More effective model checking algorithms are required for real-time and hybrid systems, and are badly in need for even more complex systems, such as stochastic hybrid systems. Moreover, there are various directions, including combining model checking and static analysis, compositional model checking of complex systems, symmetry reduction and parameterized model checking, integrating model checking and theorem proving, interpreting long and complicated counterexamples, extending CEGAR for probabilistic systems, and scaling up even more!

References

1. Abate, A.: Probabilistic reachability for stochastic hybrid systems: theory, computations, and applications. ProQuest (2007)
2. Abate, A., Katoen, J.-P., Lygeros, J., Prandini, M.: A two-step scheme for approximate model checking of stochastic hybrid systems. In: Proceedings of the 18th IFAC World Congress, IFAC (2011)
3. Abate, A., Katoen, J.-P., Mereacre, A.: Quantitative automata model checking of autonomous stochastic hybrid systems. In: Proceedings of the 14th International Conference on Hybrid Systems: Computation and Control, pp. 83–92. ACM (2011)
4. Amin, S., Abate, A., Prandini, M., Lygeros, J., Sastry, S.S.: Reachability analysis for controlled discrete time stochastic hybrid systems. In: Hespanha, J.P., Tiwari, A. (eds.) HSCC 2006. LNCS, vol. 3927, pp. 49–63. Springer, Heidelberg (2006)
5. Arnold, L.: Stochastic Differential Equations: Theory and Applications. Wiley - Interscience, New York (1974)
6. Ball, T., Rajamani, S.K.: The SLAM toolkit. In: Berry, G., Comon, H., Finkel, A. (eds.) CAV 2001. LNCS, vol. 2102, pp. 260–264. Springer, Heidelberg (2001)
7. Barrett, C., Conway, C.L., Deters, M., Hadarean, L., Jovanović, D., King, T., Reynolds, A., Tinelli, C.: CVC4. In: Gopalakrishnan, G., Qadeer, S. (eds.) CAV 2011. LNCS, vol. 6806, pp. 171–177. Springer, Heidelberg (2011)
8. Bellman, R.: A Markovian decision process. Technical report, DTIC Document (1957)
9. Biere, A., Cimatti, A., Clarke, E., Zhu, Y.: Symbolic model checking without BDDs. In: Cleaveland, W.R. (ed.) TACAS 1999. LNCS, vol. 1579, pp. 193–207. Springer, Heidelberg (1999)
10. Bloem, R., Ravi, K., Somenzi, F.: Efficient decision procedures for model checking of linear time logic properties. In: Halbwachs, N., Peled, D.A. (eds.) CAV 1999. LNCS, vol. 1633, pp. 222–235. Springer, Heidelberg (1999)
11. Blom, H.A., Bloem, E.A.: Particle filtering for stochastic hybrid systems. In: 43rd IEEE Conference on Decision and Control, vol. 3, pp. 3221–3226. IEEE (2004)
12. Blom, H.A., Lygeros, J., Everdij, M., Loizou, S., Kyriakopoulos, K.: Stochastic Hybrid Systems: Theory and Safety Critical Applications. Springer, Heidelberg (2006)
13. Brayton, R.K., et al.: VIS: a system for verification and synthesis. In: Alur, R., Henzinger, T.A. (eds.) CAV 1996. LNCS, vol. 1102, pp. 428–432. Springer, Heidelberg (1996)
14. Bryant, R.E.: Graph-based algorithms for boolean function manipulation. IEEE Trans. Comput. **100**(8), 677–691 (1986)

15. Bujorianu, M.L., Lygeros, J.: General stochastic hybrid systems. In: IEEE Mediterranean Conference on Control and Automation MED, vol. 4, pp. 174–188 (2004)

16. Burch, J., Clarke, E.M., Long, D.: Symbolic model checking with partitioned transition relations. In: Computer Science Department, p. 435 (1991)

17. Burch, J.R., Clarke, E.M., McMillan, K.L., Dill, D.L.: Sequential circuit verification using symbolic model checking. In: 27th ACM/IEEE Design Automation Conference, pp. 46–51. IEEE (1990)

18. Burch, J.R., Clarke, E.M., McMillan, K.L., Dill, D.L., Hwang, L.-J.: Symbolic model checking: 10^{20} states and beyond. In: Fifth Annual IEEE Symposium on Logic in Computer Science, pp. 428–439. IEEE (1990)

19. Cimatti, A., Clarke, E., Giunchiglia, F., Roveri, M.: NuSMV: a new symbolic model checker. Int. J. Softw. Tools Technol. Transf. **2**(4), 410–425 (2000)

20. Claessen, K., Fisher, J., Ishtiaq, S., Piterman, N., Wang, Q.: Model-checking signal transduction networks through decreasing reachability sets. In: Sharygina, N., Veith, H. (eds.) CAV 2013. LNCS, vol. 8044, pp. 85–100. Springer, Heidelberg (2013)

21. Clarke, E., Grumberg, O., Jha, S., Lu, Y., Veith, H.: Counterexample-guided abstraction refinement. In: Emerson, E.A., Sistla, A.P. (eds.) CAV 2000. LNCS, vol. 1855, pp. 154–169. Springer, Heidelberg (2000)

22. Clarke, E.M., Emerson, E.A.: Design and synthesis of synchronization skeletons using branching time temporal logic. In: Kozen, D. (ed.) Logic of Programs 1981. LNCS, vol. 131, pp. 52–71. Springer, Heidelberg (1982)

23. Clarke, E.M., Grumberg, O., Long, D.E.: Model checking and abstraction. ACM Trans. Program. Lang. Syst. (TOPLAS) **16**(5), 1512–1542 (1994)

24. Cordeiro, L., Fischer, B., Marques-Silva, J.: SMT-based bounded model checking for embedded ANSI-C software. IEEE Trans. Softw. Eng. **38**(4), 957–974 (2012)

25. D'Argenio, P.R., Jeannet, B., Jensen, H.E., Larsen, K.G.: Reachability analysis of probabilistic systems by successive refinements. In: de Luca, L., Gilmore, S. (eds.) PAPM-PROBMIV 2001. LNCS, vol. 2165, pp. 39–56. Springer, Heidelberg (2001)

26. Davis, M.H.: Piecewise-deterministic Markov processes: a general class of non-diffusion stochastic models. J. Royal Stat.Soc. Ser. B (Methodol.) **46**(3), 353–388 (1984)

27. de Moura, L., Bjørner, N.: Z3: an efficient SMT solver. In: Ramakrishnan, C.R., Rehof, J. (eds.) TACAS 2008. LNCS, vol. 4963, pp. 337–340. Springer, Heidelberg (2008)

28. Dutertre, B., De Moura, L.: The yices SMT solver. 2, 2 (2006). Tool paper at http://yices.csl.sri.com/tool-paper.pdf

29. Fränzle, M., Hahn, E.M., Hermanns, H., Wolovick, N., Zhang, L.: Measurability and safety verification for stochastic hybrid systems. In: Proceedings of the 14th International Conference on Hybrid Systems: Computation and Control, pp. 43–52. ACM (2011)

30. Fränzle, M., Hermanns, H., Teige, T.: Stochastic satisfiability modulo theory: a novel technique for the analysis of probabilistic hybrid systems. In: Egerstedt, M., Mishra, B. (eds.) HSCC 2008. LNCS, vol. 4981, pp. 172–186. Springer, Heidelberg (2008)

31. Frehse, G.: PHAVer: algorithmic verification of hybrid systems past HyTech. In: Morari, M., Thiele, L. (eds.) HSCC 2005. LNCS, vol. 3414, pp. 258–273. Springer, Heidelberg (2005)

32. Ganai, M.K., Gupta, A., Ashar, P.: Efficient SAT-based unbounded symbolic model checking using circuit co-factoring. In: Proceedings of the 2004 IEEE/ACM International Conference on Computer-Aided Design, pp. 510–517. IEEE (2004)

33. Godefroid, P.: Using partial orders to improve automatic verification methods. In: Clarke, E., Kurshan, R.P. (eds.) CAV 1990. LNCS, vol. 531, pp. 176–185. Springer, Heidelberg (1991)

34. Hahn, E.M., Norman, G., Parker, D., Wachter, B., Zhang, L.: Game-based abstraction and controller synthesis for probabilistic hybrid systems. In: 2011 Eighth International Conference on Quantitative Evaluation of Systems (QEST), pp. 69–78. IEEE (2011)

35. Hardin, R., Kurshan, R., Shukla, S., Vardi, M.: A new heuristic for bad cycle detection using BDDs. In: Grumberg, O. (ed.) CAV 1997. LNCS, vol. 1254, pp. 268–278. Springer, Heidelberg (1997)

36. Havelund, K., Shankar, N.: Experiments in theorem proving and model checking for protocol verification. In: Gaudel, M.-C., Wing, J.M. (eds.) FME 1996. LNCS, vol. 1051, pp. 662–681. Springer, Heidelberg (1996)

37. Henzinger, T.A., Jhala, R., Majumdar, R., Sutre, G.: Software verification with BLAST. In: Ball, T., Rajamani, S.K. (eds.) SPIN 2003. LNCS, vol. 2648, pp. 235–239. Springer, Heidelberg (2003)

38. Hermanns, H., Wachter, B., Zhang, L.: Probabilistic CEGAR. In: Gupta, A., Malik, S. (eds.) CAV 2008. LNCS, vol. 5123, pp. 162–175. Springer, Heidelberg (2008)

39. Holzmann, G.J.: The model checker SPIN. IEEE Trans. Softw. Eng. **23**(5), 279–295 (1997)

40. Hu, J., Lygeros, J., Sastry, S.: Towards a theory of stochastic hybrid systems. In: Lynch, N.A., Krogh, B.H. (eds.) HSCC 2000. LNCS, vol. 1790, pp. 160–173. Springer, Heidelberg (2000)

41. Katoen, J.-P., Khattri, M., Zapreev, I.S.: A Markov reward model checker. In: Second International Conference on the Quantitative Evaluation of Systems, pp. 243–244. IEEE (2005)

42. Kroening, D., Tautschnig, M.: CBMC – C bounded model checker. In: Ábrahám, E., Havelund, K. (eds.) TACAS 2014 (ETAPS). LNCS, vol. 8413, pp. 389–391. Springer, Heidelberg (2014)

43. Kwiatkowska, M., Norman, G., Parker, D.: Game-based abstraction for Markov decision processes. In: Third International Conference on Quantitative Evaluation of Systems, pp. 157–166. IEEE (2006)

44. Kwiatkowska, M., Norman, G., Parker, D.: PRISM 4.0: verification of probabilistic real-time systems. In: Gopalakrishnan, G., Qadeer, S. (eds.) CAV 2011. LNCS, vol. 6806, pp. 585–591. Springer, Heidelberg (2011)

45. Marrero, W., Clarke, E., Jha, S.: Model checking for security protocols. Technical report, DTIC Document (1997)

46. McMillan, K.L.: Symbolic Model Checking. Springer, New York (1993)

47. McMillan, K.L.: Applying SAT methods in unbounded symbolic model checking. In: Brinksma, E., Larsen, K.G. (eds.) CAV 2002. LNCS, vol. 2404, pp. 250–264. Springer, Heidelberg (2002)

48. McMillan, K.L.: Interpolation and SAT-based model checking. In: Hunt Jr., W.A., Somenzi, F. (eds.) CAV 2003. LNCS, vol. 2725, pp. 1–13. Springer, Heidelberg (2003)

49. Peled, D.: All from one, one for all: on model checking using representatives. In: Courcoubetis, C. (ed.) CAV 1993. LNCS, vol. 697, pp. 409–423. Springer, Heidelberg (1993)

50. Platzer, A.: Stochastic differential dynamic logic for stochastic hybrid programs. In: Bjørner, N., Sofronie-Stokkermans, V. (eds.) CADE 2011. LNCS, vol. 6803, pp. 446–460. Springer, Heidelberg (2011)

51. Pnueli, A.: The temporal logic of programs. In: 18th Annual Symposium on Foundations of Computer Science, pp. 46–57. IEEE (1977)
52. Queille, J.-P., Sifakis, J.: Specification and verification of concurrent systems in CESAR. In: Dezani-Ciancaglini, M., Montanari, U. (eds.) Programming 1982. LNCS, vol. 137, pp. 337–351. Springer, Heidelberg (1982)
53. Riley, D., Koutsoukos, X.D., Riley, K.: Modeling and simulation of biochemical processes using stochastic hybrid systems: the sugar cataract development process. In: Egerstedt, M., Mishra, B. (eds.) HSCC 2008. LNCS, vol. 4981, pp. 429–442. Springer, Heidelberg (2008)
54. Sebastiani, R., Tonetta, S., Vardi, M.Y.: Symbolic systems, explicit properties: on hybrid approaches for LTL symbolic model checking. In: Etessami, K., Rajamani, S.K. (eds.) CAV 2005. LNCS, vol. 3576, pp. 350–363. Springer, Heidelberg (2005)
55. Sheeran, M., Singh, S., Stålmarck, G.: Checking safety properties using induction and a SAT-solver. In: Johnson, S.D., Hunt Jr., W.A. (eds.) FMCAD 2000. LNCS, vol. 1954, pp. 108–125. Springer, Heidelberg (2000)
56. Sproston, J.: Decidable model checking of probabilistic hybrid automata. In: Joseph, M. (ed.) FTRTFT 2000. LNCS, vol. 1926, pp. 31–45. Springer, Heidelberg (2000)
57. Sproston, J.: Model checking for probabilistic timed and hybrid systems. Ph.D. thesis. School of Computer Science, University of Birmingham (2001)
58. Tijms, H.C.: A First Course in Stochastic Models. Wiley, New York (2003)
59. Tinelli, C.: SMT-based model checking. In: Goodloe, A.E., Person, S. (eds.) NFM 2012. LNCS, vol. 7226, p. 1. Springer, Heidelberg (2012)
60. Valmari, A.: Stubborn sets for reduced state space generation. In: Rozenberg, G. (ed.) APN 1990. LNCS, vol. 483, pp. 491–515. Springer, Heidelberg (1991)
61. Wachter, B., Zhang, L.: Best probabilistic transformers. In: Barthe, G., Hermenegildo, M. (eds.) VMCAI 2010. LNCS, vol. 5944, pp. 362–379. Springer, Heidelberg (2010)
62. Wang, Q., Zuliani, P., Kong, S., Gao, S., Clarke, E.M.: SReach: a bounded model checker for stochastic hybrid systems. CoRR, abs/1404.7206 (2014)
63. Wang, Q., Zuliani, P., Kong, S., Gao, S., Clarke, E.M.: SReach: combining statistical tests and bounded model checking for nonlinear hybrid systems with parametric uncertainty. Technical report, Computer Science Department, Carnegie Mellon University (2014)
64. Wimmer, R., Braitling, B., Becker, B.: Counterexample generation for discrete-time markov chains using bounded model checking. In: Jones, N.D., Müller-Olm, M. (eds.) VMCAI 2009. LNCS, vol. 5403, pp. 366–380. Springer, Heidelberg (2009)
65. Younes, H.L.S.: Ymer: a statistical model checker. In: Etessami, K., Rajamani, S.K. (eds.) CAV 2005. LNCS, vol. 3576, pp. 429–433. Springer, Heidelberg (2005)
66. Zhang, L., She, Z., Ratschan, S., Hermanns, H., Hahn, E.M.: Safety verification for probabilistic hybrid systems. Eur. J. Control 18(6), 572–587 (2012)
67. Zuliani, P., Platzer, A., Clarke, E.M.: Bayesian statistical model checking with application to simulink/stateflow verification. In: Proceedings of the 13th ACM International Conference on Hybrid Systems: Computation and Control, pp. 243–252. ACM (2010)

Big Data, Big Systems, Big Challenges: A Personal Experience

(Extended Abstract)

Vadim E. Kotov[(✉)]

Correspondent Member of the Russian Academy of Sciences,
Sunnyvale, CA, USA
vkotov@sv.cmu.edu

I have been fortunate to work in two remarkable research communities, Akademgorodok in Siberia and Silicon Valley in California, and that my professional career stretched over two very different, yet both exciting epochs of the computer systems and science evolution: steady accumulation of knowledge and technology in 1960s–1980s and, then, "Internet Big Bang" and Information Revolution in 1990s–2010s.

In this talk, I track the trends in the development of large computer systems which I witnessed working first at Hewlett-Packard Laboratories and then at Carnegie-Mellon University, Silicon Valley Campus. This is not a general survey, I exemplify those trends by the systems in the analysis or/and design of which I and my colleagues participated.

The driving force behind the computer system progress is unprecedented accumulation of complex data and huge global data traffic. "Big Data" is a popular metaphor labeling the situation. It becomes difficult to process Big Data using traditional computer systems and applications. "Big Systems" that become the main trend in the current system architecture are required. They include: powerful data centers using tens of thousands servers; enterprise IT "systems of systems" consisting of globally distribute data centers; Grid and Utility Computing; Cloud Computing; Warehouse Scale Computers, Internet of Things (IoT), and coming exascale supersystems.

Large Enterprise Systems. Actually, the story of Big Data and Big Systems began much earlier when enterprise IT systems started to have problems processing data they created. I was involved in several projects that analyzed the ways to improve the situation. For example, globalization and just-in-time delivery created in 1990s flood of packages shipped by Federal Express and the company's centralized IT system was not able to process scanned data in time. The solution was in found in a two-level distributed architecture combining small number of large data centers with large number of web-based local facilities. Or, some companies had distributed IT infrastructure that grew up several decades with no real planning. They started to have bottlenecks and low end-to-end performance. New, best-of-breed processors and large storage did not improve situation. Main reason for bad performance: bad allocation of data, applications, and resources: 90 % of time spent in the system was dedicated to moving data around, not actually manipulating data. Conclusion: systems should be designed in a systematic way as *communication structures*: federations of uniformed, well-defined components efficiently communicating and collaborating with each other.

A. Voronkov and I. Virbitskaite (Eds.): PSI 2014, LNCS 8974, pp. 41–44, 2015.
DOI: 10.1007/978-3-662-46823-4_3

New Software Paradigms. They emerged as results of those efforts. They include *service-oriented architecture, autonomous,* and *multi-agent* computing. In service-centric software organization, the basic programming entity is *service,* a well-defined procedure that does not depend on the state of other services. The services interact with each other by exchanging service requests and service results. The main challenge in such distributed dynamic systems is resource allocation and the related service placement. To overcome growing complexity of management for large-scale distributed systems, autonomous and multi-agent architecture replaces the centralized management by distributed self-management provided by *autonomic agents* that interact to manage collectively. At Hewlett-Packard Labs, we analyzed several distributed management algorithms: Random/Round Robin Load Distribution (pushes load from an overloaded server to a randomly or round robin chosen); Simple Greedy (pushes load on to the least loaded neighbor); Ant-based (a decentralized version of *Ant Colony Optimization);* Broadcast of Local Eligibility (modified highly scalable algorithm for coordination of mobile robots). They provide increased servers' utilization and reduced the overall network traffic, but differ in speed and accuracy.

Data Centers. Growing complexity of IT systems and their management pushed the creation of large *Data Centers* that concentrate large number of servers, vast storage capacity, scalability, and special processing frameworks and applications. *Utility computing* packages computing resources into metered services. *Grid* is a large network of data centers which provides computing resources that are shared and utilized for solving large complex tasks. *Cloud Computing* outsources users' local data and applications to remote servers with accessing them via internet. Users get: continuous access to their data/apps from any location at any time; ability to use the vast storage and powerful servers; automatic backup of data and applications in case of disaster. *Virtualization* allows users to access a heterogeneous computing infrastructure as if it were a single, logically unified resource.

Big Data Challenges. Four V's characterize the main Big Data challenges:

Volume: ~ 200 billions emails every day; in 2012, daily internet traffic was 40 petabytes; Facebook generates daily more than 25 terabytes data, Twitter - 12 terabytes. In 2009, the world total data was 1 zetabyte (10^{21}); it is doubling every 18 months; in 2020 it will be 40 zetabyte.

Variety: Complexity of data also growing, 90 % is unstructured data: images, video clips, musical composition, financial documents, sensor signals, barcodes, ... Their sizes vary significantly: DVD – 5 gigabytes, email – several kilobytes, barcode – 128 bytes (< 6 % of total volume in gigabytes, yet 99 % of the number of circulating files).

Value: Big Data has value if it possible to extract "Smart Data", information that actually makes sense (now it is only 3 %). Methods of converting "raw data" into sensible information:

- *Data-mining* (recognition of correlations, trends, hidden relationships and associations);
- *Data analytics* (discovery of unknown patterns, confirmation or refutation of hypotheses);
- *Machine learning* (computers acquire new knowledge on their own, without direct programming);
- *Visualization* (captures the hidden relationship between a non-quantitative and unstructured data – 70–80 % of all data; Studies show that the brain processes images 60,000x faster than text).

Velocity: Big Data should provide the right information to the right persons at the right time enabling real-time decision-making.

HANA and Hadoop. Big Data distributed among storage in a data center or in multiple data centers requires new type of database software organization and parallel frameworks for running applications. Currently, SAP *HANA* and Apache *Hadoop* are intended to help.

There are two scenarios for working online with data: OLTP (Online Transaction Processing) and OLAP (Online Analytical Processing) Traditional OLTP data bases are row-oriented, SAP *HANA* is column-oriented in-memory data base (*HANA* works for OLTP too, but its main advantages is in OLAP). Due to this, *HANA* allows users to perform quickly complex analytical queries both with structured and unstructured data.

Hadoop is programming framework that takes care about scalability and file allocation instead of programmer. Hadoop is derived from *MapReduce* developed by Google. Programming model of *MapReduce* is inspired by the *map* and *reduce* functions of Lisp: *map* applies to its arguments a given unary operation, *reduce* combines its arguments using a binary operation, thus convolving the arguments into one output value. Using these operations, *Hadoop* allocate data and distributes their processing among large number of servers and is highly scalable. *Hadoop* has also built-in fault tolerance mechanisms in case of server failures.

Graph 500. To address performance of concurrent search, optimization, and clustering of Big Data, new benchmarks are needed to replace FLOPs used in scientific computations or Transactions-Per-Minutes used in OLTP. Benchmark *Graph 500* is based on *breadth-first search* in a large undirected graph (visit a node, then visit neighboring nodes) and measures performance in *TEPS* (traversed edges per second). The benchmark has two kernels: graph generator with compressor into sparse structures and parallel *breadth-first search* of random nodes. Six possible scales of generated graphs are defined: from toy (2^{26} nodes, 17 GB of RAM) to huge (2^{42} nodes, 1.1 PB of RAM). For example, IBM *Sequoia* in Lawrence Livermore Laboratory with 98,304 nodes, 1,572,864 cores (scale: 2^{40}) reached performance of 15363 GigaTEPS on *Graph 500* benchmark.

Future of Data Centers. Data centers evolve both in the number and performance of servers. Data centers of early 2000 s were built of COTS (Commercial Off-The-Shelf) computers, switches, and racks. Around 2010, they had custom servers and switches built of commercial chips. By 2020, custom servers and switches will be built of custom systems-on-chip. Exascale systems will likely have 100,000 nodes and will require super-efficient interconnection, such as high-radix (1000?) photonic switches with narrow channels combined into routing fabrics (over low radix with broad channels). Message passing will simplify programming (over shared memory). *Warehouse Scale Computers* will become data centers in a computer with millions of 1000-core chips that runs a large variety of applications that will require new algorithms with many different levels of scalable paralellization.

Internet of Things. Those Big Systems will process Big Data produced by "Internet of Things" in which all objects and people on the Earth will be equipped with wireless identifiers to be inventoried and managed by computers. Prediction: within next six years 25–50 billion of "things" could be connected to ~ 10 billion mobile phones and PCs. Embedded computers already are becoming a key component of all kinds of complex cyber-physical systems. The current examples are Smart Homes, Smart (electrical) Grid, driverless cars, and, of course, exploding use of robots.

As computer systems play more and more important role in our life, can we trust them? System *dependability* should guarantee their availability (readiness for service), reliability (continuity of uninterrupted service), safety (no catastrophic consequences for users), integrity (no unforeseen changes), and maintainability (ability to quickly repair and modify). NASA-sponsored the High-Dependability Computing Program (HDCP), in which I participated as Director of Engineering, was an example of efforts to improve system dependability.

What is Ahead? Radically new technologies (nano- bio-)?. *Quantum computers* that will be many orders of magnitude faster? *DNA computers* that can store billions of times more data and process them many times faster? The future will show. The future has always been smarter than the present.

An Automatic Technique
for Static Deadlock Prevention

Bertrand Meyer[1,2,3(✉)]

[1] ETH Zurich, Zurich, Switzerland
Bertrand.Meyer@inf.ethz.ch
http://se.ethz.ch/
[2] Innopolis University, Kazan, Russia
http://university.innopolis.ru/en/research/selab/
[3] Eiffel Software, Goleta, USA
http://eiffel.com/

Abstract. Deadlocks remain one of the biggest threats to concurrent programming. Usually, the best programmers can expect is dynamic deadlock detection, which is only a palliative. Object-oriented programs, with their rich reference structure and the resulting presence of aliasing, raise additional problems. The technique developed in this paper relies on the "alias calculus" to offer a completely static and completely automatic analysis of concurrent object-oriented programs. The discussion illustrates the technique by applying it to two versions of the "dining philosophers" program, of which it proves that the first is deadlock-free and the second deadlock-prone.

1 Overview

Deadlock is, along with data races, one of the two curses of concurrent programming. Although other dangers — priority inversion, starvation, livelock — await concurrent programmers, these two are the most formidable. The goal of the technique presented here is to avoid deadlock entirely through static analysis, so that any program that could cause deadlock will be rejected at compile time. No implementation is available and the description is preliminary, leaving several problems open.

The general approach is applicable to any concurrency model, but its detailed application relies on SCOOP (Simple Concurrent Object-Oriented Programming) [3, 4, 7–9], a minimal concurrent extension to an OO language, retaining the usual modes of reasoning about sequential programs. One of the distinctive properties of SCOOP is that the model removes the risk of data races, but deadlocks are still possible. The goal of the approach described here is to remove deadlocks too, statically.

In today's practice, the best concurrent programmers may usually hope for is *dynamic* deadlock detection: if at run time the system runs into a deadlock, a watchdog will discover the situation and trigger an exception. Such a technique is preferable to letting the execution get stuck forever, but it is still unsatisfactory: the time of program execution is too late for detection. We should aim for *static* prevention through a technique that will analyze the program text and identify possible run-time deadlocks.

© Springer-Verlag Berlin Heidelberg 2015
A. Voronkov and I. Virbitskaite (Eds.): PSI 2014, LNCS 8974, pp. 45–58, 2015.
DOI: 10.1007/978-3-662-46823-4_4

Like many interesting problems in programming, static deadlock detection is undecidable, so the best we can expect is an over-approximation: a technique that will flag all programs that might deadlock — meaning it is *sound* — but might occasionally flag one that won't. The technique should be as *precise* as possible, meaning that the number of such false alarms is minimal. In fact an unsound technique may be of interest too, if it detects many — but not all — deadlock risks. The technique described here is intended to be sound, but no proof of soundness is available.

The approach relies on two key ideas. The first idea is that deadlock prevention means finding out if there is any set of processors whose *hold sets* and *wait sets* are mutually non-disjoint. The second idea is that in an object-oriented context, with references and hence possible aliasing, we can compute these sets by applying *alias analysis* to get a model of the processors associated with concurrent objects, and hence of their hold and wait sets. The key supporting tool in this step is the **alias calculus**, a technique developed by the author and colleagues for fully automatic alias analysis. Section 7 is a hands-on application of the resulting technique to two programs implementing solutions to the well-known "dining philosophers" problem; the analysis proves that the first version — the standard SCOOP solution of this problem — is deadlock-free, and that the second version, specifically contrived to cause potential deadlocks, can indeed result in a deadlocked execution.

The discussion begins with a general formalization of the *deadlock condition*, applicable to any concurrency framework (Sect. 2). Based on this model, a general strategy is possible for detecting deadlock statically; the principle is that deadlock may arise if the "hold sets" and "wait sets" of a set of processors are not pair-wise disjoint. This strategy is the topic of Sect. 3. After a short reminder on SCOOP in Sect. 4, Sect. 5 shows how to produce a deadlock in SCOOP; the design of the model makes such a situation rare, but not impossible. Section 6 refines the general deadlock detection technique of Sect. 3 to the specific case of SCOOP, showing the crucial role of alias analysis, as permitted by the alias calculus. Section 7 shows the application to an important and representative example problem: dining philosophers, in the case of two components. Section 8 lists the limitations of the present state of the work and the goals of its future development.

Although the literature on deadlock prevention and detection is huge, there is (to my knowledge) no precedent for an approach that, as presented here, permits static deadlock analysis for concurrent object-oriented programs by relying on alias analysis. This is the reason for the restricted nature of the bibliography.

2   General Deadlock Condition

Deadlock is, as mentioned above, only one of two major risks in traditional concurrent programming. It is closely connected to the other one, data races. A data race arises when two concurrent program elements access and modify data in an order that violates their individual assumptions; for example, if each tries to book a flight by first finding a seat then booking it, some interleavings of these operations will cause both to believe they have obtained a given seat. The remedy is to obtain exclusive access to a resource for as long as needed; but then, if concurrent elements share more than one resource and they obtain exclusive access through locking, the possibility of *deadlock* looms: the execution might run into a standstill because every element is trying to obtain a resource that one of the others has locked. In the flight example, one client might try to lock the seat list then the reservation list, and the other might try to lock them in the reverse order, bringing them to an endless "deadly embrace", as deadlocks are also called. This analysis indicates the close connection between the two plagues: to avoid data races, programmers lock resources; but the ability of multiple clients to lock multiple resources may lead to deadlock.

The two problems are, however, of a different nature. One may blame data races on the low level of abstraction of the usual concurrent programming techniques (such as threading libraries with synchronizaation through semaphores); the SCOOP model removes the risk of data races by requiring program elements to obtain exclusive access before using any shared resource. The key mechanism (Sect. 4) is the SCOOP idiom for reserving *several* resources at once, moving the task of data race avoidance from the programmer to the SCOOP implementation. As a consequence, many deadlock cases disappear naturally. But, as we will see in detail, deadlock does remain possible, and is a harder problem to eliminate statically.

Ignoring SCOOP for the moment, we will now study under what general conditions deadlock can arise. The term "processor" will denote (as in SCOOP but without loss of generality) a mechanism able to execute *sequential* computations. Concurrency arises when more than one processor is at work. Processors can be of different kinds, hardware or software; a typical example is a *thread* as provided by modern operating systems.

The deadlock scheme considered here is the "Coffman deadlock", which assumes that two or more processors need exclusive access to two or more shared resources, and all seek to obtain it through locking. Deadlock arises if at some time during execution these processors become involved in a cycle, such that every one of them is seeking to lock a resource that is held by the next processor in the cycle. This is the usual informal definition, which we may formalize (without making the cycle explicit) as follows. There is a set P of processors and a set R of resources, both finite. For each processor p, at any execution time t, there are two disjoint sets of resources:

- $H(p)$, the hold (or "has") set, containing resources that p has locked and not yet unlocked, and to which, as a result, it has exclusive access.
- $W(p)$, the wait (or "want") set, containing resources that p is trying, unsuccessfully so far, to lock.

(To avoid ambiguity, we may make the time explicit, writing $W_t(p)$ and $W_t(p)$.)

Deadlock arises between the processors in P when every one of them wants something that another has:

$$\forall p: P \mid \exists p': P \mid W(p) \cap H(p') \neq \varnothing \qquad \text{-- Deadlock condition}$$

To get the usual cycle based presentation it suffices to start from an arbitrary processor p and follow the successive p' of the condition. Since P is finite the sequence is cyclic.

It is also useful to state the reverse condition, deadlock-freedom:

$$\exists\, p: P \mid \forall\, p': P \mid W(p) \cap H(p') = \varnothing \qquad\qquad \text{-- Progress condition}$$

This condition holds in particular when $W(p)$ is empty, that is to say, p is progressing normally and not waiting for any resource. It also holds if every processor only ever needs one resource at a time, formally expressed as $\forall\, p: P \mid H(p) \neq \varnothing \Rightarrow W(p) = \varnothing$ in that case, if the deadlock condition held, the cyclic sequence obtained by the above construction would consist of processors for which neither H nor W is empty, which contradicts this assumption.

3   Deadlock Prevention Strategy

The preceding analysis leads to a general strategy for statically detecting possible deadlocks. The strategy as presented here applies to any concurrency model; the next section will describe its application to the specific case of SCOOP.

Two observations are necessary to evaluate programs for their susceptibility to the deadlock condition. First, the condition refers to processors; but processors may only be known at run time. We need to transpose the reasoning to what we can analyze statically: positions in the program text. It suffices to extend the notations $H(p)$ and $W(p)$ to p denoting a program position; they denote the run-time hold and wait sets of any processor whose execution reaches position p.

The second observation is that it is only necessary to evaluate the condition at "locking positions": program points that contain an instruction that tries to lock a resource. Locking positions mark where deadlock can occur.

The general strategy, then, is to develop techniques for:

1. Estimating the H and W sets of any locking position. (The technique may be more general, and yield these sets for any program position.)
2. Estimating, for every locking position $lp1$, the set of its "*simultaneous*" positions: all locking positions $lp2$ such that during execution a processor may reach $lp1$ and another $lp2$ at the same time. Note that $lp1$ and $lp2$ may be the same position if several processors execute the same code.
3. Computing $W(lp1) \cap H(lp2)$ for every simultaneous pair $[lp1, lp2]$.

The progress condition holds if this intersection is empty for at least one pair.

For the first two steps, the strategy "estimates" the result since it may not be possible to determine them exactly. As noted in Sect. 1, an estimation should normally be an over-approximation, as accurate as possible.

The implementation of these two steps, and the precision of the estimation, depend on the concurrency model. We now come to the application to a specific model, SCOOP.

4   SCOOP Basics

The SCOOP model simplifies the framework developed above. "Processor" is a central notion in SCOOP, and is general enough to subsume the concept of resource.

SCOOP closely connects the concurrency architecture with the object-oriented architecture of a system, through the rule that every object has an associated processor, its *handler*, which is responsible for all operations on the object (all calls of the form $x.r(\ldots)$ where r is attached to the object). The result is a partitioning of the object space into a number of regions, each associated with a handling processor:

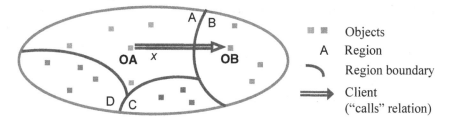

▨ ▨	Objects
A	Region
⤹	Region boundary
⇒	Client ("calls" relation)

In the figure, the object *OA* has a field x, attached (at a particular time during execution) to an object *OB* in another region. A call $x.r(\ldots)$ issued by the processor of region *A*(handler of *OA*) will be executed by the processor of region *B* (handler of *OB*).

Such a call applied to a separate object is (in the case of a procedure, rather than a function) **asynchronous**: it does not block the *A* processor. To reflect this property, a variable such as x that may represent objects in another region must be declared **separate**. But $x.r(\ldots)$ is only permitted if the processor executing this operation has obtained exclusive access to the object. The basic way to achieve exclusive access is through a procedure call with x as argument. More generally, a routine with header

> $r(x:$ **separate** $T;$ $y:$ **separate** $U;\ \ldots)$

will guarantee exclusive access to the separate arguments for the duration of the execution of r's body. A call $r(a, b, \ldots)$ may as a consequence have to wait until it has obtained exclusive access to the objects attached to $a, b, \ldots$. This is how SCOOP gets rid of data races: if you need a resource, or any number of resources, you must first obtain exclusive access to them; so a program element cannot invalidate another's assumption by messing up with shared resources.

If at the time of such a call one of the actual arguments, for example a, is already accessible under exclusive access, perhaps because a is a formal argument of the routine in which the call appears, this exclusive access is transferred to r, under "lock passing", for the duration of its execution.

As an example of simultaneous reservation of multiple resources, the following code implements the "dining philosophers" scheme. Two classes are involved, *FORK* and *PHILOSOPHER*. All we need from a fork is the ability to help us eat:

```
class FORK feature
        use do ...Use the fork to eat ...end
end
```

The creation procedure (constructor) *make* of class *PHILOSOPHER* gives a philosopher a left and a right forks, represented as separate objects. The procedure *live* capture a philosopher's behavior:

```
class PHILOSOPHER create make feature
        left, right: separate FORK

        live
                            -- Perform philosopher cycle with left and right forks.
                do
                        from until False loop
                            think
                            eat (left, right)            -- Simultaneous point (see section 7
                        end
                end
        eat (l, r: separate FORK)
                        -- Pick both l and r.
                do
                        l.use ; r.use
                end
        think do ... Not specified ... end
feature -- Initialization
        make (l, r: separate FORK)
                        -- Initialize with l as left and r as right forks.
                do left := l ; right := r end
end
```

The key element is the highlighted call *eat (left, right)* which, by virtue of the basic SCOOP processor reservation mechanism, obtains exclusive access to the two forks. No other synchronization operation is necessary. The classical problems of securing multiple resources without risking deadlock or starvation are no longer the application programmer's business; the SCOOP implementation handles them.

To set everything going we may use — in the illustrative case of two philosophers and two forks — the following "root" class. (The class text is supporting code, with no particularly deep concepts, but needed for the example analysis of the next sections):

```
class MEAL create make feature
    fork1, fork2: separate FORK
    phil1, phil2: separate PHILOSOPHER

    make
            -- Set up two philosophers sharing forks, and get them started.
        do
            -- Create the philosophers and forks:
                create fork1 ; create fork2
                create phil1.make ( fork1, fork2 )
                create phil2.make ( fork2, fork1 )
            -- Start the philosophers:
                execute (phil1, phil2)
        end
feature {NONE}
    execute (p1, p2: separate PHILOSOPHER)
            -- Perform both philosophers' lives.
        do
                p1.live
                p2.live
        end

end
```

The creation instructions for the philosophers reverse the "left" and "right" role for the two forks. It would not be possible to merge the creation procedure *make* with *execute* since it needs to perform calls such as *p1.live* on attached targets, requiring exclusive access to the corresponding objects; so we first need the creation instructions in *make* to create these objects, then *execute* to work on them.

In the version above, *make* does call *execute*, so that creating a meal object (**create** *m.make*) is enough to trigger a full system execution. As a result, *execute* is secret (private), as specified by **feature** {*NONE*}. It would also be possible to separate the two parts, removing the call to *execute* in *make* and declaring *execute* public.

The illustrated constructs are the main components of the SCOOP concurrency model. They suffice for the rest of the presentation, but for completeness it is useful to list the other properties which together with them make up all of SCOOP:

- A separate call on a *query* (function or attribute, returning a result), as in the assignment $y := x.f (...)$ is, unlike a call to a *procedure*, synchronous: since the execution needs the value, it will wait until *f* has terminated. Waiting on the result of a query is the SCOOP mechanism for re-synchronizing after an asynchronous call.
- A routine precondition of the form **require** *x.some_condition*, where *x* is a separate formal argument of the routine, will cause the execution of the routine's body to wait until the condition is satisfied. This is the SCOOP mechanism for condition synchronization.

- To work on separate targets, a program element must have exclusive access to them. The usual way to obtain it is to pass the targets as arguments to a routine, as in *execute* (*phil*1, *phil*2). If *execute* is not available separately from *make*, it is possible to avoid writing *execute* altogether and replace the call *execute* (*phil*1, *phil*2) by the "inline separate" construct

separate *phil*1 **as** *p*1, *phil*2 **as** *p*2 **do**
    *p*1. *live* ; *p*2. *live*
end

with the same effect of guaranteeing exclusive access to *phil*1 and *phil*2 under the local names *p*1 and *p*2. Inline separate avoids the writing of wrapper routines for the sole purpose of performing simple operations on separate targets. The rest of the discussion will use explicit wrapping, with no loss of generality since object reservation and access has the same semantics with inline separate as with wrapping.

5   Deadlock in SCOOP

To discuss deadlock in the SCOOP context, we do not need to distinguish between processors and resources as in the general model introduced at the beginning of this discussion. As illustrated by philosophers and forks, the notion of processor covers resources as well. A resource is an object; exclusive access to it means exclusive access to its handling processor. This unification of concepts significantly simplifies the problem.

In the practice of SCOOP programming, many deadlock risks disappear thanks to SCOOP's signature mechanism of reserving several separate targets at once by passing them as arguments to a routine (or, equivalently, using an inline separate). The most common case of deadlock other approaches arises when *p* and *q* both want to reserve *r* and *s*, but attempt to lock them in reverse order, ending up with *p* having *r* and wanting *s* while *q* has *s* and wants *r*. In SCOOP they will both execute *some_routine* (*r*, *s*); each will proceed when it gets both. No deadlock is possible. (In addition the SCOOP implementation guarantees fairness.)

Unfortunately, even though deadlock will not normally arise in proper use of SCOOP, it remains a distinct theoretical possibility. It is in fact easy to construct examples of programs that may deadlock, such as the following variant of the dining philosophers solution. The correct eating procedure in *PHILOSOPHER*, repeated here for convenience, is

```
eat (l, r. separate FORK)
            -- Pick both l and r.
        do
            l. use r. use
        end
```

Now consider the following:

```
                                  -- Features to be added to class PHILOSOPHER
eat_bad (f: separate FORK)
            -- Pick f, then the other fork.
    do
            pick_one (f)
            pick_second (f, opposite (f))
    end
pick_one (f: separate FORK)
            -- Pick f.
    do
            f.use
    end
pick_second (f1, f2: separate FORK)
            -- Already holding f1, pick f2.
    do
            f2.use
    end
opposite (f: separate FORK)
            -- The fork other than f.
            -- (With more than two forks, would be replaced by a "next" function.)
    do
            Result := if f = left then right else left end
    end
```

and replace the key call *eat* (*left*, *right*) in procedure *live* by *eat_bad* (*left*) (or *eat_bad* (*right*)).

The need for procedure *pick_second* comes from the assumptions of the dining philosophers problem: if we replaced the second instruction of *eat_bad* with just *pick_one* (*opposite* (*f*)), no deadlock would arise, but we would violate the basic condition that a philosopher requires access to both forks at once. The first argument of *pick_second* serves to maintain hold on the first fork.

If this scheme seems convoluted it is precisely because deadlock does not naturally arise in ordinary SCOOP style. With this version, however, classic dining-philosophers deadlock is possible, with a run-time scenario such as this: *eat_bad* for *phil*1 executes *pick_one* (*fork*1); *eat_bad* for *phil*2 executes *pick_one* (*fork*2); then the first *eat_-bad* tries to execute *pick_second* (*fork*1, *fork*2) and waits because *phil*2 holds *fork*2; but the second processor is also stuck, trying to execute *pick_second* (*fork*2, *fork*1) while *phil*1 holds *fork*1.

At this stage the deadlock condition of Sect. 2 holds. Identifying each processor by the program name of an object it handles:

- $H(phi1) = \{fork1\}$
- $W(phi1) = \{fork2\}$
- $H(phi2) = \{fork2\}$
- $W(phi2) = \{fork1\}$
- Hence both $H(phi1) \cap W(phi2) \neq \varnothing$ and $H(phi2) \cap W(phi1) \neq \varnothing$.

6 The SCOOP Deadlock Detection Rule

To apply the strategy of Sect. 3, we must:

- Find which pairs of locking positions are "simultaneous" (that is to say, might be executed concurrently).
- For every such pair [lp, lp'] compute the hold and wait sets of lp and lp'.
- Find out if all the intersections $H(lp) \cap W(lp')$ are non-empty.

In the SCOOP context, a locking position in SCOOP is a call $r(a, b, \ldots)$ to a routine with separate arguments. (As noted, we ignore inline separate instructions, which can be handled in the same way.)

We can define instruction simultaneity thanks to the following auxiliary concepts. Two instructions in the same routine are "*siblings*" if their closest enclosing Compounds are the same or nested within one another. (In $i1$; **if** c **then** $i2$ $i3$ **else** $i4$ **end** $i5$, all instructions are siblings except for the pairs $i2$, $i4$ and $i3$, $i4$.) In addition, a routine appearing in a loop is its own sibling. The "*dependents*" of a routine r, or a call to that routine, are r itself and all the routines that it may call directly or indirectly. A qualified call $x.r(\ldots)$ is "*separate*" if its target x is separate. Then two instructions $i1$ and $i2$ are simultaneous if $i1$ is in a dependent of a separate call c, and $i2$ is in a dependent of a sibling of c. For example in

$i1$
$sep.r(\ldots)$ -- Where sep is separate
$i2$
$x.s(\ldots)$ -- Where x may be separate or not

both $i1$ and $i2$ are simultaneous with all the instructions of r, s and their dependents.

Now the hold and wait sets. For an entity x in the program (formal argument, local variable, attribute) let $<x>$ be the handler of the object attached to x. The notation generalizes to lists: $<l>$ is the set of handlers of all the elements of a list l. Let **Current** denote the current object ("this"). Then:

For a call c with separate actual arguments *actuals*, appearing in a routine with separate formal arguments *formals*:
• $H(c) = <\textbf{Current}> \cup <Formals>$
• $W(c) = <Actuals>$

The call *c* (like any instruction in the same routine) holds the handler of the current object and the handlers of all the formal arguments of the enclosing routine. To proceed, *c* requires exclusive access to the handlers of actual arguments. This property applies both to a synchronous call, such as an unqualified call *r* (*Actuals*), for which the execution will not proceed until it has executed the body of *r*, and to an asynchronous call of the form *sep.r* (*Actuals*) for which the execution does not need to wait for *r* to complete or even to start, but does need to obtain exclusive access to the arguments.

The *W* rule ignores lock passing. To avoid the loss of generality, we may fictitiously extend the formal argument list of a routine with the separate arguments of its callers, although a more direct technique is desirable. The example discussed below does not involve lock passing.

To apply these rules, we need a way to determine the handler <*s*> of any separate entity *s*. More precisely, since the goal is to determine whether intersections of processor sets are empty, we need to determine whether <*s*> and <*t*> can be the same for two entities. This will be the case if *t* is aliased to *s*, or to *s.x* where *x* is a non-separate field of *s* (so that *s.x* has the same handler as *s*). This observation highlights *alias analysis* as the core task of deadlock analysis in an object-oriented concurrency framework.

Previous work [2, 5] has introduced an **alias calculus**. The calculus is a set of rules for computing statically, at any program point in the context of an object-oriented language with references, the *alias relation*: the set of pairs of expressions that may, be aliased when execution reaches that point. (Two expressions denoting references are aliased if they are attached to the same object.)

The rules of the alias calculus give, for every kind *c* of construct in the programming language and any alias relation *ar*, the value of *ar* » *c*: the alias relation that will hold after execution of *c* if *r* held before. For example, *ar* » (*c1*; *c2*) = (*ar* » *c1*) » *c2*). The reader may consult [2] for the full list of rules. (As may be expected, the alias relation computed by these rules is usually an over-approximation of the aliasing that may actually exist at execution time.) The present discussion assumes that we do have the alias calculus at our disposal. For the purpose of alias analysis, we add *s.x* to the aliases of *s* for all non-separate *x*.

In this framework, the above rule for computing the hold and wait sets becomes:

For a call *c* with separate actual arguments *actuals*, appearing in a routine with separate formal arguments *formals*:

- *H* (*c*) = *aliases* ({**Current**} ∪ *Formals*)
- *W* (*c*) = *aliases* (*Actuals*)

---

where *aliases* (*e*) is the set of expressions possibly aliased to *e* at the given program position. In this formulation, the *H* and *W* sets contain program expressions rather than the actual processors; the expressions act as proxies for these processors. Such an abstraction is necessary in any case since the processors only become known at execution time.

Deadlock analysis then reduces to the following steps.

Deadlock analysis strategy:
- Determine all pairs [$c1$, $c2$] of simultaneous calls with separate arguments.
- For all calls c involved, determine $H(c)$ and $W(c)$ according to the rule above, applying aliasing as necessary.
- Determine if all $H(c1) \cap W(c2)$ are non-empty.

---

7 Example Application

The following scenario illustrates deadlock analysis on the two-dining-philosophers example presented earlier.

The alias relations at each stage, resulting from the alias calculus, are assumed to come from automatic alias analysis.

In expressing these relations, we need the concept of *negative variable*, introduced in [6] to handle the changes of coordinates that characterize object-oriented programming. To understand this notion assume that a is aliased to b:

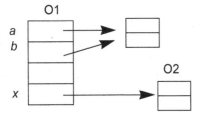

The alias relation is, in the notation of [5], $\overline{a, b}$, meaning that it contains the pair [a, b]and the symmetric pair [b, a] (an alias relation is symmetric). Also, a and b are their own aliases, but for economy we never explicitly include pairs [x, x] in an alias relation, keeping it irreflexive by convention.

At this point the program executes a qualified call $x.r(\ldots)$. The routine r may change the aliasing situation; but to determine these changes we cannot apply the alias calculus rules to the original relation $\overline{a, b}$ since a and b are fields of the original object $O1$ and mean nothing for the target object $O2$. The relation of interest is $x'.(\overline{a, b})$, equal by distributivity to $\overline{x'.a, x'.b}$. Here x', the "negation" of x, represents a back-reference to the caller as illustrated below. This reference need not exist in the implementation but is necessary for the alias computation. If ar is the alias relation obtained by the alias calculus at the end of the body of ar, then the result for the caller is $x.ar$, where any x' will cancel itself out with x since $x\tau.x' = $ **Current** and **Current**.$e = e$ for any e.

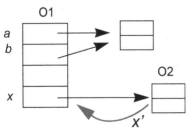

Let us now consider the deadlock analysis of the preceding section to the two versions of the dining philosopher program. In the first version, the relevant simultaneous pair is the call *eat* (*left, right*), paired with itself (since it is in a loop), in the routine *live*. Prior to aliasing, the hold and wait sets, seen from the philosopher object, are:

- $H = \{$**Current**$\}$
- $W = \{$*left, right*$\}$

Considering both calls to *live*, the reference structure is the following:

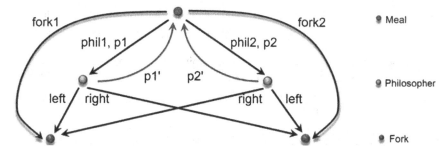

The top node is the root object, of type *MEAL*; the middle nodes are philosopher objects; the bottom nodes are fork objects. Through alias completion we get:

- $H = \{$**Current**, *p1'.phil1*, *p1'.p1*$\}$
- $W = \{$*left, right, p1'.fork1, p2'.fork2*$\}$

The intersection of these sets is empty: no deadlock. Now consider the version using *eat_bad* (*left*) instead of *eat* (*left, right*). The sets at the point of the call to *pick_second* in *eat_bad* are, at the *PHILOSOPHER* level and prior to alias completion:

- $H = \{$**Current**, $f\}$
- $W = \{$*left, right*$\}$

The reference structure is the same as above, plus aliasing of f to *left*:

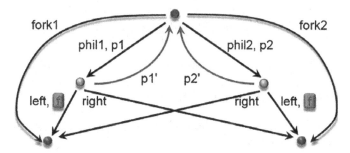

Alias completion yields:

- $H = \{$**Current**, *p1'.phil1*, *p1'.p1*, f, *left, p1'.fork1, p2'.fork2*$\}$
- $W = \{$*left, right, p1'.fork1, p2'.fork2*, $f\}$

Since *W* now includes *f*, aliased to *left*, the intersection is not empty, revealing the possibility of a deadlock.

8   Conclusion and Perspectives

The limitations of this work are clear: the technique is not modular; it has not been proved sound; its precision (avoidance of false alarms) is unknown; and it is not yet implemented.

The approach, however, seems promising. The reliance on aliasing seems to open the way for a realistic approach to static deadlock detection, applicable to modern object-oriented programs regardless of the complexity of their run-time object and reference structure.

The next step is to remedy the current limitations and make the approach fully applicable in a practical verification environment [7]. The goal is worth the effort: unleashing the full power of concurrent programming by removing an obstacle that, for decades, has been a nightmare.

Acknowledgments. The research reported here is part of the Concurrency Made Easy project at ETH, an Advanced Investigator Grant of the European Research Council (ERC grant agreement no. 29138). I am grateful to members of the CME project, particularly Scott West, Benjamin Morandi and Sebastian Nanz, for numerous comments on the research. Alexander Kogtenkov and Sergey Vedler were instrumental in the development of the alias calculus. Victorien Elvinger spotted an error in an earlier version.

References

1. EVE (Eiffel Verification Environment). http://se.inf.ethz.ch/research/eve/
2. Kogtenkov, A., Meyer, B., Velder, S.: Alias calculus, frame calculus and frame inference. Sci. Comput. Program. Part 1 **97**(1), 163–172 (2015)
3. Meyer, B.: Systematic concurrent object-oriented programming. Commun. ACM **36**(9), 56–80 (1993)
4. Meyer, B.: Object-Oriented Software Construction, 2nd edn. Prentice Hall, Upper Saddle River (1997). Chapter 32 includes a description of SCOOP
5. Meyer, B.: Steps towards a theory and calculus of aliasing. Int. J. Softw. Inform. **5**, 77–116 (2011)
6. Meyer, B., Kogtenkov, A.: Negative variables and the essence of object-oriented programming. In: Iida, S., Meseguer, J., Ogata, K. (eds.) Specification, Algebra, and Software. LNCS, vol. 8373, pp. 171–187. Springer, Heidelberg (2014)
7. Morandi, B., Schill, M., Nanz, S., Meyer, B.: Prototyping a concurrency model. In: International Conference on Application of Concurrency to System Design, pp. 177–186 (2013). http://se.inf.ethz.ch/people/morandi/publications/prototyping.pdf
8. Nienaltowski, P.: Practical framework for contract-based concurrent object-oriented programming. Ph.D. thesis, ETH Zurich (2007). http://se.inf.ethz.ch/old/people/nienaltowski/papers/thesis.pdf
9. SCOOP. http://cme.ethz.ch/

Automatically Partitioning Data to Facilitate the Parallelization of Functional Programs

Michael Dever[(⊠)] and G.W. Hamilton

Dublin City University, Dublin 9, Ireland
{mdever,hamilton}@computing.dcu.ie

Abstract. In this paper we present a novel transformation technique which, given a program defined on any data-type, automatically derives conversion functions for data of that type to and from well-partitioned *join*-lists. Using these conversion functions we employ existing program transformation techniques in order to redefine the given program into an implicitly parallel one defined in terms of well-partitioned data.

1 Introduction

The development of parallel software is inherently more difficult than that of sequential software and developers can have problems thinking in a parallel setting [16]. As the limitations of single-core processor speeds are reached, the developer has no choice but to reach for parallel implementations to obtain the required performance increases.

There are many existing automated parallelization techniques [2,3,8–11,17–19], which, while powerful, require that their inputs are defined using a *cons*-list. This is an unreasonable burden to place upon a developer as it may not be intuitive to define their program in terms of a *cons*-list. In order to remove this burden, this paper presents an automatic transformation for programs which automatically partitions the data they are defined on and uses distillation [7] to redefine these programs into implicitly parallel ones defined on the resulting well-partitioned data.

The remainder of this paper is structured as follows: Sect. 2 details the language used throughout this paper. Section 3 details the transformation which converts a given program into one defined on well-partitioned data. Section 4 presents an example program, whose data is well-partitioned using our technique and an implicitly parallel program automatically derived on this well-partitioned data. Section 5 presents a summary of related work and compares our techniques with this work. Section 6 presents our conclusions and plans for further work.

2 Language

We use a standard Haskell-like higher-order functional language throughout this paper, with the usual *cons*-list notations, where data-types are defined as shown

© Springer-Verlag Berlin Heidelberg 2015
A. Voronkov and I. Virbitskaite (Eds.): PSI 2014, LNCS 8974, pp. 59–66, 2015.
DOI: 10.1007/978-3-662-46823-4_5

$$t ::= \alpha \qquad\qquad\qquad \text{Type Variable}$$
$$\mid\; T\; t_1 \ldots t_g \qquad\qquad \text{Type Application}$$

$$\textbf{data}\; T\; \alpha_1 \ldots \alpha_k ::= c_1\; t_{1_1}\; \ldots\; t_{1_{n_1}} \qquad \text{Data-Type}$$
$$\vdots$$
$$\mid\; c_m\; t_{m_1}\; \ldots\; t_{m_{n_m}}$$

Fig. 1. Data-type definition

in Fig. 1. Within this language, a data-type T can be defined with the constructors $c_1, \ldots, c_m$. Polymorphism is supported via the use of type variables, α. We use $(e :: t)$ to denote an expression e of type t.

Within this language, *join*-lists are defined as shown in Fig. 2. The language has some useful built-in functions: *split* which takes a *cons*-list and splits it in half returning a tuple containing the left and right halves and *fst* which takes a tuple and returns its first element. The function $removeAll_\tau$, given a sequence of types, removes all occurrences of the type τ from the given sequence.

$$data\; JList\; a ::= Singleton\; a$$
$$\mid\; Join\; (JList\; a)\; (JList\; a)$$

Fig. 2. *join*-List data-type definition

3 Automatically Partitioning Data

There are many parallelization techniques which make use of well-partitioned data [1,2,8–11,13,17,18]. These can be restrictive and often require that input programs are defined on data that can be easily well-partitioned, however this may not always be intuitive. To solve this, we define a transformation technique that allows for the automatic partitioning of any data. An overview of this technique is shown in Fig. 3. The technique is combined with distillation in order to automatically convert a program into one defined on well-partitioned data. The technique consists of four steps:

1. Given a program defined on a data-type, τ, define a corresponding data-type, τ', instances of which contain the non-inductive components from data of type τ.
2. Derive a *partitioning function*, $partition_\tau$, which allows data of type τ to be converted into a well-partitioned *join*-list containing data of type τ'.
3. Derive a *rebuilding function*, $rebuild_\tau$, which converts a *join*-list containing data of type τ' into data of type τ.
4. Distill a program equivalent to the given program which is defined on a well-partitioned *join*-list.

Using these four steps, we can automatically convert a given program into an equivalent program defined on well-partitioned data.

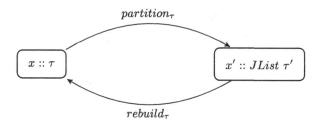

Fig. 3. Data partitioning functions

$$\mathcal{N}_\tau = \begin{cases} JList\ \tau' & \textbf{if } \tau \in \gamma \\ \tau' & \textbf{otherwise} \end{cases}$$

where

τ is defined by:
data $T\ T_1 \ldots T_k ::= c_1\ t_{1_1}\ \ldots\ t_{1_{n_1}}$

$$\vdots$$

$$\mid\ c_m\ t_{m_1}\ \ldots\ t_{m_{n_m}}$$

τ' is a new data-type defined by:
data $T' ::= c_1'\ \mathcal{N}_{t_{1_{j_1}}}\ \ldots\ \mathcal{N}_{t_{1_{k_1}}}$

$$\vdots$$

$$\mid\ c_m'\ \mathcal{N}_{t_{m_{j_m}}}\ \ldots\ \mathcal{N}_{t_{m_{k_m}}}$$

where $\langle t_{i_{j_i}}, \ldots, t_{i_{k_i}} \rangle = \begin{cases} removeAll_\tau\ \langle t_{i_{1_i}}, \ldots, t_{i_{n_i}} \rangle & \textbf{if } \tau \in \gamma \\ \langle t_{i_{1_i}}, \ldots, t_{i_{n_i}} \rangle & \textbf{otherwise} \end{cases}$

Fig. 4. Transformation rule for defining τ' using τ

3.1 Defining Partitioned Data-Types

To partition data of a given instantiated data-type, $\tau = T\ T_1 \ldots T_k$, we first define a corresponding data-type, τ', according to the rules shown in Fig. 4. In some cases it may not make sense to parallelize the processing of all data in a given program. To allow for this, we allow the developer to specify a set of *parallelizable-types*, γ, instances of which will be evaluated in parallel.

Given a program defined on a data-type, τ, $\mathcal{N}$ is applied to τ as follows:

- If τ is a parallelizable-type, its data must be well-partitioned and is therefore replaced by $JList\ \tau'$.
- If τ is not a parallelizable-type, it is replaced by τ' as it may contain data that must be well-partitioned.

When replacing τ with either τ' or $JList\ \tau'$, τ' is defined as shown in Fig. 4. For each constructor, c, in the definition of τ, a new constructor, c', is added to τ'. If τ is a parallelizable-type then any inductive components c contains are not added to c'. $\mathcal{N}$ is applied to each component of c'.

3.2 Converting Data to and From *Join*-Lists

To partition data of a given type, τ, we define a partitioning function, $partition_\tau$ as follows:

- If τ is a parallelizable-type, data of type τ is converted to a *cons*-list containing data of type τ', which is then well-partitioned into a *join*-list.
- If τ is not a parallelizable-type, data of type τ is converted to data of type τ', the components of which are also well-partitioned where necessary.

In order to convert a well-partitioned *join*-list back into its original form, we also define a rebuilding function, $rebuild_\tau$, the definition of which is simply the inverse of $partition_\tau$.

3.3 Distilling Programs on Well-Partitioned Data

Distillation [7] is a powerful fold/unfold based program transformation technique which eliminates intermediate data-structures from higher-order functional programs. It is capable of obtaining a super-linear increase in efficiency.

Given a sequential program, f, defined on a type, τ, we first define $partition_\tau$ and $rebuild_\tau$. Once these have been defined, we can convert f into an equivalent program, f_{wp}, defined on well-partitioned data. Applying distillation to $f \circ rebuild_\tau$, results in the automatic derivation of f_{wp}. A high level overview of this process is presented in Fig. 5.

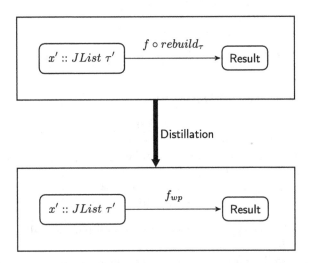

Fig. 5. Distillation of programs on well-partitioned data

As f_{wp} is defined on a well-partitioned *join*-list and f is defined on data of type τ, we must also generate the correct input for f_{wp} by applying $partition_\tau$ to the input of f.

4   Example Parallelization Using Well-Partitioned Data

Consider a function, $sumList$, which calculates the sum of a $List$ of numbers:

$$sumList = \lambda xs.\textbf{case } xs \textbf{ of}$$
$$Nil \qquad \rightarrow 0$$
$$Cons\ x\ xs \rightarrow x + sumList\ xs$$

As the input to $sumList$ is of type ($List\ Int$), the first step in the parallelization process is to define $List'$ according to the rules shown in Fig. 4, where $\gamma = \{List\ Int\}$, as shown below:

$$\cdot\ data\ List' ::= Nil'$$
$$|\ \ Cons'\ Int$$

The second step is to define both $partition_{(List\ Int)}$ and $rebuild_{(List\ Int)}$ as follows:

$$partition_{(List\ Int)} = partition \circ flatten_{(List\ Int)}$$

$$flatten_{(List\ Int)} = \lambda xs.\textbf{case } xs \textbf{ of}$$
$$Nil \qquad \rightarrow [Nil']$$
$$Cons\ x_1\ x_2 \rightarrow [Cons'\ x_1] \mathbin{+\!\!+} flatten_{(List\ Int)}\ x_2$$

$$rebuild_{(List\ Int)} = fst \circ unflatten_{(List\ Int)} \circ rebuild$$

$$unflatten_{(List\ Int)} = \lambda xs.\textbf{case } xs \textbf{ of}$$
$$(x : xs) \rightarrow \textbf{case } x \textbf{ of}$$
$$Nil' \qquad \rightarrow (Nil,\ xs)$$
$$Cons'\ x_1 \rightarrow \textbf{case } unflatten_{(List\ Int)}\ xs \textbf{ of}$$
$$(x_2,\ xs_2) \rightarrow (Cons\ x_1\ x_2, xs_2)$$

Following the definition of $rebuild_{(List\ Int)}$, we compose this with the original function, $sumList \circ rebuild_{(List\ Int)}$, and apply distillation to this composition. This allows $sumList$ to be automatically redefined into an equivalent program, $sumList_{wp}$, defined in terms of a $join$-list containing instances of $List'$, resulting in the following implicitly parallel definition:

$$sumList_{wp} = \lambda x.\textbf{case } x \textbf{ of}$$
$$Singleton\ x \rightarrow \textbf{case } x \textbf{ of}$$
$$Nil' \rightarrow 0$$
$$Join\ l\ r \quad \rightarrow \textbf{let } l' = sumList'_{wp}\ l$$
$$r' = sumList_{wp}\ r$$
$$\textbf{in } l'\ r'$$

$$sumList'_{wp} = \lambda x \; n.\textbf{case } x \textbf{ of}$$
$$Singleton \; x \rightarrow \textbf{case } x \textbf{ of}$$
$$Nil' \quad \rightarrow n$$
$$Cons' \; x \rightarrow x + n$$
$$Join \; l \; r \quad \rightarrow \textbf{let } l' = sumList'_{wp} \; l$$
$$r' = sumList'_{wp} \; r \; n$$
$$\textbf{in } l' \; r'$$

By making distillation aware of the definition of the $+$ operator, it can derive the necessary associativity that allows for each child of a *Join* to be evaluated in parallel. It is worth noting that in the case of the above program, when evaluating the left child of a *Join* we create a partial application which can be evaluated in parallel with the evaluation of the right child. This partial application is equivalent to $(\lambda r.l + r)$, where r is the result of the evaluation of the right operand. In a parallel environment the full evaluation of this partial application must be forced to ensure that the left operand has been evaluated and that parallel processes have roughly the same amount of work.

As both children are roughly equal in size, each parallel process created will have a roughly equal amount of work to do. In contrast, with respect to the original *sumList* defined on *cons*-lists, if the processing of both x and *sumList xs* are performed in parallel, one process will have one element of the list to evaluate, while the other will have the remainder of the list to evaluate, which is undesirable.

5   Related Work

There are many existing works that aim to resolve the same problem that our transformation does: mapping potentially poorly-partitioned data into a form that can be efficiently parallelized. Some work, such as list-homomorphisms and their derivative works [1,8–11,17,18] simply assume that they will use data that is well-partitioned. These techniques require that their inputs are defined using a *cons*-list, which can then be easily well-partitioned [3,5,6,19]. Restricting developers to implement their programs in these forms is an unrealistic burden.

Chin et al.'s [2] work on parallelization via context-preservation also makes use of *join*-lists as part of its parallelization process. This technique is only applicable to programs defined in the form of *list-paramorphisms* [14]. While this allows for quite a broad class of program to be parallelized, it is not realistic to force developers to define their functions in this form.

An important limitation of these techniques is that they are only applicable to lists, excluding the large class of programs that are defined on trees. One approach to parallelizing trees is that of Morihata et al.'s [15] generalization of the third homomorphism theorem [4] to trees. This approach makes use of *zippers* [12] to model the path from the root of a tree to an arbitrary leaf. While this is an interesting approach to partitioning the data contained within a binary-tree, the partitioning technique is quite complicated. It also presents no concrete methodology for generating zippers from binary-trees and assumes that the developer has provided such a function.

6 Conclusion

In this paper, we have presented a novel data-type transformation which allows for a given program to be automatically redefined into one defined on well-partitioned data. Our research is focused on automatically converting programs defined on any data-type into equivalent parallel versions defined on well-partitioned data in the form of *join*-lists. The presented data-type transformation is a significant component of that automatic parallelization system.

At a high level, by combining the outputs of the presented data-type transformation with an explicit parallelization transformation which parallelizes expressions operating on *join*-lists it is possible to automatically redefine a given sequential program defined on any data-type into an explicitly parallel one defined on well-partitioned *join*-lists.

While the presented data-type transformation is defined using *join*-lists, which appear to be the standard partitionable data-type used in automated parallelization systems [1,8–11,17,18], it is possible that *join*-lists are not the ideal data-structures to be used as part of such systems. As the data contained in a *join*-list is placed only at the leaves, it is possible that parallel processes evaluating the nodes of a *join*-list will spend much of their time waiting on the results of the parallel processes evaluating their subtrees. Further research is required to determine if there is a data structure which provides better parallel performance in general.

Where existing automated parallelization techniques are restrictive with respect to the form of their input programs and the types they are defined on, a parallelization technique defined using the presented data-type transformation should hold no such restrictions. To the best of the authors knowledge this is the first automatic data-type transformation system that will derive a well-partitioned representation of any given data-type and will redefine a given program into one defined in terms of such well-partitioned data.

Acknowledgements. This work was supported, in part, by Science Foundation Ireland grant 10/CE2/I303_1 to Lero - the Irish Software Engineering Research Centre.

References

1. Blelloch, G.E.: Scans as primitive operations. IEEE Trans. Comput. **38**(11), 1526–1538 (1989)
2. Chin, W.-N., Khoo, S.-C., Hu, Z., Takeichi, M.: Deriving parallel codes via invariants. In: Palsberg, J. (ed.) SAS 2000. LNCS, vol. 1824, pp. 75–94. Springer, Heidelberg (2000)
3. Chin, W.N., Takano, A., Hu, Z., Chin, W., Takano, A., Hu, Z.: Parallelization via context preservation. In: IEEE International Conference on Computer Languages, IEEE CS Press, pp. 153–162 (1998)

4. Gibbons, J.: The third homomorphism theorem. J. Funct. Program. **6**(4), 657–665 (1996). Earlier version appeared in Jay, C.B., (ed.), Computing: The Australian Theory Seminar, Sydney, pp. 62–69, December 1994

5. Gorlatch, S.: Systematic efficient parallelization of scan and other list homomorphisms. In: Fraigniaud, P., Mignotte, A., Robert, Y., Bougé, L. (eds.) Euro-Par 1996. LNCS, vol. 1124, pp. 401–408. Springer, Heidelberg (1996)

6. Gorlatch, S.: Systematic extraction and implementation of divide-and-conquer parallelism. In: Kuchen, H., Swierstra, S.D. (eds.) PLILP 1996. LNCS, vol. 1140, pp. 274–288. Springer, Heidelberg (1996)

7. Hamilton, G., Jones, N.: Distillation and labelled transition systems. In: Proceedings of the ACM Workshop on Partial Evaluation and Program Manipulation, pp. 15–24, January 2012

8. Hu, Z., Iwasaki, H., Takechi, M.: Formal derivation of efficient parallel programs by construction of list homomorphisms. ACM Trans. Program. Lang. Syst. **19**(3), 444–461 (1997)

9. Hu, Z., Takeichi, M., Chin, W.-N.: Parallelization in calculational forms. In: Proceedings of the 25th ACM SIGPLAN-SIGACT symposium on Principles of programming languages, POPL 1998, pp. 316–328, ACM, New York (1998)

10. Hu, Z., Takeichi, M., Iwasaki, H.: Diffusion: calculating efficient parallel programs. In: 1999 ACM SIGPLAN Workshop on Partial Evaluation and Semantics-Based Program Manipulation, pp. 85–94(1999)

11. Hu, Z., Yokoyama, T., Takeichi, M.: Program optimizations and transformations in calculation form. In: Lämmel, R., Saraiva, J., Visser, J. (eds.) GTTSE 2005. LNCS, vol. 4143, pp. 144–168. Springer, Heidelberg (2006)

12. Huet, G.: The zipper. J. Funct. Program. **7**(5), 549–554 (1997)

13. Iwasaki, H., Hu, Z.: A new parallel skeleton for general accumulative computations. Int. J. Parallel Prog. **32**, 389–414 (2004)

14. Meertens, L.: Paramorphisms. Formal Aspects Comput. **4**(5), 413–424 (1992)

15. Morihata, A., Matsuzaki, K., Hu, Z., Takeichi, M.: The third homomorphism theorem on trees: downward & upward lead to divide-and-conquer. In: Proceedings of the 36th Annual ACM SIGPLAN-SIGACT Symposium on Principles of programming languages, POPL 1909, pp. 177–185. ACM, New York (2009)

16. Skillicorn, D.: Foundations of Parallel Programming. Cambridge International Series on Parallel Computation. Cambridge University Press, Cambridge (2005)

17. Skillicorn, D.B.: Architecture-independent parallel computation. Computer **23**, 38–50 (1990)

18. Skillicorn, D.B.: The bird-meertens formalism as a parallel model. In: Kowalik, J.S., Grandinetti, L. (eds.) Software for Parallel Computation. NATO ASI Series F, vol. 106, pp. 120–133. Springer, Heidelberg (1993)

19. Teo, Y.M., Chin, W.-N., Tan, S.H.: Deriving efficient parallel programs for complex recurrences. In: Proceedings of the Second International Symposium on Parallel symbolic computation, PASCO 1997, pp. 101–110. ACM, New York (1997)

Lingva: Generating and Proving Program Properties Using Symbol Elimination

Ioan Dragan[1](✉) and Laura Kovács[2]

[1] TU Vienna, Vienna, Austria
ioan@complang.tuwien.ac.at
[2] Chalmers, Gothenburg, Sweden

Abstract. We describe the Lingva tool for generating and proving complex program properties using the recently introduced symbol elimination method. We present implementation details and report on a large number of experiments using academic benchmarks and open-source software programs. Our experiments show that Lingva can automatically generate quantified invariants, possibly with alternation of quantifiers, over integers and arrays. Moreover, Lingva can be used to prove program properties expressing the intended behavior of programs.

1 Introduction

Safety verification of programs is a challenging task especially for programs with complex flow and, in particular, with loops or recursion. For such programs one needs additional information, in the form of loop invariants, pre- and postconditions, or interpolants, that express properties to hold at certain intermediate points of the program.

In this paper we present an automated tool for generating program properties, in particular loop invariants. Our tool, called Lingva, is based on the symbol elimination method of [9]. It requires no preliminary knowledge about program behavior, and uses symbol elimination in first-order theorem proving to automatically derive complex properties, as follows. Suppose we are given a loop L over scalar and array variables. Symbol elimination first extends the loop language L to a richer language L' by additional function and predicate symbols, such as loop counters or predicates expressing update properties of arrays at different loop iterations. Next, we derive a set P of first-order loop properties expressed in L'. The derived properties hold at any loop iteration, however they contain symbols that are not in L and hence cannot yet be used as loop invariants. Therefore, in the next step of symbol elimination, logical consequences of P are derived by eliminating the symbols from $L' \setminus L$ using first-order theorem proving. As a result, first-order loop invariants in L are inferred as logical consequences of P.

This work was partially supported by Swedish VR grant D0497701 and the Austrian research projects FWF S11410-N23 and WWTF ICT C-050.

A. Voronkov and I. Virbitskaite (Eds.): PSI 2014, LNCS 8974, pp. 67–75, 2015.
DOI: 10.1007/978-3-662-46823-4_6

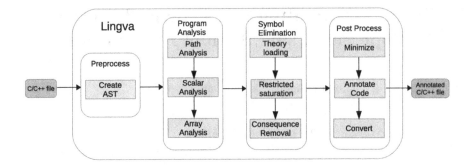

Fig. 1. The overall workflow of Lingva.

First implementation of symbol elimination was already described in [8], by using the first-order theorem prover Vampire [10]. This implementation had however various limitations: it required user-guidance for program parsing, implemented tedious translation of programs into a collection of first-order properties, had limited support for the first-order theory of arrays and the generated set of invariants could not yet be used in the context of software verification. In this paper we address these limitations and describe Lingva tool for generating loop invariants (Sect. 2). In addition to invariant generation, Lingva can also be used for proving program properties, in particular for proving program annotations from the generated set of invariants.

We evaluated Lingva on a large number of problems taken from recent research papers and open-source programs (Sect. 3). Our experiments addressed two evaluation criteria: (i) scalability, that is for how many programs Lingva successfully generated invariants; and (ii) expressiveness, that is can safety program annotation be automatically proved from the invariants generated by Lingva. The invariants inferred by Lingva are quantified properties over arrays and integers. Unlike [3,5,7,11], our invariants can express properties with quantifier alternations over the array content and exploit reasoning in the full first-order theory of arrays and integer arithmetic. In addition, in our experiments, program annotations were successfully proved by Lingva for all loops with nested conditionals. While other techniques, such as [1,6,13,14], can handle more general programs, we note that Lingva is fully automatic and requires no user guidance in the form of invariant templates, interpolants or apriori defined program properties.

2   Lingva: Tool Description

The general workflow of Lingva is summarized in Fig. 1 and detailed below. Lingva is a collection of C++ programs, glued together by Python scripts. Our implementation is available at: www.complang.tuwien.ac.at/ioan/lingva.html. Lingva can be done by executing the command: **Lingva problem.c**, where **problem.c** is a C/C++ program with loops. As a result, Lingva returns **problem.c** annotated with loop invariants.

When compared to initial implementation from [8], the preprocessing part and the code annotation and conversion parts of post processing are new features.

Further, Lingva extends that approach by more sophisticated path analysis methods and built-in support for reasoning in the first-order theory of arrays. These features allows Lingva to handle a programs with multiple loops and nested conditionals and derive quantified invariants that could not yet be obtained by [8], as arrays and integers, and their axiomatisation, were not yet supported as built-in theories in [8].

Preprocessing. Input programs of Lingva are first parsed using the Clang/LLVM infrastructure [12] and the abstract syntax tree (AST) of the input is created. Although Lingva front-end can parse arbitrary C/C++ programs, program analysis in the next step has implemented support for a restricted programming model, as follows. We only handle program loops with sequencing, assignments, and nested conditionals. Nested loops, recursive or procedure calls are thus not yet supported. Further, we only treat integers and arrays. Also we restrict program tests and assignments over integers to linear arithmetic expressions. If these restrictions are not met, Lingva terminates with an error message that provides information on the violation of the programming model.

After the AST construction, each program loop is analysed by default by Lingva. However, the user can also specify which loop or set of loops should be analysed by calling Lingva with the option `-f fn.loopNr`. Where `fn` is the name of the input's C/C++ function block and `loopNr` gives the loop number of interest within `fn`.

Example 1. Consider Fig. 2(a). It is written in C/C++ and contains multiple loops, each loop being annotated with a natural number starting from 0. For simplicity, we only show and describe Lingva on the kth loop of Fig. 2(a); analysing the other loops can be done in a similar manner. The kth loop of Fig. 2(a) takes two integer arrays aa and cc and creates an integer array bb such that each element in bb describes an array position at which the elements of aa and cc are equal. This loop is the `Partition_Init` program from Sect. 3. For running Lingva only on this loop, one should execute the command: `Lingva problem.c -f main.k`

Program Analysis. Program loops are next translated into a collection of first-order properties capturing the program behavior. These properties are formulated using the TPTP syntax [15]. Note that in TPTP, symbols starting with capital letters denote logical variables which are universally (!) or existentially (?) quantified. In the rest of the paper, we illustrate Lingva using the TPTP notation.

During program analysis, we extend the loop language with additional function and predicate symbols, as follows. For each loop, we use an extra integer constant $n \geq 0$ denoting the number of loop iterations and introduce an extra predicate $iter(X)$ expressing that the logical variable X is a valid loop iteration, that is $0 \leq X < n$. Loop variables thus become functions of loop iterations, that is a loop variable v becomes the function $v(X)$ such that $iter(X)$ holds and $v(X)$ denotes the value of v at the Xth loop iteration. For each loop variable v, we respectively denote by $v0$ and v its initial and final values. Finally, for each

Example of input file	Partial result of program analysis
```void main() { //loop 0 while (condition) { loop_body } ... //loop_k: Partition_Init int a, b, m; int *aa, *bb, *cc; while (a < m) { if (aa[a] == cc[a]) { bb[b] = a; b = b + 1; } a = a + 1; } ... }```	```... 18. ![X1]: bb(0,X1) = bb0(X1) 17. ![X0, X2, X3]: updbb(X0,X2,X3) => bb(X2) = X3 ... 9. ![X0]: iter(X0) => a(X0) = a0 + X0 8. a(0) =a0 ... 2. iter(X0) =>(let a := a(X0) in (let b := b(X0) in (let bb(X1) := bb(X0,X1) in a<m))) 1. ![X0, X1]: let a := a(X0) in (let b := b(X0) in (let bb(X1) := bb(X0,X1) in (aa(a) = cc(a) => b(X0+1) = (let bb(X1) := ite_t(b = X1,a,bb(X1)) in (let b := b +1 in (let a := a + 1 in b))))))```
(a)	(b)

Fig. 2. Program analysis with Lingva on the `Partition_Init` program of Table 2.

array variable we introduce so-called update predicates describing at which loop iteration and array position the array was updated. For example, for an array bb we write $updbb(X, Y, Z)$ denoting that at loop iteration X the array was updated at position Y by the value Z.

For each loop, we next apply path and (scalar and array) variable analysis in order to collect valid loop properties in the extended loop language. Within path analysis, loops are translated into their guarded assignment representations and the values of program variables are computed using let-in and if-then-else formulas and terms. Unlike [8], the use of let-in formulas (`let...in`) and if-then-else terms (`ite_t`) allow us to easily express the transition relations of programs. Further, (i) we determine the set of scalar and array program variables, (ii) compute monotonicity properties of scalars by relating their values to the increasing number of loop iterations, (iii) classify arrays into constant or updated arrays, and (iv) collect update array properties. As a result, for each program loop a set of valid loop properties is derived in the extended loop language.

Example 2. Consider the kth loop of Fig. 2(a). A partial set of first-order properties generated by Lingva in the extended loop language is given in Fig. 2(b). Properties 1 and 2 are derived during path analysis. They express the value of the scalar b during the program path exhibiting the then-branch of the conditional within the loop and, respectively, the loop condition. Properties 8 and 9 are derived during scalar analysis. They state that the values of a are monotonically increasing at every loop iteration; moreover, these values are exactly defined as functions of loop iterations and the initial value $a0$ of a. Properties 17 and 18 are inferred during array analysis, and express respectively, the initial and final values of the array bb.

Symbol Elimination. Within symbol elimination, for each loop we derive loop invariants. For doing so, we rely on Vampire [10] and compute logical consequences of the properties derived during program analysis. To this end, we first load the built-in theories of integers and arrays. Properties with let-in and

Generated invariants using symbol elimination	Annotated output program
⋮	...
	loop invariant
	\forall integer X0;
tff(inv3,claim,![X0 :$int]:	aa[sK1(X0)]==cc[sK1(X0)] ||
aa(sk1(X0))=cc(sk1(X0)) |	!(X0<(b-b0)) || !(0<=X0);
˜$less(X0,$sum(b,$uminus(b0))) |	loop invariant
˜$lesseq(0,X0)).	\forall integer X2, integer X1;
⋮	!(sK1(X0)=X1) || !((b0+X0)=X2) ||
	!(X0<(b-b0)) ||
tff(inv10,claim,![X0:$int, X1:$int,X2:$int]:	!(0<=X0) || || bb[X2]==X1;
˜(sk1(X0)=X1) | ˜($sum(b0,X0)=X2) |	...
˜$less(X0,$sum(b,$uminus(b0))) |	while (a < m) {
˜$lesseq(0,X0) | bb(X2) = X1)).	if (aa[a] == cc[a]) {
⋮	bb[b] = a;
	b = b + 1;}
	a = a + 1;}
	...
(c)	(d)

Fig. 3. Invariants and annotated code corresponding to Fig. 2(a).

if-then-else expressions are then translated into first-order properties with no let-in and if-then-else terms. Unlike the initial work from [8], Lingva supports now reasoning in the first-order theories of arrays and uses arrays as built-in data types. By using the theory axiomatisations of arrays and integers arithmetic within first-order theorem proving, Lingva implements theory-specific reasoning and simplification rules which allows to generate logically stronger invariants than [8] and to prove that some of the generated invariants are redundant (as explained in the post processing step of Lingva).

Next, we collect the additional function and predicate symbols introduced in the program analysis step of Lingva and specify them to be eliminated by the saturation algorithm of Vampire; to this end the approach of [9] is used. As a result, loop invariants are inferred. Symbol elimination within Lingva is run with a 5 s default time limit. This time limit was chosen based on our experiments with Lingva: invariants of interests could be generated by Lingva within a 5 s time limit in all examples we tried. The user may however specify a different time limit to be used by Lingva for symbol elimination.

Example 3. The partial result of symbol elimination on Fig. 2(b) is given in Fig. 3(c). The generated invariants are listed as typed first-order formulas (`tff`) in TPTP. The invariants `inv3` and `inv10` state that at every array position $b0 + X0$ at which the initial array $bb0$ was changed, the elements of aa and cc at position $bb(b0 + X0)$ are equal; recall that $b0$ is the initial value of b. Note that the generated invariants have skolem functions introduced: `sk1(X0)` denotes a skolem function of $X0$.

Post Processing. Some of the loop invariants generated by symbol elimination are redundant, that is they are implied by other invariants. In the post processing part of Lingva, we try to minimize the set of invariants by eliminating redundant ones. As proving first-order invariants redundant is undecidable, minimization in Lingva is performed using four different proving stratgies, with a 20 s default time limit for each of the strategy. The chosen strategies and their time limit

Table 1. Overview of experimental results obtained by Lingva.

Program	♯ loops	♯ analysed loops	Average ♯ invariants	Average ♯ minimized invariants
Academic benchmarks [4,8,14]	41	41	213	80
Open source archiving benchmarks	1151	150	198	62

were carefully selected based on our experiments, and they involve theory-specific simplifcation rules as well as special literal and selection functions within first-order reasoning.

After invariant minimization, Lingva converts the minimized set of invariants in the ACSL annotation language of the Frama-C framework [2]. The input program of Lingva is then annotated with these invariants and returned. The use of the ACSL syntax in Lingva, allows one to integrate the invariants generated by Lingva in the overall verification framework of Frama-C, formally annotate program loops with their invariants, and verify the correctness of the annotated program using Frama-C.

Example 4. Fig. 3(d) shows the kth loop of Fig. 2(a) annotated with its partial set of minimized invariants generated by symbol elimination.

Proving Program Properties. In addition to the default workflow given in Fig. 1, Lingva can be used not only for generating but also for proving properties. That is, given a program loop with user-annotated properties, such as postconditions, one can use Lingva to prove these properties as follows: (i) first, loop invariants are generated as described above, (ii) second, Lingva tries to prove the user-annotated

```
1  a = b = 0;
2  while (a < m) {
3    if aa[a] == cc[a] {
4      bb[b] = a; b = b+1;}
5    a = a+1;}
6  for j=0 to b-1 do {
7    assert(aa[bb[j]]=cc[bb[j]]);
8    j= j+1;}
```

Fig. 4. Program with assertion.

property from the set of generated invariants. For proving program properties in the combined first-order theories of integers and arrays, Lingva uses Vampire.

Example 5. Consider the simplified program given in Fig. 4.

Note that the loop between lines 2–5 corresponds to the kth loop of Fig. 2(a). The code between lines 6–8 specifies a user-given safety assertion, corresponding to the first-order property $\forall j : 0 \leq j < b \implies aa[bb[j]] = cc[bb[j]]$. This safety assertion can be proved from the invariants generated by Lingva (see Table 2).

3   Experiments with Lingva

We evaluated Lingva on examples taken from academic research papers on invariant generation [4,8,14] as well as from open source archiving packages. Our results

Table 2. Experimental results of Lingva on some academic benchmarks with conditionals.

Loop	Min. Inv.	Program annotation	Generated invariants implying annotation

`Partition [14]`
`a = 0; b = 0; c = 0;`
`while( a < m ){`
`if( aa[a] >= 0){`
`bb[b] = aa[a];`
`b = b+1;}`
`else {`
`cc[c] = aa[a];`
`c=c+1;}`
`a = a+1;}`
	647	$\forall x : 0 \le x < b \to$
		$bb[x] \ge 0 \wedge$
		$\exists y : 0 \le y < a \wedge$
		$bb[x] = aa[y]$
			`inv1:`
			$\forall x_0 : \quad aa(sk4(x_0)) \ge 0\vee$
			$\neg(0 \le x_0) \vee b \le x_0$
			`inv42:`
			$\forall x_0 : \quad 0 \le sk4(x_0) \wedge sk4(x0) < a$
			`inv81:`
			$\forall x_0 : \quad \neg(0 \le x_0) \vee b \le x_0 \vee$
			$aa(sk4(x_0)) = bb(x_0)$

`Partition_Init [8]`
`a = b = 0;`
`while( a < m ){`
`if(aa[a] == cc[a]){`
`bb[b]=a; b=b+1;}`
`a = a+1;}`
	169	$\forall x : 0 \le x < b \to$
		$aa[bb[x]] = cc[bb[x]]$
			`inv3:`
			$\forall x_0 : \quad \neg(0 \le x_0) \vee \neg(x_0 < b)\vee$
			$aa(sk1(x_0)) = cc(sk1(x_0))$
			`inv10:`
			$\forall x_0, x_1, x_2 : \neg(sk1(x_0) = x_1)\vee$
			$\neg(x_0 = x_2) \vee \neg(x_0 < b)$
			$\vee\neg(0 \le x_0) \vee bb(x_2) = x_1$

were obtained using a Lenovo W520 laptop with 8 GB of RAM and Intel Core i7 processor. All experimental results are also available on the Lingva homepage.

Table 1 summarizes our experiments. The first column lists the number of examples from each benchmark suite. The second column gives the number of problems that could be analysed by Lingva; for all these problems invariants have been generated. The third column shows the average number of generated invariants, whereas the fourth column lists the average number of invariants after minimization. Note that minimizing invariants in the post processing part of Lingva considerably decreases the number of invariants, that is 63 % in the case of academic examples and by 69 % for open source problems. In the sequel, we detail our results on each benchmark set.

Academic Benchmarks. Tables 2 and 3 describe the results of Lingva on program loops from [4,8,14], with and without conditionals. All these examples were already annotated with properties to be proven. Due to the page limit, we only list some representative examples. The first column of both tables shows the programs with their origins. The second column gives the number of generated invariants after the minimization step of Lingva. The third column states the program annotation to be proven for each program. Finally, the fourth column lists the invariants generated by Lingva which were used in proving the property of column three (similarly to Example 3). Tables 2 and 3 show that Lingva succeeded to generate complex quantified invariants over integers and arrays, some of these invariants using alternation of quantifiers[1]. We are not aware of any other tool that is able to generate invariants with quantifier alternations. We further note that all user-provided annotations were proved by Lingva, in essentially no time, by using (some of) the generated invariants.

Open Source Benchmarks. We evaluated Lingva on open source examples taken from archiving software, such as GZip, BZip, and Tar. All together we used 1151 program loops, out of which only 150 could be analysed by Lingva,

---

[1] De-skolemising skolem functions give invariants with quantifier alternations.

Table 3. Experimental results of Lingva on some academic benchmarks without conditionals.

Loop	Min.Inv.	Program annotation	Generated invariants implying annotation

Initialisation [8]
`a = 0;`
`while( a < m ){`
`  aa[a]=0; a=a+1;}`
	35	$\forall x : 0 \leq x < a \rightarrow$
		$\quad aa[x] = 0$
			inv90:
			$\forall x_0 : \quad \neg(0 \leq x_0) \vee$
			$\quad a \leq x_0 \vee aa[x_0] = 0$

Copy [14]
`a = 0;`
`while( a < m ){`
`  bb[a]=aa[a]; a=a+1;}`
	37	$\forall x : 0 \leq x < a \rightarrow$
		$\quad bb[x] = aa[x]$
			inv104:
			$\forall x_0, x_1 : \neg(0 \leq x_0) \vee a \leq x_0 \vee$
			$\quad \neg(bb[x_0] = x_1) \vee$
			$\quad aa[x_0] = x_1$

Init_non_constant [4]
`i = 0;`
`while( i < size ){`
`  aa[i]=2*i+c;i=i+1;}`
	104	$\forall x : 0 \leq x < i \rightarrow$
		$\quad aa[x] = 2 * x + c$
			inv128:
			$\forall x_3, x_4 : i \leq x_3 \vee \neg(0 \leq x_3)$
			$\quad c + (2 * x_3) = aa[x_3]$

Copy_odd [4]
`i = 0; j = 1;`
`while( i < size ){`
`  aa[j]=bb[i];`
`  j++;i+=2;}`
	214	$\forall x : 0 \leq x < j \rightarrow$
		$\quad aa(x) = bb(2 * x + 1)$
			inv206:
			$\forall x_3, x_4 : j \leq x_3 \vee \neg(0 \leq x_3) \vee$
			$\quad aa[x_4] = bb[2x_3 + 1]$

Reverse [4]
`i = 0;`
`while( i < size ){`
`  j=size-i-1;`
`  aa[i]=bb[j];`
`  i++;}`
	42	$\forall x : 0 \leq x < i \wedge \rightarrow$
		$\quad aa[x] = bb[size - x - 1]$
			inv111:
			$\forall x_4 : \quad i \leq x_4 \vee \neg(0 \leq x_4) \vee$
			$\quad bb[size - x_4 - 1] = aa[x_4]$

Strlen [4]
`i = 0;`
`while( str[i] ≠ 0 ){`
`  i=i+1;}`
	26	$\forall x : 0 \leq x < i \rightarrow$
		$\quad str(x) \neq 0.$
			inv5:
			$\forall x_0 : i \leq x_0 \vee \neg(0 \leq x_0) \vee$
			$\quad str(x_0) \neq 0$

as given in Table 1. The reason why Lingva failed on the other 1001 loops was that these programs contained nested loops, implemented abrupt termination, bitwise operations, used pointer arithmetic or procedure calls. We believe that extending and combining Lingva with more sophisticated program analysis methods, such as [6,7,14], would enable us to handle more general programs then we currently do.

The 150 loops on which Lingva has been successfully evaluated implemented array copy, initialization, shift and partition operations, similarly to the ones reported in our experiments with academic benchmarks. For these examples, Lingva generated quantified invariants, some with alternations of quantifiers, over integers and arrays. We were also interested to see the behavior of Lingva on these examples when it comes to proving program properties. To this end, we manually annotated these loops with properties expressing the intended behavior of the programs and used Lingva to prove these properties from the set of generated invariants. In all these 150 examples, the intended program behavior was proved by Lingva in essentially no time, underlining the strength of Lingva for generating complex invariants in a fully automated manner.

4   Conclusion

We described the Lingva tool for automatically generating and proving program properties. We reported on implementation details and presented experimental results on academic and open-source benchmarks. Our experiments show that Lingva can generate quantified invariants, possibly with quantifier alternations, in a fully automated manner. Moreover, the generated invariants are strong enough to prove program annotations expressing the intended behavior of programs. Further work includes extending our approach in order to better integrate theory-specific reasoning engines for improving invariant minimization.

References

1. Alberti, F., Bruttomesso, R., Ghilardi, S., Ranise, S., Sharygina, N.: Lazy abstraction with interpolants for arrays. In: Bjørner, N., Voronkov, A. (eds.) LPAR-18 2012. LNCS, vol. 7180, pp. 46–61. Springer, Heidelberg (2012)
2. Correnson, L., Cuoq, P., Puccetti, A., Signoles, J.: Frama-C user manual. In: CEA LIST (2010)
3. Cousot, P., Cousot, R., Logozzo, F.: A parametric segmentation functor for fully automatic and scalable array content analysis. In: Proceedings of POPL, pp. 105–118 (2011)
4. Dillig, I., Dillig, T., Aiken, A.: Fluid updates: beyond strong vs. weak updates. In: Gordon, A.D. (ed.) ESOP 2010. LNCS, vol. 6012, pp. 246–266. Springer, Heidelberg (2010)
5. Garg, P., Löding, C., Madhusudan, P., Neider, D.: Learning universally quantified invariants of linear data structures. In: Sharygina, N., Veith, H. (eds.) CAV 2013. LNCS, vol. 8044, pp. 813–829. Springer, Heidelberg (2013)
6. Gupta, A., Rybalchenko, A.: InvGen: an efficient invariant generator. In: Bouajjani, A., Maler, O. (eds.) CAV 2009. LNCS, vol. 5643, pp. 634–640. Springer, Heidelberg (2009)
7. Halbwachs, N., Peron, M.: Discovering properties about arrays in simple programs. In: Proceedings of PLDI, pp. 339–348 (2008)
8. Hoder, K., Kovács, L., Voronkov, A.: Invariant generation in vampire. In: Abdulla, P.A., Leino, K.R.M. (eds.) TACAS 2011. LNCS, vol. 6605, pp. 60–64. Springer, Heidelberg (2011)
9. Kovács, L., Voronkov, A.: Finding loop invariants for programs over arrays using a theorem prover. In: Chechik, M., Wirsing, M. (eds.) FASE 2009. LNCS, vol. 5503, pp. 470–485. Springer, Heidelberg (2009)
10. Kovács, L., Voronkov, A.: First-order theorem proving and VAMPIRE. In: Sharygina, N., Veith, H. (eds.) CAV 2013. LNCS, vol. 8044, pp. 1–35. Springer, Heidelberg (2013)
11. Larraz, D., Rodríguez-Carbonell, E., Rubio, A.: SMT-based array invariant generation. In: Giacobazzi, R., Berdine, J., Mastroeni, I. (eds.) VMCAI 2013. LNCS, vol. 7737, pp. 169–188. Springer, Heidelberg (2013)
12. Lattner, C., Adve, V.: LLVM: a compilation framework for lifelong program analysis and transformation. In Proceedings of CGO, pp. 75–88 (2004)
13. McMillan, K.L.: Quantified invariant generation using an interpolating saturation prover. In: Ramakrishnan, C.R., Rehof, J. (eds.) TACAS 2008. LNCS, vol. 4963, pp. 413–427. Springer, Heidelberg (2008)
14. Srivastava, S., Gulwani, S.: Program verification using templates over predicate abstraction. In: Proceedings of PLDI, pp. 223–234 (2009)
15. Sutcliffe, G.: The TPTP problem library and associated infrastructure. J. Autom. Reasoning **43**(4), 337–362 (2009)

Neutralizing Semantic Ambiguities of Function Block Architecture by Modeling with ASM

Sandeep Patil[2(✉)], Victor Dubinin[1], Cheng Pang[2], and Valeriy Vyatkin[2]

[1] Penza State University, Penza, Russia
victor_n_dubinin@yahoo.com
[2] Department of Computer Science Electrical and Space Engineering,
Luleå University of Technology, Luleå, Sweden
sandeep.patil@ltu.se,
{cheng.pang.phd,vyatkin}@ieee.org

Abstract. The Function Blocks Architecture of the IEC 61499 standard is an executable component model for distributed embedded control systems combining block-diagrams and state machines. The standard aims at the portability of control applications that is however hampered by ambiguities in its execution semantics descriptions. In recent years several execution models have been implemented in different software tools that generate mutually incompatible code.

This paper proposes a general approach to neutralizing these semantic ambiguities by formal description of the IEC 61499 in abstract state machines (ASM). The model embodies all known execution semantics of function blocks. The ASM model is further translated to the input format of the SMV model-checker which is used to verify formally properties of applications. In this way the proposed verification framework enables the portability checking of component-based control applications across different implementation platforms compliant with the IEC 61499 standard.

The paper first discusses different existing execution semantics of function blocks and the portability issues across different IEC 61499 tools. Then a modular formal model of function blocks' operational semantics in ASM is introduced and exemplified in the paper by the cyclic execution semantics case for a composite function block. Subsequently, the SMV model is generated and model-checking is illustrated for a simple test case.

Keywords: Formal semantics · Model checking · Formal verification · Abstract state machines · IEC 61499

1 Introduction

The IEC 61499 [1, 2] is an international standard that introduces an open reference architecture for distributed process measurement and control systems that is an important class of embedded systems with a strong legacy background. The standard is often nicknamed as the *function block architecture* after its main design artifact that is an event-activated function block. If one would abstract out of unnecessary details, the standard introduces quite an elegant model of distributed application that is a network

A. Voronkov and I. Virbitskaite (Eds.): PSI 2014, LNCS 8974, pp. 76–91, 2015.
DOI: 10.1007/978-3-662-46823-4_7

of function blocks connected via control and data flows. The control flow is modeled using the concept of event that is emitted from an output of one function block and can be received at one or several inputs of other function blocks.

This mechanism, however, has been interpreted differently by the implementers due to some ambiguities in the norm's text [3]. As a result, several semantic interpretations appeared. Even though the semantics gap has been tightened in the second edition of the standard in 2012, there are already a number of tools on the market reflecting the semantics ambiguities, for which portability is an important goal.

The portability of a function block application A between platforms that comply with execution semantics s_1 and s_2 can be defined as equivalence of the behavior $B(A,s_1) = B(A,s_2)$. However, brute force check of the equivalence can have prohibitive complexity. Instead, one can apply model-checking of A's model under semantic s, $M(A,s)$, against the comprehensive set of requirements R (functional and non-functional, including safety and liveness). Denoting the set of model-checking results as C $(M(A,s),R)$, we define the application A to be portable between semantics s_1 and s_2 if the model-checking gives equivalent results, i.e.:

$$P(A, s_1, s_2) \stackrel{\Delta}{=} C(M(A, s_1), R) = C(M(A, s_2), R)$$

In this paper we introduce a way of modeling function blocks that simplifies parameterization of the execution semantics, i.e. generation of model $M(A,s)$ for any known semantics s. The modeling is based on the Abstract State Machines (ASM), and SMV is assumed as a tool implementing model-checking $C(M(A,s),R)$. An example of applying model-checking to the model created in the way proposed in this paper was presented in [4] therefore it is omitted in this paper.

2   Related Facts

2.1   Function Blocks

In IEC 61499, the basic design construct is called function block (FB). Each FB consists of a graphical event-data interface and a set of executable functional specifications (algorithms), represented as a state machine (in basic FB), or as a network of other FB instances (composite FB), or as a set of services (service interface FB). FBs can be interconnected into a network using event and data connections to specify the entire control application. Execution of an individual FB in the network is triggered by the events it receives. This well-defined event-data interface and the encapsulation of local data and control algorithms make each FB a reusable functional unit of software.

There are several approaches to defining formal models of function blocks, e.g. [5–7]. In this paper, for the sake of brevity we present only informal examples of function blocks and systems built thereof. For example, the basic FB (BFB) ALU in Fig. 1 is designed to perform arithmetic operations of addition and subtraction, depending on its input events. As seen from Fig. 1, a basic FB is defined by signal interface (left hand side) and also its internal state machine (called Execution Control Chart, or ECC) on the right hand side, and definition of the three algorithms (executed in the ECC states) beneath the diagram. It also has an internal variable n initialized to the value 13.

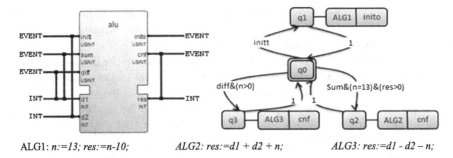

ALG1: *n:=13; res:=n-10;*   ALG2: *res:=d1 + d2 + n;*   ALG3: *res:=d1 - d2 - n;*

Fig. 1. The basic FB ALU: interface (left), ECC diagram (right), algorithms (bottom row).

A function block application is a network of FBs connected by event and data links. As an example, let us consider an application that consists of two ALU function blocks interacting with each other (Fig. 2). This example, of course, is not comprehensively covering all FB artefacts and is used for illustrative purposes [24].

The application consists of two instances of the arithmetic-logic unit (ALU) BFB type connected in closed-loop (outputs of one BFB are connected to the inputs of other BFB). Following the firing of the *initt* input of *alu*1 (Fig. 2) (emitted by hardware interface), the application enters an infinite sequence of computations consisting of alternating arithmetic operations addition and subtraction. Moreover, the input parameters are chosen such that the variables do not change, i.e. when one FB adds a certain number, the second one subtracts it, so, as a result, the state space of the system is limited.

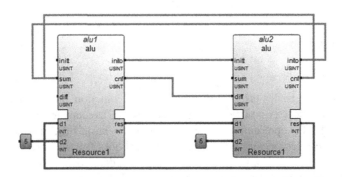

Fig. 2. FB system of two ALUs designed in the ISaGRAF development environment [8]

A composite function block (CFB) is defined by a signal interface and internal network of function block instances similar to the application in Fig. 2. The existing execution models of FB systems differ in the disciplines of FB execution scheduling and the ways of events and data passing between the FBs. For example, in the *cyclic* execution model, each FB in an application is invoked once between the update of environment variables, and its place in the order of invocations is predefined. Contrary, in the *sequential* model, the order of invocations is fully determined by the order of events arriving at the inputs of function blocks [3].

2.2 Abstract State Machines

The Abstract State Machine (ASM) paradigm was introduced by Yuri Gurevich in 1988 [9] with basic definitions presented in [10] by the same author. The ASM methodologies are practical in modeling and analyzing different sizes of systems and have been applied in different research areas such as programing languages [11, 12], hardware and software architectures [13], algorithm verification and network protocols [14, 15]. ASM's have also been successfully used in representing semantics of programming languages such as Prolog [16], C [17] and Java [18].

In this research we use ASM (in the form of functions changes' rules) to represent mathematically the execution semantics of function blocks in SMV. In particular, we consider in detail one of the execution models that is the *cyclic* execution semantics.

2.3 Formal Modeling of IEC 61499 and Cross-Platform Portability

Formal modeling of IEC 61499 has more than a decade long history [19]. There are two basic approaches to formal modeling of FB systems using: (1) a direct representation of FB in a language supported by a model-checking tool, such as SMV; and (2) modeling of FB using an intermediate formal model and its subsequent translation to a language supported by a tool. The main disadvantage of the (seldom) works in the first direction, such as [20, 21], is the lack of a systematic approach to constructing models of FB. In particular, there is no comprehensive pass-through formalization of FB models. Methods of constructing them do not reflect the system hierarchy, composite FB, algorithms and execution of FB models.

The most widely reported in the literature are the works representing the second approach. For example, [22] presents a method using net condition/event systems (NCES) as the intermediate representation and [23] presents a method of modeling NCES in SMV. Of the other papers on modeling IEC 61499 FB for the purpose of verification [7, 24, 25] can be noted. The main drawbacks of the majority of these works are limitations of model-checkers, suffering from insufficient performance or limited support of arithmetic operations. From that perspective, the SMV approach promises some breakthroughs. It should also be noted that the SMV system has been used quite successfully in industry, e.g. in the verification of the Function Blocks of the IEC 61131-3 standard [26].

Some of the authors of this paper have addressed the portability of FB applications by suggesting semantic-robust design patterns [27] and analyzing the consequences of semantic differences for portability [28]. However, the approach proposed in this paper has the potential for becoming the backend of portability certification based on formal methods.

3 Modular Formalism for FB Operational Semantics

In this section, a modular formalism for FB operational semantics definition is proposed. The formalism follows the ASM approach (further referred to as Distributed ASM – FB model, or DASM-FB) and has the following characteristic features:

1. System's state is modelled using state variables and their state functions;
2. The model is composed of modules with asynchronous behavior with respect to each other;
3. There can be shared variables in the modules;
4. Behaviour of modules are deterministic;
5. Explicit production rules are used to represent an abstract state machine (ASM) program;
6. There are special restrictions on executing the distributed ASM.

In the definition of DASM-FB, the following notations will be used. Let Z_A : $A \to Dom(A)$ be a function assigning values from a domain to the objects of A (Z_A is also called a function of values), then $[Z_A]$ denotes a set of all possible such functions. Following the concept and notation of ASM, we introduce the update operator for the functions of values, denoting it by $\leftarrow$. This operator can be defined as follows:

$$Z_A(a) \leftarrow b \triangleq (Z_A \setminus (a, x)) \cup (a, b), \tag{1}$$

where $a \in A; b, x \in Dom(A); Z_A \subseteq A \times Dom(A)$. Here the symbol '$\triangleq$' means "by definition".

A model of a FB system in DASM-FB is a linearly ordered set of asynchronously working (synchronous) modules:

$$W = (M^1, M^2, \ldots, M^n) \tag{2}$$

Each module $M^j \in W$ is defined as a tuple (for simplicity the index j (module's number) is omitted in the subscript indices).

$$M^j = \left(V, (Dom(v_i))_{v_i \in V}, (T_{v_i})_{v_i \in V}, (P_{v_i})_{v_i \in V}, \left(Z_{v_i}^0 \right)_{v_i \in V} \right), \tag{3}$$

where $V = \{v_1, v_2, \ldots, v_m\}$ is a set of module's state variables. $Dom(v_i)$ denotes the domain of values for variable $v_i \in V$. T_{v_i} is a function of updating the values of state variable $v_i \in V$. This function can be represented in a global variant or in a local one. In the first case, the function is defined as

$$T_{v_i}^G : \prod_{v_k \in V} [Z_{v_k}] \to [Z_{v_i}] \tag{4}$$

Since not all variables have influence on the change of other variables, then the global function is redundant and can be reduced to the following local variant:

$$T_{v_i}^L : \prod_{v_k \in H(v_i)} [Z_{v_k}] \to [Z_{v_i}], \tag{5}$$

where $H(v_i) = \{v_{i_1}, v_{i_2}, \ldots, v_{i_q}\}$ is a (linearly ordered) set of variables $v_{i_j} \in V, j = \overline{1, q}$ that the variable $v_i \in V$ depend on. Expression (6) is a rule for updating the value function of the variable $v_i \in V$. $Z_{v_i}^0$ is a function of initial value of variable $v_i \in V$.

$$P_{v_i} \triangleq Z_{v_i}(v_i) \leftarrow T_{v_i}\left(Z_{v_{i_1}}, Z_{v_{i_2}}, \ldots, Z_{v_{i_q}}\right) \tag{6}$$

The execution of module M^j consists in the simultaneous (synchronous) execution of all rules from $(p_{v_i})_{v_i \in V}$. A system's state is determined by the state variables that are included in all modules of W as well as by their values: $S = \prod_{v_k \in V^S} Z_{v_k}$, where $V^S = \bigcup_{i=1}^{n} V^i$ is a set of variables of the system. For definiteness, this set must be linearly ordered.

As it is known, in the theory of distributed ASM the module execution order is not defined, only restrictions on this order are given [10]. DASM-FB module execution order may be arbitrary but with only restriction – in a run of DASM-FB the executions of modules that do not change the current state are not permitted. To support this requirement the following implementation schemes are suggested:

1. To execute a module whose input data are changed that in turn can influence the change of the module's current state. From the set V^i of the M^i variables one can pick out variables shared with other modules $V_{COM}^i = V^i \cap \bigcup_{i \neq j} V^j$. Then, from those variables we select the following sets: $V_{RD}^i \subseteq V_{COM}^i$ is a set of variables which influence the change of the current state when executing the module M^i, and $V_{WR}^i \subseteq V_{COM}^i$ that is a set of variables which the module M^i changes at its execution.
   Let us use the following denotation: $Z_{RD_{curr}}^i$ is an ordered set of current values of variables from V_{RD}^i. $Z_{RD_{old}}^i$ is an ordered set of values of variables from V_{RD}^i in the previous run. Then the triggering condition for DASM-FB module is formally defined as

$$\left(Z_{RD_{curr}}^i \neq Z_{RD_{old}}^i\right) \tag{7}$$

2. After execution of the M^i module one can execute those modules whose variables directly depend on the variables of the M^i, that are, modules from the set $M_{SUCC} = \{M^j | V_{WR}^i \cap V_{RD}^j \neq \emptyset, j = \overline{1,N}\}$. This is an obvious consequence of the principle of the global state change locality at executing a module. Obviously, DASM-FB modules must be "robust" in the sense of insensitivity to the order of other modules invocation. Taking into account the robustness of modules one can assume "transactional" principle of DASM-FB module execution according to which a module is executed not only once (like in ASM) but possible repeatedly - until a fixed point, i.e. until the re-execution of the module would not lead to changes in the state variables localized in the module. This principle would not affect the final result of entire FB system execution though it may be convenient in software implementation of the system.
   DASM-FB can be used to describe the semantics of FB systems functioning in accordance with different execution models where the execution unit is one function block (for example, these are cyclic and synchronous execution models).
   The rules of changing variable's value functions (represented in DASM-FB only in general terms) will be implemented using production rules. In the simplest

case, one production rule will correspond to one rule of the function's value change. A production rule is denoted as

$$P_t^m : c \Rightarrow a, \tag{8}$$

where P_t^m is an identifier of the rule (or group of rules), c is a rule application condition, a are the actions executed on a change of the corresponding variable. The indices in the rule identifier are: t - the name of the variable to change, and m - a modifier of the rule's identifier bearing additional information about the rule.

The modifier is expressed in forms of B, C, D or B, C, where B is a number of the rule in the ordered set of rules related to value change of the variable t, C is an identifier of a module, where the rule is localized; D is an identifier of an execution model. The left hand side conditions of rules related to value change of the same variable are mutually exclusive, so rules' collisions on writing do not occur, therefore, the order of the rules in DASM-FB is not essential. For brevity of representation of the same type of rules we use the rules' parameterization and group the parameterized rules as a set.

One can arrange the use of the variable change rules into lists according their priority, e.g.: $<p_1 : c_1 \Rightarrow a_1; p_2 : c_2 \Rightarrow a_2; \ldots p_n : c_n \Rightarrow a_n >$. The priority rules' lists can be easily transformed to a non-priority group as follows:

$$<p_1 : c_1 \Rightarrow a_1; p_2 : c_2 \wedge \bar{c}_1 \Rightarrow a_2; \ldots p_n : c_n \wedge \bar{c}_1 \wedge \bar{c}_2 \wedge \ldots \wedge \overline{c_{n-1}} \Rightarrow a_n >$$

4 Model of a Composite Function Block in the Cyclic Execution Semantics

In order to apply formal methods for establishing the portability of function block applications across different execution semantics, one shall define a comprehensive model of the FB architecture in the DASM-FB.

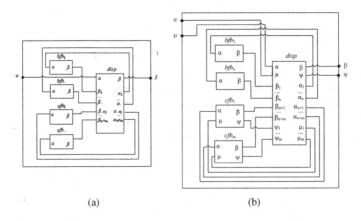

(a)   (b)

Fig. 3. Structures of composite FB operational models for (a) cyclic and (b) two-stage synchronous execution models.

In this section, we present a formal model of a composite function block which can also give idea about formal model of FB applications (since applications are FB networks same as the internals of composite FBs) and of modeling the interface part of basic FBs. A more comprehensive formal model of basic FBs is presented in [4]. Figure 3 shows the functional structure of the operational models of composite FB for cyclic and synchronous execution models. Here $bfb_1,\ldots,bfb_n$ are basic FB models, $cfb_1,\ldots,cfb_m$ are composite FB models, $disp$ is a dispatcher model. Figure 3 shows only those inputs, outputs, and connections that affect FB execution order. In the cyclic execution model (Fig. 3(a)) when FB receives the start signal α the following actions are performed: (1) the movement of signals from inputs of the composite FB module to input variables of component FB, (2) launching all the component FB by the dispatcher, (3) the movement of signals between component FB and transmission signals from outputs of component FB to outputs of the composite FB module, (4) generate finish signal β.

Figure 3(b) shows a two-stage synchronous execution model. The sequence of actions in accordance to the two-stage synchronous execution model is as follows:

Stage 1: on receiving starting signal α: (1) the movement of signals from inputs of the composite FB module to input variables of component FB, (2) launching the first execution phase in all component FB, (3) waiting for completion of the stage 1 execution of all component FB and (4) generate finish signal β.

Stage 2: on receiving starting signal μ: (5) launching the stage 2 execution in all component composite FB, (6) waiting for completion of the stage 2 execution in all component composite FB, (7) the movement of signals between component FB and transmission signals from outputs of component FB to outputs of the composite FB module and (8) generate finish signal ψ. In the rest of the paper we will only use cyclic execution semantics.

4.1 Schema Definition

A (DASM-FB) model of a composite function block (MCFB) can be represented formally as follows:

$$M_C^C = \left(Synt_C, Sem_C^C\right), \tag{9}$$

where $Synt_C$ is a syntactic and Sem_C^C is a semantic part of the definition.

The syntactic part of the definition is a tuple $Synt_C = (Interface, FB, EvConn, DataConn)$, where $Interface$ is an interface of composite FB (similar to the interface of basic FB [4]); $FB = \{fb_1, fb_2, \ldots, fb_{N_{FB}}\}$ is a set of component FBs belonging to the composite FB, $fb_i = (Interface^i, fbt^i)$, $i \in [1, NFB]$, where $Interface^i = (EI^i, EO^i, VI^i, VO^i)$ is an interface of ith component FB. This interface includes: EI^i and EO^i – sets of event input and event output variables; VI^i and VO^i- sets of input and output variables, respectively. fbt^i is a type of ith component FB. $EvConn \subseteq \left(EI \cup \bigcup_{i=1}^{N_{FB}} EO^i\right) \times \left(EO \cup \bigcup_{i=1}^{N_{FB}} EI^i\right)$ is a set of event connections, $DataConn \subseteq \left(VI \cup \bigcup_{i=1}^{N_{FB}} VO^i\right) \times \bigcup_{i=1}^{N_{FB}} VI^i \cup \bigcup_{i=1}^{N_{FB}} VO^i \times VO$ is a set of data connections.

At that, the following constraint has to be satisfied for data connections: $\forall(p,t),(q,u) \in EvConn[(t = u) \rightarrow (p = q)]$. In other words, one cannot connect more than one data output to a data input. When using event connections such topological restriction is not imposed on the structure because the use of E_SPLIT and E_MERGE FB for splitting and merging events is implied.

The semantic part of MCFB definition is given by:

$$Sem_c^c = \left(VRT_C^C, T_C^C, D_C^C\right), \tag{10}$$

where VRT_C^C is a set of variables and conditions of run-time; T_C^C is a set of MCFB transition functions; D_C^C is a scheduler which defines an execution order of component FB within its parent composite FB according to the cyclic execution model. The set of variables and conditions of run-time is determined by a tuple: $VRT_C^C = (VIB, VOB, FBD^C, \omega, \vartheta, \alpha, \beta)$, where VIB, VOB, α, and β have the same meaning as in the model of basic FB (MBFB) [4]; $\omega \triangleq \bigwedge_{eo_j^k \in \bigcup_i EO^i} Z_{EO^i}\left(eo_j^k\right)$ is a condition of termination of signal transfer from component FB' event outputs inside composite FB; $\vartheta \triangleq \bigwedge_{ei_j \in EI} Z_{EI}(ei_j)$ is a condition of existence of signals at FB event inputs; $FBD^C = \{fbd_1, fbd_2, \ldots, fbd_{N_{FB}}\}$ is a set of additional (semantic) descriptions of component FB included in the composite FB, $FB \leftrightarrow FBD^C$, $fbd_i = (\alpha_i, \beta_i)$, where α_i is a starting flag for i^{th} component FB; β_i is a finish flag for i^{th} component FB. MCFB transition functions are defined as a tuple

$$T_C = \left(t_{EI}, (t_{EI^i})_{i=\overline{1,N_{FB}}}, (t_{EO^i})_{i=\overline{1,N_{FB}}}, t_{EO}, t_{VI}, t_{VOB}\right), \tag{11}$$

where $t_{EI} : [Z_{EI}] \times [Z_\alpha] \rightarrow [Z_{EI}]$ is a function for resetting the event input variables of the MCFB (as a result of signals transfer from its inputs), $t_{EI^i} : [Z_\alpha] \times \left[\bigcup_{i=1}^{N_{FB}} Z_{EO^i}\right] \times [Z_{EI}] \rightarrow [Z_{EI^i}]$ is a function for setting the event input variables of i-th component FB, $t_{EO^i} : [Z_{EO^i}] \rightarrow [Z_{EO^i}]$ is a function for resetting the event output variables of i-th component FB, $t_{EO} : \left[\bigcup_{i=1}^{N_{FB}} Z_{EO^i}\right] \times [Z_{EI}] \rightarrow [Z_{EO}]$ is a function for setting the event output variables of the MCFB (as a result of signals transfer to its outputs), $t_{VI} : [Z_\alpha] \times [Z_{VIB}] \times [Z_{EI}] \rightarrow [Z_{VI}]$ is a function of changing the MCFB input variables (as a result of data sampling) and $t_{VOB} : \left[\bigcup_{i=1}^{N_{FB}} Z_{VO^i}\right] \times [Z_{EI}] \times \left[\bigcup_{i=1}^{N_{FB}} Z_{EO^i}\right] \rightarrow [Z_{VOB}]$ is a function of changing the output buffers (as a result of data issuing).

4.2   Model Dynamics Definition

The following summarizes the rules of composite FB functioning within a typical sequential execution model, in which the selection of an active FB is determined as a function of the execution completion of other FB. An example of this execution model type is the cyclic execution model. All actions related to signal and data transfer between component FB as well as an environment is considered to be performed in a tick.

Besides, unlike the basic FB, in this case data sampling enabled by active event inputs of composite FB is carried out simultaneously. It is so-called "synchronous data sampling". Nevertheless, this does not deny the possibility of using other modes of selection and processing of input signals including the priority ones.

There is no need in starting signal α for the transfer of signals to outputs of composite FB. Here the signal/data transfer uses "hot potato" principle according to which signals/data are passed on as soon as they appear. It should be noted that these options are an optional part and may vary. At the same time for the transfer of signals/data from inputs inside composite FB the signal α is required.

The function of signal transfer to event inputs of jth component FB can be defined as follows:

$$\{p_{EI^j}^{C,C,1}[k] : Z_\alpha(\alpha) \wedge \bigvee_{\substack{ei_m, \\ (ei_m, ei_k^j) \in EvConn}} Z_{EI}(ei_m) \vee \bigvee_{\substack{eo_n^x \in EO^x, \\ (eo_n^x, ei_k^i) \in EvConn}} Z_{EO^x}(eo_n^x) \Rightarrow$$
$$\Rightarrow Z_{EI^j}(ei_k^j) \leftarrow true | ei_k^j \in EI^j\}, j = \overline{1, N_{FB}} \tag{12}$$

where ei_k^j is k^{th} event input variable of jth component FB. In accordance with this rule an event input variable of component FB is set to "1" if there is at least one event input variable of MCFB valued to "1"("true") which is connected to this event input variable of component FB. Similarly one can define the function t_{EO} of signal transfer to MCFB event outputs:

$$\{p_{EO}^{C,C,1}[k] : Z_\alpha(\alpha) \wedge \bigvee_{\substack{ei_m, \\ (ei_m, eo_k) \in EvConn}} Z_{EI}(ei_m) \vee \bigvee_{\substack{eo_n^x \in EO^x, \\ (eo_n^x, eo_k) \in EvConn}} Z_{EO^x}(eo_n^x) \Rightarrow$$
$$\Rightarrow Z_{EO}(eo_k) \leftarrow true | eo_k \in EO\} \tag{13}$$

The function t_{VI} of data sampling can be defined by means of the following set of rules:

$$\{p_{VI}^{C,C,1}[m] : Z_\alpha(\alpha) \wedge \bigvee_{\substack{ei_k \in EI, \\ (ei_k, vi_m) \in IW}} Z_{EI}(ei_k) \Rightarrow Z_{VI}(vi_m) \leftarrow Z_{VIB}(vib_m) | vi_m \in VI\} \tag{14}$$

The function t_{VOB} of data issuing can be given by the following set of rules:

$$\{p_{VOB}^{C,C,1}[k] : \bigvee_{(eo_k, vob_m) \in OW} (Z_\alpha(\alpha) \wedge \bigvee_{\substack{ei_j \in EI, \\ (ei_j, eo_k) \in EvConn}} Z_{EI}(ei_j) \vee \bigvee_{\substack{eo_n^x \in EO^x, \\ (eo_n^x, eo_k) \in EvConn}} Z_{EO^x}(eo_n^x)) \Rightarrow$$
$$\Rightarrow Z_{VOB}(vob_m) \leftarrow Z_{VO}(repr_{Vo}(vo_m)) | vob_m \in VOB\} \tag{15}$$

Here, the argument of function Z_{VO} is not an output variable from VO but its representative. The purpose of this substitution is to minimize the number of variables in common model without loss of correctness. The function of resetting the signal sources can be represented by the following rules:

$$\{p_{EI}^{C,C,1}[j] : Z_\alpha(\alpha) \wedge Z_{EI}(ei_j) \Rightarrow Z_{EI}(ei_j) \leftarrow false | ei_j \in EI\} \tag{16}$$

$$\left\{p_{EO^j}^{C,C,1}[k] : Z_{EO^j}\left(eo_k^j\right) \Rightarrow Z_{EO^j}\left(eo_k^j\right) \leftarrow false | eo_k^j \in EO^j\right\}, j = \overline{1, N_{FB}} \tag{17}$$

4.3   Model of Scheduler

The scheduler for the cyclic execution model is defined as a tuple:

$$D_C = (V_D^C, T_D^C, Z_D^{C,0}), \tag{18}$$

where V_D^C is a set of scheduler's variables, T_D^C is a set of transition functions of the scheduler, $Z_D^{C,0}$ is a set of initial values functions of the scheduler. We assume that the scheduler is executed asynchronously with the parent FB. The set of variables of the "cyclic" scheduler is defined as follows:

$$V_D^C = \left(\alpha, \beta, (\alpha_i)_{i=\overline{1,N_{FB}}}, (\beta_i)_{i=\overline{1,N_{FB}}}\right), \tag{19}$$

where α is a flag for launching the subsystem (i.e. controlled FB network) from the upper level, β is a flag indicating the termination of the execution of controlled FB network as a whole, $(\alpha_i)_{i=\overline{1,N_{FB}}}$ are output flags for separately launching the component FB included in the controlled FB network, $(\beta_i)_{i=\overline{1,N_{FB}}}$ are input flags indicating the termination of the execution of component FB in the controlled FB network. The initial values of all flags are "false" (or "0").

The transition functions of the "cyclic" scheduler are defined as follows:

$$T_D^C = \left(t_\alpha, t_\beta, (t_{\alpha_i})_{i=\overline{1,N_{FB}}}, (t_{\beta_i})_{i=\overline{1,N_{FB}}}\right), \tag{20}$$

where $t_\alpha : [Z_\alpha] \times [Z_{EO^i}] \times [Z_{EI}] \rightarrow [Z_\alpha]$ is a function for resetting the starting flag of MCFB, $t_\beta : \left[Z_{\beta_{N_{FB}}}\right] \times [Z_{EO^i}] \rightarrow [Z_\beta]$ is a function for setting the finish flag of MCFB, $t_{\alpha_1} : [Z_\alpha] \times [Z_{EO^i}] \times [Z_{EI}] \rightarrow [Z_{\alpha_1}]$ and $t_{\alpha_i} : \left[Z_{\beta_{i-1}}\right] \times [Z_{EO^i}] \times [Z_{EI}] \rightarrow [Z_{\alpha_i}], i = \overline{2, N_{FB}}$ are functions for setting the flags α_i, $t_{\beta_i} : [Z_{\beta_i}] \times [Z_{EO^i}] \rightarrow [Z_{\beta_i}], i = \overline{1, N_{FB}}$ are functions for resetting the flags β_i. The functioning of "cyclic" scheduler of an intermediate level is determined by the following rules:

$$p_{\alpha_1}^{D,C,1} : Z_\alpha(\alpha) \wedge \omega \wedge \overline{\vartheta} \Rightarrow Z_{\alpha_1}(\alpha_1) \leftarrow true \tag{21}$$

$$\left\{p_{\alpha_i}^{D,C,2}[i] : Z_{\beta_{i-1}}(\beta_{i-1}) \wedge \omega \wedge \overline{\vartheta} \Rightarrow Z_{\alpha_i}(\alpha_i) \leftarrow true | i = \overline{2, N_{FB}}\right\} \tag{22}$$

$$\left\{p_{\beta_i}^{D,C,1}[i] : Z_{\beta_i}(\beta_i) \wedge \omega \Rightarrow Z_{\beta_i}(\beta_i) \leftarrow false | i = \overline{1, N_{FB}}\right\} \tag{23}$$

$$p_{\beta_1}^{D,C,1} : Z_{\beta_{N_{FB}}}(\hat{a}_{N_{FB}}) \wedge \omega \Rightarrow Z_\beta(\beta) \leftarrow true \tag{24}$$

$$p_\alpha^{D,C,1} : Z_\alpha(\alpha) \wedge \omega \wedge \bar{\vartheta} \Rightarrow Z_\alpha(\alpha) \leftarrow false \tag{25}$$

It should be noted that the number i determines the FB execution order assigned statically. Unlike an intermediate level scheduler, the upper level scheduler (the main scheduler) is independent of the other schedulers. At that, once the upper level scheduler executes the last FB in the execution list, it starts executing the first FB of the list. This process is repeated cyclically. The model of the upper level scheduler is defined similarly to the model of an intermediate level scheduler, but flags α and β as well as functions for their modification are not used. The set of the upper level scheduler functioning rules contains rules:

$p_{\alpha_i}^{D,C,2}[i], p_{\beta_i}^{D,C,1}[i]$ and a special rule $p_{\alpha_i}^{D,C,3}[i] : Z_{\beta_{N_{FB}}}(\beta_{N_{FB}}) \wedge \omega \Rightarrow Z_{\alpha_1}(\alpha_1) \leftarrow true.$

4.4 Implementation of DASM-FB in SMV

There are two basic approaches to developing SMV-based models of FB using the formal model of FB described in the previous sections.

The first approach uses the concept of *modules* in SMV and simultaneous local changes of variables in each module, by using the *next* statement of SMV. This approach is more intuitive, as it supports a hierarchical design and allows one to one mapping of function blocks to the hierarchy of modules SMV. In addition, it allows the use of composite verification methods supported in the SMV.

The second approach is based on the possibility of direct global transitions description using *TRANS* and *INIT* statements in SMV. Due to the complex implementation of *TRANS* and *INIT* based approach, in this paper only the first approach is presented.

In this approach all the variables of the FB model are divided into two parts: (1) a set of internal variables, which are localized in the FB, and (2) external variables that are located outside the module. Figure 4 presents the variables used in a Composite FB model (CFBM), and their relationships, solid circles denote actual variables, and

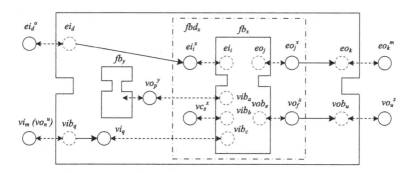

Fig. 4. Variables in Composite FB model.

dashed ones indicate parameters. Relationship of real variables and parameters are shown by dashed bidirectional arrows, while solid arrows represent signal and data transfer.

For formal matching of MBFB and MCFB functioning using the accepted buffering scheme it is necessary to use an operation of identification of variables used in neighboring FB modules. Let us introduce function $repr_{VI}$ allowing to determine representatives of input variables of component FB in MCFB:

$$repr_{vi} : \bigcup_{i=1}^{N_{FB}} VI^i \cup \bigcup_{i=1}^{N_{FB}} VO^i$$

As can be seen from the definition, input variables of component FB are identified with input variables of the composite FB itself or output variables of internal component FB.

Let us introduce function $repr_{VO}$ defining representatives of MCFB' output variables.

$$repr_{VO} : VO \rightarrow \bigcup_{i=1}^{N_{FB}} VO^i$$

Output variables of composite FB are identified with output variables of component FB. Thereby, we can assume that physically the output variables of composite FB do not exist. There exist the following one-to-one mapping between variables of i_{th} component FB and the corresponding module x:

$$EI_i \leftrightarrow EI^x; EO_i \leftrightarrow EO^x; VO_i \leftrightarrow VOB^x; \bigcup_{vi \in VI_i} repr_{VI}(vi) \leftrightarrow VIB^x.$$

5 Example: Modeling of a Simple FB Application

In this section, the "Two ALU" FB application from Fig. 2 will be modeled using the proposed modeling method. The corresponding SMV module alu is defined as follows (rules presented in [4]):

```
MODULE alu(initt, sum, diff, d1_, d2_, inito, cnf, res_,
alpha, beta).
```

We create two instances of the 'alu' module for the composite block as below.

```
VAR alu1:  process alu (initt1, add1, sub1, res2Buf, vc1,
           inito1, cnf1, res1Buf, alpha1, beta1);
VAR alu2:  process alu (initt2, add2, sub2, res1Buf, vc2,
           inito2, cnf2, res2Buf, alpha2, beta2);
```

The main part of the composite block execution is the scheduler which follows the cyclic execution semantics. The scheduler SMV module is quite small and mainly acts to schedule which instance of the BFB in the composite FB is presently executing according to the cyclic execution semantics, the rules for which were presented in Sect. 4.3:

```
MODULE  schedulerCyclic  (alpha1,    next (beta1):=case
alpha2, beta1, beta2, omega, v)              beta1& omega: 0;
ASSIGN                                       1: beta1;
next (alpha1):=case                   esac;
        beta2 & omega & !v: 1;            next (beta2):=case
        1: alpha1;                          beta2 & omega: 0;
esac;                                       1: beta2;
next (alpha2):=case                   esac;
        beta1& omega & !v: 1;
        1: alpha2;
esac;
```

The scheduler is instantiated in SMV as follows:

```
VAR disp:   process schedulerSynch (alpha1, alpha2, beta1,
            beta2, omega, v);
```

Properties of model of a system under investigation are expressed using temporal logics LTL or CTL. An example of such a CTL property in SMV is *SPEC EF alu2.beta* (with *true* result) that means alu2 module is terminated at least once.

6 Conclusions

The modeling method presented in this paper enables certification of applications portability using formal verification. It should be noted that the paper presents in detail only one model for the cyclic execution semantics of function blocks. Other execution models, for example, synchronous execution model, can be achieved by simply changing the scheduler, which we plan to present in future works.

References

1. International Standard IEC 61499 Function blocks—Part 1: Architecture, IEC Standard 61499-1 (2012)
2. Vyatkin, V.: IEC 61499 as enabler of distributed and intelligent automation: state-of-the-art review. IEEE Trans. Indus. Inf. **7**, 768–781 (2011)
3. Vyatkin, V.: The IEC 61499 standard and its semantics. Indus. Electron. Mag. IEEE **3**, 40–48 (2009)
4. Patil, S., Dubinin, V., Vyatkin, V.: Formal Modelling and Verification of IEC61499 Function Blocks with Abstract State Machines and SMV: the Cyclic Semantics Case (2014). https://pure.ltu.se/portal/en/publications/formal-modelling-and-verification-of-iec61499-function-blocks-with-abstract-state-machines-and-smv-the-cyclic-semantics-case%28a703dd4b-cd09-41ea-af45-67d8889852fe%29.html

5. Cengic, G., Akesson, K.: On formal analysis of IEC 61499 applications, part B: Execution semantics. IEEE Trans. Indus. Inf. **6**, 145–154 (2010)
6. Cengic, G., Akesson, K.: On formal analysis of IEC 61499 applications, part A: modeling. IEEE Trans. Indus. Inf. **6**, 136–144 (2010)
7. Dubinin, V., Vyatkin, V.: On definition of a formal model for IEC 61499 function blocks. EURASIP J. Embedded Syst. **2008**, 1–10 (2008)
8. ICS Triplex ISaGRAF Workbench for IEC 61499/61131, v6. http://www.icstriplex.com/
9. Gurevich, Y.: Logic and the challenge of computer science. In: Current Trends in Theoretical Computer Science, pp. 1–57 (1988)
10. Gurevich, Y.: Evolving algebras 1993: Lipari guide. In: Börger, E. (ed.) Specification and Validation Methods, pp. 9–36. Oxford University Press, Inc. (1995)
11. Stark, R.F., Borger, E., Schmid, J.: Java and the Java Virtual Machine: Definition, Verification, Validation. Springer, Heidelberg (2001)
12. Börger, E., et al.: A high-level modular definition of the semantics of C#. Theor. Comput. Sci. **336**, 235–284 (2005)
13. Börger, E., Glässer, U., Muller, W.: A formal definition of an abstract VHDL 1993 simulator by EA-machines. In: Kloos, C., Breuer, P. (eds.) Formal Semantics for VHDL, vol. 307, pp. 107–139. Springer US, New York (1995)
14. Glässer, U., Gurevich, Y., Veanes, : An abstract communication model. Technical Report MSR-TR-2002-55, Microsoft Research2002
15. Glässer, U., Gurevich, Y., Veanes, M.: High-Level Executable Specification of the Universal Plug and Play Architecture. In: Presented at the HICSS 2002
16. Börger, E., Rosenzweig, D.: A mathematical definition of full Prolog. Sci. Comput. Programm. **24**, 249–286 (1995)
17. Gurevich, Y., Huggins, J.: The semantics of the C programming language. In: Meinke, K., Börger, E., Gurevich, Y. (eds.) CSL 1993. LNCS, vol. 832, pp. 334–336. Springer, Heidelberg (1994)
18. Börger, E., Schulte, W.: A programmer friendly modular definition of the semantics of java. In: Alves-Foss, J. (ed.) Formal Syntax and Semantics of Java. LNCS, vol. 1523, pp. 353–404. Springer, Heidelberg (1999)
19. Hanisch, H.-M., et al.: One decade of IEC 61499 modeling and verification-results and open issues. In: 13th IFAC Symposium on Information Control Problems in Manufacturing, V.A. Trapeznikov Institute of Control Sciences, Russia (2009)
20. Bonfe, M., Fantuzzi, C.: Design and verification of mechatronic object-oriented models for industrial control systems. In: ETFA 2003, IEEE Conference on Emerging Technologies and Factory Automation, vol. 2, pp. 253–260 (2003)
21. Dimitrova, D., Frey, G., Bachkova, I.: Formal approach for modeling and verification of IEC 61499 function blocks. In: Advanced Manufacturing Technologies (AMTECH 2005), Russe, Bulgaria, pp. 731–736 (2005)
22. Vyatkin, V., Hanisch, H.M.: A modeling approach for verification of IEC1499 function blocks using net condition/event systems. In: 1999 7th IEEE International Conference on Emerging Technologies and Factory Automation, 1999, Proceedings, ETFA 1999, vol. 1, pp. 261–270 (1999)
23. Dubinin, V., et al.: Analysis of extended net condition/event systems on the basis of model checking. In: Presented at the Proceedings of International Conference on New Information Technologies and Systems (NITS 2010), vol. 2, pp.20–48. Penza (2010) (Originally published in Russian)
24. Dubinin, V., Vyatkin, V., Hanisch, H.M.: Modelling and verification of IEC 61499 applications using Prolog. In: IEEE Conference on Emerging Technologies and Factory Automation, ETFA 2006, pp. 774–781 (2006)

25. Schnakenbourg, C., Faure, J.M., Lesage, J.J.: Towards IEC 61499 function blocks diagrams verification. In: 2002 IEEE International Conference on Systems, Man and Cybernetics, vol. 3, p. 6 (2002)
26. Junbeom, Y., Sungdeok, C., Eunkyung, J.: A verification framework for FBD based software in nuclear power plants. In: 15th Asia-Pacific Software Engineering Conference, APSEC 2008, pp. 385–392 (2008)
27. Dubinin, V.N., Vyatkin, V.: Semantics-robust design patterns for IEC 61499. IEEE Trans. Indus. Inf. **8**, 279–290 (2012)
28. Pang, C., et al.: A portability study of IEC 61499: Semantics and Tools. In: 12th IEEE Conference on Industrial Informatics (INDIN 2014), pp. 440–445. Porto Alegre, Brazil (2014)

On Tractability of Disjoint AND-Decomposition
of Boolean Formulas

Pavel Emelyanov[1] and Denis Ponomaryov[1,2](✉)

[1] Institute of Informatics Systems, Novosibirsk, Russia
{emelyanov,ponom}@iis.nsk.su
[2] Institute of Artificial Intelligence, Ulm, Germany

Abstract. Disjoint AND-decomposition of a boolean formula means its
representation as a conjunction of two (or several) formulas having disjoint sets of variables. We show that deciding AND-decomposability is
intractable in general for boolean formulas given in CNF or DNF and
prove tractability of computing AND-decompositions of boolean formulas given in positive DNF, Full DNF, and ANF. The results follow from
tractability of multilinear polynomial factorization over the finite field of
order 2, for which we provide a polytime factorization algorithm based
on identity testing for partial derivatives of multilinear polynomials.

1 Introduction

Decomposition of boolean functions is an important research topic having a long
history and a wide range of applications. Among other application fields such as
game and graph theory, it has attracted the most attention in the logic circuit
synthesis. Decomposition is related to the algorithmic complexity and practical
issues of implementation of electronic circuits, their size, time delay, and power
consumption. The report [11] contains an extensive survey of decomposition
methods till the mid–1990's. The results of the next fifteen years of research are
presented in [2–5,7,8,15].

Typically one is interested in decompositions of the form $F = F_1 \odot \ldots \odot F_k$
where $\odot \in \{OR, AND, XOR\}$. Bi-decomposition is the most important
case of decomposition of boolean functions. Even though it may not be stated
explicitly, this case is considered in many papers: [1–4,8,9] and [5, Ch. 3–
6]. Bi-decomposition has the form: $F(X) = \pi(F_1(\Sigma_1, \Delta), F_2(\Sigma_2, \Delta))$, where
$\pi \in \{OR, AND, XOR\}$, $\Delta \subseteq X$, and $\{\Sigma_1, \Sigma_2\}$ is a partition of the variables
$X \backslash \Delta$. As a rule, a decomposition into more than two components can be obtained
by iterative computation of bi-decomposition. If $\Delta = \varnothing$ then decomposition is
called disjoint and considered as optimal for many reasons.

Bioch [2] studied computational properties of modular decompositions based
on a generalization of Shannon's Expansion. A set of variables A is called

---

An extended version of the paper containing proofs is available from http://persons.
iis.nsk.su/files/persons/pages/and-decomp-full.pdf.

A. Voronkov and I. Virbitskaite (Eds.): PSI 2014, LNCS 8974, pp. 92–101, 2015.
DOI: 10.1007/978-3-662-46823-4_8

modular set of a boolean function $F(X)$ if F can be represented as $F(X) = H(G(A), B)$, where $\{A, B\}$ is a partition of X and H, G are some boolean functions. The function $G(A)$ is called component of F and a modular decomposition is obtained from iterative decomposition into such components. It is shown that in general it is coNP-complete to decide whether a subset of variables is modular, however for monotone functions in DNF this problem is tractable.

We note that a function may have a modular or bi-decomposition, but may not be AND-decomposable, since this form of decomposition requires representation of a function strictly as a conjunction. Thus, AND–decomposition can be viewed as a special case of modular and bi-decomposition. Our results demonstrate that deciding even this special case of decomposability is coNP-complete for formulas given in CNF and DNF. On the other hand, we show tractability of computing AND-decompositions of formulas given in the forms: positive DNF, Full DNF, and ANF. It is not obvious, whether the technique used by Bioch for positive DNF is applicable to these cases of AND-decomposition. We note however that in our Lemma 1, the idea of computing decomposition components resembles the final step of constructing components in [2, Sect. 2.9].

Approaches to decomposition of boolean functions can be classified into logic and algebraic. The first are based on equivalent transformations of formulas in propositional logic. The second ones consider boolean functions as algebraic objects with the corresponding transformation rules. The most elaborated representation is polynomials, usually over finite fields, among which $\mathbb{F}_2$ (the Galois field of order 2) is the best known. Shpilka and Volkovich [14] noted the strong connection between polynomial factorization and polynomial identity testing (i.e. testing equality to the zero polynomial). It follows from their results that a multilinear polynomial over $\mathbb{F}_2$ can be factored in time that is cubic in the size of the polynomial (given as a symbol sequence). We provide a factorization algorithm for multilinear polynomials over $\mathbb{F}_2$ which runs in cubic time and is based on identity testing for partial derivatives of a product of polynomials obtained from the input one. We note however that while staying in the cubic time complexity, the same can be achieved without computing the product explicitly, thus contributing to efficiency of factorization of large input polynomials.

In our work, we follow the logic approach to decomposition, but show that tractability of multilinear polynomial factorization over $\mathbb{F}_2$ gives polytime decomposition algorithms for boolean functions in positive DNF and Full DNF.

2 Preliminaries

2.1 Basic Facts About AND-Decomposability

Let us introduce some conventions and notations. For a boolean formula φ, we denote the set of its variables by $\mathtt{var}\,(\varphi)$. If Σ is a set of propositional variables and $\mathtt{var}\,(\varphi) \subseteq \Sigma$, then we say that the formula φ is *over variables* Σ (or *over* Σ, for short); $\mathtt{taut}(\Sigma)$ denotes a valid formula over Σ. We call φ *positive* if it does not contain negative literals. If ξ and ξ' are clauses (or conjuncts, respectively), then the notation $\xi' \subseteq \xi$ means that ξ' is a subclause (subconjunct) of ξ, i.e. ξ' is given by a non-empty subset of literals from ξ. If φ is in DNF, then a conjunct ξ of φ is called *redundant* in φ if there exists another conjunct ξ' of φ such that $\xi' \subseteq \xi$.

We now define the main property of boolean formulas studied in this paper, the definition is adopted from [12], where it is given in a general form.

Definition 1 (Decomposability). *A boolean formula φ is called disjointly AND–decomposable (or decomposable, for short) if it is equivalent to the conjunction $\psi_1 \wedge \psi_2$ of some formulas ψ_1 and ψ_2 such that:*

1. $\mathsf{var}\,(\psi_1) \cup \mathsf{var}\,(\psi_2) = \mathsf{var}\,(\varphi)$;
2. $\mathsf{var}\,(\psi_1) \cap \mathsf{var}\,(\psi_2) = \varnothing$;
3. $\mathsf{var}\,(\psi_i) \neq \varnothing$, *for $i = 1, 2$.*

The formulas ψ_1 and ψ_2 are called decomposition components of φ. We say that φ is decomposable with a variable partition $\{\Sigma_1, \Sigma_2\}$ if φ has some decomposition components ψ_1 and ψ_2 over the variables Σ_1 and Σ_2, respectively.

Note that a similar definition could be given for OR–decomposability, i.e. for decomposition into the disjunction of ψ_1 and ψ_2. Clearly, a formula φ is AND–decomposable iff $\neg\varphi$ is OR–decomposable.

Observe that Definition 1 is formulated with the two components ψ_1 and ψ_2, which in turn can be decomposable formulas. Since at each decomposition step, the variable sets of the components must be proper subsets of the variables of the original formula φ, the decomposition process necessarily stops and gives formulas which are non-decomposable. The obtained formulas define some partition of $\mathsf{var}\,(\varphi)$ and the fact below (which follows from a property of a large class of logical calculi shown in [12]) says that this variable partition is unique.

Fact 1 (Uniqueness of Decompositions - Corollary of Theorem 1 in [12]). *If a boolean formula φ is decomposable, then there is a unique partition $\{\pi_1, \ldots, \pi_n\}$ of $\mathsf{var}\,(\varphi)$, $2 \leqslant n$, such that φ is equivalent to $\bigwedge\{\psi_i \mid \mathsf{var}\,(\psi_i) = \pi_i,\ i = 1, \ldots, n\}$, where each formula ψ_i is not decomposable.*

This means that *any* possible algorithm[1] for decomposing a formula into components could be applied iteratively to obtain from a given φ some formulas ψ_i, $i = 1, \ldots, n$, which are non-decomposable and *uniquely* define a partition of the variables of φ.

2.2   The Computational Problems Considered in the Paper

In the text, we omit subtleties related to efficient encoding of input sets of variables and boolean formulas (given in CNF, DNF, or ANF) assuming their standard representation as symbol sequences. The complexity of each computational problem below will be defined wrt the size of the input formula.

$\boxed{\varnothing\mathtt{Dec}}$ *For a given boolean formula φ, decide whether φ is decomposable.*

---

[1] Existence and complexity of decomposition algorithms in various logics have been studied in [6, 10, 12, 13].

$\boxed{\varnothing\text{DecPart}}$ *For a given boolean formula φ and a partition $\{\Sigma_1, \Sigma_2\}$ of $\text{var}(\varphi)$, decide whether φ is decomposable with this partition.*

It turns out that the problem $\varnothing$Dec for formulas in DNF is closely related to the problem of multilinear polynomial factorization ($\text{Dec}\mathbb{F}_2$) which we formulate below. The connection is in particular due to the fact that taking a conjunction of two formulas in DNF is quite similar to taking a product of two multivariate polynomials. We recall that a multivariate polynomial F is *linear (multilinear)* if the degree of each variable in F is 1. We denote a finite field of order 2 by $\mathbb{F}_2$ and say that a polynomial is *over the field* $\mathbb{F}_2$ if it has coefficients from $\mathbb{F}_2$. A polynomial F is called *factorable* over $\mathbb{F}_2$ if $F = G_1 \cdot G_2$, where G_1 and G_2 are non-constant polynomials over $\mathbb{F}_2$. The following important observation shows further connection between polynomial factorization and the problem $\varnothing$Dec:

Fact 2 (Factoring over $\mathbb{F}_2$). If a multilinear polynomial F is factorable over $\mathbb{F}_2$, then its factors do not have variables in common.

Clearly, if some factors G_1 and G_2 of F have a common variable then the polynomial $G_1 \cdot G_2$ is not linear and thus, is not equal to F in the ring of polynomials over $\mathbb{F}_2$.

$\boxed{\text{Dec}\mathbb{F}_2}$ *Given a non-constant multilinear polynomial F over $\mathbb{F}_2$, decide whether F is factorable over $\mathbb{F}_2$.*

3 Main Results

First, we formulate the hardness result on decomposition of formulas given in the Conjunctive Normal Form and then proceed to formulas in full DNF, positive DNF, and ANF. We note that decomposition itself is conceptually closer to the CNF representation, since it gives a conjunction of formulas. The situation with positive DNF and full DNF is more complicated, because decomposable formulas in DNF have a cartesian structure which can be recognized in polytime, but the proof of this fact relies on polynomial factorization over $\mathbb{F}_2$.

Theorem 1 (Complexity for CNF). *For boolean formulas given in CNF,*

1. *the problem $\varnothing$DecPart is coNP–complete;*
2. *the problem $\varnothing$Dec is coNP–hard and is in P^{NP}.*

Recall that the Algebraic Normal Form of a boolean formula (ANF) can be viewed as a multilinear polynomial over $\mathbb{F}_2$. Due to Fact 2, the notion of decomposability for formulas in ANF can be defined in terms of polynomial factorability over $\mathbb{F}_2$. For this reason, we use the terminology of polynomials when talking about algebraic results further in this section. We start with the complexity of decomposition for formulas in Full DNF (i.e. formulas given by the set of their satisfying assignments) and then formulate results on positive DNF and polynomial factorization over $\mathbb{F}_2$. Interestingly, the latter problem is related also to decomposition of formulas in Full DNF, even though such formulas contain negative literals. The proof of the theorem below uses the trick that negative literals can be encoded as "fresh" variables giving a positive DNF.

Theorem 2 (Complexity for Full DNF). *For boolean formulas in Full DNF,*

1. *the problem $\varnothing$DecPart is in P;*
2. *the problem $\varnothing$Dec is reducible to DecF$_2$ and hence is in P.*

In each of the cases, the corresponding decomposition components can be computed in polynomial time.

It turns out that for a positive formula φ in DNF without redundant conjuncts, decomposability is equivalent to factorability over $\mathbb{F}_2$ of the multilinear polynomial corresponding to φ. The polynomial is obtained as the sum of monomials (products of variables) corresponding to the conjuncts of φ. Observe that the positive formula $\varphi = x \vee (x \wedge y) \vee z$ with the redundant conjunct $x \wedge y$ is equivalent to $(x \vee z) \wedge \mathtt{taut}(\{y\})$ and thus, decomposable. However, the polynomial $x + xy + z$ corresponding to φ is non-factorable. Also note that if a polynomial has a factor with the constant monomial, e.g. $xy + y = (x + 1) \cdot y$, then the corresponding boolean formula in DNF contains a redundant conjunct.

Theorem 3 (Decomposition of Positive DNF and Factorization). *For positive boolean formulas in DNF without redundant conjuncts, the problem $\varnothing$Dec is equivalent to DecF$_2$.*

We formulate the main result on formulas given in DNF in the following corollary which is a consequence of Theorems 3 and 4, and the constructions from the proof of Theorem 1 given in the extended version of the paper.

Corollary 1 (Complexity for DNF).

1. *For formulas in DNF, the problem $\varnothing$DecPart is coNP-complete;*
2. *for positive boolean formulas in DNF, the problem $\varnothing$Dec is in P and the corresponding decomposition components can be computed in polynomial time.*

We now turn to tractability of the problem DecF$_2$, to which the decomposition problems in Theorem 2 and Corollary 1 are reduced. Originally, tractability of DecF$_2$ is a consequence of the results from [14], where the authors provide two solutions to polynomial decomposition over an arbitrary finite field F. The first one is a decomposition algorithm, which has a subroutine for computing a justification assignment for an input polynomial, and relies on a procedure for identity testing in F. It is proved that the complexity of this algorithm is $O(n^3 \cdot d \cdot IT)$, where n is the number of variables, d is the maximal individual degree of variables in the input polynomial, and IT is the complexity of identity testing in F. It follows that this gives a decomposition algorithm of quartic complexity for factoring multilinear polynomials over the field $\mathbb{F}_2$. The second solution proposed by the authors is a decomposition algorithm which constructs for every variable of an input polynomial f, a combination $f \cdot f_1 - f_2 \cdot f_3$ of four polynomials, where each f_i is a "copy" of f under a renaming of some variables. Every combination is tested for equality to the zero polynomial. It can be seen that this gives an algorithm of cubic complexity for factoring multilinear polynomials over $\mathbb{F}_2$.

In Theorem 4 below, we provide a solution to factorization of multilinear polynomials over $\mathbb{F}_2$, which is different from the both algorithms proposed in [14]. The only common feature between the approaches is application of identity testing, which seems to be inevitable in factorization. Our solution is based on computation of partial derivatives of polynomials obtained from the input one and gives an algorithm of cubic complexity. More precisely, the product $f_1 \cdot f_2$ is computed, where f_i are polynomials obtained from the input, and then for each variable x, the partial derivative of $f_1 \cdot f_2$ is tested for equality to zero. In particular, our algorithm operates polynomials which are smaller than the ones considered in [14]. Moreover, we note in the extended version of the paper that the same can be achieved without computing the product $f_1 \cdot f_2$ explicitly, which is particularly important on large inputs. We present the factorization algorithm as the theorem below to follow the complexity oriented style of exposition used in this paper.

Theorem 4 (Tractability of Linear Polynomial Factorization over $\mathbb{F}_2$).
The problem $\mathrm{Dec}\mathbb{F}_2$ is in P and for any factorable multilinear polynomial, its factors can be computed in polynomial time.

Proof. Let F be a non-constant multilinear polynomial over $\mathbb{F}_2$. We will describe a number of important properties which hold if F is factorable over $\mathbb{F}_2$. Based on these properties, we will derive a polynomial procedure for partitioning the variables of F into disjoints sets Σ_1 and Σ_2 such that if F is factorable, then it must have factors which are polynomials having these sets of variables. Having obtained Σ_1 and Σ_2, it suffices to check whether F is indeed factorable wrt this partition: if the answer is "no", then F is non-factorable, otherwise we obtain the corresponding factors. Checking whether F is factorable wrt a variable partition can be done efficiently due the following fact:

Lemma 1 (Factorization Under a Given Variable Partition). *In the notations above, for $i = 1, 2$, let S_i be the set of monomials obtained by restricting every monomial of F onto Σ_i (for instance, if $F = xy + y$ and $\Sigma_1 = \{x\}$, then $S_1 = \{x, 1\}$). Let F_i be the polynomial consisting of the monomials of S_i for $i = 1, 2$. Then F is factorable into some polynomials with the sets of variables Σ_1 and Σ_2 iff $F = F_1 \cdot F_2$.*

Proof of the lemma. The "if" direction is obvious, since for $i = 1, 2$, each F_i necessarily contains all the variables from Σ_i. Now assume that F has a factorization $F = G_1 \cdot G_2$ which corresponds to the partition Σ_1, Σ_2. Then every monomial of F is a product of some monomials from G_1, G_2, i.e. it either contains variables of both Σ_1 and Σ_2, or only from Σ_i for some $i = 1, 2$ iff G_{3-i} contains the constant monomial. This means that S_i is the set of monomials of G_i for $i = 1, 2$, i.e. $F_i = G_i$. □

Let us proceed to properties of factorable polynomials. Let $F_{x=v}$ be the polynomial obtained from F by setting x equal to v. Note that $\frac{\partial F}{\partial x} = F_{x=1} + F_{x=0}$.

First of all, note that if some variable x is contained in every monomial of F, then F is either non-factorable (in case $F = x$), or trivially factorable, i.e. $F = x \cdot \frac{\partial F}{\partial x}$. We further assume that there is no such variable in F. We also assume that $F \neq x + 1$, i.e. F contains at least two variables[2].

Let F be a polynomial over the set of variables $\{x, x_1, \ldots, x_n\}$. If F is factorable, then it can be represented as

$$F = (x \cdot Q + R) \cdot H, \quad \text{where}$$

- the polynomials Q,R, and H do not contain x;
- Q and R do not have variables with H in common;
- R is a non-empty polynomial (since F is not trivially factorable);
- the left-hand side of this product is a non-factorable polynomial.

Then we have $F_{x=0} = R \cdot H$ and also $\frac{\partial F}{\partial x} = Q \cdot H$. Obviously, the both polynomials can be computed in polynomial time. Let y be a variable of F different from x and consider the following derivative of the product of these polynomials:

$$\tfrac{\partial}{\partial y}(Q \cdot R \cdot H^2) = \tfrac{\partial Q}{\partial y}RH^2 + Q\tfrac{\partial}{\partial y}(RH^2) = \tfrac{\partial Q}{\partial y}RH^2 + \tfrac{\partial R}{\partial y}QH^2 + 2\tfrac{\partial H}{\partial y}QRH.$$

Since in $\mathbb{F}_2$ for all z it holds that $2z = z + z = 0$, we have:

$$\tfrac{\partial}{\partial y}(Q \cdot R \cdot H^2) = H^2 \cdot \left(\tfrac{\partial Q}{\partial y}R + \tfrac{\partial R}{\partial y}Q\right) = H^2 \cdot \tfrac{\partial}{\partial y}(Q \cdot R).$$

It follows that in case y is a variable from H, we have $\frac{\partial}{\partial y}(Q \cdot R) = 0$ and thus, $\frac{\partial}{\partial y}(Q \cdot R \cdot H^2) = 0$. Let us now show the opposite, assume that the variable y does not belong to H and prove that the derivative is not equal to zero.

Since y does not belong to H, in general, Q and R have the form

$$Q = Ay + B, \qquad R = Cy + D,$$

for some polynomials A, B, C, D not containing y. Then $Q \cdot R = ACy^2 + (AD + BC)y + BD$ and hence, $\frac{\partial}{\partial y}(Q \cdot R) = AD + BC$.

Thus, we need to show that $AD + BC \neq 0$. Assume the contrapositive, i.e. that $AD + BC = 0$. Note that AD and BC can not be zero, because otherwise at least one of the following holds: $A = B = 0$, $A = C = 0$, $D = B = 0$, or $D = C = 0$. The first two conditions are clearly not the case, since we have assumed that x and y are not contained in H, while the latter conditions yield that F is trivially factorable (wrt the variable y or x, respectively). From this we obtain that $AD + BC = 0$ holds iff $AD = BC$ (since we are in $\mathbb{F}_2$).

Let $B = f_1 \cdot \ldots \cdot f_m$ and $C = g_1 \cdot \ldots \cdot g_n$ be the (unique) factorizations of B and C into non-factorable polynomials. We have $AD = f_1 \cdot \ldots \cdot f_m \cdot g_1 \cdot \ldots \cdot g_n$, thus this may assume that $A = f_1 \cdot \ldots \cdot f_k \cdot g_1 \cdot \ldots \cdot g_l$ for some $0 \leqslant k \leqslant m$ and $0 \leqslant l \leqslant n$ (when $k = l = 0$, we assume that $A = 1$). The polynomials B, C, D can be represented in the same form. Let us denote for some polynomials U, V

---

[2] We note that besides the factors of the form x and $x + 1$, there is a number of other simple cases of factorization that can be recognized easily.

by (U, V) the greatest common divisor of U and V. Then $A = (A, B) \cdot (A, C)$, $B = (A, B) \cdot (D, B)$, similarly for C and D, and we obtain

$$x \cdot Q + R = x \cdot (Ay + B) + (Cy + D) =$$

$$= x \cdot ((A, B)(A, C)y + (A, B)(D, B)) + ((A, C)(D, C)y + (D, B)(D, C)) =$$

$$= ((A, B)x + (D, C))((A, C)y + (D, B)),$$

which is a contradiction, because we have assumed that $x \cdot Q + R$ is non-factorable. We have obtained a procedure for partitioning the variables of F into disjoint sets Σ_1 and Σ_2 in the following way. Having chosen some initial variable x from F, we first assign $\Sigma_1 = \{x\}$, $\Sigma_2 = \varnothing$ and compute the polynomial $Q \cdot R \cdot H^2$ (which equals $\frac{\partial F}{\partial x} \cdot F_{x=0}$). Then for every variable y from F (distinct from x), we compute the derivative $\frac{\partial}{\partial y}(Q \cdot R \cdot H^2)$. If it equals to zero, we put y into Σ_2, otherwise we put y into Σ_1. If at the end we have $\Sigma_2 = \varnothing$, then the polynomial F is non-factorable. Otherwise it remains to apply Lemma 1 to verify whether the obtained sets Σ_1 and Σ_2 indeed correspond to a factorization of F. If the answer is "no", then F is non-factorable, otherwise the polynomials F_1 and F_2 defined in Lemma 1 are the required factors. $\qquad\square$

If n is the size of the input polynomial as a symbol sequence, then it takes $O(n^2)$ steps to compute the polynomial $G = Q \cdot R \cdot H^2$ and test whether the derivative $\frac{\partial G}{\partial y}$ equals zero for a variable y (since identity testing is trivial in $\mathbb{F}_2$). As we must verify this for every variable $y \neq x$, we have a procedure that computes a candidate variable partition in $O(n^3)$ steps. Then it takes $O(n^2)$ time to verify by Lemma 1 whether this partition indeed corresponds to factors of F.

4   Conclusions

We have noted that decomposability is intractable in general for boolean formulas given in CNF or DNF. On the other hand, we have shown the existence of polytime algorithms for computing decomposition components of positive formulas in DNF and formulas given in Full DNF, and the Algebraic Normal Form. We believe that the tractability result on positive DNF can contribute to improving efficiency of existing model counting techniques, while the result on Full DNF can be applied in optimization of boolean functions given by lookup tables. Since AND–decomposability and OR-decomposability are the dual notions, our results are also applicable to the latter case. The factorization algorithm for multivariate polynomials over $\mathbb{F}_2$ given in this paper can be used to implement an efficient solution to disjoint AND-decomposition of formulas in DNF and ANF. It is an open question whether the algorithm can be used for obtaining decompositions of boolean formulas with a non-empty shared set of variables between the components. Further research questions include implementation of the polytime decomposition algorithms and their evaluation on industrial benchmarks for boolean circuits.

Acknowledgements. The first author was supported by the Russian Foundation for Humanities, grant No. 13-01-12003B. The second author was supported by the German Research Foundation within the Transregional Collaborative Research Center SFB/TRR 62 "Companion-Technology for Cognitive Technical Systems".

References

1. Bengtsson, T., Martinelli, A., Dubrova, E.: A fast heuristic algorithm for disjoint decomposition of Boolean functions. In: Notes of the 11th IEEE/ACM International Workshop on Logic & Synthesis (IWLS 2002), pp. 51–55 (2002)

2. Bioch, J.C.: Decomposition of boolean functions. In: Crama, Y., Hammer, P.L. (eds.) Boolean Models and Methods in Mathematics, Computer Science, and Engineering. Encyclopedia of Mathematics and its Applications, vol. 134, pp. 39–78. Cambridge University Press, New York (2010)

3. Chen, H., Janota, M., Marques-Silva, J.: QBF-based boolean function bi-decomposition. In: Proceedings of the Design, Automation & Test in Europe Conference (DATE 2012), pp. 816–819. IEEE (2012)

4. Choudhury, M., Mohanram, K.: Bi-decomposition of large boolean functions using blocking edge graphs. In: Proceedings of the 2010 IEEE/ACM International Conference on Computer-Aided Design (ICCAD 2010), pp. 586–591. IEEE Press, Piscataway (2010)

5. Khatri, S.P., Gulati, K. (eds.): Advanced Techniques in Logic Synthesis, Optimizations and Applications. Springer, New York (2011)

6. Konev, B., Lutz, C., Ponomaryov, D., Wolter, F.: Decomposing description logic ontologies. In: Proceedings of the Twelfth International Conference on Principles of Knowledge Representation and Reasoning (KR 2010). AAAI Press, Palo Alto (2010)

7. Kuon, I., Tessier, R., Rose, J.: FPGA architecture: survey and challenges. Now Publishers Inc, Boston - Delft (2008)

8. Mishchenko, A., Sasao, T.: Large-scale SOP minimization using decomposition and functional properties. In: Proceedings of the 40th ACM/IEEE Design Automation Conference (DAC 2003), pp. 149–154. ACM, New York (2003)

9. Mishchenko, A., Steinbach, B., Perkowski, M.A.: An algorithm for bi-decomposition of logic functions. In: Proceedings of the 38th ACM/IEEE Design Automation Conference (DAC 2001), pp. 103–108. ACM, New York (2001)

10. Morozov, A., Ponomaryov, D.: On decidability of the decomposability problem for finite theories. Siberian Math. J. **51**(4), 667–674 (2010)

11. Perkowski, M.A., Grygiel, S.: A survey of literature on function decomposition, Version IV. PSU Electrical Engineering Department report, Department of Electrical Engineering, Portland State University, Portland, Oregon, USA, November 1995

12. Ponomaryov, D.: On decomposability in logical calculi. Bull. Novosib. Comput. Cent. **28**, 111–120 (2008). http://persons.iis.nsk.su/files/persons/pages/delta-decomp.pdf

13. Ponomaryov, D.: The algorithmic complexity of decomposability in fragments of first-order logic, Research Note. In: Abstract appears in Proceedings Logic Colloquium (2014). http://persons.iis.nsk.su/files/persons/pages/sigdecomp.pdf

14. Shpilka, A., Volkovich, I.: On the relation between polynomial identity testing and finding variable disjoint factors. In: Abramsky, S., Gavoille, C., Kirchner, C., Meyer auf der Heide, F., Spirakis, P.G. (eds.) ICALP 2010. LNCS, vol. 6198, pp. 408–419. Springer, Heidelberg (2010)
15. Steinbach, B., Lang, C.: Exploiting functional properties of Boolean functions for optimal multi-level design by bi-decomposition. Artif. Intell. Rev. **20**(3–4), 319–360 (2003)

A Multi-agent Text Analysis Based on Ontology of Subject Domain

Natalia Garanina[✉], Elena Sidorova, and Eugene Bodin

A.P. Ershov Institute of Informatics Systems,
Lavrent'ev Av., 6, Novosibirsk 630090, Russia
{garanina,lena,bodin}@iis.nsk.su

Abstract. The paper presents a multi-agent approach for ontology population based on natural language semantic analysis. In this multi-agent model, agents of two main kinds interact: information agents correspond to meaningful units of the information being retrieved, and rule agents implement population rules of a given ontology and a semantic-syntactic model of a language.

1 Introduction

At present, ontological knowledge bases are a good solution for storing information from large quantity of documents, and automatic ontology population is necessary.

A multi-agent approach to automatic data processing and ontology population has the following advantages: (1) agents speed up process because they work in parallel; (2) they use data resources effectively, exactly what and when it is necessary; (3) agents can resolve ambiguities by competition. When we consequently process data, we have to examine analyzing rules sequentially in order to find an appropriate rule for each given data item. The multi-agent approach allows to avoid such search.

A multi-agent approach for information retrieval from heterogeneous data sources for ontology population is widespread. In particular, it is used for natural language processing [1, 2, 6, 9] and web processing [3–5]. Agents in these works have different behaviors. Usually in web processing, agents are high-level entities that manage rather data flows, using standard algorithm for knowledge retrieval, than data itself. In natural language processing, agents are either associated with conventional linguistic levels (morphological, syntactic, semantic) or targeted to recognize specific linguistic phenomena such as ellipsis, anaphora, parataxis, homonymy. These agents do not use ontological knowledge substantially. Thus they are computing processes which may speed up information retrieval due to their parallel work but they do not affect the retrieval qualitatively.

The research has been supported by Russian Foundation for Basic Research (grant 13-01-00643) and by Siberian Branch of Russian Academy of Science (Integration Grant n.15/10 "Mathematical and Methodological Aspects of Intellectual Information Systems").

A. Voronkov and I. Virbitskaite (Eds.): PSI 2014, LNCS 8974, pp. 102–110, 2015.
DOI: 10.1007/978-3-662-46823-4_9

Unlike all the above works, our approach uses two kinds of agents, collectively possessing complete information about both data being investigated and a domain-specific ontology. The agents of one kind can analyze ontological (and linguistic) features. They do not use data directly, but they process information provided by agents of the other kind. The latter agents are the most close to the ones from [8], which represent some words from a text.

The idea of our multi-agent approach is that a set of different data items is aggregated into an agent considered as an ontology instance of an object or a relation. This process is assisted by special support agents corresponding to the ontology population rules, which are defined formally. At the beginning, objects and relations significant for the ontology are recognized preliminary in given data, a text in particular. In the latter case, we call these objects *lexical objects* (they correspond to vocabulary terms) and *instance and relation agents* (they correspond to ontology concepts and relations). Let us call the latter *information agents*. Preliminary analysis evaluates some attributes of information agents. The non-evaluated objects of relations and attributes of information agents can be specified as a result of communication between information agents and support *rule agents*. In the process of interaction, the agents establish a correspondence between concepts and relations of the ontology and text units, and thus complete the ontology with specific instances of concepts and relationships.

This paper presents a multi-agent approach for natural language processing which is specialization of the approach for unstructured data processing [7]. We also introduce ways for processing ontology relations and collecting information for resolving data ambiguity. The properties of the obtained multi-agent algorithm remain the same. We give formal descriptions of information and rule agents intended for text analysis.

2   Agent Model

An outline of the approach and the multi-agent system follows. There is an ontology of a subject domain, a set of rules for completing it, a semantic-syntactic model of a sublanguage of the subject domain and a text to extract information for the ontology. The preliminary phase of text processing is executed by an external module of lexical analysis based on a vocabulary of the subject domain. This module constructs (1) a terminological cover, consisting of *lexical objects* which are tagged terms from the text, and (2) a *segment cover* which depicts structure partitions and a genre of the given text. The terminological cover is a basis for an *object cover* which is an ordered set of lexical objects and *instance* agents corresponding to ontology concepts. Lexical objects from the terminological cover are used for evaluating some attributes of instance and relation agents. The *rule* agents implement language processing and ontology population rules. According to data received from instance agents, they generate new attribute values of the instances and relations, send the obtained result to all agents interested in it, or generate new instance or relation agents. Eventually, the information agents assign values to all their attributes that can be evaluated with the information from the text, and the system stops. A special *controller* agent keeps track of system stopping. At the termination moment, the instance agents have accumulated all possible values for each of their attributes. The next stage of the data analysis is to resolve information ambiguities expressed by multiple values of instance agents' attributes. This topic is out of scope of the paper. Formal definitions of covers and agents follow.

An *object cover* OC of a text is a set of *levels*. Each level $l \in OC$ is a triple $l = (id; idx; Obj)$, where

- id is a unique level identifier;
- idx is a text index of the level;
- Obj is a set of lexical objects and instance agents starting from position idx.

This cover is ordered by positions and elements of Obj are ordered by their length. The object cover allows us to deal with homonymy and ambiguity: if this set is one-element then there is no competition for the corresponding word in the text, no homonymy. This cover is also used for checking adjacency.

A *segment cover* SC is a set of segments. Each $s \in SC$ is a triple $s = (id; idx; tp)$, where

- id is a unique segment identifier;
- idx is a text indexes (left and right) of the segment;
- tp is a type (for example, standard segments are a sentence, a paragraph, a clause; segments special for an article genre are a title, a list of authors, an annotation, a bibliography, etc.).

This cover restricts a scope of rule agents. Also rule agents use a segment cover for identifying a degree of text proximity of instance agents.

A set of *lexical objects* LO consists of vocabulary terms from the given text. Each $L \in LO$ is presented by a tuple $L = (id; trm; Cls; MCh; SA; Pos)$, where

- id is a unique object identifier;
- trm is a term from a vocabulary;
- Cls is a set of vocabulary semantic classes of the term;
- MCh is a set of morphological characters;
- SA is a set of semantic attributes;
- $Pos = (t, l, s)$ is a position in the text, where t is the text indexes of the most left and right word of the term, l is an identifier of a level including the term, and s is a set of identifiers of segments including the term.

A set of *instance agents* IA corresponds to ontological instances. Each $I \in IA$ is a tuple $I = (id; Cl; RO; Atr; Rel; SS; Pos)$, where

- id is a unique agent identifier;
- Cl is an ontological class of the agent;
- RO is a set of rule agents that use data included in this instance agent as an argument;

- $Atr = \bigcup_{j \in [1..k]} (a_j, RO_j, v_j, pos_j)$ is a set of attributes of the agent, where for each $j \in [1..k]$ (1) a_j is a name of the agent attribute; (2) every rule agent in set of rule agents RO_j requires the value of attribute a_j to get the result; (3) each value v_j can be a set of identifiers of lexical objects or instance agents; (4) pos_j is a set of closed natural intervals corresponding to the attribute position in the input text;
- Rel is a set of possible relations of the agent; for every $(r, ir) \in Rel$: ir is a set of instance identifiers of relation agent r which include this agent;
- SS is a semantic structure of the agent which is a tree consisting of agents and lexical objects used for its creating and completing of its attributes; a special *base* lexical object or instance agent is the root of this tree;
- $Pos = (t, l, s)$ is a position in the text, where t is text indexes of the most left and right attributes, l is an identifier of the base level, and s is a set of identifiers of segments including the base.

A set of *relation agents* RlA corresponds to binary ontological relations. Each $Rl \in RlA$ is a tuple $Rl = (id; Cl; IR(C_1, C_2); RO)$, where

- id is a unique agent identifier;
- R is an ontological relation of the agent;
- $IR(C_1, C_2) = \bigcup_{i \in [1..k]} ((o_1, o_2)_i, Atr_i, pos_i)$ is a set of relation instances, where for each $i \in [1..k]$ (1) relation objects o_1 and o_2 is an identifier of an instance agent belonging to a predefined ontological classes C_1 and C_2 respectively; (2) every relation attribute $(a, v, pos) \in Atr_i$ with name a has an identifier of a lexical object as attribute value v and text position pos; (3) $pos_i = (Pos_{o_1} \cup Pos_{o_2}) \bigcup (\cup_{(a,v,pos) \in Atr_i} pos)$ is a set of natural intervals corresponding to the agent position in the input data; relation instance is evaluated iff at least two relation objects are evaluated;
- RO is a set of rule agents that use this relation agent as an argument.

Let us define the set of *rule agents* RA, where each $R \in RA$ is a tuple $R = (id; Args; make\_res(args), result)$, where

- id is a unique agent identifier;
- $Args = \cup(arg_1(Cl_1), ..., arg_s(Cl_s))$ is a set of argument vectors, where for each $i \in [1..s]$: arg_i is a set of argument values determined by the corresponding instance or relation agents from ontological class Cl_i or lexical objects from semantical class Cl_i; each value from arg_i is (1) an attribute value provided with the identifier of an instance agent, or (2) an identifier of an instance agent, or (3) an identifier of an instance of a relation agent;
- $make\_res(args)$ is a function computing the result from vector $args \in Args$;
- $result$ is the result of function $make\_res(args)$ which can be (1) empty, if the argument vector is inconsistent; (2) values of some attributes with their positions for some instance agents and/or (3) tuples of values of some objects and attributes with their positions for some relation agents and/or (4) new information agents (they must differ from other agents by their classes and values of attributes).

A structure of a rule agent for natural language processing is the same as for a standard rule agent [7]. But function $make\_res(arg)$ has specialities. First, they concern conformity of arguments and their vectors.

- Restrictions on an argument: (1) semantical restrictions; (2) morphological restrictions on the base; (3) restrictions on the argument's segment.
- Restrictions on an argument vector: (1) segments: values of the vector elements are in the same segment; (2) adjacency of arguments: (a) inclusion, (b) intersection, (c) the most close text positions, (d) separated by a given sign, (e) separated by negligible words and signs, (f) not separated by other arguments of the vector; (3) relative positions of arguments: (a) any position, (b) strong preposition, (c) weak preposition, (d) strong postposition, (e) weak postposition; (4) semantic-syntactic matching: consistency of arguments' bases of an instance argument or arguments themselves of a lexical argument w.r.t. the given semantic-syntactic model of terms; (5) semantic matching: consistency of instance arguments w.r.t. the given ontology.

Second, a rule agent can deal with semantically homogenous groups. It uses the following types of binding semantically homogenous arguments into a group. Arguments can be (1) separated by a given sign; (2) separated by negligible words and signs; (3) not separated by any other arguments.

Third, a rule agent also has specific regulations for making the result. If an argument vector (or at least one of its arguments) does not satisfy the restrictions used by the rule agent then the result of $make\_res$ is empty. In the other case the argument vector is stored in special set *Success* for further forming homogenous groups if necessary. When the result includes a value of the attribute of an instance agent then we update the semantic structure of this agent. In this update its base lexical object can be changed. Let the result be a new instance agent. The base of this agent is the argument specified by the rule. Other arguments are included into the semantical structure of the new agent.

In the next section we give a brief overview of interactions of the above information and rule agents.

3   Multi-agent Algorithm for Text Analysis

Multi-agent system **MDA** for text analysis includes information agents sets, a rule agents set, and an agent-controller. The result of agent interactions by protocols below is text analysis, when the information agents determine the possible values of their attributes and objects from a given text. All agents execute their protocols in parallel. That is, all agents act in parallel until it happens that none of the rule agents can proceed. This termination event is determined by the controller agent. We use an original algorithm for termination detection which is based on activity counting. The system is dynamic because rule agents can create new information agents.

The agents are connected by duplex channels. The controller agent is connected with all agents, instance agents are connected with their relation agents, and all information agents are connected with their rule agents. Messages are transmitted instantly via a reliable medium and stored in channels until being read.

Let $IA = \{I_1, ..., I_n, ...\}$ be an instance agents set, $RlA = \{Rl_1, ..., Rl_m, ...\}$ be a relation agents set, and $RA = \{R_1, ..., R_s\}$, be a rule agents set. Let $\mathtt{Ii}$ be a protocol of actions of instance agent I_i, $\mathtt{Rlj}$ be a protocol of actions of relation agent Rl_j, and $\mathtt{Rk}$, be the protocol of actions of rule agent R_k, $\mathtt{C}$ be the protocol of actions of an agent-controller C. Then multi-agent data analysis algorithm MDA can be presented in pseudocode as follows:

```
MDA::
    parallel {I1} ...{In} ...{Rl1} ...{Rlm} ...{R1} ...{Rs} {C}
```

Here the `parallel` operator means that all execution flows (threads) in the set of braces are working in parallel. Brief descriptions of the protocols follow. Let further C be the controller agent; R, R_{ij} be rule agents; I be an instance agent; A be an information agent; `mess` be a message (special for every kind of agents); $Input$ be a set of incoming messages. For the simplicity, we suggest that rule agents produce results with at most one attribute per an instance agent and/or at most one instance of a relation per a relation agent. This case could be easily generalized for multiple results.

An informal description of the instance agent protocol. In the first phase of its activities the instance agent sends evaluated data to all rule agents interested in this data. The agent processes the received data by updating its attributes and relations, sending their fresh values to rule agents interested in. Every change of the activity is reported to the controller agent. The instance agent terminates if it receives the stop message from the controller agent.

Protocol of instance agents
$I::$
```
1.   send |RO|+1 to C;
2.   forall R ∈ RO send id to R;
3.   forall aᵢ ∈ Atr
4.       if aᵢ ≠ ∅ then { send |ROᵢ| to C;
5.           forall Rᵢⱼ ∈ ROᵢ send aᵢ to Rᵢⱼ;}
6.   send −1 to C;
7.   while (true){
8.    if Input ≠ ∅ then {
9.        mess = get_mess(Input);
10.       if mess.name = C then break;
11.       if mess.name ∈ Rel then upd_Rel(mess.name, mess.id);
12.       if mess.name = aᵢ then {
13.           upd(aᵢ, mess.val);
14.           send |ROᵢ| to C;
15.           forall Rᵢⱼ ∈ ROᵢ send aᵢ to Rᵢⱼ; }
16.       send −1 to C; } }
```

An informal description of the relation agent protocol. In the first phase of its activities the relation agent sends evaluated data to all rule agents interested in this data and instance agents involved in this data. The agent processes the received data by updating instances of its objects and attributes, sending identifiers of these fresh instances to instance agents included into evaluated tuples of data. Every change of the activity is reported to the controller agent. The relation agent terminates if it receives the stop message from the controller.

Protocol of relation agents
$Rl::$

```
1.   send 1 to C;
2.   forall ir_i ∈ IR
3.      if evaluated(ir_i) then {
4.         send |RO| + |Obj_i| to C;
5.         forall R ∈ RO send (id, ir_i) to R;
6.         forall I ∈ Obj_i send (id, ir_i) to I;
7.   send -1 to C;
8.   while (true){
9.      if Input ≠ ∅ then {
10.        mess = get_mess(Input);
11.        if mess.name = C then break;
12.        upd_Rel(mess.id, mess.value);
13.        i = mess.id
14.        send |RO| + |Obj_i| to C;
15.        forall R ∈ RO send (id, i) to R;
16.        forall I ∈ Obj_i send (id, i) to I;
17.        send -1 to C; }}
```

An informal description of the rule agent protocol. It has two parallel subprocesses: processing incoming data from information agents (`ProcInput`) and producing the outcoming result (`ProcResult`). Processing incoming data includes (1) forming argument vectors, and (2) sending argument vectors or an indication of termination to `ProcResult`. Producing the outcoming result includes (1) checking conformity of arguments and argument vectors, (2) processing semantically homogenous groups (if necessary), (3) making the result, which can include new attribute values for some information agents and/or new information agents, and (4) determining agents for sending new values to. New information agents start immediately with data given them by the rule agent at birth. Every change of the activity is reported to the controller agent. The rule agent terminates if it receives the stop message from the controller agent.

Protocol of rule agents
$R ::$

```
  SendList: set of Instance Agents = ∅;
1. parallel
2.   { ProcInput_R; ProcResult_R; }
ProcInput_R ::
```

```
args: set of vectors of Argument;
1.   while (true) {
2.       if Input ≠ ∅ then {
3.           mess = get_mess(Input);
4.           if mess.name = C then {
5.               send 'stop' to ProcResult_R;
6.               break; }
7.           if mess.name = A then {
8.               args = make_arg(mess.value, A);
9.               if (args ≠ ∅) send ( args ) to ProcResult_R;
10.              send |args| − 1 to C; }}}
ProcResult_R ::
  arg: vector of Argument∪{'stop'};
1.   while (true) {
2.       if Input ≠ ∅ then {
3.           arg = get_mess(Input);
4.           if arg = 'stop' then break;
5.           (result, SendList) = make_res(arg);
6.           if result ≠ ∅ then {
7.               start_new_information_agents;
8.               send |SendList| to C;
9.               forall A ∈ SendList send result(A) to A;}
10.          send −1 to C; }}
```

The main job of the controller agent is to sequentially calculate other agents' activities. If all agents are inactive, the agent sends them the stop message.

Protocol of agent-controller C

```
C ::
  Act: integer;
  Input: set of integer;
1.   Act = 0;
2.   while( Input = ∅ ) { }
3.   while(true){
4.     if( Input ≠ ∅ ) then Act = Act + get_mess(Input);
5.     if( Input = ∅ and Act = 0 ) then break; }
6.   send STOP to all;
```

The following proposition is a straight consequence of Proposition 1 from [7]:

Proposition 1. *Multi-agent system* **MDA** *terminates and the agent-controller determines the termination moment correctly.*

4   Conclusion

The proposed approach aims at taking advantage of the agent-based approach to knowledge representation and processing. Thus, using the agent-based technology allows to avoid unnecessary information retrieval, since at any given time, only information required for an agent is being searched for. Furthermore, due to the agents work in parallel, the speed of data processing increases.

Note that this paper presents only a basic formal model of agents' interaction that implements a model of the first stage of data analysis, which does not handle specific problems related to ambiguity of an input text. The ambiguities could be resolved by selecting the most appropriate value of every instance attribute from the values obtained at the previous stage. This selection can be made by more powerful agents able to work cooperatively, to compete, etc.

References

1. Aref, M.M.: A multi-agent system for natural language understanding. In: International Conference on Integration of Knowledge Intensive Multi-Agent Systems, p. 36 (2003)
2. Carvalho, A.M.B.R., de Paiva, D.S., Sichman, J.S., da Silva, J.L.T., Wazlawick, R.S., de Lima, V.L.S.: Multi-agent systems for natural language processing. In: Garijo, F.J., Lemaitre, C. (eds.) Multi Agent Systems Models Architecture and Appications, Proceedings of the II Iberoamerican Workshop on D.A.I. and M.A.S, pp. 61–69, Toledo, Spain, 1–2 October 1998
3. Banares-Alcantara R., Jimenez R., Aldea L.: Multi-agent systems for ontology-based information retrieval. In: European Symposium on Computer-Aided Chemical Engineering-15 (ESCAPE-15), Barcelona, Espana (2005)
4. Cheng, X., Xie, Y., Yang, T.: Study of multi-agent information retrieval model in semantic web. In: Proceedings of the 2008 International Workshop on Education Technology and Training and 2008 International Workshop on Geoscience and Remote Sensing (ETTANDGRS 2008), vol. 02, pp. 636–639 (2008)
5. Clark, K.L., Lazarou, V.S.: A multi-agent system for distributed information retrieval on the world wide web. In: Proceedings of the 6th Workshop on Enabling Technologies on Infrastructure for Collaborative Enterprises, pp. 87–93 (1997)
6. Fum, D., Guida, G., Tasso, C.: A Distributed multi-agent architecture for natural language processing. In: Proceedings of the 12th Conference on Computational Linguistics (COLING 1988), vol. 2, pp. 812–814 (1988)
7. Garanina, N., Sidorova, E., Bodin, E.: A multi-agent approach to unstructured data analysis based on domain-specific ontology. In: Proceedings of the 22nd International Workshop on Concurrency, Specification and Programming, CEUR Workshop Proceedings, Warsaw, Poland, vol. 1032, pp. 122–132, 25–27 September 2013
8. Minakov, I., Rzevski, G., Skobelev, P., Volman, S.: Creating contract templates for car insurance using multi-agent based text understanding and clustering. In: Mařík, V., Vyatkin, V., Colombo, A.W. (eds.) HoloMAS 2007. LNCS (LNAI), vol. 4659, pp. 361–370. Springer, Heidelberg (2007)
9. dos Santos, C.T., Quaresma, P., Rodrigues, I., Vieira, R.: A multi-agent approach to question answering. In: Vieira, R., Quaresma, P., Nunes, M.G.V., Mamede, N.J., Oliveira, C., Dias, M.C. (eds.) PROPOR 2006. LNCS (LNAI), vol. 3960, pp. 131–139. Springer, Heidelberg (2006)

Towards High-Level Programming for Systems with Many Cores

Sergei Gorlatch$^{(\boxtimes)}$ and Michel Steuwer

University of Muenster, Münster, Germany
{gorlatch,michel.steuwer}@wwu.de

Abstract. Application development for modern high-performance systems with many cores, i.e., comprising multiple Graphics Processing Units (GPUs) and multi-core CPUs, currently exploits low-level programming approaches like CUDA and OpenCL, which leads to complex, lengthy and error-prone programs. In this paper, we advocate a high-level programming approach for such systems, which relies on the following two main principles: (a) the model is based on the current OpenCL standard, such that programs remain portable across various many-core systems, independently of the vendor, and all low-level code optimizations can be applied; (b) the model extends OpenCL with three high-level features which simplify many-core programming and are automatically translated by the system into OpenCL code. The high-level features of our programming model are as follows: (1) memory management is simplified and automated using parallel container data types (vectors and matrices); (2) a data (re)distribution mechanism supports data partitioning and generates automatic data movements between multiple GPUs; (3) computations are precisely and concisely expressed using parallel algorithmic patterns (skeletons). The well-defined skeletons allow for semantics-preserving transformations of SkelCL programs which can be applied in the process of program development, as well as in the compilation and optimization phase. We demonstrate how our programming model and its implementation are used to express several parallel applications, and we report first experimental results on evaluating our approach in terms of program size and target performance.

1 Introduction

Modern computer systems become increasingly many-core as they comprise, in addition to multi-core CPUs, also *Graphics Processing Units* (GPUs), Intel Xeon Phi Coprocessors, FPGA, etc. with hundreds and thousands of cores.

The application programming for many-core systems is currently quite complex and error-prone. As the most prominent example, GPUs are programmed using explicit, low-level programming approaches CUDA [17] and OpenCL [13]. Even on a system with one GPU, the programmer is required to explicitly manage GPU's memory, including memory (de)allocations and data transfers, and also to explicitly describe parallelism in the application.

© Springer-Verlag Berlin Heidelberg 2015
A. Voronkov and I. Virbitskaite (Eds.): PSI 2014, LNCS 8974, pp. 111–126, 2015.
DOI: 10.1007/978-3-662-46823-4_10

For multi-GPU systems, CUDA and OpenCL make programs even more complex, as codes must explicitly implement data exchanges between the GPUs, as well as disjoint management of individual GPU's memories, with low-level pointer arithmetics and offset calculations.

In this paper, we address these main challenges of the contemporary many-core programming, and we present the *SkelCL (Skeleton Computing Language)* – our high-level approach to program many-core systems with multiple GPUs.

The SkelCL programming model extends the standard OpenCL approach with the following high-level mechanisms:

(1) *parallel container data types:* data containers (e.g., vectors and matrices) that are automatically managed on GPUs' memories in the system;
(2) *data (re)distributions:* a mechanism for specifying suitable data distributions among the GPUs in the application program and automatic runtime data re-distribution when necessary;
(3) *parallel skeletons:* pre-implemented high-level patterns of parallel computation and communication, customizable to express application-specific parallelism and combinable to larger application codes.

The high-level, formally defined programming model of SkelCL allows for semantics-preserving transformations of programs for many-cores. Transformations can be used in the process of high-level program development and in optimizing the implementation of SkelCL programs.

The remainder of the paper is structured as follows. In Sect. 2 we describe our high-level programming model and we illustrate its use for several example applications in Sect. 3. Section 4 discusses using transformations for optimizing skeleton programs, and Sect. 5 presents our current SkelCL library implementation. Section 6 reports experimental evaluation of our approach regarding program size and performance. We compare to related work and conclude in Sect. 7.

2   SkelCL: Programming Model and Library

In this section, we first explain our main design principles for a high-level programming model. We present the high-level features of the SkelCL model and illustrate them using well-known use cases of parallel algorithms.

2.1   SkeCL as Extension of OpenCL

We develop our SkelCL [21] programming model as an extension of the standard OpenCL programming model [13], which is currently the most popular approach to programming heterogeneous systems with various accelerators, independently of the vendor. At the same time, SkelCL aims at overcoming the problematic aspects of OpenCL which make its use complicated and error-prone for the application developer.

In developing SkelCL, we follow two major principles:

First, we take the existing OpenCL standard as the basis for our approach. SkelCL inherits all advantageous properties of OpenCL, including its portability across different heterogeneous parallel systems and low-lev code optimization possibilities. Moreover, this allows the application developers to remain in the familiar programming environment, develop portable programs for various many-core systems of different vendors, and apply the proven best practices of OpenCL program development and optimization.

Second, our model extends OpenCL gradually: the program developer can either design the program from the initial algorithm at a high level of abstraction while some low-level parts are expressed in OpenCL, or the developer can decide to start from an existing OpenCL program and to replace some parts of the program in a step-by-step manner by corresponding high-level constructs. In both cases, the main benefit of using SkelCL is a simplified software development, which results in a shorter, better structured high-level code and, therefore, the overall maintainability is greatly improved.

SkelCL is designed to be fully compatible with OpenCL: arbitrary parts of a SkelCL code can be written or rewritten in OpenCL, without influencing program's correctness. While the main OpenCL program is executed sequentially on the CPU – called the *host* – time-intensive computations are offloaded to parallel processors – called *devices*. In this paper, we focus on systems comprising multiple GPUs as accelerators, therefore, we use the terms CPU and GPU, rather than more general OpenCL terms host and device.

2.2   Parallel Container Data Types

The first aspect of traditional OpenCL programming which complicates application development is that the programmer is required to explicitly manage GPU's memory (including memory (de)allocations, and data transfers to/from the system's main memory). In our high-level programming model, we aim at making collections of data (containers) automatically accessible to all GPUs in the target system and at providing an easy-to-use interface for the application developer. SkelCL provides the application developer with two container classes – vector and matrix – which are transparently accessible by both, the CPU and the GPUs. The *vector* abstracts a one-dimensional contiguous memory area, and the *matrix* provides a convenient access to a two-dimensional memory area.

In a SkelCL program, a vector object is created and filled with data as in the following example (matrices are created and filled analogously):

```
Vector<int> vec(size);
for (int i = 0; i < vec.size(); ++i){ vec[i] = i; }
```

The main advantage of the parallel container data types in SkelCL as compared with the corresponding data types in OpenCL is that the necessary data transfers between the memories of the CPU and GPUs are performed by the system implicitly, as explained further in the implementation section.

2.3   Data (Re-)Distributions

To achieve scalability of applications on systems comprising multiple GPUs, it is crucial to decide how the application's data are distributed across all available GPUs. Applications often require different distributions for their computational steps. Distributing and re-distributing data between GPUs in OpenCL is cumbersome because data transfers have to be managed manually and performed via the (host) CPU. Therefore, it is important for a high-level programming model to allow both for describing the data distribution and for changing the distribution at runtime, such that the system takes care of the necessary data movements.

SkelCL offers the programmer a *distribution* mechanism that describes how a particular container is distributed among the available GPUs. The programmer can abstract from explicitly managing memory ranges which are spread or shared among multiple GPUs: the programmer can work with a distributed container as a self-contained entity.

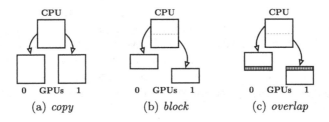

Fig. 1. Distributions of a matrix in SkelCL (without `single`).

SkelCL currently offers four kinds of distribution: *single*, *copy*, *block*, and *overlap*. Figure 1 shows how a matrix can be distributed on a system with two GPUs. The *single* distribution (omitted in the figure) means that matrix whole data is stored on a single GPU (the first GPU if not specified otherwise). The *copy* distribution in Fig. 1 copies matrix data to each available GPU. By the *block* distribution, each GPU stores a contiguous, disjoint chunk of the matrix. The *overlap* distribution splits the matrix into one chunk for each GPU; in addition, each chunk contains a number of continuous rows from the neighboring chunks. Figure 1c illustrates the overlap distribution: GPU 0 receives the top chunk ranging from the top row to the middle, while GPU 1 receives the second chunk ranging from the middle row to the bottom.

2.4   Patterns of Parallelism (Skeletons)

While the concrete operations performed in an application are (of course) application-specific, the general structure of parallelization often follows common parallel patterns that are reused in different applications. For example, operations can be performed for every entry of an input vector, which is the well-known *map* pattern of data-parallel programming, or two vectors are combined element-wise into an output vector, which is again the common *zip* pattern of parallelism.

SkelCL extends OpenCL by introducing such high-level programming patterns, called *algorithmic skeletons* [10]. Formally, a skeleton is a higher-order function that executes one or more user-defined (so-called *customizing*) functions in a pre-defined parallel manner, while hiding the details of parallelism and communication from the user. We show here for brevity the definitions of some basic skeletons on a vector data type. We do this semi-formally, with v, vl and vr denoting vectors with elements v_i, vl_i and vr_i where $0 < i \leq n$, correspondingly:

- The *map skeleton* applies a unary customizing function f to each element of an input vector v, i.e.:

$$map \ f \ [v_1, v_2, \ldots, v_n] = [f(v_1), f(v_2), \ldots, f(v_n)]$$

- The *zip skeleton* operates on two vectors vl and vr, applying a binary customizing operator $\oplus$ pairwise:

$$zip \ (\oplus) \ [vl_1, vl_2, \ldots, vl_n] \ [vr_1, vr_2, \ldots, vr_n] =$$
$$[vl_1 \oplus vr_1, vl_2 \oplus vr_2, \ldots, vl_n \oplus vr_n]$$

- The *reduce skeleton* computes a scalar value from a vector using a binary associative operator $\oplus$, i.e.:

$$red \ (\oplus) \ [v_1, v_2, \ldots, v_n] = v_1 \oplus v_2 \oplus \cdots \oplus v_n$$

These basic skeletons can be composed to express more complex algorithms. For example, the dot product of two vectors a and b of length d is defined as:

$$dotProduct(a, b) = \sum_{k=1}^{d} a_k \cdot b_k \tag{1}$$

which can be easily expressed using our basic skeletons zip and reduce, customized by multiplication and addition, correspondingly:

$$dotProduct(a, b) = red \ (+) \ (\ zip \ (\cdot) \ a \ b \ ) \tag{2}$$

As an example of a non-basic skeleton, we present here the *allpairs skeleton*. All-pairs computations occur in a variety of applications, ranging from pairwise Manhattan distance computations in bioinformatics [6] to N-Body simulations in physics [4]. These applications follow a common computation scheme: for two sets of entities, the same computation is performed for all pairs of entities from the first set combined with entities from the second set. We represent entities as d-dimensional vectors, and sets of entities as corresponding matrices.

The allpairs skeleton with a customizing binary operation $\oplus$ on vectors is defined as follows:

$$allpairs(\oplus) \left(\begin{bmatrix} a_{1,1} & \cdots & a_{1,d} \\ \vdots & & \vdots \\ a_{n,1} & \cdots & a_{n,d} \end{bmatrix}, \begin{bmatrix} b_{1,1} & \cdots & b_{1,d} \\ \vdots & & \vdots \\ b_{m,1} & \cdots & b_{m,d} \end{bmatrix} \right) \overset{\text{def}}{=} \begin{bmatrix} c_{1,1} & \cdots & c_{1,m} \\ \vdots & & \vdots \\ c_{n,1} & \cdots & c_{n,m} \end{bmatrix},$$

with entries $c_{i,j}$ computed as follows: $c_{i,j} = [a_{i,1} \cdots a_{i,d}] \oplus [b_{j,1} \cdots b_{j,d}]$.

Let us consider a first simple example application which can be expressed by customizing the allpairs skeleton with a particular function $\oplus$. The Manhattan distance (or L_1 distance) is defined for two vectors, v and w, of equal length d:

$$ManDist(v, w) = \sum_{k=1}^{d} |v_k - w_k| \tag{3}$$

In [6], the so-called Pairwise Manhattan Distance (*PMD*) is studied as a fundamental operation in hierarchical clustering for data analysis. *PMD* is obtained by computing the Manhattan distance for every pair of rows of a given matrix. This computation for arbitrary matrix A can be expressed using the allpairs skeleton customized with the Manhattan distance defined in (3):

$$PMD(A) = allpairs(ManDist)(A, A) \tag{4}$$

3   Programming in SkelCL

In original OpenCL, computations are expressed as *kernels* which are executed in a parallel manner on a GPU: the application developer must explicitly specify how many instances of a kernel are launched. In addition, kernels usually take pointers to GPU memory as input and contain program code for reading/writing single data items from/to it. These pointers have to be used carefully, because no boundary checks are performed by OpenCL.

The programming model of SkelCL differs from OpenCL: rather than writing low-level kernels, the application developer customizes suitable skeletons by providing application-specific functions which are often much simpler than kernels as they specify an operation on basic data items rather than containers. Skeletons are created as objects by providing customizing functions which, for technical reasons, must not be recursive and may only contain OpenCL C (not C++) code.

3.1   Example: Dot Product of Vectors

Equation (2) expresses the dot product of two vectors as a composition of two skeletons, zip and reduce. In SkelCL, a zip skeleton object customized by multiplication is created and then used as follows:

```
1  skelcl::init(); /* initialize SkelCL */
2  /* create skeleton objects: */
3  Zip<float>    mult(
4    "float mult(float x,float y) {return x*y;}");
5  Reduce<float> sum (
6    "float func(float x,float y) {return x+y;}");
7  /* create input vectors and fill with data: */
8  Vector<float> A(SIZE); fillVector(A);
9  Vector<float> B(SIZE); fillVector(B);
10 /* execute skeleton objects: */
11 Vector<float> C = sum( mult(A,B) );
```

Listing 1.1. A SkelCL code for computing the dot product of two vectors

$$Zip<float> mult("float func(float x,float y){ return x*y;}");$$
$$resultVector = mult(leftVector, rightVector);$$

The necessary reduce skeleton customized by addition is created similarly as an object and then called as follows:

$$Reduce<float> sum("float func(float x,float y){ return x+y;}");$$
$$result = sum(inputVector);$$

These definitions lead directly to the SkelCL code for dot product shown in Listing 1.1 (8 lines of code plus comments). The OpenCL-based implementation of dot product provided by NVIDIA [17] requires 68 lines (kernel function: 9 lines, host program: 59 lines), i.e., it is significantly longer than our SkelCL code.

3.2 Example: Matrix Multiplication

Matrix multiplication is a basic linear algebra operation, which is a building block of many scientific applications. An $n \times d$ matrix A is multiplied by a $d \times m$ matrix B, producing an $n \times m$ matrix $C = A \times B$ whose element $C_{i,j}$ is computed as the dot product of the ith row of A with jth column of B. The matrix multiplication can be expressed using the allpairs skeleton introduced in Sect. 2.4 as follows:

$$A \times B = allpairs(dotProduct)\left(A, B^T\right) \tag{5}$$

where B^T is the transpose of matrix B.

Listing 1.2 shows the SkelCL program for computing matrix multiplication using the *allpairs* skeleton; the code follows directly from the skeleton formulation (5). In the first line, the SkelCL library is initialized. Skeletons are implemented as classes in SkelCL and customized by instantiating a new object, like in line 2. The **Allpairs** class is implemented as a template class specified with the data type of matrices involved in the computation (**float**). This way the implementation can ensure the type correctness by checking the types of the arguments when the skeleton is executed in line 10. The customizing function – specified as a string (lines 3–7) – is passed to the constructor. SkelCL defines custom data types (**float_vector_t** in line 3) for representing vectors in the code of the customizing function. Helper functions are used for accessing elements from the row of matrix A and the column of matrix B (line 6). The transpose of matrix B required by the definition (5) is implicitly performed by accessing elements from the columns of B using the helper function `getElementFromCol`. After initializing the two input matrices (line 8 and 9), the calculation is performed in line 10.

4   Transformation Rules for Optimization

Our approach is based on formally defined algorithmic skeletons. This allows for systematically applying semantics-preserving transformations to SkelCL programs with the goal of their optimization. In this section, we briefly illustrate two types of transformation rules: *specialization rules* and *(de)composition rules*.

4.1   Specialization Rule: Optimizing the Allpairs Skeleton

Specialization rules enable optimizations of skeleton implementations using additional, application-specific semantical information. We illustrate specialization for our allpairs skeleton and the matrix multiplication example. If the customizing function f of the allpairs skeleton can be expressed as a sequential composition (denoted with ∘) of zip and reduce customized with a binary operator ⊙ and a binary, associative operator ⊕.:

$$f = reduce \ (\oplus) \ \circ \ zip \ (\odot) \tag{6}$$

then an optimized implementation of the allpairs skeleton for multiple GPUs can be automatically derived as described in detail in [20].

By expressing the customizing function of the allpairs skeleton as a zip-reduce composition, we provide additional semantical information about the memory access pattern of the customizing function to the skeleton implementation, thus allowing for improving the performance. The particular optimization using (6) takes into account the OpenCL programming model that organizes *work-items* (i.e., threads executing a kernel) in *work-groups* which share the same GPU local memory. By loading data needed by multiple work-items of the same work-group into the fast local memory, we can avoid repetitive accesses to the slow

```
1   skelcl::init();
2   Allpairs<float> mm(
3     "float func(float_vector_t ar, float_vector bc) {\
4     float c = 0.0f;\
5     for (int i = 0; i < length(ar); ++i) {\
6       c += getElementFromRow(ar,i) * getElementFromCol(bc,i);}\
7     return c; }");
8   Matrix<float> A(n, k); fill(A);
9   Matrix<float> B(k, m); fill(B);
10  Matrix<float> C = mm(A, B);
```

Listing 1.2. Matrix multiplication in SkelCL using the *allpairs* skeleton.

```
1  skelcl::init();
2  Zip<float> mult(
3     "float func(float x, float y) { return x*y; }");
4  Reduce<float> sum_up(
5     "float func(float x, float y) { return x+y; }");
6  Allpairs<float> mm(sum_up, mult);
7  Matrix<float> A(n, d); fill(A);
8  Matrix<float> B(d, m); fill(B);
9  Matrix<float> C = mm(A, B);
```

Listing 1.3. Matrix multiplication in SkelCL using the specialized *allpairs* skeleton.

global memory. The semantical information of the zip-reduce pattern allows the implementation to load chunks of both involved vectors into the small local memory and reduce them there, before processing the next chunks. That means that the two skeletons zip and reduce are not executed one after the other, but rather the optimized implementation interleaves these two steps. This results in a significant performance gain, as described in Sect. 6.

For the Pairwise Manhattan Distance, we can express the customizing function as a zip-reduce composition, using the binary operator $a\ominus b = |a-b|$ as customizing function for zip, and addition as customizing function for the reduce skeleton:

$$ManDist(a,b) = \sum_{i=1}^{n} |a_i - b_i| = (reduce\ (+)\ \circ zip\ (\ominus))\ [a_1 \cdots a_n]\ [b_1 \cdots b_n]$$

Similarly, as already demonstrated by (2), dot product (which is the customizing function of allpairs for matrix multiplication) can be expressed as a zip-reduce composition. The corresponding optimized SkelCL code is shown in Listing 1.3. In lines 2 and 3, the zip skeleton is defined using multiplication as customizing function and in lines 4 and 5, the reduce skeleton is customized with addition. These two customized skeletons are passed to the allpairs skeleton on its creation in line 6. This triggers our specialization rule and an optimized implementation is generated. In line 9, the skeleton is executed taking two input matrices and producing the output matrix.

Currently, SkelCL implements such customization of the allpairs skeleton by a combination of the zip and reduce skeleton as a special case. Therefore, the allpairs skeleton in Listing 1.3 accepts a zip and reduce skeleton as customizing functions instead of a string as shown earlier in Listing 1.2. We plan to generalize this in the future and allow arbitrary skeletons to be used as customizing functions of other skeletons – of course when the types match.

4.2   Composition Rules: Optimizing Scan and Reduce

In this section we present examples of composition rules which allow the application programmer to systematically apply transformations to SkelCL programs with the goal of optimization.

Our examples involve the scan skeleton (a. k. a. prefix-sum) which yields an output vector with each element obtained by applying a binary associative operator $\oplus$ to the elements of the input vector up to the current element's index:

$$scan\ (\oplus)\ [v_1, v_2, \ldots, v_n] = [v_1, v_1 \oplus v_2, \ldots, v_1 \oplus v_2 \oplus \cdots \oplus v_n]$$

The scan skeleton has been well studied and used in many parallel applications [5].

– **Scan-Reduce Composition:** This rule allows for a composition of scan followed by reduction to be expressed as a single reduction operating on pairs of values. For arbitrary binary, associative operators $\oplus$ and $\otimes$, such that $\otimes$ distributes over $\oplus$, it holds:

$$red(\oplus) \circ scan(\otimes)\ =\ \pi_1 \circ red\,(\langle\!\langle \oplus, \otimes \rangle\!\rangle) \circ map\,pair \qquad (7)$$

where function $pair$, π_1 and operator $\langle \oplus, \otimes \rangle$ are defined as follows:

$$pair\ a\ \overset{\text{def}}{=}\ (a, a), \qquad (8)$$

$$\pi_1\,(a, b)\ \overset{\text{def}}{=}\ a, \qquad (9)$$

$$(s_1, r_1)\,\langle \oplus, \otimes \rangle\,(s_2, r_2)\ \overset{\text{def}}{=}\ (s_1 \oplus (r_1 \otimes s_2), r_1 \otimes r_2) \qquad (10)$$

– **Scan-Scan Composition:** This rule allows to replace two repetitive scan skeletons by a single one.
   For associative operators $\oplus$ and $\otimes$, where $\otimes$ distributes over $\oplus$,

$$scan\,(\oplus)\ \circ\ scan\,(\otimes)\ =\ map\,\pi_1 \circ scan\,(\langle\!\langle \oplus, \otimes \rangle\!\rangle) \circ map\,pair \qquad (11)$$

Besides composing skeletons together, it also sometimes pays off to decompose them, for example to split a reduction into multiple steps (so-called decomposition rule). The motivation, proof of correctness and a discussion of the performance benefits of the composition and decomposition rules can be found in [11].

5   Implementation of SkelCL

SkelCL is implemented as a C++ library which generates valid OpenCL code from SkelCL programs. The customizing functions provided by the application developer is combined with skeleton-specific OpenCL code to generate an OpenCL kernel function, which is eventually executed on a GPU. A customized skeleton can be executed on both single- and multi-GPU systems. In case of a multi-GPU system, the calculation specified by a skeleton is performed automatically on all GPUs available in the system.

   Skeletons operate on container data types (in particular vectors and matrices) which alleviate the memory management of GPUs. The SkelCL implementation namely ensures that data is copied automatically to and from GPUs, instead of manually performing data transfers as required in OpenCL. Before performing a

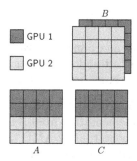

Fig. 2. Data distributions used for a system with two GPUs: matrices A and C are block distributed, matrix B is copy distributed.

computation on container types, the SkelCL system ensures that all input containers' data is available on all participating GPUs. This may result in implicit (automatic) data transfers from the CPU to GPU memory, which in OpenCL would require explicit programming. Similarly, before any data is accessed on the CPU, the implementation of SkelCL ensures that this data on the CPU is up-to-date by performing necessary data transfers implicitly and automatically.

For multi-GPU systems, the application developer can use the distributions directives of SkelCL introduced in Sect. 2.3 to specify how data is distributed across the GPUs in the system. If no distribution is set explicitly then every skeleton implementation selects a suitable default distribution for its input and output containers. Containers' distributions can be changed at runtime: this implies data exchanges between multiple GPUs and the CPU, which are performed by the SkelCL implementation implicitly. Implementing such data transfers in the standard OpenCL is a cumbersome task: data has to be downloaded to the CPU before it is uploaded to the GPUs, including the corresponding length and offset calculations; this results in a lot of low-level code which becomes completely hidden when using SkelCL.

For example, two SkelCL distributions are used in our multi-GPU implementation of the allpairs skeleton, as shown in Fig. 2: Matrix B is *copy* distributed, i.e., it is copied entirely to all GPUs in the system. Matrix A and C are *block* distributed, i.e., they are row-divided into as many equally-sized blocks as GPUs are available; each block is copied to its corresponding GPU. Following these distributions, each GPU computes one block of the result matrix C. In the example with two GPUs shown in Fig. 2, the first two rows of C are computed by GPU 1 and the last two rows by GPU 2. The allpairs skeleton uses these distributions by default; therefore, no changes to the already discussed SkelCL codes for matrix multiplication are necessary for using multiple GPUs.

The object-oriented design of SkelCL allows the developers to extend it easily: e.g., in order to add a new skeleton to SkelCL, a new class with the skeleton's implementation has to be provided, while all existing classes and concepts/data containers and data distributions) can be freely reused.

6   Experimental Evaluation

We use matrix multiplication as an example to evaluate our SkelCL implementations regarding programming effort and performance. We compare the following six implementations of the matrix multiplication:

1. the OpenCL implementation from [14] without optimizations,
2. the optimized OpenCL implementation from [14] using GPU local memory,
3. the optimized BLAS implementation by AMD [2] written in OpenCL,
4. the optimized BLAS implementation by NVIDIA [16] written in CUDA,
5. the SkelCL implementation using the generic allpairs skeleton (Listing 1.2),
6. the SkelCL implementation optimized using specialization (Listing 1.3).

6.1   Programming Effort

As the simplest criterion for estimating the programming effort, we use the program size in lines of code (LoC). Figure 3 shows the number of LoCs required for each of the six implementations. We did not count those LoCs which are not relevant for parallelization and are similar in all six implementations, like initializing the input matrices with data and checking the result for correctness. For every implementation, we distinguish between CPU code and GPU code. For the OpenCL implementations, the GPU code is the kernel definition; the CPU code includes the initialization of OpenCL, memory allocations, explicit data transfer operations, and management of the execution of the kernel. For the BLAS implementations, the CPU code contains the initialization of the corresponding BLAS library, memory allocations, as well as a library call for performing the matrix multiplication; no definition of GPU code is necessary, as the GPU code is defined inside the library function calls. For the generic allpairs skeleton (Listing 1.2), we count lines 1–2 and 8–10 as the CPU code, and the definition of the customizing function in lines 3–7 as the GPU code. For the allpairs skeleton customized with zip-reduce (Listing 1.3), lines 3 and 5 are the GPU code, while all other lines constitute the CPU code.

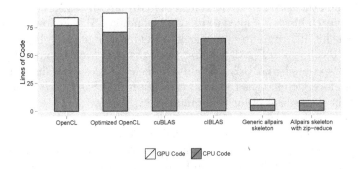

Fig. 3. Programming effort (Lines of Code) of all compared implementations.

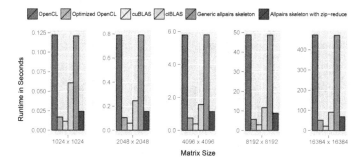

Fig. 4. Runtime of different matrix multiplication implementations on a NVIDIA system for different sizes for the matrices.

As expected, both skeleton-based implementations are clearly the shortest due to using high-level constructs, with 10 and 9 LoCs, correspondingly. The next shortest implementation is the cuBLAS implementation with 65 LoCs – 7 times longer than the SkelCL implementations. The other implementations require even 9 times more LoCs than the SkelCL implementation. Besides their length, the other implementations require the application developer to perform many low-level, error-prone tasks, like dealing with pointers or offset calculations. Furthermore, the skeleton-based implementations are more general, as they can be used for arbitrary allpairs computations, while the OpenCL and CUDA implementations perform matrix multiplication only.

6.2   Performance Experiments

We performed our performance experiments with the six different implementations of matrix multiplication on a test system using a host PC with a quad-core CPU (Intel Xeon E5520, 2.26 GHz) and 12 GB of memory, connected to a Tesla S1070 computing system equipped with 4 Tesla GPUs. Its dedicated 16 GB of memory (4 GB per GPU) is accessed with up to 408 GB/s (102 GB/s per GPU). Each GPU comprises 240 streaming processor cores running at 1.44 GHz. In all experiments, we include the time of data transfers to/from the GPU, i.e. the measured runtime consists of: (1) uploading the input matrices to the GPU; (2) performing the actual matrix multiplication; (3) downloading the computed result matrix.

Using one GPU. Figure 4 shows the runtime in seconds of all six implementations for different sizes of the matrices (note that for readability reasons, all charts are scaled differently). Clearly, the unoptimized OpenCL- and SkelCL-based implementations are the slowest, because both do not use the fast GPU local memory, in contrast to all other implementations. The SkelCL implementation optimized with specialization rule performs between 5.0 and 6.8 times faster than the implementation using the generic allpairs skeleton, but is 33 % slower on 16384×16384 matrices than the optimized OpenCL implementation using

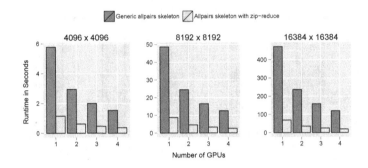

Fig. 5. Runtime of the allpairs based implementations using multiple GPUs.

local memory. However, the latter implementation works only for square matrices and, therefore, omits many conditional statements and boundary checks. Not surprisingly, cuBLAS by NVIDIA is the fastest of all implementations, as it is manually tuned for NVIDIA GPUs using CUDA. The clBLAS implementation by AMD using OpenCL is apparently well optimized for AMD GPUs but performs poorly on other hardware. Our optimized allpairs skeleton implementation outperforms the clBLAS implementation for all matrix sizes tested.

Using multiple GPUs. Figure 5 shows the runtime behavior of both implementations using the allpairs skeleton on up to four GPUs of our multi-GPU system. The other four implementations (OpenCL and CUDA) are not able to handle multiple GPUs and would have to be specially rewritten for such systems. We observe a good scalability of our skeleton-based implementations, achieving speedups between 3.09 and 3.93 when using four GPUs.

7   Conclusion and Related Work

This paper presents the SkelCL high-level programming model for multi-GPU systems and its implementation as a library. SkelCL is built on top of the OpenCL standard which provides familiar programming environment for application developers, portability across various many-core platforms of different vendors, and proven best practices of OpenCL programming and optimization. Our SkelCL approach significantly raises OpenCL's low level of abstraction: it offers parallel patterns to express computations, parallel container data types for simplified memory management and a data (re)distribution mechanism to improve scalability in systems with multiple GPUs. Our data dustributions can be viewed as instances of *covers* [15,19] which define a general framework for reasoning about possible distributions of data. Semantic-preserving transformation rules allows for systematically optimizing SkelCL programs. The SkelCL library is available as open source software from http://skelcl.uni-muenster.de.

There are other approaches to simplify GPU programming. *SkePU* [8] and *Muesli* [9] are fairly similar to SkelCL, but greatly differ in their focus and implementation, as discussed in [21]. There exist wrappers for OpenCL or CUDA as well as convenient libraries for GPU Computing, most popular of them are *Thrust* [12] and *Bolt* [3]. Compiler-based approaches similar to the popular Open-MP [18] include *OpenACC* [1] and *OmpSs-OpenCL* [7]. While reducing boilerplate in GPU-targeted applications, these approaches do not simplify the programming process by introducing high-level abstractions as done in SkelCL.

Acknowledgments. This work is partially supported by the OFERTIE (FP7) and MONICA projects. We would like to thank the anonymous reviewers for their valuable comments, as well as NVIDIA for their generous hardware donation used in our experiments.

References

1. OpenACC application program interface. Version 1.0 (2011)
2. AMD. AMD APP SDK code samples. Version 2.7, February 2013
3. AMD. Bolt – A C++ template library optimized for GPUs (2013)
4. Arora, N., Shringarpure, A., Vuduc, R.W.: Direct N-body kernels for multicore platforms. In: 2012 41st International Conference on Parallel Processing, pp. 379–387. IEEE Computer Society, Los Alamitos (2009)
5. Blelloch, G.E.: Prefix sums and their applications. In: Sythesis of Parallel Algorithms, pp. 35–60. Morgan Kaufmann Publishers Inc. (1990)
6. Chang, D.-J., Desoky, A.H., Ouyang, M., Rouchka, E.C.: Compute pairwise manhattan distance and pearson correlation coefficient of data points with GPU. In: 10th ACIS International Conference on Software Engineering, Artificial Intelligences, Networking and Parallel/Distributed Computing, pp. 501–506 (2009)
7. Elangovan, V.K., Badia, R.M., Parra, E.A.: OmpSs-OpenCL programming model for heterogeneous systems. In: Kasahara, H., Kimura, K. (eds.) LCPC 2012. LNCS, vol. 7760, pp. 96–111. Springer, Heidelberg (2013)
8. Enmyren, J., Kessler. C.: SkePU: a multi-backend skeleton programming library for multi-GPU systems. In: Proceedings 4th International Workshop on High-Level Parallel Programming and Applications (HLPP-2010), pp. 5–14 (2010)
9. Ernsting, S., Kuchen, H.: Algorithmic skeletons for multi-core, multi-GPU systems and clusters. Int. J. High Perform. Comput. Netw. **7**(2), 129–138 (2012)
10. Gorlatch, S., Cole, M.: Parallel skeletons. In: Padua, D.A. (ed.) Encyclopedia of Parallel Computing, pp. 1417–1422. Springer, US (2011)
11. Gorlatch, S., Lengauer, C.: (De)Composition rules for parallel scan and reduction. In: Proceedings of the 3rd International Working Conference on Massively Parallel Programming Models (MPPM'97), pp. 23–32. IEEE Computer Society Press (1998)
12. Hoberock, J., Bell, N.: (NVIDIA). Thrust: a parallel template, Library (2013)
13. Khronos Group. The OpenCL specification, Version 2.0, November 2013
14. Kirk, D.B., Hwu, W.W.: Programming Massively Parallel Processors - A Hands-on Approach. Morgan Kaufman, San Francisco (2010)
15. Nitsche, T.: Skeleton implementations based on generic data distributions. In: 2nd International Workshop on Constructive Methods for Parallel Programming (2000)
16. NVIDIA. CUBLAS (2013). http://developer.nvidia.com/cublas
17. NVIDIA. NVIDIA CUDA SDK code samples. Version 5.0, February 2013

18. OpenMP Architecture Review Board. OpenMP API. Version 4.0 (2013)
19. Pepper, P., Südholt. M.: Deriving parallel numerical algorithms using data distribution algebras: Wang's algorithm. In: 30th Annual Hawaii International Conference on System Sciences (HICSS), pp. 501–510 (1997)
20. Steuwer, M., Friese, M., Albers, S., Gorlatch, S.: Introducing and implementing the allpairs skeleton for programming multi-GPU systems. Int. J. Parallel Prog. **42**(4), 601–618 (2013)
21. Steuwer, M., Gorlatch, S.: SkelCL: enhancing OpenCL for high-level programming of multi-GPU systems. In: Malyshkin, V. (ed.) PaCT 2013. LNCS, vol. 7979, pp. 258–272. Springer, Heidelberg (2013)

Inductive Prover Based on Equality Saturation for a Lazy Functional Language

Sergei Grechanik[(⊠)]

Keldysh Institute of Applied Mathematics, Russian Academy of Sciences,
4 Miusskaya sq., Moscow 125047, Russia
sergei.grechanik@gmail.com

Abstract. The present paper shows how the idea of equality saturation can be used to build an inductive prover for a non-total first-order
lazy functional language. We adapt equality saturation approach to a
functional language by using transformations borrowed from supercompilation. A special transformation called merging by bisimilarity is used
to perform proof by induction of equivalence between nodes of the E-
graph. Equalities proved this way are just added to the E-graph. We
also experimentally compare our prover with HOSC and HipSpec.

1 Introduction

Equality saturation [18] is a method of program transformation that uses a
compact representation of multiple versions of the program being transformed.
This representation is based on E-graphs (graphs whose nodes are joined into
equivalence classes [4,14]) and allows us to represent a set of equivalent programs, consuming exponentially less memory than representing it as a plain set.
Equality saturation consists in enlarging this set of programs by applying certain axioms to the E-graph until there's no axiom to apply or the limit of axiom
applications is reached. The axioms are applied non-destructively, i.e. they only
add information to the E-graph (by adding nodes, edges and equivalences).

Equality saturation has several applications. It can be used for program optimization – in this case after the process of equality saturation is finished, a single
program should be extracted from the E-graph. It can also be used for proving
program equivalence (e.g. for translation validation [17]) – in this case program
extraction is not needed.

In the original papers equality saturation is applied to imperative languages.
In this paper we describe how equality saturation can be applied to the task
of proving equivalence of functions written in a lazy functional language. This
task is important for proving algebraic properties like monadic laws or some
laws concerning natural numbers and lists. Since such properties require proof
by induction, we introduce a special transformation called merging by bisimilarity which essentially proves by induction that two terms are equivalent. This

Supported by Russian Foundation for Basic Research grant No. 12-01-00972-a and
RF President grant for leading scientific schools No. NSh-4307.2012.9.

A. Voronkov and I. Virbitskaite (Eds.): PSI 2014, LNCS 8974, pp. 127–141, 2015.
DOI: 10.1007/978-3-662-46823-4_11

transformation may be applied repeatedly, which gives an effect of discovering and proving lemmas needed for the main goal.

The main contributions of this paper are: (1) we apply the equality saturation approach to a lazy functional language; (2) we propose to merge classes of the E-graph even if they represent functions equal only up to argument permutation; (3) we articulate the merging by bisimilarity transformation.

The paper is organized as follows. In Sect. 2 we briefly describe equality saturation and how functional programs and their sets can be represented by E-graphs. Then in Sect. 3 we discuss basic transformations which we apply to the E-graph. Section 4 deals with the merging by bisimilarity transformation. In Sect. 5 we present experimental evaluation of our prover. Section 6 discusses related work and Sect. 7 concludes the paper.

The source code of our experimental prover can be found on GitHub [1].

2   Programs and E-graphs

An E-graph is a graph enriched with information about equivalence of its nodes by means of splitting them into equivalence classes. In our case, an E-graph essentially represents a set of (possibly recursive) terms and a set of equalities on them, closed under reflexivity, transitivity and symmetry. If we use the congruence closure Algorithm [14], then the set of equalities will also be closed under congruence. The E-graph representation is very efficient and often used for solving the problem of term equivalence.

If we have some axioms about our terms, we can also apply them to the E-graph, thus deducing new equalities from the ones already present in E-graph (which in its turn may lead to more axiom application opportunities). This is what equality saturation basically is. So, the process of solving the problem of function/program equivalence using equality saturation is as follows:

1. Convert both function definitions to E-graphs and put both of them into a single E-graph.
2. Transform the E-graph using some axioms (transformations) until the target terms are in the same equivalence class or no more axioms are applicable. This process is called saturation.

In pure equality saturation approach axioms are applied non-destructively and result only in adding new nodes and edges, and merging of equivalence classes, but in our prover we apply some axioms destructively, removing some nodes and edges. This makes the result of the saturation dependent on the order of axiom application, so we restrict it to breadth-first order. This deviation is essential for performance reasons.

In this paper we will use a lazy first-order subset of Haskell. To illustrate how programs are mapped into graphs, let's consider the program in Fig. 1a. This program can be naturally represented as a graph, as shown in Fig. 1b. Each node represents a basic language construct (pattern matching, constructor, variable, or explicit substitution – we'll explain them in Sect. 2.1). If a node

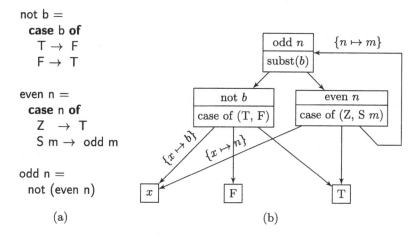

```
not b =
  case b of
    T → F
    F → T


even n =
  case n of
    Z  → T
    S m → odd m


odd n =
  not (even n)
```

         (a)   (b)

Fig. 1. A program and its graph representation

corresponds to some named function, its name is written in the top part of it. Some nodes are introduced to split complex expressions into basic constructs and don't correspond to any named functions. Recursion is simply represented by cycles. Some nodes are shared (in this example these are the variable x and the constructor T). Sharing is very important since it is one of the things that enable compactness of the representation.

Some of the edges are labeled with renamings. Actually, all edges are labeled with renamings, but identity renamings are not drawn. These renamings are very important – without them we would need different nodes for each variable, and we couldn't merge nodes representing the same function modulo renaming, which would increase space consumption (such functions often appear during transformation). Merging up to renaming will be discussed in Sect. 2.2.

Note also that we use two methods of representing function calls. If all the arguments are *distinct* variables, then we can simply use a renaming (the function odd is called this way). If the arguments are more complex, then we use explicit substitution which is very similar to function call but has more fine-grained reduction rules. We can use explicit substitutions even if the arguments are distinct variables, but it's more expensive than using renamings (and actually we have an axiom to transform such explicit substitutions to renamings). Note that we require an explicit substitution to bind *all* variables of the expression being substituted.

The same way graphs naturally correspond to programs, E-graphs naturally correspond to programs with multiple function definitions. Consider the following "nondeterministic" program:

not b = **case** b **of** { T → F; F → T }

even n = **case** n **of** { Z → T; S m → odd m }
odd n = **case** n **of** { Z → F; S m → even m }

```
odd n = not (even n)
even n = not (odd n)
```

This program contains multiple definitions of the functions even and odd, but all the definitions are actually equivalent. This program can also be represented as a graph, but there will be multiple nodes corresponding to functions even and odd. If we add the information that nodes corresponding to the same function are in the same equivalence class, we get an E-graph. We won't show here a picture of this E-graph to save space, and will use "nondeterministic" programs to describe E-graphs from here on.

E-graphs are also useful for representing compactly sets of equivalent programs. Indeed, we can extract individual programs from an E-graph by choosing a single node for each equivalence class, or in other words, a single definition for each function. However, we cannot pick the definitions arbitrarily. For example, the following program isn't equivalent to the one above:

```
not b = case b of { T → F; F → T }

odd n = not (even n)
even n = not (odd n)
```

This problem should be taken into account not only when performing program extraction, but also during certain complex transformations like merging by bisimilarity which we will discuss in Sect. 4.

2.1   Node Labels

In this section we'll discuss how node labels correspond to language constructs.

First of all, each node of an E-graph is a member of some equivalence class. We will use symbols $f, g, h, \ldots$ to denote nodes as well as corresponding functions. Each node has a label $L(f)$ and a set of input variables $V(f)$ (in the implementation variables are numbered, but in this paper we treat them as named). $V(f)$ may decrease with graph evolution, and it should be kept up to date because we need $V(f)$ to perform some transformations (keeping it up to date is beyond the scope of this paper). Each edge of an E-graph is labeled with an injective renaming, its domain being the set of input variables of the edge's destination node. We will use the notation $f = L \rightarrow \theta_1 g_1, \ldots, \theta_n g_n$ to describe a node f with a label L and outgoing edges with renamings θ_i and destinations g_i. We will write $f \cong g$ to denote that f and g are from the same equivalence class.

There are only four kinds of node labels:

- $f = x$. (Variable/identity function). We use the convention that the identity function always takes the variable x, and if we need some other variable, we adjust it with a renaming. Code example: f x = x

- $f = \text{subst}(x_1, \ldots, x_n) \rightarrow \xi h, \theta_1 g_1, \ldots, \theta_n g_n$. (Explicit substitution/function call/let expression). An explicit substitution substitutes values $\theta_i g_i$ for the variables x_i in ξh. We require it to bind *all* the variables of ξh. Explicit substitution nodes usually correspond to function calls:

  f x y = h (g1 x) (g2 y) (g3 x y)

  They may also correspond to non-recursive let expressions, or lambda abstractions immediately applied to the required number of arguments:

  f x y = **let** { u = g1 x; v = g2 y; w = g3 x y } **in** h u v w
       = (λ u v w . h u v w) (g1 x) (g2 y) (g3 x y)

  But to describe E-graph transformations we will use the following non-standard (but hopefully more readable) postfix notation:

  f x y = h u v w { u = g1 x, v = g2 y, w = g3 x y }

- $f = C \rightarrow \theta_1 g_1, \ldots, \theta_n g_n$. (Constructor). Code example:

  f x y = C (g1 x) (g2 y) (g3 x y)

- $f = \text{caseof}(C_1 \overline{x_1}, \ldots, C_n \overline{x_n}) \rightarrow \xi h, \theta_1 g_1, \ldots, \theta_n g_n$. (Pattern matching). This label is parametrized with a list of patterns, each pattern is a constructor name and a list of variables. The corresponding case bodies ($\theta_i g_i$) don't have to use all the variables from the pattern. ξh represents the expression being scrutinized. Code example:

  f x y = **case** h x **of**
          S n $\rightarrow$ g1 y n
          Z $\rightarrow$ g2 x

We will also need an operation of adjusting a node with a renaming. Consider a node $f = L \rightarrow \theta_1 g_1, \ldots, \theta_n g_n$ and a renaming ξ. Suppose, we want to create a function $f' = \xi f$ (f' is f with parameters renamed). Then we can adjust outgoing edges of f with ξ (unless $f = x$ in which case it doesn't have outgoing edges). We will use the following notation for this operation:

$$f' = \xi(L \rightarrow \theta_1 g_1, \ldots, \theta_n g_n)$$

The operation is defined as follows:

$$\xi(C \rightarrow \theta_1 g_1, \ldots, \theta_n g_n) = C \rightarrow (\xi \circ \theta_1) g_1, \ldots, (\xi \circ \theta_n) g_n$$
$$\xi(\text{subst}(\ldots) \rightarrow \zeta h, \theta_1 g_1, \ldots, \theta_n g_n) =$$
$$\text{subst}(\ldots) \rightarrow \zeta h, (\xi \circ \theta_1) g_1, \ldots, (\xi \circ \theta_n) g_n$$
$$\xi(\text{caseof}(\ldots) \rightarrow \zeta h, \theta_1 g_1, \ldots, \theta_n g_n) =$$
$$\text{caseof}(\ldots) \rightarrow (\xi \circ \zeta) h, (\xi'_1 \circ \theta_1) g_1, \ldots, (\xi'_n \circ \theta_n) g_n$$

In the last case each ξ'_i maps the variables bound by ith pattern to themselves and works as ξ on all the other variables.

2.2 Merging

One of the basic operations of the E-graph is merging of equivalence classes. Usually it is done after applying axioms that result in adding new equalities between nodes. In the case of simple equalities like $f = g$ we should simply merge the corresponding equivalence classes. But we also want to merge functions which are equal only up to some renaming, so should take into account equalities of the form $f = \theta g$ where θ is some non-identity renaming. In this case we should first adjust renamings on edges so that the equation becomes of the form $f = g$ and then proceed as usual.

Consider the equation $f = \theta g$. Let's assume that g is not a variable node (x) and it's not in the same equivalence class with a variable node (otherwise we can rewrite the equation as $g = \theta^{-1} f$, and if they both were equal to a variable node then our E-graph would be self-contradictory). Now for each node h in the same equivalence class with g (including g) we should perform the following:

1. Adjust the outgoing edges of h with θ using previously described node adjustment operation.
2. For each edge incoming into h replace its renaming, say, ξ, with a renaming $\xi \circ \theta^{-1}$

After the adjustment the equation becomes $f = g$ and we can merge the equivalence classes.

Note that this procedure works if f and g aren't in the same equivalence classes. If they are then the equation looks like $f = \theta f$ and should be modelled with an explicit substitution.

3 Axioms

3.1 Congruence

The most common cause of equivalence class merging is equivalence by congruence, that is if we know that $a = f(b)$, $c = f(d)$ and $b = d$, then we can infer that $a = c$. Note that usually this kind of merging is not explicitly formulated as an axiom, but we prefer to do it explicitly for uniformity. Also, in our case the axiom should also take into account that we want to detect equivalences up to some renaming. Here is the axiom written as an inference rule, we will later refer to it as (cong):

$$\frac{f = L \to \theta_1 h_1, \ldots, \theta_n h_n \quad \exists \xi : g = \xi(L \to \theta_1 k_1, \ldots, \theta_n k_n) \quad \forall i \; h_i \cong k_i}{g = \xi f}$$

It says that if we have a node f and a node g that is equivalent to f adjusted with some renaming ξ, then we can add the equality $g = \xi f$ to the E-graph. This axiom is advantageous to apply as early as possible since it results in merging of equivalence classes, which reduces duplication and gives more opportunities for applying axioms. Also note that to make the search for the appropriate ξ faster, it is beneficial to represent nodes in normal form:

$$f = \zeta(L \rightarrow \theta_1 g_1, \ldots, \theta_n g_n)$$

Where θ_i are as close to identity renamings as possible, so to find ξ we should just compare the ζ's.

3.2 Semantics of Explicit Substitutions

In this and the next sections we will write axioms in a less strict but more human-readable form. A rewriting rule $E_1 \mapsto E_2$ means that if we have a node f_1 representing the expression E_1, then we can add an equality $f_1 = f_2$ to the E-graph where f_2 is the node representing E_2 (which should also be added to the E-graph unless it's already there). We use the compact postfix notation to express explicit substitutions. We use letters $e, f, g, h, \ldots$ to represent nodes whose structure doesn't matter. We sometimes write them applied to variables they use $(f\ x\ y)$, but if variables don't really matter, we omit them. Note that the presented rules can be generalized to the case when pattern matchings have arbitrary number of branches and functions take arbitrary number of arguments, we just use minimal illustrative examples for the sake of readability.

In Fig. 2 four axioms of explicit substitutions are shown. All of them basically describe how to evaluate a node if it is an explicit substitution. The answer is to push the substitution down (the last three rules) until we reach a variable where we can just perform the actual substitution (the first rule, (subst-id)). The appropriate rule depends on the node we choose as the leftmost child of our substitution node – there are four kinds of nodes, so there are four rules.

(subst-id)	$x\ \{x = g\} \mapsto g$
(subst-subst)	$f\ x\ \{x = g\ y\}\ \{y = h\} \mapsto f\ x\ \{x = g\ y\ \{y = h\}\}$
(subst-constr)	$C\ (f\ x)\ (g\ x)\ \{x = h\} \mapsto C\ (f\ x\ \{x = h\})\ (g\ x\ \{x = h\})$
(subst-case-of)	$(\mathbf{case}\ f\ x\ \mathbf{of}\ C\ y \rightarrow g\ x\ y)\ \{x = h\} \mapsto$
	$\qquad \mathbf{case}\ f\ x\ \{x = h\}\ \mathbf{of}\ C\ y \rightarrow g\ x\ y\ \{x = h,\ y = y\}$

Fig. 2. Axioms of explicit substitutions

Usually substitution in the body of a function is performed as an indivisible operation, but this kind of transformation would be too global for an E-graph, so we use explicit substitutions to break it down.

There are two more rather technical but nonetheless important axioms concerning substitution. The first one is elimination of unused variable bindings:

(subst-unused)	$f\ x\ y\ \{x = g,\ y = h,\ z = k\} \mapsto f\ x\ y\ \{x = g,\ y = h\}$

When this axiom is applied *destructively* (i.e. the original node is removed), it considerably simplifies the E-graph. This axiom is the reason why we need the information about used variables in every node.

The second axiom is conversion from a substitution that substitutes variables for variables to a renaming:

$$(\text{subst-to-renaming}) \qquad f\,x\,y\,\{x = y,\ y = z\} \ \mapsto\ f\,y\,z$$

Note though that application of this axiom results in merging of the equivalence classes corresponding to the node representing the substitution and the node f, so if they are already in the same class, this axiom is inapplicable. We also apply this axiom destructively.

3.3 Semantics of Pattern Matching

The axioms concerning pattern matching are shown in Fig. 3. The first of them, (case-of-constr), is essentially a reduction rule: if the scrutinee is an expression starting with a constructor, then we just substitute appropriate subexpressions into the corresponding case branch.

(case-of-constr) $(\textbf{case}\ C\,e\ \textbf{of}\ C\,y \to f\,x\,y) \mapsto$
$\qquad\qquad f\,x\,y\,\{x = x,\ y = e\}$

(case-of-case-of) $(\textbf{case}\ (\textbf{case}\ e\ \textbf{of}\ C_1\,y \to g)\ \textbf{of}\ C_2\,z \to h) \mapsto$
$\qquad\qquad \textbf{case}\ e\ \textbf{of}\ C_1\,y \to (\textbf{case}\ g\ \textbf{of}\ C_2\,z \to h)$

(case-of-id) $(\textbf{case}\ x\ \textbf{of}\ C\,y\,z \to f\,x\,y\,z) \mapsto$
$\qquad\qquad \textbf{case}\ x\ \textbf{of}\ C\,y\,z \to f\,x\,y\,z\,\{x = (C\,y\,z),\ y = y,\ z = z\}$

Fig. 3. Axioms of pattern matching

The next two axioms came from supercompilation [16,19]. They tell us what to do when we get stuck during computation because of missing information (i.e. a variable). The axiom (case-of-case-of) says that if we have a pattern matching that scrutinizes the result of another pattern matching, then we can pull the inner pattern matching out. The axiom (case-of-id) is responsible for positive information propagation: if a case branch uses the variable being scrutinized, then it can be replaced with its reconstruction in terms of the pattern variables.

3.4 Axioms Applied Destructively

We apply some transformations destructively, i.e. remove the original nodes and edges that triggered the transformation. It is a necessary deviation from pure equality saturation. The transformations we apply destructively are (subst-id), (subst-unused), (subst-to-renaming), and (case-of-constr). We have tried to switch on and off their destructivity. Turned out that non-destructive (case-of-constr) leads to a lot of failures on our test suite due to timeouts, but helps to pass an additional test. Non-destructive (subst-unused) has a similar effect. Non-destructivity of (subst-id) and (subst-to-renaming) doesn't impede the ability of our tool to pass tests from our test suite but when either of them is non-destructive, our tool becomes about 15 % slower. We also tried to make *all* the mentioned transformations non-destructive which rendered our tool unusable.

4   Merging by Bisimilarity

The axiom of congruence can merge two functions into one equivalence class if they have the same tree representation. But if their definitions involve separate (but equal) cycles, then the congruence axiom becomes useless. Consider the following two functions:

$$f = S\ f;\ \ g = S\ g$$

If they aren't in the same equivalence class in the first place, none of the already mentioned axioms can help us equate them. Here we need some transformation that is aware of recursion.

The general idea of the transformation is to find two bisimilar subgraphs growing from the two given nodes from different equivalence classes and merge these equivalence classes if the subgraphs have been found. Note though that not every subgraph is suitable. Consider the following nondeterministic program:

$$f\ x = C;\qquad g\ x = D$$
$$f\ x = f\ (f\ x);\ g\ x = g\ (g\ x)$$

The functions f and g are different but they both are idempotent, so we have two equal closed subgraphs "defining" the functions:

$$f\ x = f\ (f\ x);\ g\ x = g\ (g\ x)$$

Of course, we cannot use subgraphs like these to decide whether two functions are equal, because they don't really define the functions, they just state that they have the property of idempotence. So we need a condition that guarantees that there is (semantically) only one function satisfying the subgraph.

In our implementation we require all the recursive calls of a subgraph to be either guarded or structural (we use the same algorithm as in Agda and Foetus [2]). These syntactic conditions are usually used in total languages, but they can nevertheless be used in languages with bottoms. Merging by bisimilarity is actually a special case of proving term equivalence by induction (in the case of structurality condition) and by coinduction (in the case of of guardedness condition). Of course, this method of ensuring uniqueness may reject some subgraphs having a single fixed point, because the problem is undecidable in general. Note also that this is not the only possible method of ensuring uniqueness. For example, we could use ticks [11,15]. Tick transformations could be encoded as axioms for equality saturation.

4.1   Algorithm Description

In this subsection we'll describe the algorithm we use to figure out if two nodes suspected of being equal have two bisimilar subgraphs growing from them and

function MERGE-BY-BISIMILARITY(m, n)
    if BISIMILAR?(m, n, $\varnothing$) **then** MERGE(m, n)

function BISIMILAR?(m, n, history)
    if $m \cong n$ **then return** true
    else if $\exists(m', n') \in$ history $: m' \cong m \wedge n' \cong n$ **then**
        if the uniqueness condition is met **then**
            return true
        else
            return false
    else if m and n are incompatible **then return** false
    else
        for $(m', n') : m' \cong m \wedge n' \cong n \wedge$ label(m') = label(n') **do**
            children_pairs = zip(children(m'), children(n'))
            if length(children(m')) = length(children(n'))
                and $\forall (m'', n'') \in$ children_pairs
                        BISIMILAR?(m'', n'', $\{(m', n')\} \cup$ history) **then**
            return true
        return false

Fig. 4. Merging by bisimilarity

meeting the uniqueness condition. First of all, the problem of finding two bisimilar subgraphs is a variation of the subgraph bisimulation problem which is NP-complete [5]. The merging by bisimilarity algorithm that we use in our implementation is outlined in Fig. 4. It checks (using the function BISIMILAR?) if there are two bisimilar subgraphs meeting the uniqueness condition, and if there are, merges the equivalence classes of the nodes. Checking for bisimilarity essentially consists in simultaneous depth-first traversal of the E-graph from the given nodes. Actually this process resembles supercompilation.

The function BISIMILAR? works as follows. If the two nodes are equal, then they are bisimilar and we return true. If we encounter a previously visited pair of nodes (up to $\cong$), we check if the uniqueness condition holds, and if it does, we return true (this case corresponds to folding in supercompilation) and otherwise we stop trying and return false (this case doesn't guarantee that there's no bisimulation, but we do it for efficiency). Then we check if the two nodes are at least compatible (again, for efficiency reasons, we could do without it in theory). That means that there are no nodes equal to them that have incompatible labels, like different constructors or a constructor and a pattern matching on a variable. If the labels are compatible, we go on and check all pairs of nodes equivalent to the original ones. If there is a pair of nodes such that their children are bisimilar, then the original pair is bisimilar.

Note that in our description of the algorithm we ignored the question of renamings. We did it for the sake of brevity, and actually (since we want to merge nodes even if they are equal only up to some renaming) we should take them into account which complicates the real implementation a little bit.

5   Experimental Evaluation

We've used a set of simple equations to evaluate our prover and compare it to similar tools. The results are shown in Table 1. We gave each tool 5 min to prove each equation. Wall-clock time in seconds is given for successful runs.

The tests can be found in our repository [1], for some of them we gave human-readable equations in the second column – note though that real equations are often a bit more complex because we have to make sure that they hold in a non-total language. The tests are divided into two groups: the upper group (kmp-eq and all the tests above it) consists of equations which can be proved simply by driving, and the rest of the tests need something more complex.

The tools we used in our benchmarking are:

- **graphsc.** It is our prover described in this paper.
- **hosc.** HOSC is a supercompiler designed for program analysis, including the problem of function equivalence [8]. It uses the following technique: first super-compile left hand side and right hand side separately and then syntactically compare the residual programs [10,13].
- **hl hosc.** Higher-level version of HOSC [9,11]. It can use lemmas which are also proved by supercompilation.
- **hipspec.** HipSpec [3] is an inductive prover for Haskell which can generate conjectures by testing, prove them using an SMT-solver, and then use them as lemmas to prove the goal and other conjectures. Since HipSpec assumes totality, it is not fair to compare other tools to pure HipSpec (the column "hipspec (total)"), so we also used a trick to encode programs operating on data with bottoms as total programs by adding additional bottom constructor to each data type. The results of HipSpec on these adjusted tests are shown in the column "hipspec (bot)".

Overall, there is no clear winner among the tested tools. Some conclusions may be drawn from the results:

- First of all, HipSpec in total mode proves most of the equalities, which is expected. Most of the equalities it doesn't prove involve infinite data structures which aren't fully supported (yet).
- HipSpec is much less powerful on tests adjusted with bottoms. Indeed, partial equalities are often a bit trickier to prove than their total counterparts. It is also possible that this particular approach of reducing a partial problem to a total one and then using a total prover is not very efficient.
- Graphsc and HipSpec don't work very well on examples that need deep driving like the KMP-test (kmp-eq). In the case of Graphsc it is concerned with its breadth-first approach to transformation.
- Graphsc cannot solve tasks that need nontrivial generalizations.
- HOSC is very fast for this task. This seems to be due to depth-first nature of traditional supercompilers. HipSpec sometimes is very fast, and sometimes it gets lost in proving irrelevant conjectures. Our tool seems to be somewhere in the middle.

Table 1. Comparison of different tools on the test set

		graphsc	hosc	hl hosc	hipspec (bot)	hipspec (total)
add-assoc	$x + (y + z) = (x + y) + z$	1.6	0.5	0.6	6.1	0.8
append-assoc	$x ++ (y ++ z) = (x ++ y) ++ z$	1.8	0.5	0.6	2.4	2.0
double-add	double (x+y) = double x + double y	2.2	0.6	0.6	14.5	0.9
even-double	even (double x) = true	1.7	0.6	0.6	38.7	48.2
ho/concat-concat	concat (concat xs) = concat (map concat xs)	3.2	0.6	0.7	85.3	43.9
ho/map-append	map f (xs ++ ys) = map f xs ++ map f ys	2.1	0.6	0.7	7.5	2.3
ho/map-comp	map (f . g) xs = (map f . map g) xs	3.4	0.6	0.6	4.6	4.9
idnat-idemp	idNat (idNat x) = idNat x	1.5	0.5	0.5	0.8	0.7
take-length	take (length x) x = x	2.3	0.6	0.6	4.5	3.5
length-concat	length (concat x) = sum (map length x)	2.8	0.7	0.8	fail	4.0
inf	fix S = fix S	1.2	0.4	0.5	fail	fail
add-assoc-bot		2.1	0.6	0.6	fail	fail
ho/church-id	unchurch (church x) = x	6.1	0.6	0.6	fail	fail
ho/church-pred		fail	0.7	0.8	fail	fail
kmp-eq		fail	1.2	1.7	fail	fail
ho/filter-append	filter p (xs ++ ys) = filter p xs ++ filter p ys	3.0	0.6	0.8	6.4	2.6
ho/fold-append	foldr f (foldr f a ys) xs = foldr f a (xs ++ ys)	2.1	0.6	0.7	176.5	3.5
ho/map-concat	map f (concat x) = concat (map (map f) x)	2.8	0.6	0.7	87.7	44.6
ho/map-filter	filter p (map f xs) = map f (filter (p . f) xs)	3.6	0.7	0.7	5.1	5.0
take-drop	drop n (take n x) = []	2.4	0.6	0.7	20.3	4.5
shuffled-let		1.5	0.5	0.5	fail	fail
mul-double	x * double y = double (x*y)	5.1	0.6	fail	91.3	77.1
mul-distrib	(x*y) + (z*y) = (x + z)*y	3.9	0.7	fail	62.0	41.9
mul-assoc	(x * y) * z = x * (y * z)	11.6	0.8	fail	85.9	15.5
deepseq-idemp	deepseq x (deepseq x y)= deepseq x y	1.8	fail	0.9	2.2	0.7
deepseq-s	deepseq x (S y) = deepseq x (S (deepseq x y))	2.1	fail	0.7	5.7	0.7
append-take-drop	take n x ++ drop n x = x	3.6	fail	1.1	71.0	5.5
double-half	double (half x) + mod2 x = x	4.6	fail	1.2	fail	fail
bool-eq		1.3	fail	fail	1.0	0.7
sadd-comm		2.1	fail	fail	2.0	6.6
dummy		1.6	fail	fail	1.1	0.7
even-slow-fast		1.8	fail	fail	1.5	1.4
or-even-odd	even x || odd x = true	3.9	fail	fail	66.3	0.9
idle-simple	idle x = idle (idle x)	1.4	fail	fail	0.7	0.7
idle	idle x = deepseq x 0	1.5	fail	fail	1.8	0.7
exp-idle		3.4	fail	fail	fail	0.9
quad-idle		1.9	fail	fail	fail	0.7
shifted-cycle	cycle [A,B] = A : cycle [B,A]	3.6	fail	fail	fail	fail
even-dbl-acc-lemma	even (doubleAcc x (S y)) = odd (doubleAcc x y)	fail	0.7	0.6	9.9	21.2
ho/map-iterate	map f (iterate f a) = iterate f (f a)	fail	0.6	0.6	fail	fail
length-intersperse	length (intersperse x xs) = length (intersperse y xs)	fail	0.6	0.7	fail	fail
ho/church-add		fail	0.7	0.7	fail	fail
even-double-acc	even (doubleAcc x 0) = true	fail	fail	0.8	fail	21.6
ho/filter-idemp	filter p (filter p xs) = filter p xs	fail	fail	fail	1.3	0.9
nrev-idemp-nat		fail	fail	fail	14.5	0.9
deepseq-add-comm		fail	fail	fail	fail	0.9
nrev-list	naiveReverse = reverse	fail	fail	fail	118.4	13.6
nrev-nat		fail	fail	fail	289.0	0.9

6   Related Work

Our work is based on the method of equality saturation, originally proposed by Tate et al. [18]. Their implementation, named Peggy, was designed to transform programs in low-level imperative languages (Java bytecode and LLVM), although internally Peggy uses a functional representation. In our work we transform lazy functional programs, so we don't have to deal with encoding imperative operations in functional representation, which makes everything much easier. Another difference is that in our representation nodes correspond to functions, not just first-order values, moreover we merge equivalence classes corresponding to functions equal up to parameter permutation, which considerably reduces space consumption. We also articulate the merging by bisimilarity transformation which plays a very important role, making our tool essentially an inductive prover. Note that Peggy have a similar (but simpler) transformation that can merge θ-nodes, but it doesn't seem to be published anywhere.

Initially our work arose from analyzing differences between overgraph supercompilation [6] and equality saturation, overgraph supercompilation being a variety of multi-result supercompilation with a flavor of equality saturation. Multi-result supercompilation was put forward by Klyuchnikov and Romanenko [12], and its idea is to produce multiple residual programs by exploring multiple transformation paths in decision-making points. Multi-result supercompilation was proposed mainly to aid higher-level supercompilation. Higher-level supercompilation is a broad term denoting systems that use supercompilation as a primitive operation, in particular supercompilers that can invent lemmas, prove them with another (lower-level) supercompiler, and use them in the process of supercompilation. Examples of higher-level supercompilation are distillation, proposed by Hamilton [7], and two-level supercompilation, proposed by Klyuchnikov and Romanenko [9,11]. We perform something similar to higher-level supercompilation, but instead of descending to lower levels when we think that we need a lemma, we start with the zeroth level and then prove more and more equalities, possibly using previously proven ones, thus gradually increasing the level.

Inductive provers use induction to prove propositions. Some inductive provers can automatically discover lemmas needed to prove the target proposition, and prove them as well. Sometimes this is done in a top-down manner, by conjecturing lemmas when the proof gets stuck or some heuristic says so. Some provers work in a bottom-up manner, for example HipSpec [3] uses theory exploration to discover lemmas. For this purpose it invokes QuickSpec, which generates all terms up to some depth, splits them into equivalence classes by random testing, and then transforms them into a set of conjectures. Then these conjectures can be proved and used as lemmas. As to our tool, we use something intermediate between the two approaches: instead of using arbitrary terms, we use the terms represented by equivalence classes of the E-graph (i.e. generated by transforming the initial term) and then try to prove them equal pairwise, discarding unfruitful pairs by comparing perfect tree prefixes that have been built in the E-graph so far, instead of testing.

HipSpec uses external SMT-solvers to prove propositions, while we maintain our own E-graph (recall that similar structures are an essential part of SMT-solvers since they are used to solve the congruence closure problem). Hence, our approach is less modular, but, on the bright side, this shared E-graph can be used for other purposes, like optimization.

7   Conclusion

In this paper we've shown how an inductive prover for a non-total first-order lazy language can be constructed on top of the ideas of equality saturation. The key ingredient is merging by bisimilarity which enables proof by induction. Another feature that we consider extremely important is the ability to merge equivalence classes even if they represent functions equal only up to some renaming.

Of course our prover has some deficiencies:

- It is limited to propositions about function equivalence, and it is not obvious how to add support for implications.
- Our prover lacks proper generalizations. We have an experimental flag that enables arbitrary generalizations, but it usually leads to combinatorial explosion of the E-graph.
- We don't support higher-order functions internally and need to perform defunctionalization if the input program contains them.
- Our internal representation is untyped, and for this reason we cannot prove some natural equalities.

Besides mitigating the above problems, another possible area of application may be optimization of functional program. Equality saturation has already been successfully applied to imperative program optimization, so some results in the functional field are to be expected. And even merging by bisimilarity may be of some use since it is known that using lemmas may lead to superlinear performance improvement.

References

1. Graphsc source code and the test suite. https://github.com/sergei-grechanik/supercompilation-hypergraph
2. Abel, A., Altenkrich, T.: A predicative analysis of structural recursion. J. Funct. Program. **12**(1), 1–41 (2002)
3. Claessen, K., Johansson, M., Rosén, D., Smallbone, N.: Automating inductive proofs using theory exploration. In: Bonacina, M.P. (ed.) CADE 2013. LNCS, vol. 7898, pp. 392–406. Springer, Heidelberg (2013)
4. Detlefs, D., Nelson, G., Saxe, J.B.: Simplify: a theorem prover for program checking. JACM: J. ACM **52**(3), 365–473 (2005)
5. Dovier, A., Piazza, C.: The subgraph bisimulation problem. IEEE Trans. Knowl. Data Eng. **5**(4), 1055–1056 (2003). Publisher: IEEE, USA

6. Grechanik, S.A.: Overgraph representation for multi-result supercompilation. In: Klimov, A., Romanenko, S. (eds.) Proceedings of the Third International Valentin Turchin Workshop on Metacomputation, pp. 48–65. Ailamazyan University of Pereslavl, Pereslavl-Zalessky (2012)
7. Hamilton, G.W.: Distillation: extracting the essence of programs. In: Proceedings of the 2007 ACM SIGPLAN Symposium on Partial Evaluation and Semantics-Based Program Manipulation, pp. 61–70. ACM Press, New York (2007)
8. Klyuchnikov, I.: Supercompiler HOSC 1.0: under the hood. Preprint 63, Keldysh Institute of Applied Mathematics, Moscow (2009)
9. Klyuchnikov, I.: Towards effective two-level supercompilation. Preprint 81, Keldysh Institute of Applied Mathematics (2010). http://library.keldysh.ru/preprint.asp?id=2010-81&lg=e
10. Klyuchnikov, I., Romanenko, S.: Proving the equivalence of higher-order terms by means of supercompilation. In: Pnueli, A., Virbitskaite, I., Voronkov, A. (eds.) PSI 2009. LNCS, vol. 5947, pp. 193–205. Springer, Heidelberg (2010)
11. Klyuchnikov, I., Romanenko, S.: Towards higher-level supercompilation. In: Second International Workshop on Metacomputation in Russia (2010)
12. Klyuchnikov, I., Romanenko, S.A.: Multi-result supercompilation as branching growth of the penultimate level in metasystem transitions. In: Clarke, E., Virbitskaite, I., Voronkov, A. (eds.) PSI 2011. LNCS, vol. 7162, pp. 210–226. Springer, Heidelberg (2012)
13. Lisitsa, A., Webster, M.: Supercompilation for equivalence testing in metamorphic computer viruses detection. In: Proceedings of the First International Workshop on Metacomputation in Russia (2008)
14. Nelson, G., Oppen, D.C.: Fast decision procedures based on congruence closure. JACM: J. ACM **27**(2), 356–364 (1980)
15. Sands, D.: Total correctness by local improvement in the transformation of functional programs. ACM Trans. Program. Lang. Syst. **18**(2), 175–234 (1996)
16. Sørensen, M., Glück, R., Jones, N.: A positive supercompiler. J. Funct. Program. **6**(6), 811–838 (1993)
17. Stepp, M., Tate, R., Lerner, S.: Equality-based translation validator for LLVM. In: Gopalakrishnan, G., Qadeer, S. (eds.) CAV 2011. LNCS, vol. 6806, pp. 737–742. Springer, Heidelberg (2011)
18. Tate, R., Stepp, M., Tatlock, Z., Lerner, S.: Equality saturation: a new approach to optimization. SIGPLAN Not. **44**, 264–276 (2009)
19. Turchin, V.: The concept of a supercompiler. ACM Trans. Program. Lang. Syst. (TOPLAS) **8**(3), 292–325 (1986)

Timed History Preserving Bisimulation and Open Maps

Nataliya S. Gribovskaya[✉]

A.P. Ershov Institute of Informatics Systems, SB RAS,
6, Acad. Lavrentiev Avenue, 630090 Novosibirsk, Russia
gribovskaya@iis.nsk.su

Abstract. The open maps approach has recently been successfully applied to structure and unify a wide range of behavior equivalences for concurrency. In this paper, we will prove that timed history preserving (thp-) bisimulation can be captured by an open maps based bisimilarity and its logical counterpart — path bisimilarity, when timed causal trees are chosen as the model category. In particular, we will construct a category of timed causal trees and a subcategory of causal timed words, for which notions of open maps and paths will be developed. Then we will define the open maps based bisimilarity and the path bisimilarity and will establish that the obtained bisimilaries coincide with thp-bisimulation.

1 Introduction

There are confusingly many models for concurrency and too many equivalences on them. It is a common practice to compare models on the basis of two antagonistic views on bisimulation semantics: interleaving – true concurrency. Interleaving models "reduce" concurrency to non-determinism and allow us to represent processes as trees. In contrast, true concurrent models use concurrency as a primitive notion extracted from partial orders, but they are not so handy and have no obvious syntactic description. In order to reconcile these views, Darondeau and Degano have recast partial ordering semantics in the framework of trees and have introduced causal trees which keep the treelike structure of the interleaving models and the descriptive power of the true concurrent models.

The category theory has been successfully used to structure models for concurrency and behavioral equivalences on them. In particular, much effort has been made in relating the models by adjunctions whose adjoints give translations of one model into another (see [3,8,13] among others). In addition, several categorical approaches to the matter have appeared in the literature as a result of attempts to explain apparent differences and to unify the extensive amount of behavioral equivalences. Two of them were initiated by Joyal, Nielsen, and Winskel in [8] where they have proposed abstract ways of capturing the notion of behavioral equivalence through open maps based bisimilarity and its logical

---

This work is supported in part by DFG-RFBR (grant No BE 1267/14-1, grant No 14-01-91334).

A. Voronkov and I. Virbitskaite (Eds.): PSI 2014, LNCS 8974, pp. 142–150, 2015.
DOI: 10.1007/978-3-662-46823-4_12

counterpart — path bisimilarity. These bisimilarities make possible a uniform definition of behavioral equivalences over different models ranging from interleaving models to partial order ones [1,3,10,13]. On the interleaving models abstract bisimilarity readily corresponds to interleaving bisimulation, but on the true concurrent models it leads to strong history preserving bisimulation. However, on causal trees it directly characterizes history preserving bisimulation.

Last years, various models and equivalences have been extended with real-time characteristics in order to handle quantitative aspects of system behaviors. Some part of the theory of untimed systems has been lifted to the real-time setting. In [6,11], an open maps based characterization is provided for interleaving bisimulation on timed transition systems and for partial order equivalences on timed event structures. The same approach was used in [5] to prove that a timed delay equivalence is indeed an equivalence relation for timed automates. In [12] it was shown how several categorical (open maps, path bisimilarity and coalgebraic) approaches to an abstract characterization of bisimulation relate to each other and to the behavioural equivalences for timed transition systems. But one model has not been developed in this direction: the causal trees.

The aim of the paper is to extend the causal trees to a new model with real-time characteristics — timed causal trees — and to provide open maps based and path bisimilarity based characterizations for a thp-bisimulation in their settings. Such characterizations and path assertions from [8] will allow us to construct the characteristic logics for the bisimulation under consideration.

2   Timed Causal Trees

In this section, we represent a timed extension of causal trees [2] and define their behavior. Causal trees are some variant of synchronization trees with labels that supply information about which transitions are causally dependent on each other. In [3], Fröschle and Lasote proved that causal trees are more basic than event structures since they capture causality without a notion of event, and they are more expressive than the latter, because their possible runs can be freely specified in terms of a tree. In contrast, event structures and their sets of runs adhere to certain axioms that express characteristics of independent events. We will define timed causal trees as generalizations of causal trees [2] and as a variant of timed transition systems [6] supplemented with the causality relation. A timed transition system is a finite transition system with a finite set of real-valued clocks. The clocks can be reset to 0 (independently of each other) with the transitions of the systems, and keep track of the time elapsed since the last reset. The transitions put certain constraints on the clock values: a transition may be taken only if the current values of the clocks satisfy the associated constraints. This model can capture several interesting aspects of real-time systems: qualitative and quantitative features.

To start with, let us introduce some auxiliary notions and notations. Let $\mathbf{R}$ be the set of non-negative reals, $\mathbf{N}$ be the set of positive integers, and Σ be a finite alphabet of actions. A *causal timed word (over Σ)* is a finite sequence of the form $\alpha_n = (\sigma_1, d_1, K_1) \ldots (\sigma_n, d_n, K_n)$, where $n \geq 0$, σ_i is an action from Σ, $d_i \in \mathbf{R}$ is the time of execution of σ_i relative to the starting time s.t. $d_i \leq d_{i+1}$ $(1 \leq i < n)$, and $K_i \subseteq \{j \in \mathbf{N} \mid j < i\}$ is a set of causes s.t. if $k \in K_i$ then $K_k \subseteq K_i$ $(i = 1, \ldots, n)$. We consider a finite set V of clock variables. A *clock valuation over* V is a mapping $\nu : V \to \mathbf{R}$ which assigns time values to the clock variables. Define $(\nu + c)(x) := \nu(x) + c$ for all $x \in V$ and $c \in \mathbf{R}$. For a subset λ of clock variables, we write $\nu[\lambda \to 0](x) := 0$, if $x \in \lambda$, and $\nu[\lambda \to 0](x) := \nu(x)$, otherwise. Given a set V, we define the set $\Delta(V)$ of *clock constraints* by the following grammar: $\delta ::= c \# x \mid x + c \# y \mid \delta \wedge \delta$, where $\# \in \{\leq, <, \geq, >, =\}$, $c \in \mathbf{R}$ and $x, y \in V$. We say that δ is *satisfied by* ν if the expression $\delta[\nu(x)/x]^1$ evaluates to true. A clock constraint δ defines a subset of $\mathbf{R}^m$ $(m = |V|)$ denoted as $\|\delta\|_V$. A clock valuation ν defines a point in $\mathbf{R}^m$ denoted as $\|\nu\|_V$. So, the clock constraint δ is satisfied by ν iff $\|\nu\|_V \in \|\delta\|_V$.

According to [6], a *timed transition system* is a tuple (S, s_0, Σ, V, T), where S is a set of states with the initial state s_0, V is a set of clock variables, $T \subseteq S \times \Sigma \times \Delta(V) \times 2^V \times S$ is a set of transitions. We write $s \xrightarrow[\delta, \lambda]{\sigma} s'$ to denote a transition $(s, \sigma, \delta, \lambda, s')$. We extend this notation to possibly empty strings of labels $v = \sigma_1 \ldots \sigma_n$ and $p = (\delta_1, \lambda_1) \ldots (\delta_n, \lambda_n)$ writing $s \xrightarrow[p]{v} s'$ to indicate that $s \xrightarrow[\delta_1, \lambda_1]{\sigma_1} s_1 \ldots s_{n-1} \xrightarrow[\delta_n, \lambda_n]{\sigma_n} s'$ for some $s_1, \ldots, s_{n-1} \in S$.

A *timed synchronization tree* is an acyclic timed transition system without backwards branching, for which every state is potentially reachable, i.e. for all $s \in S$ there are $v = \sigma_1 \ldots \sigma_n$ and $p = (\delta_1, \lambda_1) \ldots (\delta_n, \lambda_n)$ s.t. $s_0 \xrightarrow[p]{v} s$.

We are now prepared to consider the definition of timed causal trees.

Definition 1. *A* timed causal tree *$\mathcal{TC}$ (over Σ) is a tuple $(S, s_0, \Sigma, V, T, <)$, where (S, s_0, Σ, V, T) is a timed synchronization tree and $< \subseteq T \times T$ is a strict order, called the* causal dependency relation, *such that if $(s, \sigma, \delta, \lambda, s') < (s'', \sigma', \delta', \lambda', s''')$ then $s' \xrightarrow[p]{v} s''$ for some strings of labels v and p.*

Intuitively, this condition reflects a natural property of causality: if one transition is a cause of another transition, then the first transition must have happened before the second one. We say that two transitions $(s, \sigma, \delta, \lambda, s')$ and $(s'', \sigma', \delta', \lambda', s''')$, appeared on the same branch, are concurrent iff they are not identical and not related by $<$.

Definition 2. *Let $\mathcal{TC} = (S, s_0, \Sigma, V, T, <)$ be a timed causal tree. A* configuration *of $\mathcal{TC}$ is a pair $\langle s, \nu \rangle$, where $s \in S$ and ν is a clock valuation over V. A configuration $\langle s_0, \nu_0 \rangle$ of $\mathcal{TC}$, where ν_0 is the constant 0 function, is called* initial.

A *run (inducing $\alpha = (\sigma_1, d_1, K_1) \ldots (\sigma_n, d_n, K_n)$) in $\mathcal{TC}$ is a sequence $\gamma = \langle s_0, \nu_0 \rangle \xrightarrow[d_1, K_1]{\sigma_1} \langle s_1, \nu_1 \rangle \ldots \langle s_{n-1}, \nu_{n-1} \rangle \xrightarrow[d_n, K_n]{\sigma_n} \langle s_n, \nu_n \rangle$ s.t. for all $0 < i \leq n$ there is a transition $s_{i-1} \xrightarrow[\delta_i, \lambda_i]{\sigma_i} s_i$ with $\|\nu_{i-1} + (d_i - d_{i-1})\|_V \in \|\delta_i\|_V$ and $\nu_i = (\nu_{i-1} + (d_i - d_{i-1}))[\lambda_i \to 0]$ and $K_i = \{j \in \mathbf{N} \mid j \leq i-1$ and $(s_{j-1}, \sigma_j, \delta_j, \lambda_j, s_j) <$*

---

^{1} $\delta[y/x]$ is the substitution of y for x in δ.

$(s_{i-1}, \sigma_i, \delta_i, \lambda_i, s_i)\}$. Here, $\langle s_0, \nu_0 \rangle$ is the initial configuration and $d_0 = 0$. We use $Runs(TC)$ to denote the set of runs of TC. We say a run γ can be extended to some run γ' in TC iff γ is a prefix of γ'.

Example 1. To illustrate the concepts, consider the timed causal tree TC (see Fig. 1) which has four states s_0 (the initial state), s_1, s_2 and s_3, three actions a, b and c, and two clock variables x and y. Three transitions, t_1, t_2 and t_3 depicted between the states are labeled by actions, clock constraints and subsets of clocks. For instance, t_1 is labelled by an action a, a clock constraint $x \leq 1$ and a subset $\{y\}$ of clock variables. Moreover, t_1 is a cause for t_2. Clearly, $\langle s_0, \nu_0 \rangle \xrightarrow[1,\emptyset]{a} \langle s_1, \nu_1 \rangle \xrightarrow[1,\{1\}]{b} \langle s_2, \nu_1 \rangle$ with $\nu_1(x) = 1$ and $\nu_1(y) = 0$ is the run inducing $(a, 1, \emptyset)(b, 1, \{1\})$.

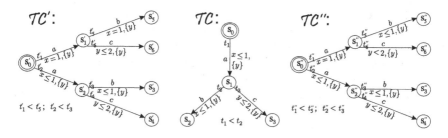

Fig. 1. Some examples of timed causal trees.

3   Timed History Preserving Bisimulation

In this section we define a timed extension of history preserving bisimulation [4] (or thp-bisimulation) in the setting of the model under consideration. Informally, two timed causal trees are bisimilar iff their behavior can be bisimulated while preserving the causal dependencies between their transitions.

Let TC_1 and TC_2 be timed causal trees. Runs $\gamma_1 \in Runs(TC_1)$ and $\gamma_2 \in Runs(TC_2)$ are synchronous iff they induce the same causal timed word. Let $SRuns(TC_1, TC_2)$ be the set of synchronous runs of TC_1 and TC_2. A relation $\mathcal{B} \subseteq SRuns(TC_1, TC_2)$ is called prefix-closed iff $(\gamma_1, \gamma_2) \in \mathcal{B}$ implies $(\gamma_1', \gamma_2') \in \mathcal{B}$ for all prefixes γ_1' and γ_2' of γ_1 and γ_2 respectively, such that $(\gamma_1', \gamma_2') \in SRuns(TC_1, TC_2)$. Following [3], we assume a thp-bisimulation to be prefix-closed, since this restriction has no effect on the induced equivalence.

Definition 3. *Let TC_1 and TC_2 be timed causal trees. Then, a thp-bisimulation between TC_1 and TC_2 is a prefix-closed relation $\mathcal{B} \subseteq SRuns(TC_1, TC_2)$ such that the pair of initial runs belongs to $\mathcal{B}$ and for all $(\gamma_1, \gamma_2) \in \mathcal{B}$, where both γ_1 and γ_2 induce α_n, the following holds: whenever γ_i ($i = 1, 2$) can be extended to the run γ_i' inducing $\alpha_{n+1}' = \alpha_n(\sigma, d, K)$ in TC_i, γ_{3-i} can also be extended to some run γ_{3-i}' inducing α_{n+1}' in TC_{3-i} and $(\gamma_1', \gamma_2') \in \mathcal{B}$. TC_1 and TC_2 are thp-bisimilar iff there is a thp-bisimulation between them.*

Example 2. To illustrate the concept, we consider three timed causal trees, $\mathcal{TC}$, $\mathcal{TC}'$ and $\mathcal{TC}''$, shown in Fig. 1. Clearly, $\mathcal{TC}$ and $\mathcal{TC}'$ are thp-bisimilar, but $\mathcal{TC}$ and $\mathcal{TC}''$ are not, because in $\mathcal{TC}''$ there exists a run inducing $(a, 1, \emptyset)$ which can not be extended by an occurrence of $(c, 3, \emptyset)$, but in $\mathcal{TC}$ we have the unique run inducing $(a, 1, \emptyset)$ which can be extended to the run inducing $(a, 1, \emptyset)(c, 3, \emptyset)$.

4   Elements of Category Theory

The concept of an open map (open morphism) appears in the paper by Joyal and Moerdijk [7], where a concept of a subcategory of open maps of a (pre)topos is defined. As reported in [8,9], the open map approach provides general concepts of bisimilarity for any categorical model of computations.

First, a category $\mathbb{M}$ whose objects represent models of computations has to be identified. A morphism $m : X \to Y$ in $\mathbb{M}$ should intuitively be thought of as a simulation of the object X in the object Y. Then, inside the category $\mathbb{M}$, we choose a subcategory of 'path objects' and 'path extension' morphisms between them. The *path subcategory* is denoted by $\mathbb{P}$. Given a path object P in $\mathbb{P}$ and a model object X in $\mathbb{M}$, a *path* is a morphism $p : P \to X$ in $\mathbb{M}$.

Second, we identify morphisms $m : X \longrightarrow Y$ which have the following path-lifting property: whenever $f : P_1 \to P_2$ in $\mathbb{P}$, $p : P_1 \to X$ and $q : P_2 \to Y$ in $\mathbb{M}$, and $m \circ p = q \circ f$, there exists a morphism $h : P_2 \to X$ in $\mathbb{M}$ s.t. $p = h \circ f$ and $q = m \circ h$. If the morphism m has this property, we will say it is $\mathbb{P}$-*open*.

Third, an abstract notion of bisimilarity is introduced. Two objects X and Y in $\mathbb{M}$ are said to be $\mathbb{P}$-*bisimilar* if there exists a span $X \xleftarrow{m} Z \xrightarrow{m'} Y$ with a common object Z of $\mathbb{P}$-open morphisms.

5   Open Maps Characterization

In this section, the category of timed causal trees and its subcategory are introduced and the open maps based characterization of thp-bisimilarity is given.

Definition 4. *Given timed causal trees* $\mathcal{TC} = (S, s_0, \Sigma, V, T, <)$ *and* $T' = (S', s_0', \Sigma, V', T', <')$, *a pair* (μ, η) *is a* morphism *between them if* $\mu : S \to S'$ *is a mapping between the states and* $\eta : V' \to V$ *is a mapping between the clock variables, s.t. for each run* $\gamma = \langle s_0, \nu_0 \rangle \xrightarrow[d_1, K_1]{\sigma_1} \langle s_1, \nu_1 \rangle \; \ldots \; \langle s_{n-1}, \nu_{n-1} \rangle \xrightarrow[d_n, K_n]{\sigma_n} \langle s_n, \nu_n \rangle$ *in* $\mathcal{TC}$, *there exist* $K_1', \ldots, K_n'$ *s.t.* $K_i' \subseteq K_i$ *for all* $1 \leq i \leq n$ *and* $\gamma' = \langle \mu(s_0), \eta^{-1}(\nu_0) \rangle \xrightarrow[d_1, K_1']{\sigma_1} \langle \mu(s_1), \eta^{-1}(\nu_1) \rangle \; \ldots \; \langle \mu(s_{n-1}), \eta^{-1}(\nu_{n-1}) \rangle \xrightarrow[d_n, K_n']{\sigma_n} \langle \mu(s_n), \eta^{-1}(\nu_n) \rangle$ *is a run in* $\mathcal{TC}'$ *called the* (μ, η)-image *of* γ.[2]

Timed causal trees and morphisms between them form a category of timed causal trees, **TCT**, in which the composition of two morphisms $(\mu, \eta) : \mathcal{TC} \to \mathcal{TC}'$ and

---

[2] Here $\eta^{-1}(\nu_i)(x') := \nu_i(\eta(x'))$ for all $x' \in V'$ and $0 \leq i \leq n$.

$(\mu',\eta') : \mathcal{TC}' \rightarrow \mathcal{TC}''$ is defined as $(\mu',\eta') \circ (\mu,\eta) := (\mu' \circ \mu, \eta \circ \eta')$, and the identity morphism is the pair of the identity functions. Following the standards of [8], a category of causal timed words has to be constructed.

Definition 5. *The full subcategory* **P** *of* **TCT** *contains the objects* $T^{\alpha_n} = (S^{\alpha_n},$ $0, \Sigma, V^{\alpha_n}, T^{\alpha_n}, <^{\alpha_n})$, *corresponding to a causal timed word* $\alpha_n = (\sigma_1, d_1, K_1)$ $\ldots (\sigma_n, d_n, K_n)$ *of the form* $0 \xrightarrow[\delta_1, \lambda_1]{\sigma_1} 1 \ldots (n-1) \xrightarrow[\delta_n, \lambda_n]{\sigma_n} n$, *where* $S^{\alpha_n} = \{0, \ldots, n\}$ *with* 0 *as the initial state,* V^{α_n} *consists of* 2^n *subsets of* $\{1, \ldots, n\}$, $T^{\alpha_n} = \{(i - 1, \sigma_i, \delta_i, \lambda_i, i) \mid i = 1 \ldots n, \lambda_i = \{x \in V^{\alpha_n} \mid i \in x\}, \delta_i = \bigwedge_{x \in V^{\alpha_n}} (x = d_i - d_{I(i,x)})\}$, *where* $I(i,x) := \max\{k \in x \cup \{0\} \mid k < i\}$,[3] $d_0 := 0$, *and* $(i - 1, \sigma_i, \delta_i, \lambda_i, i) <^{\alpha_n}$ $(j - 1, \sigma_j, \delta_j, \lambda_j, j) \iff i < j$ *and* $i \in K_j$; *and morphisms between them.*

A morphism $(\mu, \eta) : T^{\alpha_n} \rightarrow T^{\alpha'_m}$ in **P** shows how the causal timed word α'_m can extend the causal timed word α_n: by additional transitions and/or by increased concurrency. Thus, $(\mu, \eta) : T^{\alpha_n} \rightarrow T^{\alpha'_m}$ is a morphism in **P** for $\alpha_n = (\sigma_1, d_1, K_1) \ldots (\sigma_n, d_n, K_n)$ and $\alpha'_m = (\sigma'_1, d'_1, K'_1) \ldots (\sigma'_m, d'_m, K'_m)$ if and only if $n \leq m$ and for all $1 \leq i \leq n$ $\sigma_i = \sigma'_i$, $d_i = d'_i$ and $K'_i \subseteq K_i$.

The only purpose of this seemingly complex construction of **P** is that it allows us to represent the category of causal timed words with extensions inside **TCT**, and to identify the runs in $\mathcal{TC}$ with morphisms from the objects of **P** to $\mathcal{TC}$.

Lemma 1. *Let* $\mathcal{TC}$ *be an object of* **TCT**, $\alpha_n = (\sigma_1, d_1, K_1) \ldots (\sigma_n, d_n, K_n)$ *be a causal timed word and* T^{α_n} *be an object of* **P**. *Then,*

(i) there is a unique run γ_{α_n} *inducing* α_n *in* T^{α_n}, *and the set of runs in* T^{α_n} *consists of all prefixes of* γ_{α_n},

(ii) for all runs γ *inducing* α_n *in* $\mathcal{TC}$ *and for all* $\alpha'_n = (\sigma_1, d_1, K'_1) \ldots (\sigma_n, d_n, K'_n)$ *such that* $K'_i \subseteq K_i$ $(1 \leq i \leq n)$, *there is a unique morphism* $(\mu, \eta) : T^{\alpha'_n} \rightarrow$ $\mathcal{TC}$ *such that* γ *is the* (μ, η)-*image of the run in* $T^{\alpha'_n}$, *inducing* α'_n.

Next, we provide a behavioural characterization of **P**-open morphisms.

Theorem 1. *Let* $\mathcal{TC}, \mathcal{TC}'$ *be the objects of* **TCT**. *A morphism* $(\mu, \eta) : \mathcal{TC} \rightarrow$ $\mathcal{TC}'$ *in* **TCT** *is* **P**-*open iff for any run* γ *inducing* α_n *in* $\mathcal{TC}$, *the* (μ, η)-*image of* γ *is a run inducing the same causal timed word and whenever the* (μ, η)-*image of* γ *can be extended to a run* $\bar{\gamma}$ *inducing* $\alpha_n(\sigma, d, K)$ *in* $\mathcal{TC}'$, γ *can also be extended to some run* γ' *in* $\mathcal{TC}$ *such that* $\bar{\gamma}$ *is the* (μ, η)-*image of* γ'.

Proof. ($\Rightarrow$) Assume (μ, η) to be a **P**-open morphism. Take an arbitrary run γ in $\mathcal{TC}$ inducing α_n. Denote (μ, η)-image of γ as γ'. Clearly, γ' induces α'_n s.t. there is the only morphism $(q, \eta_q) : T^{\alpha_n} \rightarrow T^{\alpha'_n}$. Due to Lemma 1(i), there are unique runs r inducing α_n in T^{α_n} and r' inducing α'_n in $T^{\alpha'_n}$. By Lemma 1(ii), there are unique morphisms $(p, \eta_p) : T^{\alpha_n} \rightarrow \mathcal{TC}$ and $(f, \eta_f) : T^{\alpha'_n} \rightarrow \mathcal{TC}'$ s.t. γ is the (p, η_p)-image of r and γ' is the (f, η_f)-image of r'. It is easy to see $(\mu, \eta) \circ (p, \eta_p) = (f, \eta_f) \circ (q, \eta_q)$. Since (μ, η) is a **P**-open morphism, there

---

[3] The number returned by $I(i, x)$ is the last state before i at which x was reset.

is a morphism $(h, \eta_h) : T^{\alpha'_n} \to TC$ such that $(\mu, \eta) \circ (h, \eta_h) = (f, \eta_f)$ and $(h, \eta_h) \circ (q, \eta_q) = (p, \eta_p)$. Hence, γ is a (h, η_h)-image of r' and $\alpha_n = \alpha'_n$.

Now suppose that γ' can be extended to a run $\overline{\gamma}'$ inducing $\alpha''_{n+1} = \alpha_n(\sigma, d, K)$ in TC'. Again by Lemma 1, we have a unique run r'' inducing α''_{n+1} in $T^{\alpha''_{n+1}}$, and a unique morphism $(f', \eta_{f'}) : T^{\alpha''_{n+1}} \to TC'$ s.t. $\overline{\gamma}'$ is the $(f', \eta_{f'})$-image of r''. Due to the construction of T^{α_n} and $T^{\alpha''_{n+1}}$ there exists the only morphism $(g, \eta_g) : T^{\alpha_n} \to T^{\alpha''_{n+1}}$ s.t. the prefix of r'' inducing α_n is the (g, η_g)-image of r. Hence, $(\mu, \eta) \circ (p, \eta_p) = (f', \eta_{f'}) \circ (g, \eta_g)$. Since (μ, η) is a **P**-open morphism, there is a morphism $(l, \eta_l) : T^{\alpha''_{n+1}} \to TC$ such that $(\mu, \eta) \circ (l, \eta_l) = (f', \eta_{f'})$ and $(l, \eta_l) \circ (g, \eta_g) = (p, \eta_p)$. This implies that γ can be extended to the (l, η_l)-image of r'' and $\overline{\gamma}'$ is the (μ, η)-image of the (l, η_l)-image of r''.

($\Leftarrow$) Assume that we have morphisms $(f, \eta_f) : T^{\alpha_n} \to T^{\alpha'_m}$ in **P** and $(p, \eta_p) : T^{\alpha_n} \to TC$ and $(q, \eta_q) : T^{\alpha'_m} \to TC'$ in **TCT** such that $(\mu, \eta) \circ (p, \eta_p) = (q, \eta_q) \circ (f, \eta_f)$. Consider the proof of the case when $m = n+1$ and $\alpha'_m = \alpha_n(\sigma, d, K)$ (the proofs of the other cases are similar). According to Lemma 1(i), there are unique runs r inducing α_n in T^{α_n} and r' inducing α'_{n+1} in $T^{\alpha'_{n+1}}$, and the (f, η_f)-image of r is a prefix of r'. Define γ as the (p, η_p)-image of r, γ' as the (q, η_q)-image of the (f, η_f)-image of r, and $\overline{\gamma}'$ as the (q, η_q)-image of r'. Clearly, γ' is a prefix of $\overline{\gamma}'$. Since $(\mu, \eta) \circ (p, \eta_p) = (q, \eta_q) \circ (f, \eta_f)$, we get that γ' is the (μ, η)-image of γ. By the assumptions of the theorem, γ can be extended to some run $\overline{\gamma}$ s.t. both $\overline{\gamma}$ and $\overline{\gamma}'$ induce the same causal timed word $\overline{\alpha}_{n+1}$ and $\overline{\gamma}'$ is the (μ, η)-image of $\overline{\gamma}$. Since $\overline{\gamma}'$ is the (q, η_q)-image of r', there is a unique morphism $(h, \eta_h) : T^{\alpha'_{n+1}} \to TC$ s.t. $\overline{\gamma}$ is the (h, η_h)-image of r' by Lemma 1(ii). The commutativity properties required by **P**-openness follow from the properties listed above. $\Diamond$

Now the coincidence of **P**-bisimilarity and thp-bisimilarity is established.

Theorem 2. TC_1 and TC_2 from **TCT** are **P**-bisimilar iff they are thp-bisimilar.

Proof. ($\Rightarrow$) Assume that TC_1 and TC_2 are **P**-bisimilar with a span of **P**-open maps: $TC_1 \overset{(\mu_1, \eta_1)}{\longleftarrow} TC \overset{(\mu_2, \eta_2)}{\longrightarrow} TC_2$. Define $\mathcal{B}$ as follows: $(\gamma_1, \gamma_2) \in \mathcal{B} \iff$ there is a run γ in TC such that γ_i is the (μ_i, η_i)-image of γ $(i = 1, 2)$. Due to Theorem 1, it is routine to check that $\mathcal{B}$ satisfies the required properties of Definition 3.

($\Leftarrow$) Assume TC_1 and TC_2 to be thp-bisimilar with the relation $\mathcal{B}$ as defined in Definition refdefspshpbis and $TC_i = (S_i, s_0^i, \Sigma, V_i, T_i, <_i)$ $(i = 1, 2)$. We construct a span of **P**-open maps with a vertex TC_x induced by $\mathcal{B}$ in the following way. The states of TC_x will be pairs of runs from $\mathcal{B}$ with the pair of initial runs as the initial state. The clock variables of TC_x will be the disjoint union of V_1 and V_2. Next, for all pairs of runs (γ_n^1, γ_n^2) inducing $\alpha_n = (\sigma_1, d_1, K_1) \ldots (\sigma_n, d_n, K_n)$ from $\mathcal{B}$ $(n > 0)$, there will be an incoming transition in TC_x from the pair of runs $(\gamma_{n-1}^1, \gamma_{n-1}^2)$ inducing α_{n-1} from $\mathcal{B}$, which are prefixes of γ_n^1 and γ_n^2 respectively, of the form $\overset{\sigma_n}{\underset{\delta, \lambda}{\to}}$, where γ_{n-1}^i ends in $\langle s_{n-1}^i, \nu_{n-1}^i \rangle$ and γ_n^i ends in $\langle s_n^i, \nu_n^i \rangle$ $(i = 1, 2)$,

$$\delta = \bigwedge_{x \in V_i, i=1,2} (x = \nu_{n-1}^i(x) + (d_n - d_{n-1})); \text{ and } \lambda = \{x \in V_i \mid i = 1, 2, \nu_n^i(x) = 0\}.$$

Finally, we define the causal dependency relation $<_x$ as follows: a pair of runs

(γ_n^1, γ_n^2) from $\mathcal{B}$, inducing $\alpha_n = (\sigma_1, d_1, K_1) \ldots (\sigma_n, d_n, K_n)$, is a cause of a pair of runs $(\gamma_m'^1, \gamma_m'^2)$ from $\mathcal{B}$, inducing $\alpha_m' = (\sigma_1', d_1', K_1') \ldots (\sigma_m', d_m', K_m')$, if and only if γ_n^i is a prefix of $\gamma_m'^i$ for all $i = 1, 2$ and $n \in K_m'$.

For $i = 1, 2$, define the mappings $(\mu_i, \eta_i) : \mathcal{TC}_x \to \mathcal{TC}_i$ as follows: $\mu_i((\gamma_n^1, \gamma_n^2)) = s_n^i$, where s_n^i is the last state of γ_n^i, and η_i is the injection function. By construction, (μ_i, η_i) is a morphism, and openness follows from Theorem 1. $\diamondsuit$

6   Path Bisimilarity

To obtain a logic characteristic of bisimulation induced by open maps, Joyal, Nielsen, and Winskel [8] have proposed a second category-theoretic characterization of bisimulation — path bisimilarity.

Let $\mathbb{M}$ be a category of models, let $\mathbb{P}$ be a small category of path objects, where $\mathbb{P}$ is a subcategory of $\mathbb{M}$, let I be a common initial object[4] of $\mathbb{P}$ and $\mathbb{M}$.

Definition 6. *Two objects X_1 and X_2 of $\mathbb{M}$ are called path-$\mathbb{P}$-bisimilar iff there is a set R of pairs of paths (p_1, p_2) with common domain P, so $p_1 : P \to X_1$ is a path in X_1 and $p_2 : P \to X_2$ is a path in X_2, such that*

(o) $(i_1, i_2) \in R$, where $i_1 : I \to X_1$ and $i_2 : I \to X_2$ are the unique paths starting in the initial object, and for all $(p_1, p_2) \in R$ and for all $m : P \to Q$, where m is in $\mathbb{P}$, holds

(i) if there exists $q_1 : Q \to X_1$ with $q_1 \circ m = p_1$ then there exists $q_2 : Q \to X_2$ with $q_2 \circ m = p_2$ and $(q_1, q_2) \in R$ and

(ii) if there exists $q_2 : Q \to X_2$ with $q_2 \circ m = p_2$ then there exists $q_1 : Q \to X_1$ with $q_1 \circ m = p_1$ and $(q_1, q_2) \in R$.

Two objects X_1 and X_2 are strong path-$\mathbb{P}$-bisimilar *iff they are path-$\mathbb{P}$-bisimilar and the set R further satisfies:*

(iii) if $(q_1, q_2) \in R$, with $q_1 : Q \to X_1$ and $q_2 : Q \to X_2$ and $m : P \to Q$, where m is in $\mathbb{P}$, then $(q_1 \circ m, q_2 \circ m) \in R$.

Theorem 3. $\mathbb{P}$-*bisimilarity, path-$\mathbb{P}$-bisimilarity, strong path-$\mathbb{P}$-bisimilarity all coincide with thp-equivalence.*

Proof. According to Theorem 2, *thp*-equivalence coincides with $\mathbb{P}$-bisimilarity. The fact that $\mathbb{P}$-bisimilarity implies (strong) path-$\mathbb{P}$-bisimilarity follows from Lemma 16 [8]. Hence, it is sufficient to show that if $\mathcal{TC}_1$ and $\mathcal{TC}_2$ are path-$\mathbb{P}$-bisimilar then they are *thp*-equivalent. Suppose that $\mathcal{R}$ is a path-$\mathbb{P}$-bisimulation between $\mathcal{TC}_1$ and $\mathcal{TC}_2$. Define a relation $\mathcal{B}$ as follows: $(\gamma_1, \gamma_2) \in \mathcal{B} \iff$ there is $((\mu_1, \eta_1), (\mu_2, \eta_2)) \in \mathcal{R}$ s.t. $(\mu_i, \eta_i) : T^\alpha \to \mathcal{TC}_i$ and γ_i is (μ_i, η_i)-image of γ_α ($i = 1, 2$) where γ_α is the run inducing α in T^α. Using Lemma 1 and properties of the path-$\mathbb{P}$-bisimulation $\mathcal{R}$ it is easy to check that $\mathcal{B}$ is indeed a *thp*-bisimulation. $\diamondsuit$

---

[4] In our case the initial object I is the timed causal tree $(\{s_0\}, s_0, \Sigma, \emptyset, \emptyset, \emptyset)$.

7   Conclusion

In this paper, we have represented and investigated a timed variant of causal trees. In particular, we have integrated it into Winskel and Nielsen's framework and have shown that thp-bisimulation has an open map based and path bisimilarity based characterizations when timed causal trees are taken as the model category. This result proves that thp-bisimulation is a bisimilarity for causality while strong thp-bisimulation remains a bisimilarity for true concurrency.

The model under consideration has some advantages. For instance, it has a treelike structure and possesses a global partial order of causal dependency on transitions. Hence, the timed causal trees are a basic convenient semantic model for timed CCS. However, we think that timed causal trees also can be used in other fields of concurrency. We plan to continue our work in order to investigate this area and to examine how our model relates to the other concurrent models.

References

1. Cattani, G.L., Sassone, V.: Higher dimentional transition systems. In: Proceedings of LICS 1996, pp. 55–62 (1996)
2. Darondeau, P., Degano, P.: Causal trees interleaving + causality. In: Guessarian, I. (ed.) LITP 1990. LNCS, vol. 469, pp. 239–255. Springer, Heidelberg (1990)
3. Fröschle, S., Lasota, S.: Causality versus true-concurrency. Theor. Comput. Sci. **386**(3), 169–187 (2007)
4. van Glabbeek, R.J., Goltz, U.: Equivalence notions for concurrent systems and refinement of actions. In: Kreczmar, A., Mirkowska, G. (eds.) MFCS 1989. LNCS, vol. 379, pp. 237–248. Springer, Heidelberg (1989)
5. Gribovskaya, N., Virbitskaite, I.: Timed delay bisimulation is an equivalence relation for timed transition systems. Fundamenta Informaticae **93**(1–3), 127–142 (2009)
6. Hune, T., Nielsen, M.: Bisimulation and open maps for timed transition systems. Fundamenta Informaticae **38**, 61–77 (1999)
7. Joyal, A., Moerdijk, I.: A completeness theorem for open maps. Annu. Pure Appl. Log. **70**, 51–86 (1997)
8. Joyal, A., Nielsen, M., Winskel, G.: Bisimulation from open maps. Inf. Comput. **127**(2), 164–185 (1996)
9. Nielsen, M., Cheng, A.: Observing behaviour categorically. In: Thiagarajan, P.S. (ed.) FSTTCS 1995. LNCS, vol. 1026, pp. 263–278. Springer, Heidelberg (1995)
10. Oshevskaya, E.S.: Open Maps Bisimulations for Higher Dimensional Automata Models. In: Kutyłowski, M., Charatonik, W., Gębala, M. (eds.) FCT 2009. LNCS, vol. 5699, pp. 274–286. Springer, Heidelberg (2009)
11. Virbitskaite, I.B., Gribovskaya, N.S.: Open maps and observational equivalences for timed partial order models. Fundamenta Informaticae **60**(1–4), 383–399 (2004)
12. Virbitskaite, I.B., Gribovskaya, N.S., Best, E.: A categorical view of timed behaviours. Fundamenta Informaticae **102**(1), 129–143 (2010)
13. Winskel, G., Nielsen, M.: Models for concurrency. In: Abramsky, S., Gabbay, D., Maibaum, T. (eds.) Handbook of Logic in Computer Science, vol. 4, pp. 1–148. Oxford University Press, New York (1995)

Process Opacity for Timed Process Algebra

Damas P. Gruska[(✉)]

Institute of Informatics, Comenius University,
Mlynska Dolina, 842 48 Bratislava, Slovakia
gruska@fmph.uniba.sk

Abstract. A new security concept called *process opacity* is formalized and studied. For processes which are process opaque with respect to a given predicate over processes, an intruder cannot learn validity of this predicate for any subsequent state of computation. We discuss different extensions of this concept as well as its properties. We put some restrictions on predicates in such a way that we obtain decidable security properties.

Keywords: Process opacity · Process algebras · Information flow · Security

1 Introduction

Many security properties are based on non-interference (see [GM82]) which assumes an absence of any information flow between private and public systems activities. More precisely, systems are considered to be secure if from observations of their public activities no information about private activities can be deduced. This approach has found many reformulations for different formalisms, computational models and nature or "quality" of observations. Opacity is a general security property (see [BKR04,BKMR06]) and many security properties can be viewed as its special cases (see, for example, [Gru07]). A predicate is opaque if for any trace of a system for which the predicate holds there exists another trace for which the predicate does not hold and the both traces are indistinguishable for an observer (which is expressed by an observation function). This means that the observer (intruder) cannot say whether the predicate holds or does not hold for a trace which has been performed. Opacity is widely studied also in a process algebra framework and it represents a generalization of many traditional security properties for process algebras (see, for example, [Gru12a,Gru12b,Gru10]).

The aim of this paper is to extend the concept opacity in such a way that instead of process's traces we focus on properties of reachable states. Hence we assume an intruder who is not primarily interested whether some sequence of actions performed by a process has some given property but we consider an intruder who wants to discover whether this process reaches a state which satisfied some given (classified) predicate. It turns out that in this way we can

Work supported by the grant VEGA 1/1333/12.

A. Voronkov and I. Virbitskaite (Eds.): PSI 2014, LNCS 8974, pp. 151–160, 2015.
DOI: 10.1007/978-3-662-46823-4_13

capture some new security flaws. The resulting property, called *process opacity*, is undecidable. Hence we somehow restrict it to obtain a still meaningful but (polynomial time) decidable property. We study properties of process opacity as well as how this notion can be used for description of other information flow based security properties. Since our plan is to elaborate techniques for description of timing attacks and to verify systems security against them, we have decided to work with a timed process algebra which can be used for description of timing behavior of systems. We do not consider value-passing algebra since we focus on actions and not on communicated values. Considering also values and possible security types of variables would bring new challenges and we leave it for a further work.

The paper is organized as follows. In Sect. 2 we describe the timed process algebra TPA which will be used as a basic formalism. In Sect. 3 we present opacity and in the next section process opacity is defined and studied. Section 5 contains discussion and plans for a future work.

2   Timed Process Algebra

In this section we define Timed Process Algebra, TPA for short. TPA is based on Milner's CCS but the special time action t which expresses elapsing of (discrete) time is added. The presented language is a slight simplification of Timed Security Process Algebra introduced in [FGM00]. We omit an explicit idling operator ι used in tSPA and instead of this we allow implicit idling of processes. Hence processes can perform either "enforced idling" by performing t actions which are explicitly expressed in their descriptions or "voluntary idling" (i.e. for example, the process $a.Nil$ can perform t action since it is not contained the process specification). But in the both cases internal communications have priority to action t in the parallel composition. Moreover we do not divide actions into private and public ones as it is in tSPA. TPA differs also from the tCryptoSPA (see [GM04]). TPA does not use value passing and strictly preserves *time determinacy* in case of choice operator $+$ what is not the case of tCryptoSPA.

To define the language TPA, we first assume a set of atomic action symbols A not containing symbols τ and t, and such that for every $a \in A$ there exists $\bar{a} \in A$ and $\bar{\bar{a}} = a$. We define $Act = A \cup \{\tau\}, At = A \cup \{t\}, Actt = Act \cup \{t\}$. We assume that $a, b, \ldots$ range over A, $u, v, \ldots$ range over Act, and $x, y \ldots$ range over $Actt$. Assume the signature $\Sigma = \bigcup_{n \in \{0,1,2\}} \Sigma_n$, where

$$\Sigma_0 = \{Nil\}$$
$$\Sigma_1 = \{x. \mid x \in A \cup \{t\}\} \cup \{[S] \mid S \text{ is a relabeling function}\}$$
$$\cup \{\backslash M \mid M \subseteq A\}$$
$$\Sigma_2 = \{\mid, +\}$$

with the agreement to write unary action operators in prefix form, the unary operators $[S], \backslash M$ in postfix form, and the rest of operators in infix form. Relabeling functions, $S : Actt \to Actt$ are such that $\overline{S(a)} = S(\bar{a})$ for $a \in A, S(\tau) = \tau$ and $S(t) = t$.

The set of TPA terms over the signature Σ is defined by the following BNF notation:

$$P ::= X \mid op(P_1, P_2, \ldots P_n) \mid \mu X P$$

where $X \in Var$, Var is a set of process variables, $P, P_1, \ldots P_n$ are TPA terms, $\mu X-$ is the binding construct, $op \in \Sigma$.

The set of CCS terms consists of TPA terms without t action. We will use an usual definition of opened and closed terms where μX is the only binding operator. Closed terms which are t-guarded (each occurrence of X is within some subterm $t.A$ i.e. between any two t actions only finitely many non timed actions can be performed) are called TPA processes.

We give a structural operational semantics of terms by means of labeled transition systems. The set of terms represents a set of states, labels are actions from $Actt$. The transition relation $\rightarrow$ is a subset of TPA $\times$ $Actt$ $\times$ TPA. We write $P \xrightarrow{x} P'$ instead of $(P, x, P') \in \rightarrow$ and $P \xrightarrow{x}\!\!\!\!\!/\,$ if there is no P' such that $P \xrightarrow{x} P'$. The meaning of the expression $P \xrightarrow{x} P'$ is that the term P can evolve to P' by performing action x, by $P \xrightarrow{x}$ we will denote that there exists a term P' such that $P \xrightarrow{x} P'$. We define the transition relation as the least relation satisfying the inference rules for CCS plus the following inference rules:

$$\frac{}{Nil \xrightarrow{t} Nil} \; A1 \qquad\qquad \frac{}{u.P \xrightarrow{t} u.P} \; A2$$

$$\frac{P \xrightarrow{t} P', Q \xrightarrow{t} Q', P \mid Q \xrightarrow{\tau}\!\!\!\!\!/\,}{P \mid Q \xrightarrow{t} P' \mid Q'} \; Pa \qquad \frac{P \xrightarrow{t} P', Q \xrightarrow{t} Q'}{P + Q \xrightarrow{t} P' + Q'} \; S$$

Here we mention the rules that are new with respect to CCS. Axioms $A1, A2$ allow arbitrary idling. Concurrent processes can idle only if there is no possibility of an internal communication (Pa). A run of time is deterministic (S) i.e. performing of t action does not lead to the choice between summands of $+$. In the definition of the labeled transition system we have used negative premises (see Pa). In general this may lead to problems, for example with consistency of the defined system. We avoid these dangers by making derivations of τ independent of derivations of t. For an explanation and details see [Gro90].

For $s = x_1.x_2.\ldots.x_n, x_i \in Actt$ we write $P \xrightarrow{s}$ instead of $P \xrightarrow{x_1 x_2} \cdots \xrightarrow{x_n}$ and we say that s is a trace of P. The set of all traces of P will be denoted by $Tr(P)$. By ϵ we will denote the empty sequence of actions, by $Succ(P)$ we will denote the set of all successors of P i.e. $Succ(P) = \{P' | P \xrightarrow{s} P', s \in Actt^*\}$. If set $Succ(P)$ is finite we say that P is finite state process. We define modified transitions $\Rightarrow_M$ which "hide" actions from M. Formally, we will write $P \Rightarrow_M P'$ for $M \subseteq Actt$ iff $P \xrightarrow{s_1} \xrightarrow{x} \xrightarrow{s_2} P'$ for $s_1, s_2 \in M^*$ and $P \xrightarrow{s}_M$ instead of $P \xrightarrow{x_1}_M \xrightarrow{x_2}_M \cdots \xrightarrow{x_n}_M$. We will write $P \xrightarrow{x}_M$ if there exists P' such that $P \xrightarrow{x}_M P'$. We will write $P \xrightarrow{\hat{x}}_M P'$ instead of $P \xrightarrow{x}_M P'$ if $x \in M$. Note that $\Rightarrow_M$ is defined for arbitrary action but in definitions of security properties we will use it for actions (or sequence of actions) not belonging to M. We can the extend the definition of $\Rightarrow_M$ for sequences of actions similarly to $\xrightarrow{s}$. We conclude this section with definitions M-bisimulation and weak timed trace equivalence.

Definition 1. *Let* $(TPA, Actt, \rightarrow)$ *be a labelled transition system (LTS). A relation* $\Re \subseteq TPA \times TPA$ *is called a* M-bisimulation *if it is symmetric and it satisfies the following condition: if* $(P, Q) \in \Re$ *and* $P \xrightarrow{x} P', x \in Actt$ *then there exists a process* Q' *such that* $Q \overset{\hat{x}}{\Rightarrow}_M Q'$ *and* $(P', Q') \in \Re$. *Two processes* P, Q *are* M-bisimilar, *abbreviated* $P \approx_M Q$, *if there exists a M-bisimulation relating* P *and* Q.

Definition 2. *The set of weak timed traces of process* P *is defined as* $Tr_w(P) = \{s \in (A \cup \{t\})^\star | \exists P'.P \overset{s}{\Rightarrow}_{\{\tau\}} P'\}$. *Two process* P *and* Q *are weakly timed trace equivalent* $(P \simeq_w Q)$ *iff* $Tr_w(P) = Tr_w(Q)$.

3   Information Flow

In this section we will present motivations for new concepts which will be introduced in the next section. First we define an absence-of-information-flow property - Strong Nondeterministic Non-Interference (SNNI, for short, see [FGM00]). Suppose that all actions are divided into two groups, namely public (low level) actions L and private (high level) actions H. It is assumed that $L \cup H = A$. Process P has SNNI property (we will write $P \in SNNI$) if $P \setminus H$ behaves like P for which all high level actions are hidden (by action τ) for an observer. To express this hiding we introduce hiding operator $P/M, M \subseteq A$, for which it holds if $P \xrightarrow{a} P'$ then $P/M \xrightarrow{a} P'/M$ whenever $a \notin M \cup \bar{M}$ and $P/M \xrightarrow{\tau} P'/M$ whenever $a \in M \cup \bar{M}$. Formal definition of SNNI follows.

Definition 3. *Let* $P \in TPA$. *We say that* P *has SNNI property, and we write* $P \in SNNI$ *iff* $P \setminus H \simeq_w P/H$.

SNNI property assumes an intruder who tries to learn whether a private action was performed by a given process while (s)he can observe only public ones. If this cannot be done then the process has SNNI property. Now we generalize this idea. We do not divide actions into public and private ones at the system description level but we use a more general concept of observation and opacity. This concept was exploited in [BKR04] and [BKMR06] in a framework of Petri Nets and transition systems, respectively. Here we will work with its translation to a process algebra framework as it is done in [Gru07].

First we assume an observation function i.e. a function $\mathcal{O} : Actt^\star \rightarrow \Theta^\star$, where Θ is a set of elements called observables. Now suppose that we have some security property. This might be an execution of one or more classified actions, an execution of actions in a particular classified order which should be kept hidden, etc. Suppose that this property is expressed by a predicate ϕ over sequences. We would like to know whether an observer can deduce the validity of the property ϕ just by observing sequences of actions from $Actt^\star$ performed by system of interest. The observer cannot deduce the validity of ϕ if there are two sequences $w, w' \in Actt^\star$ such that $\phi(w), \neg\phi(w')$ and the sequences cannot be distinguished by the observer i.e. $obs(w) = obs(w')$. We formalize this concept by the notion of opacity.

Definition 4 (Opacity). *Given process P, a predicate ϕ over $Actt^*$ is opaque w.r.t. the observation function $\mathcal{O}$ if for every sequence w, $w \in Tr(P)$ such that $\phi(w)$ holds and $\mathcal{O}(w) \neq \epsilon$, there exists a sequence w', $w' \in Tr(P)$ such that $\neg\phi(w')$ holds and $\mathcal{O}(w) = \mathcal{O}(w')$. The set of processes for which the predicate ϕ is opaque with respect to $\mathcal{O}$ will be denoted by $Op_{\mathcal{O}}^{\phi}$.*

Example 1. Let us consider the processes $P_1 = h.l.Nil$, $P_2 = h.l.Nil + l.Nil$ and $P_3 = l.h.Nil$. Clearly $P_1 \notin SNNI$ and $P_2, P_3 \in SNNI$.

The most interesting case is that of P_3. The process is considered to be secure by SNNI property despite the fact that after performing public action l only private action h can be performed. On the other side this property can be captured by opacity. Note that SNNI as well as many other trace based security properties can be viewed as special cases of opacity (see, for example, [Gru07]).

Example 2. Let us consider the process $P = l.Nil + l.h_1.Nil + l.h_2.Nil + l.(h_1.Nil + h_2.Nil)$. Clearly $P \in SNNI$. Suppose that we are interested in private property ϕ defined as "process cannot perform both private actions h_1 and h_2" (note that this is the property of processes not traces). Clearly, by performing public action l we cannot say that whether process reaches a state satisfying the property hence P should be considered to be safe with respect to ϕ. Let us consider the process $P' = l.Nil + l.h_1.Nil + l.h_2.Nil$. After performing l this process always reaches a state which has the property ϕ and hence it cannot be considered as safe with respect to ϕ but, we stress, these two processes cannot be distinguished by any opacity property since the "safety" property is not a property of traces. This motivates us to a new security concept.

4   Process Opacity

Let us assume that an intruder tries to discover whether a given process reaches a state with some given property expressed by a (total) predicate. This property might be process deadlock, capability to execute only traces with time length less then n, capability to perform at the same time actions form a given set, incapacity to idle (to perform t action) etc. We do not put any restrictions on such the predicate but we only assume that it is consistent with some suitable behaviorial equivalence. The formal definition of this follows.

Definition 5. *We say that the predicate ϕ over processes is consistent with respect to relation $\cong$ if whenever $P \cong P'$ then $\phi(P) \Leftrightarrow \phi(P')$.*

As consistency relation $\cong$ we could take bisimulation ($\approx_{\emptyset}$), weak bisimulation ($\approx_{\{\tau\}}$) or any other suitable equivalence. We suppose that the intruder can only observe some activities performed by the process. We use a modified concept of observation functions to express what could be observed (motivated also by SNNI property). We suppose that there is a set of public actions which can be observed and a set of hidden (not necessarily private) actions. To model observations we exploit the relation $\overset{s}{\Rightarrow}_M$. Now formal definition of process opacity, which is inspired by opacity, follows.

Definition 6 (Process Opacity). *Given process P, a predicate ϕ over processes is process opaque w.r.t. the set M if whenever $P \overset{s}{\Rightarrow}_M P'$ for $s \in (Actt \setminus M)^*$ and $\phi(P')$ holds then there exists P'' such that $P \overset{s}{\Rightarrow}_M P''$ and $\neg\phi(P'')$ holds. The set of processes for which the predicate ϕ is process opaque w.r.t. to the M will be denoted by POp_M^ϕ.*

Example 3. Let $M = \{h_1, h_2\}$ and let the property ϕ states that a process cannot perform both actions h_1 and h_2. Then $P \in POp_M^\phi$ but $P' \notin POp_M^\phi$ where P, P' are taken from Example 2. Recall that these two processes could not be distinguished by opacity.

Note that if $P \cong P'$ then $P \in POp_M^\phi \Leftrightarrow P' \in POp_M^\phi$ whenever ϕ is consistent with respect to $\cong$ and $\cong$ is such that it a subset of the trace equivalence (defined as $\simeq_w$ but insted of $\overset{s}{\Rightarrow}_{\{\tau\}}$ we use $\overset{s}{\Rightarrow}_\emptyset$). Process opacity is the monotonic property with respect to the set of invisible actions M, anti-monotonic with respect to the strength of predicates over processes and undecidable in general, as it is stated in the following propositions.

Proposition 1. $POp_{M_1}^\phi \subseteq POp_{M_2}^\phi$ *for* $M_1 \subseteq M_2$ *and* $POp_M^{\phi_1} \subseteq POp_M^{\phi_2}$ *if* ϕ_2 *implies* ϕ_1.

Proof. Suppose that there exists P such that $P \in POp_{M_1}^\phi$ but $P \notin POp_{M_2}^\phi$. That means that there exists s such that $P \overset{s}{\Rightarrow}_{M_2} P'$ such that $\phi(P')$ holds but there is no P'' such that $P \overset{s}{\Rightarrow}_{M_2} P''$ and $\phi(P'')$ does not hold. Without loss of generality we can assume that $s|_{M_2} = \epsilon$ i.e. s does not contain actions from M_2. We know that there exist s', s'' such that $s'|_{Actt \setminus M_2} = s$, $P \overset{s'}{\rightarrow} P'$ and $s'' \in (Actt \setminus M_1)^*$ such that $s'|_{Actt \setminus M_1} = s''$. We have $P \overset{s''}{\Rightarrow}_{M_1} P'$. But hence there should exists P''' such that $P \overset{s''}{\Rightarrow}_{M_1} P'''$ for which $\phi(P''')$ does not hold what contradicts our assumption since also $P \overset{s''}{\Rightarrow}_{M_2} P'$ and $P \overset{s''}{\Rightarrow}_{M_2} P'''$ as well as since $M_1 \subseteq M_2$.

Now let $P \in POp_M^{\phi_1}$ and $P \overset{s}{\Rightarrow}_M P'$ such that $\phi_2(P')$ holds. Then also $\phi_1(P')$ holds and hence there exist P'' such that $P \overset{s}{\Rightarrow}_M P''$ and $\neg\phi_1(P'')$ holds. Then also $\neg\phi_2(P'')$ holds what means that $P \in POp_M^{\phi_2}$.

Proposition 2. *Process opacity is undecidable in general.*

Proof. Clearly process opacity is undecidable if the corresponding predicate over processes is undecidable itself. But it could be undecidable even for simple decidable predicates. Let ϕ holds for processes which can perform an action. And let $M = At$. Then the question $P \in POp_M^\phi$ corresponds to the halting problem for Turing machines (due to the universal power of TPA which results from the universal power of CCS which is its subcalculus). Note that by similar arguments undecidability of opacity has been proved (see [BKR04, BKMR06]).

To obtain a decidable variant of process opacity we put some restriction on process predicates. First we model predicates by special processes called tests.

For now we assume that action τ is not visible for an intruder, i.e. $\tau \in M$. The tests communicate with processes and produce $\sqrt{}$ action if corresponding predicates hold for the processes. In the subsequent proposition we show how to exploit this idea to express process opacity by means of appropriate M-bisimulation.

Definition 7. *We say that the process T_ϕ is the test representing predicate ϕ if $\phi(P)$ holds iff $(P|T_\phi) \backslash At \approx_t \sqrt{}.Nil$ where $\sqrt{}$ is a new action indicating a passing of the test. If T_ϕ is the finite state process we say that ϕ is the finitely definable predicate.*

Proposition 3. *Let us extend the set of actions by actions with upper indexes 1 and 2, respectively and let us introduce a new action k. Suppose that relabeling functions f_1 and f_2 map actions from A to A^1 and to A^2, respectively. Let $B = \mu X.(\sum_{l_i \in A \backslash M}(l_i^1.l_i^2.X + \bar{k}.\bar{k}.Nil))$. Then $P \in POp_M^\phi$ iff*

$$(P[f_1]|P[f_2]|B|k.T_\phi[f_1]|k.T_{\neg\phi}[f_2]) \approx_{M \cup \{t\}} \sqrt{}_1.\sqrt{}_2.Nil + \sqrt{}_2.\sqrt{}_1.Nil + \sqrt{}_2.Nil.$$

Proof. Sketch. The auxiliary process B produces visible actions for each copy of P or produces k actions which start validations of ϕ and $\neg\phi$, respectively, by corresponding tests. Then if process passes the test for validity of ϕ it has to pass also the test for validity of $\neg\phi$ (ordering is not important) or can pass only the test of validity of $\neg\phi$ or none. Note that time behaviour is checked by tests. This is the reason why we can use $\approx_{M \cup \{t\}}$ instead of $\approx_M$.

Now, thanks to the above introduced construction, we can obtain a variant of decidable process opacity. Actually, a limitation to finite states tests is practically insignificant since the most of (if not all) practically important properties can be described by them.

Proposition 4. *Let ϕ and $\neg\phi$ are finitely definable predicates. Then process opacity property POp_M^ϕ is decidable in time $O((n.m.|A|)^3)$ for finite state processes, where n and m are numbers of states of P and the maximum of numbers of states of tests corresponding to ϕ and $\neg\phi$.*

Proof. According to Proposition 3 it is enough to prove that $\approx_{M \cup \{t\}}$ can be decided in time $O((n.m.|A|)^3)$. This can be done by slight modification of the proof of complexity results for weak bisimulation (see [KS83]).

The definition of process opacity of predicate ϕ is asymmetric in the sense that if $\phi(P')$ does not hold than it is not required that there exists another process for which it holds (in general $POp_M^\phi \neq POp_M^{\neg\phi}$). This means that process opacity says something to an intruder who tries to detect only validity of ϕ (if it is process opaque, than validity cannot be detected) but nothing about its non-validity i.e. it says nothing about predicate $\neg\phi$. Hence we define a strong variant of process opacity.

Definition 8 (Strong Process Opacity). *Given process P, a predicate ϕ over processes is process opaque w.r.t. the set M if whenever $P \overset{s}{\Rightarrow}_M P_1'$ for $s \in (Actt \setminus M)^*$ and $\phi(P_1')$ holds then there exists P_1'' such that $P \overset{s}{\Rightarrow}_M P_1''$ and $\neg\phi(P_1'')$ holds. Moreover, whenever $P \overset{s'}{\Rightarrow}_M P_2'$ for $s' \in (Actt \setminus M)^*$ and $\neg\phi(P_2')$ holds then there exists P_2'' such that $P \overset{s'}{\Rightarrow}_M P_2''$ and $\phi(P_2'')$ holds. The set of processes for which the predicate ϕ is strongly process opaque w.r.t. the M will be denoted by $SPOp_M^\phi$.*

For strong process opacity we could formulate similar properties as those ones which hold for process opacity (see Proposition 1–3). But instead of that we clarify, by the following two lemmas, the relationship between strong process opacity and process opacity. Note that from computational point of view predicates ϕ and $\neg\phi$ could be different.

Lemma 1. $SPOp_M^\phi \subseteq POp_M^\phi$ *for every ϕ. Moreover, there exist ϕ and M such that $SPOp_M^\phi \subset POp_M^\phi$.*

Proof. The first part clearly follows from definitions of process opacity and strong process opacity. Now let as assume process $P = h.l.l.Nil + l.Nil$ and a property (ϕ) that process can perform an action. Then we have $P \in POp_{\{h\}}^\phi$ but $P \notin SPOp_{\{h\}}^\phi$.

Lemma 2. $SPOp_M^\phi = SPOp_M^{\neg\phi}$ *and* $SPOp_M^\phi = POp^\phi \cap POp_M^{\neg\phi}$ *for every ϕ and M.*

Proof. The proof clearly follows from definitions of process opacity and strong process opacity.

If we have a process which does not belong to SOp_M^ϕ for some ϕ and M then this means that the process could be jeopardized by an attacker who can learn validity of the secrete property expressed by ϕ. The presented framework allows us also to distinguish various types of attacks. For example, it can identify timing attacks which represent a powerful tool for "breaking" "unbreakable" systems, algorithms, protocols, etc. To describe them we could exploit time sensitive predicates, i.e. predicates for which there exist processes P, P' such that $P \approx_{\{t\}} P'$ and $\phi(P) \wedge \neg\phi(P')$ holds. That means, that validity of ϕ depends on time behaviour of processes since for two processes, which differ only in time behaviour, the predicate has different values. But timing attacks might be more subtle and also time aspects of executions might be of importance. So we formulate sensitivity for timing attacks more generally in terms of process opacity but the same can be done also for strong process opacity.

Definition 9. *We say that process P could be jeopardized by a timing attack on validity of ϕ w.r.t the set M, $t \notin M$ iff $P \in POp_{M \cup \{t\}}^\phi$ but $P \notin POp_M^\phi$.*

Example 4. Let us assume (no time sensitive) predicate ϕ which is valid if process can perform an action b. Let $P = t.a.b.Nil + a.Nil$. $P \in POp_{\{t\}}^{\phi}$ but $P \notin POp_{\emptyset}^{\phi}$ and hence it could be jeopardized by attackers who see all actions including elapsing of time. For attackers who do not see elapsing of time the process is secure.

5   Discussion and Further Work

We have presented the new security properties called process opacity and strong process opacity and we have formalized them in the timed process algebra setting. They can be used to model different security properties than traditional ones. Moreover, by careful choice of processes expressing predicates we can obtain properties which can be effectively checked. We can model security with respect to limited time length of an attack, with a limited number of attempts to perform an attack and so on. The presented approach allows us to exploit also process algebras enriched by operators expressing other "parameters" (space, distribution, networking architecture, processor, power consumption and so on). In this way also other types of attacks, which exploit information flow through various covert channels, can be described. We plan to study more sophisticated observational functions as well as compositional properties of process opacity so that bottom-up design of secure processes would be possible. In the future we also plan to further elaborate the technique which has been used for expressing timing attacks as well as to enrich the presented framework by value-passing features.

References

[BKR04]   Bryans, J., Koutny, M., Ryan, P.: Modelling non-deducibility using Petri Nets. In: Proceedings of the 2nd International Workshop on Security Issues with Petri Nets and Other Computational Models (2004)

[BKMR06] Bryans, J.W., Koutny, M., Mazaré, L., Ryan, P.Y.A.: Opacity generalised to transition systems. In: Dimitrakos, T., Martinelli, F., Ryan, P.Y.A., Schneider, S. (eds.) FAST 2005. LNCS, vol. 3866, pp. 81–95. Springer, Heidelberg (2006)

[FGM00]   Focardi, R., Gorrieri, R., Martinelli, F.: Information flow analysis in a discrete-time process algebra. In: Proceedings of 13th Computer Security Foundation Workshop. IEEE Computer Society Press (2000)

[GM04]   Gorrieri, R., Martinelli, F.: A simple framework for real-time cryptographic protocol analysis with compositional proof rules. Sci. Comput. Program. 50(1–3), 23–49 (2004)

[GM82]   Goguen, J.A., Meseguer, J.: Security policies and security Models. In: Proceedings of IEEE Symposium on Security and Privacy (1982)

[Gro90]   Groote, J.F.: Transition system specifications with negative premises. In: Baeten, J.C.M., Klop, J.W. (eds.) CONCUR 1990. LNCS, vol. 458, pp. 332–341. Springer, Heidelberg (1990)

[Gru12a] Gruska, D.P.: Informational analysis of security and integrity. Fundamenta Informaticae **120**(3–4), 295–309 (2012)

[Gru12b] Test based security: Concurrency, Specification and Verification CS&P 2012, Berlin, vol. 1 (2012)

[Gru10] Gruska, D.P.: Process algebra contexts and security properties. Fundamenta Informaticae **102**(1), 63–76 (2010)

[Gru07] Gruska, D.P.: Observation based system security. Fundamenta Informaticae **79**(3–4), 335–346 (2007)

[KS83] Kanellakis, P.C., Smolka, S.A.: CCS expressions, finite state processes, and three problems of equivalence. In: Proceedings of the Second Annual ACM Symposium on Principles of Distributed Computing, ACM (1983)

A Proof-Based Method for Modelling Timed Systems

Alexei Iliasov$^{(\boxtimes)}$ and Jeremy Bryans

Newcastle University, Newcastle, UK
alexei.iliasov@ncl.ac.uk

Abstract. We present a novel method for reasoning about time in state-based proof-oriented formalisms. The method builds on a non-classical model of time, the Leibnizian model, in which time is a relative property determined by the observations of an evolving subject, rather than one of the fundamental dimensions. It proves to be remarkably effective in the context of the Event-B formalism. We illustrate the method with a machine-checked proof of Fischer's algorithm that, to our knowledge, is simpler than other proofs available in the literature.

1 Introduction

Many systems require not only the demonstration of functional correctness but also a solid argument for the ability of a system to deliver its services in a timely manner. This is especially true for safety-critical embedded systems where formal modelling is already applied with some success. However, at the moment, the question of capturing time requirements in a real-life formal design is still largely open.

The concept of time features prominently in the field of formal verification and there is a large number of dedicated notations and semantics [2,7,16,19]. Notably, most of them are based on the *Newtonian model* where an absolute time frame determines the time coordinate of all the entities in a universe.

In this paper we present a method for modelling timed systems that makes use of the Leibnizian model of time [11]. In this model, time is not a fundamental dimension but rather a concept arising due to changes in an observed entity. Whereas in the Newtonian model, an entity in the past and an entity in the present are distinguished by consulting a common reference frame, in the Leibnizian model they are different only if some observer is able and willing to tell them apart.

The *dichotomy* of the Leibnizian model, in which two separate entities are necessary to define the notion of time, suggests that all the time-related properties may be isolated in the observer part leaving the part being observed to deal with functional properties. This has important practical implications: the formulation of timing constraints does not have to be notationally tied with the description of behaviour and so that existing methods, semantics and tools may be employed in specifying functional properties. The symmetry between observer

© Springer-Verlag Berlin Heidelberg 2015
A. Voronkov and I. Virbitskaite (Eds.): PSI 2014, LNCS 8974, pp. 161–176, 2015.
DOI: 10.1007/978-3-662-46823-4_14

and an entity observes means that an observer may also be specified using an un-timed modelling notation. The concept of time arises when two models are combined in a certain way. Crucially, with the Leibnizian model, existing modelling notations and tools may be used without any adaptations, as demonstrate in our case study.

We use the Event-B notation [4], and show how these ideas may be embedded within that. One closely related work is that of Abadi and Lamport [2] which shows that timing constraints may be expressed directly in TLA without syntactic or semantic extensions. Previous work on modelling time in B uses a clock variable which records the current value of a clock, and an operation is given to advance time [8]. This approach is taken up again for Event B in [9]. In [13] the concept of time is embedded into the B notation itself. Time is modelled by equipping a machine with a clock and assuming that an event execution is not instantaneous. Timed automata [5] offers a formal framework for specifying real-time properties by enriching the state of an automata with a number real-valued clocks. The UPPAAL [7] tool offers support for automated verification of timed automata. Timed process algebras have been researched extensively and there is a large variety of notations and semantics. Timed extensions of CSP [19] and CCS [16] are two notable examples. In particular, the elegance of the Timed CSP language was one motivating factor for this work.

Fischer's algorithm is a stock verification problem that has been verified in one way or another using almost every applicable formalism such as timed CSP [19], TLA [2] and timed automata [7]. Of particular relevance to our approach are simulation-based techniques such as [12, 14], although taking this approach leads to considerable complexity in the resultant proofs.

The paper is structured as follows. Section 2 is a brief introduction to the concepts and structures of the Leibnizian model of time. Section 3 describes a modelling notation, Event-B, employed in the definition of an observed object of our case study. In Sect. 4 we apply the discussed technique to prove Fischer's mutual exclusion algorithm, and we discuss conclusions in Sect. 5.

2   Leibnizian Time Model

Our ambition is to offer a technique to specify and verify time constraints in large-scale formal designs. Such designs are necessarily constructed in a modular, incremental way using formal refinement and typically employ theorem proving as a verification technology [6]. Industrial application of formal methods requires mature and scalable tools thus often rendering new notations and logics impractical. The proposed technique attempts to introduce discplined and systematic treatment of time into proof-oriented model-based notations such as B, Z and VDM, not otherwise equipped for dealing with time.

The rest of the section defines essential concepts of our approach to introducing time reasoning using the Leibnizian time model. For brevity, we omit proofs but these are available in the Appendix or the B model [1].

A fundamental concept is that of a process, which we define to be a transition system.

Definition 1 (Process). *A process* P *is a tuple* $(\alpha P, p, \iota P)$ *where* αP *is a set of process* states, $p \subset \alpha P \times \alpha P$ *is a transition relation and* $\iota P \subseteq \alpha P$ *is the set of initial states.*

Time appears when we put together two processes and let them interact in a certain way. The nature of the interaction is what intuitively may be regarded as an observation of one process by another.

Definition 2 (Observation Connection). *An* observation connection *between processes* C *and* S *is a relation* $\varphi \subseteq \alpha S \times \alpha C$.

A timed system is formed by a pair of processes where one process, an *observer*, is said to observe another process, a *subject*. In the definition above, C is an observer and S is a subject.

Definition 3 (Timed System). *An observer process* C, *a subject process* S *and an observation connection* φ *define a* timed system $C \cdot \varphi \cdot S$.

The following timed system *interpretation* gives a precise meaning to the observational power of an observer. It defines valid, in the sense of our timing approach, transitions of a Cartesian product of two transition systems.

Definition 4 (Interpretation of a Timed System). *Given a timed system* $C \cdot \varphi \cdot S$ *where* $S = (\alpha S, s, \iota S)$ *and* $C = (\alpha C, c, \iota C)$, *its interpretation is a process*

$$\mathbb{I}(C \cdot \varphi \cdot S) \equiv (\varphi, \tau(C \cdot \varphi \cdot S), (\iota S \times \iota C) \cap \varphi)$$

such that $(\iota S \times \iota C) \cap \varphi \neq \varnothing$ *(existence of initialisation) and every mapping* $(u \mapsto t) \mapsto (u' \mapsto t') \in (\alpha S \times \alpha C) \times (\alpha S \times \alpha C)$ *of transition relation* $\tau(C \cdot \varphi \cdot S)$ *satisfies the following properties:*

(a) $u \mapsto u' \in s$ (a valid transition of a subject process),
(b) $t \mapsto t' \in c$ (a valid transition of an observer process),
(c) $u \mapsto t, u' \mapsto t' \in \varphi$ (subject and observer transitions are in synchrony).

One may regard an observer as a historian with a preconceived notion of subject process behaviour. An observer would not tolerate a subject that does not follow a certain plan or timetable.

The following two definitions address the ability of a program to progress towards and reach a specific point in its lifetime, that is, ensuring that "eventually some good thing will happen" [2].

It may happen that a proof of some properties is solely due to a mismatch between observer and subject processes resulting in an empty interpretation with no state transitions. To ensure that this is not the case, and that proofs are not vacuously true, it is sufficient to exhibit an initialisation of the timed system.

Definition 5 (Consistency). *A timed system* $C \cdot \varphi \cdot S$ *is consistent if it holds that* $\exists x, y \cdot x \mapsto y \in \iota S \times \iota C \wedge x \mapsto y \in \varphi$.

When an observer may reject certain subject states one may not reason about liveness of a timed system on the basis of the liveness of a subject alone. In abstract models, to assist with liveness proofs, it is useful to ensure that an observer is prepared to accept any execution of a subject process. Then one knows a priori that something happens in a subject process for every point of time defined by an observer.

Definition 6 (Strictness). *A timed system* $\mathcal{A} = (\alpha C, c, \iota C) \cdot \varphi \cdot (\alpha S, s, \iota S)$ *is strict if for every* $u \mapsto t \in \alpha S \times \alpha C$ *and* $t \mapsto t' \in c$ *there exists some* u' *such that* $u' \mapsto t' \in \tau(\mathcal{A})$ *and* $\iota C \subseteq \varphi[\iota S]$.[1]

Notice that structure $\tau'(\mathcal{A}) = (\alpha C \times \alpha S, \tau(\mathcal{A}), \alpha C \times \alpha S)$ defines a new process as a product of two simpler processes. Also, observation connection φ of a strict timed system defines a simulation relation between subject and observer processes.

Watching is the observation of a timed system with another observer. Informally, an external observer makes a record of observations using its own time-keeping device.

Definition 7 (Watching). *Watching* $\xi(C \cdot \varphi \cdot S)_{T,\omega}$ *of a timed system* $\mathcal{A} = C \cdot \varphi \cdot S$ *is a process* $\xi(\mathcal{A})_{T,\omega} = (\varphi; \omega, L[\tau(T \cdot \omega \cdot \tau'(\mathcal{A}))], \iota T)$ *where* $T \cdot \omega \cdot \tau(\mathcal{A})$ *is strict,* ω *is total and functional; projection* L *removes states of process* C: $L[X] = \{((a, b), \{c\}) \mapsto (a, c) \mid ((a, b), \{c\}) \in X\}$. *Also,* $L[\iota\mathcal{A} \times \iota T] \cap \omega \neq \varnothing$.[2]

A watching is itself a transition system hence it may be possible to replace a timed system with its watching. One reason to do this is to separate the proof of logical properties relevant to timing constraints from the proof of how these properties may be expressed in a specific, implementation-oriented form, e.g., hard real-time constraints.

As a methodological principle, whenever possible, we insist that an observer C of an observed timed system is tasked with the definition of event orderings or, at a coarse granularity level, a form of scheduling policy, and just strong to proof relevant properties. Then the consideration of delays, deadlines, durations and the like may be isolated in the observer defining the watching of the original system thus allowing a modeller to reuse the core of proof when considering differing physical, be that discrete, dense or continuous.

An *animation* is a watching satisfying certain conditions. Let $B(X)$ denote the existence lower and upper bounds in X w.r.t. the relation $\prec$ of process $Y = (\alpha Y, \prec)$: $B(X) \equiv X \subseteq \alpha Y \wedge (\exists l, u \cdot l, u \in \alpha Y \wedge (\forall p \cdot p \in X \Rightarrow l \prec p \prec u))$.

Definition 8 (Animation of Timed System). *An animation of* $C \cdot \varphi \cdot S$ *is a watching* $\xi(C \cdot \varphi \cdot S)_{T,\omega}$ *such that* T *is monotone and every bounded subset of* αT *maps to a finite sequence of subject actions.*

Animation may be seen as physical device iterating through the steps of a timed system. For such a device to exist, the time flow of the animated timed system must be compatible with physical time.

---

[1] Notation $f[X]$ defines a relation image: $f[X] = \{z \mid y \in X \cap \text{dom}(f) \wedge z = f(y)\}$.
[2] $f; g$ is a forward relational composition: $f; g = \{a \mapsto b \mid a \mapsto e \in f \wedge e \mapsto b \in g\}$.

2.1   Realisability

If the aim of a development is a piece of software or hardware to be deployed in physical reality, it is necessary to check, at the level of a concrete design, that the following *realisability conditions* are respected by an observer process: (1) time advance is monotonic, and (2) an infinite number of subject steps corresponds to an infinite number of observer steps. These conditions, often embedded into the definition a timed language, e.g., [19], allow one to avoid design pitfalls such as Zeno behaviour. Existence of animation (Definition 8) is a criterion of realisability.

The following is one sufficient condition of realisability.

Theorem 1 (Criterion of Realisability, 1). *A timed system is realisable if it admits an animation based on a strict partial order with a countable alphabet.*

Realisability may also be demonstrated by exhibiting an animator process with a fixed granularity of time increments. Some Timed CSP semantics [10] rely on a similar approach while an alternative, taken in [19], is to prove the so-called finite variability condition - an equivalent of the property expressed in Definition 8. The granularity technique is applied when an observer alphabet may not be made countable, i.e., it is essential to use a dense order as the time model.

Theorem 2 (Criterion of Realisability, 2). *Let $\mathsf{T} = (\alpha\mathsf{T}, \prec, \iota\mathsf{T})$ be a metric space with metric d and $\prec$ is monotonic and irreflexive; T animates system $\mathsf{C} \cdot \varphi \cdot \mathsf{S}, \mathsf{S} = (\alpha\mathsf{S}, s, \iota\mathsf{S})$ with animation connection ω if $(\varphi; \omega)[\iota\mathsf{S}] \neq \varnothing$ and there exists δ such that for any $s_1 \mapsto s_2 \in s$ it holds that $\delta \prec d_H((\varphi; \omega)(s_1), (\varphi; \omega)(s_2))$ where d_H is the Hausdorff distance[3].*

2.2   Refinement

Refinement is an indispensable tool in the construction of large models. For brevity, we only consider the forward simulation criterion of refinement [18]. The section defines the verification conditions necessary to establish forward simulation between two timed systems.

Definition 9 (Forward Simulation). *$\mathcal{B}$ is a forward simulation of $\mathcal{A}$ if there exists relation $l \subseteq \alpha\mathcal{B} \times \alpha\mathcal{A}$ such that $\iota\mathcal{B} \subseteq l^{-1}[\iota\mathcal{A}]$ and $l^{-1}; \mathcal{B} \subseteq \mathcal{A}; l^{-1}$ where $\iota\mathcal{A}$ and $\iota\mathcal{B}$ are sets of initial states of $\mathcal{A}$ and $\mathcal{B}$.*

We write $\mathcal{A} \sqsubseteq_l \mathcal{B}$ if $\mathcal{B}$ is a forward a simulation of $\mathcal{A}$ w.r.t. simulation relation l. An important precursor to the definition of timed refinement is the following explicit form of the transition relation of an interpretation of a timed system.

Lemma 1. *Given $\mathsf{C} = (\alpha\mathsf{C}, c, \iota\mathsf{C})$ and $\mathsf{S} = (\alpha\mathsf{S}, s, \iota\mathsf{S})$, process $(\alpha\mathsf{S} \times \alpha\mathsf{C}, (s \parallel c) \cap (\varphi \times \varphi), (\iota\mathsf{S} \times \iota\mathsf{C}) \cap \varphi)$ is the least constrained interpretation of timed system $\mathsf{C} \cdot \varphi \cdot \mathsf{S}$[4].*

---

[3] $d_H(A, B) = \max\{\sup_{x \in A} \inf_{y \in B} d(x, y), \sup_{x \in B} \inf_{y \in A} d(x, y)\}$.

[4] $a \parallel b = \{(x \mapsto i) \mapsto (y \mapsto j) \mid x \mapsto y \in a \land i \mapsto j \in b\}$ *(parallel product).*

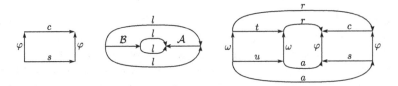

Fig. 1. Timed refinement diagrams.

Lemma 1, stating that any observation is contained in $(s \,\|\, c) \cap (\varphi \times \varphi)$, leads to the crucial *decomposability* property of timed refinement: to prove refinement of a timed system one may *separately* consider refinement of observer and subject processes. The part that makes this work is the *synchrony condition* requiring to prove that a concrete state projected into some abstract states is observed at a time similar to when the abstract state is observed. Similar condition appears, for instance, in the definition of timed automata simulation [15].

Definition 10 (Forward Simulation of Timed Systems). *Let* $\mathsf{C} = (\alpha\mathsf{C}, c, \iota\mathsf{C})$, $\mathsf{S} = (\alpha\mathsf{S}, s, \iota\mathsf{S})$, $\mathsf{T} = (\alpha\mathsf{T}, t, \iota\mathsf{T})$, $\mathsf{U} = (\alpha\mathsf{U}, u, \iota\mathsf{U})$, $a \subseteq \alpha\mathsf{U} \times \alpha\mathsf{S}$ *and* $r \subseteq \alpha\mathsf{T} \times \alpha\mathsf{C}$. *If the following conditions are satisfied:*

(a) $\mathsf{U} \sqsubseteq_a \mathsf{S}$ *(simulation of subjects w.r.t. relation $a \subseteq \alpha\mathsf{U} \times \alpha\mathsf{S}$),*
(b) $\mathsf{T} \sqsubseteq_r \mathsf{C}$ *(simulation of observers w.r.t. relation $r \subseteq \alpha\mathsf{T} \times \alpha\mathsf{C}$),*
(c) $a^{-1}; \omega; r \subseteq \varphi$ *(synchrony condition),*

then it holds that $\mathsf{T} \cdot \omega \cdot \mathsf{U} \sqsubseteq_l \mathsf{C} \cdot \varphi \cdot \mathsf{S}$ *with* $l = (a \,\|\, r) \cap (\omega \times \varphi)$.

The diagrams in Fig. 1 illustrate the structures employed in timed refinement. The first diagram depicts $(s \,\|\, c) \cap (\varphi \times \varphi)$ (commutes only in the case of a *strict* time system, see Definition 6). The second diagram shows a simulation of $\mathcal{A}$ by $\mathcal{B}$ and, according to Definition 9, it weakly commutes with $l^{-1}; \mathcal{B} \subseteq \mathcal{A}; l^{-1}$ (each l arc is doubled to help explain the third diagram). The third diagram is a fusion of the first two where $\mathcal{A}$ and $\mathcal{B}$ are instantiated by respective timed transitions (linked by observation connections φ and ω) and l is replaced with $(a \,\|\, r) \cap (\omega \times \varphi)$.

It must be the case that the conditions of Definition 10 and the identified simulation relation l satisfy Definition 9 of forward simulation.

Theorem 3. *Forward simulation of timed systems is sound.*

It is often necessary to consider an untimed model in a timed context. The following is a trivial extension of this kind where an untimed processed defines a (trivial) timed system by observing itself.

Definition 11 (Timed Extension). *A timed extension* $\bar{\mathsf{S}}$ *of a process* S *is a timed system* $\mathsf{S} \cdot \mathrm{id}(S) \cdot \mathsf{S}$.

A timed refinement of an untimed process is used to introduce time reasoning within an untimed development.

Definition 12 (Timed Refinement of an Untimed Process). *For some process* S *and timed system* T·ω·U *it is said that* S *is refined by* T·ω·U, S ⊑$_a$ T·ω·U *if it holds that the timed extension of* S *is refined by* T · ω · U: S̄ ⊑$_{a \parallel (\omega^{-1};a)}$ T · ω · U.

From our experience in using this framework, it is best to start with the specification of an untimed system (subject) deliberately making an effort to not introduce any timing or time-related ordering constraints into the model. Assuming the modelled problem requires modelling time, then either some verification conditions will be not expressible in the alphabet of the subject process or there will unprovable verification conditions. For the former case, one needs to couple the subject specification with a suitable observer model. A good starting point is to postulate the desired property in the observer model and later have it refined into a realisable time model.

For the latter, however, it is more suitable to refine an untimed (or, implicitly timed, as per Definition 11) with a timed model. This naturally introduces time as a form of scheduling policy enabling verification of stronger properties. We illustrate this technique in Sect. 4.

3   Background

To describe the subject process behaviour of the case study system we apply Event-B modelling language [4]. We choose Event-B mainly for our previous experience and the maturity of its modelling toolkit [17] which has allowed us to express both subject and observer in the same development and use the built-in automated provers and proof environment to construct all the proofs. Event-B does not allow one to define a product of two machines. Hence, for the modelling of observer process, we have to resort to specifying observer state transitions and observation connection in the algebraic style. Section 3.2 presents some fundamental constructs used in such definitions.

3.1   Event-B

Event-B is a state-based formal development method for the realisation of correct-by-construction information systems. The general form of an Event-B model (or *machine*) is shown in Fig. 2. A machine encapsulates a state space, defined by *machine variables*, and provides transitions on the state, as described by *machine events*. An event E_i is characterised by a list of parameters p_i, a state predicate G_u called an *event guard*, and a next-state relation S_i.

The **INVARIANT** clause defines the properties of a system, expressed as state predicates, that must be preserved during the system lifetime. The states defined by an invariant are called the *safe states* of a system. A correct model is proven to never leave its safe states. Data types s, constants c and relevant axioms are defined in a separate component called a *context*, and included into a machine with the **SEES** clause.

The consistency of a machine as well as the correctness of refinement steps is demonstrated by discharging relevant *proof obligations* which, collectively, define

```
MACHINE M
   SEES Context
   VARIABLES v
   INVARIANT I(c, s, v)
   INITIALISATION S_I(c, s, v')
   EVENTS
      E_i = any p_i where G_i(c, s, p_i, v) then S_i(c, s, p_i, v, v') end
END
```

Fig. 2. Event-B model structure.

the Event-B *proof semantics* [4]. The Rodin Platform [17], a tool supporting Event-B, is an integrated environment that automatically generates necessary proof obligations and providers a number of automated provers and solvers along with an interactive proof environment.

An Event-B machine defines a state transition system. Let $\Omega = \{v \mid I(c, s, v)\}$ be the (safe) states of a machine where v and $I(c, s, v)$ are the variables and the invariant of a machine. The relational form of an event e is $[e]_R \equiv \{v \mapsto v' \mid \exists p \cdot (G_e(c, s, p, v) \wedge S_e(c, s, p, v, v'))\}$.

Definition 13 (Event-B Transition System). *A machine defines a transition system* (Ω, f, ω_0) *where* $f : \Omega \rightarrow \mathbb{P}(\Omega)$ *is defined as* $f = (\bigcup_e [e]_R)$; *the set of initial states* $\omega_0 \subseteq \Omega$ *is defined by the initialisation predicate* S_I: $\omega_0 = \{v' \mid S_I(c, s, v')\}$.

The cornerstone of Event-B development method is *refinement* – the process of transforming an abstract specification by gradually introducing implementation details while preserving correctness. A number of *refinement proof obligations* implement the forward simulation criterion of refinement [4].

3.2 Observer Modelling

One important class of observers are those able to reason about duration of subject's actions. A suitable characterisation of such an observer is an ordered abelian group. *clock observer.*

Definition 14 (Additive Clock). *An additive clock* C *is a process defined by group* $(\alpha C, \prec, *, e)$ *where* $*$ *is a commutative binary operation and* $\prec$ *is a linear order. Element* $e \in \alpha C$ *is the left and right unit of* $*$.

To reason about time intervals we make use of some simple topological properties of the additive clock structure.

The relation $\preccurlyeq$ is a reflexive closure of $\prec$ and is defined as $\preccurlyeq = \prec \cup \mathrm{id}(\alpha C)$. Also, $[\![P(\omega)]\!]$ stands for the set of all time points projected from states defined by predicate $P(\omega)$: $[\![P(\omega)]\!] \equiv \varphi[\{\omega \mid P(\omega)\}]$.

Notice that $+$ and $\prec$ induce a metric space on C. The distance d between some points $i, j \in \alpha C$ is taken to be $d(i, j) = \max\{i - j, j - i\}$ where $\max\{a, b\} = a$ when $b \preccurlyeq a$ and $\max\{a, b\} = b$ otherwise. The diameter $\mathrm{diam}(A)$ of a set A is defined as $\mathrm{diam}(A) = \sup\{d(i, j) \mid i, j \in A\}$.

Relations $\prec$ and $\preccurlyeq$ may be lifted to sets in the following manner: $A \star B \Leftrightarrow \forall i, j \cdot i \in A \land j \in B \Rightarrow i \star j$, where $\star \in \{\prec, \preccurlyeq\}$.

A set A is said to be *not bigger* than some value $r \in \alpha C$, written as $A \trianglelefteq r$, if it is covered by a closed set of diameter r: $A \trianglelefteq r \Leftrightarrow \exists U \cdot \mathrm{diam}(U) \preccurlyeq r \land A \subseteq \mathrm{cl}(U)$. Symmetrically, a set is *not smaller* than r if it contains a closed set of diameter r: $A \trianglerighteq r \Leftrightarrow \exists U \cdot r \preccurlyeq \mathrm{diam}(U) \land \mathrm{cl}(U) \subseteq A$. Here $\mathrm{cl}(S)$ is a closure of S defined as the intersection of all closed sets containing set S.

Operators $\trianglerighteq$ and $\trianglelefteq$ define set measure where all points of some set of a given diameter are guaranteed to be a within or outside of the measured set without having to clarify whether the set is open, closed or neither.

4   Case Study: Fischer's Algorithm

As a case study we consider the problem of mutual exclusion: the regulation of competition among several processes for a shared resource that should be accessed by only one process at a time. In particular, we study Fischer's timing-based algorithm of mutual exclusion [2,19] that requires a single shared variable and uses execution speed constraints to ensure that a shared resource is only ever in the exclusive possession of a single process. To prove the correctness of the timed model we use an Event-B model to define an untimed, abstract mutual exclusion model that trivially possesses the desired properties. We proceed to demonstrate that a timed model realising Fischer's algorithm is a correct implementation of the abstract mutual exclusion. We achieve this by constructing subject and observer of the protocol and use our technique to link the two and construct a formal proof of correctness. We address only the basic case where, once a single process has entered the critical section, the system terminates. Following [2,19] we observe that the complete algorithm can be then be constructed in a straightforward manner.

In the remainder of this section, we give a formal definition of mutual exclusion (Sect. 4.1) as an abstract Event-B model, then outline Fischer's algorithm (Sect. 4.2). We define the subject and observer models (Sects. 4.3 and 4.4) then show the verification procedure (Sect. 4.5.)

4.1   Mutual Exclusion

We assume an entity external to the system keeping a track shared resource ownership. Let cs be the current owner of the critical section – a process number from 1 to n. Then value 0 denotes that the resource has no owner. The sole event of the model is the claiming of critical section ownership:

$$enter = \textbf{any } p \textbf{ where } p \in 1..n \land cs = 0 \textbf{ then } cs := p \textbf{ end}$$

```
1 :    if (x = 0) :
w1 :        wait(≤ δ_i);
2 :         x := i;
w2 :        wait(≥ ε_i);
3 :         if (x = i) :
4 :             // critical section
```

Fig. 3. Pseudo code of Fischer's algorithm (process i)

The model succinctly defines our verification goal. At this point, the formulation of the mutual exclusion property relies on an centralised supervisor implementing check $cs = 0$. Fischer's algorithm removes the supervisor and makes the system completely distributed.

4.2   Fischer's Algorithm

Fischer's algorithm uses a single $n + 1$ valued shared variable to implement mutual exclusion of n concurrent processes. A process may read the value of the shared variable and write its name into it (i.e., process i writes value i). The algorithm places constraints on the time delays for these actions. This permits an arrangement of test and update operations where at most one process may ever acquire the shared resource. The pseudo code for Fischer's algorithm is given in Fig. 3.

If process i discovers that the shared variable x has not been updated by another process (line 1), it waits for up to δ_i time units and then writes its name into x (line 2). It then waits again for no more then ε_i time units; this ascertains that the value of x has stabilised: any process that could have seen $x = 0$ in its history by this time must have written its name into x. We shall prove that the algorithm is correct for any delays ε_i, δ_j such that $\forall i, j \cdot \varepsilon_i > \delta_j$.

4.3   Subject Model

The algorithm correctness is established by demonstrating a timed refinement relation w.r.t. the abstract model of mutual exclusion. A pair of new variables is introduced: $x \in 0..n$ is the shared variable of the algorithm and function $s \in 1..n \rightarrow 1..4$ denotes the current execution stage of a process. Initially, all the process are at stage 1 (that is, prior to executing line 1 of the algorithm in Fig. 3), and x is initialised to 0.

The abstract statement $cs = 0$, saying that the shared resource is free, translates into a concrete statement over s that no process has obtained the resource.

$$(\forall p \cdot p \in 1..n \Rightarrow s(p) \neq 4) \Rightarrow cs = 0 \tag{1}$$

Symmetrically, the abstract condition $cs = p$, meaning that process p is the resource owner, is formulated as

$$\forall p \cdot p \in 1..n \wedge s(p) = 4 \Rightarrow cs = p \tag{2}$$

$read = $ **any** p **where** $p \in 1 \mathbin{..} n \wedge s(p) = 1 \wedge x = 0$ **then** $s(p) := 2$ **end**
$write = $ **any** p **where** $p \in 1 \mathbin{..} n \wedge s(p) = 2$ **then** $x := p \parallel s(p) := 3$ **end**
$enter = $ **any** p **where** $p \in 1 \mathbin{..} n \wedge s(p) = 3 \wedge x = p$ **then** $s(p) := 4$ **end**

Fig. 4. Event-B implementation of Fischer's algorithm (an excerpt).

which states that when a shared resource is owned by a process (i.e., $s(p) = 4$) then the name of the process agrees with the value of the abstract variable cs. These two conditions, called *gluing invariants*, provide a formal link between the states of the abstract model and its implementation by our model of Fischer's algorithm. Our proof technique is a case of data refinement, specifically forward simulation, which is an intrinsic part of the Event-B method.

The gluing invariants allow us to make certain observations about the model we are constructing. An event of the concrete model where a process claims the resource ownership (by setting $s(p) = 4$) must refine abstract event *enter* (see Stage 3 below) or it would violate Condition 2. The guard of *enter* demands that the critical section is free (predicate $cs = 0$). Consequently, the concrete behaviour implementing *enter* would have to establish that (1) holds, i.e., that there is no other process for which $s(p) = 4$. The following are the stages (events) of the model.

Stage 1: test for $x = 0$. A process starts and reads the shared variable x (Fig. 4, event *read*). If x contains the name of another process then the current process may not progress. If x contains no other process name the process updates $s(p)$ to indicate the progression to the next stage.

Stage 2: write process name into x. A process writes its name into shared variable x (Fig. 4, event *write*), and advances to stage 3.

Stage 3: test for $x = p$. A process checks if x still contains its name. If this is the case, then the process enters the critical section (Fig. 4, event *enter*). This event refines abstract event *enter*.

Stage 4: critical section. When a process reaches this point the system terminates.

The model is proven convergent – it is guaranteed to terminate. This is formally shown by proving that $4 * n - \sum_{p \in 1 \mathbin{..} n} s(p)$ is a valid model variant [3].

4.4 Observer Model

To define the timing constraints of the algorithm we use an additive clock observer (Definition 14). The observer model C is defined as $(\alpha C, \prec)$ with the usual $+$, 0 and $-$ symbols for an additive operation closed on αC, a zero of '$+$' and an inverse element operator.

Recall that the subject process state space is defined by variables $x \in 0 \mathbin{..} n, s \in 1 \mathbin{..} n \rightarrow 1 \mathbin{..} 4$. The observation connection (Definition 2) guarantees that the causality of computational steps of a subject is preserved in an observer. The following condition restates this property for Fischer's algorithm:

$$\forall p \cdot p \in 1..n \Rightarrow [\![s(p) = 1]\!] \preccurlyeq [\![s(p) = 2]\!] \preccurlyeq [\![s(p) = 3]\!] \preccurlyeq [\![s(p) = 4]\!]. \quad (3)$$

From the definition of the algorithm, while a process is at stage 2, any two time points projected from this state are no more than $\delta(p)$ units apart. We formally record this requirement by adding an axiom to the observer model stating that set $[\![s(p) = 2]\!]$ is not bigger than $\delta(p)$ (delay **w1** in Fig. 3):

$$\forall p \cdot p \in 1..n \Rightarrow [\![s(p) = 2]\!] \trianglelefteq \delta(p). \quad (4)$$

A process must spend at least $\varepsilon(p)$ time units at stage 3. Thus, the set projected from state $s(p) = 3$ is not smaller than $\varepsilon(p)$ (delay **w2** in Fig. 3):

$$\forall p \cdot p \in 1..n \Rightarrow [\![s(p) = 3]\!] \trianglerighteq \varepsilon(p). \quad (5)$$

A process may not discover that shared variable x is 0 if another process has already written its name into x. Whenever a process at stage 1 observes $x = 0$ it may not be the case that another process has updated x, i.e., is at stage 3 or 4. Because of (3), it is enough to state that $x = 0$ is not observed after some process has advanced to stage 3:

$$\forall p \cdot p \in 1..n \wedge [\![x = 0]\!] \preccurlyeq [\![s(p) = 3]\!]. \quad (6)$$

Finally, it is required that every ε is larger than any δ:

$$\forall p, q \cdot p, q \in 1..n \Rightarrow \delta(p) \prec \varepsilon(q). \quad (7)$$

Conditions 4–7 completely define the observer model.

For brevity, we omit the proof of consistency (see model in [1] for more details) and notice that due to the finite alphabet of the obser, realisability is trivially established with criterion of Definition 1. We also omit the trivial details of how this observer refines the implicit observer of the abstract mutex model.

4.5 Verification Using the Observation Model

To understand where observation process comes into the view, it is instructive to start by seeing why the untimed model of Fischer's algorithm is not a valid implementation of mutual exclusion. The Event-B toolkit [17] generates proof obligations for the demonstration of refinement between abstract and concrete models. In our example, there are proof obligations that cannot be discharged.

The first one is concerned with the satisfaction of gluing invariant (2) by event *enter*. The condition requires that upon entering the critical section, the only process that may already be in the critical section is the current process[5]:

$$p \in 1..n \wedge s(p) = 3 \wedge x = p \wedge d \in 1..n \wedge (s \mathbin{\vartriangleleft\mkern-9mu\vartriangleleft} \{p \mapsto 4\})(d) = 4 \vDash p = d. \quad (8)$$

The second condition is a guard strengthening proof obligation for event *enter*:

$$p \in 1..n \wedge s(p) = 3 \wedge x = p \wedge d \in 1..n \vDash s(d) \neq 4 \quad (9)$$

---

[5] Operator $\mathbin{\vartriangleleft\mkern-9mu\vartriangleleft}$ is defined as $f \mathbin{\vartriangleleft\mkern-9mu\vartriangleleft} g = \{x \mapsto y \mid (x \mapsto y \in f \wedge x \notin \mathrm{dom}(g)) \vee x \mapsto y \in g\}$.

The condition requires that on entering a critical section no process is already in the critical section. The similarity of the two undischarged conditions suggests the following, more general invariant condition:

$$\forall p \cdot p \in 1..n \land s(p) = 3 \land x = p \Rightarrow \neg(\exists r \cdot r \in 1..n \land r \neq p \land s(r) = 4) \qquad (10)$$

The invariant states that when a process is about to enter the critical section there does not exists another process that is already in the critical section. This invariant trivially establishes (8) and (9). There remains one open proof obligation concerned with establishing the condition of (10) by event *write*:

$$p \in 1..n \,\land\, s(p) = 2 \,\land\, r \in 1..n \,\land\, s(r) = 4 \,\land\, r \neq p \vDash \bot \qquad (11)$$

We shall prove, with the help of the observer model, that it is impossible, due to timing constraints of the algorithm, to observe any two processes in such states. Diagram in Fig. 5 illustrates how the contradiction arises.

To do the proof we need to strengthen the state model with the model of the observer. We do this by placing the definition of the observer model into an Event-B *context*: a component housing declarations of constants and axioms. The following lemma shows how to transition from reasoning about states to reasoning about times when these states are observed.

Lemma 2 (Point Merge). *Let W and P_i be non-empty subject process states such that $W = \{v \mid W(v)\}$, $P_i = \{v \mid P_i(v)\}$ where $W(v)$ and $P_i(v)$ are predicates over subject process state space and it holds that $W \Rightarrow \bigwedge_i P_i$. Then there exist time points $t_i \in [\![P_i]\!] \cap [\![W]\!]$ such that $\forall i, j \cdot t_i = t_j$.*

Using this lemma we relate the process states described in Condition 11 to the states of the observer and derive a set of hypotheses speaking about the timing constraints of the processes. The following three predicates describe the situation in the hypothesis of Condition 11.

$$W = (\exists i, j, q \cdot i, j \in 1..n \land i \neq j \land q \in 1..n \rightarrow 1..4 \land q(i) = 2 \land q(j) = 4)$$
$$P_1 = (\exists i, q \cdot i \in 1..n \land q \in 1..n \rightarrow 1..4 \land q(i) = 2)$$
$$P_2 = (\exists j, q \cdot j \in 1..n \land q \in 1..n \rightarrow 1..4 \land q(j) = 4)$$

Predicate W describes the overall the state encoded in the hypothesis while P_1 and P_2 are specific projections focusing on processes p and r so that $W \Rightarrow P_1 \land P_2$. It is trivial to prove that predicates W, P_1 and P_2 characterise non-empty states (as required by Lemma 2) by instantiating q with s, i with p and j with r in the context of Condition 11. Instantiating Lemma 2 with W, P_1 and P_2 we derive the existence of two time points G and F such that

$$G, F \in \alpha C \qquad G \in [\![P_1]\!] \qquad F \in [\![P_2]\!] \qquad G = F$$

Point G is some time when process p is at stage 2 and C is time when process r is at stage 4. We shall follow the syntactic convention of the observer model and use $[\![s(p) = 2]\!]$ and $[\![s(r) = 4]\!]$ in the place of $[\![P_1]\!]$ and $[\![P_1]\!]$.

The new hypotheses enable us to formally identify the contradiction and prove Condition 11. The following is the new form of Condition 11.

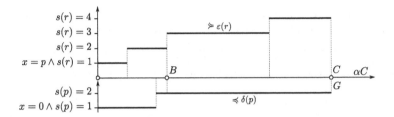

Fig. 5. Contradiction: when r is in the critical section, p may not be at stage 2.

$$G, F \in \alpha C \wedge G \in [\![s(p) = 2]\!] \wedge F \in [\![s(r) = 4]\!] \wedge G = F \vDash \bot \qquad (12)$$

with the obvious definitions of s, p and r implied. To construct the proof we involve a helper time point B with some specific properties, as shown in the diagram on Fig. 5. The following lemmata justify the existence and properties of B. The first lemma states that B is some time point at which process r is at stage 4. The value of B is selected in such a way that there are at least $\varepsilon(r)$ time units separating it from C.

Lemma 3 (Existence of B). *There exists a point B such that $B \in [\![s(r) = 3]\!]$ and $B + \varepsilon(r) \preccurlyeq F$.*

We also insist that at time B, process p is at stage 2 (see Fig. 5). From this it is concluded that the distance between B and G, which are both time points of process p's stage 2, is not more that $\delta(p)$.

Lemma 4 (Position of B). *It holds that $G \preccurlyeq B + \delta(p)$.*

The lemmata give us two new hypotheses for Condition 12.

$$\cdots \wedge B + \varepsilon(r) \preccurlyeq C \wedge G \preccurlyeq B + \delta(p) \vDash \bot$$

Since $G = C$ we have that $B + \varepsilon(r) \preccurlyeq B + \delta(p)$ or $\varepsilon(r) \preccurlyeq \delta(p)$. This statement contradicts Condition 4 of the observer model. The contradiction proves Conditions 11–12. We thus have proven the last open proof obligation and demonstrated a refinement relation between Fischer's algorithm and the abstract mutex model. This concludes the proof of the algorithm correctness.

A complete model and detailed proofs may be found in the Event-B development of the algorithm [1].

5   Conclusion

We have presented a method for modelling time in an untimed formalism using the Leibnizian, relativistic, view, rather than the classical Newtonian, absolutist, view. We believe that this a novel approach that has not been explored so far, at least in application to information systems and formal modelling. The method is compatible with the Newtonian view of time, since a model can include an

Newtonian clock. We have found the approach to be a more natural way to include time properties in state-based models: it requires no extension of the Event-B language, and the uses only existing tools and first-order logic. We have been able to demonstrate a machine checked proof of Fischer's algorithm, which, in our opinion, is simpler than anything we have seen in the literature.

The proof of Fischer's protocol is quite general and spans across a wide class of observers. In particular, it embeds proofs for an observer operating in either a discrete or a dense time domain, despite the fact that continuous numbers are not supported in Event-B.

Initial investigations suggest that this method is valuable for a variety of case studies. Possible method extensions include widening the class of observer models (e.g., cyclic time for looping models) and models of observations (e.g., a single observer and multiple subjects) and see if they present any practical advantages.

References

1. Iliasov, A., Bryans, J.: Event-B development of Fischer's algorithm. http://iliasov. org/fischer
2. Abadi, M., Lamport, L.: An old-fashioned recipe for real time. In: Huizing, C., de Bakker, J.W., Rozenberg, G., de Roever, W.-P. (eds.) REX 1991. LNCS, vol. 600, pp. 1–27. Springer, Heidelberg (1992)
3. Abrial, J.R.: The B-Book: Assigning Programs to Meanings. Cambridge University Press, New York (2005)
4. Abrial, J.-R.: Modeling in Event-B: System and Software Engineering. Cambridge University Press, New York (2010)
5. Alur, R., Dill, D.L.: Automata for modeling real-time systems. In: Paterson, M. (ed.) ICALP 1990. LNCS, vol. 443, pp. 322–335. Springer, Heidelberg (1990)
6. Behm, P., Benoit, P., Faivre, A., Meynadier, J.-M.: Météor: a successful application of B in a large project. In: Wing, J.M., Woodcock, J. (eds.) FM 1999. LNCS, vol. 1708, p. 369. Springer, Heidelberg (1999)
7. Bengtsson, J., Larsen, K., Larsson, F., Pettersson, P., Yi, W.: Uppaal - a tool suite for automatic verification of real-time systems. In: Alur, R., Sontag, E.D., Henzinger, T.A. (eds.) HS 1995. LNCS, vol. 1066, pp. 232–243. Springer, Heidelberg (1996)
8. Butler, M., Falampin, J.: An approach to modelling and refining timing properties in B. In: Refinement of Critical Systems (RCS), January 2002
9. Cansell, D., Méry, D., Rehm, J.: Time constraint patterns for event B development. In: Julliand, J., Kouchnarenko, O. (eds.) B 2007. LNCS, vol. 4355, pp. 140–154. Springer, Heidelberg (2006)
10. Davies, J.: Specification and Proof in Real-time CSP (1993)
11. Futch, M.J.: Leibniz's Metaphysics of Time and Space (2008)
12. Jensen, H.E.: Abstraction-based verification of distributed systems. Technical report, Aalborg University, Department of Computer Science (1999)
13. Lano, K.: The B Language and Method: A Guide to Practical Formal Development. Springer-Verlag New York, Inc., Secaucus (1996)
14. Luchangco, V.: Using Simulation Techniques to Prove Timing Properties (1995)

15. Lynch, N., Vaandrager, F.: Forward and backward simulations - part II: Timing-based systems. Inf. Comput. **128**, 1–25 (1996)
16. Moller, F., Tofts, C.: A temporal calculus of communicating systems. In: Baeten, J.C.M., Klop, J.W. (eds.) CONCUR 1990. LNCS, vol. 458, pp. 401–415. Springer, Heidelberg (1990)
17. RODIN. Event-B Platform (2009). http://www.event-b.org/
18. de Roever, W.-P., Engelhardt, K.: Data Refinement: Model-Oriented Proof Methods and Their Comparison (2008)
19. Schneider, S.: Concurrent and Real Time Systems: The CSP Approach. Wiley, New York (1999)

Asymptotic Speedups, Bisimulation and Distillation (Work in Progress)

Neil D. Jones[1]([✉]) and G.W. Hamilton[2]

[1] Computer Science Department, University of Copenhagen,
2100 Copenhagen, Denmark
`neil@diku.dk`
[2] School of Computing, Dublin City University, Dublin 9, Ireland
`hamilton@computing.dcu.ie`

Abstract. Distillation is a fully automatic program transformation that can yield superlinear program speedups. Bisimulation is a key to the proof that distillation is correct, i.e., preserves semantics. However the proof, based on observational equivalence, is insensitive to program running times. This paper shows *how distillation can give superlinear speedups* on some "old chestnut" programs well-known from the early program transformation literature: naive reverse, factorial sum, and Fibonacci.

1 Introduction

Distillation, supercompilation, and partial evaluation are automatic program transformations (see [7–9, 14–16]). A main goal of all three is to transform a program into an improved program. Partial evaluation has been fairly well automated [9]. In some respects supercompilation, deforestation and distillation (Turchin, Sørensen, Wadler, Hamilton [6–9, 14, 16, 17]) can make deeper transformations on program control structure. A well-known example is that deforestation can transform a multipass program into a single pass algorithm [16, 17], a feat beyond the reach of current partial evaluators.

1.1 Goal: Extend Automatic Superlinear Program Speedup

Program optimisations by hand (Burstall-Darlington and many others [1]) sometimes yield superlinear program speedups. Transformation can make substantial improvements, for instance changing a program running in time $O(n^2)$ or even $O(2^n)$ into one running in time $O(n)$. Familiar examples include naive programs for list reversal, sum of factorials, and the Fibonacci function. A goal for many years now has been how to obtain such effects *by well-automated methods*.

Classical compiler optimisations are a model of automation, though the program speedups they give are limited. Many have been proven correct using bisimulation, e.g., [12] by Lacey et al. This has led to some practical automation of compiler correctness proofs.

However it has been proven (see [9, 14]) that partial evaluation, deforestation and supercompilation (as well as classical compiler optimisations) are all limited

A. Voronkov and I. Virbitskaite (Eds.): PSI 2014, LNCS 8974, pp. 177–185, 2015.
DOI: 10.1007/978-3-662-46823-4_15

to *at most program speedups by linear constant factors*. One reason for such limited optimisation speedups is that the bisimulations of [12] all involve *one-to-one relations* between the control points of the original program and the compiler-optimised program.

In contrast, distillation [6,7]) can yield superlinear asymptotic speedups: this refinement of supercompilation can sometimes transform a program into a semantically equivalent but asymptotically faster equivalent.

1.2   Bisimulation and Program Transformation

Correctness of transformation can be proven using bisimulation [7,8,12] to relate computations by the original and the transformed programs. A question:

> How can a program running in time $O(n^2)$ (or even time $O(2^n)$) be bisimilar to a program running in time $O(n)$?

This puzzling question was the starting point of this work. It was clear at once that *1-1 relations between program control points would not suffice to explain the phenomenon*. A challenge to overcome: the system structure and techniques used in distillation as in [6–8] are complex, and hard to reason about globally.

This paper's approach to better understanding cause-and-effect in distillation is to *simplify distillation as much as possible*, while maintaining its capacity for superlinear speedups. We will describe current work on such questions, partly theoretical and partly computer experiments.

2   A Language, Observational Equivalence, and Labeled Transition Systems

Our approach is to simplify the general distillation techniques of [6–8], so its essence can be seen in a more limited context, to see what is happening abstractly. A clearer understanding of cause-and-effect could show how automatically to achieve superlinear speedup on a wider range of programs.

2.1   Source Language Syntax

Data: let Σ be an uninterpreted signature for constructors, and let T_Σ be the set of all well-formed trees over Σ, finite or infinite. Our examples use as constructors 0-ary 0, unary 1+ (successor), and binary constructors $+, *, ::$. The net effect of a program is to compute a (mathematical, partial) function $f : (T_\Sigma)^n \rightharpoonup T_\Sigma$.

Programs are first-order, built from variables x, constructors c, function calls, and **case**. Calls and constructor applications must have all their arguments, i.e., full arities. Semantics $\llbracket prog \rrbracket : (T_\Sigma)^n \rightharpoonup T_\Sigma$ is call-by-value, omitted for brevity and because of familiarity.

$$prog ::= e \text{ where } \Delta$$

Δ	$::= f_1\ x_1 \ldots x_n = e_1 \quad \ldots \quad f_m\ x_1 \ldots x_p = e_m$	Function definitions
e	$::= x \mid c\ e_1 \ldots e_k \mid call \mid case$	Expression
$call$	$::= f\ e_1 \ldots e_n$	Function call
$case$	$::= \textbf{case}\ e\ \textbf{of}\ p_1 \Rightarrow e_1 \mid \ldots \mid p_k \Rightarrow e_k$	Case expression
p	$::= c\ x_1 \ldots x_k$	Case pattern

Free variables are allowed only in the e part of program e **where** Δ. All other variables must be bound, either by function parameters or in case patterns.

Definition 1. *Denote by* $time_p(x) \in \mathbb{N} \cup \{\infty\}$ *the running time of program p on input x, e.g., the number of steps used in computing $[\![p]\!](x)$.*

Goal: automatically transform program p into program p' such that $[\![p]\!] = [\![p']\!]$, but $time_{p'} < time_p$ asymptotically, i.e., in the limit as input size grows.

2.2 Observational Equivalence and Labeled Transition Systems

For appropriate definitions of context $C[]$ and evaluation $\Downarrow$:

Definition 2 (Observational Equivalence). Programs p_1, p_2 are *observationally equivalent*, written $p_1 \simeq p_2$, if and only if they have the same termination behaviour in all closing contexts, i.e., $p_1 \simeq p_2$ iff $\forall C[]$. $C[p_1]\Downarrow$ iff $C[p_2]\Downarrow$.

Distillation transforms a program p_1 into an observationally equivalent program p_2. (Two central references: Milner and Gordon [5,13].) Observational equivalence implies semantic equivalence, i.e., $p_1 \simeq p_2$ implies $[\![p_1]\!] = [\![p_2]\!]$.

A limitation of observational equivalence Unfortunately (from this paper's perspective), observational equivalence $p \simeq p'$ tells us *nothing whatsoever* about the comparative running times of the programs involved. For instance, for each of our selection of "old chestnut" programs, the original program is observationally equivalent to its optimised version. We will attempt to clarify such relations between running times in the distillation framework.

Definition 3 (Labeled Transition Systems). *A labeled transition system (LTS for short) is a tuple $t = (\mathcal{S}, s_0, \rightarrow, Act)$ where $\mathcal{S}$ is a set of states. $s_0 \in \mathcal{S}$ is the root state, $\mathbf{0}$ is the end-of-action state, and Act is a set of actions α. The transition relation is $\rightarrow \subseteq \mathcal{S} \times Act \times \mathcal{S}$. Notation: as usual we write a transition (s, α, s') in $\rightarrow$ as $s \xrightarrow{\alpha} s'$.*

Definition 4 (Simulation). *Binary relation $\mathcal{R} \subseteq \mathcal{S}_1 \times \mathcal{S}_2$ is a simulation of LTS $t_1 = (\mathcal{S}_1, s_0^1, \rightarrow_1, Act)$ by LTS $t_2 = (\mathcal{S}_2, s_0^2, \rightarrow_2, Act)$ if $(s_0^1, s_0^2) \in \mathcal{R}$, and for every pair $(s_1, s_2) \in \mathcal{R}$ and $\alpha \in Act, s_1' \in \mathcal{S}_1$:*

$$\text{if } s_1 \xrightarrow{\alpha} s_1' \text{ then } \exists s_2' \in \mathcal{S}_2 \ .\ s_2 \xrightarrow{\alpha} s_2' \wedge (s_1', s_2') \in \mathcal{R}$$

Definition 5 (Bisimulation). *A bisimulation $\sim$ is a binary relation $\mathcal{R}$ such that both $\mathcal{R}$ and its inverse $\mathcal{R}^{-1}$ are simulations.*

Using an LTS as a program's abstract syntax. Represent a variable x by a transition $s \xrightarrow{x} \mathbf{0}$; represent $c \, e_1 \ldots e_k$ where c is a constructor by transitions $s \xrightarrow{c} \mathbf{0}, s \xrightarrow{\#1} s_1, \ldots, s \xrightarrow{\#k} s_k$, where s_i is the root of the LTS representation of expression e_i; represent **case** e_0 **of** $p_1 \Rightarrow e_1 \mid \ldots \mid p_k \Rightarrow e_k$ by transitions $s \xrightarrow{\text{case}} s_0, s \xrightarrow{p_1} s_1, \ldots, s \xrightarrow{p_k} s_k$; and represent a function call $f \, e_1 \ldots e_n$ by transitions $s \xrightarrow{\text{call}} s_0, s \xrightarrow{x_1} s_1, \ldots, s \xrightarrow{x_n} s_n$ where Δ contains function definition $f \, x_1 \ldots x_n = e_0$.

2.3 Example: "Naive Reverse" Program Representation as an LTS

Source program *nrev*:

```
nr input where
nr xs = case xs of nil => nil | (:: y ys) => (ap (nr ys) (:: y nil))
ap us vs = case us of nil => vs | (:: w ws) => (:: w (ap ws vs))
```
The LTS representation of naive reverse program is a transition set containing

$$\{2 \xrightarrow{\text{call}} 10, 2 \xrightarrow{\text{xs}} 1, 1 \xrightarrow{\text{input}} 0, 10 \xrightarrow{\text{case}} 3, 10 \xrightarrow{\text{nil}} 4, 10 \xrightarrow{::(y,ys)} 9, 3 \xrightarrow{\text{xs}} 0, 4 \xrightarrow{\text{nil}} 0, \ldots\}$$

Short form of the LTS for naive reverse (root state 2, nr *code start 10, and* ap *code start 17).* For readability we abbreviate the LTS by omitting end-of-action state $\mathbf{0}$ and variable transitions to $\mathbf{0}$, and bundling together transitions from a single state.

```
(2  -> (call 10 (input)))        ;   root = 2: call nr(input)
(10 -> (case xs ((nil).4) ((:: y ys).9))) ; start"nr"
(4  -> (nil))
(9  -> (call 17 (6 8))            ; call ap(nr(ys),...)
(6  -> (call 10 (ys)))            ; call nr(ys)
(8  -> (:: y 4))
(17 -> (case us ((nil).vs) ((:: u us1).16)))) ; start "ap"
(16 -> (:: u 15)
(15 -> (call 17 (us1 vs))         ; call ap(ws,vs)
```

An Example of Optimisation: The program above runs in time $O(n^2)$. It can, as is well known, be improved to run in time $O(n)$. Distillation does this automatically, yielding the following LTS with root state 3 and **rev** code start 10. Effect: the nested loop in **nr** has been replaced by an accumulating parameter.

```
    ;  Reverse with an accumulating parameter
(3  -> (call 10 (us 2)))
(2  -> (nil))
(10 -> (case xs ((nil) . acc) ((:: x xs1) . 9)))
(9  -> (call 10 (xs1 8)))
(8  -> (:: x acc))
```

The distilled version in source language format.

```
rev us nil where rev xs acc =
 case xs of nil => acc | (:: x xs1) => rev xs1 (:: x acc)
```

Are These Programs Bisimilar? There is no obvious bisimilarity relation between runtime states of **nr** and **rev**, e.g., because of different loop structures and numbers of variables. In the next section we will see that the *result of driving* a distilled program is always bisimilar to the *result of driving* the original program.

3   Distillation: A Simplified Version

Following the pattern of Turchin, Sørensen and Hamilton, the first step is driving.

3.1   Driving

Distillation and supercompilation of program $p = e$ **where** Δ both begin with an operation called *driving*. The result is an LTS $\mathcal{D}[\![p]\!]$, usually infinite, *with no function calls* and *with no free variables* other than those of p.

If p is closed, then driving will evaluate it completely, yielding as result an LTS for the value $[\![p]\!]$. Further, given an LTS for a program p *with* free variables, the driver will:

- compute as much as can seen to be computable;
- expand *all* function calls and
- yield as output a call-free LTS $\mathcal{D}[\![p]\!]$ equivalent to program p. (The output may be infinite if the input program has loops.)

$\mathcal{D}[\![p]\!]$ will consist entirely of constructors, together with **case** expressions whose tests could not be resolved at driving time. This is a (usually infinite) LTS to compute the function $[\![p]\!]$ (of values of p's free variables). Another perspective: $\mathcal{D}[\![p]\!]$ is essentially a "glorified decision tree" to compute $[\![p]\!]$ without calls. Input is tested and decomposed by **case**, and output is built by constructors.

Although $\mathcal{D}[\![p]\!]$ may be infinite it is executable, given initial values of any free variables. This can be realised in a lazy language, where only a finite portion of the LTS is looked at in any terminating run.

Correctness of distillation: Theorem 3.10 in [7] shows that for any p, p',

$$\mathcal{D}[\![p]\!] \sim \mathcal{D}[\![p']\!] \text{ implies } p \simeq p'$$

Bottom line: if two programs p, p' have bisimilar driven versions $\mathcal{D}[\![p]\!]$ and $\mathcal{D}[\![p']\!]$, then the programs are observationally equivalent.

3.2   A Driver for the Call-by-Value Language

The driving algorithm below transforms a program into a call-free output LTS (possibly infinite). It is essentially an extended semantics: an expression evaluator that also allows free variables in the input (transitions to **0** are generated in the output LTS for these variables); and **case** expressions that may be applied to a non-constructor value (if so, residual **case** transitions are generated in the output LTS).

Relations to the Drivers of [6–8]: We do not use silent transitions at all, and so do not need weak bisimulation. Our LTS states have no internal structure, i.e., they are not expressions as in [6–8], and have no syntactic information about the program from which it was generated, beyond function parameters and case pattern variables. (Embedding, generalisation, well-quasi-orders etc. are not discussed here, as this paper's points can be made without them.)

Another difference: the following constructs its output LTS "one state at a time": it explicitly allocates new states for constructors and for **case** expressions with unresolvable tests.[1]

One effect is an "instrumentation". For instance if p is closed, then the driven output LTS $\mathcal{D}[\![p]\!]$ will have one state for every constructor operation performed while computing $[\![p]\!]$, so $\mathcal{D}[\![\_]\!]$ yields *some intensional information* about its program argument's running time.

Our language is call-by-value, so environments map variables into states, rather than into expressions as in [6,7]. Types used in the driver:

$$\mathcal{D} : Expression \to LTS$$
$$\mathcal{D}' : Expression \to LTS \to Environment \to FcnEnv \to LTS$$
$$\theta \in Environment = Variable \to State$$
$$\Delta \in FcnEnv = FunctionName \to Variable^* \to Expression$$

Variable t ranges over LTS's, and s ranges over states. For brevity, function environment argument Δ in the definition of $\mathcal{D}'$ is elided since it is never changed.

1. $\mathcal{D}[\![e \ \textbf{where} \ \Delta]\!] = \mathcal{D}'[\![e]\!] \ \varnothing \ \{\} \ \Delta$

2. $\mathcal{D}'[\![x]\!] \ t \ \theta = \begin{cases} t \ \text{with root} \ \theta x \ \text{if} \ x \in dom(\theta) \ \textbf{else} \\ t \cup \{s \xrightarrow{x} \textbf{0}\} \quad \textbf{where} \ s \ \text{is a new root state} \end{cases}$

3. $\mathcal{D}'[\![c \ e_1 \ldots e_k]\!] \ t_0 \ \theta = \textbf{let} \ t_1 = \mathcal{D}'[\![e_1]\!] \ t_0 \ \theta, \ldots, t_k = \mathcal{D}'[\![e_k]\!] \ t_{k-1} \ \theta \ \textbf{in} \ t_k \cup \{s \xrightarrow{c}$
   $\textbf{0}, s \xrightarrow{\#1} root(t_1), \ldots, s \xrightarrow{\#k} root(t_k)\}$ **where** s is a new root state

4. $\mathcal{D}'[\![f \ e_1 \ldots e_n]\!] \ t_0 \ \theta = \textbf{let} \ t_1 = \mathcal{D}'[\![e_1]\!] \ t_0 \ \theta, \ldots, t_k = \mathcal{D}'[\![e_k]\!] \ t_{k-1} \ \theta \ \textbf{in}$
   $\mathcal{D}'[\![e^f]\!] \ t_n \ \{x_1 \mapsto root(t_1), \ldots, x_n \mapsto root(t_n)\}$ **where** $(f \ x_1 \ldots x_n = e^f) \in \Delta$

5. $\mathcal{D}'[\![\textbf{case} \ e_0 \ \textbf{of} \ p_1 \Rightarrow e_1 | \ldots | p_n \Rightarrow e_n]\!] \ t \ \theta = \textbf{let} \ t_0 = \mathcal{D}'[\![e_0]\!] \ t \ \theta \ \textbf{in}$
   if $t_0 \ni s_0 \xrightarrow{c} \textbf{0}, s_0 \xrightarrow{\#1} s_1, \ldots, s_0 \xrightarrow{\#k} s_k$ **and** $p_i = c \ x_1 \ldots x_k$
   then
   $\quad \mathcal{D}'[\![e_i]\!] \ t_0 \ (\theta \cup \{x_1 \mapsto s_1, \ldots, x_k \mapsto s_k\})$
   else

---

[1] To avoid non-termination of the program transformer itself, we assume the input does not contain nonproductive loops such as $f \ 0 \ \textbf{where} \ f \ x = f \ x$.

let $t_1 = \mathcal{D}'[\![e_1]\!] \, t_0 \; \theta \, , \ldots, t_n = \mathcal{D}'[\![e_n]\!] \, t_{n-1} \, \theta$ **in**
$t_n \cup \{s \xrightarrow{\text{case}} root(t_0), s \xrightarrow{p_1} root(t_1), \ldots, s \xrightarrow{p_n} root(t_n)\}$
where s is a new root state

4 Some Speedup Principles and Examples

4.1 On Sources of Speedup by Distillation

Speedups can be obtained for all our well-known "old chestnut" programs p as follows (where p_s is p applied to known values s of its free variables):

1. Drive: construct $\text{LTS}^{driven} = \mathcal{D}[\![p_s]\!]$ from p_s. (This is finite if p_s terminates.)
2. Remove "dead code" from LTS^{driven}: These are any states that are unreachable from its root.
3. Merge any bisimilar states in LTS^{driven}.

Step 2 must be done after constructing LTS^{driven}. Step 3 can be done either after or during driving: Elide adding a new state and transitions $s \xrightarrow{a_1} s_1, \ldots, s \xrightarrow{a_n} s_n$ to LTS^{driven} if an already-existing LTS state has the same transitions.

Two points: First, in traditional compiler construction, dead code elimination is very familiar; whereas merging bisimilar states is a form of code folding not often seen (exception: the "rewinding" by Debois [2]). Distillation accomplishes the effect of both optimisations, and in some cases more sophisticated transformations.

Second, the distiller obtains superlinear speedup for all three programs by introducing *accumulating parameters*.

4.2 Overview of the "Old Chestnut" Examples

Our goal is to relate the efficiencies of a program p and its distilled version p'. The transformation sequence involves the possibly infinite object $\mathcal{D}[\![p]\!] = \text{LTS}^{driven}$.

The following experimental results get around this problem by computing $\mathcal{D}[\![p_s]\!]$ for *fixed* input values s. The idea is to drive a version p_s of p applied to known values s of its free variables. Assuming that p_s terminates, this will yield a finite LTS whose structure can be examined.

Let n be the input size (e.g., a list length or number value). Then

1. The naive reverse algorithm $nrev$ runs in quadratic time, while its distilled version runs in linear time. Nonetheless, their driven versions are (strongly) bisimilar, and so observationally equivalent.
   Explanation of speedup: $\mathcal{D}[\![nrev_{(a_1 a_2 \ldots a_n)}]\!]$ has $O(n^2)$ states, including states for the computation of the reverse of every suffix of $(a_1 a_2 \ldots a_n)$. Among these, at the end of execution only $O(n)$ states are live, for the reverse of all of $(a_1 a_2 \ldots a_n)$.
2. The naive program to compute Factorial sum ($sumfac(n) = 0! + 1! + \ldots n!$) has running time $O(n^2)$ and allocates $O(n^2)$ heap cells, due to repeated

recomputation of $0!, 1!, 2!, \ldots$; but the distilled version is linear-time. The two are (again) observationally equivalent since their driven versions are bisimilar. The driven naive Factorial sum LTS has $O(n^2)$ states, but among these, only $O(n)$ are live at the end of execution.

This example is interesting because both source and transformed programs are purely *tail recursive*, and so typical of compiler intermediate code.

3. A more extreme example: the obvious program fib for the Fibonacci function takes exponential time and will fill up the heap with exponentially many memory cells. On the other hand, the distilled version of Fibonacci uses an accumulator and runs in linear time (counting $+, *$ as constant-time operations). Even so, the two LTS's are bisimilar.

In contrast to the examples above, the driven program $\mathcal{D}[\![fib_n]\!]$ has $O(1.7^n)$ states, all of which are live. Here speedup source number 3 (Sect. 4.1) comes into play: there are only $O(n)$ states that are distinct with respect to bisimulation.

The experiments were carried out in SCHEME. The first step was parsing: to transform the input program from the form of Sect. 2.1 into an LTS, which for clarity we will call LTS^{in}. The driver as implemented realises the one of Sect. 3.2 (except that it works on LTS^{in} rather than program p). LTS^{out} is the name of the distiller's output.

5   Conclusions

In spite of many remaining open questions, we hope the material above, particularly Sects. 3 and 4, clarifies the way that distillation yields superlinear program speedup.

The question "how can an $O(n^2)$ program or $O(2^n)$ program be bisimilar to an $O(n)$ program?" has been answered: It is not the runtime state transitions of the two programs that are bisimilar; but rather their driven versions. Further, the numbers of states in their driven versions trace the number of cons's performed, and so reflect the two programs' relative running times.

Acknowledgement. This paper has been much improved as a result of discussions with Luke Ong and Jonathan Kochems at Oxford University. Referee comments were also very useful. This work was supported, in part, by DIKU at the University of Copenhagen, and by Science Foundation Ireland grant 10/CE/I1855 to Lero - the Irish Software Engineering Research Centre (www.lero.ie).

References

1. Burstall, R., Darlington, J.: A transformation system for developing recursive programs. J. ACM **24**(1), 44–67 (1977)
2. Debois, S.: Imperative program optimization by partial evaluation. In: PEPM (ACM SIGPLAN 2004 Workshop on Partial Evaluation and Program Manipulation), pp. 113–122 (2004)

3. Ershov, A.P.: On the essence of compilation. In: Neuhold, E. (ed.) Formal Description of Programming Concepts, pp. 391–420. North-Holland, Amsterdam (1978)
4. Futamura, Y.: Partial evaluation of computation process - an approach to a compiler-compiler. High. Order Symb. Comput. **12**(4), 381–391 (1999)
5. Gordon, A.D.: Bisimilarity as a theory of functional programming. Theor. Comput. Sci. **228**(1–2), 5–47 (1999)
6. Hamilton, G.W.: Distillation: extracting the essence of programs. In: Proceedings of the ACM SIGPLAN Symposium on Partial Evaluation and Semantics-Based Program Manipulation, pp. 61–70 (2007)
7. Hamilton, G.W., Jones, N.D.: Distillation with labelled transition systems. In: PEPM (ACM SIGPLAN 2012 Workshop on Partial Evaluation and Program Manipulation), pp. 15–24. ACM (2012)
8. Hamilton, G.W., Jones, N.D.: Proving the correctness of unfold/fold program transformations using bisimulation. In: Clarke, E., Virbitskaite, I., Voronkov, A. (eds.) PSI 2011. LNCS, vol. 7162, pp. 153–169. Springer, Heidelberg (2012)
9. Jones, N., Gomard, C., Sestoft, P.: Partial Evaluation and Automatic Program Generation. Prentice Hall, New York (1993)
10. Jones, N.D.: Computability and Complexity - From a Programming Perspective. Foundations of Computing Series. MIT Press, Cambridge (1997)
11. Jones, N.D.: Transformation by interpreter specialisation. Sci. Comput. Program. **52**, 307–339 (2004)
12. Lacey, D., Jones, N.D., Wyk, E.V., Frederiksen, C.C.: Compiler optimization correctness by temporal logic. High. Order Symb. Comput. **17**(3), 173–206 (2004)
13. Milner, R.: Communication and Concurrency. PHI Series in Computer Science. Prentice Hall, Upper Saddle River (1989)
14. Sørensen, M.H., Glück, R., Jones, N.: A positive supercompiler. J. Funct. Program. **6**(6), 811–838 (1996)
15. Turchin, V.F.: Supercompilation: techniques and results. In: Bjorner, D., Broy, M., Pottosin, I.V. (eds.) PSI 1996. LNCS, vol. 1181, pp. 227–248. Springer, Heidelberg (1996)
16. Turchin, V.: The concept of a supercompiler. ACM Trans. Program. Lang. Syst. **8**(3), 90–121 (1986)
17. Wadler, P.: Deforestation: transforming programs to eliminate trees. In: Ganzinger, H. (ed.) ESOP 1988. LNCS, vol. 300, pp. 344–358. Springer, Heidelberg (1988)

Certifying Supercompilation for Martin-Löf's Type Theory

Ilya Klyuchnikov[(✉)] and Sergei Romanenko

Keldysh Institute of Applied Mathematics, Moscow, Russia
ilya.klyuchnikov@gmail.com

Abstract. The paper describes the design and implementation of a *certifying* supercompiler TT Lite SC, which takes an input program and produces a residual program and a proof of the fact that the residual program is equivalent to the input one. As far as we can judge from the literature, this is the first implementation of a certifying supercompiler for a non-trivial higher-order functional language. The proofs generated by TT Lite SC can be verified by a type checker which is independent from TT Lite SC and is not based on supercompilation. This is essential in cases where the reliability of results obtained by supercompilation is of fundamental importance. Currently, the proofs can be either verified by the type-checker built into TT Lite, or converted into Agda programs and checked by the Agda system. The main technical contribution is a simple but intricate interplay of supercompilation and type theory.

1 Introduction

Supercompilation [1,2] is a program manipulation technique that was originally introduced by V. Turchin in terms of the programming language Refal (a first-order applicative functional language) [3], for which reason the first supercompilers were designed and developed for the language Refal [4].

Roughly speaking, the existing supercompilers can be divided into two large groups: "optimizing" supercompilers that try to make programs more efficient, and "analyzing" supercompilers that are meant for revealing and proving some hidden properties of programs, in order to make programs more suitable for subsequent analysis and/or verification.

The main idea behind the program analysis by supercompilation is that supercompilation "normalizes" and "trivializes" the structure of programs by removing modularity and levels of abstraction (carefully elaborated by the programmer). Thus, although the transformed program becomes less human-friendly, it may be more convenient for *automatic* analysis.

Examples of using supercompilation for the purposes of analysis and verification are: verification of protocols [5,6], proving the equivalence of programs [7], contract checking (*e.g.* the verification of monadic laws) [8], problem solving in Prolog style by inverse computation [9], proving the correctness of optimizations (verifying improvement lemmas) [10], proving the productivity of corecursive

© Springer-Verlag Berlin Heidelberg 2015
A. Voronkov and I. Virbitskaite (Eds.): PSI 2014, LNCS 8974, pp. 186–200, 2015.
DOI: 10.1007/978-3-662-46823-4_16

functions [11]. It should be noted that the use of supercompilation for analysis and verification is based on the assumption:

> The supercompiler we use preserves the semantics of programs.

In the following we will silently assume that this requirement is satisfied[1].

At this point we are faced with the problem of correctness of supercompilation itself, which has a number of aspects. A non-trivial supercompiler is a sophisticated construction, whose proof of correctness is bound to be messy and cumbersome, involving as it does several areas of computer science. (For example, the proof of correctness of the supercompiler HOSC takes more than 30 pages [12].) Such a proof may contain some bugs and overlooks. Even if the proof is perfect, the implementation of the supercompiler may be buggy. The correctness of the implementation can be verified by means of formal methods. However, even the verification of a "toy" supercompiler is technically involved [13].

As we have seen, ensuring the correctness of a supercompiler is a difficult task. But, what we are *really* interested in is the correctness of the *results* of supercompilation. Thus we suggest the following solution.

Let the supercompiler produce a pair: a residual program, and a proof of the fact that this residual program is equivalent to the original program. The essential point is that the proof must be verifiable with a proof checker that is not based on supercompilation and is (very!) much simpler than the supercompiler.

The advantages of such *certifying supercompilation* are the following.

- The supercompiler can be written in a feature-rich programming language (comfortable for the programmer), even if programs in this language are not amenable to formal verification.
- The implementation of the supercompiler can be buggy, and yet its results can be verified and relied upon.
- The supercompiler can be allowed to apply incorrect techniques, or, more exactly, some techniques that are only correct under certain conditions that the supercompiler is unable to check. In this case, some results of supercompilation may be incorrect, but it is possible to filter them out later.

A certifying supercompiler, in general, has to deal with two languages: the programs transformed by the supercompiler are written in the *subject* language, while the *proof* language is used for formulating the proofs generated by the supercompiler. The problem is that the proof language and the subject language must be consistent with each other in some subtle respects. For example, the functions in the subject language may be partial (as in Haskell), but total in the proof language (as in Coq [14] or Agda [15]). And semantic differences of that kind may cause a lot of trouble.

The above problem can be circumvented if the subject language of the supercompiler is also used as its proof language! Needless to say, in this case the subject language must have sufficient expressive power[2].

---

[1] Note that some supercompilers are not semantics-preserving, changing as they do termination properties and/or error handling behavior of programs.

[2] Note, however, that the implementation language of the supercompiler does not need to coincide with either the subject language or the proof language.

The purpose of the present work is to show the feasibility and usefulness of certifying supercompilation. To this end, we have developed and implemented TT Lite [16], a proof-of-concept supercompiler for Martin-Löf's type theory (TT for short) [17]. The choice of TT as the subject+proof language was motivated as follows.

- The language of type theory is sufficiently feature-rich and interesting. (It provides inductive data types, higher-order functions and dependent types.)
- The type theory is easy to extend and can be implemented in a simple, modular way.
- Programs and proofs can be written in the same language.
- The typability of programs is decidable, and type checking can be easily implemented.

To our knowledge, the supercompiler described in the present work is the first one capable of producing residual programs together with proofs of their correctness. It is essential that these proofs can be verified by a type checker that is not based on supercompilation and is independent from the supercompiler.

The general idea that a certifying program transformation system can use Martin-Löf's type theory both for representing programs and for representing proofs of correctness was put forward by Albert Pardo and Sylvia da Rosa [18]. We have shown that this idea can be implemented and does work in the case of program transformations performed by supercompilation.

The TT Lite project[3] comprises 2 parts: TT Lite Core, which is a minimalistic implementation of the language of type theory (a type-checker, an interpreter and REPL), and TT Lite SC, which is a supercompiler. The results produced by TT Lite SC are verified by the type checker implemented in TT Lite Core. TT Lite Core does not depend on TT Lite SC and is not based on supercompilation[4].

TT Lite Core implements the collection of constructs and data types that can be usually found in textbooks on type theory: dependent functions, pairs, sums, products, natural numbers, lists, propositional equality, the empty (bottom) type and the unit (top) type. Also the site of the project contains a tutorial on programming in the TT Lite language with (a lot of) examples taken from [19,20].

While [16] contains full technical information about TT Lite in detail, this paper describes a small subset of TT Lite and can be regarded as a gentle, step-by-step introduction to [16]. In this paper we limit ourselves to the language which only contains dependent functions, natural numbers and identity (we use the abbreviation $\Pi\mathcal{NI}$ for this subset of TT Lite). This allows us to present and explain the fundamental principles of our certifying supercompiler without going into too much technical detail.

---

[3] https://github.com/ilya-klyuchnikov/ttlite.
[4] This design is similar to that of Coq [14] The numerous and sophisticated Coq "tactics" generate proofs written in Coq's Core language, which are then verified by a relatively small type checker. Thus, occasional errors in the implementation of tactics do not undermine the reliability of proofs produced by tactics.

```
1   plus : forall (x y : Nat). Nat;
2   plus = \(x y : Nat). elim Nat (\(n : Nat). Nat) y (\(n r : Nat). Succ r) x;
3   $x : Nat; $y : Nat; $z : Nat;
4   in1 = plus $x (plus $y $z);
5   in2 = plus (plus $x $y) $z;
6   (out1, pr1) = sc in1;
7   (out2, pr2) = sc in2;
8   id_in1_out1 : Id Nat in1 out1;
9   id_in1_out1 = pr1;
10  id_in2_out2 : Id Nat in2 out2;
11  id_in2_out2 = pr2;
12  id_out1_out2 : Id Nat out1 out2;
13  id_out1_out2 = Refl Nat out1;
14  id_in1_in2 : Id Nat in1 in2;
15  id_in1_in2 = proof_by_trans Nat in1 in2 out1 pr1 pr2;
```

Fig. 1. Proving the associativity of addition via normalization by supercompilation.

2   TT Lite SC in Action

TT Lite SC implements a supercompiler which can be called by programs written in the TT Lite input language by means of a built-in construct sc. (This supercompiler, as well as TT Lite Core, however, is implemented in Scala, rather than in the TT Lite language.) The supercompiler takes as input an expression (with free variables) in the TT Lite language and returns a pair: an output expression and a proof that the output expression is equivalent to the input one. The proof is also written in the TT Lite language and certifies that two expressions are *extensionally* equivalent, which means that, if we assign some values to the free variables appearing in the expressions, the evaluation of the expressions will produce the same result.

Both the output expression and the proof produced by the supercompiler are first-class values and can be further manipulated by the program that has called the supercompiler. Technically, the input expression is converted (reflected) to an AST, which is then processed by the supercompiler written in Scala. The result of supercompilation is then reified into values of the TT Lite language.

Let us consider the example in Fig. 1 illustrating the use of TT Lite SC for proving the equivalence of two expressions [7].

As in Haskell and Agda [15], the types of defined expressions do not have to be specified explicitly. However, type declarations make programs more understandable and easier to debug.

Lines 1–2 define the function of addition for natural numbers. Line 3 declares (assumes) 3 free variables $x, $y and $z whose type is Nat. By convention, the names of free variables start with $. Lines 4–5 define two expressions whose equivalence is to be proved.

Now we come to the most interesting point: line 6 calls the built-in function sc, which takes as input the expression in1 and returns its supercompiled version out1 along with the proof pr1 for the fact that in1 and out1 are extensionally equivalent (i.e., given $x, $y and $z, in1 and out1 return the same value). Line 7 does the same for in2, out2 and pr2.

$$
\begin{array}{ll}
p ::= (def|dec)* & \text{program} \\
def ::= id = e; \mid id : e;\ id = e; & \text{optionally typed definition} \\
dec ::= \$id : e; & \text{declaration (assumption)} \\
e ::= x & \text{variable} \\
\quad \mid \mathbf{c} & \text{built-in constant} \\
\quad \mid \mathbf{b}(x : e).\,e(x) & \text{built-in binder} \\
\quad \mid e_1\ e_2 & \text{application} \\
\quad \mid \mathbf{elim}\ e_t\ e_m\ \overline{e_i}\ e_d & \text{elimination} \\
\quad \mid (e) & \text{parenthesized expression}
\end{array}
$$

Fig. 2. TT Lite: syntax

Lines 8–9 formally state that `pr1` is *indeed* a proof of the equivalence of `in1` and `out1`, having as it does the appropriate type, and this fact is verified by the type checker built into TT Lite Core. Lines 10–11 do the same for `in2`, `out2` and `pr2`.

And now, the final stroke! Lines 12–13 verify that `out1` and `out2` are "propositionally equivalent" or, in simpler words, they are just textually the same. Hence, by transitivity (lines 14–15), `in1` is extensionally equivalent to `in2`. And this proof has been *automatically* found by supercompilation and verified by type checking [7]. The function `proof_by_trans` is coded in the TT Lite language in the file `examples/id.tt`.

3   TT Lite: Syntax and Semantics

In the following, the reader is assumed to be familiar with the basics of programming in Martin-Löf's type theory [19,20].

TT Lite Core provides a modular and extensible implementation of type theory. Technically speaking, it deals with a monomorphic version of type theory with intensional equality and universes.

TT Lite SC is based on TT Lite Core and makes heavy use of the expression evaluator (normalizer) and type checker provided by TT Lite Core. Hence, before looking into the internals of the supercompiler, we have to consider the *details* of how normalization and type checking are implemented in TT Lite Core.

The Syntax of the TT Lite language is shown in Fig. 2. A program is a list of declarations and definitions. A definition (as in Haskell) can be of two kinds: with or without an explicit type declaration. There is also a possibility to declare the type of an identifier without defining its value (quite similar to module parameters in Agda), in which case the identifier must start with $.

A TT Lite expression is either a variable, a built-in constant, a binder[5], an application, an application of an eliminator [22] or an expression enclosed in parentheses. This syntax should be familiar to functional programmers: variables and applications have usual meaning, binders are a generalization of λ-abstractions, eliminators are a "cross-breed" of `case` and `fold`.

---

[5] See [21, Sect. 1.2] describing *abstract binding trees*.

In general, an eliminator in the TT Lite language has the form $\mathtt{elim}\,e_t\ e_m\ \overline{e_i}\ e_d$ where e_t is the type of the values that are to be eliminated, e_m is a "motive" [22], e_i correspond to the cases that can be encountered when eliminating a value, and e_d is an expression that produces values to be eliminated[6].

The typing and normalization rules implemented in the $\mathit{\Pi NI}$ subset of TT Lite can be found in Fig. 3. Essentially, they correspond to the rules described in [19,20], but have been refactored, in order to be closer to their actual implementation in TT Lite.

The typing and normalization rules are formulated with respect to a context Γ, where Γ is a list of pairs of two kinds: $x := e$ binds a variable to an expression defining its value, while $x : T$ binds a variable to a type. By tradition, we divide the rules into 3 categories: *formation* (F), *introduction* (I) and *elimination* (E) rules. A rule of the form $\Gamma \vdash e : T$ means that e has the type T in the context Γ, while $[\![e]\!]_\Gamma = e'$ means that e' is the result of normalizing e in the context Γ.

Our rules mainly differ from the corresponding ones in [19,20] in that subexpressions are explicitly normalized in the process of type checking. It should be also noted that these expressions, in general, may contain free variables. If a TT Lite expression is well-typed, the normalization of this expression is guaranteed to terminate. So, any function definable in the TT Lite language is total by construction. Figure 4 gives a definition of the neutral variable [22] of an expression. Essentially, a neutral variable is the one that prevents an elimination step from being performed[7].

4   TT Lite SC: Supercompilation

The implementation of TT Lite SC is based on the MRSC Toolkit [23], which builds graphs of configurations [3] by repeatedly applying a number of graph rewrite rules. The nodes of a partially constructed graph are classified as either complete or incomplete. The supercompiler selects an incomplete node, declares it to be the *current* one, and turns it into a complete node by applying to it the rules specified by the programmer. The process starts with a graph containing a single (initial) configuration and stops when all nodes become complete[8].

Figure 5 schematically depicts the graph building operations that can be performed by the MRSC Toolkit. (Incomplete nodes are shown as dashed circles, the current node is inside a rounded box.) These operations are applied to the current node (which, by definition, is incomplete). The operation *unfold* adds child nodes to the current node. This node becomes complete, while the new nodes are declared to be incomplete. The operation *fold* adds a "folding" edge from the current node to one of its parents, and the node becomes complete. The operation *stop* just declares the current node to be complete, and does nothing else.

---

[6] By the way, application is essentially an eliminator for functional values.

[7] Recall that application is also a special case of eliminator.

[8] Or the graph is declared by the whistle to be "dangerous" (in this case the supercompiler just discards the graph), but this feature is not used by TT Lite SC.

$$(v) \ \Gamma, x : T \vdash x : [\![T]\!]_\Gamma \qquad ([\![v]\!]) \ [\![x]\!]_{\Gamma, \, x := t} = t \qquad (\mathcal{U}) \ \mathcal{U}_n : \mathcal{U}_{n+1}$$

$$(\Pi F) \ \frac{\Gamma \vdash A : \mathcal{U}_m \quad \Gamma, x : [\![A]\!]_\Gamma \vdash B(x) : \mathcal{U}_n}{\Gamma \vdash \Pi(x : A). \, B(x) : \mathcal{U}_{max(m,n)}}$$

$$(\Pi I) \ \frac{\Gamma \vdash A : \mathcal{U}_m \quad \Gamma, x : [\![A]\!]_\Gamma \vdash t(x) : B(x)}{\Gamma \vdash \lambda(x : A). \, t(x) : [\![\Pi(x : A). \, B(x)]\!]_\Gamma}$$

$$(\Pi E) \ \frac{\Gamma \vdash f : \Pi(x : A). \, B(x) \quad \Gamma \vdash t : A}{\Gamma \vdash f \, t : [\![B(x)]\!]_{\Gamma, x := [\![t]\!]_\Gamma}}$$

$$([\![\Pi F]\!]) \ [\![\Pi(x : A). \, B(x)]\!]_\Gamma = \Pi(x : [\![A]\!]_\Gamma). \, [\![B(x)]\!]_\Gamma$$

$$([\![\Pi I]\!]) \ [\![\lambda(x : A). \, t(x)]\!]_\Gamma = \lambda(x : [\![A]\!]_\Gamma). \, [\![t(x)]\!]_\Gamma$$

$$([\![\Pi E]\!]) \ [\![f \, t]\!]_\Gamma = \lceil [\![f]\!]_\Gamma \, [\![t]\!]_\Gamma \rceil_\Gamma \qquad (\lceil \Pi E \rceil) \ \lceil (\lambda(x : A). t(x)) u \rceil_\Gamma = [\![t(x)]\!]_{\Gamma, x := [\![u]\!]_\Gamma}$$

$$(\mathbb{N}F) \ \frac{}{\Gamma \vdash \mathbb{N} : \mathcal{U}_0} \qquad (\mathbb{N}I_1) \ \frac{}{\Gamma \vdash 0 : \mathbb{N}} \qquad (\mathbb{N}I_2) \ \frac{\Gamma \vdash n : \mathbb{N}}{\Gamma \vdash Succ \, n : \mathbb{N}}$$

$$(\mathbb{N}E) \ \frac{\Gamma \vdash m : [\![\Pi(x : \mathbb{N}). \, \mathcal{U}_k]\!]_\Gamma \quad \Gamma \vdash f_0 : [\![m \, 0]\!]_\Gamma}{\Gamma \vdash f_s : [\![\Pi(x : \mathbb{N}) \, (y : m \, x). \, m \, (Succ \, x)]\!]_\Gamma \quad \Gamma \vdash n : \mathbb{N}}{\Gamma \vdash elim \, \mathbb{N} \, m \, f_0 \, f_s \, n : [\![m \, n]\!]_\Gamma}$$

$$([\![\mathbb{N}I_2]\!]) \ [\![Succ \, n]\!]_\Gamma = Succ \, [\![n]\!]_\Gamma$$

$$([\![\mathbb{N}E]\!]) \ [\![elim \, \mathbb{N} \, m \, f_0 \, f_s \, n]\!]_\Gamma = \lceil elim \, \mathbb{N} \, [\![m]\!]_\Gamma \, [\![f_0]\!]_\Gamma \, [\![f_s]\!]_\Gamma \, [\![n]\!]_\Gamma \rceil_\Gamma$$

$$(\lceil \mathbb{N}E_1 \rceil) \ \lceil elim \, \mathbb{N} \, m \, f_0 \, f_s \, 0 \rceil_\Gamma = [\![f_0]\!]_\Gamma$$

$$(\lceil \mathbb{N}E_2 \rceil) \ \lceil elim \, \mathbb{N} \, m \, f_0 \, f_s \, (Succ \, n) \rceil_\Gamma = [\![f_s \, n \, (elim \, \mathbb{N} \, m \, f_0 \, f_s \, n)]\!]_\Gamma$$

$$(\mathcal{I}F) \ \frac{\Gamma \vdash A : \mathcal{U}_m \quad \Gamma \vdash t_1 : [\![A]\!]_\Gamma \quad \Gamma \vdash t_2 : [\![A]\!]_\Gamma}{\Gamma \vdash \mathcal{I} \, A \, t_1 \, t_2 : \mathcal{U}_m}$$

$$(\mathcal{I}I) \ \frac{\Gamma \vdash A : \mathcal{U}_m \quad \Gamma \vdash t : [\![A]\!]_\Gamma}{\Gamma \vdash Refl \, A \, t : [\![\mathcal{I} \, A \, t \, t]\!]_\Gamma}$$

$$(\mathcal{I}E) \ \frac{\Gamma \vdash \mathcal{I} \, A \, t_1 \, t_2 : \mathcal{U}_k \quad \Gamma \vdash m : [\![\Pi(x : A) \, (y : A) \, (z : \mathcal{I} \, A \, x \, y). \, \mathcal{U}_k]\!]_\Gamma}{\Gamma \vdash f : [\![\Pi(x : A). \, m \, x \, x \, (Refl \, A \, x)]\!]_\Gamma \quad \Gamma \vdash eq : [\![\mathcal{I} \, A \, t_1 \, t_2]\!]_\Gamma}{elim \, (\mathcal{I} \, A \, t_1 \, t_2) \, m \, f \, eq : [\![m \, t_1 \, t_2 \, eq]\!]_\Gamma}$$

$$([\![\mathcal{I}F]\!]) \ [\![\mathcal{I} \, A \, t_1 \, t_2]\!]_\Gamma = \mathcal{I} \, [\![A]\!]_\Gamma \, [\![t_1]\!]_\Gamma \, [\![t_2]\!]_\Gamma$$

$$([\![\mathcal{I}I]\!]) \ [\![Refl \, A \, t]\!]_\Gamma = Refl \, [\![A]\!]_\Gamma \, [\![t]\!]_\Gamma$$

$$([\![\mathcal{I}E]\!]) \ [\![elim \, (\mathcal{I} \, A \, t_1 \, t_2) \, m \, f \, eq]\!]_\Gamma = \lceil elim \, [\![\mathcal{I} \, A \, t_1 \, t_1]\!]_\Gamma \, [\![m]\!]_\Gamma \, [\![p]\!]_\Gamma \, [\![eq]\!]_\Gamma \rceil_\Gamma$$

$$(\lceil \mathcal{I}E \rceil) \ \lceil elim \, (\mathcal{I} \, A \, t_1 \, t_2) \, m \, f \, (Refl \, A \, t_3) \rceil_\Gamma = [\![f \, t_3]\!]_\Gamma$$

Fig. 3. TT Lite: rules

$$nv(x \, e) \qquad\qquad = x \qquad\qquad nv(elim \, \mathbb{N} \, m \, f_0 \, f_s \, e) \quad\ = nv(e)$$
$$nv(e_1 \, e_2) \qquad\qquad = nv(e_1) \qquad nv(elim \, (\mathcal{I} \, A \, t_1 \, t_2) \, m \, f \, x) = x$$
$$nv(elim \, \mathbb{N} \, m \, f_0 \, f_s \, x) = x \qquad\quad nv(elim \, (\mathcal{I} \, A \, t_1 \, t_2) \, m \, f \, e) = nv(e)$$

Fig. 4. Finding the neutral variable of a term

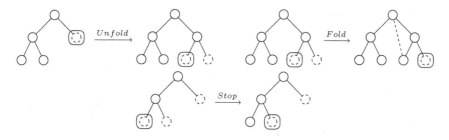

Fig. 5. Basic operations of MRSC

The MRSC toolkit allows the nodes and edges of a graph to hold arbitrary information. Information in a node is called a configuration. In the case of TT Lite SC, a configuration is a pair consisting of a term (expression) and a context. Schematically, a graph node will be depicted as follows: $\boxed{t \mid \Gamma}$. We use two kind of edge labels (I and E) in TT Lite SC. The first kind corresponds to the decomposition of a constructor, while the second kind corresponds to case analysis and (in general case) primitive recursion performed by an eliminator. In the case of recursive eliminators (such as $\mathbb{N}$, $List$) the label also holds information to be used for finding possible foldings.

We use the following notation for depicting nodes and transitions between nodes:

(a) $\boxed{t_0 \mid \Gamma_0} \xrightarrow{I(Succ)} \boxed{t_1 \mid \Gamma_1}$ (c) $\boxed{t_0 \mid \Gamma_0} \longleftarrow \boxed{t_1 \mid \Gamma_1}$

(b) $\boxed{t_0 \mid \Gamma_0} \begin{array}{c} \xrightarrow{E(y \to c_1, r)} \boxed{t_1 \mid \Gamma_1} \\ \xrightarrow{E(y \to c_1, \bullet)} \boxed{t_2 \mid \Gamma_2} \end{array}$ (d) $\boxed{t_0 \mid \Gamma_0} \longrightarrow \bullet$

An *unfolding edge* is schematically represented by a right arrow, and a *folding edge* by a left arrow. (a) represents a decomposition. (b) corresponds to case analysis performed by an eliminator. If the eliminator is a recursive one, the edge label contains a recursive term r, otherwise this position is occupied by the dummy placeholder $\bullet$. (c) represents a folding edge. (d) represents a complete node without child nodes. Sometimes, nodes will be denoted by greek letters. For example, a folding edge from β to α will be depicted as $a \leftarrow \beta$.

The rules used by TT Lite SC for building graphs of configurations are presented in Fig. 6(a). In simple cases, the left part of a rule is a pattern that specifies the structure of the nodes the rule is applicable to. But, sometimes a rule has the form of an inference rule with a number of premises ("guarded pattern matching" in programmer's terms). The rules are ordered.

Let us consider rules of various kinds in more details.

There are two kinds of rules for building graphs of configurations: type-specific and general ones. Type-specific rules determine how *driving* [24] is performed for constructions introduced by a specific type. General rules do not correspond to a specific type and ensure the finiteness of graphs of configurations. In this paper we

(a) Construction of a graph of configurations

$$\text{(Fold)} \frac{\exists \alpha \in anc(\beta) : \alpha \xrightarrow{E(y \mapsto t_1, c)} \alpha_1}{\alpha \leftarrow \beta} \qquad \text{(Stop)} \frac{depth(\beta) > n}{\boxed{c \mid \Gamma} \longrightarrow \bullet}$$

$$\text{(NI}_2') \frac{}{\boxed{Succ\; t \mid \Gamma} \xrightarrow{Succ} \boxed{t \mid \Gamma}} \qquad \text{(NE')} \frac{nv(c) = y \quad y : \mathbb{N}}{\boxed{c \mid \Gamma} \quad \begin{array}{l} \xrightarrow{y \mapsto 0, \bullet} \boxed{[\![c]\!]_{\Gamma, y := 0} \quad \mid \Gamma} \\ \xrightarrow{y \mapsto Succ\; y, c} \boxed{[\![c]\!]_{\Gamma, y := Succ\; y} \mid \Gamma} \end{array}}$$

$$\text{(Default)} \frac{}{\boxed{c \mid \Gamma} \longrightarrow \bullet}$$

(b) Code generation from a graph of configurations

$$\mathcal{C}\left[\beta \leftarrow \right]_\rho = \rho(\beta) \qquad \mathcal{C}\left[\rightarrow \bullet \right]_\rho = \alpha.e \qquad \mathcal{C}\left[\xrightarrow{I(Succ)} \alpha_1 \right]_\rho = Succ\; \mathcal{C}[\alpha_1]_\rho$$

$$\mathcal{C}\left[\begin{array}{l} \xrightarrow{E(y \mapsto 0, \bullet)} \alpha_1 \\ \xrightarrow{E(y \mapsto Succ\; y, r)} \alpha_2 \end{array} \right]_\rho = \begin{array}{l} elim\; \mathbb{N}\; (\lambda(y : \mathbb{N}).\; tp(\alpha)) \\ \mathcal{C}[\alpha_1]_\rho\; (\lambda(y : \mathbb{N})(v : tp(\alpha)).\; \mathcal{C}[\alpha_2]_{\rho + (\alpha \to v)})\; y \end{array}$$

(c) Proof generation from a graph of configurations

$$\mathcal{P}\left[\beta \leftarrow \right]_{\rho, \phi} = \phi(\beta) \qquad \mathcal{P}\left[\rightarrow \bullet \right]_{\rho, \phi} = Refl\; tp(\alpha)\; \alpha.e$$

$$\mathcal{P}\left[\xrightarrow{I(Succ)} \alpha_1 \right]_{\rho, \phi} = cong\; \mathbb{N}\; \mathbb{N}\; Succ\; \alpha_1.e\; \mathcal{C}[\alpha_1]_\rho\; \mathcal{P}[\alpha_1]_{\rho, \phi}$$

$$\mathcal{P}\left[\begin{array}{l} \xrightarrow{y \mapsto 0, \bullet} \alpha_1 \\ \xrightarrow{y \mapsto Succ\; y, r} \alpha_2 \end{array} \right]_{\rho, \phi} = \begin{array}{l} elim\; \mathbb{N}\; (\lambda(y : \mathbb{N}).\; \mathcal{I}\; tp(\alpha)\; \alpha.e\; \mathcal{C}[\alpha]_\rho) \mathcal{P}[\alpha_1]_{\rho, \phi} \\ (\lambda(y : \mathbb{N})(v : \mathcal{I}\; tp(\alpha)\; \alpha.e\; \mathcal{C}[\alpha]_\rho).\; \mathcal{P}[\alpha_2]_{\rho + (\alpha \to \mathcal{C}[\![\alpha]\!]_\rho), \phi + (\alpha \to v)}) \\ y \end{array}$$

(d) Utility function

$cong\; :\; \Pi(A : \mathcal{U}_i)(B : \mathcal{U}_j)(f : \Pi(\_ : A).B)(x : A)(y : A)(\_ : \mathcal{I}\; A\; x\; y).\; \mathcal{I}\; B\; (f\; x)\; (f\; y);$
$cong = \lambda(A : \mathcal{U}_i)(B : \mathcal{U}_j)(f : \Pi(\_ : A).B)(x : A)(y : A)(i : \mathcal{I}\; A\; x\; y).$
   $elim\; (\mathcal{I}\; A\; x\; y)\; (\lambda(x\; y : A)(\_ : \mathcal{I}\; A\; x\; y).\mathcal{I}\; B\; (f\; x)\; (f\; y))\; (\lambda(x : A).Refl\; B\; (f\; x))\; i;$

Fig. 6. Supercompilation rules

present all general rules of TT Lite SC and the driving rules for the $\Pi\mathcal{N}\mathcal{I}$ subset[9]. Rules *Fold*, *Stop* and *Default* are general ones. Rules $(\mathbb{N}I_2')$ and $(\mathbb{N}E')$ are driving rules for $\mathbb{N}$. All other driving rules can be found in [16].

Rules $(\mathbb{N}I_2')$ and $(\mathbb{N}E')$ add new nodes to the graph by applying the MRSC operation Unfold. Any driving rule in TT Lite SC can be classified as either a decomposition or a case analysis by means of an eliminator.

From the perspective of the type theory, decomposition corresponds to formation and introduction rules. The essence of decomposition is simple: we take a construct to pieces (which become the new nodes) and label the edges with some information (about the construct that has been decomposed). In the case of the $\Pi\mathcal{N}\mathcal{I}$ subset there is only one decomposition rule: $(\mathbb{N}I_2')$.

Note that, in general, for each formation and introduction rule there exists a corresponding decomposition rule, provided that the corresponding value has some internal structure. However, in the case of the type $\mathbb{N}$, the constructs $\mathbb{N}$ and 0 have no internal structure.

---

[9] In this paper the identity type is only used for constructing proofs of correctness. Thus, for brevity, we do not discuss here driving rules for identity.

Decomposition is not performed for binders Π and λ. The reason is that in this case we could be unable to generate a proof of correctness of decomposition, because the core type theory does not provide means for dealing with extensional equality.

When the supercompiler encounters an expression with a neutral variable, it considers all instantiations of this variable that are allowed by its type. Then, for each possible instantiation, the supercompiler adds a child node and labels the corresponding edge with some information about this instantiation.

When dealing with eliminators for recursive types (such as $\mathbb{N}$ and *List*), we record the expression corresponding to the "previous step of elimination"[10] in the edge label. For example, for the expression $elim\ \mathbb{N}\ m\ f_0\ f_s\ (Succ\ y)$, the expression corresponding to the previous step of elimination is $elim\ \mathbb{N}\ m\ f_0\ f_s\ y$. In the case of the subset $\Pi\mathcal{NI}$, the only rule for case analysis is ($\mathbb{N}E'$), which considers two possible instantiations of the neutral variable y of the type $\mathbb{N}$: 0 and $Succ\ y$. Note that by putting an instantiation in the context and then normalizing the expression, we perform *positive information propagation*: the key step of supercompilation. Storing "the previous step of eliminator" is crucial for folding and code generation, since the only way to introduce recursive functions in TT Lite is via eliminators.

A technical note should be done here: in TT Lite SC we generate new variables for instantiations and put them into context. So, in TT Lite SC, given a neutral variable y of type $\mathbb{N}$, the child configuration corresponding to the case $y = Succ\ y_1$ is $\boxed{\|[c]\|_{\Gamma, y := Succ\ y_1} \mid \Gamma, y_1 : \mathbb{N}}$, where y_1 is a fresh variable of the type $\mathbb{N}$. However, in this specific case we can avoid the generation of a new variable by reusing the variable y and not extending the context (since y is already in the context). This small trick allows us to make presentation of code generation and proof generation rules (given in the next sections) shorter and less cumbersome.

Note that the information stored on the edge label is enough for generating both the residual program and the proof of correctness (in a straightforward way).

Another special case is the application of a neutral variable. Since a neutral variable is bound to have a functional type, we cannot enumerate all its possible instantiations. In such situation, most supercompilers (*e.g.* HOSC [25]) perform a decomposition of the application, but, to keep the supercompiler simple, we prefer not to decompose such applications.

General rules (*Fold, Stop, Default*) are the core of TT Lite SC. In short, general rules ensure the finiteness of graphs of configurations. This is achieved either by folding the current expression to a previously encountered one or by stopping the development of the current branch of the graph.

In the rule *Fold*, $anc(\beta)$ is a set of ancestor nodes of the current node β and c is an expression in the node β. The rule itself is very simple. Suppose that the current node has an ancestor node whose "previous step of elimination" in the outgoing edge is (literally) the same as the current term. Then the rule *Fold*

---

[10] = "recursive call" of the same eliminator.

is applicable, and the current configuration can be folded to the parent one. In the residual program this folding will give rise to a function defined by primitive recursion.

Folding in TT Lite SC differs from that in traditional supercompilers. Namely, most supercompilers perform folding when the current expression is a renaming of some expression in the history. However, since TT Lite SC has to encode recursion by means of eliminators, the mixture of folding and renaming would create some technical problems. So, we prefer to separate them.

If no folding/driving rule is applicable, the rule *Default* is applied. (This rule is the last and has the lowest priority.) In this case, the current node becomes complete and the building of the current branch of the graph is stopped.

In general, the process of repeatedly applying driving rules, together with the rules *Fold* and *Default*, may never terminate. Thus, in order to ensure termination, we use the rule *Stop*, whose priority is higher than that of the unfolding rules and the rule *Default*. In this supercompiler we use a very simple termination criterion: the building of the current branch stops if its depth exceeds some threshold n. Note that, in the case of TT Lite SC, the expressions appearing in the nodes of the graph are self-contained, so that they can be just output into the residual program.

Since the graph of configurations is finitely branching, and all branches have finite depth, the graph of configurations cannot be infinite. Therefore, the process of graph building eventually terminates.

The generation of the residual program corresponding to a completed graph of configurations is performed by recursive descent. The function that implements the residualization algorithm is defined in Fig. 6(b). A call to this function has the form $\mathcal{C}[\alpha]_\rho$, where α is the current node, and ρ is an environment (mapping of nodes to variables) to "tie the knot" on "folding" edges. The initial call to the function $\mathcal{C}$ has the form $\mathcal{C}[root]_{\{\}}$, where *root* is the root node of the graph of configurations.

The function $\mathcal{C}$ performs pattern matching against the edges going out of the current node. (In the rules, the patterns are enclosed into square brackets.) We use the following conventions: the current node is α, $\alpha.e$ is an expression in the node α, $tp(\alpha)$ is the type of the expression appearing in the node α. If $e \mid \Gamma$ is the configuration in the node α, and $\Gamma \vdash e : T$, then $tp(\alpha) = T$. In the last rule (corresponding to a case analysis of a neutral var of type $\mathbb{N}$) v is a fresh variable.

Note that rules for construction of a graph of configurations take into account that residualization facilities of $\mathcal{C}$ are limited (by eliminators) and produce a graph that *can* be residualized by $\mathcal{C}$.

5   Proof Generation

The function that implements the proof generator is defined in Fig. 6(c). A call to this function has the form $\mathcal{P}[\alpha]_{\rho,\phi}$, where α is the current node, while ρ and ϕ are two environments. ρ is used for folding in residual programs (when encoding recursion), while ϕ is used for folding in proofs (when encoding proofs by induction). Technically, ϕ binds some nodes to corresponding inductive hypotheses. The initial call to the function $\mathcal{P}$ has the form $\mathcal{P}[root]_{\{\},\{\}}$, where $root$ is the root node of the graph of configurations.

Generated proofs are based on the use of propositional *equality* (*i.e.* syntactic identity of normalized expressions), functional *composition* and *induction*.

- The residual expression corresponding to a childless node is the same as the one appearing in this node. Hence, the proof amounts to the use of reflexivity of equality (*i.e.* is a call to *Refl*).
- The proofs corresponding to decompositions of configurations exploit the congruence of equality: the whole proof is constructed by combining subproofs (demonstrating that the arguments of constructors are equal) with the aid of the combinator *cong* defined in Fig. 6(d) ([16] uses more congruence combinators).
- The proofs corresponding to eliminators are by structural induction. The motive of a new eliminator is now a proof. When specifying a motive of eliminator, $\mathcal{C}[\alpha]_\rho$ is used in the same way as during code generation (using the same environment ρ). But, when generating subproofs for recursive eliminators, $\mathcal{C}[\alpha]_\rho$ is used to extend the environment ρ. Also ϕ is extended, to bind the current node to a subproof (inductive hypothesis).

Note that the same graph of configurations is used both for generating the residual program and for generating the proof. If TT Lite SC would have been implemented in "direct" style (without explicit graphs of configurations) like in [26], such reuse would be problematic, which would produce a negative effect on the modularity of our design.

Despite the fact that the rules for $\mathcal{P}$ are compact, they are technically involved since there is an intricate use of two "folding contexts" ρ and ϕ. Another technically interesting point is that code generation function $\mathcal{C}$ is used as a "type inferencer" when constructing a motive for proof term encoded via eliminators.

6   Example

Let us consider supercompilation of the expression `in2` from the Fig. 1 (which is `plus (plus $x $y) $z`). The graph of configurations for this expression is shown in Fig. 7. The generated code is shown in Fig. 8. The proof that `in2` and `out2` are equivalent is not shown here because of the lack of space (but can be found at the project website). The project site contains more examples of certifying supercompilation. In particular, TT Lite SC is capable of proving most equivalences of expressions that have been presented in the paper [7] (and proved by HOSC). The difference from HOSC, however, is that TT Lite SC generates explicit proofs, which can be verified by type checking.

7   Related Work

One of the ideas exploited by TT Lite SC is that of *supercompilation by evaluation*. As was shown in [26], supercompilation can be based on an evaluator

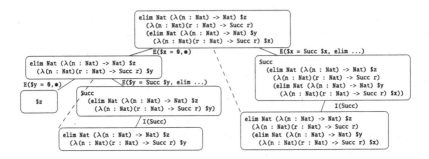

Fig. 7. Example: graph of configurations and "graph of residualization"

```
1   elim Nat (\($x : Nat) -> Nat)
2     (elim Nat (\ ($y : Nat) -> Nat) $z (\ ($y : Nat)(r2 : Nat) -> Succ r2) $y)
3       (\ ($x : Nat) (r1 : Nat) -> Succ r1) $x
```

Fig. 8. Example: residual expression (out2)

which tries to reduce an open term to head normal form. Unfortunately, if the subject language is not a total one (as in the case of Haskell), the evaluation may not terminate. For this reason, Bolingbroke and Peyton Jones had to equip their evaluator with a termination check ("local whistle"), which may interfere with global termination check in subtle ways. Hence, the evaluator had to be fused, to some extent, with other parts of their supercompiler.

In the case of TT Lite SC, the totality of the subject language has allowed us to greatly *simplify* and *modularize* the structure and implementation of our supercompiler. In particular, since the evaluation of all expressions, including expressions with free variables, terminates, the evaluator is trivialized into a standard normalizer, so that TT Lite SC just reuses the interpreter provided by TT Lite Core. Thus, the supercompiler knows nothing about the internals of the evaluator, using it as a "black box".

Another point, where we exploit the totality of the subject language, is case analysis. Since a function returns a result for *any* input, all possible instantiations of a neutral variable can be found by just examining the type of this variable. Note that supercompilers dealing with partial functions usually find instantiations of a variable by taking into account how this variable is actually used in the program. Technically, this means that driving has to be implemented as a combination of case analysis and variable instantiation. TT Lite SC, however, completely decouples case analysis from variable instantiation.

Since our goal was to investigate whether certifying supercompilation is possible *in principle*, we tried to keep our proof-of-concept certifying supercompiler as simple and comprehensible as possible. And, indeed, the ingredients of our supercompiler for the $\Pi\mathcal{N}\mathcal{I}$ subset fit on half a page! And yet, this is a supercompiler for a non-trivial language (of Martin-Löf's type theory), which is powerful enough in order to be able to prove most term equivalences from [7].

In some application areas, however, TT Lite SC is inferior even to "naïve" partial evaluators. In particular, it fails to pass the classical KMP test [24]. The reason is that, in residual programs produced by TT Lite SC, all loops and recursive functions has to be encoded in terms of eliminators. Thus, TT Lite SC can only fold a configuration to "the previous step of an eliminator". This is a restricted form of folding, which is not sufficient in the case of the KMP test. We could generalize our graph building rules to allow TT Lite SC to use more complicated forms of folding. However, in this case, residual programs would be difficult to express in terms of eliminators and, as a consequence, the generation of correctness proofs, corresponding to residual programs, would become more technically involved. This problem needs to be further investigated.

8   Conclusions

We have developed and implemented a *certifying* supercompiler TT Lite SC, which takes an input program and produces a residual program paired with a proof of the fact that the residual program is equivalent to the input one. As far as we can judge from the literature, this is the first implementation of a certifying supercompiler for a non-trivial higher-order functional language.

A proof generated by TT Lite SC can be verified by a type checker of TT Lite Core which is independent from TT Lite SC and is not based on supercompilation. This is essential in cases where the reliability of results obtained by supercompilation is of fundamental importance. For example, when supercompilation is used for purposes of program analysis and verification. Some "technical" details in the design of TT Lite SC are also of interest.

- The subject language of the supercompiler is a total, statically typed, higher-order functional language. Namely, this is the language of Martin-Löf's type theory (in its monomorphic version).
- The proof language is the same as the subject language of the supercompiler.
- Recursive functions in the subject language are written in a well-structured way, by means of "eliminators". An eliminator for an inductively defined data type performs both the case analysis and recursive calls.
- Driving is type-directed.
- There is an intricate interplay of supercompilation, type theory and limitations imposed by usage of eliminators.
- TT Lite programs (including proofs produced by supercompilation) can be exported into Agda and checked by Agda system.

References

1. Sørensen, M.H., Glück, R., Jones, N.D.: A positive supercompiler. J. Funct. Program. **6**(6), 811–838 (1996)
2. Sørensen, M.H., Glück, R.: Introduction to supercompilation. In: Hatcliff, J., Thiemann, P. (eds.) DIKU 1998. LNCS, vol. 1706, pp. 246–270. Springer, Heidelberg (1999)
3. Turchin, V.F.: The concept of a supercompiler. ACM Trans. Program. Lang. Syst. (TOPLAS) **8**(3), 292–325 (1986)

4. Turchin, V.F.: The language Refal: the theory of compilation and metasystem analysis. Technical report 20, Courant Institute of Mathematical Sciences (1980)
5. Lisitsa, A., Nemytykh, A.: Verification as a parameterized testing. Program. Comput. Softw. **33**(1), 14–23 (2007)
6. Klimov, A., Klyuchnikov, I., Romanenko, S.: Automatic verification of counter systems via domain-specific multi-result supercompilation. In: [27]
7. Klyuchnikov, I., Romanenko, S.: Proving the equivalence of higher-order terms by means of supercompilation. In: Pnueli, A., Virbitskaite, I., Voronkov, A. (eds.) PSI 2009. LNCS, vol. 5947, pp. 193–205. Springer, Heidelberg (2010)
8. Klyuchnikov, I.: Inferring and proving properties of functional programs by means of supercompilation. Ph.D. thesis, Keldysh Institute of Applied Mathematics (2010)
9. Turchin, V.F.: Supercompilation: techniques and results. In: Bjorner, D., Broy, M., Pottosin, I.V. (eds.) PSI 1996. LNCS, vol. 1181, pp. 227–248. Springer, Heidelberg (1996)
10. Klyuchnikov, I., Romanenko, S.: Towards higher-level supercompilation. In: [28]
11. Mendel-Gleason, G., Hamilton, G.: Development of the productive forces. In: [27]
12. Klyuchnikov, I.: Supercompiler HOSC: proof of correctness. Preprint 31, KIAM, Moscow (2010). http://library.keldysh.ru/preprint.asp?id=2010-31
13. Krustev, D.: A simple supercompiler formally verified in Coq. In: [28], pp. 102–127
14. Bertot, Y., Castran, P.: Interactive Theorem Proving and Program Development: Coq'Art The Calculus of Inductive Constructions. Springer, Heidelberg (2010)
15. The agda wiki (2013). http://wiki.portal.chalmers.se/agda/
16. Klyuchnikov, I., Romanenko, S.: TT Lite: A Supercompiler for Martin-Löf's Type Theory. Preprint, KIAM, Moscow (2013). http://library.keldysh.ru//preprint.asp?lg=e&id=2013-73
17. Martin-Lof, P.: Intuitionistic Type Theory. Bibliopolis, Naples (1984)
18. Pardo, A., da Rosa, S.: Program transformation in Martin-Löf's type theory. In: CADE-12, Workshop on Proof-Search in Type-Theoretic Languages (1994)
19. Nordström, B., Petersson, K., Smith, J.M.: Programming in Martin-Löf's Type Theory. Oxford University Press, Oxford (1990)
20. Thompson, S.: Type Theory and Functional Programming. Addison Wesley Longman Publishing Co. Inc., Redwood City (1991)
21. Harper, R.: Practical Foundations for Programming Languages. Cambridge University Press, New York (2012)
22. Löh, A., McBride, C., Swierstra, W.: A tutorial implementation of a dependently typed lambda calculus. Fundamenta Informaticae **21**, 1001–1032 (2010)
23. Klyuchnikov, I.G., Romanenko, S.A.: MRSC: A Toolkit for Building Multi-result Supercompilers. Preprint 77, KIAM (2011). http://library.keldysh.ru/preprint.asp?lg=e&id=2011-77
24. Jones, N.D.: The essence of program transformation by partial evaluation and driving. In: Bjorner, D., Broy, M., Zamulin, A.V. (eds.) PSI 1999. LNCS, vol. 1755, pp. 62–79. Springer, Heidelberg (2000)
25. Klyuchnikov, I.: Supercompiler HOSC 1.0: Under the Hood. Preprint 63, KIAM, Moscow (2009). http://library.keldysh.ru/preprint.asp?id=2009-63
26. Bolingbroke, M., Peyton Jones, S.: Supercompilation by evaluation. In: Proceedings of the Third ACM Haskell Symposium on Haskell, pp. 135–146. ACM (2010)
27. Klimov, A., Romanenko, S. (eds.) Third International Valentin Turchin Workshop on Metacomputation, Publishing House "University of Pereslavl", Russia (2012)
28. Nemytykh, A. (ed.) Second International Valentin Turchin Memorial Workshop on Metacomputation, Publishing House "University of Pereslavl", Russia (2010)

Index Sets as a Measure of Continuous Constraint Complexity

Margarita Korovina[1][(✉)] and Oleg Kudinov[2]

[1] A.P. Ershov Institute of Informatics Systems, Novosibirsk, Russia
rita.korovina@gmail.com
[2] Sobolev Institute of Mathematics, Novosibirsk, Russia
kud@math.nsc.ru

Abstract. We develop the theory of index sets in the context of computable analysis considering classes of effectively open sets and computable real-valued functions. First, we construct principal computable numberings for effectively open sets and computable real-valued functions. Then, we calculate the complexity of index sets for important problems such as root realisability, set equivalence and inclusion, function equivalence which naturally arise in continuous constraint solving. Using developed techniques we give a direct proof of the generalised Rice-Shapiro theorem for effectively open sets of Euclidean spaces and present an analogue of Rice's theorem for computable real-valued functions. We illustrate how index sets can be used to estimate complexity of continuous constraints in the settings of the Kleene-Mostowski arithmetical hierarchy.

1 Introduction

The present research is motivated by rapidly increasing interest in solvability and satisfiability of continuous constraints which naturally arise in program analysis, formalisations of safety-critical systems evolving in real time and real spaces. Our goal is to develop an appropriate logical framework which allows one to apply the classical recursion theory methods, originally developed for purely discrete data, to make formal reasoning about continuous data. In the previous work [10–14] we already established strong interconnection between Σ–definability and computability in real analysis. In [9] it has been illustrated how Σ_K-constraints can be used for analysing reachability problems of switched controlled systems.

In this paper we propose to consider the theory of index sets as a promising candidate for merging classical recursion theory and computable analysis. There are several reasons for doing this. One of them is that the theory of index sets provides methods for encoding problems in an effective way by natural numbers, i.e., generate the corresponding index sets which can be used for analysing

This research was partially supported by Marie Curie Int. Research Staff Scheme Fellowship project PIRSES-GA-2011-294962, DFG/RFBR grant CAVER BE 1267/14-1 and 14-01-91334.

A. Voronkov and I. Virbitskaite (Eds.): PSI 2014, LNCS 8974, pp. 201–215, 2015.
DOI: 10.1007/978-3-662-46823-4_17

their complexity in the settings of the Kleene-Mostowski arithmetical hierarchy. Another reason is that the theory of index sets has been already successfully employed in many areas in Mathematics and Computer Science. In recursion theory index sets have been applied to get both new results and new elegant proofs of classical theorems such as the Post's theorem, the density theorem [7,17,18]. In computable model theory recent advancements are closely related to index sets [4,5]. In Computer Science the Rice-Shapiro theorem provides simple description of effectively enumerable properties of program languages.

In this paper we initiate the study of the theory of index sets for computable analysis starting with index sets for classes of effectively open subsets of Euclidian spaces and strongly computable real-valued functions. In order to develop a uniform framework we use the notions of effectively enumerable space and effectively open subset recalled in Sect. 2. Previously, in [8,11] we have shown that the class of effectively enumerable spaces contains the computable metric spaces, the weakly effective ω–continuous domains as proper natural subclasses. Furthermore, for every effectively enumerable space which admits structurisation, e.g. a computable metric space, its effectively open subsets coincide with the sets which are Σ–definable without equality. This makes effectively enumerable spaces suitable for our purposes.

In Sect. 2 one of the important theorems is Theorem 3 that provides characterisation of strong computability in terms of effectively open sets. We use this result for constructing principal computable numberings of the strongly computable real-valued functions. Then, in Sect. 3 we introduce index sets for classes of effectively open subsets of Euclidian spaces and strongly computable real-valued functions. We prove a series of results on Π_2^0-completeness of several problems such as set equality, set inclusion, root realizability. One of the main theorems here is Theorem 6 which is an analog of Rice's theorem for strongly computable real-valued functions.

In Sect. 4 we prove a generalisation of the Rice-Shapiro theorem which provides simple description of effectively enumerable properties of effectively open sets of Euclidian spaces. It is worth noting that in the domain theoretical framework various versions of the theorem were proposed in pioneer papers [6,19]. In Sect. 5 we prove that index sets for computably closed, computably compact sets are Σ_3^0-complete. We also show that the index set for any class of computable compact sets is Π_2^0–hard. There results help to reveal origins of undecidability of many non-trivial problems in computable analysis.

In Sect. 6 we investigate an application of methods developed in this paper to hybrid systems. It is well-known that the most important problems such as reachability, safety, liveness are undecidable for relatively general classes of hybrid systems. In [3] it was proven that for wide classes of dynamical systems reachability sets are not computable in the sense of computable analysis. The next natural question is whether there exist properties of hybrid systems that can be decided by limit decision procedures. In this paper we give an answer for a general class of hybrid systems. The main result of this section is Theorem 14 which shows that for any non-trivial property there is no $0'$–computable, i.e., limit computable decision procedure for classes of general hybrid systems. This gives understanding of roots of undecidability for many problems in the general theory of hybrid systems, in particular, in analysis of invariants and safety properties.

2   Basic Definitions and Notions

In order to consider all Euclidean spaces and continuous real-valued functions in the same settings we recall the notion of effectively enumerable topological space. Let (X, τ, ν) be a topological space, where X is a non-empty set, $\tau^* \subseteq 2^X$ is a base of the topology τ and $\nu : \omega \to \tau^*$ is a numbering.

Definition 1 *[11]. A topological space (X, τ, ν) is effectively enumerable if the following conditions hold.*

1. *There exists a computable function $g : \omega \times \omega \times \omega \to \omega$ such that*

$$\nu(i) \cap \nu(j) = \bigcup_{n \in \omega} \nu(g(i, j, n)).$$

2. *The set $\{i \,|\, \nu(i) \neq \emptyset\}$ is computably enumerable.*

It is worth noting that Euclidean spaces and continuous real functions belong to the class of effectively enumerable topological spaces. In this paper we study the complexity of classes of effectively open sets which can be considered as continuous analogs of computable enumerable sets over natural numbers.

Definition 2 *[11]. Let X be an effectively enumerable topological space. A set $A \subseteq X$ is effectively open if there exists a computable function $h : \omega \to \omega$ such that*

$$A = \bigcup_{n \in \omega} \nu(h(n)).$$

The complement of an effectively open set is called *co-effectively closed*.

Let $\mathcal{O}_X$ denote the set of all open subsets of X and $\mathcal{O}_X^e$ denote the set of all effectively open subsets of X. We recall that for $A, B \in \mathcal{O}_{\mathbb{R}^n}$, A is way-below B, i.e., $A \ll B$, if there exists a compact K such that $A \subset K \subset B$.

A numbering $\alpha : \omega \to \mathcal{O}_X^e$ is called *computable* if there exists a computable function $H : \omega \times \omega \to \omega$ such that $\alpha(k) = \bigcup_{n \in \omega} \nu(H(k, n))$. A computable numbering α is called *principal* if any computable numbering is computably reducible to α [7].

Theorem 1. *For every effectively enumerable topological space X there exists a principal computable numbering of $\mathcal{O}_X^e$.*

Proof. Define $\alpha(e) = \bigcup_{n \in \omega} \nu(\varphi_e(n)) = \bigcup\{\nu(k) \,|\, k \in \pi_e\}$. It is easy to see that α is a computable numbering of $\mathcal{O}_X^e$. To show that α is principal we assume that $F : \omega \to \mathcal{O}_X^e$ is a computable numbering of $\mathcal{O}_X^e$. By definition, there exists a computable function H such that $F(k) = \bigcup_{n \in \omega} \nu H(k, n)$. For some computable function $\beta : \omega \to \omega$, $H(x, y) = \varphi_{\beta(x)}(y)$. Therefore, $F(k) = \alpha(\beta(k))$.

Within this paper we use closed interconnection between effective openness and Σ–definability on effectively enumerable topological spaces admitting positive predicate structurisation [8]. The real numbers and the continuous real functions are examples of such spaces. It turns out that the following properties of Σ–definability provide elegant techniques to calculate the arithmetical complexity of index sets for classes over Euclidean spaces.

Theorem 2 *[10, 13]. There is an algorithm which by a Σ–formula without equality Φ produces an effective sequence of quantifier free formulas without equality $\{\varphi_i\}_{i\in\omega}$ such that $\mathbf{HF}(\mathbb{R}) \models (\forall y \in [a,b])\Phi(\bar{x}) \leftrightarrow \mathbf{HF}(\mathbb{R}) \models \bigvee_{i\in\omega}\varphi_i(a,b,\bar{x})$. There is an algorithm which by an effective sequence of quantifier free formulas without equality $\{\psi_i\}_{i\in\omega}$ produces a Σ–formula without equality Ψ such that $\mathbf{HF}(\mathbb{R}) \models \bigvee_{i\in\omega}\psi_i(\bar{x}) \leftrightarrow \mathbf{HF}(\mathbb{R}) \models \Psi(\bar{x})$.*

The following proposition is a natural corollary of the previous theorem.

Proposition 1. *A subset of $\mathbb{R}^n$ is effectively open if and only if it is Σ–definable without equality.*

Since there is a universal Σ–predicate [13] we can define a numbering α_Σ of Σ–definable subsets in a natural way. It is easy to see that α and α_Σ are equivalent over any Euclidean space. Now we introduce the notion of strongly computable function over effectively enumerable topological spaces based on the well-known definition of enumeration operator.

Definition 3 *[17]. A function $\Gamma_e : \mathcal{P}(\omega) \to \mathcal{P}(\omega)$ is called enumeration operator if $\Gamma_e(A) = B \leftrightarrow B = \{j | \exists i\, c(i,j) \in W_e,\ D_i \subseteq A\}$, where W_e is the e-th computably enumerable set, and D_i is the i-th finite set.*

Let $\mathcal{X} = (X, \tau, \alpha)$ be an effectively enumerable topological space and $\mathbb{R} = (\mathbb{R}, \lambda, \beta)$, where β is a computable numbering of the open intervals with rational endpoints, $\emptyset$ and $\mathbb{R}$. Let us denote $A_x = \{i \in \omega | x \in \alpha(i)\}$, $B_y = \{j \in \omega | y \in \beta(j)\}$.

Definition 4. *A partial function $F : X \to \mathbb{R}$ is called strongly computable if there exists an enumeration operator $\Gamma_e : \mathcal{P}(\omega) \to \mathcal{P}(\omega)$ such that, for every $x \in X$,*

(1) for every finite set $D \subseteq \Gamma_e(A_x)$ either $\bigcap_{k\in D} \beta(k) = \emptyset$ or

$$(\exists m \in \Gamma_e(A_x))\, \beta(m) \ll \bigcap_{k\in D} \beta(k),$$

(2) if $x \in dom(F)$ then $\Gamma_e(A_x) = B_{F(x)}$,
(3) if $x \notin dom(F)$ then $\bigcap_{j\in\omega}\{\beta(j) | j \in \Gamma_e(A_x)\}$ is not a singleton.

The following theorem establishes a close relation between strongly computable functions and effectively open sets. Below we use the interval domain $\mathcal{I}_{\mathbb{R}} = \{[a,b] \subseteq \mathbb{R} \mid a, b \in \mathbb{R},\ a \le b\} \cup \{\bot\}$, the ω-continuous domain $\mathcal{I}_{\mathbb{R}}^* = \mathcal{I}_{\mathbb{R}} \cup \{\top\}$, where $x \ll \top$ for every $x \in \mathcal{I}_{\mathbb{R}}$, the standard notations $U(x) \rightleftharpoons \{y | (x,y) \in U\}$, for a binary relation $U \subseteq X \times Y$, and $O_{[a,b]} \rightleftharpoons \{x \in \mathcal{I}_{\mathbb{R}}^* | [a,b] \ll x\}$.

Theorem 3. *Let (X, τ, α) be an effectively enumerable topological space and $f : X \to \mathbb{R}$ be a partial function. The following assertions are equivalent.*

1. *The function f is strongly computable.*
2. *There exists a total computable function $F : X \to \mathcal{I}_{\mathbb{R}}^*$ such that*
   (a) $\cdot F(x) = \{f(x)\}$ for $x \in \mathrm{dom}(f)$;
   (b) $F(x) \neq \{y\}$ for $x \notin \mathrm{dom}(f)$ and any $y \in \mathbb{R}$.
3. *There exist two effectively open sets $U, V \subseteq X \times \mathbb{R}$ such that*
   (a) for all $x \in X$, $U(x)$ is closed downward and $V(x)$ is closed upward;
   (b) if $x \in \mathrm{dom} f$ then $U(x) = \{y | y < f(x)\}$ and $V(x) = \{y | y > f(x)\}$;
   (c) if $x \notin \mathrm{dom} f$ then the $\mathbb{R} \setminus (U(x) \cup V(x))$ is not a singleton.

Proof. $1 \to 2$). Let Γ_e be a enumeration operator that defines f. Denote

$$A_x \rightleftharpoons \{[q_1, q_2] | (\exists m) \beta(m) = (q_1, q_2) \wedge (\exists k)((\forall s \in D_k) \, x \in \alpha(s) \wedge c(k, m) \in W_e)\}.$$

Define

$$F(x) = \begin{cases} \bot, & \text{if } A_x = \emptyset \\ \bigcap A_x, & \text{if } A_x \neq \emptyset \text{ and } \bigcap A_x \neq \emptyset \\ \top, & \text{if } A_x \neq \emptyset \text{ and } \bigcap A_x = \emptyset. \end{cases}$$

It is clear that $F^{-1}(\top)$ and $F^{-1}(O_{[a,b]})$ are effectively open sets (uniformly in $a < b, a, b \in \mathbb{Q}$). This means that F is an effectively continuous function, therefore F is computable [11].
$2 \to 3$). Define

$$U(x) = \begin{cases} \{z | z \in \mathbb{R} \text{ and } z < F(x)\} & \text{if } F(x) \in \mathcal{I}_{\mathbb{R}} \\ \mathbb{R} & \text{if } F(x) = \top, \end{cases}$$

and

$$V(x) = \begin{cases} \{z | z \in \mathbb{R} \text{ and } z > F(x)\} & \text{if } F(x) \in \mathcal{I}_{\mathbb{R}} \\ \mathbb{R} & \text{if } F(x) = \top. \end{cases}$$

Then, $U = \{(x, a) | a \in U(x)\}$ and $V = \{(x, a) | a \in V(x)\}$. It is easy to see that U and V are open and satisfy the conditions $(a) - (c)$.
$3 \to 1$). Let $U, V \subseteq X \times \mathbb{R}$ be effectively open sets satisfying the conditions $(a) - (c)$. It is clear, that U and V are representable in the following way.

$$U = \bigcup_{i \in \omega} [\alpha h_U(i) \times (g_1(i), g_2(i))] \, ; V = \bigcup_{i \in \omega} [\alpha h_V(i) \times (g_3(i), g_4(i))]$$

for some computable functions $h_V, h_U : \omega \to \omega$ and $g_j : \omega \to \mathbb{Q}$ for $1 \leq j \leq 4$.
Define

$$W_e = \{c(k, m) | D_k = \{c(h_U(i), h_V(j))\} \wedge (\exists r_1 \in \mathbb{Q})(\exists r_2 \in \mathbb{Q})$$
$$(\beta(m) = (r_1, r_2) \wedge r_1 < g_2(i) \wedge r_2 > g_3(j))\}.$$

The function Γ_e is a required enumeration operator.

From the theorem it follows that for total functions $f : X \to \mathbb{R}$ computability [11] and strong computability coincide. For an effectively enumerable space X we denote the set of partial strongly computablefunction $f : X \to \mathbb{R}$ as $\mathcal{CFR}_X$. A numbering $\gamma : \omega \to \mathcal{CFR}_X$ is called *computable* if the sequence of functions $\{\gamma(n)\}_{n \in \omega}$ is uniformly computable.

Theorem 4. *For every effectively enumerable space X there exists a principal computable numbering of $\mathcal{CFR}_X$.*

Proof. Let us fix β a principal computable numbering of the set of pairs of effectively open subsets of $X \times \mathbb{R}$. The existence of such numbering follows from Theorem 1. Let $\beta(n) = (\widetilde{U}_n, \widetilde{V}_n)$. We can effectively construct a new pair which satisfy Condition 3 of Theorem 3. Indeed, put

$$U_n \rightleftharpoons \{(x,r) | (\exists r_1)(r_1 > r \wedge (x, r_1) \in \widetilde{U}_n)\},$$
$$V_n \rightleftharpoons \{(x,r) | (\exists r_1)(r_1 < r \wedge (x, r_1) \in \widetilde{V}_n)\}.$$

From Theorem 3 it follows that V_n, U_n define a partial strongly computablefunction $f : X \to \mathbb{R}$ such that $f(x) = y \leftrightarrow U_n(x) \cup V_n(x) = \mathbb{R} \setminus \{y\}$. Put $\gamma(n) = f$. By construction, γ is a required numbering.

3   Index Sets and Arithmetical Complexity over the Reals

Now we focus on calculating the complexity of index subsets for classes of effectively open subsets of Euclidean spaces and strongly computablereal-valued functions. We consider $(\mathcal{O}^e_{\mathbb{R}^n}, \alpha)$ and $(\mathcal{CFR}_X, \gamma)$, where α is a principal computable numbering of the effectively open subsets of the Euclidean space $\mathbb{R}^n$ and γ is a principal computable numbering of the strongly computablereal-valued functions over X. Below we use notation W_e for the computably enumerable set with Gödel number e.

Definition 5 *[17, 18].* *The set $Ix(K) = \{n | \alpha(n) \in K\}$ is called index set for the class $K = \{A | A \in \mathcal{O}^e_{\mathbb{R}}\}$.*

In the similar way we define index sets for classes of strongly computable real-valued functions. In order to calculate the complexity of index sets we use the Kleene-Mostowski arithmetical hierarchy which classifies certain sets of the natural numbers based on the complexity of formulas defining them [17,18]. Below we recall the notion of multiple m-reducibility [7] that is one of the central concepts in the classical theory of computability and introduce the notion of multiple hm-reducibility.

Definition 6. *Let A, B, C, $D \subseteq \omega$. The pair (A, B) is multiple hm-reducible to (C, D), denoted by $(A, B) \leq_{hm} (C, D)$, if there exists a computable function $f : \omega \to \omega$ such that*

$$x \in A \to f(x) \in C \ and \ x \in B \to f(x) \in D.$$

The pair (A, B) is multiple m-reducible to (C, D), denoted by $(A, B) \leq_m (C, D)$, if there exists a computable function $f : \omega \to \omega$ such that

$$x \in A \leftrightarrow f(x) \in C \ and \ x \in B \leftrightarrow f(x) \in D.$$

The function f is called reduction function.

Let $\overline{A} = \omega \setminus A$. It is easy to see that $A \leq_m B$ if and only if $(A, \overline{A}) \leq_{hm} (B, \overline{B})$.

Definition 7. *Let Γ be a class of arithmetical complexity. A set $A \subseteq \omega$ is called Γ–hard if $B \leq_m A$ for any $B \in \Gamma$. A set A is called Γ–complete if $A \in \Gamma$ and A is Γ–hard.*

Let $\perp_X$ denote the function which is undefined everywhere, $\text{Tot}_X \rightleftharpoons \{f | f \in \mathcal{CFR}_X$ and total$\}$.

Theorem 5. *Let K be a non-empty class of strongly computablereal-valued functions such that $\perp \notin K$. Then $Ix(K)$ is Π_2^0-hard.*

The proof of the theorem is based on the following lemmas, for short $\perp_X \rightleftharpoons \perp$.

Lemma 1. *Suppose $A \in \Pi_2^0$, $f \in \mathcal{CFR}_X$ and $f \neq \perp$. Then the following holds:*

$$(A, \overline{A}) \leq_m (Ix(\{f\}), Ix(\{\perp\})).$$

Proof. It is sufficient to show that the pair of Π_2^0–complete set $\{n | W_n$ is infinite$\}$ and its complement is multiple pm–reducible to the pair $(Ix(\{f\}), Ix(\{\perp\}))$. For that we construct a reduction function $g : \omega \to \omega$. From Theorem 3 it follows that there exist effectively open sets U, V such that $f(x) = y \leftrightarrow U(x) \cup V(x) = \mathbb{R} \setminus \{y\}$. Define

$$\Phi_1(x, y) \rightleftharpoons (\exists m \in W_n)(\exists z \in U(x)) \left(y < z - \frac{1}{m+1} \right) \vee (U(x, y) \wedge V(x, y)),$$

$$\Phi_2(x, y) \rightleftharpoons (\exists m \in W_n)(\exists z \in V(x)) \left(y > z + \frac{1}{m+1} \right) \vee (U(x, y) \wedge V(x, y)).$$

The formulas define effectively open sets $\widetilde{U}$ and $\widetilde{V}$ satisfying Conditions 3 of Theorem 3. Put $g(n)$ to be equal to the minimal index of the strongly computable function definable by $\widetilde{U}$ and $\widetilde{V}$. If W_n is infinite then $\gamma(g(n))(x) = f(x)$, i.e., $g(n) \in Ix(\{f\})$. If W_n is finite then $\gamma(g(n)) = \perp$, i.e., $g(n) \in Ix(\{\perp\})$. So, g is a required reduction function.

Lemma 2. *Suppose $K \subseteq \mathcal{CFR}_X$, $f \in K$ and $f \neq \perp$. Then the following holds:*

$$(Ix(\{f\}), Ix(\{\perp\})) \leq_{hm} (K, \overline{K}), \ where \ \overline{K} = \mathcal{CFR}_X \setminus K.$$

Proof. Obviously, $g \rightleftharpoons$ id is a reduction function.

Proof. (Theorem 5) It follows from Lemmas 1 and 2.

Below we prove an analog of Rice's theorem for strongly computable real functions.

Theorem 6 (Generalised Rice Theorem). *The index set for $K \subseteq \mathcal{CFR}_X$ is Δ_2^0 if and only if K is empty or coincides with $\mathcal{CFR}_X$.*

Proof. Assume K is non-empty and $\perp \notin K$. From Theorem 5 it follows that $Ix(K)$ is Π_2^0–hard. Therefore, $Ix(K) \notin \Sigma_2^0$. Assume $K \neq \mathcal{CFR}_X$ and $\perp \in K$. Then, $\perp \notin \overline{K}$. From Theorem 5 it follows that $Ix(\overline{K})$ is Π_2^0–hard. Therefore, $Ix(\overline{K}) \notin \Sigma_2^0$.

Theorem 7. *For any non-empty effectively open set $A \subseteq \mathbb{R}^n$ the index set $Ix(A) = Ix(\{B | B \in \mathcal{O}_{\mathbb{R}^n}^e$ and $B = A\}$ is Π_2^0–complete.*

Proof. Let $A \in \mathcal{O}_{\mathbb{R}^n}^e$. For proof simplicity we assume $n = 1$. First, we prove that $Ix(A) \in \Pi_2^0$. We fix a computable numbering ν of all compact intervals with rational endpoints. Then

$$n \in Ix(A) \leftrightarrow (\forall m)\,(\nu(m) \subseteq \alpha(n) \leftrightarrow \nu(m) \subseteq A)\,.$$

By Theorem 1, the sets $\alpha(n)$ and A are Σ–definable. So, $Ix(A) \in \Pi_2^0$. In order to prove Π_2^0–completeness we show that Π_2^0-complete set $\{n | W_n$ is infinite$\}$ is m–reducible to $Ix(A)$. For that we define a reduction function $g : \omega \to \omega$ using the following observation. By Theorem 2 and Proposition 1 there exists an effective sequence of quantifier free formulas $\{Q_i\}_{i \in \omega}$ such that $x \in A \leftrightarrow \mathbf{HF}(\mathbb{R}) \models \bigvee_{i \in \omega} Q_i(x)$. Without loss of generality we assume that

1. Every formula Q_i defines a non-empty interval I_i;
2. If $I_i \cap I_j \neq \emptyset$ then there exists I_k such that $I_k \supset I_i \cap I_j$.

Let $J_n = \{i | (\exists k \in W_n) k \geq i\}$. Define $\Phi_n(x) \rightleftharpoons \bigvee_{i \in J_n} Q_i(x)$. Put $g(n)$ to be equal to the minimal index of the effectively open set defined by Φ_n. If W_n is infinite then $\alpha(g(n)) = A$, i.e., $g(n) \in Ix(A)$. If W_n is finite then $\alpha(g(n)) \neq A$, i.e., $g(n) \notin Ix(A)$. Therefore, $Ix(A)$ is Π_2^0-complete.

Proposition 2. *The index set $Ix(\mathrm{Tot}_{\mathbb{R}})$ is Π_2^0–complete.*

Proof. Let us prove that $Ix(\mathrm{Tot}_{\mathbb{R}}) \in \Pi_2^0$. We fix a computable numbering ν of all compact intervals with rational endpoints. Then to say that $\nu(i) \subseteq \mathrm{dom}\, f$ we write that

$$\bigwedge_{n \in \omega} (\exists y_1 \in \mathbb{Q})(\exists y_2 \in \mathbb{Q})(\forall x \in \nu(i))((|y_1 - y_2| < \frac{1}{n}\, \wedge$$
$$(x, y_1) \in V \wedge (x, y_2) \in U \wedge \neg((\forall x \in \nu(i))(\exists y)(x, y) \in U \cap V)).$$

This has the form $(\forall)\Pi_2^0 \wedge \Pi_1^0$. It is easy to note that

$$n \in Ix(\mathrm{Tot}_{\mathbb{R}}) \leftrightarrow (\forall m)\nu(m) \subseteq \mathrm{dom}\, f.$$

By the previous observation, this has the form $(\forall)\Pi_2^0 \wedge \Pi_1^0$. Since $\Pi_2^0 \supseteq \Pi_1^0$ and the intersection of Π_2^0–relations is Π_2^0, the index set $Ix(\mathrm{Tot}_{\mathbb{R}})$ is Π_2^0. From Theorem 5 it follows that $Ix(\mathrm{Tot}_{\mathbb{R}})$ is Π_2^0-complete.

Proposition 3. *For any non-empty co-effectively closed set A the index set*

$$Ix(\mathcal{Z}ero_A) = Ix(\{f \mid f \in \text{Tot}_\mathbb{R} \text{ and } f^{-1}(0) = A\})$$

is Π_2^0-complete.

Proof. To say that $n \in Ix(\mathcal{Z}ero_A)$ we write that $n \in Ix(\text{Tot}_\mathbb{R})$ and

$$(\forall m)(\forall x \in \nu(m)) \left(x \notin A \leftrightarrow (x,0) \in V_{\beta(n)} \vee (x,0) \in U_{\beta(n)} \right),$$

where $V_{\beta(n)}$ and $U_{\beta(n)}$ are the corresponding epigraph and hypograph of $\gamma(n)$. This has the form $\Pi_2^0 \wedge (\forall)\Sigma_1^0$. Therefore, $Ix(\mathcal{Z}ero_A) \in \Pi_2^0$. From Theorem 5 it follows that $Ix(\mathcal{Z}ero_A)$ is Π_2^0-complete.

By analogy, one can prove the following theorems.

Theorem 8. *For the total strongly computablereal functions, the problems of function equivalence is Π_2^0-complete.*
For the effectively open subsets of a Euclidean space, the problem of set equivalence and the problem of set inclusion are Π_2^0-complete.

Theorem 9. *The index set $Ix(\{\perp_\mathbb{R}\})$ is Π_3^0-hard.*

4   The Rice-Shapiro Theorem Revisited

In this section we give a direct proof of the generalised Rice-Shapiro over Euclidean spaces.

Proposition 4. *Let $K \subseteq \mathcal{O}_{\mathbb{R}^n}^e$. If there exists $A \in K$ such that $B \not\ll A$ for every $B \in K$ then $Ix(K)$ is Π_2^0-hard.*

Proof. Similar to Theorem 7.

Corollary 1. *Let $K \subseteq \mathcal{O}_{\mathbb{R}^n}^e$ contain a non-empty set which is minimal by inclusion. Then $Ix(K)$ is Π_2^0-hard.*

Theorem 10 (Generalised Rice-Shapiro). *Let $K \subseteq \mathcal{O}_{\mathbb{R}^n}^e$. The index set $Ix(K)$ is computably enumerable if and only if there is a computable sequence $\{K_n\}_{n \in \omega}$ of computable compact sets such that $K = \{A \mid \exists n A \supset K_n\}$.*

Proof. ($\rightarrow$) For proof simplicity we assume $n = 1$. Let us fix a computable numbering ν of all compact intervals with rational endpoints. Below we use the notation $Int([q_1, q_2]) = (q_1, q_2)$. We define the family of computably enumerable sets $\hat{K}$ in the following way: $W \in \hat{K} \rightleftharpoons (\exists A \in K)\left(A = \bigcup_{j \in W} Int(\nu(j))\right)$. The family has the following properties.

1. $\hat{K}$ is non-empty and $Ix(\hat{K})$ is computably enumerable. Indeed, if A is effectively open, then there exists W_m such that $A = \bigcup_{j \in W_m} Int(\nu(j))$. So, $\hat{K} \neq \emptyset$. In order to prove computably enumerability let us note that there exists a $\Sigma-$ formula $\Phi_{h(m)}$ which defines A. Then $m \in Ix(\hat{K}) \leftrightarrow h(m) \in Ix(K)$, i.e., $Ix(\hat{K})$ is computably enumerable.

2. For every $A \in K$ there exists $W \in \hat{K}$ such that $A = \bigcup_{i \in W} Int(\nu(i))$. Indeed, put $W = \{n | \nu(n) \subseteq A\}$.

From the properties it follows that the family K is monotone, i.e., if $A \in K$, $B \in \mathcal{O}_{\mathbb{R}}^e$ and $B \supseteq A$, then $B \in K$. From Property (2) it follows that $A = \bigcup_{i \in W} Int(\nu(i))$ for some $W \in \hat{K}$. Then $B = \bigcup_{i \in W_1} Int(\nu(i))$ for a computably enumerable set $W_1 \supseteq W$. From Property (1) and the classical Rice-Shapiro theorem [17] it follows that $W_1 \in \hat{K}$, so $B \in K$. Since $Ix(\hat{K})$ is computably enumerable, by the classical Rice-Shapiro theorem there exists a computable sequence of finite sets $\{D_n\}_{n \in \omega}$ such that $D_n \in \hat{K}$ and $W \in \hat{K} \leftrightarrow \exists n\, W \supseteq D_n$. So, from one point all sets of the type $L_n = \bigcup_{i \in D_n} Int(\nu(i))$ and all their extensions are in K. From another point, if $A \in K$, then $A = \bigcup_{i \in W} Int(\nu(i))$ for some $W \supseteq D_n$. So, $A \supseteq L_n$. It means that K is the set of all extensions of the sets L_n. It follows from Proposition 4 that since K is computably enumerable any L_n is not of the type $A : \forall B \in K\, B \not\ll A$. So, for every L_n there exists L_m such that $L_m \ll L_n$. Put $L_n = \bigcup_{i \in D_n} \nu(i)$. The sequence $\{L_n\}_{n \in \omega}$ is required. Indeed, $A \in K \leftrightarrow \exists n\, A \supseteq L_n \leftrightarrow \exists m\, L_m \ll L_n \subseteq A \leftrightarrow K_m \subseteq A$.

$\leftarrow$) Suppose $\{K_n\}_{n \in \omega}$ is a computable sequence of computable compact sets such that $K = \{A | \exists n A \supset K\}$. Then $m \in Ix(K) \leftrightarrow \exists n \forall x \in K_n\, \Phi_{g(m)}(x)$, where g is computable function such that $\alpha = g(\alpha_\Sigma)$. By Theorem 2 we can eliminate the universal quantifiers bounded by the computable compacts. So, $m \in Ix(K) \leftrightarrow \Psi(m)$, where Ψ is a Σ-formula. So, $Ix(K)$ is computably enumerable.

Corollary 2. *For every non-trivial $K \subset \mathcal{O}_{\mathbb{R}^n}^e$ if $Ix(K)$ is computably enumerable then it is Σ_1^0-hard.*

Proof. Without loss of generality we assume that $(\alpha, \beta) \in K$. Let W be a computably enumerable set. Put

$$\Phi_{F(n)} \rightleftharpoons \begin{cases} \emptyset, & n \notin W \\ x \in (\alpha, \beta), & n \in W. \end{cases}$$

So, $n \in W \leftrightarrow F(n) \in Ix(K)$. It means that any computably enumerable set, e.g. a creative set, is m-reducible to K. So, $Ix(K)$ is Σ_1^0-hard.

Corollary 3. *The index set for $K \subset \mathcal{O}_{\mathbb{R}^n}^e$ is computable if and only if K is empty or coincides with $\mathcal{O}_{\mathbb{R}^n}^e$.*

5 Index Sets for Computable Closed and Compact Sets

In this section we calculate the complexity of the index sets of the computable closed and compact sets of Euclidean spaces. For the definitions we refer to [1]. Denote

$$CO = \{A | A \subseteq \mathbb{R}^n \text{ is co} - \text{effectively closed}\},$$
$$C = \{A | A \subseteq \mathbb{R}^n \text{ is computable closed}\},$$
$$\mathcal{K} = \{A | A \subseteq \mathbb{R}^n \text{ is computable compact}\}.$$

Below for proof simplicity we consider $n = 1$. Suppose that the set $\mathcal{CO}$ is indexed by the numbering $\alpha_{co} : \omega \to \mathcal{CO}$ defined as follows: $\alpha_{co}(n) = \mathbb{R} \setminus \alpha(n)$.

Theorem 11. *The index set for the computable closed sets of a Euclidean space is Σ_3^0-complete.*

Proof. First, we show that $Ix(\mathcal{C}) \in \Sigma_3^0$. By definition, a closed set A is computable if and only if it is co-effectively closed and its distance function d_A is computable [1]. In other words A is a computable closed set if and only if it is co-effectively closed and there exists $k \in \omega$ such that $\gamma(k) = f$, where f is a total computable function $f : \mathbb{R} \to \mathbb{R}$ satisfying the following conditions:

(1) $f \geq 0$;
(2) $f \leq d_A$ on $\mathbb{R} \setminus A$;
(3) $f \geq d_A$ on $\mathbb{R} \setminus A$;
(4) $f = 0$ on A.

We have $e \in Ix(\mathcal{C})$ iff $e \in Ix(\mathcal{CO})$ and

$$(\exists k)\,(\gamma(k) \in \mathrm{Tot}_{\mathbb{R}} \wedge \gamma(k) \geq 0 \wedge ((\forall x)\, x \notin A_e \to \gamma(k)(x) \leq d_{A_e}(x)) \wedge$$
$$((\forall x)\, x \notin A_e \to \gamma(k)(x) \geq d_{A_e}(x)) \wedge ((\forall x)\, \gamma(k)(x) > 0 \to x \notin A_e)\,).$$

From Theorems 3 and 8 it follows that the first conjunct and the second conjunct have the form Π_2^0. Now we calculate the complexity of the rest of conjuncts. First, we note that $\mathbb{R} \setminus A$ has the form $\mathbb{R} \setminus A_e = \bigcup_{n \in \omega} I_n$, where I_n is an open interval with rational endpoints. It is easy to see that $I_n = \bigcup_{m \in \omega} K_{m,n}$, where $K_{m,n}$ is a compact interval with rational endpoints and $\{K_{m,n}\}_{m,n \in \omega}$ is a computable sequence of computable compact intervals. Therefore, a formula $(\forall x)(x \notin A_e \to \Theta(x))$ is equivalent to the formula $\bigwedge_{m,n \in \omega}(\forall x \in K_{m,n})\, \Theta(x)$.

So, Condition (2), i.e., the third conjunct is equivalent to the formula

$$\bigwedge_{m,n \in \omega\ a,b \in \mathbb{Q}} \bigwedge (\forall x \in K_{m,n})([a,b] \subseteq B(x,\gamma(k)(x)) \to [a,b] \subseteq \mathbb{R} \setminus A_e),$$

where $B(x,y)$ is an open ball with the center x and the radius y. We rewrite

$$\bigwedge_{m,n \in \omega\ a,b \in \mathbb{Q}} \bigwedge (\forall x \in K_{m,n})([a,b] \not\subseteq B(x,\gamma(k)(x)) \vee \Psi_{a,b}),$$

where $\Psi_{a,b}$ is a Π_1^0-sentence. From Theorem 2 it follows that the first and the second disjuncts are Π_1^0. Therefore, Condition (2) is Π_1^0.

Condition (3), i.e., the fourth conjunct is equivalent to the following formula:

$$\bigwedge_{m,n \in \omega} ((\forall x \in K_{m,n})\neg \Psi(x,e,k),$$

where $\Psi(x,e,k) \rightleftharpoons \forall y(d(y,x) \leq \gamma(k)(k) \to y \notin A_e)$ which is rewritable as

$$(\exists a \in \mathbb{Q})(\exists b \in \mathbb{Q})(\exists c \in \mathbb{Q})(x \in (a,b) \wedge c > \sup_{z \in [a,b]} \gamma(k)(z) \wedge$$
$$(\forall y \in [a-c,b+c])\, y \notin A_e).$$

From Theorem 2 it follows that the second conjunct and the third conjunct in the formula above are equivalent to Σ–formulas. Therefore, Condition (3) is Π_1^0. Condition (4), i.e., the fifth conjunct is equivalent to the formula

$$\bigwedge_{K_m \subseteq \{y | \gamma(k)(y) > 0\}} (\forall x \in K_m)\, x \notin A_e.$$

By analogy, Conditions (4) is Π_2^0. So, the relation $e \in Ix(\mathcal{C})$ has the form Σ_3^0. It is worth noting that Σ_3^0-completeness of $Ix(\mathcal{C})$ follows from the fact that Σ_3^0-complete set $R = \{n | W_n \text{ is computable}\}$ is m-reducible to $Ix(\mathcal{C})$. Indeed, if we define $A_{\beta(n)} = \omega \setminus W_n$ then $n \in R \leftrightarrow \beta(n) \in Ix(\mathcal{C})$. Therefore, $Ix(\mathcal{C})$ is Σ_3^0–complete.

Theorem 12. *The index set for the computable compact sets of a Euclidean space is Σ_3^0–complete.*

Proof. First, we show that $Ix(\mathcal{K}) \in \Sigma_3^0$. We have $e \in Ix(\mathcal{K})$ iff $e \in Ix(\mathcal{C})$ and A_e is bounded. To say that A_e is bounded we write that

$$(\exists c \in \mathbb{Q})(\exists r \in \mathbb{Q})(\exists n \in \omega)\, (r > |c| \rightarrow r \in I_n),$$

where $\mathbb{R} \setminus A_e = \bigcup_{n \in \omega} I_n$ and I_n is an open interval with rational endpoints. This has the form $\Sigma_3^0 \wedge (\exists) \Pi_2^0$. The intersection of Σ_3^0 relations is Σ_3^0, so $Ix(\mathcal{K}) \in \Sigma_3^0$. It is worth noting that Σ_3^0–completeness of $Ix(\mathcal{K})$ follows from the fact that Σ_3^0-complete set $R = \{n | W_n \text{ is computable}\}$ is m-reducible to $Ix(\mathcal{K})$. Indeed, if we define $A_{\beta(n)} = \{x | x = \sum_{i \in \omega} \frac{2a_i}{3^i} : a_i = 0 \text{ if } i \in W_n \text{ and } a_i = 1 \text{ if } i \notin W_n\}$ then $n \in R \leftrightarrow \beta(n) \in Ix(\mathcal{K})$. Therefore, $Ix(\mathcal{K})$ is Σ_3^0–complete.

Theorem 13. *For any non-empty $K \subseteq \mathcal{K}$ the index set $Ix(X)$ is Π_2^0-hard.*

Proof. Let us fix $A \in K$. Without loss of generality we assume that $A \subseteq [0,1]$. We define a computable sequence of co-effectively closed sets as follows:

$$A_0 \leftrightharpoons A; A_n \leftrightharpoons A \bigcup_{k \geq n} [2k, 2k+1].$$

It is easy to see that for every $n > 0$, the set A_n is not compact, i.e., $A_n \notin K$ and $A = \bigcap_{n \in \omega} A_n$. Now we show that $\{n | W_n \text{ is infinite}\} \leq_m Ix(K)$. Define

$$B_n = \bigcap_{m \in W_n} A_m.$$

Since $\{B_n\}_{n \in \omega}$ is a computable sequence of co-effectively closed sets, there exists a computable function $F : \omega \rightarrow \omega$ such that $B_n = \alpha_{co}(F(n))$. We have the following equivalences: W_n is infinite $\leftrightarrow B_n \in K \leftrightarrow F(n) \in Ix(K)$. Therefore, $Ix(K)$ is Π_2^0–hard.

Corollary 4. *For any $K \subseteq \mathcal{K}$ the index set $Ix(X) \notin \Delta_2^0$.*

6   An Application to Hybrid Systems

In this section we use the techniques developed above to show that there are
no limit computable decision procedures for analysis of non-trivial properties
of classes of general hybrid systems. To illustrate we use the models of hybrid
systems proposed by Nerode, Kohn in [15], called switched controlled systems.
A hybrid system is a system which consists of a continuous plant that is disturbed
by the external world and controlled by a program implemented on a sequential
automaton. In the Nerode–Kohn modeling a hybrid system is represented by a
continuous device given by a collection of dynamical systems parameterised by
a control set along with a control automaton for switching among them.

The control automaton has input data (the set of sensor measurements) and
the output data (the set of control laws). The control automaton is modeled by
three units. The first unit converts each measurement into input symbols of an
internal control automaton. The second unit is the internal control automaton,
which has a symbolic representation of a measurement as input and produces
a symbolic representation of the next control law to be imposed on the plant
as output. The internal control automaton, in practice, is a finite state automaton with finite input and output alphabets. The third unit converts these output symbols representing control laws into the actual control laws imposed on
the plant. The plant interacts with the control automata at discrete times t_i,
where the time sequence $\{t_i\}_{i \in \omega}$ satisfies realizability requirements. At time t_i
the control automaton gets sensor data, computes the next control law, and
imposes it on the plant. The plant will continue using this control law until the
next interaction at time t_{i+1}. Below we recall the definition of **SHS** from [9].

The specification $\mathbf{SHS} = \langle TS, \mathbb{X}, \mathbb{U}, \mathbb{D}, Init, \mathcal{F}, Conv1, A, Conv2 \rangle$ of a hybrid
system consists of:

- $TS = \{t_i\}_{i \in \omega}$ is an effective sequence of rational numbers which encodes
  the times of communication of the external world, the plant and the control
  automata and satisfies realizability requirements.
- $\mathbb{X} \subseteq \mathbb{R}^n$ is a plant state space.
- $\mathbb{U} \subseteq \mathbb{R}^k$ is a set of control parameters.
- $\mathbb{D} \subseteq C(\mathbb{R})$ is a set of acceptable disturbances.
- $F \in \mathcal{F}$ is a function modeling the behaviour of the plant, where $\mathcal{F} = \{F | F : \mathbb{D} \times \mathbb{U} \times \mathbb{X} \times \mathbb{R}^+ \to \mathbb{X}\}$ is a set of strongly computable functions.
- $Conv1 : \mathbb{D} \times \mathbb{X} \to \omega$ is a weakly computable function [11]. At the time of
  communication this function converts measurements, presented by F, and
  the representation of external world f into finite words which are input words
  of the internal control automata.
- $A : \omega \to \omega$ is a Σ-definable function. The internal control automata, in practice, is a finite state automata with finite input and finite output alphabets.
  So, it is naturally modeled by Σ-definable function which has a symbolic representation of measurements as input and produces a symbolic representation
  of the next control law as output.

- $Conv2 : \omega \to \mathbb{U}$ is a computable function. This function converts finite words representing control laws into control laws imposed on the plant.
- $Init = Init_{\mathbb{U}} \times Init_{\mathbb{X}}$ is a computable compact set of initial conditions.

Definition 8. *The behaviour of a hybrid system is defined by a function $H :$ $\mathbb{D} \times \mathbb{X} \times \mathbb{R}^+ \to \mathbb{X}$ if for any external disturbance $f \in \mathbb{D}$ and an initial state $x \in Init_{\mathbb{X}}$ the function $H(f, x, \cdot) : \mathbb{R}^+ \to \mathbb{X}$ defines the trajectory of the hybrid system.*

Definition 9. *An operator $T : \mathcal{F} \times \mathcal{CO} \to [\mathbb{D} \times \mathbb{R}^n \times \mathbb{R}^+ \to \mathbb{R}]$ is called tuner if for total $F \in \mathcal{F}$ and computable compact $Init_{\mathbb{X}} \subseteq \mathbb{R}^n$*

$$T(F, Init_{\mathbb{X}})(f, x, t) = H(f, x, t) \text{ for } x \in Init_{\mathbb{X}}.$$

Informally, the tuner T defines the behaviour of the hybrid system by given plant and initial states. Let us fix T. A *non-trivial property* of **HS** is associated with $K \subseteq [\mathbb{D} \times \mathbb{X} \times \mathbb{R}^+ \to \mathbb{X}]$ such that $T^{-1}(K) \neq \emptyset$ and $T^{-1}(\overline{K}) \neq \emptyset$, where $\overline{K} = [\mathbb{D} \times \mathbb{X} \times \mathbb{R}^+ \to \mathbb{X}] \setminus K$.

Lemma 3 [18]. *For $A \subset \omega$, $\chi(A)$ is limit computable if and only if $A \in \Delta_2^0$.*

Theorem 14. *For any non-trivial property (non-trivial class K) of **HS** there is no limit computable decision procedure that recognises whether $T(\gamma(k), \alpha_{co}) \in K$, i.e., the hybrid system satisfies the property.*

Proof. Suppose contrary. There are two possible cases.
Case 1. For some fixed **Init**, there exist F_1 and F_2 such that $T(F_1, \mathbf{Init}) \in K$ and $T(F_2, \mathbf{Init}) \notin K$. By assumption and Lemma 3, $Ix(\{F | T(F, \mathbf{Init}) \in K\}) \in \Delta_2^0$. This contradicts to Theorem 6.

Case 2. For some fixed **F**, There exist $Init_1$ and $Init_2$ such that $T(\mathbf{F}, Init_1) \in K$ and $T(\mathbf{F}, Init_2) \notin K$. Then, by assumption and Lemma 3, it follows that $Ix(\{Init | T(\mathbf{F}, Init) \in K\}) \in \Delta_2^0$. This contradicts to Theorem 13.

7   Conclusion

In this paper we have shown how to construct the principal computable numberings of the effectively open subsets of Euclidean spaces. Our principal computable numberings satisfy similar properties as the Kleene numbering of computably enumerable sets in the classical computability theory. However, the situation is different for principal computable numberings of the strongly computable real-valued functions. Our results show that for strongly computable real-valued functions any non-trivial property is not limit decidable while for recursive functions there are limit decidable properties, for example, the halting problem. We believe that our results help to understand hardness of properties of continuous constraints.

References

1. Brattka, V., Weihrauch, K.: Computability on subsets of euclidean space I: closed and compact sets. Theor. Comput. Sci. **219**(1–2), 65–93 (1999)
2. Benhamou, F., Goualard, F., Languénou, E., Christie, M.: Interval constraint solving for camera control and motion planning. ACM Trans. Comput. Log. **5**(4), 732–767 (2004)
3. Collins, P.: Continuity and computability of reachable sets. Theor. Comput. Sci. **341**(1–3), 162–195 (2005)
4. Calvert, W., Fokina, E., Goncharov, S.S., Knight, J.F., Kudinov, O.V., Morozov, A.S., Puzarenko, V.: Index sets for classes of high rank structures. J. Symb. Log. **72**(4), 1418–1432 (2007)
5. Calvert, W., Harizanov, V.S., Knight, J.F., Miller, S.: Index sets of computable structures. J. Algebra Log. **45**(5), 306–325 (2006)
6. Ershov, Y.L.: Model ℂ of partial continuous functionals. In: Proceedings of the Logic Colloquium 76, pp 455–467. North-Holland, Amsterdam (1977)
7. Ershov, Y.L.: Numbering Theorey. Nauka, Moscow (1977). (in Russian)
8. Korovina, M.V., Kudinov, O.V.: Positive predicate structures for continuous data. J. Math. Struct. Comput. Sci (2015, To appear). doi:10.1017/S0960129513000315
9. Korovina, M., Kudinov, O.: Σ_K-constraints for hybrid systems. In: Pnueli, A., Virbitskaite, I., Voronkov, A. (eds.) PSI 2009. LNCS, vol. 5947, pp. 230–241. Springer, Heidelberg (2010)
10. Korovina, M.V., Kudinov, O.V.: The uniformity principle for sigma-definability. J. Log. Comput. **19**(1), 159–174 (2009)
11. Korovina, M.V., Kudinov, O.V.: Towards computability over effectively enumerable topological spaces. Electr. Notes Theor. Comput. Sci. **221**, 115–125 (2008)
12. Korovina, M.V., Kudinov, O.V.: Towards computability of higher type continuous data. In: Cooper, S.B., Löwe, B., Torenvliet, L. (eds.) CiE 2005. LNCS, vol. 3526, pp. 235–241. Springer, Heidelberg (2005)
13. Korovina, M.V.: Computational aspects of Σ-definability over the real numbers without the equality test. In: Baaz, M., Makowsky, J.A. (eds.) CSL 2003. LNCS, vol. 2803, pp. 330–344. Springer, Heidelberg (2003)
14. Korovina, M.V.: Gandy's theorem for abstract structures without the equality test. In: Vardi, M.Y., Voronkov, A. (eds.) LPAR 2003. LNCS, vol. 2850, pp. 290–301. Springer, Heidelberg (2003)
15. Nerode, A., Kohn, W.: Models for hybrid systems: automata, topologies, controllability, observability. In: Grossman, R.L., Ravn, A.P., Rischel, H., Nerode, A. (eds.) HS 1991 and HS 1992. LNCS, vol. 736, pp. 317–357. Springer, Heidelberg (1993)
16. Ratschan, S., She, Z.: Constraints for continuous reachability in the verification of hybrid systems. In: Calmet, J., Ida, T., Wang, D. (eds.) AISC 2006. LNCS (LNAI), vol. 4120, pp. 196–210. Springer, Heidelberg (2006)
17. Rogers, H.: Theory of Recursive Functions and Effective Computability. McGraw-Hill, New York (1967)
18. Shoenfield, J.R.: Degrees of Unsolvability. North-Holland Publ., New York (1971)
19. Spreen, D.: On r.e. inseparability of CPO index sets. In: Börger, E., Rödding, D., Hasenjaeger, G. (eds.) Rekursive Kombinatorik 1983. LNCS, vol. 171, pp. 103–117. Springer, Heidelberg (1984)
20. Weihrauch, K.: Computable Analysis. Springer, Berlin (2000)

Decidability and Expressiveness
of Recursive Weighted Logic

Kim Guldstrand Larsen, Radu Mardare, and Bingtian Xue[✉]

Aalborg University, Aalborg, Denmark
bingt@cs.aau.dk

Abstract. Labelled weighted transition systems (LWSs) are transition systems labelled with actions and real numbers. The numbers represent the costs of the corresponding actions in terms of resources. Recursive Weighted Logic (RWL) is a multimodal logic that expresses qualitative and quantitative properties of LWSs. It is endowed with simultaneous recursive equations, which specify the weakest properties satisfied by the recursive variables. We demonstrate that RWL is sufficiently expressive to characterize weighted-bisimilarity of LWSs. In addition, we prove that the logic is decidable, i.e., the satisfiability problem for RWL can be algorithmically solved.

Keywords: Labelled weighted transition system · Maximal fixed point · Hennessy-Milner property · Satisfiability

1 Introduction

The industrial practice has revealed lately the importance of model-driven and component-based development (MDD), in particular within the area of embedded systems. A key challenge is to handle the growing complexity of systems, while meeting requirements on correctness, predictability, performance and also resource-cost constraints. In this respect MDD is seen as a valuable approach, as it allows early design-space exploration and verification and may be used as the basis for systematic and unambiguous testing of a final product. However, for embedded systems, verification should not only address functional properties but also properties related to resource constraints. Within the area of model checking a number of state-machine based modelling formalisms have emerged, which allow for such quantitative aspects to be expressed, especially time-constraints. In particular the formalisms of timed automata [AD90], and the extensions to weighted timed automata [BFH+01, ATP01] allow for such constraints to be modelled and efficiently analyzed.

Motivated by the needs from embedded systems, we consider Recursive Weighted Logic (RWL), which is an extension of *weighted modal logic* [LM13] with maximal fixed point (and without negation), for labelled weighted transition systems (LWS). It allows us to specify and reason about not only the qualitative behaviour of a system but also its quantitative consumption of resources, and to

© Springer-Verlag Berlin Heidelberg 2015
A. Voronkov and I. Virbitskaite (Eds.): PSI 2014, LNCS 8974, pp. 216–231, 2015.
DOI: 10.1007/978-3-662-46823-4_18

encode recursive properties. Our notion of weighted transition systems is more than a simple instance of *weighted automata* [DKV09], since we also study infinite and infinitely branching systems.

RWL is a multimodal logic defined for a semantics based on LWSs. It is endowed with modal operators that predicate about both the action and the values of transition labels. While in an LWS we can have real-valued labels, the modalities only encodes rational values. Often we need to characterize a transition using an infinite convergent sequences of rationals that approximate the real resource. The logic is also endowed with maximal fixed points defined by simultaneous recursive equations [Lar90, CKS92, CS93]. They specify the weakest properties satisfied by the recursive variables.

In the non-quantitative case, the modal μ-calculus [Koz82] allows for encoding both LTL and CTL. Moreover, the modal μ-calculus is obtained by extending a simple modal logic – the Hennessy Milner Logic (HML) [HM80] having a modality for each action of the underlying transition system – with the ability to define properties recursively. In particular, it was shown that HML is *adequate* in the sense that it completely characterizes bisimilarity between image-finite labelled transition systems (LTS), i.e. two LTSs are bisimilar if and only if they satisfy the same HML properties [Sti99, SR11].

As a first result, we demonstrate that RWL is adequate with respect to weighted bisimilarity between labelled weighted transition systems, i.e. RWL is sufficiently expressive to characterize weighted-bisimilarity of LWSs.

Secondly, we prove decidability of satisfiablity for RWL. Concretely, we present a model construction algorithm, which constructs an LWS for a given RWL formula (provided that the formula is not a contradiction, i.e., without any model).

To encode various resource-constrains in RWL, we use resource-variables, similar to the clock-variables used in timed logics [ACD93, HNSY92, AILS07]. These variables can be reset, meaning that we can consider, in various states, interpretations that will map certain variable to zero. This is useful in encoding various interesting scenarios. Nevertheless, in order to prove the decidability of our logic and to be able to have the finite model property, we restrict our attention to only one variable for each type of resources. This bounds the expressiveness of our logic while it guarantees its decidability.

The remainder of this paper is organized as follows: the next section is dedicated to the presentation of the notion of labelled weighted transition system; in Sect. 3, we introduce RWL with its syntax and semantics; Sect. 4 is dedicated to the Hennessy-Milner property of RWL; in Sect. 5 we prove the decidability of the satisfiability problem for RWL and we propose an algorithm to solve it. We also present a conclusive section where we summarize the results and describe future research directions.

2   Labelled Weighted Transition Systems

An *labelled weighted transition system* (LWS) is a transition system that has the transitions labelled both with real numbers and actions - as represented in Fig. 1. The numbers are interpreted as the costs of the corresponding actions in terms of resources, e.g., energy consumption/production. Our intention is to remain as general as possible and for this reason we impose no restriction on the labels: they can be any real number, possibly negative. If the transition has a positive label, the system gains resources; negative labels encode consumption of resources.

Definition 1 (Labelled Weighted Transition System). *An labelled weighted transition system is a tuple*

$$\mathcal{W} = (M, \Sigma, \mathcal{K}, \theta)$$

where M is a non-empty set of states, Σ a non-empty set of actions, $\mathcal{K} = \{x_1, \dots, x_k\}$ is the finite set of (k types of) resource-variables and $\theta : M \times (\Sigma \times \mathbb{R}^k) \to 2^M$ is the labelled transition function.

For simplicity, hereafter we use a vector of real numbers instead of the function from the set of the resources $\mathcal{K}$ to real numbers, i.e., for $f : \mathcal{K} \to \mathbb{R}$ defined as $f(e_i) = r_i$ for all $i = 1, \dots, k$, we write $\bar{u} = (r_1, \dots, r_k) \in \mathbb{R}^k$ instead. On the other hand, for a vector of real numbers $\bar{u} \in \mathbb{R}^k$, $\bar{u}(e_i)$ denotes the i-th number of the vector $\bar{u}$, which represent the cost of the resource e_i during the transition.

Instead of $m' \in \theta(m, a, \bar{u})$ we write $m \xrightarrow{\bar{u}}_a m'$. For $r \in \mathbb{R}$ we write $r = \bar{u}(x_i)$ to denote that r is the i-th number of the vector $\bar{u}$.

An LWS is said to be *image-finite* if for each state and each action a with weight $\bar{u}$, there are finitely many outgoing a-transitions with weight $\bar{u}$.

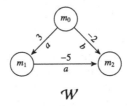

Fig. 1. Labelled weighted transition system

Example 1. Figure 1 represent the LWS $\mathcal{W} = (M, \Sigma, \mathcal{K}, \theta)$, where $M = \{m_0, m_1, m_2\}$, $\Sigma = \{a, b\}$, $\mathcal{K} = \{x\}$ and θ defined as follows: $m_0 \xrightarrow{3}_a m_1$, $m_0 \xrightarrow{-2}_b m_2$ and $m_1 \xrightarrow{-5}_a m_2$. $\mathcal{W}$ has three states m_0, m_1, m_2, one kind of resource x and two actions a, b. The state m_0 has two transitions - one a-transition which costs "3" units of x to m_1 and one b-transition which costs "−2" units of x to m_2. At m_0 the variable valuation l assigns "1" to x, which is the initial amount of the resource x at the state m_0. If the system does an a-transition from m_0 to m_1, the amount of the resource x increases with "3" units and becomes "4", which is the sum of the initial amount "1" and the value of the transition "3" - that the system gains by doing the a-transition.   ∎

The concept of *weighted bisimulation* is a relation between the states of a given LWS that equates states with identical (action- and weighted-) behaviors.

Definition 2 (Weighted Bisimulation). *Given an LWS $\mathcal{W} = (M, \Sigma, \mathcal{K}, \theta)$, a weighted bisimulation is an equivalence relation $R \subseteq M \times M$ such that whenever $(m, m') \in R$,*

- *if $m \xrightarrow{\overline{u}}_a m_1$, then there exists $m'_1 \in M$ s.t. $m' \xrightarrow{\overline{u}}_a m'_1$ and $(m_1, m'_1) \in R$;*

- *if $m' \xrightarrow{\overline{u}}_a m'_1$, then there exists $m_1 \in M$ s.t. $m \xrightarrow{\overline{u}}_a m_1$ and $(m_1, m'_1) \in R$.*

If there exists a weighted bisimulation relation R such that $(m, m') \in R$, we say that m and m' are bisimilar, *denoted by $m \sim m'$.*

As for the other types of bisimulation, the previous definition can be extended to define the weighted bisimulation between distinct LWSs by considering bisimulation relations on their disjoint union. *Weighted bisimilarity* is the largest weighted bisimulation relation; if $\mathcal{W}_i = (M_i, \Sigma_i, \mathcal{K}_i, \theta_i)$, $m_i \in M_i$ for $i = 1, 2$ and m_1 and m_2 are bisimilar, we write $(m_1, \mathcal{W}_1) \sim (m_2, \mathcal{W}_2)$. Example 2 shows the role of the weighted bisimilarity.

Example 2. In Fig. 2, $\mathcal{W}_1 = (M_1, \Sigma_1, \mathcal{K}_1, \theta_1)$ is an LWS with five states, where $M_1 = \{m_0, m_1, m_2, m_3, m_4\}$, $\Sigma_1 = \{a, b, c, d\}$, $\mathcal{K}_1 = \{x\}$ and θ_1 is defined as: $m_0 \xrightarrow{3}_a m_1$, $m_0 \xrightarrow{-2}_b m_2$, $m_1 \xrightarrow{0}_d m_2$, $m_1 \xrightarrow{3}_c m_3$, $m_2 \xrightarrow{0}_c m_1$ and $m_2 \xrightarrow{3}_c m_4$.

It is easy to see that $m_3 \sim m_4$ because neither of them can perform any transition. Besides, $m_1 \sim m_2$ because both of them can do a c-transition with cost 3 to some states which are bisimular (m_3 and m_4), and a d-action transition with cost 0 to each other. m_0 is not bisimular to any states in $\mathcal{W}_1$.

$\mathcal{W}_2 = (M_2, \Sigma_2, \mathcal{K}_2, \theta_2)$ is an LWS with three states, where $M_2 = \{m'_0, m'_1, m'_2\}$, $\Sigma_2 = \Sigma_1$, $\mathcal{K}_2 = \mathcal{K}_1$ and θ_2 is defined as: $m'_0 \xrightarrow{3}_a m'_1$, $m'_0 \xrightarrow{-2}_b m'_1$, $m'_1 \xrightarrow{0}_d m'_1$ and $m'_1 \xrightarrow{3}_c m'_2$.

We can see that: $(m_0, \mathcal{W}_1) \sim (m'_0, \mathcal{W}_2)$, $(m_1, \mathcal{W}_1) \sim (m'_1, \mathcal{W}_2)$, $(m_2, \mathcal{W}_1) \sim (m'_1, \mathcal{W}_2)$, $(m_3, \mathcal{W}_1) \sim (m'_2, \mathcal{W}_2)$, $(m_4, \mathcal{W}_1) \sim (m'_2, \mathcal{W}_2)$.

Notice that $(m''_0, \mathcal{W}_3) \not\sim (m'_0, \mathcal{W}_2)$, because $(m''_1, \mathcal{W}_3) \not\sim (m'_1, \mathcal{W}_2)$. Besides, $m''_1 \not\sim m''_2$, because m''_1 can do a d-action with weight -1 while m''_2 cannot and m''_2 can do a d-action with weight 1 while m''_1 cannot.   ∎

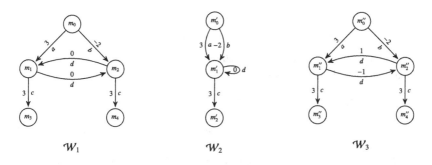

$\mathcal{W}_1$ $\qquad\qquad$ $\mathcal{W}_2$ $\qquad\qquad$ $\mathcal{W}_3$

Fig. 2. Weighted bisimulation

3   Recursive Weighted Logic

In this section we introduce a multimodal logic that encodes properties of LWSs called Recursive Weighted Logic (RWL). Our logic is endowed, in addition to the classic boolean operators (except negation), with a class of modalities of arity 0 called *state modalities* of type $x \bowtie r$ for $\bowtie \in \{\leq, \geq, <, >\}$, $r \in \mathbb{Q}$ and $x \in \mathcal{K}$, which predicates about the value of the resource x available at the current state; a class of modalities of arity 1, named *transition modalities*, of type $[x \bowtie r]_a$ or $\langle x \bowtie r \rangle_a$, for $\bowtie \in \{\leq, \geq, <, >\}$, $r \in \mathbb{Q}$, $a \in \Sigma$ and $x \in \mathcal{K}$, which approximates the transition labels; a class of modalities of arity 1, named *reset modalities*, of type x __in__, which are inspired by timed logics [ACD93, HNSY92, LLW95] and refer to the fact that the resource x is interpreted to zero at the current state; and a class of recursive (formula) variables, $X \in \mathcal{X}$.

Hereafter, we fix a set Σ of actions and a set of $\mathcal{K}$ of resource variables and for simplicity, we omit them in the description of LWSs and RWL.

Firstly we define the basic formulas of RWL and their semantics. Based on them, we will eventually introduce the recursive definitions - the maximal equation blocks - which extend the semantics of the basic formulas.

Definition 3 (Syntax of Basic Formulas). *For arbitrary* $r \in \mathbb{Q}$, $a \in \Sigma$, $x \in \mathcal{K}$ *and* $\bowtie \in \{\leq, \geq, <, >\}$, *let*

$$\mathcal{L}: \quad \phi := \top \mid \bot \mid x \bowtie r \mid \phi \wedge \phi \mid \phi \vee \phi \mid [x \bowtie r]_a \phi \mid \langle x \bowtie r \rangle_a \phi \mid x \text{ } \underline{in} \text{ } \phi \mid X.$$

Before looking at the semantics for the basic formulas, we define the notion of *variable valuation* and *extended states*.

Definition 4 (Variable Valuation). *A variable valuation is a function* $l : \mathcal{K} \to \mathbb{R}$ *that assigns a real numbers to all the resource variables in* $\mathcal{K}$.

A variable valuation assigns positive or negative values to resource-variables. The label is interpreted as the amount of resources available or required (depending of whether the number is positive or negative) in a given state of the system. We denote by L the class of variable valuations. If l is a resource valuation and $x \in \mathcal{K}$, $s \in \mathbb{R}$ we denote by $l[x \mapsto s]$ the resource valuation that associates the same values as l to all variables except x, to which it associates the value s, i.e., for any $y \in \mathcal{V}$,

$$l[x \mapsto s](y) = \begin{cases} s, & y = x \\ l(y), & \text{otherwise} \end{cases}$$

A pair (m, l) is called *extended state* of a given LWS $\mathcal{W} = (M, \mathcal{K}, \theta)$, where $m \in M$ and $l \in L$. Transitions between extended states are defined by:

$$(m, l) \to_a (m', l') \text{ iff } m \xrightarrow{\overline{u}}_a m' \text{ and } l' = l + \overline{u}.$$

Given an LWS $\mathcal{W} = (M, \mathcal{K}, \theta)$ and a class of variable valuation L, the *LWS-semantics* of RWL basic formulas is defined by the *satisfiability relation*, over an extended state (m, l) and an environment ρ which maps each recursive formula variables to subsets of $M \times L$, inductively as follows.

$\mathcal{W}, (m, l), \rho \models \top$ - always,

$\mathcal{W}, (m, l), \rho \models \bot$ - never,

$\mathcal{W}, (m, l), \rho \models x \bowtie r$ iff $l(x) \bowtie r$,

$\mathcal{W}, (m, l), \rho \models \phi \wedge \psi$ iff $\mathcal{W}, (m, l), \rho \models \phi$ and $\mathcal{W}, (m, l), \rho \models \psi$,

$\mathcal{W}, (m, l), \rho \models \phi \vee \psi$ iff $\mathcal{W}, (m, l), \rho \models \phi$ or $\mathcal{W}, (m, l), \rho \models \psi$,

$\mathcal{W}, (m, l), \rho \models [x \bowtie r]_a \phi$ iff for arbitrary $(m', l') \in M \times L$ such that $(m, l) \rightarrow_a$ (m', l') and $l' - l \bowtie r$, we have $\mathcal{W}, (m', l'), \rho \models \phi$,

$\mathcal{W}, (m, l), \rho \models \langle x \bowtie r \rangle_a \phi$ iff exists $(m', l') \in M \times L$ such that $(m, l) \rightarrow_a (m', l')$, $l' - l \bowtie r$ and $\mathcal{W}, (m', l'), \rho \models \phi$,

$\mathcal{W}, (m, l), \rho \models x \underline{\text{ in }} \phi$ iff $\mathcal{W}, (m, l[x \mapsto 0]), \rho \models \phi$,

$\mathcal{W}, (m, l), \rho \models X$ iff $m \in \rho(X)$.

Definition 5 (Maximal Equation Blocks). *Let* $\mathcal{X} = \{X_1, \ldots, X_n\}$ *be a set of recursive variables. A maximal equation block B is a list of (mutually recursive) equations:*

$$X_1 = \phi_1$$

$$\vdots$$

$$X_n = \phi_n$$

in which X_i are pairwise-distinct over $\mathcal{X}$ and ϕ_i are basic formulas over $\mathcal{X}$, for all $i = 1, \ldots, n$.

Each maximal equation block B defines an *environment* for the recursive formula variables $X_1, \ldots, X_n$, which is the weakest property that the variables satisfy. We say that an arbitrary formula ϕ is *closed with respect to a maximal equation block B* if all the recursive formula variables appearing in ϕ are defined in B by some of its equations. If all the formulas ϕ_i that appear in the right hand side of some equation in B are closed with respect to B, we say that B is *closed*.

Given an environment ρ and $\overline{\Upsilon} = \langle \Upsilon_1, \ldots, \Upsilon_n \rangle \in (2^{M \times L})^n$, let

$$\rho_{\overline{\Upsilon}} = \rho[X_1 \mapsto \Upsilon_1, \ldots, X_n \mapsto \Upsilon_n]$$

be the environment obtained from ρ by updating the binding of X_i to Υ_i.

Given a maximal equation block B and an environment ρ, consider the function

$$f_B^\rho : (2^{M \times L})^n \longrightarrow (2^{M \times L})^n$$

defined as follows:

$$f_B^\rho(\overline{\Upsilon}) = \langle [\![\phi_1]\!]\rho_{\overline{\Upsilon}}, \ldots, [\![\phi_n]\!]\rho_{\overline{\Upsilon}} \rangle,$$

where $[\![\phi]\!]\rho = \{(m, l) \in M \times L \mid \mathcal{W}, (m, l), \rho \models \phi\}$.

Observe that $(2^{M \times L})^n$ forms a complete lattice with the ordering, join and meet operations defined as the point-wise extensions of the set-theoretic inclusion, union and intersection, respectively. Moreover, for any maximal equation block B and environment ρ, f_B^ρ is monotonic with respect to the order of the lattice and therefore, according to the Tarski fixed point theorem [Tar55], it has a greatest fixed point that we denote by $\nu \overline{X}.f_B^\rho$. This fixed point can be characterized as follows:

$$\nu \overline{X}.f_B^\rho = \bigcup \{\overline{\Upsilon} \mid \overline{\Upsilon} \subseteq f_B^\rho(\overline{\Upsilon})\}.$$

When the transition system is finite-state f_B^ρ is continuous, and the fixed points also have an iterative characterization given as follows. Let

$$f_0 = \langle M \times L, \ldots, M \times L \rangle,$$
$$f_{i+1} = f_B^\rho(f_i).$$

Then, $\nu\overline{X}.f_B^\rho = \bigcap_{i=0}^\infty f_i$.

Consequently, a maximal equation block defines an environment that satisfies all its equations, i.e., $[\![B]\!]\rho = \nu\overline{X}.f_B^\rho$.

When B is closed, i.e. there is no free recursive formula variable in B, it is not difficult to see that for any ρ and ρ', $[\![B]\!]\rho = [\![B]\!]\rho'$. So, we just take $\rho = 0$ and write $[\![B]\!]$ instead of $[\![B]\!]0$. In the rest of the paper we will only discuss this kind of equation blocks. (For those that are not closed, we only need to have the initial environment which maps the free variables to subsets of the state set.)

Now we are ready to define the general semantics of RWL: for an arbitrary LWS $\mathcal{W} = (M, \theta)$ with $m \in M$, an arbitrary variable valuation $l \in L$ and arbitrary RWL-formula ϕ closed w.r.t. a maximal equation block B,

$$\mathcal{W}, (m, l) \models_B \phi \text{ iff } \mathcal{W}, (m, l), [\![B]\!] \models \phi.$$

The symbol $\models_B$ is interpreted as satisfiability for the block B. Whenever it is not the case that $\mathcal{W}, (m, l) \models_B \phi$, we write $\mathcal{W}, (m, l) \not\models_B \phi$. We say that a formula ϕ is B-*satisfiable* if there exists at least one LWS that satisfies it for the block B in one of its states under at least one variable valuation; ϕ is a B-*validity* if it is satisfied in all states of any LWS under any variable valuation - in this case we write $\models_B \phi$.

To exemplify the expressiveness of RWL, we propose the following example of a bank transaction system with recursively-defined properties.

Example 3. Consider a models of a bank transaction scenarios that involves two basic actions w (withdraw) and d (deposit). The specifications of the system are as follows:

1. The system is in a safe range, i.e., the amount of resource x is always above 0;
2. The system is never deadlocked, i.e. it should always do an w-action or a d-action;
3. There is at least one w-action in three steps;
4. Every w-action consumes at least 3 units of resource x and every d-action produces at most 2 units of resource x.

In our logic the above mentioned requirements can be encoded as follows, where $[a]\phi = \bigwedge_{x \in \mathcal{K}}([x \geq 0]_a\phi \wedge [x \leq 0]_a\phi)$ and $\langle a \rangle\phi = \bigvee_{x \in \mathcal{K}}(\langle x \geq 0\rangle_a\phi \vee \langle x \leq 0\rangle_a\phi)$, for $a = w, d$:

$$X = (x \geq 0) \wedge [w]X \wedge [d]X,$$
$$Y = (\langle w \rangle\top \vee \langle d \rangle\top) \wedge [w]Y \wedge [d]Y,$$
$$Z = [d][d][d]\bot \wedge [w]Z \wedge [d]Z,$$
$$W = [x > -3]_w\bot \wedge [w]W \wedge [d]W,$$
$$D = [x \leq 0]_d\bot \wedge [x > 2]_d\bot \wedge [w]D \wedge [d]D.$$

4 Hennessy-Milner Property

The standard theory of fixed points tells us that if f is a monotone function on a lattice, we can construct the greatest fixed point of f by repeatedly applying f on the largest element to form a decreasing chain whose limit is the greatest fixed point [Tar55]. The stages of this iteration $\nu^{\alpha}\overline{X}.f$ can be defined as follows:

$$\nu^{0}\overline{X}.f = \top$$
$$\nu^{\beta+1}\overline{X}.f = f\{\nu^{\beta}\overline{X}.f/\overline{X}\}$$
$$\nu^{\lambda}\overline{X}.f = \bigwedge_{\beta<\lambda}\nu^{\beta}\overline{X}.f$$

where $\bigwedge$ is the countable conjunction.

We use this characterization to prove that RWL satisfies the Hennessy-Milner property for LWSs. To do this we firstly define a non-recursive version of RWL in which we allow countable conjunctions.

Definition 6 (Weighted Modal Logic with Countable Conjunction).
For arbitrary $r \in \mathbb{Q}$, $a \in \Sigma$, $x \in \mathcal{K}$, $\bowtie \in \{\le, \ge, <, >\}$ and I a finite or countable set of indexes, let $\mathcal{L}^c$ be the set of the formulas inductively defined as follows:

$$\phi^c := \top \mid \bot \mid x \bowtie r \mid \bigwedge_{i\in I} \phi_i^c \mid \phi^c \vee \phi^c \mid [x \bowtie r]_a\phi^c \mid \langle x \bowtie r\rangle_a\phi^c \mid x \underline{\ in\ } \phi^c.$$

Excepting the infinite conjunction, the semantics of the above logic is defined similarly to that of RWL with no environment. In addition,

$\mathcal{W}, (m, l) \models \bigwedge_{i\in I} \phi_i^c$ iff for any $i \in I$, $\mathcal{W}, (m, l) \models \phi_i^c$.

We first demonstrate that $\mathcal{L}^c$ satisfies the Hennessy-Milner property.

Lemma 1. *Let $\mathcal{W} = (M, \mathcal{K}, \theta)$ be an image-finite labelled weighted transition system. Then, for any $m, m' \in M$:*

$m \sim m'$ *iff* $\forall \phi^c \in \mathcal{L}^c$ *and* $l \in L$, *we have* $\mathcal{W}, (m, l) \models \phi^c \Leftrightarrow \mathcal{W}, (m', l) \models \phi^c$.

Proof. "$\Longrightarrow$": Induction on ϕ^c. The cases $\top$, $\bot$ and $\phi^c \vee \psi^c$ are easy.

- **Case** $x \bowtie r$: $\mathcal{W}, (m, l) \models x \bowtie r$ implies $l(x) \bowtie r$, which implies $\mathcal{W}, (m', l) \models x \bowtie r$. Hence, $\mathcal{W}, (m, l) \models x \bowtie r$ implies $\mathcal{W}, (m', l) \models x \bowtie r$.
  Similarly $\mathcal{W}, (m', l) \models x \bowtie r$ implies $\mathcal{W}, (m, l) \models x \bowtie r$.
- **Case** $\bigwedge_{i\in I} \phi_i^c$: $\mathcal{W}, (m, l) \models \bigwedge_{i\in I} \phi_i^c$ implies for any $i \in I$, $\mathcal{W}, (m, l) \models \phi_i^c$. By inductive hypothesis, for any $i \in I$, $\mathcal{W}, (m', l) \models \phi_i^c$, which implies $\mathcal{W}, (m', l) \models \bigwedge_{i\in I} \phi_i^c$. Hence, $\mathcal{W}, (m, l) \models \bigwedge_{i\in I} \phi_i^c$ implies $\mathcal{W}, (m', l) \models \bigwedge_{i\in I} \phi_i^c$.
  Similarly $\mathcal{W}, (m', l) \models \bigwedge_{i\in I} \phi_i^c$ implies $\mathcal{W}, (m, l) \models \bigwedge_{i\in I} \phi_i^c$.
- **Case** $[x \bowtie r]_a\phi^c$: $\mathcal{W}, (m, l) \models [x \bowtie r]_a\phi^c$ implies for any $(m_1, l_1) \in M \times L$ s.t. $(m, l) \to_a (m_1, l_1)$ and $l_1 - l \bowtie r$, $\mathcal{W}, (m_1, l_1) \models \phi^c$. $(m, l) \to_a (m_1, l_1)$ implies $m \xrightarrow{\overline{u}}_a m_1$ and $l_1 = l + \overline{u}$. Since $m \sim m'$, for any $m_1' \in M$ s.t. $m' \xrightarrow{\overline{u}}_a m_1'$, there exists $m_1 \in M$ s.t. $m \xrightarrow{\overline{u}}_a m_1$ and $m_1 \sim m_1'$. By inductive hypothesis, $\mathcal{W}, (m_1', l_1) \models \phi^c$. So for any $(m_1', l_1) \in M$ s.t. $(m', l) \to_a (m_1', l_1)$ and $l_1 - l \bowtie r$, $\mathcal{W}, (m_1', l_1) \models \phi^c$. Then $\mathcal{W}, (m', l) \models [x \bowtie r]_a\phi^c$. Hence, $\mathcal{W}, (m, l) \models [x \bowtie r]_a\phi^c$ implies $\mathcal{W}, (m', l) \models [x \bowtie r]_a\phi^c$.
  Similarly $\mathcal{W}, (m', l) \models [x \bowtie r]_a\phi^c$ implies $\mathcal{W}, (m, l) \models [x \bowtie r]_a\phi^c$.

- **Case** $\langle x \bowtie r \rangle_a \phi^c$: $\mathcal{W}, (m, l) \models \langle x \bowtie r \rangle_a \phi^c$ implies there exists $(m_1, l_1) \in M \times L$ s.t. $(m, l) \to_a (m_1, l_1)$, $l_1 - l \bowtie r$ and $\mathcal{W}, (m_1, l_1) \models \phi^c$. $(m, l) \to_a (m_1, l_1)$ implies $m \xrightarrow{\overline{u}}_a m_1$ and $l_1 = l + \overline{u}$. Since $m \sim m'$, there exists m_1' s.t. $m' \xrightarrow{\overline{u}}_a m_1'$ and $m_1 \sim m_1'$. By inductive hypothesis, $\mathcal{W}, (m_1', l_1) \models \phi^c$. So we have that there exists $(m_1', l_1) \in M \times L$ s.t. $(m', l) \to_a (m_1', l_1)$, $l_1 - l \bowtie r$ and $\mathcal{W}, (m_1', l_1) \models \phi^c$, which implies $\mathcal{W}, (m', l) \models \langle x \bowtie r \rangle_a \phi^c$. Hence, $\mathcal{W}, (m, l) \models \langle x \bowtie r \rangle_a \phi^c$ implies $\mathcal{W}, (m', l) \models \langle x \bowtie r \rangle_a \phi^c$.
  Similarly $\mathcal{W}, (m', l) \models \langle x \bowtie r \rangle_a \phi^c$ implies $\mathcal{W}, (m, l) \models \langle x \bowtie r \rangle_a \phi^c$.

- **Case** $x \underline{\text{ in }} \phi^c$: $\mathcal{W}, (m, l) \models x \underline{\text{ in }} \phi^c$ implies $\mathcal{W}, (m, l[x \mapsto 0]) \models \phi^c$. By inductive hypothesis, $\mathcal{W}, (m', l[x \mapsto 0]) \models \phi^c$. Hence, $\mathcal{W}, (m, l) \models x \underline{\text{ in }} \phi^c$ implies $\mathcal{W}, (m', l) \models x \underline{\text{ in }} \phi^c$.
  Similarly $\mathcal{W}, (m', l) \models x \underline{\text{ in }} \phi^c$ implies $\mathcal{W}, (m, l) \models x \underline{\text{ in }} \phi^c$.

"$\Longleftarrow$": Let $R = \{(m, m') \mid \forall \phi^c \in \mathcal{L}^c, \mathcal{W}, (m, l) \models \phi \Leftrightarrow \mathcal{W}, (m', l) \models \phi\}$. We prove that R is a weighted bisimulation relation.

* If $m \xrightarrow{\overline{u}}_a m_1$:

  If there exists no $m_1' \in M$ s.t $m' \xrightarrow{\overline{u}}_a m_1'$, $\mathcal{W}, (m', l) \models [x \bowtie r]_a \bot$ for any $x \in \mathcal{K}$ and $r \in \mathbb{Q}$ s.t. $\overline{u}(x) \bowtie r$. Then $\mathcal{W}, (m, l) \models [x \bowtie r]_a \bot$ since $(m, m') \in R$, which contradicts the premise.

  Suppose $F = \{m_i' \mid m' \xrightarrow{\overline{u}}_a m_i'\}$ and $(m_1, m_i') \notin R$ for any i, i.e. for any i, there exists l_i and ϕ_i s.t. $\mathcal{W}, (m_1, l_i) \models \phi_i$ and $\mathcal{W}, (m_i', l_i) \not\models \phi_i$. For every $x \in \mathcal{K}(\phi^i)$, introduce x_i. Let $\phi_i' = \phi_i\{x_i/x\}$ for every ϕ_i. Let $l'(x_i) = l_i(x)$ for any i and x_i. We have: $\mathcal{W}, (m_1, l') \models \bigwedge_i \phi_i$ and $\mathcal{W}, (m_i', l') \not\models \phi_i'$ for all i. Then $\mathcal{W}, (m, l) \models [a] \bigwedge_i \phi_i'$ and $\mathcal{W}, (m', l) \not\models [a] \bigwedge \phi_i'$ - contradiction. Hence, there exists $m_1' \in M$ s.t. $m' \xrightarrow{\overline{u}}_a m_1'$ and $m_1 \sim m_1'$.

* If $m' \xrightarrow{\overline{u}}_a m_1'$: similar as above.   ∎

We previously noticed that every maximal fixed point in RWL can be translated into a formula in weighted modal logic with countable conjunction. Hence, the previous lemma ensures that RWL enjoys the Hennessy-Milner property as well.

Theorem 1 (Hennessy-Milner Theorem). *Let $\mathcal{W} = (M, \mathcal{K}, \theta)$ be an image-finite labelled weighted transition system. Then, for any $m, m' \in M$:*

$$m \sim m' \quad \text{iff}$$

for any equation block B, any ϕ closed w.r.t. B and any $l \in L$,

$$\mathcal{W}, (m, l) \models_B \phi \Leftrightarrow \mathcal{W}, (m', l) \models_B \phi.$$

Notice that in Example 2 we have already seen that $(m_1'', \mathcal{W}_3) \not\sim (m_1', \mathcal{W}_2)$. There exists, however, a RWL formula that distinguishes them. This is $[x \geq 0]_d \bot$.

5 Satisfiability of Recursive Weighted Logic

In this section we prove that it is decidable whether a given formula ϕ which is closed w.r.t. a maximal equation block B of RWL is satisfiable. We also present a decision procedure for the satisfiability problem of RWL. The results rely on a syntactic characterization of satisfiability that involves a notion of *mutually-consistent sets*.

Before going through the formal definitions, we consider the property in Example 3. Since we require that after any transition X, Y, Z, W, D still hold, X, Y, Z, W, D will hold in all the states. Let's start from the state m_0, where X, Y, Z, W, D hold and the label of x is 0. m_0 needs to do a d-action with weight at most 2 to a state m_1, since it cannot do any w-action with weight at most -3 to a state where $x \geq 0$ still holds. For m_1, the label of x can be $1, 2$ or some value in the interval $(1, 2)$. If m_0 does a d-transition with weight less than 1, after the next step there will be no next movement (no d-transition because of the constraint stated in Z and no w-transition because of the constraint stated in W). And we can also find out the transitions of m_1 and so on so forth. In this way, we can construct a finite model for the required properties. This is only a very informal discussion. We will see how to construct the model in the following.

Consider an arbitrary formula $\phi \in \mathcal{L}$ which is closed w.r.t. a maximal equation block B. In this context we define the following notions:

- For any $x \in \mathcal{K}$, let $R^B_\phi(x) \subseteq \mathbb{Q}$ be the set of all $r \in \mathbb{Q}$ such that r is in the label of some state or transition modality of type $x \bowtie r$, $\langle x \bowtie r \rangle_a$ or $[x \bowtie r]_a$ that appears in the syntax of ϕ or B. Let $Q^B_\phi(x)$ be the largest interval centred in zero that contains $R^B_\phi(x)$. If $R^B_\phi(x) = \emptyset$, then $Q^B_\phi(x) = \emptyset$.
- Let Σ^B_ϕ be the set of all actions $a \in \Sigma$ such that a appears in some transition modality of type $\langle x \bowtie r \rangle_a$ or $[x \bowtie r]_a$ in ϕ or B.
- We denoted by $G^B_\phi(x)$ the *granularity of* ϕ, defined as the least common denominator of the elements of $R^B_\phi(x)$.
- Let $I^B_\phi(x)$ be the set of all rationals of type $\frac{p}{G^B_\phi(x)}$ in $Q^B_\phi(x)$, for $p \in \mathbb{Z}$. Let

$$\Lambda^B_\phi(x) = \{\{q\} \mid q \in I^B_\phi(x)\} \cup \{(q, q + \frac{1}{G^B_\phi(x)}) \mid q, q + \frac{1}{G^B_\phi(x)} \in I^B_\phi(x)\}$$

$$\cup \{(-\infty, \min I^B_\phi(x_i))\} \cup \{(\max I^B_\phi(x_i), +\infty)\}.$$

- Let $\mathcal{R}^B_\phi = \{\bar{\delta} = (\delta_1, \ldots, \delta_k) \mid \delta_i \in \Lambda^B_\phi(x_i), \text{ where } \mathcal{K} = \{x_1, .., x_k\}\}$. For $r \in \mathbb{R}$, we write $r \in \bar{\delta}(x_j)$ to denote that $r \in \delta_j$, for arbitrary $j \in \{1, \ldots, k\}$.
- The *modal depth* of ϕ, denoted by $md(\phi, B)$, is defined inductively by

$$md(\phi, B) = \begin{cases} 0, & \text{if } \phi = \top, \phi = \bot \text{ or } \phi = x \bowtie r \\ max\{md(\psi, B), md(\psi', B)\}, & \text{if } \phi = \psi \wedge \psi' \text{ or } \phi = \psi \vee \psi' \\ md(\psi, B) + 1, & \text{if } \phi = [x \bowtie r]_a \psi \text{ or } \phi = \langle x \bowtie r \rangle_a \psi \\ md(\psi, B), & \text{if } \phi = x \text{ in } \psi \\ md(B)(X), & \text{if } \phi = X \text{ and } X = \psi \in B \\ 0, & \text{if } \phi = X \text{ and } X \notin B \end{cases}$$

$$md(B) = (md(\psi_1, B - \{X_1 = \psi_1\}), \ldots, md(\psi_n, B - \{X_n = \psi_n\}))$$

Observe that $R^B_\phi(x)$, Σ^B_ϕ, $I^B_\phi(x)$ and $\mathcal{R}^B_\phi$ are all finite (or empty). These sets will be used to construct the Fischer-Ladner closure of a given formula.

At this point we can start our model construction. We fix a formula $\phi_0 \in \mathcal{L}$ that is closed w.r.t. a given maximal equation block B and, supposing that the formula admits a model, we construct a model for it. Let

$$\mathcal{L}[\phi_0, B] = \{\phi \in \mathcal{L} \mid I_\phi^B(x) \subseteq I_{\phi_0}^B(x) \text{ for any } x \in \mathcal{K}, md(\phi, B) \leq md(\phi_0, B), \Sigma_\phi^B \subseteq \Sigma_{\phi_0}^B \}.$$

To construct the model we will use as states sets of tuples of type $(\phi, \bar{\delta}) \in \mathcal{L}[\phi_0, B] \times \mathcal{R}_{\phi_0}^B$, which are required to be maximal in a precise way. The intuition is that a state $\Gamma \subseteq \mathcal{L}[\phi_0, B] \times \mathcal{R}_{\phi_0}^B$ shall satisfy the formula ϕ in our model with the variable valuation l, whenever $(\phi, (\delta_1, .., \delta_k)) \in \Gamma$ and $l(x_j) \in \delta_j$, $j = 1, ..k$. Our construction is inspired from the region construction proposed in [LLW95] for timed automata, which adapts of the classical filtration-based model construction used in modal logics [HKT01, Wal00].

Let $\Omega[\phi_0, B] \subseteq \mathcal{L}[\phi_0, B] \times \mathcal{R}_{\phi_0}^B$. Since $\mathcal{L}[\phi_0, B]$ and $\mathcal{R}_{\phi_0}^B$ are finite, $\Omega[\phi_0, B]$ is finite.

Definition 7. *For any $\Gamma \subseteq \Omega[\phi_0, B]$, Γ is said to be maximal iff:*

1. *For any $\bar{\delta} \in \mathcal{R}_{\phi_0}^B$, $(\top, \bar{\delta}) \in \Gamma$, $(\bot, \bar{\delta}) \notin \Gamma$;*
2. *$(x \bowtie r, \bar{\delta}) \in \Gamma$ iff for any $w \in \mathbb{R}$ s.t. $w \in \bar{\delta}(x)$, $w \bowtie r$;*
3. *$(\phi \wedge \psi, \bar{\delta}) \in \Gamma$ implies $(\phi, \bar{\delta}) \in \Gamma$ and $(\psi, \bar{\delta}) \in \Gamma$; $(\phi \vee \psi, \bar{\delta}) \in \Gamma$ implies $(\phi, \bar{\delta}) \in \Gamma$ or $(\psi, \bar{\delta}) \in \Gamma$;*
4. *$(\langle x < r \rangle_a \phi, \bar{\delta}) \in \Gamma$ implies $(\langle x \leq r \rangle_a \phi, \bar{\delta}) \in \Gamma$; $(\langle x > r \rangle_a \phi, \bar{\delta}) \in \Gamma$ implies $(\langle x \geq r \rangle_a \phi, \bar{\delta}) \in \Gamma$;*
5. *$(\langle x \leq r \rangle_a \phi, \bar{\delta}) \in \Gamma$ implies $(\langle x < r + s \rangle_a \phi, \bar{\delta}) \in \Gamma$; $(\langle x \geq r \rangle_a \phi, \bar{\delta}) \in \Gamma$ implies $(\langle x > r - s \rangle_a \phi, \bar{\delta}) \in \Gamma$, for $s > 0$;*
6. *$(x \underline{in} \phi, \bar{\delta}) \in \Gamma$ implies $(\phi, \bar{\delta}[x \mapsto 0]) \in \Gamma$;*
7. *$(X, \bar{\delta}) \in \Gamma$ implies $(\phi, \bar{\delta}) \in \Gamma$, for $X = \phi \in B$.*

The maximal subsets of $\Omega[\phi_0, B]$ will be used as states in our model and for this reason we have to guarantee that their mutual relations allow us to do the construction. This is what the next lemma states.

Lemma 2. *For arbitrary $\Gamma, \Gamma' \in \Omega[\phi_0, B]$ and $r, s \in \mathbb{Q}$ with $s > 0$,*

1. *If $[([x \leq r]_a \phi, \bar{\delta}) \in \Gamma$ implies $(\phi, \bar{\delta'}) \in \Gamma']$ and there exist $w, w' \in \mathbb{R}$ s.t. $w \in \bar{\delta}(x)$, $w' \in \bar{\delta'}(x)$ and $w' - w \leq r$, then $[([x \leq r + s]_a \phi, \bar{\delta}) \in \Gamma$ implies $(\phi, \bar{\delta'}) \in \Gamma']$;*
2. *If $[([x \geq r]_a \phi, \bar{\delta}) \in \Gamma$ implies $(\phi, \bar{\delta'}) \in \Gamma']$ and there exist $w, w' \in \mathbb{R}$ s.t. $w \in \bar{\delta}(x)$, $w' \in \bar{\delta'}(x)$ and $w' - w \geq r$, then $[([x \geq r - s]_a \phi, \bar{\delta}) \in \Gamma$ implies $(\phi, \bar{\delta'}) \in \Gamma']$;*
3. *If $r \leq \inf\{t \in \mathbb{Q} \mid ([x \leq t]_a \phi, \bar{\delta}) \in \Gamma$ implies $(\phi, \bar{\delta'}) \in \Gamma$ and there exist $w, w' \in \mathbb{R}$ s.t. $w \in \bar{\delta}(x), w' \in \bar{\delta'}(x)$ and $w' - w \leq t\}$, then*

$$([x \leq r]_a \phi, \bar{\delta}) \in \Gamma \text{ implies } (\phi, \bar{\delta''}) \in \Gamma',$$

for any $\bar{\delta''}$ s.t. there exist $w, w'' \in \mathbb{R}$ with $w \in \bar{\delta}(x)$, $w'' \in \bar{\delta''}(x)$ and $w'' - w \leq r$;

4. If $r \geq \sup\{t \in \mathbb{Q} \mid ([x \geq t]_a\phi, \overline{\delta}) \in \Gamma$ implies $(\phi, \overline{\delta'}) \in \Gamma$ and there exist w, $w' \in \mathbb{R}$ s.t. $w \in \overline{\delta}(x), w' \in \overline{\delta'}(x)$ and $w' - w \geq t\}$, then

$$([x \geq r]_a\phi, \overline{\delta}) \in \Gamma \text{ implies } (\phi, \overline{\delta''}) \in \Gamma',$$

for any $\overline{\delta''}$ s.t. there exist $w, w'' \in \mathbb{R}$ with $w \in \overline{\delta}(x)$, $w'' \in \overline{\delta''}(x)$ and $w'' - w \leq r$.

Proof. 1. From Definition 7, we have that $([x \leq r + s]_a\phi, \overline{\delta}) \in \Gamma$ implies $([x \leq r]_a\phi, \overline{\delta}) \in \Gamma$. So $([x \leq r + s]_a\phi, \overline{\delta}) \in \Gamma$ implies $(\phi, \overline{\delta'}) \in \Gamma'$. Similarly for 2.

3. It is a direct consequence of case 1 when we consider the infimum. Similarly for 4. ∎

Notice that sup and inf above might be irrationals and cannot be used to index modalities. Nevertheless, they are limits of some monotone sequences of rationals.

The following definition establishes the framework on which we will define our model.

Definition 8. Let $\mathcal{C} \subseteq 2^{\Omega[\phi_0, B]}$. $\mathcal{C}$ is said to be *mutually-consistent* if whenever $\Gamma \in \mathcal{C}$:

$$[\forall \Gamma', \Gamma \xrightarrow{\overline{u}}_a \Gamma' \text{ and } \overline{u}(x) \bowtie r \Rightarrow (\phi, \overline{\delta}) \in \Gamma'] \text{ implies } ([x \bowtie r]_a\phi, \overline{\delta} - \overline{u}) \in \Gamma.$$

We say that Γ is *consistent* if it belongs to some mutually-consistent set.

Lemma 3. Let $\phi \in \mathcal{L}$ be a formula closed w.r.t. a maximal equation block B. Then ϕ is satisfiable iff there exist $\Gamma \in \Omega[\phi_0, B]$ and $\overline{\delta} \in \mathcal{R}_\phi^B$ s.t. Γ is consistent and $(\phi, \overline{\delta}) \in \Gamma$.

Proof. ($\Longrightarrow$): Suppose ϕ is satisfied in the LWS $\mathcal{W} = (M, \Sigma, \mathcal{K}, \theta)$. We construct

$$\mathcal{C} = \{\Gamma \in \Omega[\phi_0, B] \mid \exists m \in M \text{ and } l \in \overline{\delta}, \mathcal{W}, (m, l) \models_B \psi \text{ for all } (\psi, \overline{\delta}) \in \Gamma\}.$$

It is not difficult to verify that $\mathcal{C}$ is a mutually-consistent set.

($\Longleftarrow$): Let $\mathcal{C}$ be a mutually-consistent set. We construct an LWS $\mathcal{W} = (M, \Sigma, \mathcal{K}, \theta)$, where: $M = \mathcal{C}$, and the transition relation $\Gamma \xrightarrow{\overline{u}}_a \Gamma'$ is defined whenever

$$\overline{u}(x) = \sup\{r \in \mathbb{Q} \mid ([x \geq r]_a\phi, \overline{\delta}) \in \Gamma \text{ implies } (\phi, \overline{\delta'}) \in \Gamma', \text{ with } \overline{\delta'}(x) - \overline{\delta}(x) \geq r\}$$

$$= \inf\{r \in \mathbb{Q} \mid ([x \leq r]_a\phi, \overline{\delta}) \in \Gamma \text{ implies } (\phi, \overline{\delta'}) \in \Gamma', \text{ with } \overline{\delta'}(x) - \overline{\delta}(x) \leq r\} \in \mathbb{R}.$$

Let $\rho(X) = \{\Gamma \mid (X, \overline{\delta}) \in \Gamma\}$ for $X \in \mathcal{X}$. With this construction we can prove the following implication by a simple induction on the structure of ϕ, where $\Gamma \in M$ and $l \in \overline{\delta}$:

$$(\phi, \overline{\delta}) \in \Gamma \text{ implies } \mathcal{W}, \Gamma, l, \rho \models \phi.$$

We prove that ρ is a fixed point of B under the assumption that $X = \phi_X \in B$:

$\Gamma \in \rho(X)$ implies $(X, \overline{\delta}) \in \Gamma$ by the construction of ρ, which implies $(\phi_X, \overline{\delta}) \in \Gamma$. Then, by the implication we just proved above, $\mathcal{W}, \Gamma, l, \rho \models \phi_X$.

Thus ρ is a fixed point of B. Since $[\![B]\!]$ is the maximal fixed point, $\rho \subseteq [\![B]\!]$. So for any $(\psi, \overline{\delta}) \in \Gamma \in \mathcal{C}$, we have $\mathcal{W}, \Gamma, l, \nu\rho \models \psi$ with $l \in \overline{\delta}$. Then $\mathcal{W}, \Gamma, l, [\![B]\!] \models \psi$ because $\rho \subseteq [\![B]\!]$.

Hence, $(\psi, \overline{\delta}) \in \Gamma \in \mathcal{C}$ implies $\mathcal{W}, \Gamma, l \models_B \psi$ with $l \in \overline{\delta}$.   ∎

The above lemma allows us to conclude the finite model construction.

Theorem 2 (Finite Model Property). *For any satisfiable RWL formula ϕ closed w.r.t. a maximal equation block B, there exists a finite LWS $\mathcal{W} = (M, \Sigma, \mathcal{K}, \theta)$ and a variable valuation l such that $\mathcal{W}, m, l \models_B \phi$ for some $m \in M$.*

Lemma 3 and Theorem 2 provide a decision procedure for the satisfiability problem of RWL. Given a RWL formula ϕ_0 closed w.r.t. a maximal equation block B, the algorithm constructs the model with $\Sigma = \Sigma_{\phi_0}^B$:

$$\mathcal{W} = (M, \Sigma, \mathcal{K}, \theta).$$

If ϕ_0 is satisfiable, then it is contained in some consistent set. Hence, ϕ_0 will be satisfied at some state m of $\mathcal{W}$. If ϕ_0 is not satisfiable, then the attempt to construct a model will fail; in this case the algorithm will halt and report the failure.

We start with a superset of the set of states of $\mathcal{W}$, then repeatedly delete states when we discover some inconsistency. This will give a sequence of approximations

$$\mathcal{W}_0 \supseteq \mathcal{W}_1 \supseteq \mathcal{W}_2 \supseteq \cdots$$

converging to $\mathcal{W}$.

The domains M_i, $i = 0, 1, 2, \ldots$, of these structures are defined below and they are s.t.

$$M_0 \supseteq M_1 \supseteq M_2 \supseteq \cdots.$$

The transition relation for $\mathcal{W}_i$ are defined as follows: $\Gamma \xrightarrow{\overline{u}}_a \Gamma'$ whenever

$$\overline{u}(x) = \sup\{r \in \mathbb{Q} \mid ([x \geq r]_a \phi, \overline{\delta}) \in \Gamma \text{ implies } (\phi, \overline{\delta'}) \in \Gamma', \text{ with } \overline{\delta'}(x) - \overline{\delta}(x) \geq r\}$$
$$= \inf\{r \in \mathbb{Q} \mid ([x \leq r]_a \phi, \overline{\delta}) \in \Gamma \text{ implies } (\phi, \overline{\delta'}) \in \Gamma', \text{ with } \overline{\delta'}(x) - \overline{\delta}(x) \leq r\} \in \mathbb{R}.$$

Here is the algorithm for constructing the domains M_i of $\mathcal{W}_i$.

Algorithm

Step 1: Construct $M_0 = \Omega[\phi_0, B]$.
Step 2: Repeat the following for $i = 0, 1, 2, \ldots$ until no more states are deleted. Find a formula $[x \bowtie r]_a \phi \in \mathcal{L}[\phi_0, B]$ and a state $\Gamma \in M_i$ violating the property

$$[\forall \Gamma', \Gamma \xrightarrow{\overline{u}}_a \Gamma' \text{ and } \overline{u}(x) \bowtie r \Rightarrow (\phi, \overline{\delta}) \in \Gamma']$$
$$\text{implies } [([x \bowtie r]_a \phi, \overline{\delta'}) \in \Gamma \text{ and } \overline{\delta'} = \overline{\delta} - \overline{u}].$$

Pick such an $[x \bowtie r]_a \phi$ and Γ. Delete Γ from M_i to get M_{i+1}.   ∎

Step 2 can be justified intuitively as follows. To say that Γ violates the above mentioned condition, means that Γ requires an a-transition at cost $\overline{u}$ to some state that does not satisfy ϕ; however, the left-hand side of the condition above guarantees that all the outcomes of an a-transition at cost $\overline{u}$ satisfy ϕ. This demonstrates that Γ cannot be in M, since every state Γ in M satisfies ψ, whenever $(\psi, \overline{\delta}) \in \Gamma$.

The algorithm must terminate, since there are only finitely many states initially, and at least one state must be deleted during each iteration of step 2 in order to continue. Then ϕ is satisfiable if and only if, upon termination there exists $\Gamma \in M$ such that $(\phi, \overline{\delta}) \in \Gamma$. Obviously, M is a mutually-consistent set upon termination. The correctness of this algorithm follows from Lemma 3. The $\Leftarrow$ direction of the proof guarantees that all formulas in any $\Gamma \in M$ are satisfiable. The $\Rightarrow$ direction of the proof guarantees that all satisfiable Γ will not be deleted from M.

The finite model property also supported by the above algorithm demonstrates the decidability of the B-satisfiability problem for RWL.

Theorem 3 (Decidability of B-satisfiability). *For an arbitrary maximal equation block B, the B-satisfiability problem for RWL is decidable.*

6   Conclusion

In this paper we develop a recursive version of the weighted modal logic [LM13] that we call Recursive Weighted Logic (RWL). It uses a semantics based on labelled weighted transition systems (LWSs). This type of transition systems describes systems where the computations have some costs that must be paid in terms of the resources available in its states: positive transitions means that the system gains some resources during the transition, while negative ones represent resource consumption.

RWL encodes qualitative and quantitative properties of LWSs. With respect to the weighted logics studied before, RWL has recursive variables that allow us to encode circular properties. These features reflect concrete requirements from applications where liveness and safeness properties including cost information are essential.

We first prove that RWL enjoys the Hennessy-Milner property and it is consequently appropriate for describing LWSs up to bisimilarity. This result is particularly interesting because it shows that the Hennessy-Milner property can be satisfied in the absence of negation.

Our second major result is the decidability of the satisfiability problem for RWL which derives directly from our model construction. This is a novel construction that we design for RWL, which also provides a satisfiability-checking algorithm. We will discuss the complexity in a future paper.

For future work we consider to extend RWL. The current version only allows one variable for each type of resource in the syntax of the logic. This represents an important expressiveness restriction, but a necessary one if we want the satisfiability problem to be decidable. Nevertheless, we believe that one can adapt our model construction to the extended case, where we will not get a finite model any more, but one with certain types of regularity that will be properly described by some concept of weighted automata.

References

[ACD93] Alur, R., Courcoubetis, C., Dill, D.L.: Model-checking in dense real-time. Inf. Comput. **104**(1), 2–34 (1993)

[AD90] Alur, R., Dill, D.L.: Automata for modeling real-time systems. In: Paterson, M. (ed.) ICALP 1990. LNCS, vol. 443, pp. 322–335. Springer, Heidelberg (1990)

[AILS07] Aceto, L., Ingólfsdóttir, A., Larsen, K.G., Srba, J.: Reactive Systems: Modelling, Specification and Verification. Cambridge University Press, Cambridge (2007)

[ATP01] Alur, R., La Torre, S., Pappas, G.J.: Optimal paths in weighted timed automata. In: Di Benedetto, M.D., Sangiovanni-Vincentelli, A.L. (eds.) HSCC 2001. LNCS, vol. 2034, pp. 49–62. Springer, Heidelberg (2001)

[BFH+01] Behrmann, G., Fehnker, A., Hune, T., Larsen, K.G., Pettersson, P., Romijn, J.M.T., Vaandrager, F.W.: Minimum-cost reachability for priced timed automata. In: Di Benedetto, M.D., Sangiovanni-Vincentelli, A.L. (eds.) HSCC 2001. LNCS, vol. 2034, pp. 147–161. Springer, Heidelberg (2001)

[CKS92] Cleaveland, R., Klein, M., Steffen, B.: Faster model checking for the modal mu-calculus. In: von Bochmann, G., Probst, D.K. (eds.) CAV 1992. LNCS, vol. 663, pp. 410–422. Springer, Heidelberg (1993)

[CS93] Cleaveland, R., Steffen, B.: A linear-time model-checking algorithm for the alternation-free modal mu-calculus. Form. Meth. Syst. Design **2**(2), 121–147 (1993)

[DKV09] Droste, M., Kuich, W., Vogler, H. (eds.): Handbook of Weighted Automata. Springer, Heidelberg (2009)

[HKT01] Harel, D., Kozen, D., Tiuryn, J.: Dynamic Logic. The MIT Press, Cambridge (2001)

[HM80] Hennessy, M., Milner, R.: On observing nondeterminism and concurrency. In: de Bakker, J.W., van Leeuwen, J. (eds.) ICALP 1980. LNCS, vol. 85, pp. 299–309. Springer, Heidelberg (1980)

[HNSY92] Henzinger, T.A., Nicollin, X., Sifakis, J., Yovine, S.: Symbolic model checking for real-time systems. In: LICS, pp. 394–406 (1992)

[Koz82] Kozen, D.: Results on the propositional μ-calculus. In: Nielsen, M., Schmidt, E.M. (eds.) ICALP 1982. Lecture Notes in Computer Science, vol. 140, pp. 348–359. Springer, Heidelberg (1982)

[Lar90] Larsen, K.G.: Proof systems for satisfiability in hennessy-milner logic with recursion. Theor. Comput. Sci. **72**(2&3), 265–288 (1990)

[LLW95] Laroussinie, F., Larsen, K.G., Weise, C.: From timed automata to logic - and back. In: Hájek, P., Wiedermann, J. (eds.) MFCS 1995. LNCS, vol. 969, pp. 529–539. Springer, Heidelberg (1995)

[LM13] Larsen, K.G., Mardare, R.: Complete proof system for weighted modal logic. Theor. Comput. Sci. **546**, 164–175 (2013)

[SR11] Sangiorgi, D., Rutten, J. (eds.): Advanced Topics in Bisimulation and Coinduction. Cambridge University Press, Cambridge (2011)

[Sti99] Stirling, C.: Bisimulation, modal logic and model checking games. Log. J. IGPL **7**(1), 103–124 (1999)

[Tar55] Tarski, A.: A lattice-theoretical fixpoint theorem and its applications. Pac. J. Math. **5**(2), 285–309 (1955)

[Wal00] Walukiewicz, I.: Completeness of kozen's axiomatisation of the propositional μ-calculus. Inf. Comput. **157**(1–2), 142–182 (2000)

Supercompilation for Datatypes

Torben Ægidius Mogensen[(✉)]

DIKU, University of Copenhagen, Universitetsparken 5,
2100 Copenhagen O, Denmark
torbenm@diku.dk

Abstract. Supercompilation is a method of transforming programs to obtain equivalent programs that perform fewer computation steps and allocates less memory. A transformed program defines new functions that are combinations of functions from the original program, but the datatypes in the transformed program is a subset of the datatypes defined in the original program. We will change this by extending supercompilation to create new datatypes.

We do this by creating new constructors that combine several constructors from the original program in a way reminiscent of how supercompilation combines several functions to create new functions.

1 Introduction

The concept of supercompilation was introduced by Turchin [17,18] and the idea and method has been developed further by many others including [3–5,7,8,15,16].

Supercompilation has been used for *fusion*, i.e., combining functions with the aim of eliminating construction of intermediate data structures, *tupling*, i.e., combining functions with the aim of avoiding multiple traversals over the same data structure, and for *theorem proving* by composing a function with functions that define pre and post conditions. In this paper, we extend supercompilation to transform not only functions but also datatypes, using a form of constructor specialisation [2,12].

In Sect. 2, we define a small functional language and in Sect. 3, we sketch traditional supercompilation for this language using *unfolding, folding* and *special-casing*. In Sect. 4, we extend this supercompilation method to create new datatypes and constructors by modifying and extending the rules for unfolding, folding and special-casing. In Sect. 5, we show some examples of transformations and in Sect. 6, we discuss the results and future work.

2 A Simple Functional Language

To keep the presentation simple, we define a minimal functional language. The syntax of the language (which is a subset of Haskell syntax) is shown in Fig. 1.

tid represents type identifiers, **fid** represents function identifiers, **vid** variable identifiers and **cid** constructor identifiers. Constructor identifiers and type names are written with initial upper-case letters while function and variable identifiers are written with initial lower-case letters.

© Springer-Verlag Berlin Heidelberg 2015
A. Voronkov and I. Virbitskaite (Eds.): PSI 2014, LNCS 8974, pp. 232–247, 2015.
DOI: 10.1007/978-3-662-46823-4_19

$Program \rightarrow Data^* \ Rule^*$ $Data \ \rightarrow \text{data } \textbf{tid} = Cons$

$Rule \quad\ \rightarrow \textbf{fid } Patt = Exp$ $Cons \ \rightarrow \textbf{cid}$ $Exp \ \rightarrow \textbf{vid}$

$Cons \ \rightarrow \textbf{cid } Texp$ $Exp \ \rightarrow (Exps)$

$Patt \quad \rightarrow \textbf{vid}$ $Cons \ \rightarrow Cons \mid Cons$ $Exp \ \rightarrow \textbf{cid}$

$Patt \quad \rightarrow (Patts)$ $Exp \ \rightarrow \textbf{cid } Exp$

$Patt \quad \rightarrow \textbf{cid}$ $Texp \ \rightarrow \textbf{tid}$ $Exp \ \rightarrow \textbf{fid } Exp$

$Patt \quad \rightarrow \textbf{cid } Patt$ $Texp \ \rightarrow (Texps)$

$Exps \rightarrow Exp$

$Patts \quad \rightarrow Patt$ $Texps \rightarrow Texp$ $Exps \rightarrow Exp, Exps$

$Patts \quad \rightarrow Patt, Patts$ $Texps \rightarrow Texp, Texps$

Fig. 1. A first-order functional language

A program is a list of type declarations and function definitions. A type declaration is if the form data $t \ = \ cs$, where t is a type name and cs is a list of constructor declarations each of the form $c \ te$, where te is a type expression.

A function is defined by one or more *rules* of the form $f \ p = e$, where p is a pattern and e an expression. We assume *linear patterns*: No variable identifier can occur more than once in a pattern. Rules can not overlap: If there are two rules $f \ p_1 = e_1$ and $f \ p_2 = e_2$, then p_1 and p_2 can not be unified. Types are not declared for functions or variables, but we assume type inference is done to identify types, so programs are well typed and we can determine the type of any variable. We allow unspecified (externally defined) type names in type expressions. Values of externally defined types can be copied, passed as arguments and returned as results, but not deconstructed through pattern matching.

A *value* is any expression that is built only from constructors and tuples. Running a program consists of calling a function with arguments that are values and then evaluating this call to a value, which can fail due to nontermination or lack of a matching rule. We will describe evaluation more formally below.

A simple example program that defines a list type (using an externally defined integer element type) and a list-append function is shown below.

```
data List = Nil | Cons (Int, List)

append (Nil, ys) = ys
append (Cons (x, xs), ys) = Cons (x, append (xs, ys))
```

2.1   Evaluation

Evaluation of an expression in a program is done as a series of *function application* steps and continues until no further such steps are possible. If this results in a value, this is the result of the evaluation. If not, the result is considered undefined. We do not specify the order of evaluation but note that the order of evaluation can at most affect termination but not the final result (if such is obtained), as the language is purely functional.

We first need a few auxiliary definitions and functions:

A *substitution* is a set of bindings of variables to expressions. A single binding is written as $x \backslash e$, where x is a variable and e is an expression. A substitution is written as a list of bindings inside square brackets, i.e., $[x_1 \backslash e_1, \ldots, x_n \backslash e_n]$. We assume that all the variables bound in a substitution are different and that they do not occur in the expressions, i.e., $x_i = x_j \Rightarrow i = j$ and that no x_i occurs in any e_j. This means that the substitution is idempotent, so the order of bindings does not matter. We can combine two non-overlapping substitutions by the operator $+$.

We apply substitutions to expressions in the standard way, so we omit a formal definition here. Since patterns are (syntactically) a subset of expressions, we can also apply substitutions to patterns as long as all bindings in the substitution binds variables to patterns. Such a substitution can, in fact, be applied to both patterns and expressions.

We obtain substitutions by *matching* a pattern to an expression. Matching either fails (indicated by the special result value **Fail**) or produces a substitution that binds the variables in the pattern to expressions. We extend the $+$ operation on substitutions to include **Fail**, so $\Theta + \textbf{Fail} = \textbf{Fail} + \Theta = \textbf{Fail}$. $p \lhd e$ matches a pattern p to an expression e using the following rules:

$$C \lhd C = [] \qquad\qquad (C\ p) \lhd (C\ e) = p \lhd e$$
$$(p_1, \ldots, p_n) \lhd (e_1, \ldots, e_n) = (p_1 \lhd e_1) + \cdots + (p_n \lhd e_n)$$
$$x \lhd e = [x \backslash e] \qquad\qquad p \lhd e = \textbf{Fail}, \quad \text{otherwise}$$

We assume that no variable occurs more than once in p (by the linear-pattern restriction) and that no variable in p occurs in e. This ensures that any produced substitution is valid.

A function application step is replacing a function call with the body of a matching function rule. More precisely, if we have a function call $f\ e_1$, a rule $f\ p = e_2$ and $p \lhd e_1 = \Theta \neq \textbf{Fail}$, then $f\ e_1$ is replaced by $e_2 \Theta$. If p shares variables with e_1, the matching would not produce a valid substitution, so in this case we rename variables in the function rule first. Since function rules do not overlap, a function call can not match more than one rule, though it may match none. Evaluation of an expression is done by repeated use of the function application step until no calls remain or no rules match any remaining call. If no calls remain, evaluation is successful, but if calls remain and no rules match any of these calls, the result is considered undefined. There is also a possibility of nontermination through applying an infinite number of application steps.

3   Supercompilation

In this section, we will present a simple form of positive supercompilation for the language presented above. Supercompilation of a program is done in a number of transformation steps that build a new program from the original. We will use the following variables during the transformation:

- The original program P_0 as a list of datatype declarations and a list of function definitions.

- A transformed program P_1 in the same form.
- A list of function definitions Fs that defines each function that will eventually be defined in P_1 in terms of functions from P_0. All functions defined in Fs are defined by one rule only.
- A current function definition F that is being transformed.

P_0 will remain unchanged during the transformation.

Initially, the transformed program P_1 will contain the list of datatype declarations copied from P_0 and an empty list of function definitions. Fs will initially contain a list of definitions that describe the desired transformation by defining new functions in terms of the functions and datatypes in the original program. For example, if P_0 is the program shown at the end of Sect. 2, Fs may contain the definition

```
append3 (xs, ys, zs) = append (append (xs, ys), zs)
```

that defines a new function append3 in terms of the append function in P_0.

The transformation is supposed to make the new program P_1 a self-contained and optimised implementation of the functions declared in Fs, in this instance append3.

During transformation, F will contain a function definition that is originally taken from Fs and rewritten so it contains no calls to the functions defined in P_0, at which point it can be added to the transformed program P_1. Some of the steps that rewrite F may add more definitions to Fs, which will later be copied to F for transformation. We can sketch the transformation method as follows:

$P_1 : =$ the data declarations from P_0
$Fs : =$ the function definitions to be transformed
while there are definitions in Fs not defined in P_1
 Pick F from Fs
 Rewrite the right-hand side of F until it calls only functions defined in Fs
 Add F to P_1

where we note that the step "rewrite the right-hand side of F" can add definitions to Fs.

3.1   Transformation Steps

The "rewrite the right-hand side of F" part of the transformation will use *unfolding*, *folding* and *special-casing* steps, which we describe below.

Unfolding. Unfolding a call $f\ e$, where f is defined in P_0, is the same as function application as defined in Sect. 2.1 with the following restriction: We unfold only if no function call in e is duplicated or discarded by the unfolding, since discarding function calls during unfolding may change termination behaviour of the transformed program (under some evaluation orders) and duplicating function calls may have adverse effects on its runtime.

Folding. Folding is a way of replacing an expression e_0 in F by a call to a function defined in Fs. More formally:

Assume Fs defines a function by the single rule $f\ p = e_2$ where p is a pattern that does not share variables with e_0. If there are shared variables, the definition can be renamed as described in Sect. 2.1 to avoid name overlap.

If there exists an expression e_1 such that $p \lhd e_1 = \Theta \neq \mathbf{Fail}$ and $e_2\Theta = e_0$, then e_0 can be replaced by the call $f\ (e_1)$.

If we want to fold an expression e_0 to a call and there is no suitable function in Fs, we add a definition of a suitable function extracted from e_0 to Fs before folding. The name of this extracted function can not already be in use in Fs or P_0.

Folding is close to but not quite the inverse of unfolding, as folding uses a function definition in Fs and unfolding uses a function definition in P_0.

If folding is not done carefully, we risk making circular definitions such as $f\ x = f\ x$. In general, a folding step must be preceded by at least one unfolding step.

Special-Casing. Special-casing is a way of splitting a function rule into several special-case rules. In other words, given a list of substitutions $\Theta_1, \ldots, \Theta_n$, a rule $f\ p = e$ is split into the rules $f\ (p\Theta_1) = (e\Theta_1), \ldots, f\ (p\Theta_n) = (e\Theta_n)$. Note that we apply substitutions to both expressions and patterns, so we require that each Θ_i binds variables to expressions that are also valid as patterns, i.e., expressions not containing function calls.

We construct the substitutions in the following way: We select a variable x occurring in the pattern p. x must have a type t declared by a datatype declaration

$$\mathtt{data}\ t = C_1|\cdots|C_n$$

If C_i is of the form c_i, then Θ_i is the substitution $[x\backslash c_i]$. If C_i is of the form $c_i\ t$, then Θ_i is the substitution $[x\backslash c_i\ Q(t)]$, where Q maps a type expression to a pattern by replacing all type names by distinct variables. Basically, we construct substitutions that correspond to the possible top-level constructors of the value of x. The special-cased rules do not overlap, so the requirement of non-overlapping rules is preserved.

For example, given the `list` datatype shown in Sect. 2 and the definition F:
`append3 (xs, ys, zs) = append (append (xs, ys), zs)`, we can special-case F to

```
append3 (Nil, ys, zs) = append (append (Nil, ys), zs)
append3 (Cons (q, qs), ys, zs) = append (append (Cons (q, qs), ys), zs)
```

using the substitutions $\Theta_1 = [\mathtt{x}\backslash\mathtt{Nil}]$ and $\Theta_2 = [\mathtt{x}\backslash\mathtt{Cons}(\mathtt{q},\mathtt{qs})]$.

3.2 A Supercompilation Strategy

There are often cases where several of the transformation rules can apply or where a transformation rule can be applied in different ways. A supercompiler must, hence, have a strategy for which rules to apply and how. We will use the following simple strategy:

1. If a rule in F contains a function call $f\ e$, where f is defined in P_0, e does not contain any function calls, and the call to f can not be unfolded because no rules match, we special-case the rule in F on a variable x in e. If the selected call to f can now be unfolded in all the special-cased rules, we continue to step 2 below, otherwise we repeatedly special-case those rules where the selected call to f can not be unfolded until no such remain, i.e., when all calls to f can be unfolded.
2. Then, all calls $f\ e$, where the requirements for unfolding described in Sect. 3.1 are observed, are *unfolded*.
3. When no further such unfolding can be applied to F, *configurations* (see below) in F are folded against new or previous definitions in Fs until no calls to the original program P_0 remain in the modified F.
4. Add the modified F to P_1. If there are definitions in Fs not defined in P_1, pick one of these as a new F and repeat from step 1. If all definitions in Fs are defined in P_1, the transformation is complete, and P_1 contains the transformed program.

Note that, in steps 1 and 2, F can only contain calls to functions defined in P_0 and at the end of step 3, the modified F contains only calls to functions defined in Fs.

A *configuration* is an expression that is a candidate for folding. Often, a configuration consists of the entire right-hand side of a rule in F (excepting constructor applications outside function calls), but sometimes a right-hand side is split into several nested configurations that are folded individually. Splitting an expression into several nested configurations is an instance of *generalisation* and is often required to ensure termination of supercompilation. Nontermination can happen both in step 2 above, as an infinite chain of unfoldings, or by repeating the iteration over steps 1–4 above indefinitely, as an infinite sequence of definitions are added to Fs. We will not in this paper discuss how potentially infinite chains of unfoldings or definitions are detected (for that, see [14]), but only note that detection of a potentially infinite chain of unfoldings will trigger a folding step and a potential infinite chain of definitions will trigger generalisation. Nor will we discuss how it is decided how to split a right-hand side into multiple configurations: We will simply make splits that work for the examples.

3.3   Example of Supercompilation

We start with P_0 being the program at the end of Sect. 2 and add the initial definition append3 (xs, ys, zs) = append (append (xs, ys), zs) to Fs. The initial F will, hence, also be this definition. We rewrite this F using the following steps:

1. We apply *special-casing* to the rules for append3 as shown in Sect. 3.1. This yields the following new F:

   ```
   append3 (Nil, ys, zs) = append (append (Nil, ys), zs)
   append3 (Cons (q, qs), ys, zs) = append (append (Cons (q, qs), ys), zs)
   ```

2. We *unfold* three times using the definition of append in P_0, which changes F to

```
append3 (Nil, ys, zs) = append (ys, zs)
append3 (Cons (q, qs), ys, zs) = Cons (q, append (append (qs, ys), zs))
```

3. We *fold* the call `append (append (xs, ys), zs)` with the definition of `append3`
   in Fs:

```
append3 (Nil, ys, zs) = append (ys, zs)
append3 (Cons (q, qs), ys, zs) = Cons (q, append3 (qs, ys, zs))
```

4. The first rule still contains a call to a function from P_0, so we fold this
   using the definition `append2 (ys, zs) = append (ys, zs)`, which we add to
   Fs. Since F now contains no calls to functions in P_0, we can add F to P_1 and
   copy the rule for `append2` to F. We omit the (rather trivial) transformation
   steps for this rule.
5. After adding the rules for `append2` to the program, we are done. The resulting
   P_1 is

```
data List = Nil | Cons (Elem, List)

append3 (Nil, ys, zs) = append2 (ys, zs)
append3 (Cons (q, qs), ys, zs) = Cons (q, append3(qs, ys, zs))

append2 (Nil, ys) = ys
append2 (Cons (x, xs), ys) = Cons (x, append2 (xs, ys))
```

4   Supercompiling for Datatypes

We now extend the supercompilation method described in Sect. 3 to transform
datatypes as well as functions. We add to the transformation state a list of
definitions Cs that define constructors for P_1 in terms of constructors from P_0,
analogously to how Fs defines functions in P_1 in terms of functions in P_0: Each
new constructor, optionally applied to a tuple of variables, is defined by an
expression built only from variables from this tuple and constructors in the
original program. For example, Cs may contain the definitions `Nil2 = Nil` and
`Cons2 (x,y,z) = Cons (x, Cons (y, z))`.

Instead of copying all datatype declarations from P_0 to P_1, as we did in Sect. 3,
we start P_1 with empty declarations for renamed versions of the datatypes
declared in P_0 and add constructors to these during the transformation: Whenever
a constructor definition $c\ p = e$ is added to Cs, we add c to the declaration of the
renamed type of e with argument types determined by the types of the variables
in p. So, if we rename `List` from P_0 to `List2` in P_1, the Cs shown above would
yield the following datatype definition in P_1: `data List2 = Nil2 | Cons2 (Int, Int, List2)`.

Sometimes, we want to leave some datatypes unchanged. In that case, we just
copy the definitions of these to P_1 and make trivial definitions (with left-hand
side equal to right-hand side) of these in Cs.

4.1   Modified Transformation Steps

The unfold rule from Sect. 3 is unchanged, but we change folding and special-casing:

Folding. In addition to folding an expression e_0 to a function definition in Fs, as described in Sect. 3.1, we can now also fold e_0 to a constructor definition in Cs by a completely analogous process: Assume Cs defines a constructor $c\ p = e_2$. If there exists an expression e_1 such that $p \triangleleft e_1 = \Theta \neq \textbf{Fail}$ and $e_2\Theta = e_0$, then e_0 can be replaced by the constructor application $c\ (e_1)$.

If there is no suitable constructor definition in Cs, we can add one, and at the same time add the constructor to the relevant datatype declaration in P_1, as described above.

Special-Casing. The original rule for special-casing is modified as follows: We use two different substitutions for the left-hand and right-hand sides of the function rule we special-case: The left-hand substitution Θ_L binds variables to left-hand sides of definitions in Cs and the right-hand substitution Θ_R binds variables to the corresponding right-hand sides of these definitions.

For example, the Cs shown above can yield the following two pairs of substitutions:

1. $\Theta_{L1} = [\texttt{x}\backslash\texttt{Nil2}]$ and $\Theta_{R1} = [\texttt{x}\backslash\texttt{Nil}]$
2. $\Theta_{L2} = [\texttt{x}\backslash\texttt{Cons2}(\texttt{p},\texttt{q},\texttt{r})]$ and $\Theta_{R2} = [\texttt{x}\backslash\texttt{Cons}(\texttt{p},\texttt{Cons}(\texttt{q},\texttt{r}))]$

Note that we have renamed variables in the second definition in Cs to avoid overlap between variables in the domain and range of Θ_{L2}. Applying these substitutions to a definition $f\ x\ =\ \texttt{append}\ (x,\ x)$ yields the following special-cased definition

```
f Nil2 = append (Nil, Nil)
f (Cons2 (p, q, r)) = append (Cons (p, Cons (q, r)), Cons (p, Cons (q, r)))
```

4.2   A Modified Strategy

The strategy described in Sect. 3.2 is modified as follows:

1. Special-casing now uses the extended rule for special-casing.
2. Unfolding is unchanged.
3. Folding is changed in the following way: There are now two forms of configurations:
   i. Configurations with function applications at their roots and which are built from both function calls and constructor/tuple applications. These are folded against definitions in Fs as described in Sect. 3.1.
   ii. Configurations built entirely from constructor and tuple applications. These are folded against definitions in Cs, as described in Sect. 4.1.

Whenever folding causes a new constructor definition $c\ p = e$ to be added to Cs, any function definition for a function f in P_1 that was special-cased on the type of c is no longer complete, as there is no case for c. A simple way to remedy this is to remove the definition of f from P_1, so a new definition with rules for all constructors will be added later.[1]

Just as generalisation may be required when folding function configurations, generalisation may be required when folding constructor configurations. We will not address this further in this paper, except by noting that folding may involve choice of how to split a right-hand side of a rule into configurations.

A thing to note is that the output type of P_1 can be changed to a new, transformed type. In order to get output in the original type, a translation based on recursive application of the definitions in Cs must be applied to the output from P_1.

5 Examples

We now show a few examples of supercompilation of datatypes.

5.1 Combinator Reduction

Below is an interpreter for combinator reduction using the combinators K and S that have the reduction rules $(K\ x)\ y \to x$ and $((S\ x)\ y)\ z \to (x\ z)\ (y\ z)$:

```
data SK = S | K | Ap (SK, SK)

run K = K
run S = S
run (Ap (K, x)) = Ap (K, run x)
run (Ap (S, x)) = Ap (S, run x)
run (Ap (Ap (K, x), y)) = run x
run (Ap (Ap (S, x), y)) = Ap (Ap (S, run x), run y)
run (Ap (Ap (Ap (K, x), y), z)) = run (Ap (x, z))
run (Ap (Ap (Ap (S, x), y), z)) = run (Ap (Ap (x, z), Ap (y, z)))
run (Ap (Ap (Ap (Ap (p, q), x), y), z)) =
   run (Ap (run (Ap (Ap (Ap (p, q), x), y)), z))
```

The interpreter is somewhat complicated by the requirement of non-overlapping rules.

We now want to add another combinator $I = (S\ K)\ K$ to the language, so we define in Cs constructors for a new datatype SKI:

```
K1 = K
S1 = S
I = Ap (Ap (S, K), K)
Ap1 (x, y) = Ap (x, y)
```

---

[1] As an optimisation, the already transformed rules can be cached, so they do not need to be transformed once again.

Note that this gives a choice of how to fold the expression `Ap (Ap (S, K), K)`:
We can either fold it to `I` or to `Ap1 (Ap1 (S1, K1), K1)` by splitting into
single-constructor configurations that are folded individually. It is up to the
supercompilation strategy to choose which of these to use. We will use the following strategy: All occurrences of `Ap (Ap (S, K), K)` are folded to `I`, but all
other constructor configurations are split into single-constructor configurations.

We initialise P_1 to include the following datatype declaration:

```
data SKI = S1 | K1 | I | Ap1 (SKI, SKI)
```

We want to modify `run`, so we start Fs with the definition `run1 e = run e`,
which is copied to F. We then special-case this rule on the possible forms of e:

```
run1 K1 = run K
run1 S1 = run S
run1 I = run (Ap (Ap (S, K), K))
run1 (Ap1 (x, y)) = run (Ap (x, y))
```

The last rule can not be unfolded, so we special-case this on the value of x. We
need to special-case a couple of times more to ensure that unfolding is possible
in all rules:

```
run1 K1 = run K
run1 S1 = run S
run1 I = run (Ap (Ap (S, K), K))
run1 (Ap1 (K1, y)) = run (Ap (K, y))
run1 (Ap1 (S1, y)) = run (Ap (S, y))
run1 (Ap1 (I, y)) = run (Ap (Ap (Ap (S, K), K), y))
run1 (Ap1 (Ap1 (K1, q), y)) = run (Ap (Ap (K, q), y))
run1 (Ap1 (Ap1 (S1, q), y)) = run (Ap (Ap (S, q), y))
run1 (Ap1 (Ap1 (I, q), y)) = run (Ap (Ap (Ap (Ap (S, K), K), q), y))
run1 (Ap1 (Ap1 (Ap1 (K1, b), q), y)) = run (Ap (Ap (Ap (K, b), q), y))
run1 (Ap1 (Ap1 (Ap1 (S1, b), q), y)) = run (Ap (Ap (Ap (S, b), q), y))
run1 (Ap1 (Ap1 (Ap1 (I, b), q), y)) =
    run (Ap (Ap (Ap (Ap (Ap (S, K), K), b), q), y))
run1 (Ap1 (Ap1 (Ap1 (Ap1 (c, d), b), q), y)) =
    run (Ap (Ap (Ap (Ap (c, d), b), q), y))
```

At this point, all the calls to `run` can be (and are) unfolded, in some cases
repeatedly:

```
run1 K1 = K
run1 S1 = S
run1 I = Ap (Ap (S, K), K)
run1 (Ap1 (K1, y)) = Ap (K, run y)
run1 (Ap1 (S1, y)) = Ap (S, run y)
run1 (Ap1 (I, y)) = run y
run1 (Ap1 (Ap1 (K1, q), y)) = run q
run1 (Ap1 (Ap1 (S1, q), y)) = Ap (Ap (S, run q), run y)
run1 (Ap1 (Ap1 (I, q), y)) = run (Ap (q, y))
```

```
run1 (Ap1 (Ap1 (Ap1 (K1, b), q), y)) = run (Ap (b, y))
run1 (Ap1 (Ap1 (Ap1 (S1, b), q), y)) = run (Ap (Ap (b, y), Ap (q, y)))
run1 (Ap1 (Ap1 (Ap1 (I, b), q), y)) = run (Ap (Ap (b, q), y))
run1 (Ap1 (Ap1 (Ap1 (Ap1 (c, d), b), q), y)) =
   run (Ap (run (Ap (Ap (Ap (c, d), b), q)), y))
```

We can now fold using the definitions in *Cs* and *Fs*:

```
run1 K1 = K1
run1 S1 = S1
run1 I = I
run1 (Ap1 (K1, y)) = Ap1 (K1, run y)
run1 (Ap1 (S1, y)) = Ap1 (S1, run y)
run1 (Ap1 (I, y)) = run1 y
run1 (Ap1 (Ap1 (K1, q), y)) = run1 q
run1 (Ap1 (Ap1 (S1, q), y)) = Ap1 (Ap1 (S1, run q), run y)
run1 (Ap1 (Ap1 (I, q), y)) = run1 (Ap1 (q, y))
run1 (Ap1 (Ap1 (Ap1 (K1, b), q), y)) = run1 (Ap1 (b, y))
run1 (Ap1 (Ap1 (Ap1 (S1, b), q), y)) = run1 (Ap1 (Ap1 (b, y), Ap1 (q, y)))
run1 (Ap1 (Ap1 (Ap1 (I, b), q), y)) = run1 (Ap1 (Ap1 (b, q), y))
run1 (Ap1 (Ap1 (Ap1 (Ap1 (c, d), b), q), y)) =
   run1 (Ap1 (run1 (Ap1 (Ap1 (Ap1 (c, d), b), q)), y))
```

These rules are added to P_1, and since nothing was added to *Fs* or *Cs*, we are done. The resulting program (which includes the declaration of the SKI datatype from above) is a natural extension of the original interpreter to include the *I* combinator with the reduction rule $I\ x \to x$.

5.2   A Lambda-Calculus Reducer

The example above did not add new constructors to any datatype during the transformation, so we will now show an, admittedly somewhat contrived, example that does that. We first define a datatype for lambda expressions that uses De Bruijn indexes [1] instead of named variables and two mutually recursive datatypes to represent closures and environments:

```
data expr = Lam expr | App (expr, expr) | Var index
data index = Z | S index
data closure = C (expr, env)
data env = Em | Bind (closure, env)
```

Since an environment is just a list of closures, we can use the same datatype for a stack of closures. The lambda reducer is based on Krivine's abstract machine [10]:

```
run e = do (e, Em, Em)

do (Lam e, r, Em) = C (e, r)
do (Lam e, r, Bind (c, s)) = do (e, Bind (c, r), s)
do (App (f, e), r, s) = do (f, r, Bind (C (e, r), s))
do (Var i, r, s) = look (i, r, s)

look (Z, Bind (C (e, r1), r), s) = do (e, r1, s)
look (S i, Bind (c, r), s) = look (i, r, s)
```

We will now specialise the reducer to expressions of the form $f\ (\lambda x.x\ x)$, where f is an unknown expression. We do this by initialising Fs (and F) with the definition

```
run1 f = run (App(f, Lam (Var Z, Var Z)))
```

We only want to specialise closures, so we copy the other datatypes unchanged to P_1 while creating an empty datatype definition for a renamed closure datatype called closure1.

Our strategy for folding will be to specialise the closure-building constructor C with respect to its expression argument. We start by unfolding the call to run a couple of times:

```
run1 f = do (f, Em, Bind (C (Lam (App (Var Z, Var Z)), Em), Em))
```

We now fold to the definition run1 f = do1(f, Em, Bind(C1 Em, Em)), which adds the following definitions to Fs and Cs, respectively:

```
do1 (f, r, s) = do (f, r, s)
C1 r = C (Lam (App (Var Z, Var Z)), r)
```

We now transform the definition of do1 by special-casing and unfolding:

```
do1 (Lam e, r, Em) = C (e, r)
do1 (Lam e, r, Bind (c, s)) = do (e, Bind (c, r), s)
do1 (App (f, e), r, s) = do (f, r, Bind (C (e, r), s))
do1 (Var i, r, s) = look (i, r, s)
```

We fold this to

```
do1 (Lam e, r, Em) = C2 (e, r)
do1 (Lam e, r, Bind (c, s)) = do1 (e, Bind (c, r), s)
do1 (App (f, e), r, s) = do1 (f, r, Bind (C2 (e, r), s))
do1 (Var i, r, s) = look1 (i, r, s)
```

while adding the definitions

```
look1 (i, r, s) = look (i, r, s)
C2 (e, r) = C (e, r)
```

While transforming the definition for look1, we special-case on the new closure constructors:

```
look1 (Z, Bind (C1 r1, r), s) = do (Lam (App (Var Z, Var Z)), r1, s)
look1 (Z, Bind (C2 (e, r1), r), s) = do (e, r1, s)
look1 (S i, Bind (c, r), s) = look (i, r, s)
```

We fold this to

```
look1 (Z, Bind (C1 r1, r), s) = do2 (r1, s)
look1 (Z, Bind (C2 (e, r1), r), s) = do1 (e, r1, s)
look1 (S i, Bind (c, r), s) = look1 (i, r, s)
```

which adds the definition do2 (r, s) = do (Lam (App (Var Z, Var Z)), r, s) to *Fs*. We transform do2 by special-casing on the stack s and unfolding:

```
do2 (r, Em) = C (Lam (App (Var Z, Var Z)), r)
do2 (r, Bind (c, s1)) = look (Z, Bind (c, r), Bind (C (Var Z, Bind (c, r)), s1))
```

We fold this to

```
do2 (r, Em) = C1 r
do2 (r, Bind (c, s1)) = look1 (Z, Bind (c, r), Bind (C3 (Bind (c, r)), s1))
```

which adds the definition C3 r = C (Var Z, r) to *Cs*. Since this adds more constructors to the new closure datatype, the definition of look1 in the transformed program is incomplete, so we must remove this and redo the transformation. The redone transformation recreates the rules for look1 shown above[2] and adds one more special case:

```
look1 (Z, Bind (C3 r1, r), s) = do (Var Z, r1, s)
```

which transforms to

```
look1 (Z, Bind (C3 r1, r), s) = look1 (Z, r1, s)
```

Since the transformed program is now complete with respect to all definitions in *Fs* and *Cs*, we are done and end up with the following transformed program (omitting the unchanged datatype definitions):

```
datatype closure1 = C1 env | C2 (exp, env) | C3 env

run1 f = do1(f, Em, Bind(C1 Em, Em))

do1 (Lam e, r, Em) = C2 (e, r)
do1 (Lam e, r, Bind (c, s)) = do1 (e, Bind (c, r), s)
do1 (App (f, e), r, s) = do1 (f, r, Bind (C2 (e, r), s))
do1 (Var i, r, s) = look1 (i, r, s)

do2 (r, Em) = C1 r
do2 (r, Bind (c, s)) = look1 (Z, Bind (c, r), Bind (C3 (Bind (c, r)), s))

look1 (Z, Bind (C1 r1, r), s) = do2 (r1, s)
look1 (Z, Bind (C2 (e, r1), r), s) = do1 (e, r1, s)
look1 (Z, Bind (C3 r1, r), s) = look1 (Z, r1, s)
look1 (S i, Bind (c, r), s) = look1 (i, r, s)
```

Note that the result of run1 is of type closure1. If we want to see the result of evaluation in terms of the original type closure, we must apply the definitions in *Cs*:

---

[2] If a cache of transformed rules is used, they can just be copied from this.

```
C1 r = C (Lam (App (Var Z, Var Z)), r)
C2 (e, r) = C (e, r)
C3 r = C (Var Z, r)
```

to all occurrences of the new constructors in the output of the transformed program.

6 Conclusion

The suggested method overcomes a current limitation of supercompilation: Datatypes are unchanged by supercompilation. We do this by combining groups of constructor applications to single constructor applications in a way that is analogous to how supercompilation combines groups of function calls to single function calls.

Supercompilation for datatypes can reduce the number of constructor applications and destructions in the transformed program compared to normal supercompilation. For example, normal supercompilation can not achieve an effect similar to the optimised extension of the SK-combinator reducer to include the I combinator.

One issue with the method is that a transformed function definition does not have the same type as the original. For example, the input and output of the SKI-reducer are of a different type than the input and output of the SK-reducer. This may not be a problem if the new type (as in this example) is completely specified before the transformation, so the user of the transformed program knows the meaning of the new constructors, but if the transformation invents new constructors, these need to be related to the original.

The constructor definitions in Cs can be used to translate input and output of the transformed program from and to the original types, so the transformed program can be used in a context that uses and expects the original types. But in some cases it can be an advantage to use the transformed types without translation. For example, the SKI reducer is not useful unless the I combinator is used in the input, and it is natural to expect the I combinator in the output.

Consider, also, two programs p and q running as a pipeline: The output of p becomes the input to q. If p is supercompiled, the definitions in Cs for the output type of p can be used to transform q. In essence, q is specialised to the transformed output type of p. For example, assume p is a translator from a high-level language into an abstract machine M having a set of small instructions defined by a datatype. Transforming p can transform the abstract machine-code datatype into a new datatype where each constructor corresponds to a sequence of instructions from the original abstract machine. If q is an interpreter for M, transforming q with respect to the definitions of the modified datatype will construct an interpreter for this modified abstract machine. Essentially, a new abstract machine is "invented" by the supercompilation process. This is analogous to the process used in [9] to "invent" a Prolog abstract machine.

6.1 Future Work

The method described in this paper has not been implemented in an actual supercompiler, so this remains to do. There is also a need for a more formal definition of the relation between the original and the transformed program, including a formal correctness criterion.

A limitation of the described method is that each original datatype is transformed into a single new datatype. It can happen that some specialised constructors can only occur in some contexts within the transformed program, so it might be advantageous to split the single transformed datatype into two or more disjoint datatypes. This can avoid special-casing a function on constructors that can not actually ever occur as arguments to this function. Avoiding this can lead to shorter transformed programs. The analogous issue for constructor specialisation is discussed in [13] and partially solved in [2]. Not that the transformation described in [6], though called "constructor specialisation", does not specialise constructors, but functions to constructor patterns. Hence, it is not directly related to the constructor specialisations described in [2,13], but rather to specialisation of functions to partially static structures [11] or to traditional supercompilation [3–5,7,8,15–18].

References

1. de Bruijn, N.G.: Lambda calculus notation with nameless dummies, a tool for automatic formula manipulation, with application to the church-rosser theorem. Indagationes Math. (Proc.) **75**(5), 381–392 (1972)
2. Dussart, D., Bevers, E., De Vlaminck, K.: Polyvariant constructor specialisation. In: Proceedings of ACM Conference on Partial Evaluation and Program Manipulation, pp. 546–5 (1995)
3. Glück, R., Klimov, A.V.: Klimov. Occam's razor in metacomputation: the notion of a perfect process tree. In: Cousot, P., Falaschi, M., Filé, G., Rauzy, A. (eds.) Static Analysis. LNCS, vol. 724, pp. 112–123. Springer, Berlin Heidelberg (1993)
4. Glück, R., Sørensen, M.H.: A roadmap to metacomputation by supercompilation. In: Danvy, O., Thiemann, P., Glück, R. (eds.) Dagstuhl Seminar 1996. LNCS, vol. 1110, pp. 137–160. Springer, Heidelberg (1996)
5. Hamilton, G.W.: Distillation: extracting the essence of programs. In: Proceedings of the 2007 ACM SIGPLAN Symposium On Partial Evaluation And Semantics-based Program Manipulation, PEPM 2007, pp. 61–70. ACM, New York (2007)
6. Jones, S.L.P.: Call-pattern specialisation for haskell programs. In: Hinze, R., Ramsey, N. (eds.) ICFP, pp. 327–337. ACM (2007)
7. Klimov, A.V.: Solving coverability problem for monotonic counter systems by supercompilation. In: Clarke, E., Virbitskaite, I., Voronkov, A. (eds.) PSI 2011. LNCS, vol. 7162, pp. 193–209. Springer, Heidelberg (2012)
8. Klyuchnikov, I., Romanenko, S.: Proving the equivalence of higher-order terms by means of supercompilation. In: Pnueli, A., Virbitskaite, I., Voronkov, A. (eds.) PSI 2009. LNCS, vol. 5947, pp. 193–205. Springer, Heidelberg (2010)
9. Kursawe, P.: How to invent a prolog machine. New Gener. Comput. **5**, 97–114 (1987). doi:10.1007/BF03037460

10. Krivine, J.L.: A call-by-name lambda-calculus machine. In Higher Order and Symbolic Computation, (2004)

11. Mogensen, T.: Partially static structures in a self-applicable partial evaluator. In: Bjorner, D., Ershov, A.P., Jones, N.D. (eds.) Partial Eval. Mixed Comput., pp. 325–347. North-Holland, Amsterdam (1988)

12. Mogensen,T.Æ. Constructor specialization. In: Partial Evaluation and Semantics-Based Program Manipulation (PEPM 1993), pp. 22–32. ACM, New York (1993)

13. Mogensen, T.Æ.: Evolution of partial evaluators: removing inherited limits. In: Danvy, O., Thiemann, P., Glück, R. (eds.) Dagstuhl Seminar 1996. LNCS, vol. 1110. Springer, Heidelberg (1996)

14. Mogensen, T.Æ.: A comparison of well-quasi orders on trees. Electron. Proc. Theor. Comput. Sci. **129**, 30–40 (2013)

15. Nemytykh, A.P.: The Supercompiler SCP4: general structure. In: Broy, M., Zamulin, A.V. (eds.) PSI 2003. LNCS, vol. 2890, pp. 162–170. Springer, Heidelberg (2004)

16. Sorensen, M.H., Glück, R., Jones, N.D.: A positive supercompiler. J. Funct. Program. **6**, 465–479 (1993)

17. Turchin, V.F.: A supercompiler system based on the language refal. SIGPLAN Not. **14**(2), 46–54 (1979)

18. Turchin, V.F.: The concept of a supercompiler. ACM Trans. Program. Lang. Syst. **8**(3), 292–325 (1986)

More Type Inference in Java 8

Martin Plümicke[(✉)]

Department of Computer Science, Baden-Wuerttemberg Cooperative
State University Stuttgart, Florianstraße 15, 72160 Horb, Germany
pl@dhbw.de

Abstract. Java is extended in version eight by lambda expressions and
functional interfaces, where functional interfaces are interfaces with one
method. Functional interfaces represent the types of lambda expressions.
The type inference mechanism will be extended, such that the types of
the parameters of lambda expressions can be inferred. But types of complete lambda expressions will still not be inferable. In this paper we give
a type inference algorithm for complete lambda expressions. This means
that fields, local variables, as well as parameters and return types of
lambda expressions do not have to be typed explicitly.

We therefore define for a core of Java 8 an abstract syntax and formalize the functional interfaces. Finally, we give the type inference algorithm.

Keywords: Java · Language design · Type system · Type inference

1 Introduction

In the Project lambda[1] a new version (version 8) of Java has been developed. The
most important goal is to introduce programming patterns that allow modeling
code as data [1]. The version includes the new features *lambda expressions, functional interfaces as target types, method and constructor references* and *default
methods*. An essential enhancement is the introduction of lambda expressions.
The following example from [1] illustrates lambda expressions.

Example 1.

```
(int x, int y) -> x + y
() -> 42
(String s) -> System.out.println(s);
```

The first expression takes two integer arguments, named x and y, and returns
their sum. The second takes no arguments and returns the integer 42, while the
third takes a string and prints it to the console, returning nothing.

In Java 8 lambda expressions have no explicit types. Instead, they are type-
checked using *target types* taken from syntactic context. Functional interfaces,
interfaces with only one abstract method, are used as target types. Target types
of the above examples could be

---

[1] http://openjdk.java.net/projects/lambda.

© Springer-Verlag Berlin Heidelberg 2015
A. Voronkov and I. Virbitskaite (Eds.): PSI 2014, LNCS 8974, pp. 248–256, 2015.
DOI: 10.1007/978-3-662-46823-4_20

```
interface intOp { int op (int x, int y); }
interface retInt { int ret (); }
interface stringVoid { void put (String s); }
```

The reason for this construction is that Java's library contains many interfaces that merely serve to specify callbacks. Lambda expressions implement such interfaces. This is a very convenient abbreviation for an anonymous inner class, which needed to be used in Java until version 7. E.g. in Java 8 it is possible to write: `Callable<String> c = () -> "done";`

This approach has, however, some disadvantages, the first is the type of the lambda expression is deduced from the context. In the above example `Callable<String>`. But in another context the same lambda expression might get a completely different type, e.g. `PrivilegedAction<String> a = () -> "done";` Secondly, types can be deduced from the context but the lambda expression itself has no explicit type. This means for a declaration `c = () -> "done";` no type can be inferred.

Third, types cannot even be deduced for all contexts. E.g. for

$$\text{Object } o = ()->\{\text{System.out.println}(``\text{hi"});\};$$

no type can be determined, as `Object` is no functional interface.

In this paper we present an approach where all lambda expressions have unambiguous types that are inferred automatically. This approach solves all highlighted problems, by the three following steps:

1. We collect all correct deducible functional interfaces for a lambda expression in an equivalence class.
2. We introduce a canonical functional interface as a representative of each equivalence class, which is defined as the explicit type of the lambda expression.
3. We give a type inference algorithm that determines the respective canonical interfaces.

Beyond circumventing the mentioned restrictions of target types the algorithm also allows us to write Java 8 programs without any type declarations. All types are determined by the type inference algorithm. Let us consider the following example:

```
interface Fun1<R,T1> { R apply(T1 arg1); }
interface Fun2<R,T1,T2> { R apply(T1 arg1, T2 arg2); }

class Matrix extends Vector<Vector<Integer>> {

  Fun1<Fun1<Matrix, Fun2<Matrix, Matrix,Matrix>>, Matrix>
  op = (m) -> (f) -> f.apply(this, m); }
```

`op` takes first a matrix resulting in a function. This function takes another function which has as arguments two matrices and returns another matrix. The resulting type `Fun1<Fun1<Matrix, Fun2<Matrix,Matrix,Matrix>>, Matrix>` is not obvious.

$$
\begin{aligned}
source &:= class* \\
class &:= \mathsf{Class}(type, [\ \mathsf{extends}(\ type\ ),]\ fielddecl*) \\
fielddecl &:= \mathsf{Field}(\ [\boldsymbol{type},]var[,expr]\ ) \\
block &:= \mathsf{Block}(\ stmt*) \\
stmt &:= block\ |\ \mathsf{Return}(\ expr\ )\ |\ \mathsf{While}(\ bexpr, stmt\ )\ |\ \mathsf{LocalVarDecl}(\ [\boldsymbol{type},]var\ ) \\
&\quad\ |\ \mathsf{If}(\ bexpr, stmt[, stmt]\ )\ |\ \mathsf{EmptyStmt}\ |\ stmtexpr \\
lambdaexpr &:= \mathsf{Lambda}(\ ((var[:\ \boldsymbol{type}]))*, (stmt\ |\ expr)\ ) \\
stmtexpr &:= \mathsf{Assign}(\ vexpr, expr\ )\ |\ \mathsf{MethodCall}(\ iexpr, \mathtt{apply}, expr*)\ |\ \mathsf{New}(\ type\ ) \\
vexpr &:= \mathsf{LocalVar}(\ var\ )\ |\ \mathsf{InstVar}(\ iexpr, var\ ) \\
iexpr &:= vexpr\ |\ stmtexpr\ |\ \mathsf{Cast}(\ type, iexpr\ )\ |\ \mathtt{this}\ |\ \mathtt{super} \\
expr &:= lambdaexpr\ |\ iexp\ |\ bexp\ |\ sexp^3
\end{aligned}
$$

Fig. 1. The abstract syntax of a core of Java 8

E.g. `Fun1<Fun1<aapp, Fun2<a3, Vector<? extends Vector<Integer>>, a2>>, am>`
is also a correct type. We will see in Sect. 3 that both types are not principal. Our
type inference algorithm would allow to leave out the type and determine principal
types, automatically.

In [2] we have presented for an earlier version of Java with lambda expressions
[3] that we have called Java$_\lambda$, a type inference algorithm. This algorithm has been
oriented at [4]. The main problem of [4] is that the results are *well-typings*[2],
which are not contained in the Java type system.

The new algorithm, presented in this paper, solves this problem, as its result
is a set of typed Java programs. This is done by replacing the function **MATCH**,
SIMPLIFY and **CONSISTENT** by our type unification [5].

This improvement is supported by the property, that real function types,
included in Java$_\lambda$, becomes in Java 8 functional interfaces Fun$N$ [6].[3]

The paper is structured as follows. In Sect. 2 we define the abstract syntax
for a core of Java 8 and present a formal definition for the inferred functional
interfaces. In Sect. 3 we give the type inference algorithm. In Sect. 4 we consider
related work. Finally, in Sect. 5 we close with a summary and an outlook.

2   The Language

2.1   Abstract Syntax

The language (Fig. 1) we treat in this paper is an abstract representation of a
core of Java 8. The new feature is the lambda expressions. A lambda expression
is an anonymous function and consists of optionally typed parameters and either
a statement or an expression.

---

[2] A well-typing is a conditional type for an expression, where the conditions are given
by a set of consistent coercions (constraints).

[3] *sexp* and *bexp* stands for simple and boolean expressions, which are expressions of
the base types `int` and `boolean`, respectively.

For the purpose of this paper we reduce Java 8 by omitting exceptions and without loss of generality by omitting method declarations and overloading.

The concrete syntax in this paper of the lambda expressions is oriented at [1].

The optional type annotations [*type*] are the types, which can be inferred by our type inference algorithm.

2.2 Canonical Representatives of Functional Interfaces

In this section we introduce a collection of standard functional interfaces into Java 8, which can simulate function types.

First, we define the equivalence of two functional interfaces.

Definition 1 (Equivalent functional interfaces). *Two functional interfaces are equivalent (in sign: $\sim_{fi}$) if for its single methods holds:*

- *The number of arguments are equal and its types are either equal or if they are functional interfaces, they are equivalent*
- *The result types are equal or if they are functional interfaces, they are equivalent*

Lemma 1. *The relation $\sim_{fi}$ is an equivalence relation.*

Finally, we will introduce the following collection of interfaces into Java 8.

Definition 2 (Interface Fun$N$). *The language* Java 8 *is extended for all N by*

interface Fun$N <$ R, T1 $, \ldots,$ T$N >$ { R apply(T1 arg1 $, \ldots,$ TN arg$N$); }

This leads directly to the following theorem.

Theorem 1 (Canonical representative). *For each functional interface there is an unique N, such that an instance of* Fun$N$ *is an equivalent functional interface. This instance is called* canonical representative *of the equivalence class of functional interfaces.*

Example 2. The canonical representative of the compatible types of the lambda expression () -> "done" from the introduction is Fun0<String>.

3 Type Inference

The base of many type inference algorithms is the algorithm $\mathcal{W}$ that was presented by Damas and Milner [7]. The fundamental idea of the algorithm is to determine types by type term unification [8]. In [9] we have presented a type inference algorithm for Java5.0 which is based on $\mathcal{W}$ and our type unification algorithm for Java5.0 types [5]. In [2] we have presented a type inference algorithm for Java$_\lambda$ which is based on the type inference algorithm that was presented by Fuh and Mishra [4] for a λ–calculus with subtyping. Our contribution in this paper is a new type inference algorithm, which is an improvement of [2]: First, the well-typings from [4] are replaced by Java types. Secondly, the algorithm is adapted to Java 8's type system extended by the functional interfaces Fun$N$. Finally, our type unification [5] replaces three unwieldy functions.

The type inference algorithm for core Java 8 determines for each declared field respectively its defining expression a principal type.

First, we define the argument and result types of **TYPE** and **SOLVE**:

Set of type assumptions TypeAssumptions: contains two different forms of elements:
  $v : \theta$: Assumptions for fields or local variables of the actual class.
  $\tau.v : \theta$: Assumptions for fields of the class τ.
Set of Java classes, expressions and statements Class, Expr, Stmt: contains respectively all core Java 8 elements as defined in Fig. 1.
Set of constraints ConstraintsSet: contains pairs of types $ty_1 \lessdot ty_2$, and $ty_1 \doteq ty_2$, which declares the conditions that ty_1 must be a subtype of ty_2 respectively ty_1 must be equal to ty_2.

Additionally, there are the sets TClass, TExpr and TStmt, which means that in the respective Java elements all expressions and statements are type annotated.

In the following we define the functions **TYPE** and **SOLVE**. F inally, we give the whole algorithm **TI**. We present the algorithms in a functional style.

The Function TYPE. The function **TYPE** inserts type annotations, widely type variables as placeholders, in the Java class and determines a set of type constraints.

TYPE: TypeAssumptions $\times$ Class $\to$ TClass $\times$ ConstraintsSet
TYPE(Ass, Class(τ, extends(τ'), $fdecls$)) = **let**

  $\underline{fdecls} = [\text{Field}(f_1, lexpr_1), \dots, \text{Field}(f_n, lexpr_n)]^4$
  $\underline{ftypeass} = \{\, \text{this}.f_i : a_i \mid a_i \text{ fresh type variables} \,\}$

  $\qquad\qquad \cup \{\, \text{this} : \tau, \text{super} : \tau' \,\} \cup \{\, visible \; types \; fields \; of \; \tau' \,\}$
  $\underline{AssAll} = Ass \cup ftypeass$
  Forall $1 \leqslant i \leqslant n : (lexp_{i_t} : rtyF_i, ConSF_i) = \textbf{TYPEExpr}(AssAll, lexpr_i)$
  $\underline{fdecls_t} = [\text{Field}(a_1, f_1, lexpr_{1_t} : rtyF_1), \dots, \text{Field}(a_n, f_n, lexpr_{n_t} : rtyF_n)]$

  in(Class(τ, extends(τ'), $fdecls_t$), $(\bigcup_i ConSF_i \cup \{\, (rtyF_i \lessdot a_i) \mid 1 \leqslant i \leqslant n \,\}))$

The function **TYPEExpr** is given as:

TYPEExpr: TypeAssumptions $\times$ Expr $\to$ TExpr $\times$ ConstraintsSet
TYPEExpr(Ass, Lambda($(x_1, \dots, x_N), expr|stmt$)) =
  let $AssArgs = \{\, x_i : a_i \mid a_i \text{ fresh type variables} \,\}$
  $\quad \underline{(expr_t : rty, ConS)} = \textbf{TYPEExpr}(Ass \cup AssArgs, expr)$
  $\mid \underline{(stmt_t : rty, ConS)} = \textbf{TYPEStmt}(Ass \cup AssArgs, stmt)$
  in (Lambda($(x_1 : a_1, \dots, x_N : a_N), expr_t : rty | stmt_t : rty$) : Fun$N$<$a, a_1, \dots, a_N$>,
  $\quad ConS) \cup \{\, rty \lessdot a) \,\}$), *where a is a fresh type variable*

---

4 We assume without loss of generality that all fields are declared typeless and that all fields are initialized by expressions.

TYPEExpr$(\textit{Ass}, \mathsf{Assign}(\textit{ve}, e)) =$
  let $\underline{(e_t : rty_2, ConS_2)} = \mathbf{TYPEExpr}(\textit{Ass}, e)$
    $\overline{(\textit{ve}_t : rty_1, ConS_1)} = \mathbf{TYPEExpr}(\textit{Ass}, \textit{ve})$
  in $\overline{(\mathsf{Assign}(\textit{ve}_t : rty_1, e_t : rty_2) : rty_1, ConS_1} \cup ConS_2 \cup \{(rty_2 \lessdot rty_1)\})$

TYPEExpr$(\textit{Ass}, \mathsf{MethodCall}(\textit{re}, \mathsf{apply}, (e_1, \ldots, e_n))) =$
  let $\underline{(\textit{re}_t : rty, ConS)} = \mathbf{TYPEExpr}(\textit{Ass}, \textit{re})$
    $\overline{(e_{i_t} : rty_i, ConS_i)} = \mathbf{TYPEExpr}(\textit{Ass}, e_i), \forall 1 \leqslant i \leqslant n$
  in $(\mathsf{MethodCall}(\textit{re}_t : rty, \mathsf{apply}, (e_{1_t} : rty_1, \ldots, e_{n_t} : rty_n))) : a,$
    $(ConS \cup \bigcup_i ConS_i) \cup \{rty \doteq \mathsf{FunN}{<}a, a_1, \ldots, a_N{>}\}$
    $\cup \{rty_i \lessdot a_i \mid 1 \leqslant i \leqslant N\}$
    where $a_1, \ldots, a_N$ *and* a *are fresh type variables*

TYPEExpr$(\textit{Ass}, \mathsf{LocalVar}(v)) = \mathbf{let} \ (v : \theta) \in \textit{Ass} \ \mathbf{in} \ (\mathsf{LocalVar}(v) : \theta, \emptyset)$

TYPEExpr$(\textit{Ass}, \mathsf{InstVar}(\textit{re}, v)) =$

  $\mathbf{let}(rty, ConS) = \mathbf{TYPEExpr}(\textit{Ass}, \textit{re})$
  $\mathbf{in} \ (\mathsf{InstVar}(\textit{re} : rty, v) : \tilde{\theta}, \ ConS \cup \{\{(rty \doteq \tau)\}\}), \textit{where } \tau.v : \theta \in \textit{Ass}$
  and $\tilde{\theta} = \theta, \ \textit{if } \tau = \mathbf{ass}(\mathsf{this})^5, \ \textit{otherwise } \tilde{\theta} = \mathbf{fresh}(\theta)^6$

We omit the remaining cases of **TYPEExpr** for New, Cast, This and Super and the **TYPEStmt** rules. These are given analogously.

Example 3. We consider again the method op of the class `Matrix` from the introduction.

```
class Matrix extends Vector<Vector<Integer>> {
  op = (m) -> (f) -> f.apply(this, m);
}
```

In **TYPE** the function **TYPEExpr** is called with the arguments:
$AssAll = \{\texttt{this.op} : a_{\mathrm{op}}, \texttt{this} : \texttt{Matrix}, \texttt{super} : \texttt{Vector<Vector<Integer>>}\}$
$lexpr_1 = \mathsf{Lam}(\texttt{m}, \mathsf{Lam}(\texttt{f}, \mathsf{MCall}(\mathsf{LoVar}(\texttt{f}), \mathsf{apply}, (\textit{this}, \mathsf{LoVar}(\texttt{m}))))).$

The result consists of the typed lambda expression:
$lexpr_{1_t} =$
  $\mathsf{Lam}(\texttt{m} : a_m,$
    $\mathsf{Lam}(\texttt{f} : a_f,$
      $\mathsf{MCall}(\mathsf{LoVar}(\texttt{f}) : a_f,$
        $\mathsf{apply}, (\textit{this} : \texttt{Matrix},$
          $\mathsf{LoVar}(\texttt{m}) : a_m)) : a_3) : \mathsf{Fun1}{<}a_{app}, a_f{>}) : \mathsf{Fun1}{<}a_{\lambda f}, a_m{>}$
and the set of constraints:
$\{(\mathsf{Fun1}{<}a_{\lambda f}, a_m{>} \lessdot a_{\mathrm{op}}), (\mathsf{Fun1}{<}a_{app}, a_f{>} \lessdot a_{\lambda f}), (a_f \doteq \mathsf{Fun2}{<}a_3, a_1, a_2{>}),$
$(\texttt{Matrix} \lessdot a_1), (a_m \lessdot a_2), (a_3 \lessdot a_{app})\}.$

---

[5] The function $\mathbf{ass}(\mathsf{this})$ gives the type assumption of the actual class.
[6] The function **fresh** refreshes the type variables.

The Function SOLVE. The function **SOLVE** determines the solutions of the set of constraints. In **SOLVE** the type unification **TUnify** from [5] is called. There are two cases of results of the type unification. Either the results are in solved form, which means that all instances of the remaining type variables are correct solutions. Otherwise, besides the solutions there are remaining constraints of the form $a\,R\,a'$, where a and a' are type variables. In this case all instances of type variables are correct, if they fulfill these constraints.

SOLVE: `ConstraintsSet` $\rightarrow$ `ConstraintsSet`
SOLVE(ConS) = let $\underline{subs}$ = **TUnify**(ConS) **in**
   if (there are $\sigma \in subs$ in solved form) **then**
      $\{\,c \in subs \mid c$ is in solved form $\}$
   if (there are $\sigma \in subs$, which has the form
      $\{\,v\,R\,v' \mid v, v'$ are type vars $\} \cup \{\,v \doteq \theta \mid v$ is a type var $\})$ **then**
      $\{\,c \in subs \mid c$ has the given form $\}$
   else *fail*

Finally, both functions **TYPE** and **SOLVE** are combined to the type inference algorithm by the function **TI**.

The Type Inference Algorithm TI. The type inference algorithm for Java 8 **TI** calls first the function **TYPE**. The function **TYPE** inserts type annotations, widely type variables as placeholders, in the Java class and determines a set of type constraints. Secondly, the function **SOLVE** solves the type constraints by type unification. Finally, the set of substitutions, which are results of **SOLVE**, are applied to the type annotated Java class. The result of **TI** is a set of pairs of a remaining set of constraints and a typed Java 8 class.

TI: `TypeAssumptions` $\times$ `Class` $\rightarrow \{\,(\texttt{Constraints}, \texttt{TClass})\,\}$

TI$(\mathit{Ass}, \mathsf{Class}(\tau, \mathsf{extends}(\tau'), \mathit{fdecls})) =$
   let $\underline{(\mathsf{Class}(\tau, \mathsf{extends}(\tau'), \mathit{fdecls_t}), \mathit{ConS})} =$
      TYPE$(\mathit{Ass}, \mathsf{Class}(\tau, \mathsf{extends}(\tau'), \mathit{fdecls}))$
      $\{\,(cs_1, \sigma_1), \ldots, (cs_n, \sigma_n)\,\} =$ **SOLVE**(ConS)
   in $\{\,(cs_i, \sigma_i(\mathsf{Class}(\tau, \mathsf{extends}(\tau'), \mathit{fdecls_t})))\mid 1 \leqslant i \leqslant n\,\}$

The result of **TI** is a set of typed Java 8 classes with constraints. As Java allows only a restricted form of type constraints (bounded type parameters), either this mechanisms must be extended such any constraint of cs_i could be given, or the elements of cs_i must be set equal, which means that the result is less general.

Example 4. We continue Example 3. The set of constraints was given as:

$$\mathit{ConS} = \{\,(\texttt{Fun1}<a_{\lambda f}, a_m> \lessdot a_{\mathrm{op}}), (\texttt{Fun1}<a_{app}, a_f> \lessdot a_{\lambda f}),$$
$$(a_f \doteq \texttt{Fun2}<a_3, a_1, a_2>), (\texttt{Matrix} \lessdot a_1), (a_m \lessdot a_2), (a_3 \lessdot a_{app})\,\}$$

With step 4 of **TUnify** we get:

$$\{\{a_{op} \doteq \mathtt{Fun1}{<}a_{\lambda f}, a_m{>}, a_{\lambda f} \doteq \mathtt{Fun1}{<}a_{app}, a_f{>}, a_f \doteq \mathtt{Fun2}{<}a_3, a_1, a_2{>},$$
$$a_1 \doteq X, a_m \lessdot a_2, a_3 \lessdot a_{app}\} \mid \mathtt{Matrix} \ is \ a \ subtype \ of \ X\}$$

With step 5 (subst) and step 6 of **TUnify** we get:

$$\{ \ (\ \{ \ a_m \lessdot a_2, a_3 \lessdot a_{app} \},$$
$$\{ \ a_{op} \doteq \mathtt{Fun1}{<}\mathtt{Fun1}{<}a_{app}, \mathtt{Fun2}{<}a_3, X, a_2{>>}, a_m{>},$$
$$a_{\lambda f} \doteq \mathtt{Fun1}{<}a_{app}, \mathtt{Fun2}{<}a_3, X, a_2{>>},$$
$$a_f \doteq \mathtt{Fun2}{<}a_3, X, a_2{>}, a_1 \doteq X\})\} \mid \mathtt{Matrix} \ \text{is a subtype of} \ X\}$$

The results of **SOLVE** applied to the result program of **TYPE** gives the result set:

```
{ class Matrix extends Vector<Vector<Integer>> {
    <a2, aapp, am extends a2, a3 extends aapp>⁷
    Fun1<Fun1<aapp, Fun2<a3, X,a2>>, am>
    op = (m) -> (f) -> f.apply(this, m); }      | Matrix is a subtype of X }
```

If we compare this result with the example in the introduction we see that the types are more general.

4   Related Work

The programming language Scala [10] allows functional programming features. In addition to Java, Scala allows real function types as in our Java$_\lambda$ [2], currying and pattern-matching.

Scala contains, however, a type-inference system. But in comparison to our approach, the type-inference system is restricted to *local type inference*. For complete lambda expressions and recursive methods, it is not possible to infer the complete types.

In C# (e.g. [11]) lambda expressions are also included. Function types are given as *delegates*. A delegate defines a type that encapsulates a method with argument types and a return type. A delegate plays the role of functional interfaces in Java 8. In C# there is no type inference.

In C++11 [12] there are also lambda expressions. There is a possibility to leave out type declarations by using the predefined keyword auto. In some cases then the types can be inferred automatically.

5   Conclusion and Future Work

We have presented a type inference algorithm for a core of Java 8 that allows to write Java programs without any type annotation. The types are determined by the type inference algorithm.

---

[7] The constraints are here given as bounded type variables for fields, which is in original Java only allowed for methods.

This extension simplifies Java programming as complex and confusing type annotations with functional interfaces and wildcards are not longer necessary.

The central point is the treatment of lambda expressions. Here, for lambda expressions a canonical representative functional interface is inferred that is equivalent to all other compatible target types of the lambda expression.

The canonical representative fits into Java 8 smoothly. In original Java 8, lambda expressions have no explicit type. Now the lambda expressions have the canonical representatives as types. In Java 8, for a lambda expression the type checker must check if it is compatible to the context type. Now the type checker must check if the inferred type of the lambda expression is equivalent to the context type. This check is normally much easier, as the argument and the result types of the lambda expression are already determined.

In future work, we plan to extend the principal type property from expressions to Java methods in the sense of [13].

Furthermore we develop an IDE, which supports the user by automatic type inference, similar as we have introduced it for Java5.0 [14].

References

1. Goetz, B.: State of the lambda, September 2013
2. Plümicke, M.: Well-typings for Java$_\lambda$. In: Proceedings of the 9th International Conference on Principles and Practice of Programming in Java, PPPJ 2011, pp. 91–100. ACM New York (2011)
3. Lambda: Project lambda: Java language specification draft Version 0.1.5 (2010)
4. Fuh, Y.C., Mishra, P.: Type inference with subtypes. In: Proceedings 2nd European Symposium on Programming (ESOP 1988) pp. 94–114 (1988)
5. Plümicke, M.: Java type unification with wildcards. In: Seipel, D., Hanus, M., Wolf, A. (eds.) INAP 2007. LNCS, vol. 5437, pp. 223–240. Springer, Heidelberg (2009)
6. Plümicke, M.: Functional interfaces vs. function types in java with lambdas - extended abstract. In: CEUR Workshop Proceedings (CEUR-WS.org) of the Tagungsband der Arbeitstagung Programmiersprachen (ATPS 2014), vol. 1129 (2014)
7. Damas, L., Milner, R.: Principal type-schemes for functional programs. In: Proceedings of 9th Symposium on Principles of Programming Languages (1982)
8. Robinson, J.A.: A machine-oriented logic based on the resolution principle. J. ACM **12**(1), 23–41 (1965)
9. Plümicke, M.: Typeless programming in java 5.0 with wildcards. In: Amaral, V., Veiga, L., Marcelino, L., Cunningham, H.C. (eds.) Proceedings of 5th International Conference on Principles and Practices of Programming in Java. ACM International Conference Proceeding Series, vol. 272, pp. 73–82, September 2007
10. Odersky, M.: The Scala Language Specification Version 2.8, Draft November 2013
11. Skeet, J.: C# in Depth, 3rd edn. Manning Publications Co., Newyork (2013)
12. Stroustrup, B.: The C++ Programming Language, 4th edn. Addison-Wesley, UK (2013)
13. van Bakel, S.: Principal type schemes for the strict type assignment system. J. Logic Comput. **3**(6), 643–670 (1993)
14. Plümicke, M., Bäuerle, J.: Typeless programming in Java 5.0. In: Gitzel, R., Aleksey, M., Schader, M., Krintz, C. (eds.) Proceedings of 4th International Conference on Principles and Practices of Programming in Java. Volume 178 of ACM International Conference Proceeding Series. pp. 175–181. August 2006

Polynomial-Time Optimal Pretty-Printing Combinators with Choice

Anton Podkopaev[1]([⊠]) and Dmitri Boulytchev[2]

[1] Intellij Labs Co. Ltd, Universitetskaya emb., 7-9-11/5A,
199034 St.Petersburg, Russia
Anton.Podkopaev@jetbrains.com
[2] St.Petersburg State University, Universitetski pr., 28,
198504 St.Petersburg, Russia
dboulytchev@math.spbu.ru

Abstract. We describe pretty-printing combinators with choice which provide optimal document layout in polynomial time. Bottom-up tree rewriting and dynamic programming (BURS) is used to calculate a set of possible layouts for a given output width. We also present the results of suggested approach evaluation and discuss its application for the implementation of pretty-printers.

Keywords: Pretty-printing · Combinators · Bottom-up rewriting systems

1 Introduction

Pretty-printing is a transformation which provides a human-readable text from some internal program representation (for example, AST). The need for pretty-printing arises in a wide variety of applications, for example IDEs [7], reengineering tools [9] etc. In its utter form pretty-printer has to implement a reverse transformation to parsing, i.e. to generate text which can further be edited and parsed back.

The general requirement for pretty-printer to provide human-readable text decomposes into many additional requirements most of which are hard to formalize. For example, the resulting text must be *observable* (not *too wide* and not *too long*), it should reflect the structure of a program, it has to respect the coding style conventions for a given project, etc. As a result, pretty-printers, which try to fulfill these requirements, become hard to implement, maintain and reason about.

In the realm of functional programming the natural approach to pretty-printing is *pretty-printing combinators*: source representation of a program is transformed into a structured *document* using relatively small set of constructors. Then, this document is interpreted by a pretty-printing algorithm providing string representation.

© Springer-Verlag Berlin Heidelberg 2015
A. Voronkov and I. Virbitskaite (Eds.): PSI 2014, LNCS 8974, pp. 257–265, 2015.
DOI: 10.1007/978-3-662-46823-4_21

The mainstream set of pretty-printer combinators originates from the works of Wadler [15] and Hughes [6], who in turn referred to the approach developed by Oppen [11]. The basic document constructors in this approach[1] are:

- atomic string which is printed as is;
- *separator*;
- sequential composition of two documents;
- scoping.

The definitive characteristic of this approach is the interpretation of separators: all separators within a given scope can *coherently* be turned into either spaces or newline symbols by a pretty-printing algorithm. The choice for separators is determined by the requirement to respect given line width using as few lines as possible (hence optimality property).

The original Oppen's algorithm is essentially imperative; it works in a time linear on an input program length and provides optimal result. Pretty-printer combinators of Wadler and Hughes use backtracking and therefore less efficient; in addition Hughes' combinators do not provide optimality. More elaborated versions with linear-time optimal implementation are presented in [4,10,12,13]. However, these works contribute more to functional programming than to pretty-printing as such since all of them provide more advanced functional implementations of the same approach.

The problem with mainstream pretty-printer combinators is their weak expressivity. They treat pretty-printing programs *too uniformly* which sometimes can result in undesirable (or even incorrect) output. For example, if we pretty-print Python programs, then we have to handle printing two operators on the same line essentially differently since in this case additional separator character ("``;``") is required. However, mainstream pretty-printer combinators do not provide any means to specify such a behavior. Another example is layout-based syntax which is generally cannot be generated by mainstream pretty-printers since they treat vertical and horizontal spaces uniformly. It is impossible for mainstream pretty-printer combinators to adopt various project-specific layouts — they always generate text in a single hardcoded style. While some of these problems can be handled with other approaches [14] the resulting solutions utilize much more advanced machinery then a small set of high-order functions.

The aforementioned deficiencies can be alleviated if the set of pretty-printing primitives is extended by the notion of *choice* between various layouts. Thus, instead of making it possible to freely break line at arbitrary space, we may describe different *variants* of layouts and let pretty-printing algorithm choose the best one. The ability to choose between different layouts gives rise to the ability to support various code styles since each of them can be expressed as a set of patterns to choose from.

Pretty-printing frameworks with choice are already considered in the literature; however, none of them are optimal and efficient at the same time.

---

[1] The sets of combinators suggested by Hughes and Wadler slightly differ in details; however both of them share a similar relevant properties.

Pretty-printers described in [8, 9] make use of the "ALT" operator which gives an opportunity to express non-trivial layout variations. However, provided implementation does not deliver optimal layout because the choice is based on the first document fitting in the given width. In contrast, pretty-printer combinators described in [2] have no lack in expressiveness and generate optimal layout but proposed algorithm has exponential complexity. Though authors later [3] discuss some heuristic, this doesn't change the worst-case behavior.

The contribution of this paper is optimal and polynomial-time re-implementation of combinators with choice described in [2]. We utilize bottom-up tree rewriting and dynamic programming (BURS) [1,5] to provide an optimal pretty-printing algorithm which has linear complexity on the number of nodes in the document, polynomial on the width of output and exponential only on the document tree degree (which we consider a constant). Our implementation does not make use of lazy evaluation and can be natively expressed in both strict and non-strict languages.

2   Pretty-Printing Combinators with Choice

Pretty-printer combinators with choice were introduced in [2]; the implementation we refer to (and compare with) is a part of Utrecht Tools Library[2] (there are some negligible differences between published and implemented versions).

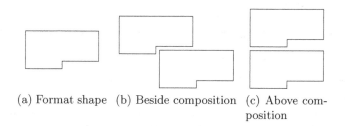

(a) Format shape   (b) Beside composition   (c) Above composition

Fig. 1. Format primitives

Output text in this approach is built from blocks shaped as rectangles with possibly incomplete last line (Fig. 1a). In Haskell implementation blocks are represented by the values of type `Format`:

```
data Format = Elem {height        :: Int
                   , lastLineWidth :: Int
                   , width         :: Int
                   , txtstr        :: Int → String → String
                   }
```

The first three fields specify the geometric properties of the block; the last one is a content-generation function which is needed to provide a linear-time block-to-text conversion in a functional settings. The first integer argument of `txtstr` is an indentation of the whole block (so blocks can be moved right horizontally).

[2] http://www.cs.uu.nl/wiki/HUT/WebHome.

Table 1. Format and document manipulation primitives

s2fmt	::	String → Format		text	::	String → Doc
indentFmt	::	Int → Format → Format		indent	::	Int → Doc → Doc
aboveFmt	::	Format → Format → Format		beside	::	Doc → Doc → Doc
besideFmt	::	Format → Format → Format		above	::	Doc → Doc → Doc

There are four primitives working with formats (see Table 1, left column). Function s2fmt creates a single-line Format from an atomic string; indentFmt moves the whole block right by a given number of positions. Two composition primitives besideFmt and aboveFmt combine two layouts as shown on the Fig. 1b, 1c.

The next notion in the framework is *document*. We may consider document as a set of various layouts for the same text. Documents are represented by the values of type Doc which we leave abstract by now. The right column in the Table 1 shows four primitives for documents which are dual for those for formats.

In addition there is fifth operator for documents:

choice :: Doc → Doc → Doc

which denotes the *union* of two sets of layouts. Note that choice is the only primitive which can produce multi-variant layouts from the single-variant arguments.

From an end-user perspective, first, the document is created by means of these five combinators. Then, the document can be rendered using the function

pretty :: Int → Doc → String

which takes the output width and the document and provides optimal layout.

The original implementation essentially relies on lazy evaluation. In [2] Doc data type is represented as a (lazy) list of all possible layouts for a given width. This list is sorted so "better" layouts come first. In the case of "beside" or "above" document composition the complexity of the new document construction is $O(n \times m)$ where n and m are lengths of the first and the second layout lists. The new document also has length $O(n \times m)$.

The document rendering function just takes the head of the document layouts list. So, at the moment of rendering we need only its first element. Due to lazy evaluation this may reduce the overall complexity. However, the implementation of beside combinator in [2] triggers the full calculation of its both parameters which compromises the benefits of lazy evaluation. Thus, the calculation of layout in [2] has the worst-case exponential complexity on the number of combinators used to construct the document. We do not see any way to avoid this drawback while preserving list-based representation.

Despite a poor worst-case behavior optimal pretty-printing combinators with choice can be used in many practical cases.

3 Bottom-Up Rewrite Systems

Bottom-up rewrite systems (BURS) [1] is a dynamic programming framework initially developed in the context of research on instruction selection problem for machine code generation. The core notion of BURS is a weighted regular tree grammar [5] i.e. a grammar with the following two kinds of rules:

$$N : \alpha \ [c] \text{ and } N : \alpha \ (K_1, \ldots, K_n) \ [c]$$

Here N, K_i are nonterminals, α — terminal, c — cost functions (one per rule, see below). Similar to the ordinary *"linear"* (or *"word"*) grammar we distinguish certain starting nonterminal S and say that terminal-labeled *tree* is derivable in the given grammar if it can be constructed from a single node labeled by S using repetitive substitutions. Each substitution replaces (arbitrary) leaf labeled by a nonterminal N with a tree $\alpha \ (K_1, \ldots, K_n)$ if there is a rule $N : \alpha \ (K_1, \ldots, K_n)$ in the grammar. The cost functions are used to calculate the overall cost of a certain derivation. Each cost function can depend on the terminal label (α) and derivation costs for each subtree.

In the context of BURS we are interested in (arbitrary) least-cost derivation of a certain tree provided by a certain grammar. This derivation can be found by a two-pass algorithm.

The first pass (*labeling*) traverses the subject tree bottom-up and calculates for each its node the set of all triplets (K, R, c), where K — nonterminal from which the subtree rooted at the given node can be derived, R — the first rule of the minimal derivation from K, c — the cost of this derivation. The labeling process is performed as follows:

- for each leaf node labeled by a terminal α we add into the set for this node a triplet (K, R, $c \ (\alpha)$) for each rule $R = K : \alpha \ [c]$;
- for an intermediate node labeled by a terminal α with immediate successors $v_1, \ldots, v_n$ we add into the set for this node a triplet (K, R, $c(\alpha, c_1, \ldots, c_n)$) for each rule $R = K : \alpha \ (K_1, \ldots, K_n) \ [c]$ such that there is a triplet (K_i, R_i, c_i) in the labeling for the node v_i; if there are different suitable rules for the same nonterminal K then we choose that delivering minimal cost.

The second pass (*reduce*) is a top-down traversal which makes use of the constructed labeling. The first rule of minimal derivation is that from the triplet (S, R, c) for the root node (if there is no such a triplet, then there is no derivation from S). This rule unambiguously determines nonterminals K_i for each direct subtree of the root node and the process repeats.

To perform labeling we potentially need to try each rule of the grammar for each node of the tree; given the fixed grammar this results in $O(|R|)$ complexity, where $|R|$ is the number of rules (the size of the set of triples is limited by the number of nonterminals which in turn is not greater than the number of rules). Reduce is linear as well.

4   Pretty-Printing via BURS

The reduction of the optimal pretty-printing problem to a BURS is based on the following observations. Let w be the output width. Since the approach in question deals with formats (rectangular boxes of a certain shape, see Sect. 2), the rendered text is in turn always shaped as a box. Let parameters of this box are n, k, h, where n — its width, $k \leq n$ — the length of its last line, h — its height. Under these considerations an *optimal* rendering is that with the minimal h over all pairs (n, k) such that $k \leq n \leq w$. So for a fixed width w we may try to render the text as no more than w^2 boxes and then simply choose the best one.

The document for pretty-printing can be considered as a tree built of primitives text, indent, beside, above, and choice. The main question is whether the rendering can be done *compositionally* by the tree structure (i.e. by reusing renderings for the subtrees of each node). It can be done if we memoize for each node and each pair (n, k), where $k \leq n \leq w$, the minimal h such that the subtree rooted at that node can be rendered as a box with parameters n, k and h. Having optimal renderings for each possible box shape for each subtree of some node we can in turn calculate optimal rendering for each possible box shape for the node itself *et cetera*. For each node of the tree we thus need to calculate no more then w^2 renderings which means that (under the assumption that w is fixed) the number of renderings is linear on the number of nodes in the tree.

Once all these renderings are calculated in a bottom-up manner we may then reconstruct the optimal one by a top-down traversal. For the root of the tree we choose the rendering with the minimal height. This choice immediately provides us with the renderings for immediate subtrees *et cetera*. Note that generally speaking the optimal rendering for a tree is not necessarily combined from optimal renderings for its subtrees.

These considerations boil down to the following BURS specification. Given output width w we introduce a family of nonterminals T_n^k for all $k \leq n \leq w$. We are going to define a BURS grammar in such a way that a derivation of cost h of some document tree from the nonterminal T_n^k corresponds to the optimal rendering of that document into a box with parameters n, k and h. Once we have a grammar with this property the labeling stage will calculate all (interesting) renderings while reduce stage will provide the optimal one.

The grammar in question can be constructed by the case analysis:

1. For a terminal node [text s][3] we have two cases:
   – if $|s| \leq w$ (where $|s|$ is the length of the string s) we introduce the single rule $T_{|s|}^{|s|} :$ [text   s] with cost 1; for all other $k, n \neq |s|$ we have $T_n^k :$ [text   s] with cost ∞;
   – if $|s| > w$ then we have $T_n^k :$ [text s] with cost ∞ for all k, n.
   Indeed, a (single-line) string of length $|s|$ can only be rendered as a box with parameters $|s|$ (width), $|s|$ (length of the last line) and 1 (height). All other renderings are not possible — hence "∞" cost.

---

[3] We use square brackets to denote multi-symbol terminals.

2. For a node [indent m] we introduce two sets of rules:
   (a) T_{n+m}^{k+m} : [indent m] (T_n^k) with identity cost function for each n and k such that $n + m \leq w$ and $k \leq n$;
   (b) T_n^k : [indent m] (T_j^i) with cost ∞ for all other cases.
   Clearly, shifting a box with parameters n, k and h by m positions to the right transforms it into the box with parameters $n + m$, $k + m$, h. This box represents an admissible rendering if $n + m \leq w$ (and hence $k + m \leq w$).
3. For a node [above] we have the rule $T_{\max(n_1,n_2)}^{k_2}$: [above] $(T_{n_1}^{k_1}, T_{n_2}^{k_2})$ with the cost function which sums the costs of both subtree derivations for each $k_1 \leq n_1 \leq w$ and $k_2 \leq n_2 \leq w$. Indeed, when we combine boxes with parameters n_1, k_1, h_1 and n_2, k_2, h_2 we obtain the box with parameters $\max(n_1, n_2), k_2, h_1 + h_2$. Vertical combination of two admissible boxes is always admissible.
4. For a node [beside] we have the rule $T_{\max(n_1, k_1+n_2)}^{k_1+k_2}$: [beside] $(T_{n_1}^{k_1}, T_{n_2}^{k_2})$ for each combination of n_1, n_2, k_1, k_2 such that $k_1 + k_2 \leq \max(n_1, k_1 + n_2) \leq w$. The cost function for these rules calculates the sum of costs for subtree derivations minus 1. This can be validated by elementary geometric considerations.
5. Finally, for [choice] we have the rule T_n^k : [choice] (T_n^k, T_n^k) for all $k \leq n \leq w$. The cost function is minimum between two derivations for subtrees. Clearly, between two layouts with the same shape but different height we have to choose the shortest one.

To complete the construction we have to provide rules for the starting non-terminal S. We can either add a rule S : r with identity cost function for each right-hand side r of each rule constructed so far or introduce a chain rule S : T_n^k with identity cost function for each nonterminal T_n^k (the latter requires a trivial extension of BURS description presented in Sect. 3).

The number of nonterminals in the constructed grammar is $O(w^2)$; the number of rules, however, is $O(w^4)$ since there are nodes of degree 2 in the tree. So our BURS implementation of the optimal pretty-printer works in linear time on the number of nodes in the document tree for fixed width; the complexity on width is of fourth degree. Clearly, given reduction can be scaled to document construction primitives of arbitrary degree at the cost of exponential growth.

5 Implementation and Evaluation

We implemented our approach in Haskell as a pretty-printing combinator library[4] Our implementation borrows some basic underlying types and functions from the original library [2] with top-level types and combinators re-implemented.

In our implementation we do not follow BURS reduction literally; we do not make any use of BURS grammar, sets of nonterminals or standard algorithm. Instead, we calculate for each node of the document a map from pairs of integers (n, k) to the best ("shortest") format with the parameters n and k (if any). Thus, an entry (n, k) in the map corresponds to the cost of optimal derivation from T_n^k

---

[4] http://github.com/anlun/polynomialPPCombinators.

Table 2. Time of layout calculation (in seconds)

Height	Nodes	W=25		W=50		W=100		W=150	
7	10921	0.07	0.18	0.12	0.69	0.06	0.97	0.06	1.01
8	43689	1.28	0.73	287.55	4.03	97.79	14.92	38.99	20.75
9	174761	6.47	2.86	294	17.93	179	88.71	59	204.51
10	699049	18.46	11.58	284	71.70	172	390.45	58.25	1026.44

and the first rule for that derivation. At the top level we choose the least-cost element from the map.

Since we are interested in the worst-case behavior we evaluate our implementation on the number of artificial automatically-generated documents. Given a tree of type `Ast`, we then generate a document in a bottom-up manner. For each intermediate node we combine its subtrees' layouts both vertically and horizontally and generate a choice between them in the following manner:

```
data Ast = T String | N String Ast Ast
astToDoc (T s)     = text s
astToDoc (N s l r) = make beside 'choice' make above where
    make f = foldl f (text s) (map astToDoc [l, r])
```

The results of comparison of our implementation against the original one are shown on the Table 2. Here "Height" stands for the height of the initial tree, "Nodes" — for the number of nodes in the generated document, "W" — for the output width. For each width the left sub-column shows the running time of the original implementation, while the right — of ours (in seconds). We can see that starting from some combination of width/number of nodes the original implementation was not able to calculate the layout. Table entries like **59** show the time when a stack overflow occurred.

Our implementation sometimes does not demonstrate linear behavior (as it is expected since the number of nodes is virtually quadrupled from line to line). We performed additional experiments and found that this phenomenon is due to the irregular sparsity of calculated layouts for the larger widths. In other words, for a small tree the number of non-empty entries in the layout maps is far below the upper bound. As the tree grows this number also grows non-linearly until the upper bound is reached.

6   Conclusions and Future Work

Despite our approach is better in asymptotic sense, the constant factor of w^4 makes it still unusable in a direct form for large widths. Several ways to reduce this factor may be considered as directions for future research. For example, we may try to factorize output width into smaller number of values or to perform auxiliary heuristic search to prevent too many layouts from being considered.

On the other hand, the presented approach has an interesting "relocation" property: if we once calculated layouts for some tree, then we can instantly pretty-print it in arbitrary context (e.g. from arbitrary position or as a subtree of arbitrary tree). This property opens some perspectives for incremental pretty-printing in the context of IDEs.

Another issue which we have to mention is a conversion from AST into documents. Generally speaking the direct conversion might provide a document of an exponential size since at each node we might try to choose from various compositions ("beside" or "above") of layouts of its descendants. While this does not compromise our approach, it still has practical impact. To cope with this issue an additional level of memoization is needed to prevent shared document nodes from being processed several times. The original set of combinators [2] seem to face the same problem.

References

1. Aho, A.V., Ganapathi, M., Tjiang, S.W.K.: Code generation using tree matching and dynamic programming. ACM Trans. Program. Lang. Syst. **11**(4), 491–516 (1989)
2. Azero, P., Swierstra, S.D.: Optimal Pretty-Printing Combinators. http://www.cs.ruu.nl/groups/ST/Software/PP, (1998)
3. Swierstra, S.D., Alcocer, P.R.A., Saraiva, J.: Designing and implementing combinator languages. In: Swierstra, S.D., Oliveira, J.N., Henriques, P.R. (eds.) AFP 1998. LNCS, vol. 1608. Springer, Heidelberg (1999)
4. Chitil, O.: Pretty printing with lazy dequeues. ACM Trans. Program. Lang. Syst. **27**, 163–184 (2005)
5. Comon, H., Dauchet, M., Gilleron, R. et al.: Tree Automata Techniques and Applications. http://www.grappa.univ-lille3.fr/tata, (2007)
6. Hughes, J.: The design of a pretty-printing library. In: Jeuring, J., Meijer, E. (eds.) AFP 1995. LNCS, vol. 925. Springer, Heidelberg (1995)
7. Jackson, S., Devanbu, P., Ma, K.: Stable, flexible, peephole pretty-printing. J. Sci. Comput. Program. **72**(1–2), 40–51 (2008)
8. De Jonge, M.: A pretty-printer for every occasion. In: Proceedings of the 2nd International Symposium on Constructing Software Engineering Tools (2000)
9. De Jonge, M.: Pretty-printing for software reengineering. In: Proceedings of the International Conference On Software Maintenance (2002)
10. Costanzo, D., Shao, Z.: A case for behavior-preserving actions in separation logic. In: Jhala, R., Igarashi, A. (eds.) APLAS 2012. LNCS, vol. 7705, pp. 332–349. Springer, Heidelberg (2012)
11. Oppen, D.C.: Pretty-printing. ACM Transact. Program. Lang. Syst. **2**(4), 465–483 (1980)
12. Swierstra, S.D.: Linear, Online, Functional Pretty Printing (corrected and extended version). Technical report, UU-CS-2004-025a. Institute of Information and Computing Sciences, Utrecht University (2004)
13. Swierstra, S.D., Chitil, O.: Linear, bounded, functional pretty-printing. J. Funct. Program. **19**, 1–16 (2009)
14. van den Brand, M., Visser, E.: Generation of formatters for context-free languages. ACM Trans. Softw. Eng. Methodol. **5**(1), 1–41 (1996)
15. Wadler, P.: A Prettier Printer: The Fun of Programming. Palgrave MacMillan (2003)

The Study of Multidimensional R-Tree-Based Index Scalability in Multicore Environment

Kirill Smirnov, George Chernishev$^{(\boxtimes)}$, Pavel Fedotovsky,
George Erokhin, and Kirill Cherednik

Saint-Petersburg University, Saint Petersburg, Russia
{kirill.k.smirnov,chernishev,pavel.v.fedotovsky,
george.erokhin,kirill.cherednik}@gmail.com

Abstract. In this paper we consider the scalability issues of a classical data structure used for multidimensional indexing: the R-Tree. This data structure allows for an efficient retrieval of records in low-dimensional spaces and is de facto standard of the industry. Following the design guidelines of the GiST model we have implemented a prototype which supports concurrent (parallel) access and provides read committed isolation level. Using our prototype we study the impact of threads and cores on the performance of the system. In order to do this, we evaluate it in several scenarios which may occur during the course of DBMS operation.

Keywords: Threads · Scalability · Databases · Multidimensional indexing · In-memory index · R-Tree · GiST · Experimental evaluation

1 Introduction

R-Tree is a de facto standard of the database industry for multidimensional indexing: PostgreSQL, Oracle, Informix, SQLite and MySQL follow this approach [1]. However, the problem of efficient multidimensional indexing is very far from being solved. Moreover, the problem becomes challenging when one considers it in a transactional environment. This means that, inter alia, a programmer should provide [2]:

- A concurrency control mechanism to ensure the integrity of a data structure during multithreaded access. The index must preserve its internal structure, i.e. broken links or dangling pointers must not appear.
- Some guarantees for the outcome of conflicting operations. These guarantees are specific to the area of databases and are defined by the specified isolation level.

Performance and correctness of parallel access are not the only important characteristics. This access should also be scalable, e.g. the performance of such system should benefit from the addition of new processing elements (processors, cores).

This work is partially supported by Russian Foundation for Basic Research grant 12-07-31050.

A. Voronkov and I. Virbitskaite (Eds.): PSI 2014, LNCS 8974, pp. 266–272, 2015.
DOI: 10.1007/978-3-662-46823-4_22

The goal of this paper is to explore the scalability issues of such system and to study the effect of adding more cores in a variety of scenarios. We consider a multidimensional indexing system in a transactional environment.

This work uses a prototype implementation of transactional, in-memory, multidimensional indexing system based on R-Tree and the GiST model [3]. This system is the follow-up of the ACM SIGMOD Contest 2012, where initial version was created. It was ranked 5th on the public (preliminary) tests[1]. Detailed description of the system can be found in the report [4].

2   Considered Problems

The considered question is "How does plugging more cores and threads into a system affect its performance?". Intuitively, working with an index in parallel should bring benefits, e.g. decrease index construction time. However this may not be the case due to implementation-specific software issues (latch interference, node splits, etc.) or hardware limitations.

We have considered the following scenarios which we deem the most important for the evaluation:

1. Index construction. During this scenario we measure the time it takes to construct the index.
2. Query execution: an update intensive workload. This scenario includes a big portion of queries with update statements. Such queries may trigger conflicts and eventually lead to formation of queues of waiting transactions, which may adversely affect query performance.
3. Query execution: a select intensive workload. In this scenario the selection operations constitute a substantional fraction of all operations.

These scenarios are considered for several synthetic datasets. We consider low-dimensional data because it is a well-known fact that R-Tree performs poorly with high-dimensional data [5] and thus is not used with it.

Also, it is necessary to mention that our problem formulation involves in-memory index. This approach, contrary to disk-based one doesn't keep transient index data on a hard drive. This type of systems is becoming increasingly popular due to the vast amounts of cheap memory being available and it is believed that these systems will dominate the OLTP market soon [6,7].

3   The Prototype

In order to explore the problem stated in the previous section we have decided to empirically evaluate these scenarios. One might think that such a popular data structure must have a variety of implementations which could be reused. Unfortunately, existing open-source systems are not suitable due to the following reasons:

---

[1] http://web.archive.org/web/20120424201336/http://wwwdb.inf.tu-dresden.de/ sigmod2012contest/leaderboard/ last accessed: 26/04/2014.

1. They don't have any support for concurrency [8,9] and thus, are not suitable for our purposes at all.
2. They are tuned for disk I/O [10]. This also diverges from our goals, because in-memory systems behave differently from disk-based ones.

The general reason of such unsuitability is the disparity in system purposes. For example, the system [8] is dedicated to evaluation of clustering techniques (and access methods, including R-Tree) and this problem considerably differs from ours. To the best of our knowledge there is no study or prototype which considers scalability issues and impact of concurrency on R-Tree. Thus, we had to implement our own prototype. Our system follows classical design guidelines and contains several high-level features:

– An R-Tree data structure, which is built upon GiST [3], a popular template index structure which allows to "abstract" various tree data structures.
– We used a mechanism adapted from [2] with locks, latches and Node Sequence Numbers. Also we provided deadlock resolution mechanism. Eventually, we ensured the read committed isolation level. Details see in [4].
– Our prototype is designed for in-memory indexing.
– Currently our prototype lacks logging and recovery components.
– In our implementation we don't delete records, instead, we mark them as "deleted" and take this into account during the processing. This kind of processing (called logical deletion) is a widely-used approach for handling deletions in database systems [2].

We validated our implementation in two ways:

– First, we used public third-party unit-tests, provided by [11]. We also had extended this test set with our own cases. These unit-tests ensured correctness of an isolation level (read committed) and other implementation issues.
– An evaluation of our prototype with industrial systems PostgreSQL and Berkeley DB was presented in the reference [12]. This evaluation showed that the system's performance is comparable to the industrial ones.

More details of the system and algorithms can be found in the report [4].

4   Experiments

Benchmark and Parameters. In our evaluations we used the benchmark suite, which allows us to specify a variety of parameters constituting the data (data type, distribution, number of dimensions) and queries (query distributions and their parameters). We used our custom benchmark suite [4], because of lack of the standard multidimensional transactional indexing benchmarks and the general inapplicability of the analogues.

The workload parameters were the following: uniform data distribution, 4 dimensions, integer (8 bytes) datatype used. R-tree parameters were: plain R-Tree with 32 fan-out with Guttman Quadratic split algorithm [13].

Experimental Setup. Our hardware and software setup was the following: hardware — 2 x Intel(R) Xeon(R) CPU E5-2670 0 @ 2.60 GHz (32 cores total), 120 GB RAM; software — Linux Ubuntu 3.13.0-30-generic x86_64, GCC 4.8.2.

Measurements. In our work we simulate addition of a processing element via addition of a new thread and a core. To evaluate the scalability of R-Tree-based multidimensional transactional index we used the following metrics [14]:

– Speed up, i.e. the performance improvement gained by adding extra processing elements (in our case a core and a thread).
– Scale up, i.e. the ability to handle the larger tasks by increasing the degree of parallelism (in our case we both increase the size of the task and number of cores). More precisely, we are going to study data scale up.

We built our charts using 95 % confidence intervals. Now, lets describe the considered scenarios and their respective parameters.

Index Construction Phase. We have explored the impact of parallelism on the index construction time. The first considered metric was data scale up. In order to study it we conducted a series of experiments in which we increased both the data size and number of threads. The Figs. 1 and 2 show the data scale up during the index construction.

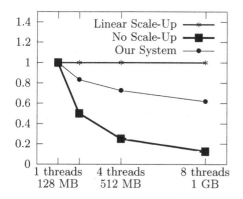 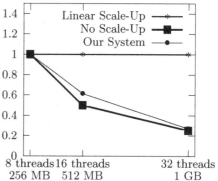

Fig. 1. Data scale up of our system (small number of working threads).

Fig. 2. Data scale up of our system (large number of working threads).

As we can see from Fig. 2, we get almost no scale up from using a lot of threads. However, we get more promising results from the experiment described on Fig. 1. The second considered metric was the speed up. The Fig. 3 shows the speed up which may be achieved by increasing the number of working threads participating in index construction. In the next experiments we use 512 MB index, 4 dimensions, uniform data distribution. Dataset sizes are relatively small since our goal is to obtain credible numerical results in a reasonable amount of time.

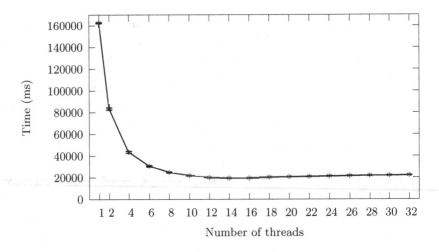

Fig. 3. Speed up of our system during index construction phase.

With a fair degree of certainty we can assert that increasing the number of working threads will decrease the index construction time. This tendency will manifest itself until we increase the number of working threads to 10–12. Then, index construction time stabilizes despite the fact that the system has idle hardware processing elements.

Query Execution Phase. We also considered two query execution modes: update intensive and select intensive. The parameters for update intensive are: 20 % range, 40 % update, 20 % insert, 20 % delete. Select intensive is as follows: 85 % range, 5 % update, 5 % insert, 5 % delete.

We have to mention that we don't consider wildcard queries, i.e. queries which request all values for one attribute. Also, unlike our previous study [12], here a sorted output is not required.

The considered scenarios describe two extremes of possible situations encountered in DBMS during the course of operation. The first one (update intensive) may be less prone to scale up due to the amount of locks and the second one should scale more easily.

The Fig. 4 shows the performance of update intensive and select intensive workloads. Both series of experiments show growth of the system throughput while increasing the number of working threads up to 18–20. Increasing it further slows growth down significantly. Update intensive workload is characterized by slower growth. Select intensive workload demonstrates larger relative errors. The latter fact makes the analysis considerably harder. This behavior can be explained by considering it as the result of intensive use of XLatch (rwlock). Then, select intensive workload shows almost linear increase in performance and demonstrates relatively smaller error bars.

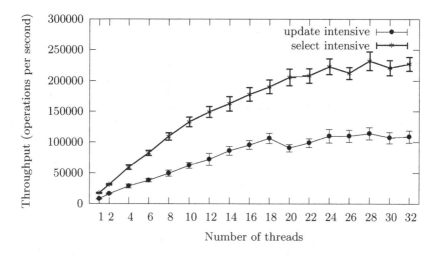

Fig. 4. Performance of our system during query execution phase.

5 Conclusions

In this paper we have evaluated the scalability of the multidimensional transactional index based on R-Tree. First, we have developed and implemented a novel transactional isolation algorithm based on the one proposed in [2]. The proposed algorithm ensures the read committed isolation level [4]. Next, we have studied the scalability of R-Tree in a transactional environment. We have examined both index construction and query execution scenarios. The results show the lack of scalability on index construction, we do not gain any scalability past 10-12 working threads. This may happen due to lock or latch contention. However, during the query execution mode we benefit from any additional cores up to 18-20 threads. Also, we can see that the amount of updates negatively impacts the scalability potential of the aforementioned index. The applicability of the observed behaviour to an arbitrary R-Tree-based system is the matter for further inquires.

Acknowledgements. We would like to thank organizers of ACM SIGMOD Programming Contest'12 for providing a base for benchmark, data generator and unit tests. This work is partially supported by Russian Foundation for Basic Research grant 12-07-31050.

References

1. Beckmann, N., Seeger, B.: A revised R*-tree in comparison with related index structures. In: Proceedings of the 2009 ACM SIGMOD International Conference on Management of data, SIGMOD 2009, New York, NY, USA, pp. 799–812. ACM (2009)
2. Kornacker, M., Mohan, C., Hellerstein, J.M.: Concurrency and recovery in generalized search trees. SIGMOD Rec. **26**(2), 62–72 (1997)

3. Hellerstein, J.M., Naughton, J.F., Pfeffer, A.: Generalized search trees for database systems. In: Proceedings of the 21th International Conference on Very Large Data Bases, VLDB 1995, San Francisco, CA, USA, pp. 562–573. Morgan Kaufmann Publishers Inc. (1995)

4. Smirnov, K., Chernishev, G., Fedotovsky, P., Erokhin, G., Cherednik, K.: R-tree re-evaluation effort: a report. Technical report (2014) http://www.math.spbu.ru/user/chernishev/papers/r-tree-scalability2014.pdf

5. Papadopoulos, A.N., Corral, A., Nanopoulos, A., Theodoridis, Y.: R-Tree (and Family). In: Liu, L., Özsu, M.T. (eds.) Encyclopedia of Database Systems, pp. 2453–2459. Springer, New York (2009). doi:10.1007/978-0-387-39940-9_300

6. Stonebraker, M., Madden, S., Abadi, D.J., Harizopoulos, S., Hachem, N., Helland, P.: The end of an architectural era: (it's time for a complete rewrite). In: Proceedings of the 33rd International Conference on Very Large Data Bases, VLDB 2007, pp. 1150–1160. VLDB Endowment (2007)

7. Harizopoulos, S., Abadi, D.J., Madden, S., Stonebraker, M.: Oltp through the looking glass, and what we found there. In: Proceedings of the 2008 ACM SIGMOD International Conference on Management of Data, SIGMOD 2008, New York, NY, USA, pp. 981–992. ACM (2008)

8. Achtert, E., Goldhofer, S., Kriegel, H.P., Schubert, E., Zimek, A.: Evaluation of clusterings - metrics and visual support. In: Proceedings of the 2012 IEEE 28th International Conference on Data Engineering, ICDE 2012, Washington, DC, USA, pp. 1285–1288. IEEE Computer Society (2012)

9. Kornacker, M., Shah, M., Hellerstein, J.M.: AMDB: an access method debugging tool. SIGMOD Rec. **27**(2), 570–571 (1998)

10. Arge, L., Procopiuc, O., Vitter, J.S.: Implementing i/o-efficient data structures using TPIE. In: Möhring, R.H., Raman, R. (eds.) ESA 2002. LNCS, vol. 2461, pp. 88–100. Springer, Heidelberg (2002)

11. ACM SIGMOD Programming Contest 2012. http://wwwdb.inf.tu-dresden.de/sigmod2012contest/. Accessed: 9th November 2012

12. Chernishev, G., Smirnov, K., Fedotovsky, P., Erokhin, G., Cherednik, K.: To sort or not to sort: the evaluation of R-tree and B^+-tree in transactional environment with ordered result set requirement. In: SYRCoDIS, pp. 27–34 (2013)

13. Guttman, A.: R-trees: a dynamic index structure for spatial searching. SIGMOD Rec. **14**(2), 47–57 (1984)

14. Taniar, D., Leung, C.H.C., Rahayu, W., Goel, S.: High Performance Parallel Database Processing And Grid Databases. Wiley Publishing, New York (2008)

Skeblle: A New Kind of Diagramming Tool with Programmable Active Diagrams

Vinodh Kumar Sunkara$^{(\boxtimes)}$ and Aamod Sane

Yahoo Inc., Sunnyvale, CA, USA
{vinsun,aamod}@yahoo-inc.com

Abstract. Diagramming tools range from manual free-form drawing tools to pre-programmed notation specific tools for UML or SDL, and further to fully programmatic tools like Pic or TikZ. In such tools, the diagrams are the end product, not available for further use, unaware of relations between diagrams or the ability to express one diagram as a function of another. We propose a new kind of tool based on programmable active diagrams, where diagrams are active entities to be operated upon and connected to systems they depict. Our tool, Skeblle, implements this approach for box-line diagrams. In Skeblle, every diagram drawn by a user is backed by a graph, and both the diagram and the underlying graph can be manipulated manually or with a command language. Manipulations of the graph are reflected in the diagram and vice versa, and the graph can link real systems to diagram nodes via urls. In combination, these facilities give us a novel tool that feels like a simple diagramming tool, but is capable of creating diagrams that better capture the domain they represent. Diagrams can change to reflect changes in systems they depict, and may be operated upon to compute related diagrams.

We describe how Skeblle may be used to draw software deployment and architecture diagrams, explain distributed protocols, and visualize chemical reactions. We show that Skeblle makes it simple to compute diagrams to illustrate differences in system states due to component failures, data flows, and chemical interactions.

Keywords: Software architecture · Software visualization · Graph drawing · Graph rewriting · MDA · Model-based diagrams

1 Introduction

Graphs as an underlying model for simple diagrams of systems have been implicit in tools such as structured graphics applications like Idraw [19] and Visio [2], programmatic tools like Pic [14], as well as domain specific tools for ER diagrams or UML. More recently, Graphviz [7] and derived systems like PlantUML [4] have made graphs the basis of diagrams, while Graph transformation tools Groove [9], GrGen [12] and others [13] encourage users to compute graphs and render them visually. While diagramming tools like Visio leave the graphs

© Springer-Verlag Berlin Heidelberg 2015
A. Voronkov and I. Virbitskaite (Eds.): PSI 2014, LNCS 8974, pp. 273–287, 2015.
DOI: 10.1007/978-3-662-46823-4_23

implicit and inaccessible to users, graph transformation tools require the users to understand formalisms like rewrite rules before they can use the tool successfully. Furthermore, designers of transformation tools do not put a premium on visual appearance of graphs. In our work with diagramming various software systems, we found neither alternative entirely comfortable to use.

For example, suppose we wish to illustrate failure handling of a system spanning two data centers. In such a system, the subsystems in each data center are identical, except that some components might be "cold" in one while being "hot" in another. In case of failover from one data center to another, the components switch their states. A diagram for such a system has a great deal of structure: it consists of a pair of sub diagrams, one for each data center, such that normally the diagram for one data center should be "the same as the other, except for ...", while after a failure, the respective component states shown in the sub diagrams will be reversed. An ordinary diagramming tool cannot model such structure at all, while the level of effort needed to use graph transformation tools for simple models like these is not easy to justify.

Thus we were led toward "programmable active diagrams", an approach that combines diagrams with structural models of the system being depicted. In this approach, a user draws a diagram, and the tool automatically generates an associated model that "backs" diagram. When needed, the user can start thinking in terms of the underlying model and manipulate it, while the tool reflects changes to the model in the diagram. Visual aspects of a diagram are also treated with a similar mix of manual and programming options. A user starts by specifying visual properties manually as in an ordinary drawing tool, but internally visual specifications are captured using markup attached to the underlying model. This markup can be edited manually or programmatically to affect the diagram. In Skeblle, we have implemented the active diagrams approach for box and line diagrams backed by graph models. The model graph is manipulated with graph operators, and markup is used to describe graph structure as well as visualization styles attached to nodes and edges.

Besides creating the diagrams, we are interested in using the diagrams to interact with the systems they represent. Our tool, Skeblle[1], allows diagrams to be connected to live systems via urls. Data fetched by querying the urls can be used to affect the represented systems. Skeblle enables rich visual presentations using the full power of Javascript and browsers. We are also interested in Skeblle being comfortable to use. Given the considerable familiarity of web tools like Firebug [15], we have given Skeblle a similar interface. Taken together, these facilities make for a novel tool that takes diagramming in a new direction.

The contributions of this work are as follows:

– We present a new approach, programmable active diagrams, that makes visualization tools more useful. In this approach, diagrams are not just structured pixels, but are backed by a model that captures aspects of the domain that the diagram represents. The underlying model is revealed by the tool and may

---

[1] A portmanteau of Sketch and Bubble.

be operated upon to yield new diagrams. The operators are carefully chosen for the domain at hand and suffice for most uses, and may be extended as needed.

– Existing visual tools for working with graphs have relied on declarative or logical languages. We show that a simple imperative language can be very effective as a high level tool for working with graphs. We complement this language with declarative markup for visual appearance.

– Our technique of creating a tool that feels as light as a manual diagramming tool while being backed by a formal model appears to be novel. To the best of our knowledge, existing systems do not combine these two aspects.

– We present a new application of the bidirectional visual and textual interfaces developed in web browser debuggers like Firebug [15], as discussed in Sect. 2. This is a powerful interface model that should find more applications.

In the rest of the paper, we begin by describing the tool interface (Sect. 2), followed by a series of case studies, each illustrating an interesting use of high level graph operations (Sect. 3, 4, 5 and 6). These cases give evidence that the "programmable active diagrams" approach gives a powerful versatile tool. Next we look at design considerations (Sect. 7), with details of graph operations (Sect. 8) and visual customization (Sect. 9) via markup and our simple layout mechanism. Finally (Sect. 10) we show how the ability to link diagrams to external data sources, and arbitrary customization with javascript lets the tool connect with live systems. We close with a discussion of related work and possible futures.

2   Skeblle and its User Interface

Skeblle is implemented as a client side Javascript program. Its interface is in part inspired by Firebug [15], a web development tool for understanding and manipulating structure and behavior of web pages.

The Skeblle interface (Fig. 1) offers three ways to create and manipulate diagrams. At the top left is a drawing board with a conventional direct manipulation interface, where a user can create, delete, and move nodes and edges. The top right is a command shell – an unusual feature for a drawing tool. The command shell proves to be an extremely fast way to create diagrams and manipulate it with high level graph operators. Details of the operators are discussed in Sect. 8. The bottom two areas show two aspects of the same diagram in stylized JSON, used as a markup language: the left area is a description of the graph, while the right area contains markup for visual aspects. The structure markup is analogous to HTML while visual is analogous to CSS, as discussed in Sect. 9.

We show case studies of usage of Skeblle in the following sections, and consider details of the command language (Sect. 8) and markup languages (Sect. 9) afterward. We also provide some layout assistance, discussed in Sect. 9. The case studies illustrate how the command language enables easy, high-level manipulation of diagrams.

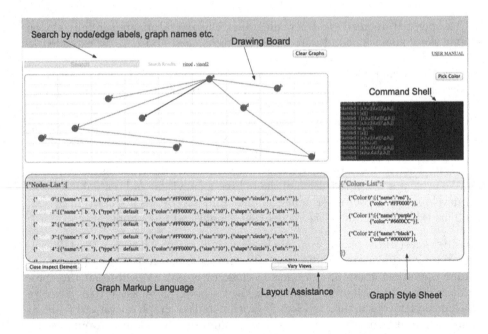

Fig. 1. Skeblle interface: DrawingBoard, Command Shell, and Markup areas

3   Case I: Request Flow in a Deployment Diagram

In this section, we show how Skeblle can model logical structures in a diagram.
Our example, Fig. 2, is the deployment architecture of a typical website where
users upload text, image, and video data. Such systems have a logical structure.
There are nodes such as traffic splitters that serve to segregate different kinds
of traffic, frontend systems that render web pages, middle tiers that multiplex
various backend systems, and a number of different storage systems depending
on media they store. Skeblle provides several ways in which this structure can
be captured in the diagram.

Construction: During diagram construction, Skeblle users combine use of commands and manual controls. We start by creating a graph (command 'cg'). Given
the context of a graph, the following commands create the nodes (command 'cn'),
associate the types "external" and "service" with them, and lays them out in
two columns (command 'lc').

```
cg sitedeployment
cn external Users,Api
cn service Frontend,MiddleTier,Moderation,Search
lc service,external
```

Using commands provides a far faster way to initially create the graphs. Fine
adjustments of layout are then done manually. Further columns and nodes

eventually get us the complete graph in Fig. 2. The types capture related groups of nodes, and find use in operators that govern layout and other graph manipulations.

Visual Appearance: We use type labels to associate styles with the nodes. For an example, see Sect. 9. In addition, we can manually change the appearance. In these diagrams, we distinguish the shape MiddleTier node since it plays a significant role in the system. All storage nodes are squares, while the rest are left as circles.

Diagram Explanation: Diagrams like these are understood by looking at slices of the diagram, for instance, moving left to right column by column, or by following the flow of particular requests. Skeblle shines in this use, since we can show interesting slices, and create urls that point to diagram of the different slices. We use high-level graph operations for this purpose. We show one example, a project operation that highlights the request flow for video content. The commands are as follows:

```
sn videorequest Users,Splitter,Proxy,VideoConverter,VideoStore
hp videorequest url videorequest
```

The first command 'sn' (subgraph of nodes) creates a subgraph called "videorequest", and the second command ('hp') projects out the relevant graph. See Sect. 8 for details. The last command, 'url' creates the url http://<siteurl>/ diagram/sitedeployment/videorequest that we can use to refer to the current diagram. Other such diagrams that highlight different aspects of the system are equally simple to construct (Fig. 3).

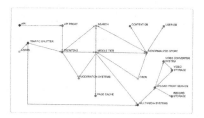

Fig. 2. Deployment of a user generated content website.

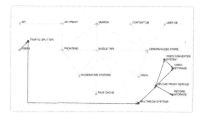

Fig. 3. Understanding video request flow.

4 Case II: BCP and Failure Handling

In our second example, we discuss the use of high level operators in constructing and displaying diagrams, and the power of customizing the tool using Javascript to add new facilities.

Our example is another diagram of the website in Sect. 3. This diagram concentrates on another aspect of the system that deals with failure management. Such sites have systems that are replicated in two data centers, both of which serve read traffic, while one, called a "master", serves traffic that creates, updates, or deletes content. Here we use Skeblle in a manner similar to the Sect. 3.

Construction: We construct the left hand side graph in Fig. 4, and construct the right side (Fig. 5) with a copy operator:

```
cg failover
cn external Users
cn edge WVip,RVip
cn store DB
cn service MiddleTier
```

We adjust the nodes, then draw the edges by hand, and next we copy the graph with a high level operator:

```
sn master WVip,RVip,DB,MiddleTier
hcp slave master
```

With this command, we first create a group of nodes that constitute the master, and copy the group to create the slave system diagram.

Explaining Diagrams: To show the master and slave states, we can use the knowledge of structure from the copy operation. The following commands lead to the diagram in Fig. 5.

```
scm nonmaster master
hp nonmaster
url failedstate
```

The scm "complement" command subtracts the master from the entire graph. Next we project the complement to create the diagram. Once created the current state of the diagram can be referred to with a url as before: http://<skebllesite>/diagram/failover/failedstate

5   Case III: Chemical Reactions

Any situation where node-edge graphs are useful is fair game for Skeblle. In this example, we see a rather different application, where the figures are customized to show chemical reactions. In this particular case, there are many custom tools that can be used for diagramming, for instance, Chemtube [1]. We included this example to show that Skeblle can be nearly as useful without much effort.

In our example, we show stages in the reaction

$$CH_4 + 2O_2 \longrightarrow CO_2 + 2H_2O$$

In the first figure, Fig. 6, we see the initial state. As heat increases the bonds break to give us Fig. 7, and later the reaction completes to yield Fig. 8. For these diagrams, Skeblle is used as follows.

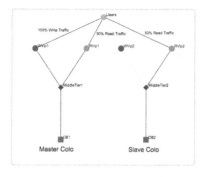

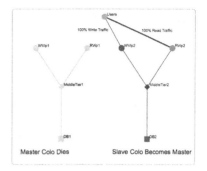

Fig. 4. Master read/write, slave read-only

Fig. 5. Master failed, slave becomes master

Visual Appearance: We use type labels to associate styles with elements of the graphs as discussed in Sect. 9. We customize these for appearance of the atoms. Once the style is available, we can create nodes with types and apply the style as follows

```
cn -n 4 oatom O
sty oxy oatom
```

cn creates 4 nodes of type oatom with label O, while sty associates nodes of type oatom with style oxy. In turn, the style oxy is defined in JGSS.

Deriving New Graphs: The chemical reaction example involves significant graph changes. Graphs in the first diagram are split to get the second diagram:

```
hs ch4,o21,o22
```

where the operator split (hs) splits the graphs mentioned. It turns out that for the third diagram, we ended up defining a new operator, cstar, for "create star".

```
cstar O1,h1,h2
cstar O2,h3,h4
cstar C,O3,O4
cstar C,O3,O4
```

We have since found many uses for the cstar operator, which joins the first node to the other nodes.

6   Case IV: Routing Protocols for Wireless Sensor Networks

Our last case illustrating routing protocols hinges on another interesting use of a high-level operator, the quotient [5]. A quotient operator takes a graph, collapses the graph to a single representative node, and changes edges leading out

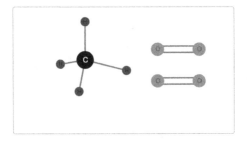

Fig. 6. Methane and oxygen molecules before the reaction

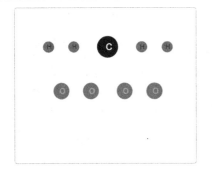

Fig. 7. Atoms after bonds break in methane and oxygen molecules

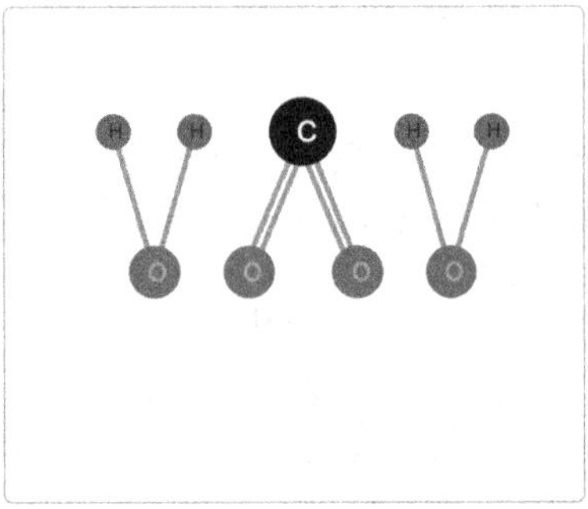

Fig. 8. New bonds formation giving in carbon dioxide and water

of the graph to the new representative node. In many applications that involve hierarchical structures, the quotient operation provides a useful transformation.

Our example is a protocol called LEACH [10] – low energy adaptive clustering hierarchy protocol – for use with wireless sensors. If sensor nodes near one another all communicate with a base station, they send similar and so redundant data while expending energy. The LEACH protocol reduces such transmission by limiting base station communication to "cluster heads", special nodes that represent other nodes in a neighborhood and aggregate their data. The "headship" rotates among cluster members so that no particular sensor bears the energy cost of communication.

The Skeblle figures illustrate states in this protocol. In the first diagram (Fig. 9), all nodes are their own cluster. The second diagram is created using the star operators

```
cstar 2, 3-8
```

The last diagram is created by the quotient operator, followed by a star

```
hq A 2-8
hq B 9-12
...
cstar SINK, A-F
```

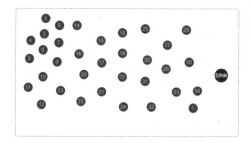

Fig. 9. Network with nodes arranged in random

These diagrams are, of course, static. However, the underlying Javascript libraries can be used to program such diagrams to show further protocol states, relying on the regularity inherent in these graphs (Figs. 10 and 11).

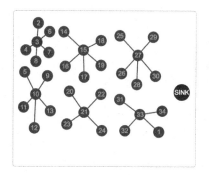

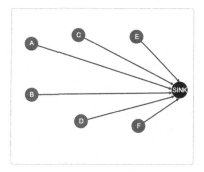

Fig. 10. Cluster formation   **Fig. 11.** Quotient graph on clusters

7 Design of Skeblle

In this section, we motivate the design at a high level, and in subsequent sections discuss some aspects in depth.

The basic elements of Skeblle, the combination of diagramming and a command language for manipulating the underlying model, are intrinsic to the programmable active diagram approach. The need to connect the diagrams to the underlying systems naturally suggests a web browser as the platform. Browsers suffice for diagramming, given libraries like JSXGraph [8].

The remaining questions center around what graph operators to choose, and how to describe the graphs and their appearance.

To describe graphs we use markup languages in analogy with HTML and CSS, and allow users to edit either the graph or the markup, following the approach of tools like Firebug [15]. The next design question is what markup to use. In principle, one should use a standard such as GraphML [6], but for implementation simplicity, we use stylized JSON.

The choice of graph operators in Skeblle was guided by applications. CRUD operations on individual nodes and edges as well as subgraphs arose in many cases, while operations such as quotient graphs arise due to the hierarchical nature of many systems. We are still exploring what is possible with Skeblle, and eventually hope to discover a more principled approach for choosing operators.

8   Graph Operations in Skeblle

Graph operations in Skeblle are available either manually, via the command line scripting language, or directly as a library in Javascript. It is much faster to create and operate on graphs via the command line, while operations like layout and label editing are simpler via the UI – with Skeblle, the user may choose whichever feels convenient. Skeblle offers simple but effective layout assistance that makes command line usage pleasant. In this section we will discuss graph operations, leaving layout for Sect. 9.

8.1   Nodes, Edges, and Types

The simplest of operations create and delete nodes, edges and their types in the context of a particular graph. The command `cg` <graphname> creates a graph, `dg` <graphname> deletes it, and `ct` <graphname> makes it the current graph for subsequent commands. A graph name also doubles as a namespace for subsequent names.

Command	Typename	Entityname	Notes
cn	frontend	abc,pqr,..	Nodes with labels abc, pqr
cn	memcache	[a-n]	Nodes a through n
cn	sensor	1-10	Nodes 1 through 10
ce	request	abc=>pqr,...	Edge from abc to pqr
ce	request	(x,y)abc=>pqr	Edges x and y from abc to pqr

Having created a graph, we can now create and delete nodes and edges with commands like `cn` or `ce`. Node names can be specified in various ways, either explicit list of labels or generic labels as in the following table. Node and Edge commands take optional type names used to address groups of nodes and edges. Type names identify kinds of nodes depicted in various systems in our examples. For instance, "memcache" nodes are servers that represent caches in a web application, while "sensor" type nodes represent sensors in a wireless sensor network. Edge operations take explicit specification via label pairs, and can also take optional types. In our example, edge types are the edges that indicate the processing of a request in a web site. Along similar lines, we can specify deletions and updates:

dn frontend   – Delete all frontend nodes
un memcache a=>a1   – Update node label a to $a1$ if type memcache

Commands for deletions and updates are especially useful when modifying sets of nodes. For individual nodes, it is expected that users will manually change nodes as in common drawing tools.

8.2   Derived Graphs and High-level Operators

As discussed in Sect. 7, we have chosen graph operators based on experience. The simplest high level operations define subgraphs, and other operations operate on these derived graphs. The commands can also define virtual subgraphs, whose nodes and edges need not be defined. Such virtual subgraphs are useful in high level operations as discussed below. Once named, the subgraphs can be used in commands that operate on graphs. The following high level operators are available. All high level operators can be seen either as queries or as modifiers. When used as a query, these operators change the visualization of the graph, and used as a mutator they alter graphs.

Command	Graphname	Entitynames	Definition
sn/svn	edge	abc,pqr	Subgraph by Node set
se/sve	bridge	a=>b,m=>n	Subgraph by Edge set
sp/svp	flow	a=>b=>c	Subgraph by path

- *Project* (hp) separates a graph into a subgraph and its complement. As a query, it highlights a subgraph, and grays out the complement. The meaning of highlight and gray are defined in GSS as discussed below. As a mutator, it deletes the complement.
- *Quotient* (hq) as a query visually replaces groups of nodes by a single quotient node, and collapses any edges. As a mutator, it deletes nodes and replaces them by the quotient node.
- *Split* (hs) removes edges between the graphs mentioned, either hiding them or actually modifying a graph.
- *Join* (hj) takes a set of virtual edges that do not actually exist and adds or displays them.

Query/mutate	Graphs	Definition
hp/hmp	g1 g2	Project subgraphs
hq/hmq	g1 g2	Quotient by subgraphs
hs/hms	g1	Split subgraph
hj/hmj	g1	Join subgraph

Lastly, we have a simple mutating operation, copy:

```
hcp copygraph origgraph
```

Copy (hcp) takes a graph and makes a copy, renaming the node labels with an instance number (See Sect. 4).

9 Visual Aspects: Layout and Markup

Our approach to layout is very simple. By default, given a command like cn edge WVip, RVip, we divide the drawing board into a 2×2 grid, and place the two nodes randomly into the grid cells with disjoint rows and columns. As more nodes get added, the grid expands to create more rows and columns. A sample is shown in Fig. 12. At any time, a user may adjust the layout, and the users adjustments will be remembered even as other nodes are added. Surprisingly, this simple approach is not too bad in actual use.

We provide for further support by allowing a user to divide the drawing area into rows and columns, adjust their sizes, and within each subarea, we place nodes randomly without row-column overlap. An example appears in Fig. 13. We expect to support layout algorithms and as well as L^AT_EX style tabular layouts in the future.

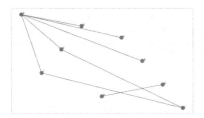

Fig. 12. Default layout: pseudo random with disjoint rows and columns

Fig. 13. Layout from command lc [a,b,c] [d,e] [f,g,h,j]

```
{"Nodes-List":[
 { "Node0":[
  {"label":"FRONTEND"},
  {"type":"server"},
  {"urls":"http://front.."}
 ]}
]}
{ "Edges-List":[
 { "Edge0":[
  {"startNode":"Node0"},
  {"endNode":"Node1"},
  { "type":"request"},
 ]}
]}
```

Listing 1.1. Graph markup

```
{"Node-Type-List":[
 {"server":[
  {"shape":"circle"},
  {"size":"10"},
  {"color":"brown"},
 ]}
]}
{"Edge-Type-List":[
 {"request":[
  {"width":"2"},
  {"color":"red"},
  {"dash":"0"},
 ]}
]}
```

Listing 1.2. Styles

As discussed in Sect. 7, we used stylized JSON for markup. Listing 1.1 shows markup for Fig. 2 in Sect. 3. A user can directly modify markup via Skeblle interface (Fig. 1), and such modifications will be mirrored in the diagram.

The markup for a Skeblle diagram are sufficient to describe a diagram, and is used as the notation for persisting diagrams to disk.

10   Connecting Skeblle to Live systems

The nodes and edges of a Skeblle diagram can hold references to external resources using urls. The architecture diagram from Sect. 3 is actually connected to real servers, whose statistics are available from the diagram, as shown in Fig. 14. Besides this simple use case, we can add Javascript code that fetches data using URLs, and can combine that data with the graph operations.

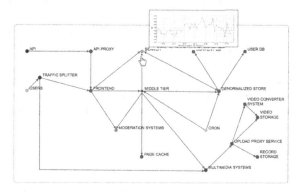

Fig. 14. Deployment diagram connected to servers

11   Related Work

Current industrial tools for diagramming like Visio [2] are intended for manual use, although they include support for style sheets, templates, and scripting languages. Tools like TikZ [3] and Pic [14] and Graphviz [7] are languages for diagramming. Skeblle takes inspiration from these tools, but forges a distinct path: an imperative, high level command language for drawing graphs, combined with declarative markup for visualization, and a bidirectional editing system.

Tools like Matplotlib [11] are also programmatic diagram tools, but with a focus on viewing existing data. Others like [17,18] require explicit programs that generate diagrams from underlying data. Skeblle can be used for viewing existing models, but it is more common to create a diagram first, either manually or by commands, implicitly generating an underlying model *from* the diagram.

Bidirectional editing in Skeblle and feel of the Skeblle interface is inspired by similar tools in web browsers, especially Firebug [15]. From HTML and CSS we take the idea of separating structure and appearance, but others graph tools also use similar ideas. Graph markups like GraphML [6], an interchange language for tools and GSS [16] for layout of RDF graphs, are in use. At present, we use ad-hoc stylized-JSON as markup for simplicity, but in time Skeblle will move to a standard markup.

Our other major inspiration comes from the world of Graph Rewriting, especially tools like Groove [9], GrGen [12] and others [13]. We tried to use some of these tools and found that while the tools have enormous power, we needed a system that could be used as a simple drawing tool, and when needed manipulate the drawing formally. Skeblle is, to our knowledge, unique in this capability.

12   Conclusion

Structured diagramming tools are simple to use, but the diagrams become pixels and the connection to the domain is lost. On the other hand, tools based on formalisms like graph rewriting excel at graph manipulation, but require considerable investment. Programmable active diagrams is an approach that marries the simplicity of a diagramming tool to the manipulation power of a powerful formalism, as shown in Skeblle.

The Skeblle implementation builds on interface design ideas that evolved with Web tools, but are rarely seen outside this context. We have shown that ideas from web tools like bidirectional edit are convenient in other contexts. We add to this set of ideas the notion of an imperative language in the tradition of Unix languages like Pic. The resulting tool has proven convenient to use, although the idea of a command line driven diagramming tool sounds strange at first glance.

In conclusion, we believe that future toolmakers will benefit from these ideas: web style interfaces for tools, marriage of command line and manual manipulation, and diagrams that are both easy to create and backed by formal models.

Acknowledgments. We thank our colleagues at Yahoo for their support of this work, and the JSXGraph [8] team for their library.

References

1. Chemtube3d. http://www.chemtube3d.com
2. Microsoft Visio. http://en.wikipedia.org/wiki/Microsoft_Visio
3. PGF/TikZ. http://en.wikipedia.org/wiki/TikZ
4. PlantUML tool. http://plantuml.sourceforge.net/
5. Quotient set. http://en.wikipedia.org/wiki/Quotient_set
6. Brandes, U., Eiglsperger, M., Lerner, J., Pich, C.: Graph markup language (GraphML) (2013)
7. Ellson, J., Gansner, E.R., Koutsofios, L., North, S.C., Woodhull, G.: Graphviz - open source graph drawing tools. In: Mutzel, P., Jünger, M., Leipert, S. (eds.) GD 2001. LNCS, vol. 2265, pp. 483–484. Springer, Heidelberg (2002)
8. Gerhauser, M., Valentin, B., Wassermann, A.: JSXGraph-dynamic mathematics with javascript. Int. J. Technol. Math. Educ. **17**(4), 211–215 (2010)

9. Ghamarian, A.H., de Mol, M., Rensink, A., Zambon, E., Zimakova, M.: Modelling and analysis using groove. STTT **14**(1), 15–40 (2012)
10. Heinzelman, W.R., Chandrakasan, A., Balakrishnan, H.: Energy-efficient communication protocol for wireless microsensor networks. In: HICSS (2000)
11. Hunter, J.D.: Matplotlib: a 2D graphics environment. Comput. Sci. Eng. **9**(3), 90–95 (2007)
12. Jakumeit, E., Buchwald, S., Kroll, M.: GrGen.NET - the expressive, convenient and fast graph rewrite system. STTT **12**(3–4), 263–271 (2010)
13. Jakumeit, E., Buchwald, S., Wagelaar, D., Dan, L., Hegedüs, Á., Herrmannsdörfer, M., Horn, T., Kalnina, E., Krause, C., Lano, K., Lepper, M., Rensink, A., Rose, L., Wätzol, S.: A survey and comparison of transformation tools based on the transformation tool contest. Sci. Comput. Program. **85**, 41–99 (2013)
14. Kernighan, B.W.: Pic-a language for typesetting graphics. Softw. Pract. Exper. **12**(1), 1–21 (1982)
15. Luthra, C., Mittal, D.: Firebug 1.5: Editing, Debugging, and Monitoring Web Pages. Packt Publishing, New Delhi (2010)
16. Pietriga, E.: Graph style sheets in IsaViz (2001). http://www.w3.org/2001/11/IsaViz/gss/gssmanual.html
17. Sefika, M., Sane, A., Campbell, R.H.:Architecture-oriented visualization. In: ACM SIGPLAN Notice, vol. 31, pp. 398–405. ACM (1996)
18. Sefika, M., Sane, A., Campbell, R.H.: Monitoring compliance of a software system with its high-level design models. In: Proceedings of the 18th International Conference on Software Engineering, pp. 387–396. IEEE Computer Society (1996)
19. Vlissides, J.M., Linton, M.A.: Unidraw: a framework for building domain-specific graphical editors. ACM Trans. Inf. Syst. **8**(3), 237–268 (1990)

The Role of Indirections in Lazy Natural Semantics

Lidia Sánchez-Gil[1], Mercedes Hidalgo-Herrero[2], and Yolanda Ortega-Mallén[3]([✉])

[1] Facultad de Informática, Universidad Complutense de Madrid, Madrid, Spain
[2] Facultad de Educación, Universidad Complutense de Madrid, Madrid, Spain
[3] Facultad de CC. Matemáticas, Universidad Complutense de Madrid, Madrid, Spain
yolanda@ucm.es

Abstract. Launchbury defines a natural semantics for lazy evaluation and proposes an alternative version which introduces indirections, eliminates blackholes and does not update closures. Equivalence of both semantics is not straightforward. In this paper we focus on the introduction of indirections during β-reduction and study how the heaps, i.e., the sets of bindings, obtained with this kind of evaluation do relate with the heaps produced by substitution. As a heap represents the context of evaluation for a term, we first define an equivalence that identifies terms with the same meaning under a given context. This notion of *context* equivalence is extended to heaps. Finally, we define a relation between heap/term pairs to establish the equivalence between Launchbury's alternative natural semantics and its corresponding version without indirections.

1 Motivation

More than twenty years have elapsed since Launchbury first presented in [9] a natural semantics for lazy evaluation (*call-by-need*), a key contribution to the semantic foundation for non-strict functional programming languages like Haskell or Clean. Throughout these years, Launchbury's semantics has been cited frequently and has inspired many further works as well as several extensions like in [2,8,10,13,17,20]. The success of Lanchbury's proposal resides in its simplicity. Expressions are evaluated with respect to a *context*, which is represented by a heap of *bindings*, that is, (variable, expression) pairs. This heap is explicitly managed to make possible the sharing of bindings, thus, modeling laziness.

In order to prove that this lazy (operational) semantics is *correct* and *computationally adequate* with respect to a standard denotational semantics, Launchbury introduces some variations in the operational semantics. On the one hand, the update of bindings with their computed values is an operational notion without counterpart in the standard denotational semantics, so that the alternative natural semantics does no longer update bindings and becomes a *call-by-name* semantics. On the other hand, functional application is modeled denotationally by extending the environment with a variable bound to a value. This new variable represents the formal parameter of the function, while the value corresponds

A. Voronkov and I. Virbitskaite (Eds.): PSI 2014, LNCS 8974, pp. 288–303, 2015.
DOI: 10.1007/978-3-662-46823-4_24

to the actual argument. For a closer approach to this mechanism, in the alternative semantics applications are carried out by introducing *indirections*, i.e., variables bound to variables, instead of by performing the β-reduction through substitution. Besides, the denotation "undefined" indicates that there is no value associated to the expression being evaluated, but there is no indication of the reason for that. By contrast, in the operational semantics there are two possibilities for not reaching a value: either the reduction gets blocked if no rule is applicable, or the reduction never stops. The first case occurs in the original semantics when reducing self-references (*blackhole*). The rules in the alternative semantics guarantee that reductions never reach a blackhole.

Alas, the proof of the equivalence of the natural semantics and its alternative version is detailed nowhere, and a simple induction turns out to be insufficient. The *context-heap* semantics is too sensitive to the changes introduced by the alternative rules. Intuitively, both reduction systems should lead to the same results. However, this cannot be directly established since final values may contain free variables that are dependent on the context of evaluation, which is represented by the heap of bindings. The lack of update leads to the duplication of bindings, but is awkward to prove that duplicated bindings, as well as indirections, do not add relevant information to the context. Therefore, our challenge is to establish a way of relating the heaps and values obtained with each reduction system, and to prove that the semantics are equivalent, so that any reduction of a term in one of the systems has its counterpart in the other. To facilitate this task we consider separately the no updating and the introduction of indirections.

In this paper we investigate the effect of introducing indirections in a setting without updates, and we analyze the similarities and differences between the reductions proofs obtained with and without indirections. Indirections have also been used in [8] to model communication channels between processes.

We want to identify terms up to α-conversion, but dealing with α-equated terms usually implies the use of Barendregt's variable convention [3] to avoid the renaming of bound variables. However, the use of the variable convention is sometimes dubious and may lead to *faulty* results (as it is shown by Urban et al. in [18]). Moreover, we intend to formalize our results with the help of some proof assistant like Coq [4] or Isabelle [11]. Looking for a binding system susceptible of formalization, we have chosen a *locally nameless* representation (as presented by Charguéraud in [6]). This is a mixed notation where bound variable names are replaced by de Bruijn indices [7], while free variables preserve their names. This is suitable in our case because context heaps collect free variables whose names we are interested in preserving in order to identify them more easily. A locally nameless version of Launchbury's natural semantics has been presented by the authors in [14,15].

Others are revisiting Launchbury's semantics too. For instance, Breitner has formally proven in [5] the correctness of the natural semantics by using Isabelle's nominal package [19], and presently he is working on the formalization of the adequacy. While Breitner is exclusively interested in formalizing the proofs, we have a broader objective: To analyze the effect of introducing indirections in the context heaps, and the correspondence between heap/value pairs obtained with

$$x \in Id \qquad i,j \in \mathbb{N}$$

$$x \in Var$$
$$v \in Var \quad ::= \mathbf{bvar}\ i\ j \mid \mathbf{fvar}\ x$$
$$e \in Exp ::= x' \mid \lambda x.e \mid (e\ x) \mid$$
$$t \in LNExp ::= v \mid \mathbf{abs}\ t \mid \mathbf{app}\ t\ v \mid$$
$$\mathbf{let}\ \{x_i = e_i\}_{i=1}^n\ \mathbf{in}\ e$$
$$\mathbf{let}\ \{t_i\}_{i=1}^n\ \mathbf{in}\ t$$

(a) Named representation
(b) Locally nameless representation

Fig. 1. Extended λ-calculus

update and those produced without update. Furthermore, we want to prove the equivalence of the two operational semantics.

The main contributions of the present work are:

1. An equivalence relation to identify heaps that define the same free variables but whose corresponding closures may differ on *undefined free variables*;
2. A preorder that relates two heaps whenever the first can be transformed into the second by *eliminating indirections*;
3. An extension of the previous preorder relation for heap/term pairs expressing that two terms are equivalent if they have the same structure and their free variables, defined in the context of the respective heaps, are the same except for some indirections.
4. An equivalence theorem for Launchbury's alternative semantics and a version without indirections (and without update and blackholes).

The paper is structured as follows: In the next section we give a locally nameless version of Launchbury's semantics and its alternative rules. In Sect. 3 we define equivalence and preorder relations on terms, heaps and also on heap/term pairs. We include a number of interesting results concerning these relations and, finally, we prove the equivalence of Launchbury's alternative semantics and an intermediate semantics without update, without blackholes and without indirections. In the last section we draw conclusions and outline our future work.

2   A Locally Nameless Representation

The language described in [9] is a normalized lambda calculus extended with recursive local declarations. The abstract syntax, in the *named representation*, appears in Fig. 1a. Normalization is achieved in two steps. First an α-conversion is performed so that all bound variables have distinct names. In a second phase, it is ensured that arguments for applications are restricted to be variables. These static transformations make more explicit the sharing of closures and, thus, simplify the definition of the reduction rules.

Since there are two name binders, i.e., λ-abstraction and `let`-declaration, a quotient structure respect to α-equivalence is required. We avoid this by employing a *locally nameless representation* [6]. As mentioned above, our locally nameless representation has already been presented in [14,15]. Here we give only a brief overview avoiding those technicalities that are not essential to the contributions of the present work.

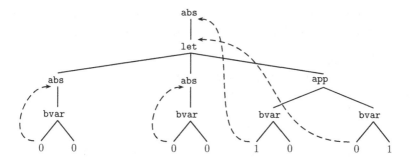

Fig. 2. Syntactic tree for a locally nameless term

2.1 Locally Nameless Syntax

The locally nameless version of the abstract syntax is shown in Fig. 1b. *Bound variables* and *free variables* are distinguished. Since let-declarations are multi-binders, we have followed Charguéraud [6] and bound variables are represented with two natural numbers: the first number is a de Bruijn index that counts how many binders (abstraction or let) have been passed through in the syntactic tree to reach the corresponding binder for the variable, while the second refers to the position of the variable inside that binder. Abstractions are seen as multi-binders that bind one variable, so that the second number should be zero.

Example 1. Let $e \in Exp$ be a λ-expression given in the named representation: $e \equiv \lambda z.\text{let } \{x_1 = \lambda y_1.y_1, x_2 = \lambda y_2.y_2\} \text{ in } (z\ x_2)$. The corresponding locally nameless term $t \in LNExp$ is:
$t \equiv \text{abs } (\text{let } \{\text{abs } (\text{bvar } 0\ 0), \text{abs } (\text{bvar } 0\ 0)\} \text{ in app } (\text{bvar } 1\ 0)\ (\text{bvar } 0\ 1))$.
Notice that x_1 and x_2 denote α-equivalent expressions in e. This is more clearly seen in t, where both expressions are represented with syntactically equal terms. The syntactic tree corresponding to t is shown in Fig. 2. $\qquad \square$

This locally nameless syntax allows to build terms that have no corresponding named expression in *Exp*. For instance, when bound variables indices are out of range. Those terms in *LNExp* that do match expressions in *Exp* are called *locally-closed*, written lc t.

   In the following, a list like $\{t_i\}_{i=1}^n$ is represented as $\bar{t}$, with length $|\bar{t}| = n$. Later on, we use $[t : \bar{t}]$ to represent a list with head t and tail $\bar{t}$; the empty list is represented as $[\,]$, a unitary list as $[t]$, and $+\!\!+$ stands for list concatenation.

   We denote by $\text{fv}(t)$ the set of *free variables* of a term t. A name $x \in Id$ is *fresh in a term* $t \in LNExp$, written fresh x in t, if x does not belong to the set of free variables of t, i.e., $x \notin \text{fv}(t)$. Similarly, for a list of names, fresh $\bar{x}$ in t if $\bar{x} \notin \text{fv}(t)$, where $\bar{x}$ represents a list of pairwise-distinct names in *Id*. We say that two terms have the *same structure*, written $t \sim_S t'$, if they differ only in the names of their free variables.

Since there is no danger of name capture, *substitution* of variable names is trivial in the locally nameless representation. We write $t[y/x]$ for replacing the occurrences of x by y in the term t.

A *variable opening* operation is needed to manipulate locally nameless terms. This operation turns the outermost bound variables into free variables. The opening of a term $t \in LNExp$ with a list of names $\overline{x} \subseteq Id$ is denoted by $t^{\overline{x}}$. For simplicity, we write t^x for the variable opening with a unitary list $[x]$. We illustrate this concept and its use with an example:

Example 2. Let $t \equiv$ abs (let bvar 0 1, bvar 1 0 in app (abs bvar 2 0) (bvar 0 1)). Hence, the body of the abstraction is:

$$u \equiv \text{let bvar 0 1, } \boxed{\text{bvar 1 0}} \text{ in app (abs } \boxed{\text{bvar 2 0}} \text{) (bvar 0 1).}$$

But then in u the bound variables referring to the outermost abstraction of t (shown squared) point to nowhere. The opening of u with variable x replaces with x the bound variables referring to an hypothetical binder with body u:
$u^x = $ let bvar 0 1, fvar x in app (abs fvar x) (bvar 0 1). □

Inversely to variable opening, there is an operation to transform free names into bound variables. The *variable closing* of a term is represented by $\backslash^{\overline{x}}t$, where $\overline{x}$ is the list of names to be bound (recall that the names in $\overline{x}$ are distinct).

Example 3. We close the term obtained by opening u in Example 2.
Let $t \equiv$ let bvar 0 1, fvar x in app (abs fvar x) (bvar 0 1), then
$\backslash^x t = $ let bvar 0 1, bvar 1 0 in app (abs bvar 2 0) (bvar 0 1). □

Notice that in the last example the closed term coincides with u, the body of the abstraction in Example 2 that was opened with x, although this is not always the case. Only under some conditions variable closing and variable opening are inverse operations: If the variables are fresh in t, then $\backslash^{\overline{x}}(t^{\overline{x}}) = t$; and if the term is locally closed, then $(\backslash^{\overline{x}}t)^{\overline{x}} = t$.

2.2 Locally Nameless Semantics

In the natural semantics defined by Launchbury [9] judgements are of the form $\Gamma : t \Downarrow \Delta : w$, that is, the term t in the context of the heap Γ reduces to the value w in the context of the (modified) heap Δ. *Values* ($w \in Val$) are terms in weak-head-normal-form (*whnf*) and *heaps* are collections of *bindings*, i.e., pairs (variable, term). A binding (fvar x, t) with $x \in Id$ and $t \in LNExp$ is represented by $x \mapsto t$. In the following, we represent a heap $\{x_i \mapsto t_i\}_{i=1}^n$ as $(\overline{x} \mapsto \overline{t})$, with $|\overline{x}| = |\overline{t}| = n$. The set of the locally-nameless-heaps is denoted as *LNHeap*.

The *domain* of a heap Γ, written $\text{dom}(\Gamma)$, collects the set of names defined in the heap, so that $\text{dom}(\overline{x} \mapsto \overline{t}) = \overline{x}$. By contrast, the function names returns the set of all names that appear in a heap, i.e., the names occurring either in the domain or in the terms on the right-hand side of the bindings. This is used to define a freshness predicate for heaps: fresh $\overline{x}$ in $\Gamma \overset{\text{def}}{=} \overline{x} \notin \text{names}(\Gamma)$.

$$\text{LNLam} \quad \frac{\{\text{ok } \Gamma\} \qquad \{\text{lc } (\text{abs } t)\}}{\Gamma : \text{abs } t \Downarrow \Gamma : \text{abs } t}$$

$$\text{LNVar} \quad \frac{\Gamma : t \Downarrow \Delta : w \qquad \{x \notin \text{dom}(\Gamma) \cup \text{dom}(\Delta)\}}{(\Gamma, x \mapsto t) : \text{fvar } x \Downarrow (\Delta, x \mapsto w) : w}$$

$$\text{LNApp} \quad \frac{\Gamma : t \Downarrow \Theta : \text{abs } u \qquad \Theta : u^x \Downarrow \Delta : w \qquad \{x \notin \text{dom}(\Gamma) \Rightarrow x \notin \text{dom}(\Delta)\}}{\Gamma : \text{app } t \ (\text{fvar } x) \Downarrow \Delta : w}$$

$$\text{LNLet} \quad \frac{\begin{array}{c} \forall \overline{x}^{|\overline{t}|} \notin L \subseteq Id.[(\Gamma, \overline{x} \mapsto \overline{t}^{\overline{x}}) : t^{\overline{x}} \Downarrow (\overline{x} +\!\!+ \overline{z} \mapsto \overline{s}^{\overline{x}}) : w^{\overline{x}} \\ \wedge \ ^{\backslash \overline{x}}(\overline{s}^{\overline{x}}) = \overline{s} \wedge \ ^{\backslash \overline{x}}(w^{\overline{x}}) = w] \\ \{\overline{y}^{|\overline{t}|} \notin L\} \end{array}}{\Gamma : \text{let } \overline{t} \text{ in } t \Downarrow (\overline{y} +\!\!+ \overline{z} \mapsto \overline{s}^{\overline{y}}) : w^{\overline{y}}}$$

Fig. 3. Natural semantics with locally nameless representation

$$\text{ALNVar} \quad \frac{(\Gamma, x \mapsto t) : t \Downarrow \Delta : w}{(\Gamma, x \mapsto t) : \text{fvar } x \Downarrow \Delta : w}$$

$$\text{ALNApp} \quad \frac{\begin{array}{c} \Gamma : t \Downarrow \Theta : \text{abs } u \\ \forall y \notin L \subseteq Id.[(\Theta, y \mapsto \text{fvar } x) : u^y \Downarrow ([y : \overline{z}] \mapsto \overline{s}^y) : w^y \\ \wedge \ ^{\backslash y}(\overline{s}^y) = \overline{s} \wedge \ ^{\backslash y}(w^y) = w] \\ \{x \notin \text{dom}(\Gamma) \Rightarrow x \notin [z : \overline{z}]\} \qquad \{z \notin L\} \end{array}}{\Gamma : \text{app } t \ (\text{fvar } x) \Downarrow ([z : \overline{z}] \mapsto \overline{s}^z) : w^z}$$

Fig. 4. Alternative rules with locally nameless representation

In a well-formed heap names are defined at most once and terms are locally closed. We write $\text{ok } \Gamma$ to indicate that a heap is well-formed.

Figure 3 shows our locally nameless representation of the rules for the natural semantics for lazy evaluation. For clarity, in the rules we put in braces the side-conditions to better distinguish them from the judgements.

To prove the computational adequacy of the natural semantics with respect to a standard denotational semantics, Launchbury introduces alternative rules for variables and applications, whose locally nameless version is shown in Fig. 4. Observe that the ALNVar rule does not longer update the binding for the variable being evaluated, namely x. Besides, the binding for x does not disappear from the heap where the term bound to x is to be evaluated; therefore, any further reference to x leads to an infinite reduction. The effect of ALNApp is the addition of an indirection $y \mapsto \text{fvar } x$ instead of performing the β-reduction by substitution, as in u^x in LNApp.

In the rules LNLet and ALNApp we use *cofinite quantification*, which is an alternative to "exists-fresh" quantification that provides stronger induction and inversion principles [1]. In LNLet the notation $\overline{x}^{|\overline{t}|} \notin L$ indicates that $\overline{x}$ is a list of length $|\overline{t}|$ of (distinct) names not belonging to the finite set L. Hence, although there are not explicit freshness side-conditions in the rules, the finite set L represents somehow the names that should be avoided during a reduction proof. Among infinite possible combinations for $\overline{x}$, the set of names $\overline{y}$ is chosen for the reduction. The list $\overline{z}$ represents the rest of names defined in the heap which is obtained after the reduction. Notice how variable opening is used to express that the final heap and value may depend on the names that have been chosen. For instance, in LNLET, $w^{\overline{x}}$ indicates that it depends on the names $\overline{x}$, but there is a common basis w . Moreover, it is required that this basis does not contain occurrences of $\overline{x}$; this is expressed by $\backslash^{\overline{x}}(w^{\overline{x}}) = w$. A detailed explanation of these semantic rules can be found in [14–16].

In the following, the natural semantics (rules in Fig. 3) is referred as NS, and the alternative semantics (rules LNLAM, LNLET and those in Fig. 4) as ANS. We write $\Downarrow^A$ for reductions in ANS. Launchbury proves in [9] the correctness of NS with respect to a standard denotational semantics, and a similar result for ANS is easily obtained (as the authors of this paper have done in [12]). Therefore, NS and ANS are "denotationally" equivalent in the sense that if an expression is reducible (in some heap context) by both semantics then the obtained values have the same denotation. But this is insufficient for our purposes, because we want to ensure that if for some (heap : term) pair a reduction exists in any of the semantics, then there must exist a reduction in the other too and the final heaps must be related. The changes in ANS might seem to involve no serious difficulties to prove the latter result. Unfortunately things are not so easy. On the one hand, the alternative rule for variables transforms the original call-by-need semantics into a call-by-name semantics because bindings are not updated and computed values are no longer shared. Moreover, in the original semantics the reduction of a self-reference gets blocked (*blackhole*), while in the alternative semantics self-references yield infinite reductions. On the other hand, the addition of indirections complicates the task of comparing the (heap : value) pairs obtained by each reduction system, as one may need to follow a chain of indirections to get the term bound to a variable. We deal separately with each modification and introduce two intermediate semantics: (1) the *No-update Natural Semantics* (NNS) with the rules of NS (Fig. 3) except for the variable rule, that corresponds to the one in the alternative version, i.e., ALNVAR in Fig. 4; and (2) the *Indirection Natural Semantics* (INS) with the rules of NS but for the application rule, that corresponds to the alternative ALNAPP rule in Fig. 4. We use $\Downarrow^N$ to represent reductions of NNS and $\Downarrow^I$ for those of INS.

The following table summarizes the characteristics of the four natural semantics defined above:

	NS - $\Downarrow$	INS - $\Downarrow^I$	NNS - $\Downarrow^N$	ANS - $\Downarrow^A$
Indirections	✗	✓	✗	✓
Update	✓	✓	✗	✗
Blackholes	✓	✓	✗	✗

It is guaranteed that the judgements produced by the locally nameless rules given in Figs. 3, 4 involve only well-formed heaps and locally closed terms. Furthermore, the reduction systems corresponding to these rules verify a number of interesting properties proved in [15]. We include here some new results that comprehend the alternative rules. In the four reduction systems, definitions are not lost during reduction, i.e., heaps only can grow with new names. But in the case of non updating (NNS and ANS) the bindings in the initial heap are preserved during the whole reduction:

Lemma 1. $\Gamma : t \Downarrow^K \Delta : w \Rightarrow \Gamma \subseteq \Delta$, where $\Downarrow^K$ represents $\Downarrow^N$ and $\Downarrow^A$.

During reduction, names might be added to the heap by the rules LNLET and ALNAPP. However, there is no "spontaneous generation" of names, i.e., any name occurring in a final (heap : value) pair must either appear already in the initial (heap : term) pair or be defined in the final heap. The freshness of the names introduced by the rules LNLET and ALNAPP is determined as follows:

Lemma 2. *1.* $\Gamma : t \Downarrow^N \Delta : w \wedge x \in \mathrm{dom}(\Delta) - \mathrm{dom}(\Gamma) \Rightarrow \mathtt{fresh}\ x\ \mathrm{in}\ \Gamma.$
2. $\Gamma : t \Downarrow^A \Delta : w \wedge x \in \mathrm{dom}(\Delta) - \mathrm{dom}(\Gamma) \Rightarrow \mathtt{fresh}\ x\ \mathrm{in}\ (\Gamma : t).$

The following *renaming* lemma ensures that the evaluation of a term is independent of the names chosen during the reduction process. Further, any name defined in the context heap can be replaced by a fresh one without changing the meaning of the terms evaluated in that context. In fact, reductions for (heap : term) pairs are unique up to α-conversion of the names defined in the heap.

Lemma 3. *(Renaming)*

1. $\Gamma : t \Downarrow^K \Delta : w \wedge \mathtt{fresh}\ y\ \mathrm{in}\ \Gamma, \Delta, t, w \Rightarrow \Gamma[y/x] : t[y/x] \Downarrow^K \Delta[y/x] : w[y/x].$
2. $\Gamma : t \Downarrow^K \Delta : w \wedge \mathtt{fresh}\ y\ \mathrm{in}\ \Gamma, \Delta, t, w \wedge x \notin \mathrm{dom}(\Gamma) \wedge x \in \mathrm{dom}(\Delta)$
$\Rightarrow \Gamma : t \Downarrow^K \Delta[y/x] : w[y/x],$

where $\Gamma[y/x]$ indicates that name substitution is done in the left and right hand sides of the heap Γ, and $\Downarrow^K$ represents $\Downarrow$, $\Downarrow^A$, $\Downarrow^I$, and $\Downarrow^N$.
    Detailed proofs are given in [15], and also in [16] that is an extended version of the present paper including detailed proofs for all the lemmas and propositions.

3   Indirections

The aim in this section is to prove the equivalence of NNS and ANS. After the evaluation of a term in a given context, each semantics yields a different binding heap. It is necessary to analyze their differences, which lie in the indirections introduced by ANS. An *indirection* is a binding of the form $x \mapsto \mathtt{fvar}\ y$, that is, it just redirects to another variable name. The set of indirections of a heap Γ is denoted by $\mathtt{Ind}(\Gamma)$.

Example 4. Let us evaluate $t \equiv \mathtt{let\ abs\ (bvar\ 0\ 0)\ in\ app\ (abs\ s)\ (bvar\ 0\ 0)}$, where $s \equiv \mathtt{let\ abs\ (bvar\ 0\ 0)}, \mathtt{app\ (bvar\ 0\ 0)\ (bvar\ 1\ 0)\ in\ abs\ (bvar\ 0\ 0)}$, in the empty context $\Gamma = \emptyset$:

$$\Gamma : t \Downarrow^N \{x_0 \mapsto \mathtt{abs\ (bvar\ 0\ 0)}, x_1 \mapsto \mathtt{abs\ (bvar\ 0\ 0)}, x_2 \mapsto \mathtt{app\ (fvar\ }x_1\mathtt{)\ (fvar\ }x_0\mathtt{)}\}$$
$$: \mathtt{abs\ (bvar\ 0\ 0)}$$
$$\Gamma : t \Downarrow^A \{x_0 \mapsto \mathtt{abs\ (bvar\ 0\ 0)}, x_1 \mapsto \mathtt{abs\ (bvar\ 0\ 0)}, x_2 \mapsto \mathtt{app\ (fvar\ }x_1\mathtt{)\ (fvar\ }y\mathtt{)},$$
$$y \mapsto \mathtt{(fvar\ }x_0\mathtt{)}\} : \mathtt{abs\ (bvar\ 0\ 0)}$$

The value produced is the same in both cases. Yet, when comparing the final heap in $\Downarrow^A$ with that in $\Downarrow^N$, we observe that there is an extra indirection, $y \mapsto \mathtt{fvar\ }x_0$. This indirection corresponds to the binding introduced by ALNAPP to reduce the application in the term t. □

The previous example gives a hint of how to establish a relation between the heaps that are obtained with NNS and those produced by ANS. Two heaps are related if one can be obtained from the other by eliminating some indirections. For this purpose we define how to remove indirections from a heap, while preserving the evaluation context represented by that heap.

$$(\emptyset, x \mapsto \mathtt{fvar\ }y) \ominus x = \emptyset$$
$$((\Gamma, z \mapsto t), x \mapsto \mathtt{fvar\ }y) \ominus x = ((\Gamma, x \mapsto \mathtt{fvar\ }y) \ominus x, z \mapsto t[y/x])$$

This is generalized to remove a sequence of indirections from a heap:

$$\Gamma \ominus [\,] = \Gamma \qquad \Gamma \ominus [x : \overline{x}] = (\Gamma \ominus x) \ominus \overline{x}$$

3.1 Context Equivalence

The meaning of a term depends on the meaning of its free variables. However, if a free variable is not defined in the context of evaluation of a term, then the name of this free variable is irrelevant. Therefore, we consider that two terms are equivalent in a given context if they only differ in the names of the free variables that do not belong to the context.

Definition 1. *Let* $V \subseteq Id$, *and* $t, t' \in LNExp$. *We say that* t *and* t' *are* context-equivalent *in* V, *written* $t \approx^V t'$, *when*

$$\text{CE-BVAR} \quad \frac{}{(\mathtt{bvar}\ i\ j) \approx^V (\mathtt{bvar}\ i\ j)} \qquad \text{CE-FVAR} \quad \frac{x, x' \notin V \lor x = x'}{(\mathtt{fvar}\ x) \approx^V (\mathtt{fvar}\ x')}$$

$$\text{CE-ABS} \quad \frac{t \approx^V t'}{(\mathtt{abs}\ t) \approx^V (\mathtt{abs}\ t')} \qquad \text{CE-APP} \quad \frac{t \approx^V t' \quad v \approx^V v'}{(\mathtt{app}\ t\ v) \approx^V (\mathtt{app}\ t'\ v')}$$

$$\text{CE-LET} \quad \frac{|\overline{t}| = |\overline{t'}| \quad \overline{t} \approx^V \overline{t'} \quad t \approx^V t'}{(\mathtt{let}\ \overline{t}\ \mathtt{in}\ t) \approx^V (\mathtt{let}\ \overline{t'}\ \mathtt{in}\ t')}$$

Fixed the set of names V, $\approx^V$ is an equivalence relation on *LNExp*.

Proposition 1.

CE_REF	$t \approx^V t$
CE_SYM	$t \approx^V t' \Rightarrow t' \approx^V t$
CE_TRANS	$t \approx^V t' \wedge t' \approx^V t'' \Rightarrow t \approx^V t''$

Based on this equivalence on terms, we define a family of relations on heaps, where heaps are equivalent when they have the same domain and corresponding closures differ only in the free variables not defined in a given context:

Definition 2. *Let* $V \subseteq Id$, *and* $\Gamma, \Gamma' \in LNHeap$. *We say that* Γ *and* Γ' *are heap-context-equivalent in* V, *written* $\Gamma \approx^V \Gamma'$, *when*

$$\text{HCE-EMPTY} \frac{}{\emptyset \approx^V \emptyset} \qquad \text{HCE-CONS} \frac{\Gamma \approx^V \Gamma' \quad t \approx^V t' \quad \text{lc } t \quad x \notin \text{dom}(\Gamma)}{(\Gamma, x \mapsto t) \approx^V (\Gamma', x \mapsto t')}$$

The relations defined above are equivalences on well-formed heaps.

Proposition 2.

HCE_REF	ok $\Gamma \Rightarrow \Gamma \approx^V \Gamma$
HCE_SYM	$\Gamma \approx^V \Gamma' \Rightarrow \Gamma' \approx^V \Gamma$
HCE_TRANS	$\Gamma \approx^V \Gamma' \wedge \Gamma' \approx^V \Gamma'' \Rightarrow \Gamma \approx^V \Gamma''$

Moreover, if two heaps are heap-context-equivalent, then both are well-formed, have the same domain, and have the same indirections.

There is an alternative characterization for heap-context-equivalence which expresses that heaps are context-equivalent whenever they are well-formed, have the same domain, and each pair of corresponding bound terms is context-equivalent.

Lemma 4. $\Gamma \approx^V \Gamma' \Leftrightarrow$
ok $\Gamma \wedge$ ok $\Gamma' \wedge \text{dom}(\Gamma) = \text{dom}(\Gamma') \wedge (x \mapsto t \in \Gamma \wedge x \mapsto t' \in \Gamma' \Rightarrow t \approx^V t')$.

Considering context-equivalence on heaps, we are particularly interested in the case where the context coincides with the domain of the heaps:

Definition 3. *Let* $\Gamma, \Gamma' \in LNHeap$. *We say that* Γ *and* Γ' *are* heap-equivalent, *written* $\Gamma \approx \Gamma'$, *if they are heap-context-equivalent in* $\text{dom}(\Gamma)$, *i.e.,* $\Gamma \approx^{\text{dom}(\Gamma)} \Gamma'$.

The following lemmas establish the uniqueness (up to permutation) of the set of indirections that sets up the equivalence of two heaps. First, we have that the order in which two indirections are removed from a heap can be exchanged, producing equivalent heaps.

Lemma 5. ok $\Gamma \wedge x, y \in \text{Ind}(\Gamma) \wedge x \neq y \Rightarrow \Gamma \ominus [x, y] \approx \Gamma \ominus [y, x]$.

Next, the previous result is generalized so that any permutation of a sequence of indirections produces equivalent heaps. Moreover, if equivalent heaps are obtained by removing different sequences of indirections, then these must be the same up to permutation.

Lemma 6. ok $\Gamma \wedge \overline{x}, \overline{y} \subseteq \text{Ind}(\Gamma) \Rightarrow (\Gamma \ominus \overline{x} \approx \Gamma \ominus \overline{y} \Leftrightarrow \overline{y} \in \mathcal{S}(\overline{x}))$,
where $\mathcal{S}(\overline{x})$ *denotes the set of all permutations of* $\overline{x}$.

3.2 Indirection Relation

Coming back to the idea of Example 4, where a heap can be obtained from another by removing some indirections, we define the following relation on heaps:

Definition 4. *Let* $\Gamma, \Gamma' \in LNHeap$. *We say that* Γ *is indirection-related to* Γ', *written* $\Gamma \succsim_I \Gamma'$, *when*

$$\text{IR-HE} \quad \frac{\Gamma \approx \Gamma'}{\Gamma \succsim_I \Gamma'} \qquad\qquad \text{IR-IR} \quad \frac{\text{ok } \Gamma \quad \Gamma \ominus x \succsim_I \Gamma' \quad x \in \text{Ind}(\Gamma)}{\Gamma \succsim_I \Gamma'}$$

There is an alternative characterization for the relation $\succsim_I$ which expresses that a heap is indirection-related to another whenever the later can be obtained from the former by removing a sequence of indirections.

Proposition 3. $\Gamma \succsim_I \Gamma' \Leftrightarrow \text{ok } \Gamma \wedge \exists \, \overline{x} \subseteq \text{Ind}(\Gamma) \,.\, \Gamma \ominus \overline{x} \approx \Gamma'$.

By Lemma 6, the sequence of indirections is unique up to permutations, and it corresponds to the difference between the domains of the related heaps.

Corollary 1. $\Gamma \succsim_I \Gamma' \Rightarrow \Gamma \ominus (\text{dom}(\Gamma) - \text{dom}(\Gamma')) \approx \Gamma'$.[1]

The *indirection-relation* is a preorder on the set of well-formed heaps.

Proposition 4.

IR_REF $\text{ok } \Gamma \Rightarrow \Gamma \succsim_I \Gamma$

IR_TRANS $\Gamma \succsim_I \Gamma' \wedge \Gamma' \succsim_I \Gamma'' \Rightarrow \Gamma \succsim_I \Gamma''$

We extend Definition 4 to (heap : term) pairs. Again we use cofinite quantification instead of adding freshness conditions on the new name z.

Definition 5. *Let* $\Gamma, \Gamma' \in LNHeap$, *and* $t, t' \in LNExp$. *We say that* $(\Gamma : t)$ *is indirection-related to* $(\Gamma' : t')$, *written* $(\Gamma : t) \succsim_I (\Gamma' : t')$, *when*

$$\text{IR-HT} \quad \frac{\forall z \notin L \subseteq Id.(\Gamma, z \mapsto t) \succsim_I (\Gamma', z \mapsto t')}{(\Gamma : t) \succsim_I (\Gamma' : t')}$$

We illustrate these definitions with an example.

Example 5. Let us consider the following heap and term:

$\Gamma = \{x_0 \mapsto \text{fvar } x_1, x_1 \mapsto \text{abs (bvar 0 0)}, x_2 \mapsto \text{abs (app (fvar } x_0) \text{ (bvar 0 0))},$
$\qquad y_0 \mapsto \text{fvar } x_2\}$
$t = \text{abs (app (fvar } x_0) \text{ bvar 0 0)}$

The (heap : term) pairs related with $(\Gamma : t)$ are obtained by removing the sequences of indirections $[\,]$, $[y_0]$, $[x_0]$, and $[x_0, y_0]$:

---

[1] Since the ordering of indirections is irrelevant, $\text{dom}(\Gamma) - \text{dom}(\Gamma')$ represents any sequence with the names defined in Γ but undefined in Γ'.

(a) $\{x_0 \mapsto$ fvar $x_1, x_1 \mapsto$ abs (bvar 0 0)$, x_2 \mapsto$ abs (app (fvar x_0) (bvar 0 0)),
$\quad\ y_0 \mapsto$ fvar $x_2\}$
$\quad$: abs (app (fvar x_0) (bvar 0 0))

(b) $\{x_0 \mapsto$ fvar $x_1, x_1 \mapsto$ abs (bvar 0 0)$, x_2 \mapsto$ abs (app (fvar x_0) (bvar 0 0))$\}$
$\quad$: abs (app (fvar x_0) (bvar 0 0))

(c) $\{x_1 \mapsto$ abs (bvar 0 0)$, x_2 \mapsto$ abs (app (fvar x_1) (bvar 0 0))$, y_0 \mapsto$ fvar $x_2\}$
$\quad$: abs (app (fvar x_1) (bvar 0 0))

(d) $\{x_1 \mapsto$ abs (bvar 0 0)$, x_2 \mapsto$ abs (app (fvar x_1) (bvar 0 0))$\}$
$\quad$: abs (app (fvar x_1) (bvar 0 0)) $\square$

Notice that in Example 4 the (heap : term) pair obtained with ANS is indirection-related to the pair obtained with NNS by removing the indirection $y \mapsto$ fvar x.

Now we are ready to establish the equivalence between ANS and NNS in the sense that if a reduction proof can be obtained with ANS for some term in a given context heap, then there must exist a reduction proof in NNS for the same (heap : term) pair such that the final (heap : value) is indirection-related to the final (heap : value) obtained with ANS, and vice versa.

Theorem 1 *(Equivalence ANS-NNS).*

1. $\Gamma : t \Downarrow^A \Delta_A : w_A \Rightarrow$
$\exists \Delta_N \in LNHeap . \exists w_N \in Val . \Gamma : t \Downarrow^N \Delta_N : w_N \wedge (\Delta_A : w_A) \succsim_I (\Delta_N : w_N).$

2. $\Gamma : t \Downarrow^N \Delta_N : w_N \Rightarrow$
$\exists \Delta_A \in LNHeap . \exists w_A \in Val . \exists \overline{x} \subseteq dom(\Delta_N) - dom(\Gamma) . \exists \overline{y} \subseteq Id .$
$|\overline{x}| = |\overline{y}| \wedge \Gamma : t \Downarrow^A \Delta_A : w_A \wedge (\Delta_A : w_A) \succsim_I (\Delta_N[\overline{y}/\overline{x}] : w_N[\overline{y}/\overline{x}]).$

Notice that in the second part of the theorem, i.e., from NNS to ANS, a renaming may be needed. This renaming only affects the names that are added to the heap during the reduction process. This is due to the fact that in NNS names occurring in the evaluation term (that is t in the theorem) may disappear during the evaluation and, consequently, they may be chosen on some application of the rule LNLET and added to the final heap. This cannot happen in ANS due to the introduction of indirections (see Lemma 2).

To prove this theorem by rule induction, a generalization is needed. Instead of evaluating the same term in the same initial heap, we consider indirection-related initial (heap : term) pairs:

Proposition 5. $(\Gamma_A : t_A) \succsim_I (\Gamma_N : t_N)$

1. $\forall \overline{x} \notin L \subseteq Id . [\Gamma_A : t_A \Downarrow^A (\Gamma_A, \overline{x} \mapsto \overline{s}_A{}^{\overline{x}}) : w_A{}^{\overline{x}} \wedge {}^{\backslash \overline{x}}(\overline{s}_A{}^{\overline{x}}) = \overline{s}_A \wedge {}^{\backslash \overline{x}}(w_A{}^{\overline{x}}) = w_A]$
$\Rightarrow \exists \overline{y} \notin L . \exists \overline{s}_N \subset LNExp . \exists w_N \in LNVal .$
$\Gamma_N : t_N \Downarrow^N (\Gamma_N, \overline{z} \mapsto \overline{s}_N{}^{\overline{z}}) : w_N{}^{\overline{z}} \wedge {}^{\backslash \overline{z}}(\overline{s}_N{}^{\overline{z}}) = \overline{s}_N \wedge {}^{\backslash \overline{z}}(w_N{}^{\overline{z}}) = w_N \wedge \overline{z} \subseteq \overline{y} \wedge$
$((\Gamma_A, \overline{y} \mapsto \overline{s}_A{}^{\overline{y}}) : w_A{}^{\overline{y}}) \succsim_I ((\Gamma_N, \overline{z} \mapsto \overline{s}_N{}^{\overline{z}}) : w_N{}^{\overline{z}})$

2. $\forall \overline{x} \notin L \subseteq Id . [\Gamma_N : t_N \Downarrow^N (\Gamma_N, \overline{x} \mapsto \overline{s}_N{}^{\overline{x}}) : w_N{}^{\overline{x}} \wedge {}^{\backslash \overline{x}}(\overline{s}_N{}^{\overline{x}}) = \overline{s}_N \wedge {}^{\backslash \overline{x}}(w_N{}^{\overline{x}}) = w_N]$
$\Rightarrow \exists \overline{z} \notin L . \exists \overline{s}_A \subset LNExp . \exists w_A \in LNVal .$
$\Gamma_A : t_A \Downarrow^A (\Gamma_A, \overline{y} \mapsto \overline{s}_A{}^{\overline{y}}) : w_A{}^{\overline{y}} \wedge {}^{\backslash \overline{y}}(\overline{s}_A{}^{\overline{y}}) = \overline{s}_A \wedge {}^{\backslash \overline{y}}(w_A{}^{\overline{y}}) = w_A \wedge \overline{z} \subseteq \overline{y} \wedge$
$((\Gamma_A, \overline{y} \mapsto \overline{s}_A{}^{\overline{y}}) : w_A{}^{\overline{y}}) \succsim_I ((\Gamma_N, \overline{z} \mapsto \overline{s}_N{}^{\overline{z}}) : w_N{}^{\overline{z}})$

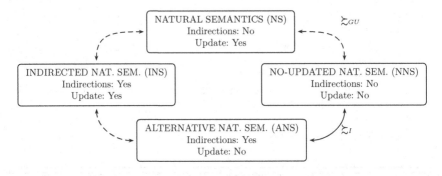

Fig. 5. The relations between the semantics

Once more, cofinite quantification replaces freshness conditions. For instance, in the second part of the proposition it is required that the names introduced during the reduction for NNS do not collide with names that are already defined in the initial heap for ANS. The cofinite quantification expresses that if there is an infinite number of "similar" reduction proofs for $(\Gamma_N : t_N)$, each introducing alternative names in the heap, one can chose a reduction proof such that the new bindings do not interfere with $(\Gamma_A : t_A)$.

Since there is update neither in ANS nor in NNS (Lemma 1), a final heap can be expressed as the initial heap plus some set of bindings, such as $(\Gamma_A, \overline{x} \mapsto \overline{s}_A{}^{\overline{x}})$. In this case, $\overline{x}$ represents the list of new names, i.e., those that have been added during the reduction of local declarations, as well as the indirections introduced by the alternative application rule. Since the terms bound to these new names are dependent on $\overline{x}$, they are represented as $\overline{s}_A{}^{\overline{x}}$. Similarly for the final value $w_A{}^{\overline{x}}$. The proposition indicates that it is possible to construct reductions for NNS whose set of new defined names is a subset of the set of new names of the corresponding ANS reduction (NNS only adds new names with the rule LNLET). Detailed proofs of the theorem and the proposition are given in [16].

4   Conclusions and Future Work

Launchbury natural semantics (NS) has turned out to be too much sensitive to the changes introduced by the alternative semantics (ANS), i.e., indirections and no-update. These changes should lead to the same values, but this cannot be directly established since values may contain free variables which are dependent on the context of evaluation, represented by the heap. And, precisely, the changes introduced by the ANS do affect deeply the heaps. In fact, the equivalence of the values produced by the NS and the ANS is based on their correctness with respect to a denotational semantics. Although indirections and duplicated bindings (consequence of not updating) do not add new information to the heap, it is not straightforward to prove it formally.

Since the variations introduced by Launchbury in the ANS do affect two rules, i.e. the variable rule (no-update) and the application rule (indirections), we have defined two intermediate semantics to deal separately with the effect of each modification: The NNS (without update) and the INS (with indirections). A schema of the semantics and how to relate them is included in Fig. 5.

In this paper we have compared NNS with ANS, that is, substitution vs. indirections. We have started by defining an equivalence $\approx$ such that two heaps are considered equivalent when they have the same domain and the corresponding closures may differ only in the free variables not defined in the heaps. We have used this equivalence to define a preorder $\succsim_I$ expressing that a heap can be transformed into another by eliminating indirections. Furthermore, the relation has been extended to (heap : terms) pairs, expressing that two terms can be considered equivalent when they have the same structure and their free variables (only those defined in the context of the corresponding heap) are the same except for some indirections. We have used this extended relation to establish the equivalence between NNS and ANS (Theorem 1).

At present we are working on the equivalence of NS and NNS, which will close the path from NS to ANS. In order to compare NS with NNS, that is, update vs. no-update, new relations on heaps and terms have to be defined. No updating the bindings in the heap corresponds to a call-by-name strategy, and implies the duplication of evaluation work, that leads to the generation of duplicated bindings. More precisely, duplicated bindings come from several evaluations of the same let-declarations, so that they form *groups* of equivalent bindings. Therefore, we first define a preorder $\succsim_G$ that relates two heaps whenever the first can be transformed into the second by eliminating duplicated groups of bindings. Afterwards, we define a relation $\sim_U$ that establishes when a heap is an updated version of another heap. Finally, both relations must be combined to obtain the *group-update* relation $\succsim_{GU}$ that, extended for (heap : terms), will allow us to formulate an equivalence theorem for NS and NNS, similar to Theorem 1.

Although the relations $\succsim_I$ and $\succsim_{GU}$ are sufficient for proving the equivalence of NS and ANS, it would be interesting to complete the picture by comparing NS with INS, and then INS with ANS. For the first step, we have to define a preorder similar to $\succsim_I$, but taking into account that extra indirections may now be updated, thus leading to "redundant" bindings. For the second step, some version of the group-update relation is needed. Dashed lines indicate future work.

We have used a locally nameless representation to avoid problems with the α-equivalence, while keeping a readable formalization of the syntax and semantics. This representation allow us to deal with heaps in a convenient and easy way, avoiding the problems that arise when using the de Bruijn notation (indexes do change when bindings are introduced in or eliminated from heaps; moreover, the formalization becomes unreadable). We have also introduced cofinite quantification (in the style of [1]) in the evaluation rules that introduce fresh names, namely the rule for local declarations (LNLET) and for the alternative application (ALNAPP). Moreover, this representation is more amenable to formalization in proof assistants. In fact we have started to implement the semantic rules given in Sect. 2.2 using Coq [4], with the intention of obtaining a formal checking of our proofs.

Acknowledgments. This work is partially supported by the projects: TIN2012-39391-C04-04 and S2009/TIC-1465.

References

1. Aydemir, B.E., Charguéraud, A., Pierce, B.C., Pollack, R., Weirich, S.: Engineering formal metatheory. In: ACM Symposium on Principles of Programming Languages, POPL 2008, pp. 3–15. ACM Press (2008)

2. Baker-Finch, C., King, D., Trinder, P.W.: An operational semantics for parallel lazy evaluation. In: ACM-SIGPLAN International Conference on Functional Programming (ICFP 2000), Montreal, Canada, pp. 162–173, September 2000

3. Barendregt, H.P.: The Lambda Calculus: Its Syntax and Semantics. Studies in Logic and the Foundations of Mathematics, vol. 103. North-Holland, Amsterdam (1984)

4. Bertot, Y.: Coq in a hurry. CoRR, abs/cs/0603118 (2006)

5. Breitner, J.: The correctness of launchbury's natural semantics for lazy evaluation. Archive of Formal Proofs, January 2013. Formal proof development, Amended version May 2014. http://afp.sf.net/entries/Launchbury.shtml

6. Charguéraud, A.: The locally nameless representation. J. Autom. Reason. **46**(3), 363–408 (2012)

7. de Bruijn, N.G.: Lambda calculus notation with nameless dummies, a tool for automatic formula manipulation, with application to the Church-Rosser theorem. Indag. Math. **75**(5), 381–392 (1972)

8. Hidalgo-Herrero, M., Ortega-Mallén, Y.: An operational semantics for the parallel language Eden. Parallel Process. Lett. (World Scientific Publishing Company) **12**(2), 211–228 (2002)

9. Launchbury, J.: A natural semantics for lazy evaluation. In: ACM Symposium on Principles of Programming Languages, POPL 1993, pp. 144–154. ACM Press (1993)

10. Nakata, K., Hasegawa, M.: Small-step and big-step semantics for call-by-need. J. Funct. Program. **19**(6), 699–722 (2009)

11. Nipkow, T., Paulson, L.C., Wenzel, M.: Isabelle/HOL. LNCS, vol. 2283. Springer, Heidelberg (2002)

12. Sánchez-Gil, L., Hidalgo-Herrero, M., Ortega-Mallén, Y.: Call-by-need, call-by-name, and natural semantics. Technical report UU-CS-2010-020, Department of Information and Computing Sciences, Utrech University (2010)

13. Sánchez-Gil, L., Hidalgo-Herrero, M., Ortega-Mallén, Y.: An operational semantics for distributed lazy evaluation. In: Trends in Functional Programming, pp. 65–80, vol. 10. Intellect (2010)

14. Sánchez-Gil, L., Hidalgo-Herrero, M., Ortega-Mallén, Y.: A locally nameless representation for a natural semantics for lazy evaluation. Technical report 01/12, Dpt. Sistemas Informáticos y Computación. Univ. Complutense de Madrid (2012). http://federwin.sip.ucm.es/sic/investigacion/publicaciones/pdfs/SIC-1-12.pdf

15. Sánchez-Gil, L., Hidalgo-Herrero, M., Ortega-Mallén, Y.: A locally nameless representation for a natural semantics for lazy evaluation. In: Roychoudhury, A., D'Souza, M. (eds.) ICTAC 2012. LNCS, vol. 7521, pp. 105–119. Springer, Heidelberg (2012)

16. Sánchez-Gil, L., Hidalgo-Herrero, M., Ortega-Mallén, Y.: The role of indirections in lazy natural semantics (extended version). Technical report 13/13, Dpt. Sistemas Informáticos y Computación. Univ. Complutense de Madrid (2013). http://federwin.sip.ucm.es/sic/investigacion/publicaciones/pdfs/TR-13-13.pdf

17. Sestoft, P.: Deriving a lazy abstract machine. J. Funct. Program. **7**(3), 231–264 (1997)

18. Urban, C., Berghofer, S., Norrish, M.: Barendregt's variable convention in rule inductions. In: Pfenning, F. (ed.) CADE 2007. LNCS (LNAI), vol. 4603, pp. 35–50. Springer, Heidelberg (2007)

19. Urban, C., Kaliszyk, C.: General bindings and alpha-equivalence in nominal Isabelle. Log. Methods Comput. Sci. **8**(2:14), 1–35 (2012)

20. van Eekelen, M., de Mol, M.: Proving lazy folklore with mixed lazy/strict semantics. In: Barendsen, E., Capretta, V., Geuvers, H., Niqui, M. (eds.) Reflections on Type Theory, λ-calculus, and the Mind. Essays dedicated to Henk Barendregt on the Occasion of his 60th Birthday, pp. 87–101. Radboud University Nijmegen (2007)

Model Checking Value-Passing Modal Specifications

Maurice H. ter Beek[(⊠)], Stefania Gnesi, and Franco Mazzanti

ISTI–CNR, Via G. Moruzzi 1, Pisa, Italy
{terbeek,gnesi,mazzanti}@isti.cnr.it

Abstract. Formal modelling and verification of variability concepts in product families has been the subject of extensive study in the literature on Software Product Lines. In recent years, we have laid the basis for the use of modal specifications and branching-time temporal logics for the specification and analysis of behavioural variability in product family definitions. A critical point in this formalization is the lack of a possibility to model an adequate representation of the data that may need to be described when considering real systems. To this aim, we now extend the modelling and verification environment that we have developed for specifications interpreted over Modal Transition Systems, by adding the possibility to include data in the specifications. In concert with this, we also extend the variability-specific modal logic and the associated special-purpose model checker VMC. As a result, it offers the possibility to efficiently verify formulas over possibly infinite-state systems by using the on-the-fly bounded model-checking algorithms implemented in the model checker. We illustrate our approach by means of a simple yet intuitive example: a bike-sharing system.

1 Introduction

Product Line Engineering (PLE) is a paradigm for the development of a variety of products from a common product platform. Its aim is to lower the production costs of individual products by letting them share an overall reference model of a product family, while allowing them to differ with respect to specific features to serve, e.g., different markets. Software Product Line Engineering (SPLE) has translated this paradigm into a software engineering approach aimed at the development, in a cost-effective way, of a variety of software-intensive products that share an overall reference model, i.e., that together form a product family [34]. Usually, the commonality and variability of a product family are defined in terms of features, and managing variability is about identifying variation points in a common family design to encode exactly those combinations of features that lead to valid products. The actual configuration of the products during application engineering then boils down to selecting desired options in the variability model.

Research partly supported by the EU FP7-ICT FET-Proactive project QUANTI-COL (600708) and by the Italian MIUR project CINA (PRIN 2010LHT4KM).

A. Voronkov and I. Virbitskaite (Eds.): PSI 2014, LNCS 8974, pp. 304–319, 2015.
DOI: 10.1007/978-3-662-46823-4_25

Since many software-intensive systems are embedded, distributed and safety-critical, there is a need for rigour and formal modelling and verification (tools). Our contribution to make the development of product families more rigorous consists of an ongoing research effort to elaborate a suitable formal modelling structure to describe behavioural product variability, together with a temporal logic that can be interpreted over that structure [3,4]. We opted for Modal Transition Systems (MTSs) [1,29], which were recognized in [22,28,30] as a useful formal method to describe in a compact way the possible operational behaviour of all products of a product family and in [26] to generate component-level MTSs from system level specifications. The most closely related approach is based on Featured Transition Systems (FTSs) [16], where actions are labelled with features and an associated feature model expresses feature constraints. A detailed comparison is given in [4]. We moreover defined an action-based branching-time CTL-like temporal modal logic over MTSs and we developed efficient algorithms to derive valid products from families and to model check properties over products and families alike. We implemented these algorithms in an experimental tool: the Variability Model Checker (VMC) [6,8,9]. Our approach thus differs from the more widespread use of LTL model checking MTSs [13,20].

A critical point in the formalization by means of MTSs is the lack of a possibility to model an adequate representation of the data that may need to be described when considering real systems. To this aim, in this paper we extend the modelling and verification environment we developed so far by adding the possibility to include data in the specifications. In concert with this, we also extend the logic and the tool. As a result, VMC offers the possibility to efficiently verify properties over possibly infinite-state systems by means of explicit-state on-the-fly bounded model checking. We illustrate our approach by means of a simple yet intuitive example: a bike-sharing system.

2   Background

Definition 1. *A* Labelled Transition System *(LTS) is a 4-tuple* $(Q, A, \overline{q}, \delta)$, *with set Q of states, set A of actions, initial state $\overline{q} \in Q$, and transition relation $\delta \subseteq Q \times A \times Q$; we may write $q \xrightarrow{a} q'$ if $(q, a, q') \in \delta$.*

An MTS is an LTS which distinguishes between *may* and *must* transitions.

Definition 2. *A* Modal Transition System *(MTS) is a 5-tuple* $(Q, A, \overline{q}, \delta^{\diamond}, \delta^{\square})$ *such that $(Q, A, \overline{q}, \delta^{\diamond} \cup \delta^{\square})$ is an LTS and $\delta^{\square} \subseteq \delta^{\diamond}$. An MTS distinguishes the* may *transition relation $\delta^{\diamond}$, expressing* admissible *transitions, and the* must *transition relation $\delta^{\square}$, expressing* necessary *transitions; we may write $q \xrightarrow{a}_{\diamond} q'$ for $(q, a, q') \in \delta^{\diamond}$ and $q \xrightarrow{a}_{\square} q'$ for $(q, a, q') \in \delta^{\square}$.*

The inclusion $\delta^{\square} \subseteq \delta^{\diamond}$ formalizes that necessary transitions are also admissible. Graphically, an MTS is a directed edge-labelled graph where nodes model states and action-labelled edges model transitions: solid edges are necessary ones (i.e., $\delta^{\square}$) and dotted edges are admissible but not necessary ones (i.e., $\delta^{\diamond} \setminus \delta^{\square}$).

A *full path* is a path that cannot be extended further, i.e., it is infinite or it ends in a state without outgoing transitions. A *must path* is a full path that consists of only must transitions, i.e., it consists of only solid edges.

An MTS can provide an abstract description of the set of (valid) products of a product family, defining both the behaviour that is common to all products and the behaviour that varies among different products. This requires an interpretation of the requirements of a product family and its constraints with respect to certain features as may and must transitions labelled with actions, and a temporal ordering among these transitions. The idea is that the family's products are the ordinary LTSs that can be obtained by resolving the variability modelled through admissible (may) but not necessary (must) transitions (i.e., the aforementioned dotted edges). Resolving variability then boils down to deciding for each particular optional behaviour whether it is to be included in a specific product LTS, whereas all mandatory behaviour is included by definition.[1] This thus differs from the usual notion of MTS refinement [1,22,35].

Definition 3. *Let* $\mathcal{F} = (Q, A, \overline{q}, \delta^{\diamond}, \delta^{\square})$ *be an MTS. The set* $\{\mathcal{P}_i = (Q_i, A, \overline{q}, \delta_i) \mid i > 0\}$ *of derived product LTSs of* $\mathcal{F}$ *is obtained from* $\mathcal{F}$ *by considering each pair of* $Q_i \subseteq Q$ *and* $\delta_i \subseteq \delta^{\diamond} \cup \delta^{\square}$ *to be defined such that:*

1. *every* $q \in Q_i$ *is reachable in* $\mathcal{P}_i$ *from* $\overline{q}$ *via transitions from* δ_i *and*
2. *there exists no* $(q, a, q') \in \delta^{\square} \setminus \delta_i$ *such that* $q \in Q_i$.

2.1 A Modal Process Algebra

Rather than directly specifying the behaviour of a complex system in an MTS, it is often convenient to describe it in an abstract high-level language interpreted over MTSs. We consider a process algebra in which the parallel composition operator is parametrized by a set of actions to be synchronized, which contrasts the recent approaches in [7,24,31]. A system can then be defined inductively by composition, with the additional distinction between may and must actions.

Definition 4. *Let* $\mathcal{A}$ *be a set of* actions, *let* $a \in \mathcal{A}$ *and let* $L \subseteq \mathcal{A}$. *Processes are built from terms and actions according to the abstract syntax:*

$$
\begin{aligned}
N &::= [P] & T &::= nil \mid K \mid A.T \mid T + T \\
P &::= K \mid P/L/P & A &::= a \mid a(may)
\end{aligned}
$$

where $[P]$ *denotes the complete system and* K *is a process identifier from the set of process definitions of the form* $K \overset{def}{=} T$.

If $L = \varnothing$, then we may also write $P // P$. The set $\{M, N, \ldots\}$ of *systems* is denoted by $\mathcal{N}$ and the set $\{P, Q, \ldots\}$ of *processes* is denoted by $\mathcal{P}$.

A process can thus be one of the following:

---

[1] Actually, each product moreover needs to satisfy assumptions of *coherence* and *consistency* and *variability constraints* of the form alternative, excludes, and requires [9].

nil : a terminated process that has finished execution;

K : a process identifier that is used for modelling recursive sequential processes;

$A.P$: a process that can execute action A and then behave as P;

$P+Q$: a process that can non-deterministically choose to behave as P or as Q;

$P\,/L\,/\,Q$: a process formed by the parallel composition of P and Q that can synchronize on actions in L and interleave other actions.

Note that we distinguish between *must* actions a and *may but not must* actions $a(may)$. Each action type is treated differently in the rules of the SOS semantics.

Definition 5. *The* operational semantics *of a system* $N \in \mathcal{N}$ *is given over the MTS* $(\mathcal{N}, \mathcal{A}, N, \delta^\diamond, \delta^\square)$, *where* $\delta^\diamond$ *and* $\delta^\square$ *are defined as the least relations that satisfy the set of axioms and transition rules in Figs. 1 and 2.*

As usual, inference rules are defined in terms of a (possibly empty) set of premises (above the line) and a conclusion (below the line). The reduction relation is defined in SOS style (i.e., by induction on the structure of the terms denoting a process) modulo the structural congruence relation $\equiv \subseteq \mathcal{P} \times \mathcal{P}$ defined in Fig. 2. Considering terms up to a structural congruence allows identifying different ways of denoting the same process and the expansion of recursive process definitions.

Note that when restricted to must actions (i.e., LTSs) the rules for non-deterministic choice and parallel composition collapse onto the standard ones [33]. As is common for MTSs, synchronizing $a(may)$ with a results in $a(may)$ [1,35].

$$(\text{SYS}_\square)\quad \frac{P \xrightarrow{a} P'}{[P] \xrightarrow{a} [P']} \qquad\qquad (\text{SYS}_\diamond)\quad \frac{P \dashrightarrow{a} P'}{[P] \dashrightarrow{a} [P']}$$

$$(\text{ACT}_\square)\quad \frac{}{a.P \xrightarrow{a} P} \qquad\qquad (\text{ACT}_\diamond)\quad \frac{}{a(may).P \dashrightarrow{a} P}$$

$$(\text{OR}_\square)\quad \frac{P \xrightarrow{a} P'}{P+Q \xrightarrow{a} P'} \qquad\qquad (\text{OR}_\diamond)\quad \frac{P \dashrightarrow{a} P'}{P+Q \dashrightarrow{a} P'}$$

$$(\text{INT}_\square)\quad \frac{P \xrightarrow{\ell} P'}{P\,/L/\,Q \xrightarrow{\ell} P'\,/L/\,Q}\,\ell\notin L \qquad (\text{INT}_\diamond)\quad \frac{P \dashrightarrow{\ell} P'}{P\,/L/\,Q \dashrightarrow{\ell} P'\,/L/\,Q}\,\ell\notin L$$

$$(\text{PAR}_\square)\quad \frac{P \xrightarrow{a} P' \quad Q \xrightarrow{a} Q'}{P\,/L/\,Q \xrightarrow{a} P'\,/L/\,Q'}\,a\in L \qquad (\text{PAR}_\diamond)\quad \frac{P \dashrightarrow{a} P' \quad Q \dashrightarrow{a} Q'}{P\,/L/\,Q \dashrightarrow{a} P'\,/L/\,Q'}\,a\in L$$

$$(\text{PAR}_\boxtimes)\quad \frac{P \xrightarrow{a} P' \quad Q \dashrightarrow{a} Q'}{P\,/L/\,Q \dashrightarrow{a} P'\,/L/\,Q'}\,a\in L$$

Fig. 1. The SOS semantics of the modal process algebra, with $a, \ell \in \mathcal{A}$

$$P+Q \equiv Q+P \qquad P+(Q+R) \equiv (P+Q)+R \qquad P \equiv P+0$$
$$P\,/L/\,Q \equiv Q\,/L/\,P \qquad P\,/L/\,(Q\,/L/\,R) \equiv (P\,/L/\,Q)\,/L/\,R \qquad P \equiv P[^Q/_K] \text{ iff } K \overset{\text{def}}{=} Q$$

Fig. 2. Structural congruence relation $\equiv \subseteq \mathcal{P} \times \mathcal{P}$

3   Dealing with Data

A critical point in the approach presented so far is the lack of a possibility to model an adequate representation of the data that may need to be described when considering realistic systems. We present a case study to makes this clear.

3.1   Case Study: Bike-Sharing Systems

An increasing number of cities worldwide are adopting fully automated public bike-sharing systems (BSS) as a green urban mode of transportation [17]. The concept is simple and their benefits multiple, including the reduction of vehicular traffic (congestion), pollution, and energy consumption. A BSS consists of parking stations distributed over a city, typically in close proximity to other public transportation hubs such as subway and tram stations. (Subscribed) users may rent an available bike from one of the stations, use it for a while and then drop it off at any (other) station. BSS offer a number of challenging run-time optimization problems aimed at improving the efficiency and user satisfaction. A primary example is balancing the load between the different stations, e.g., by using incentive (reward) schemes that may change the behaviour of users but also by efficient (dynamic) redistribution of bikes between stations.

A side-study of the EU FP7 project QUANTICOL (http://www.quanticol. eu) concerns the quantitative analysis of BSS seen as so-called Collective Adaptive Systems (CAS). The design of CAS must be supported by a powerful and well-founded framework for quantitative modelling and analysis. CAS consist of a large number of spatially distributed entities, which may be competing for shared resources even when collaborating to reach common goals. The nature of CAS, together with the importance of the societal goals they address, mean that it is imperative to carry out thorough analyses of their design to investigate all aspects of their behaviour before they are put into operation. In the context of QUANTICOL, we collaborate with "PisaMo S.p.A. azienda per la mobilità pisana", an in-house public mobility company of the Municipality of Pisa. They recently introduced the public BSS *CicloPi* in the city of Pisa, which currently consists of some 150 bikes and 15 stations and thus forms a perfect test case for our research and an interesting benchmark for the QUANTICOL project.

Inspired by [23], we consider a BSS with N stations and a fleet of M bikes. Each station i has a capacity K_i. The dynamic behaviour of the system is then:

1. Users arrive at station i.
2. If a user arrives at a station and there is no available bike, then (s)he leaves the system.
3. Otherwise, (s)he takes a bike and chooses station j to return the bike.
4. When (s)he arrives at station j, if there are less than K_j bikes in this station, (s)he returns the bike and leaves the system.
5. If the station is full the user chooses another station, say k, and goes there.
6. A redistribution activity of bikes *may* be asked and *may* possibly be satisfied.
7. The user rides like this again until (s)he can return the bike.

This list contains a mix of a kind of static constraints defining the differences in configuration (features), like the optional possibility to have a redistribution mechanism in our BSS, between products as well as more operational constraints defining the behaviour of products through admitted sequences (temporal orderings) of actions or operations implementing features according to certain values.

4   Value-Passing Modelling and Verification Environment

We now extend the modelling and verification environment of Sect. 2 to handle data. First, we extend the modal process algebra of Sect. 2.1 with values and parameters.

4.1   A Value-Passing Modal Process Algebra

Definition 6. *Let $\mathcal{A}$ be a set of actions, let $a \in \mathcal{A}$ and let $L \subseteq \mathcal{A}$. Processes are built from terms and actions according to the abstract syntax:*

$$N ::= [P]$$
$$P ::= K(e) \mid P\,/L/\,P$$

where $[P]$ denotes a closed system and $K(e)$ is a process identifier from the set of process definitions of the form $K(v) \stackrel{def}{=} T$, and

$$T ::= nil \mid K(e) \mid A.T \mid T+T \mid [e \bowtie e]\,T$$
$$A ::= a(e) \mid a(may,e) \mid a(?v) \mid a(may,?v)$$
$$e ::= v \mid \textbf{int} \mid e \pm e$$

where $\bowtie \in \{<, \leq, =, \neq, \geq, >\}$ is a comparison relation, v is a variable, $\textbf{int}$ is an integer, and $\pm \in \{+, -, \times, \div\}$ is an arithmetic operation.

Also the semantics of this value-passing modal process algebra is given over MTSs, but we only provide the SOS rules for the must actions (in Fig. 3); the others follow straightforwardly from those in Fig. 1. In the structural congruence relation $\equiv \subseteq \mathcal{P} \times \mathcal{P}$ defined in Fig. 2, the addition of value passing is reflected by replacing $P \equiv P[Q/_K]$ iff $K \stackrel{def}{=} Q$ with $P \equiv P[Q[^e/v]/_{K(e)}]$ iff $K(v) \stackrel{def}{=} Q$.

Note that the SYS rule implies that we assume a closed-world semantics, i.e., a system cannot evolve on input actions of the form $a(?v)$.

The intuition of parallel composition is that both partners must fully and deterministically agree on the actual parameter values for the synchronization to occur. The rules in Fig. 3 refer to the case of just two parameters. In general, e.g., $a(X,2).nil$ and $a(3,Y).nil$ can synchronize and perform the action $a(3,2)$.

4.2   A Value-Passing Logic to Express Variability

We define value-passing v-ACTL, an action-based branching-time temporal logic for *variability* in the style of (action-based) CTL [15,18] and Hennessy–Milner

$$(\text{SYS}) \quad \frac{P \xrightarrow{a(e)} P'}{[P] \xrightarrow{a(e)} [P']}$$

$$(\text{ACT}_\Box) \quad \frac{}{\alpha.P \xrightarrow{\alpha} P} \;\; \alpha \in \{a(e),a(?v)\}$$

$$(\text{OR}_\Box) \quad \frac{P \xrightarrow{\alpha} P'}{P+Q \xrightarrow{\alpha} P'} \;\; \alpha \in \{a(e),a(?v)\}$$

$$(\text{INT}_\Box) \quad \frac{P \xrightarrow{\ell} P'}{P/L/Q \xrightarrow{\ell} P'/L/Q} \;\; \ell \notin L$$

$$(\text{PAR}_\Box) \quad \frac{P \xrightarrow{a(e_1)} P' \quad Q \xrightarrow{a(e_2)} Q'}{P/L/Q \xrightarrow{a} P'/L/Q'} \;\; a \in L, e_1 = e_2$$

$$(\text{PAR}_\Box) \quad \frac{P \xrightarrow{a(?v)} P' \quad Q \xrightarrow{a(e)} Q'}{P/L/Q \xrightarrow{a} P'[^e/_v]/L/Q'} \;\; a \in L$$

$$(\text{GUARD}) \quad \frac{}{[e_1 \bowtie e_2]\, P(e_3) \longrightarrow P(e_3)} \;\; e_1 \bowtie e_2$$

Fig. 3. The SOS semantics of the value-passing modal process algebra, with $a \in \mathcal{A}$

Logic (HML) with Until defined in [19,27]. Next to the operators of propositional logic, v-ACTL contains the classical box and, by duality, diamond modal operators from HML, the existential and universal path quantifiers and next operator from CTL and the (action-based) F and, by duality, G operators from ACTL, as well as the (action-based) Until and Weak until operators U and W drawn from those firstly introduced in [18] and elaborated in [32]. For the box, diamond and F operators, v-ACTL also contains a *deontic* interpretation that takes the modality (or 'deonticity') of the transitions (may or must) into account. In the SPLE context, these deontic interpretations allow to suitably capture behavioural properties over MTSs that are inherited by all its product LTSs. More on this and on *deontic logic* [2] below. v-ACTL defines action formulas (denoted by ψ), state formulas (denoted by ϕ), and path formulas (denoted by π).

Definition 7. *Action formulas are built over a set $\mathcal{A}$ of actions, where $a \in \mathcal{A}$:*

$$\psi ::= true \mid a \mid a(e) \mid \neg\psi \mid \psi \wedge \psi$$

Action formulas are thus Boolean compositions of actions. As usual, *false* abbreviates $\neg true$, $\psi \vee \psi'$ abbreviates $\neg(\neg\psi \wedge \neg\psi')$ and $\psi \Longrightarrow \psi'$ abbreviates $\neg\psi \vee \psi'$.

Definition 8. *Let $a, b \in \mathcal{A}$. The satisfaction of formula ψ by $a(e)$, denoted by $a(e) \models \psi$, is defined as:*

$a(e) \models true$ *always holds* $a(e) \models b(e')$ *iff $a = b$ and $e = e'$*
$a(e) \models b$ *iff $a = b$* $a(e) \models \neg\psi$ *iff $a(e) \not\models \psi$*
$a(e) \models b(*)$ *iff $a = b$* $a(e) \models \psi \wedge \psi'$ *iff $a(e) \models \psi$ and $a(e) \models \psi'$*

Definition 9. *The syntax of v-ACTL is:*

$$\phi ::= true \mid \neg\phi \mid \phi \wedge \phi \mid [\psi]\phi \mid [\psi]^\Box \phi \mid E\pi \mid A\pi \mid \mu Y.\phi(Y) \mid \nu Y.\phi(Y)$$
$$\pi ::= [\phi \{\psi\} U \{\psi'\} \phi'] \mid [\phi \{\psi\} U \phi'] \mid [\phi \{\psi\} W \{\psi'\} \phi'] \mid [\phi \{\psi\} W \phi'] \mid$$
$$X\{\psi\} \phi \mid F\phi \mid F^\Box \phi \mid F\{\psi\}\phi \mid F^\Box \{\psi\}\phi$$

where Y is a propositional variable and $\phi(Y)$ is syntactically monotone in Y.

The least and greatest fixed-point operators μ and ν provide a semantics for recursion, used for "finite looping" and "looping" (or "liveness" and "safety"), respectively. It is well known that the path formulas (e.g., the Until and F and G operators) can be derived from the least and greatest fixed-point operators. We however prefer to represent some of them explicitly to make their understanding simpler. The intuitive interpretation of the remaining nonstandard operators is:

$[\psi]\,\phi$: in all next states reachable by a *may* transition executing an action satisfying ψ, ϕ holds.

$[\psi]^{\square}\,\phi$: in all next states reachable by a *must* transition executing an action satisfying ψ, ϕ holds.

$X\{\psi\}\,\phi$: in the next state of the path, reached by an action satisfying ψ, ϕ holds.

$F\,\phi$: there exists a future state in which ϕ holds.

$F^{\square}\,\phi$: there exists a future state in which ϕ holds and all transitions until that state are must transitions.

$F\{\psi\}\,\phi$: there exists a future state, reached by an action satisfying ψ, in which ϕ holds.

$F^{\square}\{\psi\}\,\phi$: there exists a future state, reached by an action satisfying ψ, in which ϕ holds and all transitions until that state are must transitions.

$\phi\,\{\psi\}\,U\,\{\psi'\}\,\phi'$: in a future state (reached by an action satisfying ψ'), ϕ' holds, while ϕ holds from the current state until that state is reached and all actions executed in the meantime along the path satisfy ψ.

$\phi\,\{\psi\}\,W\,\{\psi'\}\,\phi'$: either $\phi\,\{\psi\}\,U\,\{\psi'\}\,\phi'$ or ϕ holds from the current state onwards and all actions executed along the path satisfy ψ.

The semantics of v-ACTL is interpreted over MTSs. Let $path(q)$ denote the set of all full paths from a state q. Moreover, for a path $\sigma = q_1 a_1(e_1) q_2 a_2(e_2) q_3 \cdots$, we denote its ith state (i.e., q_i) by $\sigma(i)$ and its ith action (i.e., $a_i(e_i)$) by $\sigma\{i\}$.

Definition 10. *Let $(Q, A, \overline{q}, \delta^{\diamond}, \delta^{\square})$ be an MTS, with $q \in Q$ and $\sigma \in path(q)$. The satisfaction relation $\models$ of v-ACTL is defined as:*

$q \models$ *true always holds*

$q \models \neg\,\phi$ *iff* $q \not\models \phi$

$q \models \phi \wedge \phi'$ *iff* $q \models \phi$ *and* $q \models \phi'$

$q \models [\psi]\,\phi$ *iff* $\forall q' \in Q$ *such that* $q \xrightarrow{a(e)}_{\diamond} q'$ *and* $a(e) \models \psi$, *we have* $q' \models \phi$

$q \models [\psi]^{\square}\,\phi$ *iff* $\forall q' \in Q$ *such that* $q \xrightarrow{a(e)}_{\square} q'$ *and* $a(e) \models \psi$, *we have* $q' \models \phi$

$q \models E\,\pi$ *iff* $\exists \sigma' \in path(q)\colon \sigma' \models \pi$

$q \models A\,\pi$ *iff* $\forall \sigma' \in path(q)\colon \sigma' \models \pi$

$q \models \mu\,Y.\phi(Y)$ *iff* $\bigvee_{i \geq 0}\phi^{i}(false)$

$q \models \nu\,Y.\,\phi(Y)$ *iff* $\bigwedge_{i \geq 0}\phi^{i}(true)$

$q \models X\,\{\psi\}\,\phi$ *iff* $\sigma\{1\} \models \psi$ *and* $\sigma(2) \models \phi$

$q \models F\,\phi$ *iff* $\exists j \geq 1\colon \sigma(j) \models \phi$

$q \models F^{\square}\,\phi$ *iff* $\exists j \geq 1\colon \sigma(j) \models \phi$ *and* $\forall 1 \leq i < j\colon (\sigma(i), \sigma\{i\}, \sigma(i+1)) \in \delta^{\square}$

$q \models F\,\{\psi\}\,\phi$ *iff* $\exists j \geq 1\colon \sigma\{j\} \models \psi$ *and* $\sigma(j+1) \models \phi$

$q \models F^\Box \{\psi\} \, \phi \;\; \textit{iff} \;\; \exists j \geq 1 : \sigma\{j\} \models \psi \; \text{and} \; \sigma(j+1) \models \phi,$

$\qquad\qquad\qquad\qquad \text{and} \; \forall 1 \leq i \leq j : (\sigma(i), \sigma\{i\}, \sigma(i+1)) \in \delta^\Box$

$\sigma \models \phi \, \{\psi\} \, U \, \{\psi'\} \, \phi' \;\; \textit{iff} \;\; \exists j \geq 1 : \sigma(j) \models \phi', \; \sigma\{j\} \models \psi', \text{and} \; \sigma(j+1) \models \phi',$

$\qquad\qquad\qquad\qquad \text{and} \; \forall 1 \leq i < j : \sigma(i) \models \phi \; \text{and} \; \sigma\{i\} \models \psi$

$\sigma \models \phi \, \{\psi\} \, W \, \{\psi'\} \, \phi' \;\; \textit{iff} \; \sigma \models \phi \, \{\psi\} \, U \, \{\psi'\} \, \phi' \; \textit{or} \; \forall j \geq 1 : \sigma(j) \models \phi \; \text{and} \; \sigma\{j\} \models \psi$

$\langle \psi \rangle \, \phi$ abbreviates $\neg \, [\psi] \, \neg \, \phi$: a next state exists, reachable by a *may* transition executing an action satisfying ψ, in which ϕ holds; $\langle \psi \rangle^\Box \, \phi$ abbreviates $\neg \, [\psi]^\Box \, \neg \, \phi$: a next state exists, reachable by a *must* transition executing an action satisfying ψ, in which ϕ holds; $G \, \phi$ abbreviates $\neg F \, \neg \phi$: the path is a full path on which ϕ holds in all states; $AG \, \phi$ abbreviates $\neg EF \, \neg \phi$: in all states on all paths, ϕ holds.

v-ACTL thus interprets some classical modal and temporal operators in a deontic way by considering the modalities of the transitions of an MTS. Deontic logic formalises notions like violation, obligation, permission, and prohibition [2].

4.3   Model Checking Value-Passing Modal Specifications

The modelling and verification environment described so far has been implemented in the Variability Model Checker (VMC) [6,8,9], which is freely usable online (http://fmt.isti.cnr.it/vmc/). VMC accepts as input a model specified in the value-passing modal process algebra presented in Sect. 4.1 and it allows to verify properties expressed in the value-passing v-ACTL logic presented in Sect. 4.2.

We are unaware of other model-checking tools for MTSs that support value passing. MTSA [20] is a prototype, built on top of the LTS Analyser LTSA, for the analysis of MTSs specified in an extension of the process algebra FSP (Finite State Processes). MTSA allows 3-valued FLTL (Fluent LTL) model checking of MTSs by reducing the verification to two FLTL model-checking runs on LTSs.

VMC is the most recent product of a family of model checkers we developed at ISTI–CNR over the past two decades, including UMC [5] and CMC [21]. Each allows the efficient verification by means of explicit-state on-the-fly model checking of functional properties expressed in a specific action- and state-based branching-time temporal logic derived from the family of logics based on CTL [15], including ACTL [18]. The on-the-fly nature of this family of model checkers means that in general not the whole state space needs to be generated and explored. This feature improves performance and allows to deal with infinite-state systems.

In the case of infinite-state systems, a bounded model-checking approach is adopted, i.e., the evaluation is started by assuming a certain value as a maximum depth of the evaluation. If the evaluation of a formula reaches a result within the requested depth, then the result holds for the whole system; otherwise the maximum depth is increased and the evaluation is retried (preserving all useful partial results already found). This approach, initially introduced in UMC [5] to address infinite state spaces, happens to be quite useful also for another reason: by setting a small initial maximum depth and a small automatic increment of this bound at each re-evaluation failure, once a result is finally found then we also have a reasonable (almost minimal) explanation for it.

On the basis of the algorithms presented in [5], on-the-fly model checking v-ACTL formulas (without fixed points) over MTSs can be achieved in a complexity that is linear w.r.t. the size of the state space. It is beyond the scope of this paper to give detailed descriptions of the model-checking algorithms and architecture underlying this family of model checkers (for which we refer to [5]).

5   Modelling and Analyzing the Case Study

We first specify the behaviour of a family of bike-sharing stations in the value-passing modal process algebra, taking into account the possibility of having a dynamic redistribution scheme as an optional feature of the BSS. Without loss of generality, we assume a bike-sharing station with 2 as its maximum capacity:

```
Station(X) = request.StationBikeRequested(X)
StationBikeRequested(Y) =
  [Y<1] ( nobike.Station(Y) +
          redistribute(may).Station(Y+2) ) +
  [Y>0] givebike.Station(Y-1)

net BSS = Station(2)
```

From this specification of a family of bike-sharing stations, VMC generates the MTS depicted in Fig. 4(a) and its possible products depicted in Figs. 4(b)–(c).

If we want also user behaviour, we might specify the following family of BSS:

```
User = request.(givebike.User + nobike.User + redistribute.User)

net BSS = Station(2) /request,givebike,nobike,redistribute/ User
```

Due to the synchronous parallel composition, this specification of course results in the same family MTS and product LTSs depicted in Fig. 4.

To illustrate what kind of variability analyses can be performed with the extended value-passing modelling and verification environment introduced in Sect. 4, we now present a few properties and the result of model checking them with VMC against the above family of BSS (i.e., on the MTS depicted in Fig. 4(a)):[2]

Eventually it must occur that no more bike is available: $EF^\square \{nobike\}$ *true*. This formula obviously is true.

It is always the case that eventually it must occur that no bike is available: $AG\,EF^\square \{nobike\}$ *true*. Also this formula is obviously true.

---

[2] In VMC, ¬, ∨, ∧, $[]^\square$, μ, ν, and $F^\square$ are written as **not**, **or**, **and**, **[]#**, **min**, **max**, and **F#**, respectively, whereas ' * ' can be used as 'don't care' symbol for parameter values.

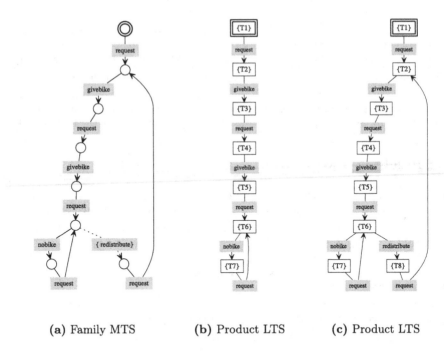

(a) Family MTS   (b) Product LTS   (c) Product LTS

Fig. 4. (a)–(c) A family MTS and its product LTSs generated by VMC

It is possible for a user to request and receive a bike for three times in a row: ⟨*request*⟩ ⟨*givebike*⟩ ⟨*request*⟩ ⟨*givebike*⟩ ⟨*request*⟩ ⟨*givebike*⟩ *true*. This formula is of course false.

Formulas without negation and only composed from *false*, *true* and the operators ∧, ∨, [], ⟨⟩□, μ, ν, $EF^\square$, $EF^\square\{\}$, $AF^\square$, $AF^\square\{\}$ and AG that are valid for a family MTS are valid for all its product LTSs [4]. Dually, formulas without negation and only composed from *false*, *true* and the operators ∧, ∨, ⟨⟩, μ, ν, EF and $EF\{\}$ that are false for a family MTS are false for all its product LTSs.

As a final example, we model a possibly infinite number of users that take a bike from station I to station J. Initially, station I has N bikes, which it gives (when available) to a requesting user or accepts from a returning user. If the station receives more than M bikes, the exceeding $N - M$ bikes are distributed to station J. Station I must accept all bikes distributed by other stations or returned by a user (possibly for redistribution). It could easily be extended to N stations and K groups of users that take a bike from one station to another.

```
Station(I,N,J,M) =
  request(I).
  ( [N=0] nobike(I).Station(I,N,J,M) +
    [N>0] givebike(I).Station(I,N-1,J,M) ) +
  return(I).Station(I,N+1,J,M) +
```

```
    redistribute(may,?FROM,?TO,?K).
    ( [TO = I] Station(I,N+K,J,M) +
      [TO /= I] Station(I,N,J,M) ) +
    [N > M] redistribute(may,I,J,N-M).Station(I,M,J,M)

-- two stations:
net STATIONS =
  Station(s1,2,s2,2) /redistribute/ Station(s2,2,s1,2)

Users(I,J) =
  request(I).
    ( givebike(I).return(J).Users(I,J) +
      nobike(I).Users(I,J) )

--   one or two groups of users
net USERS = Users(s1,s2) -- // Users(s2,s1)

net BSS = STATIONS /request,givebike,nobike,return/ USERS
```

From this specification of a family of bike-sharing stations, VMC generates the MTS with 18 states depicted in Fig. 5 in case of a BSS with only one user group (i.e., `net USERS = Users(s1,s2)`); in case of a BSS with two user groups (i.e., `net USERS = Users(s1,s2) // Users(s2,s1)`) the MTS has 224 states.[3]

For the family of BSS with one user group, we present some properties and the result of model checking them with VMC (i.e., on the MTS depicted in Fig. 5):

Eventually it must occur that station 1 has no bikes: $EF^{\Box} \{nobike(s1)\} \; true$.
This formula is of course true.

Eventually it may occur that station 2 has no more bikes: $EF \{nobike(s2)\} \; true$.
This formula however is false. (Note that it is true in case of two user groups.)

For all products, if redistribution is implemented, then it is always the case that eventually station 1 gives the user a bike: $(\neg \, EF \{redistribute(*,s1,*)\} true)$ $\lor (AG \, EF \{givebike(s1)\} \; true)$. This formula is actually true for all products (LTS) of the family (MTS in Fig. 5). However, it does not make much sense to verify this formula over the MTS, since it is not expressed in the specific fragment of v-ACTL that has the characteristic that any formula expressed in it and which is true for the MTS, is also true for all its products (cf. [9]).

---

[3] In VMC, text or code can be commented out by prefixing it with `--`.

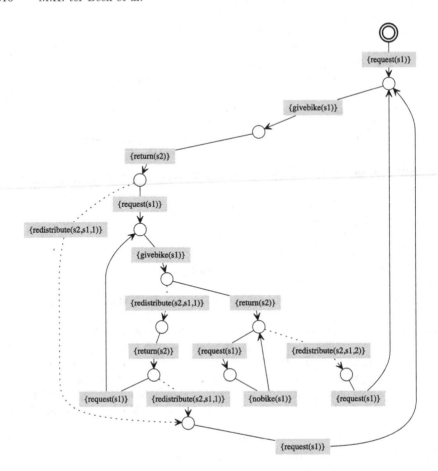

Fig. 5. A family MTS of a BSS with 2 stations and 1 group of users generated by VMC

6   Conclusions and Future Work

In this paper we have presented some of the recent developments concerning our ongoing research effort to elaborate a rigorous modelling and verification environment for behavioural variability analyses of product families. These developments, which concern the extension of both the input language of VMC and its logic to be able to deal with (integer) value-passing, stem from the fact that we realized that a major limitation for applying our approach to realistic case studies from industry is the lack of a possibility to model an adequate representation of the data that may need to be described.

This paper is only a first contribution to removing this limitation as it defines an extension of the environment that can deal with data in the form of integer value-passing. In particular, VMC now accepts models specified in a value-passing modal process algebra and allows explicit-state on-the-fly model checking of properties expressed in a value-passing action-based branching-time modal temporal logic.

It thus remains to extend the data handling in VMC to more than just integers. to this aim, we might turn to the mCRL2 toolset (http://www.mcrl2.org) for inspiration, since it allows to model actions parametrized with user-defined abstract datatypes and to verify formulas in the modal μ-calculus, thus allowing to quantify over data [25]. Moreover, also mCRL2 is recently being used for product family analysis [10–12].

In this paper we furthermore illustrated the new features of VMC by means of simple yet intuitive examples from a case study on bike-sharing systems originating from the EU FP7 project QUANTICOL (http://www.quanticol.eu).

In the future, we intend to further investigate the application of the modelling and verification environment presented in this paper to the behavioural analysis of product families, such as the preservation of properties from families to their products, in particular in the presence of the complex constraints that usually exist between the various features that can be distinguished in a product family. A promising starting point could be the results on generalized model checking [14].

We also intend to address the scalability of our approach, which is of utmost importance for any variability analysis technique to be succesful in SPLE, since a product family's variability is exponential in the number of available features.

Acknowledgments. We thank Marco Bertini from PisaMo S.p.A. for generously sharing with us his knowledge on bike-sharing systems in general and *CicloPi* in particular.

References

1. Antonik, A., Huth, M., Larsen, K.G., Nyman, U., Wąsowski, A.: 20 Years of modal and mixed specifications. Bull. EATCS **95**, 94–129 (2008)
2. Åqvist, L.: Deontic logic. Handbook of Philosophical Logic, 2nd edn, pp. 147–264. Kluwer, Dordrecht (2002)
3. Asirelli, P., ter Beek, M.H., Fantechi, A., Gnesi, S.: A logical framework to deal with variability. In: Méry, D., Merz, S. (eds.) IFM 2010. LNCS, vol. 6396, pp. 43–58. Springer, Heidelberg (2010)
4. Asirelli, P., ter Beek, M.H., Fantechi, A., Gnesi, S.: Formal description of variability in product families. In: SPLC 2011, pp. 130–139. IEEE (2011)
5. ter Beek, M.H., Fantechi, A., Gnesi, S., Mazzanti, F.: A state/event-based model-checking approach for the analysis of abstract system properties. Sci. Comput. Program. **76**(2), 119–135 (2011)
6. ter Beek, M.H., Gnesi, S., Mazzanti, F.: Demonstration of a model checker for the analysis of product variability. In: SPLC 2012, pp. 242–245. ACM (2012)
7. ter Beek, M.H., Lluch Lafuente, A., Petrocchi, M.: Combining declarative and procedural views in the specification and analysis of product families. In: SPLC 2013, Vol. 2, pp. 10–17. ACM (2013)

8. ter Beek, M.H., Mazzanti, F., Sulova, A.: VMC: a tool for product variability analysis. In: Giannakopoulou, D., Méry, D. (eds.) FM 2012. LNCS, vol. 7436, pp. 450–454. Springer, Heidelberg (2012)

9. ter Beek, M.H., Mazzanti, F.: VMC: recent advances and challenges ahead. In: SPLC 2014, Vol. 2, pp. 70–77. ACM (2014)

10. ter Beek, M.H., de Vink. E.P.: Using mCRL2 for the analysis of software product lines. In: FormaliSE 2014, IEEE (2014)

11. ter Beek, M.H., de Vink, E.P.: Software product line analysis with mCRL2. In: SPLC 2014, vol. 2, pp. 78–85. ACM (2014)

12. ter Beek, M.H., de Vink, E.P.: Towards modular verification of software product lines with mCRL2. In: Margaria, T., Steffen, B. (eds.) ISoLA 2014, Part I. LNCS, vol. 8802, pp. 368–385. Springer, Heidelberg (2014)

13. Beneš, N., Černá, I., Křetínský, J.: Modal transition systems: composition and LTL model checking. In: Bultan, T., Hsiung, P.-A. (eds.) ATVA 2011. LNCS, vol. 6996, pp. 228–242. Springer, Heidelberg (2011)

14. Bruns, G., Godefroid, P.: Generalized model checking: reasoning about partial state spaces. In: Palamidessi, C. (ed.) CONCUR 2000. LNCS, vol. 1877, pp. 168–182. Springer, Heidelberg (2000)

15. Clarke, E.M., Emerson, E.A., Sistla, A.P.: Automatic verification of finite state concurrent systems using temporal logic specifications. ACM TOPLAS 8(2), 244–263 (1986)

16. Classen, A., Cordy, M., Schobbens, P.-Y., Heymans, P., Legay, A., Raskin, J.-F.: Featured transition systems: foundations for verifying variability-intensive systems and their application to LTL model checking. IEEE TSE 39(8), 1069–1089 (2013)

17. DeMaio, P.: Bike-sharing: history, impacts, models of provision, and future. J. Public Transp. 12(4), 41–56 (2009)

18. De Nicola, R., Vaandrager, F.W.: Action versus state based logics for transition systems. In: Guessarian, I. (ed.) LITP 1990. LNCS, vol. 469, pp. 407–419. Springer, Heidelberg (1990)

19. De Nicola, R., Vaandrager, F.W.: Three logics for branching bisimulation. J. ACM 42(2), 458–487 (1995)

20. D'Ippolito, N., Fischbein, D., Chechik, M., Uchitel, S.: MTSA: the modal transition system analyser. In: ASE 2008, pp. 475–476. IEEE (2008)

21. Fantechi, A., Lapadula, A., Pugliese, R., Tiezzi, F., Gnesi, S., Mazzanti, F.: A logical verification methodology for service-oriented computing. ACM TOSEM 21(3), 1–46 (2012). Article 16

22. Fischbein, D., Uchitel, S., Braberman, V.A.: A foundation for behavioural conformance in software product line architectures. In: ROSATEA 2006, pp. 39–48. ACM (2006)

23. Fricker, C., Gast, N.: Incentives and redistribution in homogeneous bike-sharing systems with stations of finite capacity. EURO J. Transp. Logistics, 1–31 (2014)

24. Gnesi, S., Petrocchi, M.: Towards an executable algebra for product lines. In: SPLC 2012, Vol. 2, pp. 66–73. ACM (2012)

25. Groote, J.F., Mateescu, R.: Verification of temporal properties of processes in a setting with data. In: Haeberer, A.M. (ed.) AMAST 1998. LNCS, vol. 1548, pp. 74–90. Springer, Heidelberg (1998)

26. Krka, I., Edwards, G., Brun, Y., Medvidovic, N.: From system specifications to component behavioral models. In: ICSE 2009, pp. 315–318. IEEE (2009)

27. Larsen, K.G.: Proof systems for satisfiability in Hennessy-Milner logic with recursion. Theoret. Comput. Sci. 72(2–3), 265–288 (1990)

28. Larsen, K.G., Nyman, U., Wąsowski, A.: Modal I/O automata for interface and product line theories. In: De Nicola, R. (ed.) ESOP 2007. LNCS, vol. 4421, pp. 64–79. Springer, Heidelberg (2007)
29. Larsen, K.G., Thomsen, B.: A modal process logic. In: LICS 1988, pp. 203–210. IEEE (1988)
30. Lauenroth, K., Pohl, K., Töhning, S.: Model checking of domain artifacts in product line engineering. In: ASE 2009, pp. 269–280. IEEE (2009)
31. Leucker, M., Thoma, D.: A formal approach to software product families. In: Margaria, T., Steffen, B. (eds.) ISoLA 2012, Part I. LNCS, vol. 7609, pp. 131–145. Springer, Heidelberg (2012)
32. Meolic, R., Kapus, T., Brezocnik, Z.: ACTLW: an action-based computation tree logic with unless operator. Inf. Sci. **178**(6), 1542–1557 (2008)
33. Milner, R.: Communication and Concurrency. Prentice Hall (1989)
34. Pohl, K., Böckle, G., van der Linden, F.J.: Software Product Line Engineering: Foundations, Principles, and Techniques. Springer, Heidelberg (2005)
35. Sibay, G.E., Uchitel, S., Braberman, V., Kramer, J.: Distribution of modal transition systems. In: Giannakopoulou, D., Méry, D. (eds.) FM 2012. LNCS, vol. 7436, pp. 403–417. Springer, Heidelberg (2012)

Towards Specializing JavaScript Programs

Peter Thiemann[(✉)]

University of Freiburg, Freiburg im Breisgau, Germany
`thiemann@acm.org`

Abstract. Program specialization is an effective tool for transforming interpreters to compilers. We present the first steps in the construction of a specialization tool chain for JavaScript programs. We report on an application of this tool chain in a case study that transforms a realistic interpreter implemented in JavaScript to a compiler.

The difference to previous work on compiling with program specialization is threefold. First, the interpreter has not been written with specialization in mind. Second, instead of specializing the interpreter, we transform it into a generating extension, which replaces parts of the interpreter's code by a corresponding code generator. Third, the implementation language of the interpreter is not a restricted toy language, but full JavaScript.

1 Introduction

Program specialization [10,14] is an effective tool for transforming interpreters into compilers. A program specializer may be applied to a program where the input can be partitioned into *static* and *dynamic* arguments. Static and dynamic are the prime examples for *binding times*: The static parts are known before the dynamic parts. Applying the specializer transforms the program such that all computations that solely depend on the static parts are executed and code is generated for the rest. The resulting *residual program* accepts the dynamic parts and computes the same results as the original program on all arguments.

Considering the arguments of an interpreter, its program-text argument is static whereas its program-input argument is dynamic. Specializing the interpreter translates the program text into a residual program in the implementation language of the interpreter, thus performing some kind of compilation. The quality of compilation depends on the structure of the interpreter. If it keeps static and dynamic data nicely apart, then the specializer can perform many computations statically. Some styles of interpreters are known to specialize badly [15].

Related Work. The Futamura projections have been the main inspiration for pushing the state of the art in program specialization and for building compilers and compiler generators [9]. However, they require a self-applicable specializer to start with and much effort has been invested in constructing such specializers, but mostly for relatively small and clean languages, e.g., [4,5,16]. Jørgensen's thesis presents a number of examples [17]. Recent work applies these ideas to

© Springer-Verlag Berlin Heidelberg 2015
A. Voronkov and I. Virbitskaite (Eds.): PSI 2014, LNCS 8974, pp. 320–334, 2015.
DOI: 10.1007/978-3-662-46823-4_26

generating JIT compilers [3]. For various reasons, later work on more realistic languages has taken up the *cogen approach*, which essentially shortcuts two steps in the Futamura projections [2,6,13].

Applying the cogen approach directly maps a program (to be specialized) into a so-called *generating extension*. This generating extension is a specializer tailored to specialize just this one program. It accepts the static arguments and returns the corresponding residual program. Using this approach greatly simplifies the specialization for typed languages and it speeds up the specialization because static computations are guaranteed to run natively at full speed. The cogen approach is also very suitable for an experiment like ours because new ideas can be tested by transforming existing programs instead of implementing a full-blown specializer.

The ultimate goal of our work is to obtain a cogen-based program specialization system for JavaScript. The present investigation is a first step in this direction. It presents a case study, in which part of a sophisticated interpreter is manually turned into a compiler, that is, the generating extension of the interpreter. Our subject is the JSFlow JavaScript interpreter. It is written in JavaScript with the extra twist that it performs low-level information-flow control at run time. It has been developed by Hedin, Sabelfeld, and others [11,12], who report that "Compared to a fully JITed JavaScript engine, JSFlow is slower by two orders of magnitude". So, the ultimate goal is to see how this slowdown can be amended.

Contribution. Our case study investigates the potential of specialization in a realistic JavaScript program, obtains a preliminary toolbox for writing generating extensions, identifies the specialization techniques needed for obtaining satisfactory results, and explores the requirements for automatizing our manual transformation. Ideally, we would be able to state the requirements for a binding-time analysis, a static analysis that classifies all program parts as either static or dynamic, the results of which guide an automatic transformation from program to generating extension (i.e., from interpreter to compiler).

Our main result is that an offline approach to transforming the interpreter is successful and yields a speedup between 1.1 and 1.8. This small number is nevertheless remarkable because the architecture of the interpreter is not chosen with specialization in mind. Our experiments further indicate that a pure offline approach, where the generating extension just executes instructions from a binding-time analysis, is unlikely to give satisfactory results so that a hybrid approach that integrates offline with online techniques is called for. Encouragingly, inspection of the residual code for example programs indicates that there is scope for further improvements using online techniques.

The concrete outcome of this work is a compiler for a subset of JavaScript based on JSFlow. The subset comprises all expressions and statements, but it does not handle built-in objects, yet. The compiler transforms a JavaScript program into an instrumented program that performs information-flow control. Technically, it inlines a reference monitor. A further outcome is a JavaScript library for various code generation and specialization tasks. The functions of this library are reusable building blocks for generating extensions.

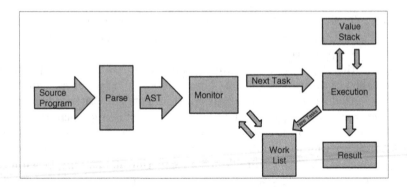

Fig. 1. Architecture of the JSFlow interpreter.

2   Architecture of the JSFlow Interpreter

Figure 1 gives a rough overview of the architecture of the JSFlow interpreter. After parsing the source code into an abstract syntax tree (AST), a monitor takes control. It pushes the root node of the AST on a *worklist*, the manipulation of which implements all control structures of the interpreted language. The monitor repeatedly pulls the top entry from the worklist, acts on it, checks the current information-flow state after the action, and continues as long as the state does not indicate a violation of the information-flow policy. A worklist entry may be a node of the syntax tree or a function inside the interpreter. A worklist action puts new entries on the worklist according to the required control flow.

The other main datastructure of the interpreter is the *value stack*. It contains intermediate results during the evaluation of expressions. These results are represented by *value objects*. A value object is a pair of a raw value and an information-flow label. Thus, each manipulation of a value in the interpreter entails repeated wrapping and unwrapping of the value objects involved along with the corresponding manipulation of the information-flow labels.

3   Specializing the JSFlow Interpreter

The first task in any application of specialization is to figure out the binding-time assumptions of the datastructures in the program. In specializing an interpreter, the traditional division of binding times states that the source program is static and that all run-time data is dynamic.

In JSFlow the AST is static as it only depends on the source programs. Likewise, the initial worklist is static. However, as the worklist is used to implement control structures, it is a datastructure under dynamic control and thus it cannot remain static! Unfortunately, if the worklist is not static, then the dispatch on the nodes of the syntax tree cannot be static either. But that means that the execution component cannot be specialized, either!

The textbook solution to this problem is program point specialization [14]. While the worklist is under dynamic control, it only assumes finitely many different

```
function unaryExpression (node ,wl ,vs ) {
  var ip = wl.top();
  ip.then(node.argument);
  ip.then(unarytbl[node.operator]);
}
function unaryMinus (wl ,vs ) {
  var ref = vs.pop();
  var n   = conversion.ToNumber(GetValue(ref));
  n.value = -n.value;
  vs.push(n);
}
```

Fig. 2. Interpreting unary operations.

static shapes after discarding the dynamic values. Program point specialization creates a mutually recursive set of residual functions indexed by these static shapes. However, this solution is not applicable in our context. First, the worklist may contain functions, so we would have to modify the interpreter to use a standardized function representation that admits comparison. Second, the resulting set of functions would look artificial as it would contain many very short functions.

The solution is to change the meaning of the worklist from scheduling interpretation to scheduling specialization. This change enables us to regard the worklist as static, so that the syntax dispatch can be static.

The second important datastructure is the value stack. Initially, we consider the value stack as dynamic as it is truly under dynamic control, but this assumption results in atrocious, inefficient code.

3.1 Specializing Unary Operations

Figure 2 contains the interpreter's implementation of unary operations. As this code only manipulates static data, it remains unchanged in the compiler! The use of ip requires some explanation: its then method installs a queue interface on top of the worklist such that the "tasks" are executed in the order in which they are added. The unarytbl dispatches on the particular operator.

The function unaryMinus is a potential target of this dispatch. As it handles the dynamic value stack, it needs to be changed. It even turns out that *all* instructions of unaryMinus need to be executed at run time because they all depend on the value on top of the value stack.

3.2 Generating Code for Expressions and Assignments

Initially, we take a very simple approach to code generation, which is encapsulated in a module GEN that we developed. Its named method sets a stub for subsequent name generation and returns the module for chaining. Figure 3 contains the code-generating variant of unaryMinus. Calling this code generator in the context of translating the expression -(42) yields the (last four lines of the) code in Fig. 4.

```
function unaryMinus(wl,vs) {
    var ref = GEN.named("ref").Expr("^d^.pop()", vs);
    var n   = GEN.named("n").
              Expr("conversion.ToNumber(GetValue(^d^))", ref);
    GEN.Stmt("^d^.value = -^d^.value;", n, n);
    GEN.Stmt("^d^.push(^d^);", vs, n);
}
```

Fig. 3. Compiling unary minus.

```
// generated code for literal 42
var v_res_0_ = new Value(42,bot);
vs.push(v_res_0_);
// generated code for unary minus
var v_ref_1_ = vs.pop();
var v_n_2_ = conversion.ToNumber(GetValue(v_ref_1_));
v_n_2_.value = -v_n_2_.value;
vs.push(v_n_2_);
```

Fig. 4. Compiled code for -(42).

This approach to code generation works by supplying template strings with holes indicated by ^s^ and ^d^ for static and dynamic data, respectively. For expressions, the GEN.Expr function generates a fresh variable binding, instantiates the template from the remaining arguments, and returns the name of the fresh variable that stands for the result of the generated computation. For assignments, GEN.Stmt just instantiates the template.

This simple principle can be applied (almost) throughout the interpreter and leads to executable code. However, the quality of this code is quite bad and it results in almost no speedup.

3.3 Making the Value Stack Static

The first improvement is to make the value stack *partially static* [18]. That means that the stack manipulation is to happen at specialization time, but the actual values on the stack are run-time values, i.e., dynamic. The interesting point about this change in bining time is that the revised generating extension is closer to the original than before!

Figure 5 contains the revised code. Instead of generating code for push and pop, the code creates a stack and also performs the push and pop operations at compile time. The generated code improves substantially by this change as shown in Fig. 6.

However, there is a catch. The value stack is actually needed at run time for evaluating some kinds of expressions. As an example, consider the conditional expression (b?e1:e2), where depending on the value of b the result is either the value of e1 or the value of e2.

```
function unaryMinus(wl,vs) {
  var ref = vs.pop();
  var n   = GEN.named("n").
            Expr("conversion.ToNumber(GetValue(^d^))", ref);
  GEN.Stmt("^d^.value = -^d^.value;", n, n);
  vs.push(n);
}
```

Fig. 5. Compiling unary minus with partially static stack.

```
var v_res_4_ = new Value(42,bot);
var v_n_5_ = conversion.ToNumber(GetValue(v_res_4_));
v_n_5_.value = -v_n_5_.value;
```

Fig. 6. Compiled code for -(42).

Figure 7 contains the gist of the implementation of the conditional expression. It reads the evaluated condition from the top of the value stack into lb. Because lb.value is dynamic, code must be generated for both branches of the conditional. Compiling each branch leaves a separate entry on top of the stack, but the expected effect is to leave just one entry for the result of the conditional.

One way to fix this problem is to improve binding times with "The Trick" [8]. As the end of each branch, we pop its value from the specialization-time stack and push it on the run-time stack. After specializing both branches, we pop the run-time stack and push its top on the compile-time stack as shown in Fig. 8.

The implemented code generator elides the run-time stack entirely by representing its top-level entry by a new variable. This choice renders the generated push operation an assignment to the variable and eliminates the dynamic pop operation entirely: The code generator just pushes the new variable after processing the conditional. Figure 9 shows a code fragment generated in this manner.

3.4 Making Values Static

A closer look at Fig. 6 reveals that this code still contains some churn. JavaScript's object dereference operation returns a Reference object instead of the dereferenced value. For that reason, an operation first has to obtain the underlying value by invoking GetValue. For non-Reference arguments, GetValue is the identity. In consequence, the GetValue operation in Fig. 6 may be elided as its argument is certainly not a Reference object.

Unlike the value stack, value objects cannot simply be allocated statically. The main reason is that there are different types of objects on the value stack and inter-converting them between a static and a dynamic representation (as for the value stack) is much more involved.

For this reason, we adopt a *new strategy* to represent specialization-time knowledge about data. Instead of keeping static values objects, we maintain known properties of dynamic values. This approach is dual to the usual partially static values and might be dubbed *smart dynamic values*.

```
function conditionalExpressionChoose (wl,vs) {
  var ip = wl.top ();
  var lval = GetValue (vs.pop ());
  var lb   = conversion.ToBoolean (lval);
  if (lb.value) {
    ip.then (this.node.consequent );
  } else {
    ip.then (this.node.alternate );
  }
}
```

Fig. 7. Interpreting conditional expressions (simplified).

```
function conditionalExpressionChoose (wl,vs) {
  var ip = wl.top ();
  var lval = GetValue_s (vs.pop ());
  var lb   = conversion.ToBoolean_s (lval);
  GEN.If (lb.value);
    ip.then (this.node.consequent );
    ip.then (function () { var v = vs.pop ();
                           GEN.Stmt ("^d^.push (^d^)", vs, v);})
  ip.then (GEN.Else );
    ip.then (this.node.alternate );
    ip.then (function () { var v = vs.pop ();
                           GEN.Stmt ("^d^.push (^d^)", vs, v);})
  ip.then (GEN.Endif );
  ip.then (function ()    { var r = GEN.Expr ("^d^.pop ()", vs);
                            vs.push (r);});
}
```

Fig. 8. Compiling conditional expressions.

Each value object is created dynamic from the start and represented by a variable like all other dynamic values. However, when it is created, the properties of the value are stored with the variable. For example, it is known that the variable contains a value object at run time and its components are also recorded.

By exploiting this extra information, the GetValue function can be adapted to statically check whether its argument is definitely not a Reference object. This check effectively elides many occurrences of GetValue in the generated code. In particular, it can be elided from Fig. 6.

Similar exploitation of the properties of a value object enables a specializing version of conversion.ToNumber, which is the identity on numbers like 42. Taking all these optimization steps together, the compiled code for -(42) boils down to just two statements.

```
var v__7_ = new Value (42, bot);
v__7_.value = -v__7_.value;
```

It is possible to get down to just one line:

```
var v__7_ = new Value (-42, bot);
```

```
var v_temp_10_;
if(v_lb_8_.value) {
  var v_res_11_ = new Value(42, bot);
  v_temp_10_ = v_res_11_;
} else {
  var v_res_12_ = new Value("a string", bot);
  v_temp_10_ = v_res_12_;
}
var v_val_13_ = GetValue(v_temp_10_);
```

Fig. 9. Generated code fragment for conditional expression `b?42:'a string'`.

It requires replacing the assignment `n.value = -n.value` in `unaryMinus` (Fig. 2) by the construction of a new value as follows.

```
var t = new Value (-n.value, n.label);
vs.push(t);
```

3.5 Variables and the Environment

In the current approach, the environment structure is dynamic so that all variable accesses are handled at run time. The code generated for, say, `n-1` looks like this:

```
var v_temp_66_ = env.
    GetIdentifierReference(v_c_42_.lexicalEnv,''n'');
var v_temp_67_ = GetValue(v_temp_66_);
var v__71_ = conversion.ToNumber(v_temp_67_);
var v__73_ = v__71_.value - 1;
```

The motivation is twofold. First, the representation of the `lexicalEnv` provides the mutable object structure needed for variables at run time. Second, the interpreter also handles the notorious `with` statement, which pushes an arbitrary (run-time) object on top of the environment. That means, the environment structure is only static *most of the time*, but with intermittent dynamic sections.

3.6 Function Expressions *

A JavaScript function expression creates a function object in the interpreter. Hence, the compiled code also creates a function object. The invocation of a function object happens via its `Call` method. In the interpreter, the method fetches the AST of the function body and recursively invokes the interpreter loop with a new worklist instance etc. In contrast, the compiled code should contain a suitably *specialized* `Call` method that does not refer to the AST, anymore.

For that reason, the transformed interpreter equips the function object with a `Call_s` method that generates a specialized `Call` method for a function object. The code generator for a function expression needs to be extended (with respect to the interpreter) with an assignment that overwrites the generic `Call` method with the result of invoking Call_s. Code generation for the corresponding call expression constructs the argument object from the argument list and invokes the Call method of the function object.

3.7   Control Structures

Code generation for loops required the most invasive changes to the interpreter. To understand why requires a look at the implementation of control structures in JSFlow using the while statement as an example.

Initially, each looping statement gathers the labels attached to it. The labels serve as marks for break and continue statements occurring in the loop's body. These statements are implemented by setting a flag in the result of the statement. The outer execution loop in the monitor checks this flag and unwinds the worklist down to the first entry that wants to process the flag. This intent is indicated by an annotation of the worklist entry.

The second subtask of the looping statement is to process breaks and continues that are signalled by the execution loop. Next, it schedules the execution of the loop test and the potential execution of the loop body.

If the loop test yields true, then the third subtask schedules another execution of the loop body followed by the second subtask.

In principle, a specializer could generate code from this pattern. However, it would require to specialize each iteration of the execution loop in the monitor with respect to its current worklist, an instance of *program point specialization* [14]. This approach is theoretically more pleasing, but it has a number of drawbacks. First, specialization with respect to the worklist requires to compare different worklists. Unfortunately, this comparison is expensive because it involves comparison of fragments of the AST, but on top of that the worklist also contains functions created on the fly by function expressions, which cannot be reliably compared. Second, the specialization would result in many small

```
var x = 10;
var n = 0;
while (x>0) {
    x--;
    n++;
}
```
Listing 1.1. While

```
var x = 68;
var n = 0;
while (x>1){
    if (x%2==0) {
        x = x/2;
    } else {
        x = 3*x+1;
    }
    n++;
}
```
Listing 1.2. Collatz

```
var i,j,n=0;
for (j=1; j<=10; j++) {
    for (i=1; i<=10; i++) {
        n+=i*j;
    }
}
```
Listing 1.3. NestedFor

```
var myPower = function power (b, n){
    return (n===0) ? 1 : b * power (b, n-1);
}
var b = 2; var n = 10;   myPower(b, n);
```
Listing 1.4. Power

mutually recursive functions, each corresponding to the compilation of a worklist entry. Many of these functions are called only once and aggressive inlining would be required to assemble them back together to larger, more efficient functions. Third, specialization with respect to the worklist also requires to specialize with respect to the current configuration of the value stack, which potentially leads to a further explosion of specialized variants of the worklist entry functions.

Hence, we decided to shortcut this mechanism for the time being and to generate a suitably labeled `while(true)` loop for all control structures. All exits from the loop are implemented via generated `break` statements. Explicit `break` and `continue` statements are copied to the generated code.

The third subtask above is modified for code generation. The loop test compiles to a conditional statement that executes the loop body in the true-branch and performs a `break` in the other. The second subtask is *not* rescheduled, as the code generation for the loop only needs to happen once and for all.

This approach works mutatis mutandis for all looping statements as well as for the `switch` statement. One problem of the latter is that cases fall through unless they are terminated with a `break`, `continue`, or `return` statement. The current implementation does not detect whether the transition from one case to the next is dead. Therefore, it generates duplicate code for consecutive cases.

4 Results

This section reports the results from running the JSFlow interpreter (version 1.0.0) on selected micro benchmarks and comparing it with the code generated by two versions of our compiler.

All programs were run on *node.js*[1] version v0.10.20 on an Apple MacBook with intel Core 2 Duo 2.26 GHz processor and 2 GB RAM.

This section considers four micro benchmark programs shown in Listings 1.1 (While), 1.2 (Collatz), 1.3 (NestedFor), and 1.4 (Power). The programs While and Collatz are run with different values of x, Power is run with different values of n, and NestedFor is run with different ranges for i and j.

Table 1. Execution times for execution environment setup

Setup	Interpreter	Compiler	Compiled code
Time/ms	151	156	145

To interpret a program, to compile a program, and to run a compiled program all requires a pre-execution setup that consists of reading a number of utility modules from the local disk. The execution time for this setup is different for the interpreter, the compiler, and the residual program because they depend on different sets of modules. Essentially, the compiler needs to load all interpreter

---

[1] http://nodejs.org/.

dependencies and a code-generating module, whereas the residual program only needs a subset of the interpreter modules. Table 1 shows these setup times in milliseconds. They are not included in the timings reported subsequently.

In the following, the execution time of the interpreter is measured without the setup time and without reading the source file. The execution time of the compiler is measured without setup and without reading the source, but it includes creating the output file and writing the generated code. The execution time of a residual program is measured without the setup time.

4.1 Benchmark Results

When specializing an interpreter, we hope that the residual program runs faster than the interpretation of the source program. To determine the speedup from specialization, we run four different JavaScript source programs on the interpreter, we compile them, and run the residual programs to measure the execution time for each step.

The compiler and the residual programs run in two modes. In *dynamic-stack* mode, the entire manipulation of the value stack is done at run time with residual code as shown in Fig. 4. In *static-stack* mode, the value stack is manipulated at compile time as much as possible as explained in Sect. 3.3. In addition, the static value optimization is also applied (Sect. 3.4). The difference between these numbers indicates the effectiveness of the static-stack optimization.

Table 2 shows the execution time of a single iteration (compilation) for each program. It demonstrates that the compile times are up to 20 % slower than the execution of one iteration in the interpreter. There is no discernible difference in compile time between the dynamic-stack and the static-stack modes.

Table 2. Execution time (in ms) for one iteration.

Benchmark	Interpreter	Compiler (*Dynamic stack*)	Compiler (*Static stack*)
While	15	15	15
Collatz	16	18	18
NestedFor	17	18	18
Power	20	26	26

Table 3. Number of source code lines for each benchmark.

Benchmark	Source	RP	ORP	Improvement	ORP/Source
While	7	110	94	17 %	13.4
Collatz	10	194	135	43 %	13.5
NestedFor	6	233	181	28 %	30.2
Power	6	325	266	22 %	44.3

Table 3 shows the size of the benchmark programs, residual programs (RP), and optimized residual programs (ORP) measured in the number of lines. As the compiler in dynamic stack mode generates code for many push and pop operations, the unoptimized programs are on average (geometric mean) 26 % longer than the optimized ones. Compilation expands the program by a factor of 22.2 (geometric mean). The Power benchmark expands by a factor 44 because it contains a compiled function.

Benchmark While. Table 4 shows execution times for the While benchmark in Listing 1.1. The first column contains the number of loop iterations. Column (Int) shows the execution time of the unmodified interpreter. Column (RP) shows the execution time of the residual program with dynamic stack. The nexts columns show the speedup = interpreter/RP of the residual program and the amortized speedup (A Speedup) = interpreter/(compile time + RP). Column OPR contains the run time for the Optimized Residual Program compiled with static value stack. The seventh and eighth columns contain the corresponding speedup and amortized speedup. Compile times for computing the amortized speedup are taken from Table 2.

Benchmark Collatz. Table 5 presents the execution times for the Collatz benchmark (Listing 1.2). Unfortunately, modifying the input x only indirectly affects the number n of loop iterations, which determines the run time. The columns of the table are analogous to Table 4.

Benchmark NestedFor. Table 6 presents the measurements for Listing 1.3. The columns are the same as before, only in this case we are varying the number of inner and outer iterations.

Benchmark Power. This program (Listing 1.4) takes a base number and a positive integer as an exponent and calculates the power. Instead of using loops, this program uses recursion to calculate the power of a number.

To obtain the execution times in Table 7, the base number $b = 2$ is fixed but the exponent n varies for different measurments. The columns in the table are analogous to the previous tables.

Table 4. Execution times for While (milliseconds).

n	Int	RP	Speedup	A Speedup	ORP	Speedup	A Speedup
10	19	8	2.37	0.82	6	3.16	0.90
10^2	46	29	1.58	1.04	25	1.84	1.15
10^3	177	132	1.34	1.21	116	1.53	1.36
10^4	1174	932	1.26	1.24	810	1.45	1.42
10^5	11081	8865	1.25	1.25	7650	1.45	1.45
10^6	111930	90266	1.24	1.24	79890	1.40	1.40

Table 5. Execution times for Collatz (milliseconds).

x	n	Int	RP	Speedup	A Speedup	ORP	Speedup	A Speedup
10	6	20	8	2.5	0.76	6	3.33	0.83
10^2	25	31	15	2.06	0.93	14	2.21	0.96
10^3	111	64	36	1.77	1.18	34	1.88	1.23
10^5	128	67	38	1.76	1.17	36	1.86	1.24
10^6	152	75	45	1.66	1.19	42	1.78	1.25

4.2   Analysis

The results from the four micro benchmarks indicate a speedup between 1.1 and 1.6 (geometric mean: 1.28) for the programs compiled with dynamic stack. After the stack optimization, the speedup ranges between 1.1 and 1.8 (geometric mean: 1.36). This change indicates that the stack optimization speeds up program by about 6 %. As expected, the amortized speedup converges against the raw speedup. All programs exhibit an amortized speedup greater than 1 after about 100 iterations, which indicates the break-even point of compilation.

5   Assessment

The positive message is that we successfully applied program specialization techniques to transform a realistic interpreter into a compiler. We achieve a moderate speedup by a factor of at most 1.8, which is only a small improvement on the 100 fold slowdown incurred by using the interpreter (cf. introduction). However, there is a lot of scope for improvement.

The code generated by running the interpreter transformed to a generating extension is still far from optimal. In particular, much more information could be propagated at specialization time (compile time). The propagation of the structure of values (Sect. 3.4) is just a first step. In many places, the interpreter checks the type of the arguments of an operation, which generates lengthy code fragments. By propagating type information, these checks could be elided.

Another point is to shift handling of the environment to compile time as much as possible. However, it must be possible to switch between a compile-time version and a run-time version, in case the with statement occurs in a program. There are proposals how to handle such situations in the literature [19,20].

Right now, it is not clear if program point specialization is required beyond the trivial instances where the Call method is specialized. However, the current strategy for handling function objects relies on handling the environment at run time. It probably must be revised when using compile time environments.

A main design goal of the transformation strategy is to keep the changes to the underlying interpreter as small as possible. In many cases, we succeeded in doing so. For example, the final compiler function for unaryMinus (not shown) looks almost identical to the interpreter code in Fig. 2. In other places, we were

Table 6. Execution times for NestedFor (milliseconds)

j	i	Int	RP	Speedup	A Speedup	ORP	Speedup	A Speedup
10	10^2	67	37	1.82	1.20	36	1.86	1.24
10^2	10^3	1574	1202	1.31	1.18	1280	1.23	1.21
10^3	10^4	147327	123804	1.19	1.17	118812	1.24	1.24

Table 7. Execution times for Power

n	Int	RP	Speedup	A Speedup	ORP	Speedup	A Speedup
10	48	25	1.92	0.94	24	2.00	0.96
10^2	143	112	1.28	1.02	111	1.27	1.03
10^3	990	900	1.10	1.06	885	1.12	1.09

less successful. For example, it would be interesting to investigate whether program point specialization would enable to dismiss the shortcuts for implementing control structures (Sect. 3.7).

One technique to keep the source code of a generating extension close to the original program is to use overloading [1]. In JavaScript, we might employ proxies to achieve similar goals, but unfortunately the proxy API only applies to objects, not to primitve values and their operations.

6   Conclusion

We successfully built a program specialization toolchain for constructing generating extensions in JavaScript. This toolchain enabled us to transform an existing JavaScript interpreter into a compiler. While the compiler realizes a modest speedup, there is still a lot of potential for future improvements. We regard it as a first step to evaluate the use of program specialization in such a task. The final goal of our work is to obtain a low-overhead compiler, where the generated code could be fed directy into eval and executed. For that reason, we are interested in good amortized speedup.

Thanks to Daniel Hedin and Andrei Sabelfeld for giving us access to the JSFlow implementation and for discussions. Further thanks to Javed Sarwar for his work on transforming the interpreter, for building the testing infrastructure, and for performing measurements.

References

1. Andersen, L.O.: Program analysis and specialization for the c programming language. Ph.D. thesis, DIKU, University of Copenhagen (DIKU report 94/19) May 1994
2. Birkedal, L., Welinder, M.: Partial evaluation of Standard ML. Rapport 93/22, DIKU, University of Copenhagen (1993)

3. Bolz, C.F., et al.: Allocation removal by partial evaluation in a tracing JIT. In: PEPM 2011, Austin, TX, USA, pp. 43–52. ACM, January 2011
4. Bondorf, A.: Automatic autoprojection of higher order recursive equations. Sci. Comput. Program. **17**, 3–34 (1991)
5. Consel, C.: A tour of schism. In: Proceedings of the 1993 ACM Workshop Partial Evaluation and Semantics-Based Program Manipulation, Copenhagen, Denmark, pp. 134–154. ACM Press, June 1993
6. Consel, C., Lawall, J., Le Meur, A.-F.: A tour of tempo: a program specializer for the C language. Sci. Comput. Program. **52**(1–3), 341–370 (2004)
7. Danvy, O., Thiemann, P., Glück, R. (eds.): Dagstuhl Seminar 1996. LNCS, vol. 1110. Springer, Heidelberg (1996)
8. Danvy, O., Malmkjær, K., Palsberg, J.: Eta-expansion does the trick. ACM TOPLAS **18**(6), 730–751 (1996)
9. Futamura, Y.: Partial evaluation of computation process – an approach to a compiler-compiler. Syst. Comput. Controls **2**(5), 45–50 (1971)
10. Hatcliff, J., Thiemann, P. (eds.): DIKU 1998. LNCS, vol. 1706. Springer, Heidelberg (1999)
11. Hedin, D., et al.: JSFlow: tracking information flow in JavaScript and its APIs. In: ACM Symposium on Applied Computing (SAC 2014), Gyeongju, Korea, March 2014
12. Hedin, D., Sabelfeld, A.: Information-flow security for a core of JavaScript. In: Chong, A.S. (ed.) CSF 2012, pp. 3–18. IEEE (2012)
13. Helsen, S., Thiemann, P.: Polymorphic specialization for ML. ACM TOPLAS **26**(4), 1–50 (2004)
14. Jones, N., Gomard, C., Sestoft, P.: Partial Evaluation and Automatic Program Generation. Prentice-Hall, New Jersey (1993)
15. Jones, N. D.: What not to do when writing an interpreter for specialisation. In: Danvy et al. [7], pp. 216–237
16. Jones, N.D., Sestoft, P., Søndergaard, H.: An experiment in partial evaluation: the generation of a compiler generator. In: Jouannaud, J.-P. (ed.) RTA 1985. LNCS, vol. 202, pp. 124–140. Springer, Heidelberg (1985)
17. Jørgensen, J.: Compiler generation by partial evaluation. Master's thesis, DIKU, University of Copenhagen (1991)
18. Mogensen, T.Æ.: Partially static structures in a self-applicable partial evaluator. In: Partial Evaluation and Mixed Computation, pp. 325–347. North-Holland, Amsterdam (1988)
19. Sperber, M.: Self-applicable online partial evaluation. In: Danvy et al. [7], pp. 465–480
20. Sumii, E., Kobayashi, N.: A hybrid approach to online and offline partial evaluation. Higher-Order Symbol. Comput. **14**(2/3), 101–142 (2001)

Symbolic String Transformations with Regular Lookahead and Rollback

Margus Veanes[(✉)]

Microsoft Research, Redmond, USA
margus@microsoft.com

Abstract. Implementing string transformation routines, such as encoders, decoders, and sanitizers, correctly and efficiently is a difficult and error prone task. Such routines are often used in security critical settings, process large amounts of data, and must work efficiently and correctly. We introduce a new declarative language called Bex that builds on elements of regular expressions, symbolic automata and transducers, and enables a compilation scheme into C, C# or JavaScript that avoids many of the potential sources of errors that arise when such routines are implemented directly. The approach allows correctness analysis using symbolic automata theory that is not possible at the level of the generated code. Moreover, the case studies show that the generated code consistently outperforms hand-optimized code.

1 Introduction

Recent focus on string analysis is motivated by the fact that strings play a central role in all aspects of web programming. As soon as you visit a web page or read a file, several encoders, decoders and sanitizers launch for different purposes. Some coders are related to data integrity and format, such as UTF8 encoding and decoding that translates between standard text file representation (UTF8) and standard runtime memory representation (UTF16) of Unicode characters. Other encoders, called sanitizers, are used to prevent cross-site scripting (XSS) attacks; typical examples are Html encoder and Css encoder. While for such coders, basic functional correctness criteria is often vital for security, it may be notoriously difficult to implement them correctly or even reason about such correctness criteria [3,13]. One reason behind this difficulty is the subtle semantics resulting from a combinaton of *arithmetic* with *automata theory*. Individual characters are represented by integers and operations over characters often involve arithmetic operations such as bit-shifting and modulo arithmetic. Automata theory, on the other hand, is used overs strings (sequences of characters) to check for possible input or output patterns that may cause security vulnerabilities. Encoding related security vulnerabilities have been exploited for example through over-encoding [18,20], double-encoding [19], and XSS attacks. Some recent work has studied sanitizer correctness by utilizing automata techniques [6,16,17], including Bek [13] that our current work builds on.

Here we introduce a language called *Bex*. The main features of Bex that make it more expressive and succinct than Bek are: (1) *regex lookahead* for pattern

© Springer-Verlag Berlin Heidelberg 2015
A. Voronkov and I. Virbitskaite (Eds.): PSI 2014, LNCS 8974, pp. 335–350, 2015.
DOI: 10.1007/978-3-662-46823-4_27

matching that removes the burden of having to explicitly encode state machines; (2) *default rules* to specify what happens when a normal rule fails. In contrast, Bek supports only single-character guards and construction of default rules is then trivial by using the disjunction of all the negated guards from a given state as the guard of the default rule from that state.

Example 1. Consider the following Bex program B. B decodes two-digit html decimal encodings. The first rule, with pattern P_0 = "&#00;", states that the null character must not be decoded. The second rule, with pattern P_1 = "&#[0--9]{2};", is the normal decoding case. The third rule, with pattern P_2 = "&#$", uses the end-anchor $ so it applies only if the match occurs at the end of the input. The fourth rule is a default rule, it applies only when no other rule applies and it always reads a single character while a normal rules read k characters at a time with k being the length of the matched input.

```
program B { "&#00;"    ==> "&#00;";
            "&#\d\d;" ==> [(10*(x2-48))+(x3-48)];
            "&#$"      ==> "&#";
            else       ==> [x0]; }
```

Consider the input u = "&&#00;&&#". No pattern matches initially, both P_0 and P_1 match from position 1, P_1 matches from position 6, and P_2 matches from position 11. For the overlapping case, P_i has priority over P_j for $i < j$. So

$$B(u) = \text{"\&"} + \text{"\&#00;"} + [(10*('3'-48))+('8'-48)] + \text{"\&#"} = \text{"\&\&#00;\&\&#"}$$

where the ASCII character codes are '&' = 38, '3' = 51 and '8' = 56.   ⊠

Bek programs were originally compiled into *symbolic finite transducers* or SFTs [13]. Unlike sanitizers, a direct representation of *decoders* with SFTs is highly impractical due to state space explosion [24]. Even when registers are added to Bek and symbolic transducers with *registers* (STs) are being used, direct representation with Bek and STs is still very cumbersome and error prone, as illustrated by the representation of HTMLdecode (corresponding to B) in [24, Fig. 7]. The need to read several characters at once without storing them in registers and without introducing intermediate states, motivated the introduction of *extended* symbolic finite transducers (ESFTs) [8], that add support for *lookahead*. However, unlike in the classical case where lookahead can effectively be eliminated [26, Theorem 2.17], analysis of ESFTs does not reduce to analysis of SFTs and requires, for decidability, further restriction to the *Cartesian* case [7] where *guards* are conjunctions of unary predicates. Regexes such as P_1 in Example 1 naturally give rise to Cartesian guards, e.g., P_1 represents the guard $\lambda\bar{x}.(x_0 = \text{'\&'} \wedge x_1 = \text{'\#'} \wedge \text{'0'} \leq x_2 \leq \text{'9'} \wedge \text{'0'} \leq x_3 \leq \text{'9'} \wedge x_4 = \text{';'})$. The guard is Cartesian because it has the form $\lambda\bar{x}. \bigwedge_{i=1}^{|\bar{x}|} \varphi_i(x_i)$.

Cartesian ESFTs are still a powerful extension of SFTs because *outputs* may depend on multiple variables and use nonunary functions. For example, the second rule of B in Example 1 has the output function $\lambda\bar{x}.[10 * (x_2 - 48) + x_3 - 48]$.

The main difficulty with Bex is how to efficiently deal with default rules. A naive implementation of the semantics of bex, e.g., by using a regex matching library, is far too inefficient. For example, the full version of HtmlDecode requires 280 rules. One approach would be to eliminate default rules by adding more normal rules in an attempt to transform Bex programs to ESFTs. For example, we could add the rule `"&[^#&]"` ==> `['&',x1]` to cover the case when the matched subsequence starts with & but is not followed by # or &. Continuing this transformation quickly leads to an explosion of cases and requires intermediate states, obfuscating the semantics and defeating the purpose of the concise declarative style of Bex.

Instead, we provide here a novel compilation scheme from Bex programs to an intermediate form called *symbolic rollback transducers* SRTs that are subsequently compiled into STs. SRTs use *lookback* to avoid state space explosion. For example, an SRT may treat the pattern `"&#\d{6};"` of an html decoder using nine transitions rather than $100\,k$ transitions required by an SFT; once it successfully matches the pattern it refers back to the characters in the matched input, similar to k-SLTs [5]. SRTs incorporate the notion of *rollback* in form of *rollback*-transitions not present in STs [24], ESFTs [8] or k-SLTs [5], to accommodate default or exceptional behavior.

To summarize, this paper makes the following contributions:

– *Bex*: a new declarative language for specifying string coders;
– *SRTs*: a variant of ESFTs with the capability of rewinding the input tape;
– Algorithm for compiling bex programs into SRTs.

As a key component the algorithm makes use of the recent algorithm for minimizing SFAs [9].

2 Symbolic Automata

In this section we introduce the basic concepts of symbolic automata that we are using in this paper. A key role is played by symbolic representation of alphabets as effective Boolean algebras. An *effective Boolean algebra* $\mathcal{A}$ has components $(\mathfrak{D}, \Psi, \llbracket\_\rrbracket, \bot, \top, \vee, \wedge, \neg)$. $\mathfrak{D}$ is a nonempty r.e. (recursively enumerable) set of *domain elements*. Ψ is an r.e. set of *predicates* closed under the Boolean connectives and $\bot, \top \in \Psi$. The *denotation function* $\llbracket\_\rrbracket : \Psi \to 2^{\mathfrak{D}}$ is r.e. and is such that, $\llbracket\bot\rrbracket = \emptyset$, $\llbracket\top\rrbracket = \mathfrak{D}$, for all $\varphi, \psi \in \Psi$, $\llbracket\varphi \vee \psi\rrbracket = \llbracket\varphi\rrbracket \cup \llbracket\psi\rrbracket$, $\llbracket\varphi \wedge \psi\rrbracket = \llbracket\varphi\rrbracket \cap \llbracket\psi\rrbracket$, and $\llbracket\neg\varphi\rrbracket = \mathfrak{D} \setminus \llbracket\varphi\rrbracket$. For $\varphi \in \Psi$, we write $IsSat(\varphi)$ when $\llbracket\varphi\rrbracket \neq \emptyset$ and say that φ is *satisfiable*. The intuition is that $\mathcal{A}$ is represented programmatically as an API with corresponding methods implementing the components. We use the following symbolic alphabets.

$\mathbf{2}^k$ is the powerset algebra with domain $\{n \mid 0 \leq n < 2^k\}$. Case $k = 0$ is trivial and is denoted 1. For $k > 0$, a predicate in Ψ_{2^k} is a BDD of depth k.[1]

---

[1] The variable order of the BDD is the reverse bit order of the binary representation of a number, thus, the most significant bit has the lowest ordinal.

The Boolean operations are the BDD operations. The denotation $[\![\beta]\!]$ is the set of all n, $0 \leq n < 2^k$, whose binary representation is a solution of β.

$\mathcal{U}$ We let $\mathcal{U} \stackrel{\text{def}}{=} 2^{16}$ denote the basic *Unicode* alphabet. We use standard regex character class notation to describe predicates in $\Psi_{\mathcal{U}}$. For example $[\![\text{A}]\!] = [\![\backslash\text{x41}]\!] = \{65\}$, $[\![\text{01}]\!] = \{48, 49\}$, and $[\![[\backslash\text{0-}\backslash\text{xFF}]]\!] = \{n \mid 0 \leq n \leq 255\}$.

We use the following construct for alphabet extensions. Given a domain D we write D' for an injective renaming of all elements in D, $D' = \{a' \mid a \in D\}$. Similarly for D''. One concrete definition of D' is $D \times \{1\}$ and of D'' is $D \times \{2\}$. In particular, $D' \cap D'' = \emptyset$.

Definition 1. The *disjoint union* $\mathcal{A}+\mathcal{B}$ of two effective Boolean algebras $\mathcal{A}$ and $\mathcal{B}$, is the effective Boolean algebra $(\mathfrak{D}'_{\mathcal{A}} \cup \mathfrak{D}''_{\mathcal{B}}, \Psi_{\mathcal{A}} \times \Psi_{\mathcal{B}}, [\![\_]\!], \bot, \top, \vee, \wedge, \neg)$ where,

$$[\![\langle \alpha, \beta \rangle]\!] \stackrel{\text{def}}{=} [\![\alpha]\!]'_{\mathcal{A}} \cup [\![\beta]\!]''_{\mathcal{B}}, \quad \langle \alpha, \beta \rangle \diamond \langle \alpha_1, \beta_1 \rangle \stackrel{\text{def}}{=} \langle \alpha \diamond_{\mathcal{A}} \alpha_1, \beta \diamond_{\mathcal{B}} \beta_1 \rangle, \quad (\diamond \in \{\vee, \wedge\})$$
$$\neg \langle \alpha, \beta \rangle \stackrel{\text{def}}{=} \langle \neg_{\mathcal{A}} \alpha, \neg_{\mathcal{B}} \beta \rangle, \quad \bot \stackrel{\text{def}}{=} \langle \bot_{\mathcal{A}}, \bot_{\mathcal{B}} \rangle, \quad \top \stackrel{\text{def}}{=} \langle \top_{\mathcal{A}}, \top_{\mathcal{B}} \rangle.$$

It is straightforward to prove that $\mathcal{A}+\mathcal{B}$ is still an effective Boolean algebra. Observe that the implementation of $\mathcal{A}+\mathcal{B}$ is trivial given the implementations of $\mathcal{A}$ and $\mathcal{B}$, e.g., extension of $\mathcal{A}$ with a new element can be defined as $\mathcal{A}+1$.

Given a word $u \in \mathfrak{D}^*_{\mathcal{A}}$ we write u' for the word $[u|'_0, u|'_1, \ldots, u|'_{|u|-1}]$ in $\mathfrak{D}^*_{\mathcal{A}+\mathcal{B}}$. Similarly for the second subdomain.

Definition 2. A *symbolic finite automaton* (*SFA*) M is a tuple $(\mathcal{A}, Q, q^0, F, \Delta)$ where $\mathcal{A}$ is an effective Boolean algebra, called the *alphabet*, Q is a finite set of *states*, $q^0 \in Q$ is the *initial state*, $F \subseteq Q$ is the set of *final states*, and $\Delta \subseteq Q \times \Psi_{\mathcal{A}} \times Q$ is a finite set of *moves* or *transitions*. Elements of $\mathfrak{D}_{\mathcal{A}}$ are called *characters* and finite sequences of characters are called *words*. ⊠

A word w of length $|w|$, is denoted by $[a_0, a_1, \ldots, a_{|w|-1}]$ where all the a_i are characters. Given a position $i < |w|$, $w|_i$ denotes the i'th character a_i of w. The empty word is $[]$. Given two words u and v, $u.v$ denotes their concatenation. In particular, $u.[] = [].u = u$.

A move $\rho = (p, \varphi, q)$ *from* p *to* q is also denoted by $p \xrightarrow{\varphi} q$ where p is the *source* state $Src(\rho)$, q is the *target* state $Tgt(\rho)$, and φ is the *guard* or *predicate* of the move $Grd(\rho)$. A move is *feasible* if its guard is satisfiable. In the following let $M = (\mathcal{A}, Q, q^0, F, \Delta)$ be a fixed SFA.

Definition 3. A word $w \in \mathfrak{D}^*_{\mathcal{A}}$, is *accepted at state* q of M, $w \in \mathscr{L}_q(M)$, if there exists a set of moves $\{q_i \xrightarrow{\varphi_i} q_{i+1}\}_{i<k} \subseteq \Delta$ where $k = |w|$, $q_0 = q$, $q_k \in F$, and $w|_i \in [\![\varphi_i]\!]$ for $i < k$. The *language* of M is $\mathscr{L}(M) \stackrel{\text{def}}{=} \mathscr{L}_{q^0}(M)$.

For $q \in Q$, we use the definitions

$$\Delta(q) \stackrel{\text{def}}{=} \{\rho \in \Delta \mid Src(\rho) = q\}, \quad \Delta^{-1}(q) \stackrel{\text{def}}{=} \{\rho \in \Delta \mid Tgt(\rho) = q\}.$$

A state q of M is a *deadend* when $\mathscr{L}_q(M) = \emptyset$. A *deadend-move* is a move whose target is a deadend. A state q of M is *partial* if $\neg \bigvee \{Grd(\rho) \mid \rho \in \Delta(q)\}$ is satisfiable. A move is *feasible* if the guard of the move is satisfiable. The following terminology is used to characterize various subclasses of SFAs.

- M is *deterministic*: for all $p \xrightarrow{\varphi} q, p \xrightarrow{\varphi'} q' \in \Delta$, if $IsSat(\varphi \wedge \varphi')$ then $q = q'$.
- M is *partial (incomplete)*: there is a partial state.
- M is *clean*: all moves are feasible and all states are reachable from q^0,
- M is *trim*: M is clean and has no deadend-moves,
- M is *normalized*: forall $p, q \in Q$, there is at most one move from p to q.
- M is *minimal*: M is deterministic, trim, and normalized, and forall $p, q \in Q$, $p = q$ if and only if $\mathscr{L}_p(M) = \mathscr{L}_q(M)$.
- M is a *prefix acceptor* if M is minimal, M has a single final state q_M^f and either $\Delta_M(q_M^f) = \emptyset$, or $\Delta_M(q_M^f) = \{q_M^f \xrightarrow{\top} q_M^f\}$, and all paths from q_M^0 to q_M^f without passing through q_M^f have a fixed length K, the *length of M*.

Regexes used here range over the Unicode alphabet $\mathcal{U}$ and support character classes, the syntax and the semantics is the same as in C# or JavaScript.[2] Given a regex P we write ^P for P prepended with the start anchor. We write $\mathscr{L}(P)$ for the regular language over $\mathfrak{D}_{\mathcal{U}}$ accepted by P. Given a regular language L, we write $SFA_{\min}(L)$ for a minimal SFA accepting L.

Anonymous functions. We write $\Lambda(D \rightarrow R)$ for some well-defined effective representation of functions, or λ-*terms*, with domain D and range R. A λ-term $f \in \Lambda(D \rightarrow R)$ denotes the mathematical function $\boldsymbol{f} : D \rightarrow R$.

Let the alphabet $\mathcal{A}$ be fixed and let $\mathfrak{D}$ stand for $\mathfrak{D}_{\mathcal{A}}$ and let Ψ stand for $\Psi_{\mathcal{A}}$. We let $\mathfrak{D}^k \stackrel{\text{def}}{=} \{w \in \mathfrak{D}^* \mid |w| = k\}$.[3] We write Λ for $\bigcup_{m>0,n\geq 0} \Lambda(\mathfrak{D}^m \rightarrow \mathfrak{D}^n)$, i.e., Λ is the set of λ-terms denoting functions from *nonempty* fixed length words to fixed length words (the range may be $\{[]\}$). Given $f \in \Lambda$, let $\natural(f)$ denote the *input rank m* of $f \in \Lambda(\mathfrak{D}^m \rightarrow \mathfrak{D}^n)$.

Example 2. Consider $\mathcal{A} = \mathcal{U}$. Let $h \in \Lambda(\mathfrak{D} \rightarrow \mathfrak{D})$ be $\lambda x.(x < 10 \, ? \, x + 48 : x + 55)$. Then $\boldsymbol{h}$ encodes every nibble (value in $\{0, \ldots, 15\}$) as the corresponding hexadecimal (ASCII) digit,[4] e.g., $\boldsymbol{h}(11) = $ 'B' and $\boldsymbol{h}(7) = $ '7'. Let $f \in \Lambda(\mathfrak{D}^1 \rightarrow \mathfrak{D}^2)$ be $\lambda x.[h(x|_0 \gg 4), h(x|_0 \, \& \, 15)]$ ($\gg$ is *shift-right* and $\&$ is *bitwise-and*). Then $\boldsymbol{f}$ encodes every single-byte-word as a word of two hexadecimal digits, e.g., $\boldsymbol{f}(\texttt{"K"}) = \boldsymbol{f}([4B_{16}]) = [\boldsymbol{h}(4B_{16} \gg 4), \boldsymbol{h}(4B_{16} \, \& \, 15)] = [\text{'4'}, \text{'B'}] = \texttt{"4B"}$.   ⊠

3   Symbolic Rollback Transducers

Symbolic transducers (STs) are a generalization of symbolic *finite* transducers or SFTs; STs were originally introduced in [24]. An ST may use *registers* in addition to a finite set Q of states. In general, registers can hold arbitrary values and the use of registers is unrestricted. Here we introduce another extension of

---

[2] Regular Expression Language - Quick Reference: http://msdn.microsoft.com/en-us/library/az24scfc.aspx.

[3] Observe that $\mathfrak{D}^0 = \{[]\}$ and $\mathfrak{D}^1 = \{[a] \mid a \in \mathfrak{D}\}$.

[4] No semantic distinction is made between characters and their numeric codes. Thus '0', '\x30', and 48 all denote number 48.

$$
\begin{array}{|c|c|c|}
\hline
\alpha & \beta & \cdots\ rest\ of\ input\ tape\ \cdots \\
\hline
\end{array}
$$

Fig. 1. Intuition behind a snapshot $\langle\alpha, q, \beta\rangle$ of an SRT.

SFTs called SRTs that do not allow explicit use of registers but allow *lookback* and *rollback* of input. SRTs have *three* kinds of transitions, defined below.

To formally define the semantics of transitions we introduce the notion of a *snapshot* $\mathfrak{s}$, that is a triple $\langle\alpha, q, \beta\rangle \in \mathfrak{S} = \mathfrak{D}^* \times Q \times \mathfrak{D}^*$ with *argument store* α, *state q* and *buffer* β. We say *current character* for the first character of the buffer if it is nonempty, else for the first character in the rest of the input. The unread portion of the input tape is not part of the snapshot. The idea behind the concept of a snapshot is illustrated in Fig. 1. The buffer is intended to be a *prepending* to the rest of the input; the semantics enforces that the buffer must be empty before any more characters are read from the rest of the input.

An *input-transition* $p \overset{\varphi}{\longrightarrow} q \in Q \times \Psi \times Q$ has the following semantics. From source state p it reads and enqueues the current character a into the argument store, provided that $a \in [\![\varphi]\!]$, and enters the target state q, formally:

$$
[\![p \overset{\varphi}{\longrightarrow} q]\!] \overset{\text{def}}{=} \{\langle\alpha, p, []\rangle \xrightarrow{[a]/[]} \langle\alpha.[a], q, []\rangle \mid a \in [\![\varphi]\!],\ \alpha \in \mathfrak{D}^*\} \cup
$$
$$
\{\langle\alpha, p, [a].\beta\rangle \xrightarrow{[]/[]} \langle\alpha.[a], q, \beta\rangle \mid a \in [\![\varphi]\!],\ \alpha, \beta \in \mathfrak{D}^*\}
$$

An *output-transition* $p \overset{f}{\mapsto} q \in Q \times \Lambda \times Q$ has the following semantics. From state p it consumes the argument store α outputs the word $\boldsymbol{f}(\alpha)$ and enters state q. The transition is enabled when the length of α matches the arity of f.

$$
[\![p \overset{f}{\mapsto} q]\!] \overset{\text{def}}{=} \{\langle\alpha, p, \beta\rangle \xrightarrow{[]/\boldsymbol{f}(\alpha)} \langle[], q, \beta\rangle \mid \beta \in \mathfrak{D}^*,\ \alpha \in \mathfrak{D}^{\natural(f)}\}
$$

A *rollback-transition* $p \overset{\varphi}{\dashrightarrow} q$ has the following semantics. From state p, if the current character $a \in [\![\varphi]\!]$, it "rewinds the input tape" by pushing the current character and the argument store (back) into the buffer, and enters state q.

$$
[\![p \overset{\varphi}{\dashrightarrow} q]\!] \overset{\text{def}}{=} \{\langle\alpha, p, []\rangle \xrightarrow{[a]/[]} \langle[], q, \alpha.[a]\rangle \mid a \in [\![\varphi]\!],\ \alpha \in \mathfrak{D}^*\} \cup
$$
$$
\{\langle\alpha, p, [a].\beta\rangle \xrightarrow{[]/[]} \langle[], q, \alpha.[a].\beta\rangle \mid a \in [\![\varphi]\!],\ \alpha, \beta \in \mathfrak{D}^*\}
$$

The idea is that a rollback-transition is taken when a normal input sequence cannot be completed, the target state q is then an "exception handling" state.

Definition 4. A *Symbolic Rollback Transducer (SRT)* is a tuple $(\mathcal{A}, Q, q^0, F, \Delta)$, where $\mathcal{A}$, Q, q_0, and F are as in Definition 2, and Δ is a finite set of *transitions* as defined above.   ⊠

The semantics of an SRT B is defined using a transducer $(\mathfrak{s}_0, \mathfrak{S}, \mathfrak{T})$ that is the unwinding of B, where $\mathfrak{s}_0$ is the initial snapshot $\langle[], q^0, []\rangle$ of B, $\mathfrak{S}$ is the set $\mathfrak{D}^* \times Q \times \mathfrak{D}^*$ and $\mathfrak{T} \subseteq \mathfrak{S} \times \mathfrak{D}^* \times \mathfrak{D}^* \times \mathfrak{S}$ is the set $\bigcup_{\rho \in \Delta} [\![\rho]\!]$.

The relation $\mathfrak{s} \xrightarrow{u/v} \mathfrak{t}$ for $\mathfrak{s}, \mathfrak{t} \in \mathfrak{S}$ and $u, v \in \mathfrak{D}^*$ is defined as the least relation such that $\mathfrak{s}_0 \xrightarrow{[]/[]} \mathfrak{s}_0$ and if $\mathfrak{s} \xrightarrow{u/v} \mathfrak{s}_1$ and $\mathfrak{s}_1 \xrightarrow{u_1/v_1} \mathfrak{t} \in \mathfrak{T}$ then $\mathfrak{s} \xrightarrow{u.u_1/v.v_1} \mathfrak{t}$. The *transduction* of B is now defined as the following function from $\mathfrak{D}^*$ to $2^{\mathfrak{D}^*}$.

$$\mathscr{T}_B(u) \overset{\text{def}}{=} \{v \mid \exists q \in F \, \langle [], q^0, [] \rangle \xrightarrow{u/v} \langle [], q, [] \rangle \}$$

As a minimal requirement, we want the transition relation $\mathfrak{T}$ to be *well-founded* in the following sense: there is no infinite chain $\{\mathfrak{s}_i \xrightarrow{[]/v_i} \mathfrak{s}_{i+1}\}_{i<\omega}$ in $\mathfrak{T}$. For example, if there is a rollback-transition $p \overset{\top}{\dashrightarrow} p$ then $\mathfrak{T}$ is not well-founded, because $\langle [], p, [a] \rangle \xrightarrow{[]/[]} \langle [], p, [a] \rangle \in \mathfrak{T}$. A sufficient condition to ensure well-foundedness of $\mathfrak{T}$ is that the SRT is not *ill-defined*:

Definition 5. An SRT is *ill-defined* if there exists a path of states $(q_i)_{i \le n}$ and states p_1 and p_2 such that, $p_1 \dashrightarrow q_0$, (for $0 \le i < n$) $q_i \rightarrow q_{i+1}$, and $q_n \dashrightarrow p_2$. The SRT is *well-defined* otherwise. $\boxtimes$

In a well-defined SRT, any two rollback-transitions must be separated by at least one output-transition. For example, if $p \overset{\top}{\dashrightarrow} p$ then the SRT is ill-defined. An *output-state* is a state that has an outgoing output-transition.

Definition 6. An SRT B is *deterministic* if every output-state has exactly one outgoing transition and for every other state q, all transitions from q have mutually disjoint guards. B is *single-valued* if, for all u, $|\mathscr{T}_B(u)| \le 1$. $\boxtimes$

Proposition 1. *Every deterministic SRT is single-valued.*

Proof. Determinism implies that for any snapshot and current character there can be at most one resulting snapshot. Thus, for any given $u \in \mathfrak{D}^*$, there can be at most one path $\{\mathfrak{s}_i \xrightarrow{u_i/v_i} \mathfrak{s}_{i+1}\}_{i<n}$ such that $u = u_0.u_1.\cdots.u_{n-1}$. Thus, either $\mathscr{T}_B(u) = \emptyset$ or $\mathscr{T}_B(u) = \{v_0.v_1.\cdots.v_{n-1}\}$. $\boxtimes$

We treat a deterministic SRT B as a partial function and we write $B(u) = v$ for $\mathscr{T}_B(u) = \{v\}$.

Example 3. Let f be defined as in Example 2. Let B be the SRT

$$(\mathcal{U}, \{q_0, q_1\}, q_0, \{q_0\}, \{q_0 \xrightarrow{[\backslash 0 - \backslash xFF]} q_1, q_1 \overset{f}{\mapsto} q_0)\}$$

Since there are no rollback-transitions the buffer is never used. We have

$$\langle [], q_0, [] \rangle \xrightarrow{\text{"o"}/[]} \langle \text{"o"}, q_1, [] \rangle \xrightarrow{[]/\text{"6F"}} \langle [], q_0, [] \rangle \xrightarrow{\text{"k"}/[]} \langle \text{"k"}, q_1, [] \rangle \xrightarrow{[]/\text{"6B"}} \langle [], q_0, [] \rangle$$

Thus $\langle [], q_0, [] \rangle \xrightarrow{\text{"ok"}/\text{"6F6B"}} \langle [], q_0, [] \rangle$, so $B(\text{"ok"}) = \text{"6F6B"}$. $\boxtimes$

End anchors. Given an alphabet $\mathcal{A}$, in order to detect the end of the input string over $\mathfrak{D}_\mathcal{A}$, we can lift $\mathcal{A}$ to $\mathcal{A}+1$ and lift all $u \in \mathfrak{D}_\mathcal{A}^*$ to $u'.[0''] \in \mathfrak{D}_{\mathcal{A}+1}^*$ where the character $0'' \in \mathfrak{D}_{A+1}$ is used only as the last input character. Such end-of-input character can then be used to trigger a final output-transition that empties the store (when the store is nonempty).

4   Bex

The alphabet is fixed to $\mathcal{U}$ here, $\mathfrak{D}$ stands for $\mathfrak{D}_{\mathcal{U}}$. A bex program consist of a nonempty sequence of *pattern rules* $(P_i \implies f_i)_{0 \le i < k}$ and a *default output* f_d, where all P_i are regexes, called *patterns*, and all f_i and f_d are *output expressions* such that the following well-formedness criteria hold.

- $SFA_{\min}(\mathcal{L}(\hat{\ }P_i))$ is a prefix acceptor of some length $K_i > 0$.
- $f_i \in \Lambda$ and $\natural(f_i) = K_i$.
- f_d is undefined or $f_d \in \Lambda$ and $\natural(f_d) = 1$.

The first well-formedness condition ensures that all patterns have fixed lengths. The second condition ensures that the output functions are in scope: depend only on the characters matched by the pattern. The third condition ensures that the default output function only depends on one character (the current one).

The formal semantics of bex programs is as follows. The intent is to support straightforward specification of how typical encoders and decoders work in practice. Given a word u and indices i and j, $0 \le i \le j < |u|$, we write $u[i..]$ for the suffix $[u|_i, \dots, u|_{|u|-1}]$ and $u[i..j]$ for the subsequence $[u|_i, \dots, u|_j]$ of u.

Definition 7. Given a bex program $B = ((P_i \implies f_i)_{0 \le i < k}, f_d)$. The *denotation* of B, $\boldsymbol{B}$, is a (partial) function from $\mathfrak{D}_{\mathcal{U}}^*$ to $\mathfrak{D}_{\mathcal{U}}^*$. Let $u \in \mathfrak{D}_{\mathcal{U}}^*$ be the input sequence. Let $n := 0$ and $v := []$. Let $M_i = SFA_{\min}(\mathcal{L}(\hat{\ }P_i))$ and let K_i be the length of M_i. Repeat the following until $n = |u|$:

1. Let $I = \{i \mid u[n..] \in \mathcal{L}(M_i)\}$.
2. If $I \ne \emptyset$ let $i = \min\{i \in I \mid K_i = \min\{K_j \mid j \in I\}\}$ and $(m, f) = (K_i, f_i)$
3. If $I = \emptyset$ let $(m, f) = (1, f_d)$.
4. Let $v := v + f(u[n..n + m - 1])$ and $n := n + m$.

Then $\boldsymbol{B}(u) = v$. ($\boldsymbol{B}(u)$ is undefined if f_d is used but is undefined). ⊠

Example 1 is a simplified version of an Html decoder. Its purpose is to illustrate the use and the semantics of typical pattern rules and the default rule. It is used as a running example in the rest of the paper. In the next section we describe an algorithm that converts a bex program into an equivalent SRT.

5   Bex to SRT Compiler

The purpose of the bex to SRT compiler is, given a well-formed bex program $B = ((P_i \implies f_i)_{0 \le i < k}, f_d)$ as input, to generate a well-defined deterministic SRT that is equivalent to B. We assume that the default output f_d is defined. The case when f_d is undefined amounts to a trivial modification of the compiler.

The compiler works in two main phases. First, all the patterns of the rules are combined into a single pattern automaton N that is then minimized. The alphabet of N is $\mathcal{U}2 \overset{\text{def}}{=} \mathcal{U}+\mathcal{U}$. The first subuniverse $\mathcal{U}'$ serves the purpose of the Unicode alphabet, while the second subuniverse $\mathcal{U}''$ serves the purpose of bex rule identifiers.

Second, the pattern automaton N is (essentially) extended with output-transitions and rollback-transitions to form the final SRT. It follows from minimality of N and the construction of the additional transitions that the resulting SRT is well-defined and deterministic and preserves the semantics of the original bex program.

The alphabet of the generated SRT is going to be $\mathcal{U} + 1$. The new element $0'' \in \mathfrak{D}_{\mathcal{U}+1}$ is used as the end-of-input symbol of words. Observe that $\mathfrak{D}_{\mathcal{U}+1} = \mathfrak{D}'_{\mathcal{U}} \cup \{0''\}$. The main correctness theorem is the following.

Theorem 1. *Given a bex program B, $SRT(B)$ is a well-defined deterministic SRT such that, for all $u, v \in \mathfrak{D}^*_{\mathcal{U}}$, $B(u) = v$ iff $\mathscr{T}_{SRT(B)}(u'.[0'']) = \{v'.[0'']\}$.*

Proof. Formal proof is by induction over the length of computations, relating the points in Definition 7 to the constructs below and by using basic properties of

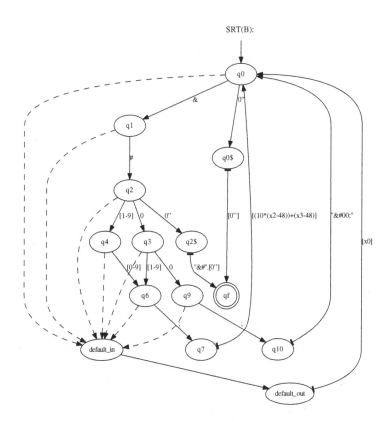

Fig. 2. Sample SRT with rollback-transitions.

N and SFAs operations. The construction of the SFA N itself uses an algorithm for minimizing SFAs [9].   ⊠

Detailed descriptions of the compilation phases are given below. The following example illustrates a small but realistic example.

Example 4. Consider the bex program B in Example 1. Figure 2 shows the generated $SRT(B)$. The rollback-transitions have a guard (not shown) that is the complement of the disjunction of all the guards from all other transitions from the source state. E.g., $q_2 \xrightarrow{\langle [\char94 0\text{-}9],\bot\rangle} \text{default}_{\text{in}}$ and $q_1 \xrightarrow{\langle [\char94 \#],\top\rangle} \text{default}_{\text{in}}$ ⊠

5.1   Pattern Automaton Construction

1. Let $\mathcal{E} := \emptyset$; $\mathcal{E}$ is computed as the set of all pattern ids having *end anchors*.
2. For $\imath = 0, \ldots, k-1$:
   (a) Let $M_\imath = SFA_{\min}(\mathcal{L}(\char94 P_\imath))$. (Recall that $M_\imath$ is a prefix acceptor.)
       Let $K_\imath$ be the length of $M_\imath$.
       If $\Delta_{M_\imath}(q^{\mathrm{f}}_{M_\imath}) = \emptyset$ then $\mathcal{E} := \mathcal{E} \cup \{\imath\}$.
   (b) Let $q^\imath$ be a new state not it $Q_{M_\imath}$. Lift $M_\imath$ into $N_\imath$:

$$N_\imath = (\mathcal{U}2, Q_{M_\imath} \cup \{q^\imath\}, q^0_{M_\imath}, \{q^\imath\}, \Delta),$$

$$\text{where } \Delta = \{p \xrightarrow{\langle\varphi,\bot\rangle} q \mid p \xrightarrow{\varphi} q \in \Delta_{M_\imath}, p \neq q^{\mathrm{f}}_{M_\imath}\} \cup \{q^{\mathrm{f}}_{M_\imath} \xrightarrow{\langle\bot,\imath\rangle} q^\imath\}$$

3. Let

$$N := SFA_{\min}(\bigcup_\imath \mathcal{L}(N_\imath)).$$

N has a single final state, say $F_N = \{q^{\mathrm{f}}_N\}$, and $\Delta_N(q^{\mathrm{f}}_N) = \emptyset$. A move $p \xrightarrow{\langle\bot,\beta\rangle} q^{\mathrm{f}}_N$ is a *final move*; let $\imath = \min[\![\beta]\!]$, the state p is $\imath$-*final*.
4. *Cleanup:*
   (a) If a state p is $\imath$-final but $\imath \notin \mathcal{E}$ then delete all non-final moves from p.
   (b) Remove unreachable states from N.

Cleanup removes unreachable cases: shorter patterns override longer ones (for the overlapping cases) and for patterns of the same length the ones with smaller id have priority (see Definition 7.2). The following are key properties of N.

Proposition 2. *For all* $w \in \mathfrak{D}^*_{\mathcal{U}2}$ *the following statements are equivalent:*

- $w \in \mathcal{L}(N)$
- *for some* $u \in \mathfrak{D}^*_{\mathcal{U}}$ *and* $\imath \in \mathfrak{D}_{\mathcal{U}}$, $w = u'.[\imath'']$ *and* $w \in \mathcal{L}(N_\imath)$
- *for some* $u \in \mathfrak{D}^*_{\mathcal{U}}$ *and* $\imath \in \mathfrak{D}_{\mathcal{U}}$, $w = u'.[\imath'']$ *and* $u \in \mathcal{L}(M_\imath)$ *and* $|u| = K_\imath$

Proposition 3. *If* $q^0_N \xrightarrow{v} q$ *and* $q \xrightarrow{\langle\bot,\psi\rangle} q^{\mathrm{f}}_N \in \Delta_N$ *then for all* $\imath \in [\![\psi]\!]$, $|v| = K_\imath$.

Proof. Fix $\imath, \jmath \in [\![\psi]\!]$. Then $v + \imath^{(2)}, v + \jmath^{(2)} \in \mathcal{L}(N)$. So, by Proposition 2, $v = u^{(1)}$ for some $u \in \mathfrak{D}^*_{\mathcal{U}}$ such that $u \in \mathcal{L}(M_\imath) \cap \mathcal{L}(M_\jmath)$ and $|u| = K_\imath = K_\jmath$.   ⊠

The purpose of N is going to be that N is used to construct a control flow graph of the SRT. N takes care of selecting the correct rule for a given input.

Example 5. Consider the bex program B in Example 1. The SFAs N_0, N_1, N_2 and N are as follows:[5]

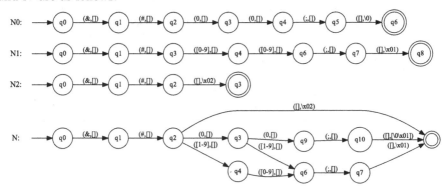

In N the overlapping patterns are reflected in the final move $q_{10} \xrightarrow{\langle [], [\backslash 0\backslash x01]\rangle} q_N^f$ where $[\![[\backslash 0\backslash x01]]\!] = \{0, 1\}$. $\mathcal{E} = \{2\}$. If the end anchor was removed from P_2 then $\mathcal{E}$ would be empty and the cleanup step would delete the moves from q_2 to q_3 and q_4. Then the states $\{q_3, q_4, q_6, q_7, q_9, q_{10}\}$ would become unreachable. ⊠

5.2   Compute Normal Transitions

We will now use N as a starting point for constructing an SRT $SRT(B)$ from B.

We lift functions f over the universe $\mathfrak{D}_\mathcal{U}$ implicitly to functions over the universe $\mathfrak{D}_{\mathcal{U}+1}$ by lifting elements in $\mathfrak{D}_\mathcal{U}$ to elements in the first subuniverse $\mathfrak{D}'_\mathcal{U}$ of $\mathfrak{D}_{\mathcal{U}+1}$. Let Δ^{in} be the following set of input-transitions.

$$\Delta^{\mathrm{in}} = \{p \xrightarrow{\langle \varphi, \perp \rangle} q \mid p \xrightarrow{\langle \varphi, \perp \rangle} q \in \Delta_N\}$$

In other words, all nonfinal moves of N become input-transitions. Let Δ^{out} be the following set of output-transitions, where $q^0 = q_N^0$,

$$\Delta^{\mathrm{out}} = \{p \xrightarrow{f_\imath} q^0 \mid p \xrightarrow{\langle \perp, \beta \rangle} q_N^f \in \Delta_N, \ \imath = \min[\![\beta]\!], \ \imath \notin \mathcal{E}\}$$

In other words, if a state p is $\imath$-final and the pattern $P_\imath$ is not a suffix pattern of the input ($\imath \notin \mathcal{E}$) then, upon reaching the state p, the input store contains a word s of length $K_\imath$ matching the pattern $P_\imath$. The output function $f_\imath$ is applied to the matched word s committing to the output word $f_\imath(s)$. The process is repeated from the initial state q^0.

---

[5] Predicates in $\Psi_\mathcal{U}$ are denoted by regex character classes, or individual characters. The predicate $\perp$ is denoted by the empty character class [].

5.3 Compute Ending Transitions

When a regex pattern $P_\imath$ ends with an end anchor ($ or \z) then this is reflected in N by the fact that there is a state p that is $\imath$-final and $\imath \in \mathcal{E}$. This means that the match must end with the end-of-input character $0''$ because all valid input words have the form $u'.[0'']$ for $u \in \mathfrak{D}_\mathcal{U}^*$. There are new output states $p_\$^\imath$ for all $\imath \in \mathcal{E}$, with the following input-transitions leading to them.

$$\Delta^{\mathrm{in}\$} = \{p \xrightarrow{\langle \perp, \top \rangle} p_\$^\imath \mid p \xrightarrow{\langle \perp, \beta \rangle} q_N^\mathrm{f} \in \Delta_N,\ \imath = \min[\![\beta]\!],\ \imath \in \mathcal{E}\}$$

There are output-transitions from each $p_\$^\imath$ that apply the corresponding final output function to the final stored input word in each case, append the ending character $0''$, so that all output words are also $0''$-terminated, and transition to the final state $q^\mathrm{f} = q_N^\mathrm{f}$ of the SRT.

$$\Delta^{\mathrm{out}\$} = \{p_\$^\imath \xrightarrow{\lambda x.(f_\imath(x).[0''])} q^\mathrm{f} \mid p \xrightarrow{\langle \perp, \beta \rangle} q_N^\mathrm{f} \in \Delta_N,\ \imath = \min[\![\beta]\!],\ \imath \in \mathcal{E}\}$$

There are also transitions from the initial state $q^0 = q_N^0$ leading to the final state (upon end of input), where $q_\$^0$ is a new output state:

$$\Delta^0 = \{q^0 \xrightarrow{\langle \perp, \top \rangle} q_\$^0 \xrightarrow{\lambda x.[0'']} q^\mathrm{f}\}$$

There are no transitions outgoing from the final state q^f.

5.4 Compute Default Transitions

The default behavior kicks in from a state p when the current character does not match any of the possible guards of the outgoing input-transitions from p. Formally, let $G(p)$ be the disjunction of all the guards from transitions exiting from p. Here p is an *input state* that is a non-output state and not q^f.

$$G(p) \overset{\mathrm{def}}{=} \bigvee \{\varphi \mid \exists q(p \xrightarrow{\varphi} q \in \Delta^{\mathrm{in}} \cup \Delta^{\mathrm{in}\$} \cup \Delta^0)\}, \qquad \gamma_p \overset{\mathrm{def}}{=} \neg G(p).$$

Predicate γ_p describes all characters that break all possible patterns at state p. If γ_p is satisfiable then, for all current characters in $[\![\gamma_p]\!]$, roll back the input tape back to the position before the match was started, then apply the default function to the first character in the input tape (it cannot be $0''$ because the input store is nonempty when $p \neq q^0$ and $0'' \notin [\![\gamma_{q^0}]\!]$), and finally continue the process from state q^0 and the next input position. This corresponds to Definition 7.3. Formally, the following transitions are added to capture this default behavior.

$$\Delta^{\mathrm{default}} = \{p \dashrightarrow^{\gamma_p} \mathrm{default}_{\mathrm{in}} \mid p \text{ is an input state},\ [\![\gamma_p]\!] \neq \emptyset\}$$
$$\cup \{\mathrm{default}_{\mathrm{in}} \xrightarrow{\top} \mathrm{default}_{\mathrm{out}} \xrightarrow{f_\mathrm{d}} q^0\}$$

where $\mathrm{default}_{\mathrm{in}}$ and $\mathrm{default}_{\mathrm{out}}$ are fixed new states. Observe that the well-definedness criterion (see Definition 5) is trivially satisfied. Let Q be the set of all states that occur in the transitions. The final result of the compilation is the SRT:

$$SRT(B) \stackrel{\text{def}}{=} (\mathcal{U} + 1, Q, q^0, \{q^f\}, \Delta^{\text{in}} \cup \Delta^{\text{out}} \cup \Delta^{\text{in\$}} \cup \Delta^{\text{out\$}} \cup \Delta^0 \cup \Delta^{\text{default}})$$

Moreover, a well-defined SRT can be further translated into an equivalent ST without rollback-transitions by performing a symbolic partial evaluation of the default cases. Generation of C# or JavaScript code is straightforward from either well-defined deterministic SRTs or deterministic STs.

6   Implementation and Experiments

The bex language and the algorithm for generating symbolic transducers from bex programs has been implemented and is available in an online toolkit and tutorial [4]. The tutorial includes several samples, such as base64 encoding and decoding, allows online editing, and enables JavaScript generation from the bex programs. The generated JavaScript can also be directly executed online.

We have built a prototype implementation of the compiler. In a final phase the compiler converts the generated SRT into an ST without rollback-transitions. It does so by symbolically forward executing the rollback-cases and by optimizing the generated code through a combination of SFA techniques and SMTlib representation of terms using Z3 [10, 27]. Z3 terms are used to simplify arithmetic expressions and to prune unsatisfiable predicates. The STs are then converted into either C# or JavaScript implementations.

We have applied this technique to a variety of different encoders and decoders such as: Utf16Encoder and Decoder, Base32Encoder and Decoder, Base64Encoder and Decoder, CssEncoder, JavaScriptEncoder, JsonEncoder, and HtmlEncoder and Decoder. They all fall into a category of string transformation routines that can be very naturally expressed and analyzed in bex.

So far our largest case study is a bex program for the complete version of *HtmlDecode* that uses over 280 rules. The full bex program is less than 300 lines of code including comments. The large number of rules is due to many special cases of patterns such as `"&lt;"` $\implies$ `"<"` and `"&le;"` $\implies$ `"\u2264"` in addition to rules that decode numeric (decimal or hexadecimal) encodings of characters. The resulting *minimal* pattern automaton N has in this case 920 states and the generated C# code is just shy of 20 k lines of code (with sparsely generated code). The end-to-end compilation time was around 8 s that includes preprocessing as well as some analysis of the generated code. A key factor here was an efficient minimization algorithm of SFAs [9]. The minimization algorithm is used repeatedly in the loop where the SFAs N_i are being constructed during the pattern automaton construction phase of the bex compiler. For the alphabet algebra we use $\mathcal{U}2$ for most parts, but for dealing with λ-terms and satisfiability checking of linear arithmetic formulas in the final phases of the compiler we use SMT2lib representation of terms and Z3 [27].

We compared the running time of the bex generated HtmlDecoder in C# against the *hand-optimized* HtmlDecoder in the .NET System.Net.WebUtility library. As input to both decoders we used maximally encoded input (with hexadecimal encoding of all non-ASCII) texts over various parts of the Unicode alphabet. In this experiment, the bex coder *outperformed* the System coder by 2 times on average.

7   Related Work

Symbolic finite transducers (SFTs) and the BEK language were originally introduced in [13] and formally studied in [24]. SFTs were also extended to STs in [24] to allow the use of registers for increased expressive power. A common usage pattern that often occurs in the context of string decoders is that of a finite window of characters that are grouped and processed together. For such a class of problems, SFTs are too weak, while STs sacrifice analyzability. Two related formalisms have been proposed to address this issue, ESFTs [8] and k-SLTs [5]. The former uses bounded *lookahead* and reads several characters at once, while the latter uses bounded *lookback* and reads one character at a time. Further properties of ESFTs are studied in [7].

The formalism of SRTs is in spirit related to k-SLTs, because output-transitions refer to earlier characters as a form of lookback. However, once an output happens (is "committed"), there is no way to refer back to those input characters that were used, in later transitions; this is similar to the sematic of ESFTs. The aspect that is new in SRTs, is the notion of a *rollback*-transition that allows the input tape to be rewound or rolled back conditionally. As we demonstrated with bex, this aspect greatly simplifies the task of programming typical encoders and decoders, HtmlDecoder being a perfect example, where default rules are used extensively when pattern matching fails.

Automata over infinite alphabets have received a lot of interest [21], starting with the work on *register automata* [14]. A different line of work on automata with infinite alphabets called *lattice automata*, originates from verification of symbolic communicating machines [11]. *Streaming transducers* [1] provide a recent symbolic extension of finite transducers. Extended Finite Automata, or XFAs, is a succinct representation of DFAs that use registers, are introduced in [22] for network packet inspection. XFAs support only finite alphabets. History-based finite automata [15] are another extension of DFAs that have been introduced for encoding regular expressions in the context of network intrusion detection systems. Finite state transducers have been used for dynamic and static analysis to validate sanitization functions in web applications [17,25].

Symbolic transductions can also be considered over infinite strings. For finite alphabets, a study of transformations of infinite strings is proposed in [2]. Yet a different extension is symbolic transductions over trees [23].

We use the SMT solver Z3 [10] for incrementally solving and simplifying constraints in the process of composing predicates that arise during bex compilation. Similar applications of SMT techniques have been introduced in the context of symbolic execution of programs by using path conditions [12].

References

1. Alur, R., Cerný, P.: Streaming transducers for algorithmic verification of single-pass list-processing programs. In: POPL 2011, pp. 599–610. ACM (2011)
2. Alur, R., Filiot, E., Trivedi, A.: Regular transformations of infinite strings. In: LICS, pp. 65–74. IEEE (2012)
3. Balzarotti, D., Cova, M., Felmetsger, V., Jovanovic, N., Kirda, E., Kruegel, C., Vigna, G.: Saner: composing static and dynamic analysis to validate sanitization in web applications. In: SP 2008, pp. 387–401. IEEE (2008)
4. Bex (2013). http://www.rise4fun.com/Bex/tutorial
5. Botincan, M., Babic, D.: Sigma*: symbolic learning of input-output specifications. In: POPL 2013, pp. 443–456. ACM (2013)
6. Christensen, A.S., Møller, A., Schwartzbach, M.I.: Precise analysis of string. In: Cousot, R. (ed.) SAS 2003. LNCS, vol. 2694, pp. 1–18. Springer, Heidelberg (2003)
7. D'Antoni, L., Veanes, M.: Equivalence of extended symbolic finite transducers. In: Sharygina, N., Veith, H. (eds.) CAV 2013. LNCS, vol. 8044, pp. 624–639. Springer, Heidelberg (2013)
8. D'Antoni, L., Veanes, M.: Static analysis of string encoders and decoders. In: Giacobazzi, R., Berdine, J., Mastroeni, I. (eds.) VMCAI 2013. LNCS, vol. 7737, pp. 209–228. Springer, Heidelberg (2013)
9. Dantoni, L., Veanes, M.: Minimization of symbolic automata. In: POPL 2014. ACM (2014)
10. de Moura, L., Bjørner, N.S.: Z3: an efficient SMT solver. In: Ramakrishnan, C.R., Rehof, J. (eds.) TACAS 2008. LNCS, vol. 4963, pp. 337–340. Springer, Heidelberg (2008)
11. Le Gall, T., Jeannet, B.: Lattice automata: a representation for languages on infinite alphabets, and some applications to verification. In: Riis Nielson, H., Filé, G. (eds.) SAS 2007. LNCS, vol. 4634, pp. 52–68. Springer, Heidelberg (2007)
12. Godefroid, P.: Compositional dynamic test generation. In: POPL 2007, pp. 47–54(2007)
13. Hooimeijer, P., Livshits, B., Molnar, D., Saxena, P., Veanes, M.: Fast and precise sanitizer analysis with Bek. In: USENIX Security, August 2011
14. Kaminski, M., Francez, N.: Finite-memory automata. TCS **134**(2), 329–363 (1994)
15. Kumar, S., Chandrasekaran, B., Turner, J., Varghese, G.: Curing regular expressions matching algorithms from insomnia, amnesia, and acalculia. In: ANCS 2007, pp. 155–164. ACM/IEEE (2007)
16. Livshits, B., Nori, A.V., Rajamani, S.K., Banerjee, A.: Merlin: specification inference for explicit information flow problems. In: PLDI 2009, pp. 75–86 (2009)
17. Minamide, Y.: Static approximation of dynamically generated web pages. In: WWW 2005, pp. 432–441 (2005)
18. NVD. http://web.nvd.nist.gov/view/vuln/detail?vulnId=CVE-2008-2938
19. OWASP. https://www.owasp.org/index.php/Double_Encoding
20. SANS. http://www.sans.org/security-resources/malwarefaq/wnt-unicode.php
21. Segoufin, L.: Automata and logics for words and trees over an infinite alphabet. In: Ésik, Z. (ed.) CSL 2006. LNCS, vol. 4207, pp. 41–57. Springer, Heidelberg (2006)
22. Smith, R., Estan, C., Jha, S., Kong, S.: Deflating the big bang: fast and scalable deep packet inspection with extended finite automata. In: SIGCOMM 2008, pp. 207–218. ACM (2008)
23. Veanes, M., Bjørner, N.: Symbolic tree transducers. In: Clarke, E., Virbitskaite, I., Voronkov, A. (eds.) PSI 2011. LNCS, vol. 7162, pp. 377–393. Springer, Heidelberg (2012)

24. Veanes, M., Hooimeijer, P., Livshits, B., Molnar, D., Bjørner, N.: Symbolic finite state transducers: algorithms and applications. In: POPL 2012, pp. 137–150 (2012)
25. Wassermann, G., Yu, D., Chander, A., Dhurjati, D., Inamura, H., Su, Z.: Dynamic test input generation for web applications. In: ISSTA (2008)
26. Yu, S.: Regular languages. In: Rozenberg, G., Salomaa, A. (eds.) Handbook of Formal Languages, vol. 1, pp. 41–110. Springer, Heidelberg (1997)
27. Z3. http://research.microsoft.com/projects/z3

Towards Symbolic Execution in Erlang

Germán Vidal$^{(\boxtimes)}$

MiST, DSIC, Universitat Politècnica de València,
Camino de Vera, S/n, 46022 Valencia, Spain
gvidal@dsic.upv.es

1 Introduction

The concurrent functional language Erlang [1] has a number of distinguishing features, like dynamic typing, concurrency via asynchronous message passing or hot code loading, that make it especially appropriate for distributed, fault-tolerant, soft real-time applications. The success of Erlang is witnessed by the increasing number of its industrial applications. For instance, Erlang has been used to implement Facebook's chat back-end, the mobile application Whatsapp or Twitterfall—a service to view trends and patterns from Twitter—, to name a few. The success of the language, however, also requires the development of powerful testing and verification techniques.

Symbolic execution is at the core of many program analysis and transformation techniques, like partial evaluation, test-case generation or model checking. In this paper, we introduce a symbolic execution technique for Erlang. We discuss how both an overapproximation and an underapproximation of the concrete semantics can be obtained. We illustrate our approach through some examples. To the best of our knowledge, this is the first attempt to formalize symbolic execution in the context of this language, where previous approaches have only considered exploring different schedulings but have not dealt with symbolic data. More details can be found in the companion technical report [17].

2 Erlang Syntax

In this section, we present the basic syntax of a significant subset of Erlang. In particular, we consider a slightly simplified version of the language where some features are excluded (basically, we do not consider modules, exceptions, records, binaries, monitors, ports or process links, most of which are not difficult to deal with but would encumber the notations and definitions of this paper). Nevertheless, this is still a large subset of Erlang and covers its main distinguishing features, like pattern matching, higher-order functions, process creation, message sending and receiving, etc.

This work has been partially supported by the Spanish *Ministerio de Economía y Competitividad (Secretaría de Estado de Investigación, Desarrollo e Innovación)* under grant TIN2013-44742-C4-1-R and by the *Generalitat Valenciana* under grant PROMETEO/2011/052.

A. Voronkov and I. Virbitskaite (Eds.): PSI 2014, LNCS 8974, pp. 351–360, 2015.
DOI: 10.1007/978-3-662-46823-4_28

$$\text{Program} \ni pgm ::= f(\overline{X_n}) \to e. \quad | \quad pgm \; pgm$$

$$\text{Exp} \ni e ::= bv \quad | \quad [e_1|e_2] \quad | \quad \{\overline{e_n}\} \quad | \quad X \quad | \quad e(\overline{e_n}) \qquad (n \geq 0)$$
$$| \quad \text{case } e \text{ of } cl \text{ end} \quad | \quad e_1 \,!\, e_2 \quad | \quad \text{receive } cl \text{ end}$$
$$| \quad p = e \quad | \quad e_1, e_2$$

$$\text{BasicValue} \ni bv ::= \text{a} \quad | \quad \text{n} \quad | \quad \text{p} \quad | \quad [] \quad | \quad \{\,\}$$
$$\text{Value} \ni v ::= bv \quad | \quad [v_1|v_2] \quad | \quad \{\overline{v_n}\} \qquad (n > 0)$$

$$\text{Pattern} \ni p ::= bv \quad | \quad X \quad | \quad [p_1|p_2] \quad | \quad \{\overline{p_n}\} \qquad (n > 0)$$
$$\text{Clauses} \ni cl ::= p_1 \text{ when } g_1 \to e_1; \ldots; p_n \text{ when } g_n \to e_n \qquad (n > 0)$$

where a $\in$ Atom,   n $\in$ Number,   p $\in$ Pid, $X \in$ Var, $g \in$ Guard

Fig. 1. Erlang syntax rules

The syntax of the language can be found in Fig. 1. We denote by $\overline{o_n}$ the sequence of syntactic objects $o_1, \ldots, o_n$. Programs are sequences of function definitions, where each function f/n is defined by a rule $f(X_1, \ldots, X_n) \to e.$ with $X_1, \ldots, X_n$ distinct variables and the body of the function, e, an expression that might include basic values, lists, tuples, variables, function applications, case expressions, message sending and receiving, pattern matching and sequences.

Besides the functions defined in the program, we consider some of the usual *built-in* functions (logical and relational operators, arithmetic operators, etc.), together with the functions self, that returns the pid of the current process, and spawn, that is used to create new processes. E.g., spawn(*foo*, [a, 42]) creates a new process that starts calling the function *foo*(a, 42) and returns the new (fresh) pid assigned to this process. Only the concurrent actions have side effects. We assume that *guards* can only contain calls to built-in functions without side effects.

Example 1. Consider the program in Fig. 2 which follows a very simple client-server scheme. Here, the first process is called with $start(N)$, where N is the maximum number of requests accepted by the server. Then, it creates a client (a new concurrent process) and starts the server. A client request just includes its own pid and the request number. If the request number is smaller than N, the server answers "ok"; otherwise, it answers "last" and terminates. The client keeps asking the server with increasing numbers until it gets the reply "last".

We do not consider I/O in this paper. Therefore, input parameters must be provided through the initial function.

3   Concrete Semantics

The semantics of Erlang is informally described, e.g., in [1]. The past years have witnessed an increasing number of works aimed at defining a formal semantics for the language. Some of the first attempts were done by Huch [9] and, more extensively, by Fredlund [6]. More recent approaches focus on the definition of the distributed aspects of the Erlang semantics, like [4]; this semantics was later

$$start(N) \rightarrow S = \mathsf{self}(), \ C = \mathsf{spawn}(client, [1, S]), \ server(N).$$

$$server(N) \rightarrow \mathsf{receive}$$
$$\{Pid, M\} \ \mathsf{when} \ M < N \rightarrow Pid \,!\, \mathsf{ok}, \ server(N);$$
$$\{Pid, M\} \ \mathsf{when} \ M >= N \rightarrow Pid \,!\, \mathsf{last}$$
$$\mathsf{end}.$$

$$client(N, Pid) \rightarrow Pid \,!\, \{\mathsf{self}(), N\},$$
$$\mathsf{receive} \ Atom \rightarrow \mathsf{case} \ Atom \ \mathsf{of}$$
$$\mathsf{ok} \rightarrow client(N + 1, Pid);$$
$$\mathsf{last} \rightarrow \mathsf{ok}$$
$$\mathsf{end}$$
$$\mathsf{end}.$$

Fig. 2. Simple client-server example in Erlang

refined in [15] and [14], where some assumptions on the future of the language design are proposed. Other approaches have formalized the semantics of Erlang by defining its semantics in the framework of rewriting logic [10,11].

Unfortunately, there is no commonly accepted semantics and, moreover, most of the above papers only cover part of the language semantics (e.g., [4,14,15] are mainly oriented towards the concurrent features of the language). Therefore, we have recently introduced a semantics for a subset of Erlang in [16]. In the following, we present a more elegant and general version of this semantics that follows some of the ideas in [14].

Erlang follows a leftmost innermost operational semantics. Following, e.g., [6,9], every expression $C[e]$ can be decomposed into a context $C[]$ with a (single) hole and a subexpression e where the next reduction can take place:

$$C ::= [] \ \mid \ C, e \ \mid \ \mathsf{case} \ C \ \mathsf{of} \ cl \ \mathsf{end} \ \mid \ C \,!\, e \ \mid \ v \,!\, C \ \mid \ p = C \ \mid \ C(e_1, \ldots, e_n)$$
$$\mid \ f(v_1, \ldots, v_i, C, e_{i+2}, \ldots, e_n) \ \mid \ op(v_1, \ldots, v_i, C, e_{i+2}, \ldots, e_n)$$
$$\mid \ [v_1, \ldots, v_i, C | e] \ \mid \ \{v_1, \ldots, v_i, C, e_{i+2}, \ldots, e_n\}$$

An Erlang *process* is denoted by a tuple $\langle p; e; q \rangle$, where p is a the process identifier, e is the expression to be evaluated, and q is the process mailbox. An Erlang *system* is a pair $(\Pi, \mathcal{Q})$, where Π is a pool of processes and $\mathcal{Q}$ is the system mailbox (analogous to the *ether* in the semantics of [14]). We assume no order in Π since it is not relevant to our purposes (i.e., we will be interested in exploring *all* possible schedulings within symbolic execution). For implementing actual scheduling policies, an ordering would be required. The system mailbox $\mathcal{Q}$ is a set of triples (p, p', q), where q is a list of messages (values) sent from the process with pid p to the process with pid p'. The system mailbox is needed to correctly model a multi-node distributed system (see the discussion in [14]). Basically, Erlang only requires that the messages sent *directly* between two processes must arrive in the same order. However, if the messages follow different paths, say one message is sent directly from p to p'', while another message is sent from p to p'' via p', then there is no guarantee regarding which message arrives first to p''.

(seq)	$\dfrac{}{(\langle \mathrm{p}; C[v,e]; q\rangle\ \&\ \Pi, \mathcal{Q}) \xrightarrow{\tau} (\langle \mathrm{p}; C[e]; q\rangle\ \&\ \Pi, \mathcal{Q})}$
(self)	$\dfrac{}{(\langle \mathrm{p}; C[\mathsf{self}()]; q\rangle\ \&\ \Pi, \mathcal{Q}) \xrightarrow{\tau} (\langle \mathrm{p}; C[\mathrm{p}]; q\rangle\ \&\ \Pi, \mathcal{Q})}$
(builtin)	$\dfrac{eval(op(\overline{v_n})) = v}{(\langle \mathrm{p}; C[op(\overline{v_n})]; q\rangle\ \&\ \Pi, \mathcal{Q}) \xrightarrow{\tau} (\langle \mathrm{p}; C[v]; q\rangle\ \&\ \Pi, \mathcal{Q})}$
(fun)	$\dfrac{f(\overline{X_n}) \to e. \in pgm}{(\langle \mathrm{p}; C[f(\overline{v_n})]; q\rangle\ \&\ \Pi, \mathcal{Q}) \xrightarrow{\tau} (\langle \mathrm{p}; C[\widehat{e}\{\overline{X_n \mapsto v_n}\}]; q\rangle\ \&\ \Pi, \mathcal{Q})}$
(match)	$\dfrac{\exists \sigma.\ p\sigma = v}{(\langle \mathrm{p}; C[p=v]; q\rangle\ \&\ \Pi, \mathcal{Q}) \xrightarrow{\tau} (\langle \mathrm{p}; (C[v])\sigma; q\rangle\ \&\ \Pi, \mathcal{Q})}$
(case)	$\dfrac{match(v, cl) = (e, \sigma)}{(\langle \mathrm{p}; C[\mathsf{case}\ v\ \mathsf{of}\ cl\ \mathsf{end}]; q\rangle\ \&\ \Pi, \mathcal{Q}) \xrightarrow{\tau} (\langle \mathrm{p}; (C[e])\sigma; q\rangle\ \&\ \Pi, \mathcal{Q})}$
(receive)	$\dfrac{matchrec(q, cl) = (e, \sigma, q')}{(\langle \mathrm{p}; C[\mathsf{receive}\ cl\ \mathsf{end}]; q\rangle\ \&\ \Pi, \mathcal{Q}) \xrightarrow{\tau} (\langle \mathrm{p}; (C[e])\sigma; q'\rangle\ \&\ \Pi, \mathcal{Q})}$
(spawn)	$\dfrac{\mathrm{p}'\ \text{is a fresh pid}}{(\langle \mathrm{p}; C[\mathsf{spawn}(f, \overline{v_n})]; q\rangle\ \&\ \Pi, \mathcal{Q}) \xrightarrow{\tau} (\langle \mathrm{p}; C[\mathrm{p}']; q\rangle\ \&\ \langle \mathrm{p}', f(\overline{v_n}), [\,]\rangle\ \&\ \Pi, \mathcal{Q})}$
(send)	$\dfrac{v_1 = \mathrm{p}' \in Pid\ \wedge\ add\_msg(\mathrm{p}, \mathrm{p}', v_2, \mathcal{Q}) = \mathcal{Q}'}{(\langle \mathrm{p}; C[v_1\,!\,v_2]; q\rangle\ \&\ \Pi, \mathcal{Q}) \xrightarrow{\tau} (\langle \mathrm{p}; C[v_2]; q\rangle\ \&\ \Pi, \mathcal{Q}')}$
(sched)	$\dfrac{(\mathrm{p}, \mathrm{p}') \in sched(\Pi, \mathcal{Q})\ \wedge\ delivery(\mathrm{p}, \mathrm{p}', \Pi, \mathcal{Q}) = (\Pi', \mathcal{Q}')}{(\Pi, \mathcal{Q}) \xrightarrow{\alpha} (\Pi', \mathcal{Q}')}$

Fig. 3. Concrete semantics

The operational semantics is defined by the labelled transition relation $\to$ shown in Fig. 3. Here, we use the notation $\langle \mathrm{p}; e; q\rangle\ \&\ \Pi$ to denote an arbitrary pool of processes that contains the process $\langle \mathrm{p}; e; q\rangle$. The initial system has the form $(\langle \mathrm{p}_0; e; [\,]\rangle, [\,])$. Most rules are self-explanatory. Let us just explain the more involved ones:

In rule builtin, we assume a function $eval$ that evaluates all built-in's without side effects (i.e., arithmetic or relational expressions, etc.).

In rule fun, we assume that the program pgm is a global parameter of the transition system. Moreover, we let $\widehat{e}$ denote a copy of e with local variables renamed with fresh names. The notation $\{\overline{X_n \mapsto v_n}\}$ denotes a substitution binding variables $X_1, \ldots, X_n$ to values $v_1, \ldots, v_n$. The application of a substitution σ to an expression e is denoted by $e\sigma$.

In rule case, we assume an auxiliary function $match$ that takes a value v and the clauses p_1 when $g_1 \to e_1; \ldots; p_n$ when $g_n \to e_n$ and returns a pair (e_i, σ) if i is the smaller number such that $p_i\sigma = v$ and $eval(g_i\sigma) = true$.

The case of rule receive uses a similar auxiliary function $matchrec$ that takes a mailbox queue q and the clauses cl, determines the first message v such that $match(v, cl) = (e, \sigma)$, and returns (e, σ, q'), where q' is obtained from q by deleting message v.

In rule send, the message is stored in the system mailbox, together with the source and target pids, using the auxiliary function add_msg, whose definition is straightforward. Note that the message is not actually delivered to the process with pid p' until the sched rule is applied (see below).

Finally, rule sched uses the auxiliary function *sched* to model a particular scheduling policy. Basically, it selects two pids (p, p') from Π (source and target processes, which might be the same) such that $(p, p', q) \in \mathcal{Q}$ and q is not empty. Then, function *delivery* moves the first message of q to the local mailbox of the process with pid p', thus returning a new pair $(\Pi', \mathcal{Q}')$.

Observe that all rules are labeled with τ except for the last one. This is explained by the fact that we are interested in a particular type of computations that we call *normalized* computations. In the following, given a state s, we denote by $s{\downarrow}^\tau$ the state that results from s by only applying transitions labeled with τ until no more transitions labeled with τ are possible, i.e., if $s \equiv s_0 \xrightarrow{\tau} s_1 \xrightarrow{\tau} \ldots \xrightarrow{\tau} s_n \not\xrightarrow{\tau}$, then $s{\downarrow}^\tau = s_n$.

Definition 1 (Normalized Computation). Let s_0 be the initial system. Then, we say that a computation is *normalized* if it has the form
$$s_0 \xrightarrow{\tau}{}^* s_0{\downarrow}^\tau \xrightarrow{\alpha} s_1 \xrightarrow{\tau}{}^* s_1{\downarrow}^\tau \xrightarrow{\alpha} s_2 \xrightarrow{\tau}{}^* s_2{\downarrow}^\tau \xrightarrow{\alpha} s_3 \ldots$$

In the following, we only consider normalized computations in order to reduce the search space.

Example 2. Consider again the program of Ex. 1. A computation with this program is shown in Fig. 4, where the expression selected for reduction is underlined.

$$
\begin{aligned}
&(\langle p_0; \mathit{start}(1); [\,] \rangle, [\,]) \\
\xrightarrow{\tau}\; &(\langle p_0; S = \underline{\mathsf{self}()}, C = \mathsf{spawn}(\mathit{client}, [1, S]), \mathit{server}(1); [\,] \rangle, [\,]) \\
\xrightarrow{\tau}\; &(\langle p_0; \underline{S = p_0}, C = \mathsf{spawn}(\mathit{client}, [1, S]), \mathit{server}(1); [\,] \rangle, [\,]) \\
\xrightarrow{\tau}\; &(\langle p_0; \underline{p_0}, C = \mathsf{spawn}(\mathit{client}, [1, p_0]), \mathit{server}(1); [\,] \rangle, [\,]) \\
\xrightarrow{\tau}\; &(\langle p_0; \underline{C = \mathsf{spawn}(\mathit{client}, [1, p_0])}, \mathit{server}(1); [\,] \rangle, [\,]) \\
\xrightarrow{\tau}\; &(\langle p_0; \underline{C = p_1}, \mathit{server}(1); [\,] \rangle \;\&\; \langle p_1; \mathit{client}(1, p_0); [\,] \rangle, [\,]) \\
\ldots \\
\xrightarrow{\tau}\; &(\langle p_0; \mathsf{receive} \ldots \mathsf{end}; [\,] \rangle \;\&\; \langle p_1; \mathsf{receive} \ldots \mathsf{end}; [\,] \rangle, [(p_1, p_0, [\{p_1, 1\}])]) \\
\xrightarrow{\alpha}\; &(\langle p_0; \underline{\mathsf{receive} \ldots \mathsf{end}}; [\{p_1, 1\}] \rangle \;\&\; \langle p_1; \mathsf{receive} \ldots \mathsf{end}; [\,] \rangle, [(p_1, p_0, [\,])]) \\
\xrightarrow{\tau}\; &(\langle p_0; \underline{p_1 \,!\, \mathsf{last}}; [\,] \rangle \;\&\; \langle p_1; \mathsf{receive} \ldots \mathsf{end}; [\,] \rangle, [(p_1, p_0, [\,])]) \\
\xrightarrow{\tau}\; &(\langle p_0; \mathsf{last}; [\,] \rangle \;\&\; \langle p_1; \mathsf{receive} \ldots \mathsf{end}; [\,] \rangle, [(p_1, p_0, [\,]), (p_0, p_1, [\mathsf{last}])]) \\
\xrightarrow{\alpha}\; &(\langle p_0; \mathsf{last}; [\,] \rangle \;\&\; \langle p_1; \underline{\mathsf{receive} \ldots \mathsf{end}}; [\mathsf{last}] \rangle, [(p_1, p_0, [\,]), (p_0, p_1, [\,])]) \\
\xrightarrow{\tau}\; &(\langle p_0; \mathsf{last}; [\,] \rangle \;\&\; \langle p_1; \underline{\mathsf{case\ last\ of}} \ldots \mathsf{end}; [\,] \rangle, [(p_1, p_0, [\,]), (p_0, p_1, [\,])]) \\
\xrightarrow{\tau}\; &(\langle p_0; \mathsf{last}; [\,] \rangle \;\&\; \langle p_1; \mathsf{ok}; [\,] \rangle, [(p_1, p_0, [\,]), (p_0, p_1, [\,])])
\end{aligned}
$$

Fig. 4. Computation for the program of example 1

4   Symbolic Execution Semantics

In this section, we introduce a symbolic execution semantics for Erlang. Firstly, one could consider the semantics in Fig. 3 and just define a function *sched* that returns all feasible combinations of processes in the considered system. This is useful to explore all possible schedulings and detect errors (e.g., deadlocks) that only occur in a particular scheduling. This is the aim, e.g., of the model checker McErlang [7]. Basically, McErlang is today a mature tool that combines the use of random test cases (using, e.g., a tool like QuickCheck [2]) with a semantics that explores possible schedulings.

Here, we plan to also cope with missing input data (analogously to the tool Java Pathfinder [12] for model checking of Java bytecode). Our *symbolic systems* are now triples of the form $(\Pi, \mathcal{Q}, \mathcal{C})$, where the new element $\mathcal{C}$ is the so called *path constraint* (initialized to *true*). Loosely speaking, $\mathcal{C}$ contains some constraints on the symbolic values that represent the missing input data, such that the system $(\Pi, \mathcal{Q})$ is reachable (using the concrete semantics) when the input data in the initial system satisfies the constraint $\mathcal{C}$.

(seq)
$$\frac{}{(\langle p; C[p,e];q\rangle\ \&\ \Pi,\mathcal{Q},\mathcal{C}) \xrightarrow{\tau} (\langle p; C[e];q\rangle\ \&\ \Pi,\mathcal{Q},\mathcal{C})}$$

(self)
$$\frac{}{(\langle p; C[\mathsf{self}()];q\rangle\ \&\ \Pi,\mathcal{Q},\mathcal{C}) \xrightarrow{\tau} (\langle p; C[p];q\rangle\ \&\ \Pi,\mathcal{Q},\mathcal{C})}$$

(builtin1)
$$\frac{eval(op(\overline{v_n})) = v}{(\langle p; C[op(\overline{v_n})];q\rangle\ \&\ \Pi,\mathcal{Q},\mathcal{C}) \xrightarrow{\tau} (\langle p; C[v];q\rangle\ \&\ \Pi,\mathcal{Q},\mathcal{C})}$$

(builtin2)
$$\frac{\exists i.\ p_i \text{ is not a value}, X \text{ is a fresh variable}}{(\langle p; C[op(\overline{p_n})];q\rangle\ \&\ \Pi,\mathcal{Q},\mathcal{C}) \xrightarrow{\tau} (\langle p; C[X];q\rangle\ \&\ \Pi,\mathcal{Q},\mathcal{C} \wedge (X = op(\overline{p_n})))}$$

(fun)
$$\frac{f(\overline{X_n}) \to e. \in pgm}{(\langle p; C[f(\overline{p_n})];q\rangle\ \&\ \Pi,\mathcal{Q},\mathcal{C}) \xrightarrow{\tau} (\langle p; C[\widehat{e}\{\overline{X_n \mapsto p_n}\}];q\rangle\ \&\ \Pi,\mathcal{Q},\mathcal{C})}$$

(match)
$$\frac{\exists\sigma.\ p_1\sigma = p_2\sigma}{(\langle p; C[p_1 = p_2];q\rangle\ \&\ \Pi,\mathcal{Q},\mathcal{C}) \xrightarrow{\tau} (\langle p; (C[p_2])\sigma;q\rangle\ \&\ \Pi,\mathcal{Q},\mathcal{C})}$$

(case)
$$\frac{(e,\sigma,\mathcal{C}') \in unify(\mathcal{C}, p, cl),\ \mathcal{C}'' = \widehat{\sigma} \wedge \mathcal{C}'}{(\langle p; C[\mathsf{case}\ p\ \mathsf{of}\ cl\ \mathsf{end}];q\rangle\ \&\ \Pi,\mathcal{Q},\mathcal{C}) \xrightarrow{\tau} (\langle p; (C[e])\sigma;q\rangle\ \&\ \Pi,\mathcal{Q},\mathcal{C} \wedge \mathcal{C}'')}$$

(receive)
$$\frac{(e,\sigma,q',\mathcal{C}') \in unifyrec(\mathcal{C}, q, cl),\ \mathcal{C}'' = \widehat{\sigma} \wedge \mathcal{C}'}{(\langle p; C[\mathsf{receive}\ cl\ \mathsf{end}];q\rangle\ \&\ \Pi,\mathcal{Q},\mathcal{C}) \xrightarrow{\tau} (\langle p; (C[e])\sigma;q'\rangle\ \&\ \Pi,\mathcal{Q},\mathcal{C} \wedge \mathcal{C}'')}$$

(spawn)
$$\frac{p' \text{ is a fresh pid}}{(\langle p; C[\mathsf{spawn}(f,\overline{p_n})];q\rangle\ \&\ \Pi,\mathcal{Q},\mathcal{C}) \xrightarrow{\tau} (\langle p; C[p'];q\rangle\ \&\ \langle p', f(\overline{p_n}), [\,]\rangle\ \&\ \Pi,\mathcal{Q},\mathcal{C})}$$

(send)
$$\frac{v = p' \in Pid\ \wedge\ add\_msg(p,p',p,\mathcal{Q}) = \mathcal{Q}'}{(\langle p; C[v\,!\,p];q\rangle\ \&\ \Pi,\mathcal{Q},\mathcal{C}) \xrightarrow{\tau} (\langle p; C[p];q\rangle\ \&\ \Pi,\mathcal{Q}',\mathcal{C})}$$

(sched)
$$\frac{(p,p') \in sched(\Pi,\mathcal{Q})\ \wedge\ delivery(p,p',\Pi,\mathcal{Q}) = (\Pi',\mathcal{Q}')}{(\Pi,\mathcal{Q},\mathcal{C}) \xrightarrow{\alpha} (\Pi',\mathcal{Q}',\mathcal{C})}$$

Fig. 5. Symbolic execution

An Overapproximation. First, we consider that symbolic execution must *overapproximate* the concrete semantics. This is useful, e.g., in the context of partial evaluation or when a property that holds for *all* states must be verified. The symbolic execution semantics is shown in Fig. 5. Let us briefly explain the main differences w.r.t. the concrete semantics:

Rule builtin considers now two cases: builtin1, which is equivalent to the previous rule in the concrete semantics, and builtin2 that considers the case when some argument is not a value. In the latter case, the built in function cannot be evaluated and we reduce it to a fresh variable and add the corresponding constraint to the system. E.g., given the expression $3+Y$, we reduce it to a fresh variable X and add the constraint $X = 3+Y$ to the system constraint.

Rule fun remains unchanged. Applications of the form $X(p_1, \ldots, p_n)$ are not considered since it would involve calling every function and built-in of the program to keep the symbolic execution complete, which is not acceptable. If such an expression is reached, we give up and stop symbolic execution with a failure.

Rule match is similar to the original rule in the concrete semantics but replaces matching with unification. Analogously, rules case and receive mainly replaces the auxiliary functions *match* and *matchrev* with *unify* and *unifyrev* where unification replaces matching as follows. Function *unify* takes a constraint $\mathcal{C}$, a pattern p and the clauses p_1 when $g_1 \rightarrow e_1; \ldots; p_n$ when $g_n \rightarrow e_n$ and returns a triple $(e_i, \sigma, \mathcal{C}')$ for each i such that $p_i\sigma = p\sigma$ (i.e., σ is a *unifier* of p_i and p) and $\mathcal{C} \Rightarrow \neg g_i\sigma$ cannot be proved (i.e., the unsatisfiability of $g_i\sigma$ cannot be proved); here, $\mathcal{C}'$ is the constraint $\mathcal{C} \wedge g_i\sigma$ (when $g_i\sigma$ is different from *true*). Function *unifyrec* proceeds analogously. Note that we also add the computed unifier to the path constraint (where $\hat{\sigma}$ denotes the equational representation of a substitution σ). This will be required in the next section. The new functions return a *set* since the pattern might unify with more than one clause whose guard is also satisfiable. Note that this strategy is complete but typically not sound since (besides the limitations of the constraint solver) we might follow several paths while the original, concrete semantics only considers the first clause even if a value matches several clauses.

Rule spawn, analogously to the case of rule fun, does not consider an expression like spawn$(X, [\overline{p_n}])$, which will be considered a failure. A similar situation happens with rule send. Here, we consider the case where the message is a pattern and, thus, might be a variable. However, we do not consider that the pid of the target process is a variable, since it would involve broadcasting the message to all processes to keep the symbolic execution complete, which is not acceptable.

Finally, rule sched just considers a scheduling function *sched* that returns all possible combinations in order to explore all feasible schedulings.

We assume that the system constraint is checked for *unsatisfiability* at every step. When unsatisfiability cannot be proved we continue with the symbolic execution (which is complete, but a potential source of unsoundness).

As in the previous case, only *normalized* symbolic executions are considered.

Example 3. Consider again the program of Ex. 1. Now, Fig. 6 shows a normalized symbolic execution starting with an unknown number K of maximum requests.

An Underapproximation. So far, we have put the emphasis on completeness (i.e., producing an overapproximation of the original Erlang computations). For this purpose, we had to take a number of decisions that make the resulting search space too huge to scale to real world Erlang applications with thousands or millions of processes. Moreover, there are a number of situations in which we have to give up (i.e., variable applications, process spawning with an unknown function or sending a message to an unknown pid) because dealing with them is simply intractable.

$(\langle p_0; start(K); [\,] \rangle, [\,], \; true)$
$\xrightarrow{\tau} (\langle p_0; S = \underline{self()}, C = spawn(client, [1, S]), server(K); [\,] \rangle, [\,], \; true)$
$\ldots$
$\xrightarrow{\alpha} (\langle p_0; \underline{receive \ldots end}; [\{p_1, 1\}] \rangle \; \& \; \langle p_1; receive \ldots end; [\,] \rangle, \; [(p_1, p_0, [\,])], \; true)$
$\xrightarrow{\tau} (\langle p_0; \underline{p_1 \,!\, ok}, server(K); [\,] \rangle \; \& \; \langle p_1; receive \ldots end; [\,] \rangle, \; [(p_1, p_0, [\,])], \; 1 < K)$
$\xrightarrow{\tau} (\langle p_0; \underline{ok, server(K)}; [\,] \rangle \; \& \; \langle p_1; receive \ldots end; [\,] \rangle, \; [(p_1, p_0, [\,]), (p_0, p_1, [ok])], \; 1 < K)$
$\xrightarrow{\tau} (\langle p_0; receive \ldots end; [\,] \rangle \; \& \; \langle p_1; receive \ldots end; [\,] \rangle, \; [(p_1, p_0, [\,]), (p_0, p_1, [ok])], \; 1 < K)$
$\ldots$

Fig. 6. Partial symbolic execution for the program of example 1

As an alternative, we propose in this section a *sound* symbolic execution that computes an *underapproximation* of the concrete semantics. This is useful for many applications (like test case generation or model checking), and it is often more scalable and avoids false positives. Here, we follow the approach of [8,13] to so called *concolic execution* and consider the following scheme:

Processes are slightly extended as follows: $\langle p, e_c, e_s, q \rangle$, where p is a pid, e_c is a concrete expression, e_s is a symbolic expression, and q is the mailbox queue. The symbolic expression is only used to compute the corresponding path constraint.

Now, one starts the execution with a random test input data and execute the program using basically the symbolic execution semantics of Fig. 5 using an initial system like $\langle p_0, start(1), start(K), [\,], true \rangle$.

Then, when the computation terminates, we produce a sequence of the form $E_0, E_1, E_2, \ldots, E_n$ where each E_i is either a constraint C_i (associated to the i-th computation step) or the symbol α denoting one application of the sched rule. We now traverse this sequence starting from the last element and either negate a constraint or consider alternative schedulings, depending on the type of the considered element. In the case of a negated constraint, we use a constraint solver to produce a new set of input data. Either way, a new concolic execution is considered and the process starts again. Usually, backtracking can be used to explore all possibilities.

If the algorithm terminates and the constraint solver is always able to generate a new set of input data, concolic execution is both sound and complete; otherwise, it is only sound (an underapproximation). Termination can be ensured using, e.g., a maximum depth for symbolic execution.

Example 4. Consider again the program of Example 1 and the initial call $start(1)$. The initial system is thus $(\langle p_0, start(1), start(K), [\,] \rangle, [\,], \; true)$. Here, we would basically perform the same computation shown in Example 2 but using the rules of Fig. 5 to also obtain the following sequence of constraints and scheduling steps: $(\alpha, \; 1 >= K)$ (only the constraints relevant to the symbolic input data, K, have to be considered). Now, by negating the constraint $1 >= K$, we produce a new value, e.g., $K = 5$, and consider a new symbolic execution starting from the system $(\langle p_0, start(5), start(K), [\,] \rangle, [\,], \; true)$. Finally, one should consider alternative schedulings (because we reach a symbol α) but no alternative exists. Therefore, we conclude that executing $start(1)$ and $start(5)$ is sufficient to cover all possible execution paths for the source program.

5   Discussion

In this paper, we have introduced a high-level concrete semantics for the functional and concurrent language Erlang, and have explored the definition of an associated symbolic execution technique. We proposed both an overapproximation and an underapproximation—based on a variant of symbolic execution called concolic execution—. In principle, it seems that the underapproximation will be more practical and scalable in order to design a tool for model checking and/or test case generation. We are only aware of the approach of [3] to symbolic execution in Erlang, though no formalization is introduced in this paper (it is only explained informally). Hence we think that our approach is a promising step towards defining a practical symbolic execution technique for Erlang, which can be used in different contexts like model checking or test case generation.

References

1. Armstrong, J., Virdig, R., Williams, M.: Concurrent Programming in Erlang, 2nd edn. Prentice Hall, Englewood Cliffs (1996)
2. Arts, T., Hughes, J., Johansson, J., Wiger, U.T.: Testing telecoms software with quviq QuickCheck. In: Proceedings of the Erlang Workshop, pp. 2–10. ACM (2006)
3. Benac Earle, C.: Symbolic program execution using the Erlang verification tool. In: Proceedings of the 9th Int'l Workshop on Functional and Logic Programming (WFLP 2000), pp. 42–55 (2000)
4. Claessen, K., Svensson, H.: A semantics for distributed Erlang. In: Proceedings of the 2005 ACM SIGPLAN Workshop on Erlang, pp. 78–87. ACM (2005)
5. Felleisen, M., Friedman, D.P., Kohlbecker, E.E., Duba, B.F.: A syntactic theory of sequential control. Theor. Comput. Sci. **52**, 205–237 (1987)
6. Fredlund, L.-A.: A framework for reasoning about Erlang code. Ph.D. thesis, The Royal Institute of Technology, Sweeden (2001)
7. Fredlund, L.-A., Svensson, H.: McErlang: a model checker for a distributed functional programming language. In: Proceedings of ICFP 2007, pp. 125–136. ACM (2007)
8. Godefroid, P., Klarlund, N., Sen, K.: DART: directed automated random testing. In: Proceedings of PLDI 2005, pp. 213–223. ACM (2005)
9. Huch, F.: Verification of Erlang programs using abstract interpretation and model checking. In: Proceedings of ICFP 1999, pp 261–272. ACM (1999)
10. Noll, T.: A Rewriting Logic Implementation of Erlang. Electr. Notes Theor. Comput. Sci. **44**(2), 206–224 (2001)
11. Noll, T.: Equational Abstractions for Model Checking Erlang Programs. Electr. Notes Theor. Comput. Sci. **118**, 145–162 (2005)
12. Pasareanu, C.S., Visser, W., Bushnell, D.H., Geldenhuys, J., Mehlitz, P.C., Rungta, N.: Symbolic PathFinder: integrating symbolic execution with model checking for Java bytecode analysis. Autom. Softw. Eng., 20(3), 391–425 (2013)
13. Sen, K., Marinov, D., Agha, G.: CUTE: a concolic unit testing engine for C. In: Proceedings of ESEC/SIGSOFT FSE 2005, pp. 263–272. ACM (2005)
14. Svensson, H., Fredlund, L.-A., Benac Earle, C.: A unified semantics for future Erlang. In: Proceedings of the Erlang Workshop, pp. 23–32. ACM (2010)

15. Svensson, H., Fredlund, L.-A.: A more accurate semantics for distributed Erlang. In: Proceedings of the Erlang Workshop, pp. 43–54. ACM (2007)
16. Vidal, G.: Towards erlang verification by term rewriting. In: Gupta, G., Peña, R. (eds.) LOPSTR 2013, LNCS 8901. LNCS, vol. 8901, pp. 109–126. Springer, Heidelberg (2014)
17. Vidal, G.: Symbolic execution in Erlang. Technical report, DSIC, UPV (2014). http://users.dsic.upv.es/~gvidal/

Bonsai: Cutting Models Down to Size

Stefan Vijzelaar[(⊠)], Kees Verstoep, Wan Fokkink, and Henri Bal

VU University Amsterdam, Amsterdam, The Netherlands
{s.j.j.vijzelaar,c.verstoep,w.j.fokkink,h.e.bal}@vu.nl

Abstract. In model checking, abstractions can cause spurious results, which need to be verified in the concrete system to gain conclusive results. Verification based on multi-valued model checking can distinguish conclusive and inconclusive results, while increasing precision over traditional two-valued over- and under-abstractions. This paper describes the theory and implementation of multi-valued model checking for Promela specifications. We believe our tool Bonsai is the first four-valued model checker capable of multi-valued verification of parallel models, i.e. consisting of multiple concurrent processes. A novel aspect is the ability to only partially abstract a model, keeping parts of it concrete.

1 Introduction

The ubiquitous problem of state space explosion, i.e. a combinatorial blow-up of behaviour, is a central theme in the verification of systems. While abstraction can reduce the impact of state space explosion, it can also introduce spurious results [5]. By combining over- and under-abstraction, it is possible to identify abstract behaviour which is guaranteed to match the concrete behaviour of the system. This can be implemented using three-valued semantics [2,15]: properties can be either *true, false,* or *unknown*; any result which would have been spurious in the over- or under-abstraction is represented by the *unknown* value.

An elegant way to model abstract transitions is to use a four-valued logic [1]. The truth values of the logic form a bilattice [8], the elements of which are in both a truth ordering and an orthogonal information ordering. Operations of the logic map to operations over the truth ordering, while abstractions of the system can be mapped to operations over the information ordering. An added benefit of this strong relation between the logic and truth ordering is a natural definition of existing temporal logics in terms of lattice operations [3,16]. These definitions can be reused for other multi-valued logics [11], conceivably resulting from new abstraction or modelling techniques.

Techniques based on a four-valued logic have been successfully used in symbolic trajectory evaluation for verification of logical circuits [17], and abstract model checking of software [13]. In this paper we are interested in applying the multi-valued approach to concurrent software systems, for which to our knowledge there are no tools available at this point. We generalise the abstraction technique used in [12] to use operations in the information ordering of the bilattice, and implement this technique in a tool for concurrent processes.

© Springer-Verlag Berlin Heidelberg 2015
A. Voronkov and I. Virbitskaite (Eds.): PSI 2014, LNCS 8974, pp. 361–375, 2015.
DOI: 10.1007/978-3-662-46823-4_29

Since we prefer to extend on existing work, we focus on concurrent Promela models as used by the SPIN [14] model checker. For these models we implement four-valued abstraction, combining two-valued over- and three-valued under-abstraction, in a tool called Bonsai. Abstractions are constructed using predicate abstraction [9], which is a special case of abstract interpretation [6].

The implementation is written in Java, and based on the SpinJa model checker [7] and the SMTInterpol satisfiability solver [4]. The two-valued semantics of the SpinJa model checker can be reused by decomposing the four-valued model checking problem into two, classical, two-valued problems [11] using the satisfiability solver for abstraction. This method can be extended to model check other higher-valued logics.

The paper is structured as follows. Section 2 gives an introduction to multi-valued model checking; it shows the four-valued logic used in our abstraction, a method for constructing the multi-valued abstraction, and the decomposition applied by our tool. In Sect. 3 we detail the implementation and show that the decomposed problems can share results: it is not required to calculate two completely separate abstractions to get a multi-valued result. Section 4 demonstrates the tools effectiveness at some typical examples for abstraction, while in Sect. 5 we conclude and consider future applications.

The long term goal of this tool is to investigate four-valued and other higher-valued logics for concurrent processes. Specifically logics which separately model steerable and unsteerable non-determinism can prove to be interesting: results of multi-valued abstract verification could be combined with runtime steering to guarantee correct execution of software for which verification would otherwise have been intractable.

2   Multi-valued Model Checking

2.1   Preliminaries

A lattice is a partially ordered ($\sqsupseteq$) set, in which any two elements have a least upper bound (supremum or join), and a greatest lower bound (infimum or meet). By induction, a non-empty finite lattice has a join and meet for each subset of elements. Therefore, the set as a whole is bounded, and has a greatest element (top or $\top$), and least element (bottom or $\bot$).

Lattices can be used to define quasi-boolean algebras which can be applied when verifying temporal properties. Model checking typically uses classical boolean logic: transitions between states either exist (are *true*) or do not exist (are *false*); and atomic propositions used by temporal properties either hold for a state (are *true*) or do not hold (are *false*). It is customary to only draw *true* transitions in a state space graph; missing transitions are assumed to be *false*.

The classical boolean logic used to verify properties can be described in the more general framework of lattice theory: a lattice consisting of two elements, with *true* being the supremum, and *false* being the infimum. The boolean conjunction and disjunction operations map respectively to the meet ($\sqcap$) and join ($\sqcup$) of lattice theory.

In multi-valued model checking, instead of classical boolean logic, more general quasi-boolean logics can be used. The truth values of a quasi-boolean logic are the elements of a finite distributive lattice. Conjunction and disjunction map to meet ($\sqcap$) and join ($\sqcup$) respectively, while negation ($\sim$) needs to adhere to De Morgan's laws and the law of double negation. Distributivity of the lattice ensures that the meet and join distribute over each other, similar to conjunction and disjunction in classical boolean logic.

The strong relation between boolean operations and lattice operations ensures that the verification of temporal properties remains the same for different quasi-boolean logics. Classical definitions of temporal properties can easily be translated to lattice operations, and are then applicable to the more general class of quasi-boolean logics instead of just classical boolean logic.

2.2 A Lattice for Under- and Over-Abstraction

We can use a quasi-boolean logic, based on a lattice, to model both under- and over-abstraction at the same time. The interlaced bilattice [8] used for this purpose in [12] not only defines the required truth ordering of the logic, but also an orthogonal information ordering; see Fig. 1a. As a consequence of this additional ordering, the $\top$ and $\bot$ elements should not be interpreted as the top and bottom of the logic: they are used to model the top and bottom of the information ordering.

One way to characterise the additional two truth values is to interpret *bottom* ($\bot$) as neither true nor false, and *top* ($\top$) as both true and false. In other words, the elements of the information ordering can be seen as sets, which can contain an item for truth (t) and an item for falsity (f). Truth values no longer map to a single items of the set $\{t, f\}$, as is the case for classical logic, but to its subsets. This allows for values which contain none ($\bot$) or both ($\top$) of the elements in $\{t, f\}$, as can be seen in Fig. 1b.

We can apply this interpretation to the atomic propositions and transitions of a transition system, and by extension to temporal properties evaluated over this system. Each of these concepts can be modelled using the same four-valued

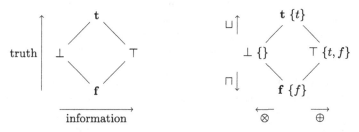

(a) Orthogonal information ordering (b) Operations and interpretations

Fig. 1. Multi-valued lattice for under- and over-abstraction

logic, but this does not mean that all truth values are meaningful for every context. Depending on the context, some values should not occur.

Atomic propositions can be *true* (**t**), *false* (**f**) or *unknown* ($\perp$). The *unknown* value for a proposition is represented as the absence of knowledge by using the bottom element of the information ordering ($\perp$). It can be used to express a loss of information due to abstraction: we conclude neither true nor false for an atomic proposition which has been assigned this value. Conversely, the value *top* ($\top$) will never be assigned to a proposition, since atomic propositions cannot be both true and false at the same time.

Transitions can be *may* transitions ($\perp$), *must* transitions ($\top$), both (**t**), or neither (**f**). This requires a more general definition of *may* and *must* transitions than is used by modal transition systems which only recognise *must* transitions as a subset of *may* transitions (e.g. [10]). We define *may* transitions as those transitions that are at least not false (i.e. of value $\perp$ or **t**), and *must* transitions as those transitions that are at least true (i.e. of value $\top$ or **t**). The use of the *top* ($\top$) value allows us to express that for a set of states, some states are reachable while others are not.

By extension of the atomic propositions and transitions of the system we can evaluate temporal properties over the system. Temporal properties use the same values as atomic propositions: *true* (**t**), *false* (**f**) or *unknown* ($\perp$). Similar to atomic propositions they express a property of a state: the reachability of behaviour from said state. Even though transitions can take on the value *top* ($\top$), this value should never result in a temporal property of the same value: a temporal property cannot be both true and false at the same time.

Note that while *bottom* and *top* behave similarly in the logic, i.e. when only using operations on the truth ordering, they are not interchangeable when taking into account operations on the information ordering, which we will be using when constructing abstractions. It is however possible to obtain a similar construction if also the operations used for the abstraction method are interchanged.

2.3   Multi-valued Abstraction

Using the notion of an information ordering, it is no longer necessary to separately reason about under- and over-abstraction. It is possible to use a single generic multi-valued method of abstraction which captures both types of abstraction using operations on the information ordering. For this purpose we will be using the meet ($\otimes$) and join ($\oplus$) operations on the information ordering. See Fig. 1b for an overview of the operations on the truth and information ordering.

Assume we have defined equivalence classes over a set of concrete states of a Kripke structure, e.g. using predicates. Figure 2a shows a concrete example system: source states are on the left and destination states on the right. The lines are used to indicate how predicates divide the concrete states into equivalence classes. An abstract state is formed by those concrete states which have the same evaluation for all predicates. To complete the abstraction we want to lift the transitions between concrete states to transitions between abstract states.

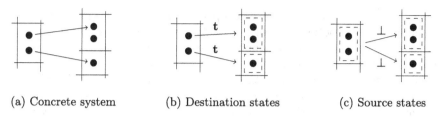

<table>
<tr><td>(a) Concrete system</td><td>(b) Destination states</td><td>(c) Source states</td></tr>
</table>

Fig. 2. Abstraction with individual abstract states

Our abstraction method to lift transitions starts by applying an induction hypothesis. It is assumed that we are able to correctly express the behaviour of the abstract destination states; therefore, we can replace any transition to a concrete state by a transition to the abstract state it belongs to. The results are shown in Fig. 2b. The induction hypothesis ensures that we do not have to differentiate between constituent states of the abstract destination state, and any possible loss of information is caused solely by the abstraction of behaviour for the abstract destination state.

To complete the induction hypothesis, we need to determine the behaviour of the abstract source state. For this purpose we calculate the consensus of the concrete source states on the reachability of specific abstract destinations; we do this by using the meet of the information ordering ($\otimes$). Stated differently, since we will lose the ability to differentiate between concrete source states for a given abstract source state, the best we can do is to describe the behaviour they agree on. In the example of Fig. 2b each abstract destination state is reachable (**t**) by one concrete source state, and unreachable (**f**, not drawn) by the other. This gives us the value *bottom* (**t** $\otimes$ **f** $= \perp$) for each abstract destination state, as can be seen in Fig. 2c above.

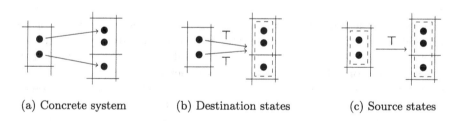

<table>
<tr><td>(a) Concrete system</td><td>(b) Destination states</td><td>(c) Source states</td></tr>
</table>

Fig. 3. Abstraction with a set of abstract states

This method in itself would be sufficient to create a multi-valued abstract model, a model containing aspects of both under- and over-abstraction, but we can do better. To increase precision we can merge abstract states by using the meet operator of the information ordering ($\otimes$). Take two or more abstract destination states that have different valuations for one or more properties and combine their valuations using the meet operator. The result is a merged abstract state with the value *bottom* ($\bot$) for any predicate the original abstract states did not agree on. It models the possibility of these predicates being either true or false: their actual value is unknown.

Using these merged abstract states, we can model the reachability of sets of abstract states. While concrete source states might not agree on the reachability of *individual* abstract destination states, they could still agree on the reachability of a *set* of abstract destination states. We create sets by merging abstract states, with the provision that the resulting sets are limited to a cartesian product of predicate values by construction. Transitions to merged abstract states model whether any individual abstract state in the set is reachable, but without specifying *which* particular states are reachable.

To calculate the correct value of a transition from a concrete state to a set of abstract states, we combine the information of the states in the set using the join operator of the information ordering ($\oplus$). Since we are interested in the reachability of the set of abstract states as a whole, we want to aggregate the knowledge we have for reachability of the individual abstract states. This can be contrasted to the meet operator of the information ordering ($\otimes$) which calculates the consensus. In Fig. 3b it can be seen how this gives us the value *top* ($\mathbf{t} \oplus \mathbf{f} = \top$), since the merged abstract state contains both reachable and unreachable abstract states.

The behaviour of abstract source states is calculated in the usual manner, using the meet operator ($\otimes$). This also applies to sets of abstract source states, since we cannot distinguish between abstract source states in a set any more than we can distinguish between concrete states in an abstract state. The best we can do is to describe the behaviour the abstract source states in the set agree on. Figure 3c shows how this results in *top* ($\top \oplus \top = \top$) for the case of a single abstract source state as used in the example.

We can generalise the abstraction method by considering individual abstract states as sets containing just one abstract state. The resulting generic method constructs a multi-valued abstract system with transitions between sets of abstract states.

The generic method can be summarised as follows. Start by calculating the reachability of abstract destination states from concrete source states. Subsequently use the join operator ($\oplus$) to aggregate all transitions to members of the abstract destination set. Finally use the meet operator ($\otimes$) to reach consensus for all concrete states contained by members of the abstract source set. Repeat the last two steps for other abstract source and destination sets.

2.4 Multi-valued Through Classical Model Checking

A multi-valued model checking problem can be reduced to multiple classical model checking problems [11]. This is done by identifying the join-irreducible elements J in the lattice of truth values. (Join-irreducible elements are those elements, except for the bottom element, which cannot be expressed as the join of two other elements.) The multi-valued model checking problem for a temporal property can then be split into $|J|$ classical model checking problems. For an LTL property φ, a trace π, and the partial lattice ordering $\sqsupseteq$, this gives the following identity:

$$[\varphi]_\pi = \bigsqcup_{j \in J} (j \sqcap ([\varphi]_\pi \sqsupseteq j))$$

All truth values can be expressed as a combination of join operations on join-irreducible elements, or more precisely as a join of those join-irreducible elements which are smaller than or equal to that specific truth value. The expression $[\varphi]_\pi \sqsupseteq j$ is either *true* or *false*, ensuring that $j \sqcap ([\varphi]_\pi \sqsupseteq j)$ is either j or *false*. The end result is a join over a join-irreducible value smaller than or equal to $[\varphi]_\pi$ and *false* otherwise, and since *false* has no influence on the join operation, we get $[\varphi]_\pi$.

The identity above allows us to evaluate inequalities over $[\varphi]_\pi$ and combine the results, instead of determining $[\varphi]_\pi$ directly. To calculate $[\varphi]_\pi \sqsupseteq j$, the cut operator $\Uparrow$ is introduced [11] to syntactically distribute the inequality over the temporal property (after which it can be evaluated using classical model checking over a modified model):

$$[\varphi \Uparrow j]_\pi = [\varphi]_\pi \sqsupseteq j$$

We assume LTL formulas to be in release positive normal form (PNF):

$$\varphi_n = true \mid false \mid p \mid \neg p \mid \varphi_1 \wedge \varphi_2 \mid \varphi_1 \vee \varphi_2 \mid \varphi_1 \cup \varphi_2 \mid \varphi_1 \mathrel{R} \varphi_2$$

This ensures only atomic propositions can be negated, and allows for a simple reduction. (The implicit universal quantification of an LTL formula could complicate this reduction [11], was it not for the fact that we check for language emptiness using the negated LTL formula. That is, we apply the reduction to the negated LTL formula in PNF.)

$$
\begin{aligned}
true \Uparrow j &= \mathbf{t} \sqsupseteq j & false \Uparrow j &= \mathbf{f} \sqsupseteq j \\
p \Uparrow j &= p \sqsupseteq j & \neg p \Uparrow j &= \neg p \sqsupseteq j \\
(\varphi \wedge \psi) \Uparrow j &= (\varphi \Uparrow j) \wedge (\psi \Uparrow j) & (\varphi \vee \psi) \Uparrow j &= (\varphi \Uparrow j) \vee (\psi \Uparrow j) \\
(\varphi \cup \psi) \Uparrow j &= (\varphi \Uparrow j) \cup_{\sqsupseteq j} (\psi \Uparrow j) & (\varphi \mathrel{R} \psi) \Uparrow j &= (\varphi \Uparrow j) \mathrel{R}_{\sqsupseteq j} (\psi \Uparrow j)
\end{aligned}
$$

This reduction leaves us with some inequalities over j, and the operators $X_{\sqsupseteq j}$, $U_{\sqsupseteq j}$ and $R_{\sqsupseteq j}$. The values of $\mathbf{t} \sqsupseteq j$ and $\mathbf{f} \sqsupseteq j$ can be put directly into the property, while the inequalities $p \sqsupseteq j$ and $\neg p \sqsupseteq j$ will need to be encoded into the model. The semantics of the $X_{\sqsupseteq j}$, $U_{\sqsupseteq j}$ and $R_{\sqsupseteq j}$ operators are identical to their LTL counterparts for a classical boolean logic by only considering transitions with a value $v \sqsupseteq j$ to be true. Keeping only those transitions in the model allows us to use the classical X, U and R operators.

In general, we can evaluate the reduced property $\varphi \Uparrow j$ for each $j \in J$ separately, by creating an appropriate transition system for each $j \in J$ respectively. Instead of evaluating φ over multi-valued paths, we evaluate $\varphi \Uparrow j$ over classical paths, by only modelling whether literals and transitions are $\sqsupseteq j$. This is sufficient to evaluate the inequalities and $X_{\sqsupseteq j}$, $U_{\sqsupseteq j}$ and $R_{\sqsupseteq j}$ operators introduced by the reduction.

3   Implementation

The theory presented above can be used to implement a multi-valued model checker by decomposing problems into multiple classical model checking problems. We implement our multi-valued model checker Bonsai on top of the SpinJa model checker [7], and use the SMTInterpol satisfiability solver [4] to construct the decomposition.

3.1   Modifications to SpinJa

To abstract a Promela model with Bonsai, predicates can be added directly to the Promela specification by using the special type `pred`. These predicates are then automatically used during the subsequent abstraction process. For example, to add the predicate $x < 4$ to the specification, we write `pred x < 4` in the declaration list of either the specification itself, or one of its processes. By allowing declarations in both the specification and its processes, predicates can be made either global for the whole specification or local to a specific process type; this allows predicates to reference both global and local variables without breaking scoping rules. Note that a local predicate can reference global variables.

The version of the SpinJa model checker we use, has been slightly modified to parse predicates in a similar way to standard variables. In the original implementation, variables are stored by the SpinJa parser in a VariableStore; this design is copied to store predicates in a PredicateStore. Predicates in the PredicateStore can reference variables in the VariableStore, but do not yet have a variable associated with them for storing the actual value of the predicate. The PredicateStore simply acts as a bookkeeping device for keeping track of which predicates have been added to the specification. Together with the introduction of the `pred` type, this is the only required modification to the SpinJa model checker.

3.2   Overview of the Abstraction

Parsing a specification with the modified SpinJa model checker, creates a *promela model* containing multiple automata. These automata are object-based representations of the processes as defined in the Promela specification. Since automata are a type of program graph, we can use them to create abstract program graphs: one abstract automata for each concrete automata of the specification. Together they form an *abstract model* of the specification with respect to the given predicates.

This abstraction is done in two passes. Before we create the completed *abstract model*, we traverse the automata created by SpinJa one transition at a time. Transitions not influenced by abstraction (e.g. goto's) are copied directly

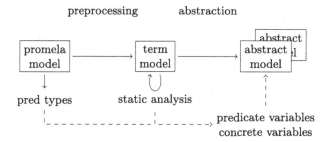

Fig. 4. An overview of the implementation

into the *abstract model*, but other transitions (e.g. assignments) require pre-processing to create a *term transition* containing the metadata required for static analysis and abstraction. These *term transitions* are stored in a separate *term model*, which is a kind of scaffolding over the still incomplete *abstract model*.

The *term model* has additional facilities for static analysis. In some cases it is useful to not abstract away from all concrete actions and variables of the original specification; for example, we might want to keep variables when they are part of the control flow. Static analysis can be used to determine which concrete variables, used by *term transitions*, need to be kept in the abstract automaton. Only after static analysis of the *term transitions*, do we add the actual variables to the *abstract model* for tracking concrete variables and predicates. To differentiate between them, all variable names in the *abstract model* have a prefix with their type. Predicates additionally have a unique number and a short descriptive string as a part of their name.

Using the *term model* we can generate the final over- and under-abstractions of the specification, which correspond to the two join-irreducible elements of the four-valued logic. For every *term transition* in the automaton, we generate two decision diagrams: one diagram for each abstraction. The diagrams are then encoded as transitions in an *abstract model* using only standard Promela if-statements and assignments. Together with the transitions already present, this completes the *abstract model*. For an overview see Fig. 4.

The resulting two *abstract models*, one for each join-irreducible element, can be compiled and verified using the default SpinJa tool stack. Each partial result indicates whether the multi-valued result is larger or equal to one of the join-irreducible elements. By combining them, we get a multi-valued result of the complete model checking problem.

3.3   Constructing SMT Terms for Transitions

Promela transitions consist of one or more actions, and each action can be modelled using two terms: a guard term, and an effect term. See Fig. 5 for an example of an effect term being constructed from code: type definitions are shown for completeness. The guard term indicates whether the action is enabled, while the effect term models the relation between source and destination states.

```
int x;                    x_0:Int, x_1:Int,
int y;                    y_0:Int, y_1:Int,
x = x + 1;                x_1 == x_0 + 1 && y_1 == y_0
   (a) Promela code           (b) SMT term
```

Fig. 5. Constructing an effect term

Even though only the first action in a transition is allowed to block, we cannot ignore the guard terms of the other actions. It depends on whether we are going to model the actions of a transition separately, or as one big abstract action; we might need the guard terms to detect blocking of subsequent actions in the transition, and report an error. The end result for a transition is a list of *term actions*, each containing a guard and effect term for the corresponding action.

To create terms for the individual actions we make use of the theories supported by the SMT solver, in this case the theory of integers. There is, however, no support for arrays in the solver we use, therefore any array encountered in the specification needs to be backed by separate term variables for each index; these are combined using an if-then-else construction based on the index term to model an array. At the same time we assume abstractions over indices may be unwanted, and keep track of any terms used as an index. One can argue that indices are at times part of the control flow of the program, i.e. a defining part of the program graph, and do not need be abstracted. Static analysis can then be applied to do a form of taint analysis: any variable used in an assignment to a concrete variable, also needs to be a concrete variable.

Using concrete values in a term can cause difficulties when abstracting transitions using the SMT solver. Concrete variables can store a large range of values; enumerating all of them in the SMT solver can make the abstraction intractable. As a first step, we ensure that assignments to concrete variables are never abstracted; such assignments are handled by concrete transitions, since we can assume that all referenced variables are also concrete. This assumption is guaranteed by the taint analysis, since concrete information cannot be created from abstract information.

Mixing concrete and abstract information is only allowed in specific cases. Either all variables used in a predicate are concrete, making the solution trivial since we can simply evaluate the predicate at runtime; or we require the concrete parts of the predicate to be somehow in a bounded domain, making the solution tractable. This is specifically the case when using a concrete value as the index of an array.

When constructing *term transitions* with concrete indices, we keep track of the possible range of these indices. This ensures that the SMT solver is bounded when enumerating all possible values of the index. This bound is over the complete expression which is used as an index, and can also be used to detect out-of-bound conditions. Note that the use of concrete indices is useful when predicates reference specific indices in an array, but should only be used for small arrays, lest the abstraction would become intractable.

3.4   Abstracting SMT Terms Using Predicates

Given a list of *term actions* for a concrete transition, we want to generate an over- and under-abstraction of this transition. Each *term action* contains a guard and effect term. Since a guard is a simple boolean expression, we can easily over- and under-approximate this guard using the SMT solver. This leaves the effect term, for which we effectively want the following results: for the over-abstraction, we want to over-approximate the post-image of each abstract pre-state; and for the under-abstraction, we want to under-approximate the pre-image of each abstract post-state. While the over-approximation poses no problems, since over-approximation is a natural operation for an SMT solver, the under-approximation is not that straight forward.

We can calculate an under-approximation of a guard term, by negating the term, over-approximating it, and negating the result. For the effect term we want to under-approximate the pre-image of a specific abstract post-state; however, the pre-image is defined only implicitly by the combination of the effect term and the abstract post-state. As can be seen in Fig. 6, negating the effect term does not give the desired result, and negating the post-state only works when the effect relation is total.

One solution is to ensure that the effect relation is total by extending it, and to rely on an under-approximation of the guard term to filter out unwanted transitions. Then we could safely negate the post-state to calculate the required under-approximation of pre-states; however, this use of a guard in combination with a total function allows for a better solution. When trying to under-abstract the effect relation, we have the guarantee that all enabled concrete states have outgoing transitions: the under-approximated guard term reduces the domain of the effect relation to only enabled states and ensures it is total over this domain. In addition we only abstract individual deterministic transitions. We can use these facts to our advantage.

As a consequence of the above, the over- and under-abstraction can share results of the SMT solver. We start by over-approximating the effect function, which can be done using a single allSAT call to the SMT solver. This result can be shared between both abstractions. Next we respectively over- and under-approximate the guard and subsequently remove these pre-states from the over-approximation of the effect function. This gives us the two-valued over- and under-abstraction of the transition.

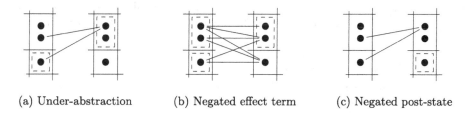

(a) Under-abstraction   (b) Negated effect term   (c) Negated post-state

Fig. 6. Under-abstraction by over-approximation

For an over-abstraction, the result can be used as-is to generate *abstract transitions*. A transition is created for each possible post-state. Pre-states related to this post-state can be identified using boolean conjunctions; their disjunction is the first action of the transition, and will act as a guard. The post-state can be constructed using a series of assignments, which will change the pre-state into the requested post-state; together with the guard action, these assign actions complete the transition. The construction of multiple transitions, allows the model checker to non-deterministically explore all possible post-states during verification.

For an under-abstraction, the result needs some additional processing. All post-states reachable from a given pre-state are flattened into a single new post-state. This is done by combining the predicate values of these post-states: if the post-states agree on the value of a predicate, that value is used; but if they disagree, the *unknown* value is used. This creates the most precise must transition for a fully specified pre-state, since we only abstract individual deterministic transitions. To include under-specified pre-states, we flatten sets of existing pre-states to form new pre-states, while we flatten their respective post-states to form a new post-state. By relating these new states, we can handle any possible pre-state in the under-abstraction. This results in a deterministic transition for each pre-state with outgoing transitions.

Since the method above already supports partial relations, we can further increase precision by also taking into account the guard term when abstracting the effect relation. We can actually ignore any concrete pre-state, which is not part of the guard. For an over-abstraction, the guard term can reduce the number of post-states reachable from a pre-state: removing impossible concrete transitions can reduce the number of may-transitions. For an under-abstraction, the guard term can reduce the number of post-states used by the flattening operations: preventing disagreement on predicate values can increase the amount of information in states after must-transitions.

3.5   Storing SMT Results in Decision Diagrams

After abstracting the SMT terms, we need to store the results in some way. We also require support for different kinds of operations on these results, like the flattening operation described above. For this purpose we use a multi-valued decision diagram, allowing storage of predicate values and bounded concrete values. Predicate values are multi-valued: they can be *true, false* or *unknown*. Concrete values need to be part of some, preferably small, domain; this is not only to prevent large enumerations by the SMT solver, but also to allow tractable negation of a result, e.g. for under-approximation. Finally we allow for the value *skip*, which is used to optimise assignments when predicate values are the same for both the pre- and post-state.

The diagrams we use are refined in multiple steps: we start by creating a generic decision diagram, which works for any type of value. It supports simple operations like union and intersection of diagrams. This is subsequently extended to a bounded term diagram by storing terms and their bounds at each node.

Operations requiring multi-valued term information, like the flatten operation, are implemented at this level. Relations between sets of states are stored by creating nested term diagrams, which split the diagram into one outer and multiple inner diagrams: for each state in the outer diagram it contains an inner diagram containing related states. Finally we use assign diagrams to optimise the encoding of the diagram into actual transitions of the model; for example, values which do not change can be skipped when implementing a transition.

4 Experimental Results

We use two mutual exclusion algorithms to demonstrate our implementation: Lamport's bakery algorithm, and Fischer's algorithm. Both algorithms use shared memory, and have potentially very large state spaces; they respectively model ticket numbers and discrete time, which can have domains of arbitrary size. These algorithms make typical examples for demonstrating the strengths of abstraction.

In Lamport's bakery algorithm, a process intending to enter its critical section picks a ticket number higher than any of the numbers used by other processes. It then waits until its number is the smallest of the waiting processes before starting its critical section. Due to concurrency, multiple processes can pick the same number, in which case the process id's are used as a tie-breaker.

For Fischer's algorithm, a single shared variable is used to keep track of reservations. A process reads the variable, and if it is zero, overwrites it with its own id. It then reads the variable for a second time, and can enter its critical section if its identity is still contained by the variable. Since concurrent processes can overwrite each others values, there is a timing constraint. It is required that after writing, a process waits a specified time before reading. This wait period needs to be longer than the time between reading zero and writing an id.

The abstractions used, map ticket numbers and discrete time values to smaller bounded domains. Enough information is retained to model check the algorithm. For Lamport's bakery algorithm, it is sufficient to map the relative ordering of ticket numbers, instead of their absolute values. Similarly, for Fischer's algorithm it is sufficient to keep track of remaining wait time, instead of absolute values of the clock and timers.

The concrete state spaces can be made arbitrarily large by increasing the maximum value for tickets or time after which the algorithm halts. In contrast, the abstract state space has a fixed size, irrespective of these values. In our tests we demonstrate this effect by varying the maximum value, and showing its effect on the running time.

Tests are performed on a 2.66 GHz Intel Core 2 Duo, with 4 GB of RAM. The Java virtual machine is given 2 GB of heap space. Parameters for the SpinJa model checker are -m1000000 for the search depth and -DNOREDUCE to prevent partial order reduction. For the cases of more than 2^{14} ticket numbers or clock ticks, we use -m10000000 to increase the depth by a factor of 10 for the concrete model. During compilation we use -o3 to disable statement merging. Source code and model are available at http://www.cs.vu.nl/~sjj.vijzelaar/spinja/.

Abstracting the algorithms give typical examples of collapsing a large state space, an effect which shows clearly in the results (Tables 1 and 2). Parsing and compiling of the abstract model takes significantly longer than for the concrete model, since parsing for the abstract model includes the construction of two abstract models. Any performance lost during construction, however, is easily gained during model checking. The state spaces of the concrete models grow with each increase of the model bounds. In the case of Fischer's algorithm, this even causes the model checker to run out of memory for more than 2^{15} clock ticks; the abstract model has no such problem.

Table 1. Verifying Lamport's bakery algorithm (seconds)

	Parse	Compile	Model checking (numbers)			
			2^{12}	2^{14}	2^{16}	2^{18}
Abstract	12.35	5.81	0.33			
Concrete	0.39	1.36	1.64	5.85	23.85	121.61

Table 2. Verifying Fischer's algorithm (seconds)

	Parse	Compile	Model checking (ticks)			
			2^{12}	2^{13}	2^{14}	2^{15}
Abstract	30.41	8.20	1.47			
Concrete	0.36	1.85	11.16	22.58	50.01	108.08

5   Conclusion

This paper gives an overview of the theory required to implement multi-valued verification on top of a classical two-valued model checker. We have used this theory to implement four-valued abstract verification using the SpinJa model checker and SMTInterpol satisfiability solver. By doing so, we can now leverage the strength of the Promela language in modelling concurrent processes, and explore the benefits of multi-valued model checking in this context.

As far as we know, this tool is the first to implement multi-valued model checking of a quasi-boolean logic for concurrent processes. Additionally our model checker has the ability to apply abstraction to only parts of the concrete model. We want to apply these strengths to future research in the areas of runtime verification and execution steering.

References

1. Belnap, N.D.: Modern Uses of Multiple-Valued Logics, pp. 30–56. Reidel, Dordrecht (1977)
2. Bruns, G., Godefroid, P.: Model checking partial state spaces with 3-valued temporal logics. In: Halbwachs, N., Peled, D.A. (eds.) CAV 1999. LNCS, vol. 1633, pp. 274–287. Springer, Heidelberg (1999)
3. Chechik, M., Devereux, B., Easterbrook, S.M., Gurfinkel, A.: Multi-valued symbolic model-checking. ACM TOSEM 12(4), 371–408 (2003)
4. Christ, J., Hoenicke, J., Nutz, A.: SMTInterpol: an interpolating SMT solver. In: Donaldson, A., Parker, D. (eds.) SPIN 2012. LNCS, vol. 7385, pp. 248–254. Springer, Heidelberg (2012)
5. Clarke, E.M., Grumberg, O., Jha, S., Jha, Y., Veith, H.: Counterexample-guided abstraction refinement. In: Allen Emerson, E., Sistla, A.P. (eds.) CAV 2000. LNCS, vol. 1855, pp. 154–169. Springer, Heidelberg (2000)
6. Cousot, P., Cousot, R.: Abstract interpretation: A unified lattice model for static analysis of programs by construction or approximation of fixpoints. In: POPL, pp. 238–252. ACM (1977)
7. de Jonge, M., Ruys, T.C.: The SPINJA model checker. In: van de Pol, J., Weber, M. (eds.) Model Checking Software. LNCS, vol. 6349, pp. 124–128. Springer, Heidelberg (2010)
8. Fitting, M.: Bilattices and the theory of truth. J. Philos. Logic 18, 225–256 (1989)
9. Graf, S., Saïdi, H.: Construction of abstract state graphs with PVS. In: Grumberg, Orna (ed.) CAV 1997. LNCS, vol. 1254, pp. 154–169. Springer, Heidelberg (1997)
10. Grumberg, O.: 2-valued and 3-valued abstraction-refinement in model checking. In: Logics and Languages for Reliability and Security, pp. 105–128. IOS Press (2010)
11. Gurfinkel, A., Chechik, M.: Multi-valued model checking via classical model checking. In: Amadio, R.M., Lugiez, D. (eds.) CONCUR 2003. LNCS, vol. 2761, pp. 266–280. Springer, Heidelberg (2003)
12. Gurfinkel, A., Chechik, M.: Why waste a perfectly good abstraction? In: Hermanns, H., Palsberg, J. (eds.) TACAS 2006. LNCS, vol. 3920, pp. 212–226. Springer, Heidelberg (2006)
13. Gurfinkel, A., Wei, O., Chechik, M.: YASM: a software model-checker for verification and refutation. In: Ball, T., Jones, R.B. (eds.) CAV 2006. LNCS, vol. 4144, pp. 170–174. Springer, Heidelberg (2006)
14. Holzmann, G.J.: The SPIN Model Checker - primer and reference manual. Addison-Wesley, Reading (2004)
15. Huth, M., Jagadeesan, R., Schmidt, D.A.: Modal transition systems: a foundation for three-valued program analysis. In: Sands, D. (ed.) ESOP 2001. LNCS, vol. 2028, pp. 155–169. Springer, Heidelberg (2001)
16. Konikowska, B., Penczek, W.: Reducing model checking from multi-valued CTL* to CTL*. In: Brim, L., Jančar, P., Křetínský, M., Kučera, A. (eds.) CONCUR 2002. LNCS, vol. 2421, pp. 226–239. Springer, Heidelberg (2002)
17. Seger, C.J.H., Bryant, R.E.: Formal verification by symbolic evaluation of partially-ordered trajectories. Formal Methods Sys. Des. 6(2), 147–189 (1995)

Comparing Semantics Under Strong Timing of Petri Nets

Irina Virbitskaite[1,2] and Dmitry Bushin[1(✉)]

[1] A.P. Ershov Institute of Informatics Systems,
SB RAS 6, Acad. Lavrentiev avenue, 630090 Novosibirsk, Russia
dima.bushin@gmail.com
[2] Novosibirsk State University, 2, Pirogov Avenue,
630090 Novosibirsk, Russia

Abstract. The intention of the note is towards a framework for developing, studying and comparing observational semantics in the setting of a real-time true concurrent model. In particular, we introduce trace and bisimulation equivalences based on interleaving, step and causal net semantics in the setting of Petri nets with strong timing, i.e. Petri nets whose transitions are labeled with time firing intervals, can fire only if their lower time bounds are attained, and are forced to fire when their upper time bounds are reached. We deal with the relationships between the equivalences showing the discriminating power of the approaches of the linear-time – branching-time and interleaving – partial order spectra. This allows studying in complete detail the timing behaviour in addition to the degrees of relative concurrency and nondeterminism of processes.

1 Introduction

In the core of every theory of systems lies a notion of equivalence between systems: it indicates which particular aspects of systems behaviors are considered to be observable. In concurrency theory, a variety of observational equivalences have been promoted, and the relationships between them have been quite well-understood.

In order to investigate the performance of systems (e.g. the maximal time used for the execution of certain activities and average waiting time for certain requests), many time extensions have been defined for a non-interleaving model of Petri nets. On the other hand, there are few mentions of a fusion of timing and partial order semantics, in the Petri net literature. In [6], processes of timed Petri nets (under the asap hypothesis) have been defined by an algebra of the so-called weighted pomsets. The paper [5] has provided and compared timed step sequence and timed process semantics for timed Petri nets. A method to compute all valid timings for a causal net process of a time Petri net has been put forward in [1]. Branching processes (unfoldings) of time Petri nets have been constructed in [4].

This work is supported in part by DFG-RFBR (project CAVER, grants BE 1267/14-1 and 14-01-91334).

© Springer-Verlag Berlin Heidelberg 2015
A. Voronkov and I. Virbitskaite (Eds.): PSI 2014, LNCS 8974, pp. 376–384, 2015.
DOI: 10.1007/978-3-662-46823-4_30

To the best of our knowledge, the incorporation of timing into equivalence notions on Petri nets is even less advanced. In this regard, the paper [2] is a welcome exception, where the testing approach has been extended to Petri nets with associating clocks to tokens and time intervals to arcs from places to transitions. Also, it is worth mentioning the paper [3] that compares different subclasses of timed Petri nets with strong timing semantics on the base of timed interleaving language and bisimulation equivalences.

The intention of the note is towards developing, studying and comparing trace and bisimulation equivalences based on interleaving, step, and partial order (causal net) semantics in the setting of Petri nets with strong timing (elementary net systems whose transitions are labeled with time firing intervals, can fire only if their lower time bounds are attained, and are forced to fire when their upper time bounds are reached).

2   Time Petri Nets

In this section, we define some terminology concerning time Petri nets which were introduced in [1] and extend elementary net systems with timing constraints (time intervals) on the firings of transitions.

The domain $\mathbb{T}$ of time values is the set of natural numbers. We denote by $[\tau_1, \tau_2]$ the closed interval between two time values $\tau_1, \tau_2 \in \mathbb{T}$. Infinity is allowed at the upper bounds of invervals. Let $Interv$ be the set of all such intervals. We use Act to denote an alphabet of actions.

Definition 1. A (labeled over Act) time Petri net *is a tuple* $\mathcal{TN} = ((P, T, F, M_0, L), D)$, *where* (P, T, F, M_0, L) *is a* Petri net *with a set P of places, a set T of transitions* $(P \cap T = \emptyset)$, *a flow relation* $F \subseteq (P \times T) \cup (T \times P)$, *an initial marking* $\emptyset \neq M_0 \subseteq P$, *a labeling function* $L : T \to Act$, *and* $D : T \to Interv$ *is a static timing function* associating with each transition a time interval.

For $x \in P \cup T$, let ${}^\bullet x = \{y \mid (y, x) \in F\}$ and $x^\bullet = \{y \mid (x, y) \in F\}$ be the *preset* and *postset* of x, respectively. For $X \subseteq P \cup T$, define ${}^\bullet X = \bigcup_{x \in X} {}^\bullet x$ and $X^\bullet = \bigcup_{x \in X} x^\bullet$. For a transition $t \in T$, the boundaries of the interval $D(t) \in Interv$ are called the earliest firing time Eft and latest firing time Lft of t.

A *marking* M of $\mathcal{TN}$ is any subset of P. A transition t is *enabled* at a marking M if ${}^\bullet t \subseteq M$ (all its input places have tokens in M), otherwise the transition is *disabled*. Let $En(M)$ be the set of transitions enabled at M. We call a non-empty subset $U \subseteq T$ a *step enabled at a marking* M, if $(\forall t \in U \diamond t \in En(M))$ and $(\forall t \neq t' \in U \diamond {}^\bullet t \cap {}^\bullet t' = \emptyset)$.

Consider the *behavior* of the time Petri net $\mathcal{TN}$. A *state* of $\mathcal{TN}$ is a triple (M, I, GT), where M is a marking, $I : En(M) \longrightarrow \mathbb{T}$ is a *dynamic timing function*, and $GT \in \mathbb{T}$ is a *global time moment*. The *initial state* of $\mathcal{TN}$ is a triple $S_0 = (M_0, I_0, GT_0)$, where M_0 is an initial marking, $I_0(t) = 0$, for all $t \in En(M_0)$, and $GT_0 = 0$.

A step $U \subseteq T$ enabled at a marking M is *fireable from a state* $S = (M, I, GT)$ *after a delay time* $\theta \in \mathbb{T}$ if $(\forall t \in U \diamond Eft(t) \leq I(t) + \theta)$ and $(\forall t' \in En(M) \diamond$

$I(t') + \theta \le Lft(t'))$. Let $Contact(S) = \{t \in U \mid U$ is a step fireable from a state $S = (M, I, GT)$ after some delay time $\theta \in \mathbb{T}$ and $(M \setminus {}^\bullet t) \cap t^\bullet \ne \emptyset)\}$.

The *firing* of a step U fireable from a state $S = (M, I, GT)$ after a delay time θ *leads* to the new state $S' = (M', I', GT')$ given as follows:

(i) $M' = (M \setminus {}^\bullet U) \cup U^\bullet$,

(ii) $\forall t' \in T \circ I'(t') = \begin{cases} I(t') + \theta, & \text{if } t' \in En(M \setminus {}^\bullet U), \\ 0, & \text{if } t' \in En(M') \setminus En(M \setminus {}^\bullet U), \\ \text{undefined}, & \text{otherwise}, \end{cases}$

(iii) $GT' = GT + \theta$.

In this case, we write $S \xrightarrow{(U, \theta)} S'$, and, moreover, $S \xrightarrow{(A, \theta)} S'$, if $A = L(U) = \sum_{t \in U} L(t)$. A finite or infinite sequence of the form: $S = S^0 \xrightarrow{(U_1, \theta_1)} S^1 \xrightarrow{(U_2, \theta_2)} S^2$ ..., is a *step firing sequence of* $\mathcal{TN}$ from the state S. Then, $(U_1, \theta_1)(U_2, \theta_2) \cdots$ is called a *step firing schedule of* $\mathcal{TN}$ *from* S. The sequence is an *interleaving firing schedule of* $\mathcal{TN}$ *from* S, if $|U_i| = 1$, for all $i \ge 1$. Define the *step (interleaving) language of* $\mathcal{TN}$ as follows: $\mathcal{L}_{s(i)}(\mathcal{TN}) = \{(A_1, \theta_1) \cdots (A_k, \theta_k) \mid (U_1, \theta_1) \cdots (U_k, \theta_k)$ is a step (interleaving) firing schedule of $\mathcal{TN}$ from the initial state S_0, and $A_k = L(U_k)$ $(k \ge 0)\}$.

A state S of $\mathcal{TN}$ is *reachable* if it appears in some step firing sequence of $\mathcal{TN}$ from the initial state S_0. Let $RS(\mathcal{TN})$ denote the set of all reachable states of $\mathcal{TN}$. We call $\mathcal{TN}$ *T-restricted* if ${}^\bullet t \ne \emptyset \ne t^\bullet$ for all transitions $t \in T$; *contact-free* if $Contact(S) = \emptyset$ for all $S \in RS(\mathcal{TN})$; *time-progressive* if for every infinite step firing schedule $(U_1, \theta_1)(U_2, \theta_2)(U_3, \theta_3) \cdots$ of $\mathcal{TN}$ from some $S \in RS(\mathcal{TN})$, the series $\theta_1 + \theta_2 + \theta_3 + \cdots$ diverges. In what follows, we will consider only T-restricted, contact-free and time-progressive time Petri nets.

Example 1. Figure 1 shows a time Petri net $\mathcal{TN}$. Both $\sigma = (\{t_1, t_3\}, 3)$ and $\sigma' = (\{t_1, t_3\}, 3)(\{t_2\}, 2)(\{t_1, t_3\}, 2)(\{t_4, t_5\}, 2)$ are step firing schedules of $\mathcal{TN}$ from $S_0 = (M_0, I_0, GT_0)$, where $M_0 = \{p_1, p_2\}$, $I_0(t) = \begin{cases} 0, & \text{if } t \in \{t_1, t_3\}, \\ \text{undefined}, & \text{otherwise}, \end{cases}$ and $GT_0 = 0$. Furthermore, $\hat{\sigma} = (\{t_2\}, 2)(\{t_1, t_3\}, 2)(\{t_4, t_5\}, 2)$ is a step firing schedule of $\mathcal{TN}$ from $S = (M, I, GT)$, where $M = \{p_3, p_4\}$, $GT = 3$, and

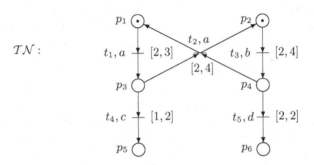

Fig. 1. An example of a time Petri net

$$I(t) = \begin{cases} 0, & \text{if } t \in \{t_2, t_4, t_5\} \\ undefined, & \text{otherwise.} \end{cases}$$ It is easy to see that $\mathcal{TN}$ is really T-restricted, contact-free and time-progressive.

3 Time Process Semantics

First, consider definitions related to time partial orders.

Definition 2. *A (labeled over Act) time partial order is a tuple $\eta = (X, \prec, \lambda, \tau)$ consisting of a set X; a transitive, irreflexive relation $\prec$; a labeling function $\lambda : X \to Act$; and a timing function $\tau : X \to \mathbb{T}$ such that $e \prec e' \Rightarrow \tau(e) \leq \tau(e')$. As usual, we write $x \preceq y$ for $x \prec y$ or $x = y$. Often $\prec$ is called a strict partial order, while $\preceq$ is a partial order, i.e. a reflexive, antisymmetric and transitive relation.*

Time partial order sets over Act, $\eta = (X, \prec, \lambda, \tau)$ and $\eta' = (X', \prec', \lambda', \tau')$, are *isomorphic* (denoted $\eta \sim \eta'$) iff there is a bijective mapping $\beta : X \to X'$ such that (i) $x \prec y \iff \beta(x) \prec' \beta(y)$, for all $x, y \in X$; (ii) $\lambda(x) = \lambda'(\beta(x))$ and $\tau(x) = \tau'(\beta(x))$, for all $x \in X$. The isomorphic class of a time partial order over Act, η, is called a *time pomset over Act* and denoted as $pom(\eta)$.

Next, define the concept of a time causal net.

Definition 3. *A (labeled over Act) time causal net is a finitary, acyclic net $TN = (B, E, G, l, \tau)$ with a set B of conditions, a set E of events, a flow relation $G \subseteq (B \times E) \cup (E \times B)$ such that $\{e \mid (e, b) \in G\} = \{e \mid (b, e) \in G\} = E$, and, for any $b \in B$, $|\{e \mid (e, b) \in G\}| = |\{e \mid (b, e) \in G\}| \leq 1$, a labeling function $l : E \to Act$, and a time function $\tau : E \to \mathbb{T}$ such that $e \, G^+ \, e' \Rightarrow \tau(e) \leq \tau(e')$. Let $\tau(TN) = \sup\{\tau(e) \mid e \in E\}$.*

Time causal nets over Act, $TN = (B, E, G, l, \tau)$ and $TN' = (B', E', G', l', \tau')$, are *isomorphic* (denoted $TN \simeq TN'$) iff there exists a bijective mapping $\beta : B \cup E \to B' \cup E'$ such that (i) $\beta(B) = B'$ and $\beta(E) = E'$; (ii) $x \, G \, y \iff \beta(x) \, G' \, \beta(y)$, for all $x, y \in B \cup E$; (iii) $l(e) = l'(\beta(e))$ and $\tau(e) = \tau'(\beta(e))$, for all $e \in E$.

Specify additional notions and notations for a time causal net TN. Let ${}^\bullet x = \{y \mid (y, x) \in G\}$ and $x^\bullet = \{y \mid (x, y) \in G\}$, for $x \in B \cup E$; ${}^\bullet X = \bigcup_{x \in X} {}^\bullet x$ and $X^\bullet = \bigcup_{x \in X} x^\bullet$, for $X \subseteq B \cup E$; and ${}^\bullet TN = \{b \in B \mid {}^\bullet b = \emptyset\}$, $TN^\bullet = \{b \in B \mid b^\bullet = \emptyset\}$. Also, $\prec = G^+$ and $\preceq = G^*$. For a downward-closed (w.r.t. $\preceq$) subset $E' \subseteq E$, define the set $Cut(E') = (E'^\bullet \cup {}^\bullet TN) \setminus {}^\bullet E'$. A downward-closed subset $E' \subseteq E$ is called *timely sound* if $\tau(e') \leq \tau(e)$, for all $e' \in E'$ and $e \in E \setminus E'$. Clearly, $\eta(TN) = (E, \prec \cap (E \times E), l, \tau)$ is a time partial order. For $x, x' \in B \cup E$, $x \smile x' \iff \neg((x \prec x') \vee (x' \prec x) \vee (x = x'))$ *(concurrency)*. A subset $\emptyset \neq E' \subseteq E$ is a *step* of TN iff $e \smile e'$ and $\tau(e) = \tau(e')$, for all $e, e' \in E'$. In this case, let $\tau(E') = \tau(e)$ for some $e \in E'$. An *s-linearization* of a time causal net TN is a finite or infinite sequence $\rho = V_1 V_2 \ldots$ of steps of TN, such that every event of TN is included in the sequence exactly once, and both causal and time orders are preserved: $(e_i \prec e_j \vee \tau(e_i) < \tau(e_j)) \Rightarrow i < j$, for all $e_i \in V_i$

and $e_j \in V_j$ $(i, j \geq 1)$. An s-linearization ρ of TN is called an i-linearization of TN, if $|V_i| = 1$, for all $i \geq 1$. For an s-linearization $\rho = V_1 V_2 \ldots$ of TN, define $E_\rho^k = \bigcup_{1 \leq i \leq k} V_i$ $(k \geq 0)$. Clearly, E_ρ^k is a downward-closed subset of E.

Given time causal nets $TN = (B, E, G, l, \tau)$, $\widehat{TN} = (\widehat{B}, \widehat{E}, \widehat{G}, \widehat{l}, \widehat{\tau})$ and $TN' = (B', E', G', l', \tau')$, TN is a *prefix of* TN' (denoted $TN \longrightarrow TN'$) if $B \subseteq B'$, E is a finite, downward-closed and timely sound subset of E', $G = G' \cap (\times E \cup E \times B)$, $l = l' \mid_E$, and $\tau = \tau' \mid_E$; $\widehat{TN}$ is a *suffix of* TN' w.r.t. TN if $\widehat{E} = E' \setminus E$, $\widehat{B} = B' \setminus B \cup TN^\bullet$, $\widehat{G} = G' \cap (\widehat{B} \times \widehat{E} \cup \widehat{E} \times \widehat{B})$, $\widehat{l} = l' \mid_{\widehat{E}}$, and $\widehat{\tau} = \tau' \mid_{\widehat{E}}$. We write $TN \xrightarrow{\widehat{TN}} TN'$ iff $TN \longrightarrow TN'$ and $\widehat{TN}$ is a suffix of TN' w.r.t. TN.

We are now ready to define the notion of a time process of $\mathcal{TN}$ enabled at some marking.

Definition 4. *Given a time Petri net* $\mathcal{TN} = (P, T, F, M_0, L, D)$ *with its marking* M*, a pair* $\pi = (TN, \varphi)$ *with a time causal net* $TN = (B, E, G, l, \tau)$ *and a mapping* $\varphi : B \cup E \to P \cup T$ *is a time process of* $\mathcal{TN}$ *enabled at* M *iff the following conditions hold:*

- $\varphi(B) \subseteq P$, $\varphi(E) \subseteq T$,
- *the restriction of* φ *to* $^\bullet e$ *is a bijection between* $^\bullet e$ *and* $^\bullet \varphi(e)$ *and the restriction of* φ *to* $e^\bullet$ *is a bijection between* $e^\bullet$ *and* $\varphi(e)^\bullet$*, for all* $e \in E$*,*
- *the restriction of* φ *to* $^\bullet TN$ *is a bijection between* $^\bullet TN$ *and* M*,*
- $l(e) = L(\varphi(e))$*, for all* $e \in E$*.*

We use $\mathcal{EN}(\mathcal{TN})$ $(\mathcal{EN}(\mathcal{TN}, M))$ to denote the set of time processes of $\mathcal{TN}$ enabled at the initial marking M_0 (a marking M).

Given a time process $\pi = (TN, \varphi) \in \mathcal{EN}(\mathcal{TN}, M)$, a state $S = (M, I, GT)$ of $\mathcal{TN}$, and a subset $B' \subseteq B_{TN}$, the latest global time moment when tokens appear in all input places of the transition $t \in En(\varphi(B'))$ is defined as follows:

$$\mathbf{TOE}_{\pi,S}(B', t) = \max \left(\{\tau_{TN}(^\bullet b) \mid b \in B'_{[t]} \setminus {}^\bullet TN\} \cup \{\overline{GT}\} \right),$$

where $B'_{[t]} = \{b \in B' \mid \varphi_{TN}(b) \in {}^\bullet t\}$, $\overline{GT} = GT - I(t)$, if $B'_{[t]} \subseteq {}^\bullet TN$, and $\overline{GT} = GT$, otherwise. Notice that the above is an extension of the definition of $\mathbf{TOE}(\cdot, \cdot)$ from [1] to the case of time processes of $\mathcal{TN}$ enabled at an arbitrary marking and not only at the initial one.

Definition 5. *A time process* $\pi = (TN, \varphi) \in \mathcal{EN}(\mathcal{TN}, M)$ *is fireable from a state* S *iff for all* $e \in E$ *it holds:*

- (i) $\tau(e) \geq GT$,
- (ii) $\tau(e) \geq \mathbf{TOE}_{\pi,S}(^\bullet e, \varphi(e)) + Eft(\varphi(e))$,
- (iii) $\forall t \in En(\varphi(C_e)) \diamond \tau(e) \leq \mathbf{TOE}_{\pi,S}(C_e, t) + Lft(t)$,
  where $C_e = Cut(Earlier(e) = \{e' \in E \mid \tau(e') < \tau(e)\})$.

The time process $\pi_0 = (TN_0 = (B_0, \emptyset, \emptyset, \emptyset, \emptyset), \varphi_0)$ of $\mathcal{TN}$ fireable from the initial state is called the *initial time process* of $\mathcal{TN}$. We use $\mathcal{FI}(\mathcal{TN})$

$(\mathcal{FI}(\mathcal{TN}, S))$ to denote the set of time processes of $\mathcal{TN}$ fireable from the initial state (a state $S \in RS(\mathcal{TN})$). The *pomset language of* $\mathcal{TN}$ is given by $\mathcal{L}_{pom}(\mathcal{TN}) = \{pom(\eta(TN)) \mid \pi = (TN, \varphi) \in \mathcal{FI}(\mathcal{TN})\}$.

We now intend to realize for a time Petri net the relationships between its firing schedules from reachable states and its time processes fireable from the states. For $\pi = (TN, \varphi) \in \mathcal{FI}(\mathcal{TN}, S)$, define the function $FS_{\pi,S}$ which maps any s-linearization $\rho = V_1 V_2 \ldots$ of TN to the sequence of the form: $FS_{\pi,S}(\rho) = (\varphi(V_1), \tau(V_1) - GT)\ (\varphi(V_2), \tau(V_2) - \tau(V_1))\ \ldots$.

Lemma 1.   – *Given* $\pi = (TN, \varphi) \in \mathcal{FI}(\mathcal{TN}, S = (M, I, GT))$ *and an* $s(i)$-*linearization* $\rho = V_1 V_2 \ldots$ *of* TN, $FS_{\pi,S}(\rho)$ *is a step (interleaving) firing schedule of* $\mathcal{TN}$ *from the state* S.
– *For any step (interleaving) firing schedule* σ *of* $\mathcal{TN}$ *from a state* $S \in RS(\mathcal{TN})$, *there is a unique (up to an isomorphism) time process* $\pi = (TN, \varphi) \in \mathcal{FI}(\mathcal{TN}, S)$ *such that* $FS_{\pi,S}(\rho) = \sigma$, *where* ρ *is an* $s(i)$-*linearization of* TN.

Notice that the items of the Lemma are extensions of Theorems 19 and 21 from [1] to the cases of s-linearizations on time processes of $\mathcal{TN}$ fireable from arbitrary reachable states and step firing schedules of $\mathcal{TN}$ from the states.

For $\pi = (TN, \varphi), \pi' = (TN', \varphi') \in \mathcal{FI}(\mathcal{TN})$, we write $\pi \xrightarrow{\widehat{\pi} = (\widehat{TN}, \widehat{\varphi})} \pi'$ iff $TN \xrightarrow{\overline{TN}} TN'$, $\varphi = \varphi'|_{B \cup E}$, and $\widehat{\varphi} = \varphi'|_{\widehat{B} \cup \widehat{E}}$.

Theorem 1. *If* $\pi = (TN, \varphi), \pi' = (TN', \varphi') \in \mathcal{FI}(\mathcal{TN})$ *such that* $\pi \xrightarrow{\widehat{\pi}} \pi'$, *then* $\widehat{\pi} = (\widehat{TN}, \widehat{\varphi}) \in \mathcal{FI}(\mathcal{TN}, S = (M, I, GT))$, *where* $M = \varphi(TN^{\bullet})$, $I(t) = \begin{cases} \tau(TN) - \mathbf{TOE}_{\pi,S_0}(TN^{\bullet}, t), & \text{if } t \in En(M) \\ \text{undefined}, & \text{otherwise}, \end{cases}$ *and* $GT = \tau(TN)$.

From now on, we write $\pi \xrightarrow{u} \pi'$ iff $\pi \xrightarrow{\widehat{\pi}} \pi'$ and $u = pom(\eta(\widehat{TN}))$.

Example 2. The time causal net $TN' = (B', E', G', l', \tau')$ is depicted in Fig. 2, where the net elements are accompanied by their names, and the values of the functions l' and τ' are indicated nearby the events. Define the time causal nets $TN = (B, E, G, l, \tau)$, with $B = \{b_1, \ldots, b_4\}$, $E = \{e_1, e_3\}$, $G = G' \cap (B \times E \cup E \times B)\}$, $l = l'|_E$, $\tau = \tau'|_E$, and $\widehat{TN} = (\widehat{B}, \widehat{E}, \widehat{G}, \widehat{l}, \widehat{\tau})$, with $\widehat{B} = B' \setminus B \cup \{b_3, b_4\}$, $\widehat{E} = E' \setminus E$, $\widehat{G} = G' \cap (\widehat{B} \times \widehat{E} \cup \widehat{E} \times \widehat{B})$, $\widehat{l} = l'|_{\widehat{E}}$, $\widehat{\tau} = \tau'|_{\widehat{E}}$.

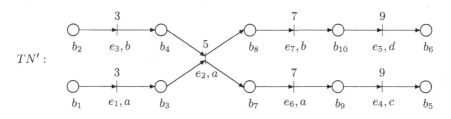

Fig. 2. An example of a time causal net

It is easy to see that TN is a prefix of TN', $\widehat{TN}$ is a suffix of TN' w.r.t. TN, and, moreover, $TN \xrightarrow{\widehat{TN}} TN'$.

Define a mapping φ' from the time causal net TN' to the time Petri net $\mathcal{TN}$ (see Fig. 1) as follows: $\varphi'(b_i) = p_i$ $(1 \leq i \leq 6)$, $\varphi'(b_i) = p_{i-6}$ $(7 \leq i \leq 10)$, and $\varphi'(e_i) = t_i$ $(1 \leq i \leq 5)$, $\varphi'(e_6) = t_1$, $\varphi'(e_7) = t_3$. Next, for the time causal nets TN and $\widehat{TN}$, set $\varphi = \varphi' \mid_{E \cup B}$ and $\widehat{\varphi} = \varphi' \mid_{\widehat{E} \cup \widehat{B}}$, respectively. Obviously, $\pi' = (TN', \varphi')$ and $\pi = (TN, \varphi)$ are time processes of $\mathcal{TN}$ enabled at M_0.

Take $S = (M, I, GT)$ as specified in Example 1, $\widetilde{B} = \{b_3, b_4\}$, and $t_2 \in En(\varphi'(\widetilde{B}))$. Calculate $\mathbf{TOE}_{\pi', S}(\widetilde{B}, t_2) = \max\left(\{\tau_{TN'}(^\bullet b) \mid b \in \widetilde{B}_{[t_2]} \setminus {}^\bullet TN'\} \cup \{\overline{GT}\}\right) = \max\left(\{\tau'(e_1) = 3, \tau'(e_3) = 3\} \cup \{3\}\right) = 3$.

It is not difficult to check that $\pi' = (TN', \varphi')$, $\pi = (TN, \varphi) \in \mathcal{FI}(\mathcal{TN})$. For the s-linearization $\rho = \{e_1, e_3\} \{e_2\} \{e_6, e_7\} \{e_4, e_5\}$ of TN', we get $FS_{\pi', S_0}(\rho) = \sigma' = (\{t_1, t_3\}, 3) (\{t_2\}, 2) (\{t_1, t_3\}, 2) (\{t_4, t_5\}, 2)$ (see Example 1), in support of Lemma 1. Furthermore, we can write $\pi \xrightarrow{\widehat{\pi} = (\widehat{TN}, \widehat{\varphi})} \pi'$ because $TN \xrightarrow{\widehat{TN}} TN'$, $\varphi = \varphi' \mid_{E \cup B}$ and $\widehat{\varphi} = \varphi' \mid_{\widehat{E} \cup \widehat{B}}$. Then, $\widehat{\pi} \in \mathcal{FI}(\mathcal{TN}, S)$, due to Theorem 1.

4   Hierarchy of Equivalences

We start with defining interleaving, step and partial order equivalences for time Petri nets.

Definition 6. *Time Petri nets $\mathcal{TN}$ and $\mathcal{TN}'$ labeled over Act are:*

- *interleaving (step) trace equivalent (denoted $\mathcal{TN} \equiv_{i(s)} \mathcal{TN}'$) iff $\mathcal{L}_{i(s)}(\mathcal{TN}) = \mathcal{L}_{i(s)}(\mathcal{TN}')$,*
- *interleaving (step) bisimilar (denoted $\mathcal{TN} \underset{i(s)}{\leftrightarrow} \mathcal{TN}'$) iff there is a relation $R \subseteq RS(\mathcal{TN}) \times RS(\mathcal{TN}')$ such that $(S_0, S_0') \in R$ (S_0 and S_0' are the initial states of $\mathcal{TN}$ and $\mathcal{TN}'$, respectively) and for all $(S, S') \in R$ it holds:*
  - *if $S \xrightarrow{\omega} S_1$ with $\omega \in (Act \times \mathbb{T})^*$ (with $\omega \in (\mathbb{N}^{Act} \times \mathbb{T})^*$) in $\mathcal{TN}$, then $S' \xrightarrow{\omega} S_1'$ in $\mathcal{TN}'$ and $(S_1, S_1') \in R$,*
  - *and vice versa,*
- *pom-trace equivalent (denoted $\mathcal{TN} \equiv_{pom} \mathcal{TN}'$) iff $\mathcal{L}_{pom}(\mathcal{TN}) = \mathcal{L}_{pom}(\mathcal{TN}')$,*
- *pom-bisimulation equivalent (denoted $\mathcal{TN} \underset{pom}{\leftrightarrow} \mathcal{TN}'$) if there is a relation $R \subseteq \mathcal{FI}(\mathcal{TN}) \times \mathcal{FI}(\mathcal{TN}')$ such that $(\pi_0, \pi_0') \in R$ (π_0 and π_0' are the initial time processes of $\mathcal{TN}$ and $\mathcal{TN}'$, respectively) and for all $(\pi, \pi') \in R$ it holds:*
  - *if $\pi \xrightarrow{u} \pi_1$ (u is a time pomset over Act) in $\mathcal{TN}$, then $\pi' \xrightarrow{u} \pi_1'$ in $\mathcal{TN}'$ and $(\pi_1, \pi_1') \in R$,*
  - *and vice versa.*

Finally, we state the relationships between the equivalences.

Theorem 2. *Let $\leftrightarrow, \rightleftharpoons \in \{\equiv, \leftrightarrow\}$ and $\star, * \in \{i, s, pom\}$. Then,*

$$\mathcal{TN} \leftrightarrow_\star \mathcal{TN}' \Rightarrow \mathcal{TN} \rightleftharpoons_* \mathcal{TN}'$$

iff there is a directed path from $\leftrightarrow_\star$ to $\rightleftharpoons_*$ in Fig. 1.

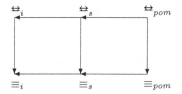

Fig. 3. A hierarchy of equivalences

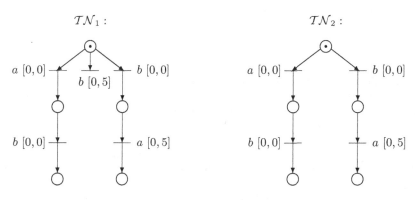

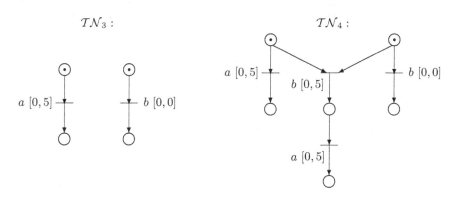

Fig. 4. Examples of equivalent and non-equivalent time Petri nets

Proof. '⇐' All the implications in Fig. 1 follow from the Definitions, Lemma and Theorems given above.

'⇒' We now demonstrate that it is impossible to draw any arrow from one equivalence to the other such that there is no directed path from the first equivalence to the second one in the graph in Fig. 3. For this purpose, we contemplate the time Petri nets depicted in Fig. 4. It is easy to see that $\mathcal{TN}_1$ and $\mathcal{TN}_2$ are $\equiv_{pom}$-equivalent but not $\leftrightarrow_i$-equivalent because in $\mathcal{TN}_2$, for example, the execution of an action a after time moment 5 is always possible from the state reachable by the execution of an action b after time moment 0 but it is not the case in $\mathcal{TN}_1$. Next, $\mathcal{TN}_2$ and $\mathcal{TN}_3$ are $\underleftrightarrow{}_i$-equivalent but not $\equiv_s$-equivalent because, for example, in $\mathcal{TN}_3$ the execution of the step consisting of an action a and b from the initial state after time moment 0 is possible but it is not the case in $\mathcal{TN}_2$. Finally, $\mathcal{TN}_3$ and $\mathcal{TN}_4$ are $\underleftrightarrow{}_s$-equivalent but not $\equiv_{pom}$-equivalent because, for example, there is a time process of $\mathcal{TN}_4$ fireable from the initial state where the execution of an action b at time moment 0 causally precedes the execution of an action a at time moment 5 but it is not the case in $\mathcal{TN}_3$.

References

1. Aura, T., Lilius, J.: Time processes for time Petri nets. In: Azéma, P., Balbo, G. (eds.) ICATPN 1997. LNCS, vol. 1248, pp. 136–155. Springer, Heidelberg (1997)
2. Bihler, E., Vogler, W.: Timed Petri nets: efficiency of asynchronous systems. In: Bernardo, M., Corradini, F. (eds.) SFM-RT 2004. LNCS, vol. 3185, pp. 25–58. Springer, Heidelberg (2004)
3. Boyer, M., Vernadat, R.: Language and bisimulation relations between subclasses of timed Petri nets with strong timing semantics. Technical report No. 146, LAAS (2000)
4. Chatain, T., Jard, C.: Time supervision of concurrent systems using symbolic unfoldings of time Petri nets. In: Pettersson, P., Yi, W. (eds.) FORMATS 2005. LNCS, vol. 3829, pp. 196–210. Springer, Heidelberg (2005)
5. Valvero, V., De Frutos, D., Cuartero, F.: Timed processes of timed Petri nets. In: DeMichelis, G., Díaz, M. (eds.) ICATPN 1995. LNCS, vol. 935, pp. 490–509. Springer, Heidelberg (1995)
6. Winkowski, J.: Algebras of processes of timed Petri nets. In: Jonsson, B., Parrow, J. (eds.) CONCUR 1994. LNCS, vol. 836, pp. 194–209. Springer, Heidelberg (1994)

Probabilistic Formal Concepts with Negation

E.E. Vityaev[1,2]($\boxtimes$) and V.V. Martinovich[2]

[1] Sobolev Institute of Mathematics, Novosibirsk, Russia
evgenii.vityaev@math.nsc.ru
[2] Novosibirsk State University, Novosibirsk, Russia
vilco@ya.ru

Abstract. The probabilistic generalization of formal concept analysis, as well as it's comparison to standard formal analysis is presented. Construction is resistant to noise in the data and give one an opportunity to consider contexts with negation (object-attribute relation which allows both attribute presence and it's absence). This generalization is obtained from the notion of formal concepts with its definition as fixed points of implications, when implications, possibly with negations, are replaced by probabilistic laws. We prove such fixed points (based on the probabilistic implications) to be consistent and wherefore determine correct probabilistic formal concepts. In the end, the demonstration for the probabilistic formal concepts formation is given together with noise resistance example.

Keywords: Formal concept analysis · Probability · Data mining · Association rules · Noise

1 Introduction

In the formal concept analysis (FCA) [1,2], formal concepts are used as classification units. The main task of FCA consists in construction of a complete lattice of formal concepts. But FCA induces a potentially dreadful combinatorial complexity and the structures obtained even from small-sized datasets can become prohibitively huge. Noise in data constitutes a primary factor of complication as it favors the existence of many similar but distinct concepts, which may excessively inflate the lattice with superfluous information that significantly impaired readability. Hence, the translation of empirical data into clean and relatively readable structures remains the most important problem. There are some works where concepts formation considered in the presence of noise [3,4]. But all these papers base on the complete lattice of formal concepts.

In this paper we consider the problem: is it possible to construct the clean and relatively readable structure of idealized or refined concepts directly without the construction of complete lattice of formal concepts. If we consider the complete lattice of formal concepts as a "photo" of data, then the structure of "idealized" concepts may be considered as a "picture" of data.

© Springer-Verlag Berlin Heidelberg 2015
A. Voronkov and I. Virbitskaite (Eds.): PSI 2014, LNCS 8974, pp. 385–399, 2015.
DOI: 10.1007/978-3-662-46823-4_31

For solution of this problem we introduce the probabilistic generalization of formal concepts. The first step was made in [5,6], where the probabilistic generalization of the formal concepts without negations was developed. Here we introduce the probabilistic generalization of the formal concepts with negations for many-valued contexts. For that purpose we utilize, as in [5,6], the definition of a formal concept in terms of fix-points of implications. Then we define a probability measure and generalize implications into probabilistic implications, so that they minimize the intent of concepts and eliminate random attributes. After that we define a probabilistic formal concept as a fix-point of probabilistic implications. For that purpose we prove the consistency of these fixed points. Resulting fixed points don't directly depend on data and are defined in pure probabilistic terms and thus produce a "picture" of data. At the end of paper the results of the experiment that illustrate the formation of probabilistic formal concepts are presented.

2   Formal Concept Analysis

Here we give a short review of the formal concept analysis. For details we refer to [1,2]. FCA examines the set of objects G, which have properties from a fixed set M. We say that "the object g has the property m" by using a relation $I \subseteq G \times M$.

Definition 1. *Formal context is a triple (G, M, I), where G and M are sets of the arbitrary nature and $I \subseteq G \times M$ is a binary relation.*

On the formal context (or simply context) we define the operation $'$ as follows:

Definition 2. $A \subseteq G$, $B \subseteq M$, $g \in G$. *Then:*

1. $A' = \{m \in M \mid \forall g \in A, (g, m) \in I\}$
2. $B' = \{g \in G \mid \forall m \in B, (g, m) \in I\}$
3. $g' = \{g\}' = \{m \in M \mid (g, m) \in I\}$

Definition 3. *Pair (A, B) is called a formal concept, if B expresses all common features for objects in A, and A - objects that have all attributes from B. In other words, $A' = B$ and $B' = A$.*

Here and further we delve a bit into the theory of FCA [1,2,7], but only just as much as it is necessary for the design of construction, proposed in the article.

Lemma 1. *Suppose $A_1 \subseteq A_2 \subseteq G, B_1 \subseteq B_2 \subseteq M$. Then*

1. $A_2' \subseteq A_1', B_2' \subseteq B_1'$
2. $A \subseteq A'', B \subseteq B''$
3. (A, B) - *concept* $\Rightarrow B'' = B$.

In fact, usually objects are not formed from attributes in a completely arbitrary manner. Attributes form numerous relationships, which can be described in terms of implications. In definitions below B, C are subsets of attributes $\subseteq M$.

Definition 4. *Implication is a pair (B, C) which we write as $B \rightarrow C$. Implication $B \rightarrow C$ is true on $K = (G, M, I)$, if $\forall g \in G(B \nsubseteq g'$ or $C \subseteq g')$. The set of all true implications will be denoted as $Imp(K)$.*

Definition 5. *Implication $B \rightarrow C$ is called a non-trivial on K, if $C \nsubseteq B$ and $B' \neq \varnothing$. The set of all non-trivial truth implications on K we denote as $ntImp(K)$.*

Definition 6. *For any set of implications L we can construct the operator of direct inference f_L that add conclusions of all implications to the set-operand*

$$f_L(X) = X \cup \{C \mid B \subseteq X, \; B \rightarrow C \in ntImp(K)\}$$

Successively applying the operator of direct inference to any set X, we are gradually approaching it's closure [1,6].

Definition 7. *Operator cl_L, closing the set X relative to the operator of direct inference is $cl_L(X) = f_L^\infty(X)$.*

Theorem 1. *For any set $B \subseteq M$ the following is accomplished [2]:*

1. $f_{Imp(K)}(B) = B \Leftrightarrow B'' = B$;
2. *If $B' \neq \varnothing$, then $f_{ntImp(K)}(B) = B \Leftrightarrow B'' = B$.*

3   Many-Valued Contexts. Formulae on Binary Contexts

Definitions of the previous section present in a set-theoretical notions about attributes and objects. In variety of practical problems this hardly limits the space of possible models and reality interpretations, and sometimes as well - results [6,8]. This is a case for combinations of attributes and reasoning in terms of implications [8].

There are several different approaches to extend the I relation. Some classic examples can be found in [7,8]. In this chapter we enrich contexts, providing for each pair (g, m) the degree of belonging the attribute to the object.

We extend context I relation with value-dependent component. Let each attribute m has its own domain V_m. To describe the degree of belonging the attribute to object we need to know the value $v \in V_m$ of the attribute m on object g. For such value we assume that $(g, m, v) \in I$.

Definition 8. *Let G - set of objects and M - set of attributes, and each attribute has a set of possible attribute values V_m. Many-valued context K is a triple*

$$(G, M, \{I_m : G \rightarrow V_m \mid m \in M\})$$

In fact $I_m(g)$ maps the object g to value of the attribute m on g. It is not difficult to envision how the many-valued contexts and ordinary contexts are connected. Each attribute with its specific value can be considered as a new independent attribute. That is, for each attribute m, consider the set of pairs (m, v) where $m \in M$ and $v \in V_m$. Relation of the object g to take quality v on m attribute can now be described as $(g, (m, v)) \in I$.

Definition 9. *As a nominally scaled context of $K = (G, M, \{I_m\})$ we call $K^* = (G, M^*, \cup I_m^*)$, where $M^* = \{(m, v) \mid m \in M, v \in V_m\}$, and $I_m^* = \{(g, (m, v)) \mid I_m(g) = v\}$. For brevity, we say that $g \in G$ has the attribute m_v, if $I_m(g) = v$ or, equivalently, $(m, v) \in g'$ within the K^*.*

All constructions naturally transeferred to the nominally scaled K^*, as well as statements and theorems, which are presented in classic analysis of formal concepts. Particularly we can talk about formal concepts, defined on many-valued contexts. It is enough to replace occurrences of m by m_v in the relevant cases. Further referring to the classic's structures on K, we mean exactly the same constructions relative to K^*. For example,

Definition 10. *Formal concept on many-valued context K is a pair (A, B), where $A \subseteq G$, $B \subseteq M^*$, such that (A, B) - formal concept for K^*.*

It is natural to consider the proposed structure in the simplest case. In this case, each attribute we interpret in the form of predicate, identifying the a value of 1 with presence of corresponding attribute and 0 - with its absence.

Definition 11. *Binary context is a many-valued context, where $\forall m(V_m = \{0, 1\})$. Here and further m and $\overline{m}$ stay for $(m, 1)$ and $(m, 0)$ respectively.*

Our immediate task is to build on an arbitrary binary context of a formal system based on the first-order logic.

Definition 12. *For a binary context $K = (G, M)$ define a signature $\sigma = (R, F, \rho)$:*

1. *Set of predicates R - precisely the set of all I_m, stating the presence of the corresponding attribute or its negation;*
2. *Empty set of functional symbols $F = \varnothing$ (and so does ρ);*

All notions, such as atom, term, letter, formula and so on, are determined in a classical manner of formal systems. Formula of defined signature operates with logical connectives $\&, \vee, \rightarrow, \neg$ and predicates. We denote the resulting sets of atoms, letters, formulae and sentences as $At(K)$, $Lit(K)$, $For(K)$, $Sen(K)$, respectively.

Basic set $\mathcal{D} = \{g\}$ together with the predicates forms a model, futher labelled with K_g. The fact of truth of the formula Φ on the model of an object g we denote as follows: $g \vDash \Phi \Leftrightarrow K_g \vDash \Phi$. $G_\Phi \subseteq G = \{g \in G \mid g \vDash \Phi\}$ is called the support for Φ. If $G_\Phi = G$, then Φ - contextual tautology.

Lemma 2. *Note that $G_{\neg\Phi} = G \setminus G_\Phi$, $G_{\Phi\&\Psi} = G_\Phi \cap G_\Psi$, $G_{\Phi\vee\Psi} = G_\Phi \cup G_\Psi$.*

4   Probability and Rules on the Context

Now we need the definition of probability on binary context.

Definition 13. *Consider probability measure μ on the set G in the Kolmogorov meaning, so G can be interpreted as a set of elementary events. Let us introduce the contextual probability measure:*

$$\nu : For(K) \to [0,1], \nu(\Phi) = \mu(G_\Phi) = \mu(\{g \mid g \vDash \Phi\})$$

Definition 14. *By statistically insignificant objects (subsets) we call $g \in G$ ($A \subset G$) such that $\mu(g) = 0$ ($\mu(A) = 0$). Formula Φ is called a ν-consistent, if $\nu(\Phi) > 0$. Formula Φ is called an almost tautology, if $\nu(\Phi) = 1$.*

Proposition 1. *Context measure ν has the following properties:*

1. *If Φ - is a classical tautology, then Φ – contextual tautology, $\nu(\Phi) = 1$;*
2. *If $\neg(\Phi\&\Psi)$ is almost a tautology on K, then $\nu(\Phi \vee \Psi) = \nu(\Phi) + \nu(\Psi)$;*
3. *$\nu(\Phi\&\Psi) \leq \nu(\Phi)$.*

■ 1. Φ - is generally valid, so it is true on any model. In particular, $\forall g \in G(K_g \vDash \Phi)$, so $\Vdash \Phi$. Therefore $\nu(\Phi) = \mu(\{g \mid g \vDash \Phi\}) = \mu(G) = 1$.

2. Remember that $\nu(\Phi \vee \Psi) = \mu(G_{\Phi\vee\Psi}) = \mu(G_\Phi \cup G_\Psi)$. Inclusion-exclusion principle asserts $\mu(G_\Phi \cup G_\Psi) = \mu(G_\Phi) + \mu(G_\Psi) - \mu(G_\Phi \cap G_\Psi)$. The last one is zero due to the fact of $\neg(\Phi\&\Psi)$ is almost a tautology: $\mu(G_\Phi \cap G_\Psi) = \mu(G_{\Phi\&\Psi}) = \nu(\Phi\&\Psi) = 0$. At last, $\nu(\Phi \vee \Psi) = \mu(G_\Phi) + \mu(G_\Psi) = \nu(\Phi) + \nu(\Psi)$.

3. $G_{\Phi\&\Psi} = G_\Phi \cap G_\Psi \subseteq G_\Phi$; due to the axioms of measure: $\nu(\Phi\&\Psi) = \mu(G_{\Phi\&\Psi}) \leq \mu(G_\Phi) = \nu(\Phi)$. $\square$

In this section, we always assume that $L = Lit(K)$, K - binary context and ν - contextual measure on it. We follow the way proposed in [9–11].

Definition 15. *For the set of letters $M \subseteq L$ we construct the composition: $\&M = \underset{P \in M}{\&} P$. For the case of $M = \varnothing$ let $\& M = 1$. Similarly, we construct the negation: $\neg M = \{\neg P \mid P \in M\}$.*

Formulae of the form of simple conjunctions $F = m_{i_1}\&m_{i_2}\ldots\& m_{i_k}$ have one property that interlinks formulae structure and derivation operator of the classical FCA. In fact, the carrier G_F coincides with $\{m_{i_j}\}'$. In this sense, we can identify the set of letters with their representation in the form of a set of attributes $\{m_{i_j}\}$.

Moreover, the formula $m_{i_1} \& m_{i_2} \ldots \& m_{i_k} \to m = \& \{m_{i_j}\} \to m$ describes the same process as the implication on the context in classical sense, $(\{m_{i_j}\}, \{m\})$. According to this it is natural to define a class of implications similar to the FCA, but inside the class of formulae. We call them as rules.

Definition 16

1. *Rule is the formula $R = (H_1\&H_2\ldots\&H_k \Rightarrow T)$, where $T, H_i \in L$, $T \notin \{H_1, H_2, \ldots H_k\}$.*
2. *For the rule R under $\mathrm{head}(R)$ we mean the set $\{H_1, H_2 \ldots, H_k\}$, and $\mathrm{tail}(R) = T$. If $\mathrm{head}(R_1) = \mathrm{head}(R_2)$ and $\mathrm{tail}(R_1) = \mathrm{tail}(R_2)$, then $R_1 = R_2$.*
3. *The length of the rule is a power of its premise: $\mathrm{len}(R) = |\mathrm{head}(R)|$.*

Definition 17. *The probability of the rule R is the value*

$$\eta(R) = \nu(\text{tail}(R)|\text{head}(R)) = \frac{\nu(\&\text{head}(R)\&\text{tail}(R))}{\nu(\&\text{head}(R))}$$

The rule is global if the expression in the denominator equals to one. If the expression in the denominator is zero, the probability of rule remains undefined.

Definition 18. *Rule R_1 is a sub-rule of R_2, or R_1 is more general then R_2, if head$(R_1) \subset$ head(R_2) and tail$(R_1) =$ tail(R_2). This fact we denote as $R_1 \succ R_2$.*

Definition 19. *The rule R_1 is a generalization of the rule R_2, i.e. $R_1 \succeq R_2$, when $R_1 \succ R_2$ or $R_1 = R_2$.*

Definition 20. *The rule R_1 is a refinement of the rule R_2, $R_1 > R_2$, if $R_2 \succ R_1$ and $\eta(R_1) > \eta(R_2)$.*

Theorem 2. *Let R is a non-global rule on the context K with measure ν.*

1. *Probability of R is less or equal of the probability of corresponding implication:*

$$\eta(R) \le \nu(\text{head}(R) \rightarrow \text{tail}(R))$$

2. *R is almost a tautology if $\Leftrightarrow \eta(R) = \nu(R) = 1$.*

■ Let $H = \&\text{head}(R)$, $T = \text{tail}(R)$ and consider the difference $\nu(H)(\eta(R) - \nu(H \rightarrow T))$. Note that $H \rightarrow T = T \vee \neg H = (T\&H) \vee \neg H$, while $(T\&H)\&\neg H = 0$. Hence, by lemma 4, $\nu(H \rightarrow T) = \nu(T\&H) + \nu(\neg H)$. Thus the difference can be transformed as

$$\nu(H)(\eta(R) - \nu(H \rightarrow T)) = \nu(H\&T) - \nu(H\&T)\nu(H) - \nu(\neg H)\nu(H) =$$
$$\nu(H\&T)\nu(\neg H) - \nu(H)\nu(\neg H) = -\nu(H\&\neg T)\nu(\neg H) \le 0$$

Further, equality to 0 is achieved only if $\nu(H\&\neg T) = 0$. However, this is equivalent to the $\nu(H\&T) = \nu(H) - \nu(H\&\neg T) = \nu(H)$ and $\eta(R) = \frac{\nu(H\&T)}{\nu(H)} = 1$. Here we conclude that R is almost a tautology.   □

Corollary 1. *If the measure μ does not permit insignificant objects, then the set of almost tautologies turns into a set of tautologies, and $\eta(R) = 1 \Leftrightarrow R$ - contextual tautology.*

Definition 21. *R is a probability law, if it is a refinement of every of its sub-rule, i.e. $(R' \succ R) \Rightarrow (R > R')$.*

Now we prove some technical points we need to continue our working with the rules.

Lemma 3. *If addition of the letter H into the premise of the rule R reduces it's probability, $\eta(\&\text{head}(R) \& H \Rightarrow \text{tail}(R)) < \eta(R)$, then $\neg H$ increases it.*

Lemma 4. *For any rule R there exists its generalization R' such that R' is probabilistic law, and $\nu(R') \geq \nu(R)$.*

■ Consider the set $\Pi = \{A \mid \nu(A) \geq \nu(R),\ A \succeq R\}$. So as $R \in \Pi$, then $\Pi \neq \varnothing$. Hence, there is a minimal element in the sense of relation $\succeq$, call it $S = \min \Pi$. Condition 2 of the lemma holds for S by construction of Π.

Suppose S is not a law, i.e. here exists sub-rule S', such that $\nu(S') \geq \nu(S)$ and $S' \succ S$, given $S \succeq R$ we conclude that $S' \succ R$. From the other side, $\nu(S') \geq \nu(S) \geq \nu(R)$, where it follows that $S' \in \Pi$, contradicting the minimality of S. □

5   Refinement Theorem

Now we apply the proposed in [10, 12] technics to defined rules.

Definition 22. *Pseudo rule is a formula $R = ((P_1 \& \ldots \& P_k) \,\&\, \neg(N_1 \& \ldots \& N_s)$ $\Rightarrow T)$; for pseudo rule R, $\mathrm{head}(R) = (P_1 \& \ldots \& P_k) \,\&\, \neg(N_1 \& \ldots \& N_s)$ and $\mathrm{tail}(R) = T$; letters P_i we call the positive part of the premise and letters N_j we call the negative part; probability of the pseudo rule R is the value*

$$\eta(R) = \nu(\mathrm{tail}(R)|\mathrm{head}(R)) = \frac{\nu(\&\mathrm{head}(R)\ \&\ \mathrm{tail}(R))}{\nu(\&\mathrm{head}(R))}$$

Theorem 3. *(about refinement) Let $S = ((\&A)\&\neg(\&B)) \Rightarrow T)$ be a pseudo rule, $R = ((\&A) \Rightarrow T)$ the corresponding rule without negative part and moreover $\eta(S) > \eta(R)$. Then for R there is refinement rule $R' > R$ formed with the help of the negative part of pseudo rule S.*

■ For brevity, we denote $\overline{A} = \&A$, $\overline{B} = \&B$. Let us write the probability of pseudo rule S as:

$$\eta(S) = \nu(T \mid \overline{A} \,\&\, \neg\overline{B}) = \nu(T \mid \overline{A} \,\&\, (\neg B_1 \vee \ldots \vee \neg B_m)) \tag{1}$$

Next we represent the disjunction as disjunction of conjunctions:

$$\neg B_1 \vee \ldots \vee \neg B_m = \bigvee_{i=(0,\ldots,0)}^{i=(1,\ldots,1,0)} (B_1^{i_1} \,\&\, \ldots \,\&\, B_m^{i_m})$$

where 0 in multi-index indicates the presence of negation, and 1 - its absence. All multi-indices are included in a lexicographic order except for the last $(1,\ldots,1)$, which corresponds to the conjunction $B_1 \& \ldots \& B_m$.

Then the conditional probability (1) can be rewritten as

$$\eta(S) = \nu(T \mid \bigvee_{i=(0,\ldots,0)}^{i=(1,\ldots,1,0)} (\overline{A} \,\&\, B_1^{i_1} \,\&\, \ldots \,\&\, B_m^{i_m})) \tag{2}$$

Suppose the theorem's statement is false and any generalization $R' \succ R$, formed via appending some subset from $\{B_1, \ldots, B_m\}$ to premise, will fail as a refinement. This means that all inequalities like $\nu(T \mid \overline{A} \,\&\, B_1^{i_1} \,\&\, \ldots \,\&\, B_m^{i_m}) \leq \nu(T \mid \overline{A})$

are true, if corresponding probabilities are defined. Since $\nu(\overline{A}\,\&\,\neg\overline{B}) \neq 0$, there is at least one multi-index $(i_1, \ldots, i_m)$, for which it is true. Then

$$\nu(T\,\&\,\overline{A}\,\&\,B_1^{i_1}\,\&\,\ldots\,\&\,B_m^{i_m}) \leq \nu(T \mid \overline{A})\nu(\overline{A}\,\&\,B_1^{i_1}\,\&\,\ldots\,\&\,B_m^{i_m});$$

$$\nu(T \mid \overset{i=(1,\ldots,1,0)}{\underset{i=(0,\ldots,0)}{\vee}} (\overline{A}\,\&\,B_1^{i_1}\,\&\,\ldots\,\&\,B_m^{i_m})) = \frac{\nu(\vee\, T\,\&\,\overline{A}\,\&\,B_1^{i_1}\,\&\,\ldots\,\&\,B_m^{i_m})}{\nu(\vee\,\overline{A}\,\&\,B_1^{i_1}\,\&\,\ldots\,\&\,B_m^{i_m})} =$$

$$\frac{\sum \nu(T\,\&\,\overline{A}\,\&\,B_1^{i_1}\,\&\,\ldots\,\&\,B_m^{i_m})}{\sum \nu(\overline{A}\,\&\,B_1^{i_1}\,\&\,\ldots\,\&\,B_m^{i_m})} \leq \frac{\nu(T \mid \overline{A}) \sum \nu(\overline{A}\,\&\,B_1^{i_1}\,\&\,\ldots\,\&\,B_m^{i_m})}{\sum \nu(\overline{A}\,\&\,B_1^{i_1}\,\&\,\ldots\,\&\,B_m^{i_m})} = \nu(T \mid \overline{A});$$

The last, according to (2), means that $\eta(S) \leq \eta(R)$ – is a contradiction with the theorem premise. So, our assumption is false and for one of the rules we have $\nu(T \mid \overline{A}\,\&\,B_1^{i_1}\,\&\,\ldots\,\&\,B_m^{i_m}) > \nu(T \mid \overline{A})$.   □

6   Semantic Probabilistic Inference

We define another key concept for this work - the ratio of semantic probabilistic inference on the set of rules [10, 11, 13].

Definition 23. *The rule R is semantically probabilistic inferred from the rule R', $R' \sqsubset R$ if: R, R' - probabilistic laws, $\text{len}(R) = \text{len}(R') + 1$, $R > R'$.*

Definition 24. *Probabilistic law R is the strongest, if $\forall R'\ \neg(R \sqsubset R')$.*

Definition 25. *Semantic Probabilistic Inference (SPI) is a sequence of rules $R_0 \sqsubset R_1 \sqsubset R_2 \ldots \sqsubset R_m$, such that: $\text{len}(R_0) = 0$, R_m – the strongest probabilistic law.*

In other words, SPI requires the procedure of inference from start to finish.

Definition 26. *A maximal specific law for the predicate T is called as the strongest probabilistic law, if it has the maximal conditional probability among all the other strongest probabilistic laws with the conclusion T.*

The set of maximal specific laws on the context K we denote as MSR_K or MSR, if there is no ambiguity. Designation $\text{MSR}(T)$ stays for those subsets from MSR for which the conclusion is T.

Lemma 5. *For any rule R with $\text{tail}(R) = T$, which probability is defined, there always exists a maximal specific law W with the same conclusion T, such that $\eta(R') \geq \eta(R)$.*

■ By lemma 4 there is a generalization R' for the rule R which is a probabilistic law. But for R' there exists the strongest probabilistic law R'' such that $\eta(R'') \geq \eta(R')$. For R'', there is a maximum of the set of the strongest probabilistic laws, i.e. maximal specific law R''' and $\eta(R''') \geq \eta(R'') \geq \eta(R') \geq \eta(R)$. $W = R'''$ still has same $\text{tail}(W) = T$ and so it is the sough for.   □

7 Classes of Rules

In [10,14] classes of rules presented. They are used to justify the correctness of the semantic probabilistic inference. Slightly modifying these definitions, we will receive the comparable results.

Definition 27. $R \in M_1(T) \Leftrightarrow ((\varnothing \Rightarrow T) \succ R \Rightarrow R > (\varnothing \Rightarrow T))$

Definition 28. $R \in M_2(T) \Leftrightarrow R \in M_1(T)$ and $(\forall R' \in M_1(T))[R \succ R' \Rightarrow \eta(R') \leq \eta(R)]$

Definition 29. $M_1 = \bigcup_{T \in Lit(K)} M_1(T); \quad M_2 = \bigcup_{T \in Lit(K)} M_2(T)$

In other words, class M_1 requires rules to be meaningful, thus enable them to make sense compared with the unconditional approval of T. Class M_2 requires that the rule can not be more specific (no matter how we have expanded the rule R, we can never improve the estimation of its probability). We have the following relationship:

Proposition 2. MSR $\subset M_2 \subset M_1$.

■ The second inclusion is obvious. Let $R \in$ MSR. There is some SPI for R according to definition 27, starting with the unconditional rule $R' = \varnothing \Rightarrow \text{tail}(R)$. If the premise of R is not empty, then $\varnothing \Rightarrow \text{tail}(R) \succ R$ and from the chain of semantic probabilistic inference relations it follows that $R > R'$ and $R \in M_1$. If the premise R is empty, then the last is automatically fulfilled.

Consider $R \succ R' \in M_1$ and assume that $\eta(R') > \eta(R)$. Lemma 5 implies that there exists $S \in$ MSR : $\eta(S) \geq \eta(R') > \eta(R)$. This contradicts the maximal specificity of R and therefore $\eta(R') \leq \eta(R)$. Hence $R \in M_2$. □

Definition 30. *As a system of the rules we will call any $\Pi \subseteq M_2$.*

To investigate the formal concept of the binary context of K in the spirit of the approach indicated in [5,6], it is sufficient to understand the structure of corresponding prediction operator's fixed points on the nominally scaled context K^*. Here we aim to study the fixed points for the probabilistic operator of prediction on K, accounting the availability of negations in the formulae of a special kind. Let $L \subset Lit(K)$ be a arbitrary set of letters from context formal system.

The definition is completely similar to deterministic one (compare with defenition 6). We strictly follows the generelization idea and the only difference will be the nature of used implications: they are turned in probabilistic entities.

Definition 31. *Operator of direct predictions on the system Π works as follows:*

$$\text{Pr}_\Pi(L) = L \cup \{T \mid \exists R \in \Pi : \text{head}(R) \subseteq L, \text{tail}(R) = T\}$$

so Pr_Π adds conclusions of all the implications, the premise of which is contained in L and fullfilled on it, to the operand.

Definition 32. *Closure of a set of letters L is the smallest fixed point of operator of direct prediction: $\text{PR}_\Pi(L) = \text{Pr}_\Pi^\infty(L)$.*

8   Consistency Theorem

The correctness for construction proposed in the previous section needs to be proven, as in [10,14,15]. Correctness here is understood in two senses: in probabilistic and logical. We show that both they are satisfied.

Definition 33. *Set of letters L is called compatible, if $\& L - \nu$-consistent on K.*

In fact, the set is compatible when there is a set of statistically significant objects of G_K, on which the formula $\& L$ is fulfilled. On "normal" probability contexts K (with no more than countable set of objects G, each of which is statistically significant), the compatible sets L will be those sets (and with them also the corresponding sets of attributes L from M_{K*}) for which $L' \neq \varnothing$.

Object can not have both $m \in M_{K*}$ and $\overline{m} \in M_{K*}$ simultaniously. It can either possess or lack any attribute accordingly to binary context defenition. Such attribute combinations looks very suspecious and leads to known logical problems, consistency of attribute sets is a desirable property here.

Definition 34. *Set of letters L – consistent, if it does not contain any atom T simultaneously with its negation $\neg T$.*

Proposition 3. *If L – compatible, then L – consistent.*

∎ Otherwise $\exists T\colon T \in L$ and $\neg T \in L$, so $\nu(\& L) \leq \nu(T \,\&\, \neg T) = 0$.   □

Let Π be any rule system and Pr be according prediction operator Pr_Π. We first show that the direct prediction retains the property of compatibility.

Theorem 4. *(Compatibility) If L is compatible, then $\mathrm{Pr}(L)$ is also compatible.*

∎ The proof is easy to obtain by looking at the refinement theorem. Consider all rules that contribute to the formation of the direct prediction based on L:

$T = \{R \in \Pi \mid \mathrm{head}(R) \subseteq L\}$. We enumerate all the elements of T in an arbitrary manner, $T = \{T_1, \dots T_m\}$, and consider the sequence of sets $U_i = U_{i-1} \cup \{\mathrm{tail}(T_i)\}, U_0 = L$. We show that each U_i is compatible.

$U_0 = L$ is obviously compatible by the premise of the theorem.

Let U_i is compatible. For brevity, let $U = U_i, W = U_{i+1}, R = R_{i+1}$ and $T = \mathrm{tail}(R), H = \mathrm{head}(R), N = U \setminus H$. Suppose that W is inconsistent, i.e. $\nu(\& W) = 0$. Similarly to the refinement theorem, consider pseudo rule $F = (\& H \,\&\, \neg(\& N)) \Rightarrow T$. There are two cases:

1. case: $\nu(\&\mathrm{head}(F)) \neq 0$. Then the probability of F is defined and

$$\eta(F) = \frac{\nu(\& H \,\&\, \neg(\& N) \,\&\, T)}{\nu(\& H \,\&\, \neg(\& N))} = \frac{\nu(\& H \,\&\, T) - \nu(\& H \,\&\, (\& N) \,\&\, T)}{\nu(\& H) - \nu(\& H \,\&\, (\& N))} =$$

$$\frac{\nu(\& H \,\&\, T) - \nu(\& W)}{\nu(\& H) - \nu(\& U)} = \frac{\nu(\& H \,\&\, T)}{\nu(\& H) - \nu(\& U)} > \frac{\nu(\& H \,\&\, T)}{\nu(\& H)} = \eta(R) > 0.$$

According to the refinement theorem, there is a rule S such that $S > R$, which contradicts that the R is non-refineable (i.e., the fact that $R \in M_2$).

2. case: $\nu(\&\text{head}(F)) = 0$. Then

$$\nu(\&\text{head}(F)) = \nu(\&H \;\&\; \neg(\&N)) = 0 \Rightarrow \nu(\&H \;\&\; \neg(\&N) \;\&\; T) = 0;$$
$$0 = \nu(\&H \;\&\; (\&N) \;\&\; T) = \nu(\&H \;\&\; T) - \nu(\&H \;\&\; \neg(\&N) \;\&\; T) = \nu(\&H \;\&\; T).$$

The last means that $\eta(R) = 0$, which contradicts $R \in M_1$ ($0 = \eta(R) > \eta(\varnothing \Rightarrow T) \geq 0$).   □

Corollary 2. *If L – compatible, then $\mathrm{PR}(L)$ – also compatible.*

Corollary 3. *If L is compatible, then $\mathrm{PR}(L)$ – consistent.*

9   About Incompatible Sets

The situation is quite clear for compatible sets. Direct prediction on the compatible set L and the closure of this set are compatible and consistent.

Let's try to understand the structure of incompatible sets L. We will start with a fairly trivial statement, which is the opposite to the compatibility theorem.

Proposition 4. *If L – incompatible, then $\mathrm{PR}(L)$ – is also incompatible.*

■ Assuming compatibility $\mathrm{PR}(L)$ we find that any subset, and in particular L, is compatible.   □

Somewhat more difficult is the question of the inconsistency of such closures. For a more detailed study of the structure of incompatible systems of letters we need the following concept.

Definition 35. *We say that M is ν-maximal in L, $M \subseteq_\nu L$, when M is maximal by inclusion subset of L and M is compatible.*

Definition 36. *System of rules Π is called complete, if $\mathrm{MSR} \subset \Pi$.*

The following discussion focuses only on complete systems of rules. Requirement of completeness can be slightly relaxed, as it can be seen from the theorem below, but we restrict ourselves to the most specific rules in this article. This means we consider only $PR = PR_\Pi$ operators, where Π is complete system. It should be noted, that according to proposition 2 the system containing M_2 are complete.

Theorem 5. *Let $M \subseteq_\nu L$. Then $M \cup \neg(L \setminus M) \subseteq \mathrm{PR}(M)$.*

■ Let x belong to the left side of the formula. Case $x \in M$ is obvious. Here $x \in \mathrm{PR}(M)$ according to the definition of the closure.

Now let $x \in L \setminus M$. By definition, ν-maximal subsets of the set $M \cup \{x\}$ is incompatible (otherwise obtain a new maximal set by inclusion). This means that

$$\nu(\&M \;\&\; x) = 0;$$
$$\nu(\&M \;\&\; \neg x) = \nu(\&M) - \nu(\&M \;\&\; x) = \nu(\&M);$$

Let $R = (\&M \Rightarrow \neg x)$. From the relations above it is easy to calculate the probability of rule R:

$$\eta(R) = \frac{\nu(\&M \ \& \ \neg x)}{\nu(\&M)} = 1;$$

Lemma 11 asserts there is a rule $S \in \mathrm{MSR} \subset \Pi$, which is MSR-rule with conclusion equal $\neg x$, so that for S is fulfilled $\nu(S) \geq 1$. Thus, the rule S inevitably add $\neg x$ into direct prediction of $\mathrm{Pr}(L)$.   □

Theorem 6. *Consider* $M \subseteq_{\nu} L$, $N \subseteq_{\nu} L$ *and* $M \neq N$. *Then*

1. $\exists x \ : \ x \in \mathrm{PR}(M)$ *and* $\neg x \in \mathrm{PR}(N)$;
2. $\mathrm{PR}(M) \supseteq \mathrm{PR}(M \cap N) \subseteq \mathrm{PR}(N)$ *and* $\mathrm{PR}(M) \neq \mathrm{PR}(N)$.

■ 1. $M \neq N$ means, that $\exists x \in M \setminus N$ (indeed $M \subset N$ would be contrary to the maximality of M). $x \in M \Rightarrow \mathrm{PR}(M)$ and similarly to Theorem 6 $\neg x \in \mathrm{PR}(N)$.
   2. $\mathrm{PR}(N)$ – is compatible and consistent, and $\neg x \in \mathrm{PR}(N)$; it means $x \notin \mathrm{PR}(N)$ and $x \in \mathrm{PR}(M) \setminus \mathrm{PR}(N)$. Then, $M \cap N \subset M$, so $\mathrm{PR}(M \cap N) \subseteq \mathrm{PR}(M)$.
     □

The last two theorems conclude that there exists an injective mapping from ν-maximal subsets of L to fixed points set, each completely covering the entire set of atoms in L (containing them or their negations).
   Inconsistency and compatibility of fixed points for compatible sets proved in section above. For incompatible sets following theorem tends to be an answer.

Theorem 7. *If* L *is incompatible, then* $\mathrm{PR}(L)$ *– inconsistent.*

■ Find ν-maximal subset of L and denote it as M. $M \neq L$, otherwise L would have been compatible. Therefore, there exists $x \in L \setminus M$. Set $\{x\}$ is extended to a maximal compatible $N \subseteq_{\nu} L$. By construction, $x \in N \setminus M \Rightarrow M \neq N$. By Theorem 6, there exists y, such that $y \in \mathrm{PR}(M)$ and $\neg y \in \mathrm{PR}(N)$:

$$\left.\begin{array}{r} M \subseteq L \\ N \subseteq L \end{array}\right\} \Rightarrow \left.\begin{array}{r} y \in \mathrm{PR}(M) \subseteq \mathrm{PR}(L) \\ \neg y \in \mathrm{PR}(N) \subseteq \mathrm{PR}(L) \end{array}\right\} \Rightarrow \mathrm{PR}(L) \text{ - contradictory.} \qquad □$$

10 Probabilistic Formal Concepts

The fixed points of PR operator are rather interesting and promising. However, the purpose for their consideration was the motive of introduction of the probabilistic analogous of formal concepts. Using the idea of Theorem 1, it is easy to offer as candidates [5,6] for inclusion in intent of such concepts. We mean exactly the fixed points of PR.
   Selection for concept extent is a bit more complicated. But since all the sets of letters, such that $\mathrm{PR}(M) = B$, have a real connection to the closure, it is logical to propose to collect all objects falling under them. That is:

Definition 37. *By probabilistic formal concept on K we denote (A, B), such that:*

$$\text{PR}(B) = B, \quad A = \bigcup_{\text{PR}(C)=B} G_C$$

To distinguish probabilistic concepts from the usual ones in the sense of the context of K^*, the last ones we call strict formal concepts. Our selection justified by the following statement, relating probabilistic and strict formal concepts on the same context.

Theorem 8. *Let K be a binary context.*

1. *If (A, B) is strict concept on K, then there is a probabilistic concept (N, M) such that $A \subseteq N$, and $B \subseteq M$.*
2. *If (N, M) is the probabilistic concept on K, then there is a set of strict notions C, such that*

$$\forall (A, B) \in C \ (\text{PR}(B) = M),$$

$$N = \bigcup_{(A,B) \in C} A.$$

∎ Suppose $S = \{S \mid \text{PR}(S) = M\}$.
  1. Let $M = \text{PR}(B)$. Then $B \in S$ and $A = G_B \subseteq \bigcup_S G_S = N$. Hence (A, B) is
desired.
  2. On S we make a set of strict concepts $C = \{(S''', S'') \mid S \in S\}$. From lemma 1 it is easy to understand that $B''' = B'$, that is $C = \{(S', S'') \mid S \in S\}$ and all $(A, B) \in C$ - are strict concepts. Hence $N = \bigcup_S S' = \bigcup_{(A,B) \in C} A$ It should
be added that $M \in S$ and hence $C \neq \varnothing$.   □

Probabilistic concept is like cluster unifying set of poorly distinguishable strict concepts in terms of a system of rules Π.

11 Probabilistic Concepts Search

In this section we restrict ourselves to the case of finite context K. From the last one, we can drop out statistically insignificant objects without loss of generality.
  Assume that the system of rules Π on context K has already been found by one of the algorithms, for example [11,13]. Probabilistic concept definition implies the following search procedure.

1. On step $k = 1$ we generate the set $C^{(1)} = \{\text{PR}(\text{head}(R)) \mid R \in \Pi\}$.
2. On step $k > 1$ in case of $C^{(k-1)} = \varnothing$ algorithm finishes its execution and output a list of detected probability concepts.
3. Else on step $k > 1$ the set $A = \{g \in G \mid \text{PR}(g' \cap B) = B\}$ is calculated for each $B \in C^{(k-1)}$. If $A \neq \varnothing$, pair (A, B) is added to list of found concepts.

4. The set $C^{(k)} = \{\mathrm{PR}(B \cup C) \mid B, C \in C^{(k-1)}, \mathrm{PR}(B \cup C) \notin C^{(k-1)}\}$ is generated.
5. Let $k := k+1$ and go to step 2.

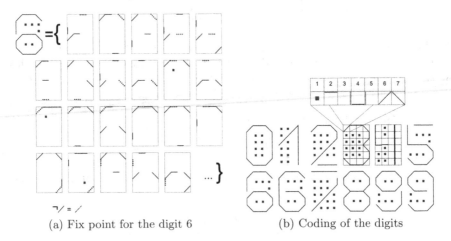

(a) Fix point for the digit 6　　　　　　(b) Coding of the digits

Finally, we present one of many examples. Real example can be found in [16]. In [17] there is experiment for analyzing of postal envelopes digits. The data contains 12 digits (2 options for each "6" and "9"). The context is based on 24 attributes, each of which has 7 values (for different shapes in the relevant sector of the digit partition). Set G consists of 360 objects (30 copies of each digit) with gap in information (each digit misses one randomly deleted attribute), which are mixed, plus negative sample of 1050 objects with random attributes. There is no attribute that designate which digit is the object representing. On these data, 73458 rules was found. Then the all fixed points were computed using set of all rules, which turn up just 14. From them, 12 digits were exactly our numbers, and for each of "6" and "9" were still two fixed points containing an extra space in the features that distinguishes 2 options of those digits ("6" and "9" are not mixed up due to fixing top-bottom orientation while coding procedure).

12　Conclusion

Negations (and, in general, the values for attributes) in formal contexts, produce a much more expressive system of concepts. This provides such properties (in some sense) as correctness and completeness to proposed method.

Our considerations and algorithm allows us to find consistent probabilistic concepts, and, at the same time, do not lose strict concepts. Moreover, the proposed method preserves a binary noise - the random binary noise imposed into the values of attributes don't change the set of concepts [5,6].

The concept of fixed points may be rather natural applied for formalization of classtering [17]. Therefore, the fix point theory and probabilistic formal concepts may be used for the new Data Mining method development.

References

1. Ganter, B.: Formal Concept Analysis: Methods, and Applications in Computer Science. TU Dresden, Germany (2003)
2. Ganter, B., Wille, R.: Formal concept analysis - Mathematical Foundations. LNCS (LNAI). Springer, Heidelberg (1999)
3. Klimushkin, M., Obiedkov, S., Roth, C.: Approaches to the selection of relevant concepts in the case of noisy data. In: Kwuida, L., Sertkaya, B. (eds.) ICFCA 2010. LNCS, vol. 5986, pp. 255–266. Springer, Heidelberg (2010)
4. Kuznetsov, S.O.: On stability of a formal concept. Ann. Math. Artif. Intell. **49**, 101–115 (2007)
5. Demin, A., Ponomaryov, D., Vityaev, E.: Probabilistic concepts in formal contexts. In: Proceedings of ARCOE Workshop at IJCAI 2011, pp. 31–35. Barcelona (2011)
6. Vityaev, E.E., Demin, A.V., Ponomaryov, D.K.: Probabilistic generalization of formal concepts. Program. Comput. Softw. **38**(5), 219–230 (2012)
7. Ganter, B., Obiedkov, S.: Implications in Triadic Formal Contexts. TU Dresden, Springer (2004)
8. Missaoui, R., Kwuida, L.: Implications in triadic formal contexts. In: 9th International Conference, ICFCA 2011, Nicosia, Cyprus. Springer (2011)
9. Vityaev, E., Kovalerchuk, B.: Empirical theories discovery based on the measurement theory. Mind Mach. **14**(4), 551–573 (2004)
10. Vityaev, E.E.: The logic of prediction. Mathematical Logic in Asia. In: Proceedings of the 9th Asian Logic Conference Mathematical Logic in Asia, pp. 263–276. World Scientific, Singapore (2006)
11. Vityaev, E.E.: Knowledge Discovery. Computational Cognition. Cognitive Process Models. Novosibirsk State University Press, Novosibirsk (2006). (in Russian)
12. Vityaev, E., Smerdov, S.: On the problem of prediction. In: Wolff, K.E., Palchunov, D.E., Zagoruiko, N.G., Andelfinger, U. (eds.) KONT 2007 and KPP 2007. LNCS, vol. 6581, pp. 280–296. Springer, Heidelberg (2011)
13. Kovalerchuk, B., Vityaev, E.: Data Mining in Finance: Advances in Relational and Hybrid methods. Kluwer Academic Publishers, Boston (2000)
14. Speransky, S.O.: On the logical consistency of probabilistic predictions. Messenger of NGU. Series: Mathematics, Mechanics, Informatics **11**, 99–115 (2011). (in Russian)
15. Speransky, S.O.: Logic of probability and probability logic. Novosibirsk State University, Novosibirsk, Ph.D. thesis (2013). (in Russian)
16. Vityaev, E.E., Lapardin, K.A., Khomicheva, I.V., Proskura, A.L.: Transcription factor binding site recognition by regularity matrices based on the natural classification method. Intell. Data Anal. **12**(5), 495–512 (2008)
17. Vityaev, E.E., Neupokoev, N.V.: Formal model of perception and pattern as fix point of anticipations. In: Approaches to the thinking modeling, pp. 155–172. URSS, Moscow, Editorial (2014). (in Russian)

Modeling Environment for Static Verification of Linux Kernel Modules

Alexey Khoroshilov, Vadim Mutilin, Evgeny Novikov, and Ilja Zakharov$^{(\boxtimes)}$

Institute for System Programming of the Russian Academy of Sciences,
Moscow, Russia
{khoroshilov,mutilin,novikov,ilja.zakharov}@ispras.ru

Abstract. Linux kernel modules operate in an event-driven environment. Static verification of such software has to take into consideration all feasible scenarios of interaction between modules and their environment. The paper presents a new method for modeling the environment which allows to automatically generate an environment model for a particular kernel module on the base of analysis of module source code and a set of specifications describing patterns of possible interactions. In specifications one can describe both generic patterns that are widespread in the Linux kernel and detailed patterns specific for a particular subsystem. This drastically reduces a specification size and thus helps to verify more modules with less efforts. The suggested method was implemented in Linux Driver Verification Tools and was successfully used for static verification of modules from almost all Linux kernel subsystems.

Keywords: Operating system kernel · Kernel module · Software quality · Static verification · Environment model

1 Introduction

The Linux kernel is a base for various operating systems. Depending on their utilization and on underlying hardware these operating systems require specific sets of features to be supported by the kernel. Usually the Linux kernel provides just some common functions, e.g. memory and process management. To extend kernel functionality with new features one can dynamically load corresponding modules into the kernel.

The Linux kernel is shipped with a large set of modules for specific device drivers, file systems, network protocols, etc. Subsets of modules available for loading depend on a system architecture and a kernel configuration. For instance on architecture x86_64 in configuration `allmodconfig` current versions of the Linux kernel contain about 4 thousand modules.

Linux kernel modules operate in the same address space and have the same level of privileges as the kernel itself. But by a number of reasons they have much less quality in comparison with the rest of the kernel [1]. About a half of all typical bugs in modules are caused by incorrect usage of the Linux kernel API [2].

© Springer-Verlag Berlin Heidelberg 2015
A. Voronkov and I. Virbitskaite (Eds.): PSI 2014, LNCS 8974, pp. 400–414, 2015.
DOI: 10.1007/978-3-662-46823-4_32

The given paper focuses on this sort of bugs and suggests to find them with help of static verification, since this technique allows to analyze all possible execution paths, even hard-to-reproduce ones.

Modern static verifiers [3–7] already can check middle-sized programs. So they can be applied for Linux kernel modules that usually have a size of about several thousand lines of code. It was shown that static verifiers need rather accurate environment models for checking programs [8]. Without these models the tools can produce a large number of false alarms because they assume that some infeasible scenarios of interaction are possible. Also environment models should not omit scenarios that may happen in practice. Otherwise static verifiers can miss actual bugs.

The rest of the paper is organized as follows. In Sect. 2 we consider typical scenarios of interaction between Linux kernel modules and their environment. In Sect. 3 we present a method which allows to define a specification of the environment in the formal notation of π-processes. The main contribution is that this method introduces pattern specifications that allow to describe scenarios of interaction between modules from different subsystems and their environment in a compact form. This drastically reduces a specification size and thus helps to verify more modules with less efforts. A method implementation is outlined in Sect. 4. Section 5 presents experimental results. Related work is considered in Sect. 6. Section 7 makes a conclusion.

2   Environment of Linux Kernel Modules

Linux kernel modules operate in an event-driven environment which is reflected in Fig. 1. For simplicity hereinafter we suggest that each module interacts with user-space applications and with hardware only through the so-called *kernel core*. Below we consider a lifecycle of a typical Linux kernel module.

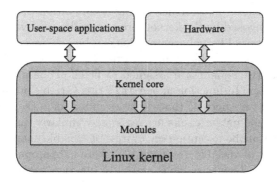

Fig. 1. Interaction of Linux kernel modules with their environment.

Figure 2 presents snippets of the USB CDC Phonet module from Linux kernel 3.2 (original source code was simplified). One can see that this module does

```
1 static int usbpn_open(struct net_device *dev) { ... };
2 static int usbpn_close(struct net_device *dev) { ... };
3 static const struct net_device_ops usbpn_ops = {
4         .ndo_open = usbpn_open, .ndo_stop = usbpn_close
5 };
6 int usbpn_probe(struct usb_interface *intf, ...) {
7         struct net_device *dev;
8         struct usbpn_dev *pnd;
9         ...
10        dev->netdev_ops = &usbpn_ops;
11        spin_lock_init(&pnd->tx_lock);
12        usb_set_intfdata(intf, pnd);
13        pnd->dev = dev;
14        err = register_netdev(dev);
15        ...
16 }
17 static void usbpn_disconnect(struct usb_interface *intf) {
18        struct usbpn_dev *pnd = usb_get_intfdata(intf);
19        unregister_netdev(pnd->dev);
20 }
21 static struct usb_driver usbpn_driver = {
22        .probe = usbpn_probe, .disconnect = usbpn_disconnect
23 };
24 static int usbpn_init(void) { return usb_register(&usbpn_driver); }
25 static void usbpn_exit(void) { usb_deregister(&usbpn_driver); }
26 module_init(usbpn_init);
27 module_exit(usbpn_exit);
```

Fig. 2. Snippents of the USB CDC Phonet module.

not have function main. Instead it registers via macro module_init (line 26) initialization function usbpn_init (defined at line 24) that is called in loading the module. On initialization and further during its operation the module registers callbacks that are invoked by the kernel core to handle such events as interrupts, system calls and internal kernel events. This can be achieved in different ways.

On initialization of variable usbpn_driver (lines 21–23), callbacks usbpn_probe and usbpn_disconnect are assigned to fields probe and disconnect of structure usb_driver. In function usbpn_init this variable address is passed to function usb_register (line 24) that registers callbacks in the kernel core. Callbacks usbpn_open and usbpn_close are registered similarly (lines 3–5). But during callback usbpn_probe execution an address of variable usbpn_ops is assigned to field netdev_ops of variable dev (line 10) where usbpn_ops holds pointers to considered callbacks. That variable is passed to function register_netdev (line 14) registering those callbacks.

Deregistration of callbacks is performed as follows. Callbacks usbpn_open and usbpn_close are deregistered in function usbpn_disconnect (line 19), callbacks usbpn_probe and usbpn_disconnect — in function usbpn_exit (line 25).

Below we call a group of callbacks whose pointers assigned to fields of the same structure as a *callback group*. Corresponding structure types will be referred to as a *group types*. Therefore there are two callback groups of types usb_driver and net_device_ops in Fig. 2.

Modules interact with their environment in conformance with a strict contract which imposes restrictions on possible interaction scenarios. For instance, for the USB CDC Phonet module (Fig. 2) the kernel core calls initialization function usbpn_init at module loading. Then the module tries to register the callback group of type usb_driver via function usb_register. This function returns 0 if the kernel core successfully registers callbacks and an error code otherwise. In the same way, function usbpn_init returns 0 if it succeeds to initialize the module and an error code otherwise.

If function usbpn_init succeeded, the kernel core can invoke callback usbpn_probe to initialize one or more USB CDC Phonet devices. During device initialization the module initializes a spinlock with help of function spin_lock_init (line 11) and tries to register the callback group of type net_device_ops. After successful registration the kernel core becomes able to call callback usbpn_open. Callbacks from group of type net_device_ops use the initialized spinlock. So a callbacks invocation order does matter. If one will invoke callbacks from group of type net_device_ops before callback usbpn_probe succeeded he or she will catch a false alarm in verification of correct initialization of spinlocks before usage.

Usually the kernel core invokes callbacks in parallel. So it can simultaneously initialize several USB CDC Phonet devices with callback usbpn_probe or open several network devices for a given USB CDC Phonet device.

The kernel core can invoke callback usbpn_close only if callback usbpn_open returns 0. Callback usbpn_disconnect can be invoked just after callback usbpn_probe returns 0 and if either callback usbpn_open was not called at all or all opened network devices were closed. Function usbpn_exit can be called by the kernel core after function usbpn_init returns 0 and if either callback usbpn_probe callback was not invoked or all USB CDC Phonet devices were disconnected.

It is worthwhile to mention that the kernel core passes pointers to the same objects (*resources*) as parameters to callbacks of the same group. For instance, callback usbpn_probe stores all necessary information on initialization of a particular USB CDC Phonet device to its parameter intf that will be later passed to callback usbpn_disconnect.

Analysis of source code of wide range of Linux kernel subsystems shows that callbacks from groups of the same type are usually invoked similarly for different modules. So we say that corresponding callbacks have the same *roles*. In the example above callbacks usbpn_probe and usbpn_disconnect has roles usb_driver.probe and usb_driver.disconnect respectively. This observation will be used in a method for modeling environment suggested below.

3   Environment Modeling

Environment models required for static verification of Linux kernel modules should be complete and correct. Completeness means that models should contain all interaction scenarios possible in the real environment. If an environment model is incomplete, static verifiers may miss actual bugs. Correctness means that environment models should not contain scenarios which are impossible in the real environment. If an environment model is incorrect the tools may report false alarms.

π-calculus [9,10] suits well to specify environment models, since it allows to describe arbitrary high-parallel systems completely and correctly in terms of message passing and parallel composition of processes. Below we propose the environment modeling method based on π-calculus which allows to reduce efforts required for development of environment models.

3.1 Definitions

In π-calculus [9,10] we have processes, operations of parallel composition, synchronous communication between processes through channels, creation of fresh channels, replication of processes and nondeterminism. Each channel has a name also called label $\alpha \in A$.

We use definitions from [9] with a polyadic extension described in [10] where labels have vectors of labels as parameters, denoted by x.

Processes are described in the following manner:

$$P ::= P|Q(\text{parallel composition}) \mid !P(\text{replication})$$

$$\mid (\nu\alpha)P(\text{new label creation}) \mid N(x)$$

where $N(x) ::= 0 \mid K_1(x) + \cdots + K_n(x) \mid [x = v]K(x)$

- 0 is an empty process;
- $K_1(x) + \cdots + K_n(x)$ is a choice of
  - $\alpha(y_i).K_i(x, y_i)$ - receiving vector of input parameters y_i over channel $\underline{\alpha}$;
  - $\alpha(x).K_i(x)$ - sending vector x over channel α;
  - $\tau.K_i(x)$ - a silent action;
- $[x = v]K(x)$ is a match. The process behaves like $K(x)$ if x and v are equal, and otherwise like $\mathbf{0}$.

For convenience we add operator $[x \neq v]$ which is the same as $[x = v]$, but it tests inequality.

3.2 π-Model for Kernel Module and Environment

A Linux kernel module and its environment can be considered as a parallel composition of processes in π-calculus. We suppose that there is process P_{fcall} which has the same behavior as implementation in C language for all callbacks of the kernel module. Process P_{fcall} receives requesting callback invocation messages $\overline{f(ret_i, f_i, ctx_i, params_i)}$, where ret_i is a channel name for a response, f_i is a callback function, ctx_i is a calling context and $params_i$ are callback function parameters. As far as callbacks can be executed in parallel, process P_{fcall}

is replicated for each call. On function return P_{fcall} replies with return value $ret_i(result)$.

Hence the kernel module can be seen as a composition:

$$Module_\pi ::= P_{init}|P_{exit}|!P_{fcall}$$

Processes P_{init} and P_{exit} represent module initialization and exit functions correspondingly. They are not replicated as far as these functions cannot be called simultaneously by the environment. These processes receive messages $init(ret)$ and $exit(ret)$, and send $\overline{ret(x)}$, $\overline{ret()}$.

The environment is represented as a composition:

$$Env_\pi ::= P_{g_i} \ldots |P_{v_i} \ldots |P_{module}|P_{a_i} \ldots$$

where processes P_{g_i} represent kernel core functions $g_1(ret_1, params_1), \ldots,$ $g_l(ret_l, params_l)$ and P_{v_i} represent global variables with $set_{v_i}(x)$, $\overline{get_{v_i}(x)}$. These processes model functions and variables of the environment which can be used by the kernel module during initialization, exit and execution of callbacks.

An active part of the environment modeling interaction scenarios with the kernel module includes main process P_{module} calling initialization and exit functions and a set of P_{a_i} processes calling callbacks of the module.

The environment model is not required to be equivalent to the real environment of a particular kernel version. On the contrary, the model should allow as many interaction scenarios as possible within the contract between the environment and the module.

The environment model is divided into parts according to group types. The first group is a special group modeling initialization and exit of the module as a parallel composition: $P_{module}|P_{trymoduleget}$. P_{module} starts interaction with the module:

$P_{module} ::= (\nu ret)L0$
$L0 ::= \overline{init(ret)}.ret(r).[r = 0]L1$
$L1 ::= \overline{mstop}.\overline{exit(ret)}.ret.0$

Process $L0$ sends $init$ message to the module. The module performs initialization, e.g. it registers callback groups. If initialization is successful, $L0$ sends 0 to channel ret, and continues as $L1$. Otherwise, $init$ sends an error code and execution is finished. The environment interacts with the module until message $exit$. On receiving it the module deregisteres callback groups.

$P_{trymoduleget}$ is an auxiliary process specifying the module cannot be unloaded, i.e. the environment cannot call exit function. The process acquiring the module sends $\overline{tmg}$ message and receives $tmg^{ret}(true)$ answer in case of success. $mstop$ is required for disabling all acquirements when unloading the module.

$P_{trymoduleget} ::= M_0$
$M_0 ::= \overline{tmg}.tmg^{ret}(true).M_1 + mstop.MD$
$MD ::= mstop.MD + tmg.\overline{tmg^{ret}(false)}.MD$
For each $i \geq 1$ we define the process:
$M_i ::= tmg.\overline{tmg^{ret}(true)}.M_{i+1} + mput.\overline{mput^{ret}}.M_{i-1}$

3.3 Group Type Specifications

We define a group type specification as a π-process parametrized with callback roles of the group type. The process should model actions performed at calling registration/deregistration functions and should invoke callbacks with certain roles according to the contract.

In the example in Fig. 2 function usb_register is called with a pointer to variable usbpn_driver of type usb_driver, containing pointers to callbacks usbpn_probe and usbpn_disconnect with roles usb_driver.probe and usb_driver.disconnect.

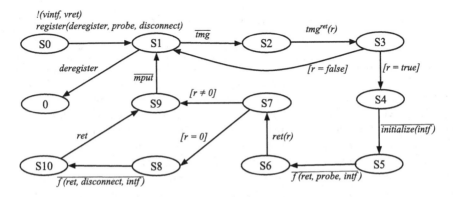

Fig. 3. Example of P_{usb_driver} modeling callback group of type *usb_driver*.

For each callback group a registration function model creates instances of group processes parametrized by callback roles (Fig. 3). The number of created instances depends on resources the group is operating with. For instance, if group file_operations is operating with file resources a separate instance for each file may be created.

A usb_driver specification has parameters *probe* and *disconnect* for roles usb_driver.probe and usb_driver.disconnect. In the example for each registered callback group we create one instance of process and a new resource intf which is initialized with *initialize*. Then this resource is passed to callbacks usbpn_probe and usbpn_disconnect as a parameter.

P_{usb_driver} is defined as follows (we use Si to denote notes shown in Fig. 3).
$P_{usb\_driver} ::= S0$
$S0 ::= !(\nu intf, \nu ret)register(deregister, probe, disconnect).S1$
$S1 ::= deregister.0 + \overline{tmg}.\langle S2 \rangle tmg^{ret}(r).\langle S3 \rangle ([r = true]S4 + [r = false]S1)$
$S4 ::= \overline{initialize(intf)}.S5$
$S5 ::= \overline{f(ret, probe, intf)}.\langle S6 \rangle ret(r).\langle S7 \rangle ([r = 0]S8 + [r \neq 0]S9)$
$S8 ::= \overline{f(ret, disconnect, intf)}.\langle S10 \rangle ret.S9$
$S9 ::= \overline{mput}.S1$

Semantics of π-process interactions allow to define both dependencies between groups and dependencies with initialization and exit functions. In the example in

Fig. 3 the module cannot be unloaded after the process came to state $S4$ where it is ready to call callbacks usbpn_probe and then usbpn_disconnect. For the environment it means that we cannot call the exit function in process P_{module}. Process $P_{trymoduleget}$ stores the number of module acquirements. Before calling any callbacks process P_{usb_driver} sends $\overline{tmg}$. In case of success it goes to process $S4$. Otherwise, if the module is unloading ($r = false$), it goes to $S1$ and waits for deregistration.

3.4 Group Pattern Specifications

We analyzed a plenty of Linux kernel modules and found that there are similar restrictions for different roles of different group types. For example, in Fig. 4 we have callback group 2430_driver of type platform_driver. It has two roles platform_driver.probe and platform_driver.remove. The roles are the same as usb_driver.probe and usb_driver.disconnect of group type usb_driver. The groups are operating with different resources of types usb_interface and platform_device in the same manner. We say that two group types have the same *group pattern specification* in case of correspondence between roles and resources, i.e. contracts for the groups are equivalent.

```
static int omap2430_probe(struct platform_device *pdev) { ... }
static int omap2430_remove(struct platform_device *pdev) { ... }
struct platform_driver omap2430_driver = {
        .probe = omap2430_probe, .remove = omap2430_remove
};
```

Fig. 4. Example of platform_driver group type from drivers/usb/musb/omap2430.c.

We define a group pattern specification as a pair of a group pattern and a parametrized π-process. The group pattern is defined as *abstract roles* and an *abstract resource type*, which describe a set of concrete roles and a set of concrete resource types. In the example we have two abstract roles *probe* describing concrete roles platform_driver.probe and usb_driver.probe, and *disconnect* describing concrete roles platform_driver.remove and usb_driver.disconnect. The *abstract resource type* represents a set of concrete resource types. Usually it is determined by resources used in callbacks with abstract roles. Abstract resources are usually passed as parameters. In the example the abstract resource is passed as a first parameter to functions with abstract roles *probe* and *disconnect*.

For group pattern specifications we have π-processes parametrized by abstract roles, abstract resource types, registration and deregistration functions. Abstract roles may be set as optional, in this case a callback with a concrete role may be absent.

For the example, behavior may be described by the process similar to P_{usb_driver} with addition of registration and deregistration functions for groups containing callbacks for abstract roles *probe* and *disconnect*. Abstract resource *intf* is described as a first parameter of callbacks.

The presented specification pattern describes callback groups of such types as usb_driver, platform_driver, sdio_driver, pcmcia_driver, etc. (see source code of Linux kernel version 3.12). Note, that these group types can have additional roles, e.g. *suspend* and *resume*. If a group has callbacks with roles which are not matched by the group pattern then it is not applicable.

3.5   Method for Environment Modeling

With help of π-processes it is possible to describe precise models of the Linux kernel modules environment. In practice development of precise models for all group types takes too much time. Moreover, the majority of bugs in modules can be found with less precise models. That is why we propose a method for modeling the kernel modules environment that provides means to specify patterns which are applicable to many group types. Also the method still allows to define a specific model for a particular group to meet requirements on completeness and correctness.

An individual environment model is constructed for each kernel module. It is composed of π-processes that model an active piece of the environment for each callback group identified in the module.

The method for modeling the environment consists of three steps. On the **first step** the environment model developer defines a *kernel activity specification* (TS, PS, DS, KS), where

1. TS is a map from a group type to a group type specification;
2. PS is a set of group pattern specifications;
3. DS is a default group specification;
4. KS is a set of kernel core specifications.

Group type specifications describe precise models of group types. Where it is possible group pattern specifications are used to describe sets of callback groups of corresponding types. The default group specification describes a process that invokes callbacks in an arbitrary order. Kernel core specifications contain descriptions of kernel core functions and additional processes shared between group specifications, e.g. $P_{trymoduleget}$.

On the **second step** a π-model of the environment is constructed for a particular kernel module. First of all, source code of the kernel module is analyzed to identify callback groups used in it. For each callback group extracted information includes callback roles, each with an associated callback function if it is identified, registration/deregistration functions if present and concrete resource types.

For each callback group either a precise group type specification is found or the most relevant group pattern specification is searched for.

To select a group pattern abstract roles are matched with concrete ones, abstract resources are matched with concrete resources passed as parameters to registration functions or to callbacks with abstract roles. Each non-optional abstract role in the specification should have a corresponding concrete role.

Among all matching patterns a pattern having the largest set of abstract roles is chosen. The pattern is applied to callback groups of the kernel module by replacing abstract roles with concrete ones, and replacing abstract resource types by concrete ones. If a relevant group pattern specification is not found then the default group specification is applied.

Finally, all π-processes of each callback group identified in the module are combined by parallel composition with the kernel core specification KS into a π-model of the module environment.

On the **third step** the π-model of the environment is translated into the input format of static verifiers (see the next Section for details).

4 Driver Environment Generator

The suggested approach was implemented as a part of Linux Driver Verification (LDV) Tools [11]. LDV Tools allow to check that Linux kernel modules do not violate rules of correct usage of the Linux kernel API.

LDV Tools prepare a verification task on the basis of kernel module source code and apply various reachability static C verification tools - static verifiers. Currently LDV Tools support the following static verifiers: CPAchecker [3], BLAST [4,5], CBMC [6] and UFO [7] based on Counter-Example Guided Abstraction Refinement (CEGAR) and Bounded Model Checking (BMC). These tools proved their efficiency on annual competitions on software verification [12].

Environment model generation is one of the most important operations which is performed during verification task preparation. Driver Environment Generator (DEG) prepares an environment model for a given Linux kernel module according to the suggested method. The first step requires manual development of the kernel activity specification which is used by DEG during following steps.

The second step of the method is implemented in DEG as preliminary source code analysis of the kernel module. The aim of the analysis is to determine particular callback groups defined in the module. To perform such analysis DEG uses another LDV Tools component called C Instrumentation Framework (CIF) [13] which allows C source code querying. Currently CIF supports queries to get information on function calls, macro expansions, global variable declarations, including structure initialization, parameters passed to registration functions and macros. On the third step of the method DEG generates a C program from the π-model, because of this is an input language for the most of static verifiers. DEG implements approach described in detail in [14].

On practice DEG cannot generate precise models for all kernel modules because of restrictions of preliminary source code analysis and specific requirements of static verifiers. The most important issues are the following:

1. Not all callback groups can be extracted correctly with CIF from module source code. For instance, currently the analysis misses dynamically assigned callbacks.

2. If extracted data does not allow to accurately define a π-process on the base of specifications and data obtained from module source code, DEG adapts specifications when it is possible. DEG can add default registration or function stubs for missed roles heuristically.

3. The majority of static verifiers can analyze only sequential C code, yet original environment models are parallel in the notation of π-calculus. The restriction is dramatically important, since it requires translation of parallel π-models into sequential source code. To do this DEG uses a method for translating π-models into sequential C program described in detail in [14]. This method throws off simultaneous execution of callbacks. Thus, it reduces completeness of environment models. As consequence sequential models does not allow to find specific bugs like race conditions.

4. All static verifiers need an *entry point* function as a starting point of analysis. Function `main` is an example of entry point in user-space programs.

5. Most of static verifiers based on BMC need significantly accurate models with minimum uninitialized variables. This obstacle increases manual work for specifying kernel core functions in DEG specifications and also makes application of group pattern specifications less effective (less callback groups are matched with callback pattern specifications). That is why currently LDV Tools yield better results for CEGAR based static verifiers like CPAchecker or BLAST.

6. Most of static verifiers have restricted support of function pointers. If DEG extracts a function name for a concrete role instead of a function pointer, it replaces a corresponding parameter of the process by that function name. In this case generated code becomes much more friendly for static verifiers.

7. Static verifiers have restricted support of pointer arithmetic. The issue carries great weight for code generation since without lists or other dynamically allocated structures it is too hard to describe in C code all feasible scenarios from π-models. DEG does not support replication of processes from π-models while an approach in [14] suggested to store a state of process instances in a list. Nevertheless, several process instances can be defined manually in specifications.

Although considered issues currently does not allow to generate precise environment models for Linux kernel modules, experimental results demonstrate that models are already sufficiently precise.

5   Experimental Results

In this paper we present results of verification of Linux kernel 3.13-rc1 modules (3289 modules on architecture x86-64 in configuration `allmodconfig`). DEG was able to successfully generate environment models for 2972 modules (approximately 80 % of the total number of modules). It failed on the rest 317 modules mostly because of lacks of callback groups which DEG tool can extract with preliminary source code analysis.

Table 1. Actual bugs and false alarms yielded by the BLAST static verifier.

	Mutexes	Clocks	Spinlocks	Atomic memory allocation
Actual bugs	6	3	1	2
False alarms not because of DEG	8	9	11	0
False alarms because of DEG	17	32	6	7
Preliminary analysis	1	10	1	1
Kernel core specification	16	5	5	6
Unknown handler roles	0	17	0	0

5.1 Model Correctness

To evaluate correctness of generated environment models we verified all modules against rules which specify how to use correctly mutexes, clocks, spinlocks and memory allocation in atomic context. Table 1 shows the number of false alarms and actual bugs yielded for them by the BLAST static verifier [5].

The first three lines show the total number of actual bugs, false alarms not due to incorrect environment models and false alarms due to incorrect environment models respectively. Last three lines present distribution of false alarms by reasons of incorrect environment model generation. The first reason represents the cases where preliminary source code analysis extracted less data than DEG needed for accurate matching of π-process parameters. The second reason is incompleteness of kernel core specifications, i.e. new kernel core functions are to be specified. And false alarms from the last category need improvements in DEG to better determine group types and callback roles after source code analysis for several particular cases.

Overall, the number of false alarms because of incorrect models is minuscule in comparison with the number of all verified modules (0.5 %). The data shows that correctness of generated environment models is good enough, although the current implementation still misses some features.

5.2 Model Completeness

To evaluate completeness of generated environment models we checked whether already fixed bugs can be found by LDV Tools. For the benchmark we had chosen 34 different bugs from a wide range of Linux kernel subsystems. LDV Tools found 15 bugs, while environment model incompleteness caused missing of 8 bugs (24 %). A reason for missing 4 bugs is that environment models do not model interaction between several modules (currently we model only interaction of modules with the kernel core). 2 bugs were missed because of preliminary source code analysis cannot extract information on dynamically assigned callbacks. Last 2 of 8 bugs were missed due to lack of specifications. The rest 11 bugs were missed because of issues in the BLAST static verifier and in rule specifications as well as exhaustion of memory or time limits.

5.3 Callback Pattern Matching

The kernel activity specification used in evaluation consists of 7 group pattern specifications, 8 group type specifications for callback group types and the default specification.

Table 2 shows how many callback groups and corresponding group types are presented in Linux kernel 3.13-rc1 and how they were matched. The data demonstrates that group pattern specifications matched a lot of callback groups and group types.

Table 2. Matching of callback groups and group types with DEG specifications.

Matched with	Callback groups	Group types
Group type specifications	818	8
Group pattern specifications	5678	297
Default group specification	9876	434
Total	16372	739

An average size of a group type specification is 140 lines in XML notation. A size of group pattern specifications and the default group specification is about 1500 lines in total. It means that specification of all 731 imprecisely specified group types can be estimated in 102 thousand lines. Therefore the proposed method allowed to reduce the total specification size approximately in 68 times.

6 Related Work

Existing approaches for modeling environment of kernel modules significantly differ by required efforts and theirs means to specify precise models. For the Linux kernel there are two approaches implemented in DDVerify [15] and Avinux [16].

DDVerify requires manual development of environment models. It allows to specify models with any precision, since all possible C expressions are available, yet this approach requires a lot of effort. In DDVerify only 4 group types were specified for Linux kernel 2.6.19. Developed models highly depended on kernel headers, that complicates migration to next versions of the Linux kernel.

The developers used state variables to define an order and parameters for callback invocations. Models for registration functions transfer pointers to callbacks into state variables. Callback invocations were implemented via function pointers. This makes environment model code complicated for CEGAR based static verifiers. Model precision allowed to effectively apply just BMC based static verifiers like CBMC [6]. Environment models developed for DDVerify are fully covered by environment models specified in LDV Tools.

Avinux extracts some information on callbacks by analysis of modules source code. It does not impose any restrictions on an invocation order of callbacks and provides only initialization of their parameters.

SDV [17] was developed for verification of Windows device drivers. The Windows driver developers who want to check their drivers with SDV have to write annotations for driver callbacks manually. In contrast to Linux where we could not force the community to annotate drivers it is convenient for Windows.

7 Conclusion

The paper proposed a new method for generating environment models for Linux kernel modules on the base of specifications that describe patterns of possible scenarios of interaction between modules and their environment. The approach allowed to achieve sufficient level of model correctness and completeness minimizing the total specification size by two orders of magnitude at the same time. As a result it aided to perform large-scale verification of Linux kernel modules with static verifiers that require precise environment models.

References

1. Palix, N., Thomas, G., Saha, S., Calvès, C., Lawall, J., Muller, G.: Faults in Linux: ten years later. In: Proceedings of the 16th International Conference on Architectural Support for Programming Languages and Operating Systems, ASPLOS XVI, pp. 305–318. ACM (2011)
2. Mutilin, V., Novikov, E., Khoroshilov, A.: Analysis of typical faults in Linux operating system drivers (in Russian). In: Proceedings of the Institute for System Programming of RAS, vol. 22, pp. 349–374 (2012)
3. Beyer, D., Keremoglu, M.E.: CPACHECKER: a tool for configurable software verification. In: Gopalakrishnan, G., Qadeer, S. (eds.) CAV 2011. LNCS, vol. 6806, pp. 184–190. Springer, Heidelberg (2011)
4. Beyer, D., Henzinger, T., Jhala, R., Majumdar, R.: The software model checker BLAST. Int. J. Softw. Tools Technol. Transfer. 9(5–6), 505–525 (2007)
5. Shved, P., Mandrykin, M., Mutilin, V.: Predicate analysis with BLAST 2.7. In: Flanagan, C., König, B. (eds.) TACAS 2012. LNCS, vol. 7214, pp. 525–527. Springer, Heidelberg (2012)
6. Clarke, E., Kroning, D., Lerda, F.: A tool for checking ANSI-C programs. In: Jensen, K., Podelski, A. (eds.) TACAS 2004. LNCS, vol. 2988, pp. 168–176. Springer, Heidelberg (2004)
7. Albarghouthi, A., Gurfinkel, A., Li, Y., Chaki, S., Chechik, M.: UFO: verification with interpolants and abstract interpretation. In: Piterman, N., Smolka, S.A. (eds.) TACAS 2013 (ETAPS 2013). LNCS, vol. 7795, pp. 637–640. Springer, Heidelberg (2013)
8. Engler, D., Musuvathi, M.: Static analysis versus software model checking for bug finding. In: Steffen, B., Levi, G. (eds.) VMCAI 2004. LNCS, vol. 2937, pp. 191–210. Springer, Heidelberg (2004)
9. Milner, R., Parrow, J., Walker, D.: A calculus of mobile processes, I. Inf. Comput. 100(1), 1–40 (1992)
10. Milner, R.: The Polyadic π-Calculus: a Tutorial. Department of Computer Science, University of Edinburgh, LFCS (1991)

11. Khoroshilov, A., Mutilin, V., Novikov, E., Shved, P., Strakh, A.: Towards an open framework for C verification tools benchmarking. In: Clarke, E., Virbitskaite, I., Voronkov, A. (eds.) PSI 2011. LNCS, vol. 7162, pp. 179–192. Springer, Heidelberg (2012)
12. Beyer, D.: Second competition on software verification. In: Piterman, N., Smolka, S.A. (eds.) TACAS 2013 (ETAPS 2013). LNCS, vol. 7795, pp. 594–609. Springer, Heidelberg (2013)
13. Novikov, E.: An approach to implementation of aspect-oriented programming for C. Program. Comput. Softw. **39**(4), 194–206 (2013)
14. Zakharov, I., Mutilin, V., Novikov, E., Khoroshilov, A.: Environment modeling of Linux operating system device drivers (in Russian). In: Proceedings of the Institute for System Programming of RAS, vol. 25, pp. 85–112 (2013)
15. Witkowski, T., Blanc, N., Kroening, D., Weissenbacher, G.: Model checking concurrent Linux device drivers. In: Proceedings of the 22nd IEEE/ACM International Conference on Automated Software Engineering, pp. 501–504. ACM, New York (2007)
16. Post, H., Küchlin, W.: Integrated static analysis for linux device driver verification. In: Davies, J., Gibbons, J. (eds.) IFM 2007. LNCS, vol. 4591, pp. 518–537. Springer, Heidelberg (2007)
17. Ball, T., Bounimova, E., Cook, B., Levin, V., Lichtenberg, J., McGarvey, C., Ondrusek, B., Rajamani, S.K., Ustuner, A.: Thorough static analysis of device drivers. SIGOPS Oper. Syst. Rev. **40**(4), 73–85 (2006)

Author Index

Printed in the United States
By Bookmasters